Deltic Dynasty

By Paul Gildersleve

A comprehensive archive and anecdotal record of the lives of British Railways' 'Deltic' Class 55 English Electric Locomotives 1961-1982

Published by A&C **Services (Enterprise Publications)**

Deltic Dynasty

By Paul Gildersleve

Published by
A&C Services
(Enterprise Publications)
3 Peddars Way
Longthorpe
Peterborough
Cambs
PE3 9NQ.

www.westernclass52.com

Designed and edited by
Christine Curtis
Researched and written by
Paul Gildersleve
Copyright
©A&C Services (Enterprise Publications) 2002

All rights reserved. No part of this book may be reproduced or transmitted in any form or by any means electronic or mechanical including photocopying recording or any information storage and retrieval system without prior permission in writing from the Publishers.

Also available from the publisher: 'The Western Collection'
A critically-acclaimed series of booklets detailing the lives of all 74 Western Class 52 locomotives from 1961-1977 and:
'Cast of Thousands' (ISBN 0954021304); 'Western Dawn' (ISBN 0954021371); 'Hymek Dawn' (ISBN 095402138X); 'Western Liveries' (ISBN 0954021312)
Please contact the publishers for a catalogue.

A catalogue record for this book is available from the British Library.

ISBN 0-9540213-4-7

Printed and bound in Great Britain by: Fisherprint, Padholme Road East, Peterborough, Cambs. PE1 5UL

* *

A SPECIAL THANKS TO:

My beloved wife and daughter, Jayne & Sophie Gildersleve, for patience in my absence whilst seeking out information on the Deltics and understanding whilst many hours were spent hidden away working at the computer.

* *

THIS BOOK IS DEDICATED TO THE MEMORY OF MY FATHER
(Albert Vernon Gildersleve 17/12/1922 - 31/12/1998)

He introduced me to railways and was responsible for all my earliest railway experiences. He pointed me in the direction of Deltics in 1965 and in 1977.
Thanks Dad

Acknowledgments

The Deltic Preservation Society Ltd;
The Deltic Study Group;
The National Railway Museum;
The Public Records Office, Kew;
Mark Alden;
Paul Bettany;
Dave Bugg;
Richard Campbell;
Martin Clark;
Les Feasby;
Russell Hallam;
L. A. Harper;
David Heywood;
Phil Hodgson;
Richard MacLennan;
Pete Manning;
Steve McFarlane;
Steve Philpott;
Nigel Rollings;
Chris Short;
Tony Wardle;
Phil Wormald and Neil Young.

CONTENTS

1 INTRODUCTION *(7-9)*

✱ ✱ ✱ ✱ ✱ ✱

2 MEMOIRS OF AN OLD FOOL *(10-38)*

✱ ✱ ✱ ✱ ✱ ✱

3 FACT FILES *(39-50)*

✱ ✱ ✱ ✱ ✱ ✱

4 DESIGN & LIVERY — ARCHIVE REVELATIONS *(51-70)*

✱ ✱ ✱ ✱ ✱ ✱

5 THE LAST MONTHS OF THE DELTICS *(71-154)*

✱ ✱ ✱ ✱ ✱ ✱

6 DELTIC PICTORIAL *(135-150)*

✱ ✱ ✱ ✱ ✱ ✱

7 DELTIC HIGHLIGHTS *(155-166)*

✱ ✱ ✱ ✱ ✱ ✱

8 DELTIC NAMES *(167-179)*

✱ ✱ ✱ ✱ ✱ ✱

9 DELTICS ON WORKS *(180-342)*

✱ ✱ ✱ ✱ ✱ ✱

Left: The author found some new revelations about the naming of the Deltics as he researched this book. Here is the plate from D9016 Gordon Highlander. Picture: L. P. Gater

INTRODUCTION
Dreams do come true...

It has taken me about two years to research and compile the information contained in this book. However, its origins can really be traced back some 25 years. When I first developed a serious interest in Deltics, I would keep a note of which members of the class I had recorded on film, what trains they had worked and of course the date. Initially this information was recorded for those members of the class that I photographed but after a while I would also make the same notes for all Deltics seen during the length of my visits to the ECML.

By 1979 my notes had become very comprehensive as I was trying to collate as much information as possible as regards Deltic workings. This culminated in my effort to record all Deltic workings for 1980. This was no easy task. I was, by this time however, spending nearly every free moment chasing Deltics and therefore I was able to keep on top of the job. However, if I was away from the line for more than a couple of days at a time it became extremely difficult to make up the lost ground. The fact I did stands as a great testament to the many friends I had and their assistance in helping me to achieve my goal. By the end of the year I would estimate that I had recorded approximately 95% of all Deltic workings and I was able to sit back and look at a job well done. By this time more and more people were starting to keep records of Deltic workings and therefore I decided not to do the same for 1981, as, based on experience, I was aware of just what an enormous task it was.

During the early 1990s, I started to do some research into the lives of the diesel hydraulics. This was primarily based on the Warships, although a certain amount was done on the other types as well. After a few years of this, a one-off magazine entitled 'Diesels' was published. This was just the sort of magazine I had been waiting for, as it revealed many interesting facts never before published about our beloved boxes on wheels. I wrote a letter to Adrian Curtis, the man behind the magazine, to congratulate him on providing the diesel enthusiast with a breath of fresh air. A few months later I met up with Adrian and he revealed that the library at the National Railway Museum (NRM) along with the Public Records Office at Kew (PRO) were the places to go if I wished to further my interest in railway research. When I visited the NRM to do some very interesting research into the hydraulics, I also noticed that they had plenty of material to interest the Deltic enthusiast. I stored this information at the back of my mind for a future project. By late 1999 I had secured most of the hydraulic information available and so turned my attention to the Deltics. However, my computer would not be up to the task of storing all the information and so the project was put on hold.

During the early part of 2000 the opportunity arose for me to purchase a much more up to date computer and that the internet would also now be a viable proposition. I thought that my priority should be to type out all those workings I had recorded during 1980 and finally give them the treatment they deserved. After that was done I was able, through some old Deltic friends to obtain a copy of all the 1981 workings for the fleet as well. I soon discovered that people I hadn't seen for years could be contacted via e-mail and so friends were able to give me the addresses of former Deltic chasing colleagues I knew from years ago. Although the workings for 1980 and 1981 were extremely comprehensive there were the inevitable missing workings. I made a list for each Deltic of what information was required and then started contacting everyone I could and sent them a list of what I needed to know. A lot of people replied by saying they were sorry as they could only help me with one or two missing pieces of information. However, when you are contacting 10 or more people who all respond with just one or two workings suddenly a large proportion of what was missing was filled in. One of my band of helpers, long standing friend Chris Short, also mentioned that he had a large proportion of Deltic workings for 1977. Once I had gone as far as I could with the 1980 and 1981 workings I contacted Chris and he sent me the workings for 1977. I then had to write them all out in diary form to ensure that everything made sense. There were the inevitable conflicting workings but for a couple of months Chris and I battled away before we were satisfied that we had got as much sorted out as we possibly could. There was just not enough space to use them in this volume, but hopefully they will see the light of day in a follow-up publication to this one. In between all this I was making regular trips to the NRM to go through the information they had. The bulk of this surrounded the files that contained information on work carried out on the fleet at Doncaster Works. Each locomotive had about three files each, listing all power units, bogies and boilers carried by each member of the class and quite often reasons for repair. This was to be an enormous project, however, the Deltic Study Group had beaten me to it. Three people had formed this group, John Scott, Ken Hackling and Mike Notley. They had been through all the files and done the bulk of the work for me. However, I still had to check through the files for myself as when I cross-checked their work I found plenty of discrepancies that needed sorting out. The work they had done though was certainly of great assistance and I am indebted to them for the hours they put in. Having gained access to the internet I was able to find more Deltic information but even though I was building up quite a supply, there was little new stuff to be found. Whilst searching the internet I discovered a site called 'The Definitive Deltic Library'. This quite superb website is run by Paul Bettany, who has since become a firm friend. Getting to know Paul was very advantageous as he was able to pass on plenty of information to me that people regularly sent him for inclusion on his website. I also started to collate as much information as I could on the earlier years of Deltic operation as well to try and look at the bigger picture. What was I planning to do with all this information I was gathering? Initially I had planned to distribute it amongst Deltic minded friends that had contributed, but the amount of information was getting extremely large. I had considered a book but the unknown world of publishing made me slightly apprehensive in going down that avenue. Then one day I received an e-mail from Adrian Curtis asking me if I would be prepared to do a book about Deltics. I said I would and when we met up to discuss the project Adrian was amazed that I had almost finished it! My Deltic information and his knowledge of the publishing world was the perfect combination. I believe there is still a lot more information on the Deltics that has never before been published. We have had the books with the technical details and how the class came to be, but what about some factual information from the depots and from Doncaster Works in relation to what work was carried out and how.

I have not included some Deltic performances for you to savour although this sort of information would create enough interest to warrant an in depth look at the way Deltics actually performed from day to day. I also believe that some people have gathered together information in relation to the smaller details. For example when did each member of the fleet lose the double windscreen wipers? There really is a lot more that can be done. I hope this book whets your appetite for more of the 'King' of diesels. I feel I should pick out a few individuals for special mentions and thanks on the completion of this project.

First, my late father. He was the one who took a photograph that is almost legendary among my friends as I have shown it to them so many times. It is a colour photograph of me and my Mum standing next to 'Nimbus' at King's Cross in 1965. It was also my Dad who suggested to me in 1977 that Deltics were where I should point my camera and from that day on I haven't looked back.

To Chris Short. By providing me with a bulk of workings, which will hopefully be the mainstay of another Deltic volume in the near future, and for spending all that time when we were trying to make sense of it all. Thanks Chris, I owe you a pint. David 'Fred Flintstone' Heywood, for lending me his book of Deltic workings for 1981 and also for providing me with much of the information relating to the early years. To Paul Bettany. A new friend, who unselfishly assisted in all matters where ever possible, but most of all for his enthusiasm for the Deltics and that stunning website. To my wife Jayne and daughter Sophie. They are more than aware of what a Deltic is, in fact their training is coming along very nicely! Well done girls.

Finally, to all my old friends who rode with me behind those East Coast legends, we had some memorable times and we all have a story to tell. So now the project has come to fruition with the publication of this book. I hope you enjoy reading it as much as I did in putting it all together and may the legend live on.

Paul Gildersleve
Leighton Buzzard
December 2002

1 Memoirs of an Old Fool

I was always destined to have an interest in railways in one form or another. My Dad and two older brothers had been bitten by the bug before me and there had always been a model railway in the house. Dad would regularly take us trainspotting from our Wembley home to Southall or Paddington to see the green and maroon diesels the Western Region were offering. My eldest brother Alan was more of a steam fan at the time but I do remember him liking a Hornby-Dublo diesel we called, 'Deltic'.

However, my other brother, Colin, who is eight years older than me, seemed to be more interested in the Western Region diesels, particularly the 'Westerns'. So I followed his liking for things Western and many trips ensued with our Dad to see these machines at work and, as a result of these sojourns, I developed a liking for the 'Warship' locomotives.

My first ride on a main line train came in August 1965 when Mum and Dad took my sister and I to Newcastle to visit relations. I can still remember making our way along the platform at King's Cross and naturally enough my Dad led us to the very end to see what was going to pull our train. As we approached I could see this great big green thing making the most frightening of noises – frightening that is to a four-year old! It was photograph time of course, my sister ran a mile, but I was brave enough to stand beside this thing, but only with Mum between it and me! I was determined that this monster called 'NIMBUS', wasn't going to eat me, so I held on to Mum for all I was worth! So I had my first run behind a Deltic Apart from a very rare visit to King's Cross a couple of years later and a few more trips to Newcastle it was that first encounter that is the most vivid memory of my early railway years and one that would prove significant at a later stage in my life.

During the late 1960's and early 1970's the regular family holiday haunt was Dawlish Warren, where I would develop a big liking for all things hydraulic. So for the next ten years my interest was a few spotting trips around the country and all things Western. Unfortunately I was too young to be able to spend much time chasing the last Westerns but I did make some trips from Paddington to Reading to see and travel behind the class. It was during one of my trips to Reading that I saw an evening commuter train arrive behind one of the last surviving Hymeks. Suddenly people appeared from everywhere to photograph the loco, this, I decided was what I wanted to do — photography.

However, paper-round money wouldn't stretch to a decent camera, but I did get a black and white Polaroid camera for Christmas and if it was a very bright day then some reasonable photos were possible. Our last Dawlish Warren holiday was in 1975 and I was able to get some reasonable shots of Westerns, but on the whole it was disappointing. It wasn't until I started work in August 1977 that I finally bought a 'Zenith E', cheap and cheerful but an excellent camera to start with. But I was at a loss as to what to point the lens at now the Westerns had finished. I remember sitting at home and saying to my Dad that now I had got a decent camera I didn't know what to photograph. So he said to me, "It's got to be Deltics, they're the best things left". Of course, he was right. So the next day I headed for King's Cross to photograph these machines. I spent a short time at the Cross and took my first two photographs with 55019 and 55015 obliging me. After a few more trips I realised this needed a rethink, as I had used up just about every vantage point available. I therefore set myself a goal of trying to take two photographs at every station between King's Cross and York. The first location would be Peterborough and I decided to catch the 10:05 King's Cross-Leeds. As I walked along platform six to board the train I noticed two plumes of exhaust coming from the sharp end. This was an added bonus I thought as I photographed 55015 'Tulyar. I hadn't thought about riding behind Deltics to get to my destinations but this would add to the appeal. A successful day was had at Peterborough, but when I tried the 10:05 Leeds train for future trips it produced a class 47 each time.

I continued to make regular trips to King's Cross but I wanted more, so January and February 1978 saw me travel on two 'Railway Pictorial Publications Railtours' with 55018 'Ballymoss'. The first trip was 'Deltic Dragon' from Paddington to Cardiff for a pair of class 20's into the Welsh Valleys. This told me that I was purely and simply into Deltics as I found it totally boring behind the 20's. The following month I went on the 'Deltic Ranger' again from Paddington to Paignton for a run behind D1013 Western Ranger on the Torbay Steam Railway. However, due to blizzard weather conditions, the southwest was cut off, so the train terminated at Bristol and returned to Paddington. Shortly after this I spent a day photographing the class at York — travelling out on 1N08 09:00 King's Cross-Newcastle behind 55009 'Alycidon'. My journey home was behind my old friend 55020 'Nimbus'. I wasn't to know it at the time but within a month she would be laid up at Gateshead awaiting a trip to Doncaster Works for a power unit change that would never come. So it turned out to be the last time I saw 55020 in traffic.

The following month, March 1978, I travelled on 'Deltic Ranger re-run' behind 55003 Meld. I believe 55020 was the chosen motive power but was undergoing exam at Finsbury Park and therefore wasn't available. This time the weather was much better, with bright sunshine, however, due to engineering work on the TSR D1013 was not able to run, but at least we saw it at Paignton.

Soon after this I thought it was time I got out into the suburbs to photograph Deltics on their way into and out of London. I spent an afternoon just north of Potters Bar at a lineside path that offers good views of the line through the overhead masts. By this time I was beginning to get familiar with what trains were likely to produce Deltics and therefore when I travelled further north I began to make sure that I would travel out and back behind them. The end of April saw me spend a day at Newcastle, as I arrived behind 55006 I noticed that outside Gateshead shed was my old friend 'Nimbus', however, when I returned home she had gone. At the time I didn't think too much of this, I later discovered that this was the day she was towed to Doncaster Works never to emerge.

I was out most days by now if only to take a few photos at the Cross and it became quite noticeable how Deltics were few and far between on some days. This was the period of poor availability of repaired power units from Doncaster, as I was to find out at a later date. The beginning of May 1978 saw the last runs of the Deltic hauled 'Flying Scotsman'. I could not allow this event to go by without travelling throughout on the final 10:00 King's Cross-Edinburgh, so I duly purchased a ticket and travelled behind 55010 on what could be said to have been the beginning of the end. The following week I was back at King's Cross for my first look at the new timetable. I was pleasantly surprised to see six Deltics at the Cross in a three-hour period. This was a good sign as many locos had previously been laid up in Doncaster Works awaiting replacement power units, but now there seemed to be plenty of locos in traffic.

On May 20th 1978 I travelled behind 55012 'Crepello' on the 'East Coast Pullman Salute' from King's Cross to Leeds on board the last Pullman train on the ECML. On arrival at Leeds the Deltic was replaced by a pair of Class 37's and 55012 worked forward on another rail tour — 'Thames Forth Express'. A lot of books regularly make the mistake of not realising that 'Crepello' worked two rail tours on this date and the Pullman rail tour doesn't always get a mention. The following week I was once again out photographing Deltics in the London suburbs at Harringay, Hornsey, Wood Green, New Southgate and New Barnet. Deltics were out in abundance with nine members of the fleet seen in a five-hour period. Eventually, at the end of June I embarked on a week-long Eastern Rover to visit various locations and try to ride behind some members of the fleet. In a six-day period I had about twenty runs behind Deltics but best of all I was able to photograph them at Leeds, Darlington and Edinburgh to name just a few previously unvisited locations.

With my old friend, 'Nimbus' ensconced in Doncaster Works I needed a second favourite Deltic, although this was never on my mind, it just happened that we were drawn together. It was the last day of my week with the Deltics and I stood at York awaiting the arrival of (1S31) 15:00 King's Cross-Aberdeen, a regular turn for the fleet. I would take this train to Newcastle for a connection of about 10 minutes into 1E21 17:00 Edinburgh-King's Cross – the last daytime train home. When the 15:00 arrived it was almost 20 minutes late and the train was a complete wedge. The only space available was in the leading vestibule right behind the loco. As we headed north from York across the legendary 'racing stretch' towards Darlington, I was treated to a very lively ride and it was quite superb to see the bouncing nose of the loco through the small windows of the corridor connection. On from Darlington we stormed and I knew I should probably have left the train there to be certain of catching my train back home, but as I was enjoying the run so much, I thought I'd go for it. As we rounded the curve off of the King Edward Bridge and into Newcastle, 55015 'Tulyar' and my train home was also arriving. We drew to a stand alongside the 17:00, which was at the adjacent platform, I'd made it.

An exhilarating run had ensured the connection was made and as I left the 15:00 I glanced back for an appreciative look at 55005 'The Prince of Wales's own Regiment of Yorkshire'. This loco had completely won me over and it was destined to become my favourite Deltic once the fate of 'Nimbus' had been sealed. As the summer wore on Deltics seemed to remain regular performers, confirming that perhaps for the time being at least, that the power unit crisis was over.

Towards the end of July I noticed a leaflet at King's Cross proclaiming "A trip behind a Deltic". I read the leaflet and it said that a special train would be running on August 13th 1978 taking a Deltic to Skegness and a later trip going to Lowestoft. I decided I would travel on the Skegness trip and duly purchased a ticket for the run. A very clean 55015 'Tulyar' was the motive power, having received a recent repaint she looked superb sitting at the head of the train on that sunny Sunday morning. We headed off initially for Lincoln for a break where I was fortunate to get some photos of Deltics on diverted trains due to engineering work on the main line. We then headed off to old Skeggy where I was able to sample fish, chips and for the first time, mushy peas!

On the return run I was sitting with a like-minded Deltic enthusiast who I had spoken to during the day, when his girlfriend asked me if I travelled behind Deltics for mileage (she was obviously in the know). For mileage, I thought about that for a while before realising that was the way forward for me. I had never heard of this before but it seemed a great idea to try and amass as many miles as possible behind each individual loco and therefore behind the class as a whole. Fortunately arrival back at King's Cross that evening coincided with my next Eastern Rover behind the Deltics whilst photography, still playing an important part, took on a secondary role in my bid to travel behind the fleet. A new age was about to begin. It was during this week that I started to meet fellow Deltic bashers, some of whom remain friends to this day. I started my week by travelling on 1N12 23:55 King's Cross-Newcastle behind 55003 'Meld', arrival at Newcastle was at 05:47 and fortunately the station buffet was open so I could grab a bite and a drink. Soon after my arrival I watched 55015 'Tulyar' arrive with 1N00 01:00 King's Cross-Newcastle. Being August it was possible to take photographs of the two racehorses at the head of their trains in the early morning sunshine. Whilst admiring 55015 the driver invited me into the cab where I spent about 20 minutes chatting to him. This was most pleasing as even though it was still summer it was a cool morning and feeling slightly rundown after my nights doss in a MK1 compo the warm cab was most welcome. After watching 55015 take the stock out to Heaton I awaited the arrival of the coaches to form (1A11) 08:20 Newcastle-King's Cross, the first 'up' loco-hauled train. Soon after 08:00, 55011 arrived from Heaton with the train and I settled down to enjoying more Deltic haulage. I travelled regularly overnight to Newcastle during that week as I began to get familiar with Deltic diagrams and what the best moves were so as to maximise Deltic mileage. Whilst waiting at Peterborough for a 'down' service during the week I got talking to another Deltic basher I had seen earlier in the week.

I believe he became known as 'The Goat' (due to his beard) and he told me a story where someone he knew had a run behind 55012 'Crepello' earlier in the week between Darlington and York and they had timed number twelve at 118mph. This got me thinking again, I liked the sound of this, timing Deltics. Once my week chasing Deltics was over, I made some enquiries about what I needed to time Deltics. I read the articles that appeared regularly in the 'Railway Magazine' and eventually decided I needed two stopwatches, one to record the start to stop and passing times and one that would display fractions of seconds so as to calculate the speed. I worked out the necessary formula for converting times into mph so I could note the speed on the road rather than waiting until I got home and then convert it.

So I was now ready to try it out behind a Deltic. My first train would be (1S17) 09:00 King's Cross-Edinburgh, a train that became a favourite with me, on this particular day 55 009 'Alycidon' would have the distinction of being my first timed Deltic. I was only able to go to Peterborough as I didn't really have any time to do anything more, I wouldn't normally have come out on that day but I was keen to time a Deltic, logging as it was known. I was pleased with that first run and I recorded a maximum speed of 107 mph behind number nine. However, I soon realised I needed to gain more knowledge of the route, such as the position of closed stations, their names and any other relevant information I could find out. This turned out to be an ongoing process and when I look back it probably took me more than a year to become completely competent at this art and also to identify the site of many closed stations, yards, signal boxes etc. I continued my quest to photograph Deltics at all the stations between King's Cross and York so that by the end of 1978 I had completed it. Also by the end of the year I was seeing the same faces regularly on Deltic-hauled trains and it was about this time when I was christened as 'Mr Wembley'. Several people were known by the name of the place where they came from rather than their actual name, hence my name. Once I got to know various people it became easier to track down Deltics as we would all pass on 'the gen' to each other and of course it became more enjoyable to be in the company of like-minded people. The first Deltic bashers I remember meeting were Steve Philpott, Pete Toulson, Andy Young (Mr Boston) and Pete 'The Captain' Manning. These fellow Deltic bashers would regularly join (1S17) 09:00 King's Cross-Edinburgh at Peterborough where I would usually let them know what was following us on 1L03 09:04 King's Cross-Leeds, also a regular Deltic working. They would then choose which train to take and where to go based on this info. Steve Philpott and 'The Captain' were old hands with stopwatches and regularly we would sit together with just one of us logging while maybe another would note the passing times, in fact we did just this on a recent Deltic rail tour. I was also able to learn a bit more about the route and indeed the Deltics by listening to them. In a way they had been brought up on Deltics, they lived at Grantham and Newark respectively and so they were an everyday site in their towns, where as I had almost an hours journey to King's Cross, (although some people had several hours to travel to get to the ECML). The new year of 1979 saw me continue to travel regularly behind the Deltics with photography still playing its part. At the end of February I made my first overnight trip of the year and Edinburgh was to be my destination. I had chosen to go to Edinburgh because I had heard through the grapevine that all trains were being diverted via Carlisle and this was to be my first opportunity to travel behind a Deltic over Beattock. However, on arrival at King's Cross that evening I was told that there was some kind of industrial dispute taking place that may affect the overnight trains. This was not good news, we then discovered that all trains to Scotland had been cancelled and then reinstated as additional services. Therefore the train I had been intending to travel on, (1S66) 21:00 King's Cross-Edinburgh, became (1F66) and ran in the same path. Fortunately it produced 55010 'The King's own Scottish Borderer', which I was happy to take to Edinburgh. We left the Cross at 21:00 and were diverted via the 'Joint Line' through Lincoln and further on via Stockton. However, on arrival at Newcastle the site of a class 47 waiting to take over from the Deltic greeted us. We were not amused; there must have been about 15 Deltic bashers who got off to await developments. There was talk that no Deltics would go via Beattock and that we would probably have to take a Deltic on an 'up' working back to the Cross. This was turning out to be a disappointment as I had been looking forward to my Scottish trip, but we did have one more train to cover that might just produce a Deltic. This was (1S72) 22:30 King's Cross-Edinburgh, it was running as (1F67) due to the earlier mentioned industrial action. When the train finally arrived at Newcastle it had come in off the High Level Bridge and under the arched roof of the station twin Napiers could be heard. There were no other replacement locomotives about so we all boarded the train behind the ever reliable 55 018 'Ballymoss'.

Sure enough, The Moss didn't let us down as we headed off along the Tyne Valley in the wee small hours. We all got down to some doss in various compartments and I awoke as we approached Carlisle. However, I was unable to find the energy to get up, find my stopwatch and log the run over Beattock. I thought that could wait as trains were to be diverted this way all day Sunday as well. When we arrived at Edinburgh breakfast was called for so we all headed for 'The Talisman' buffet for a good old fried breakfast. Our train to head back south on was expected to be (1E11) 10:30 Aberdeen-King's Cross, which wasn't due to leave Edinburgh until 14:10.

We had over four hours to kill once we had finished our breakfast so a walk to Haymarket depot seemed in order. When we arrived at the depot 'Ballymoss' was seen standing outside the shed basking in the sunlight. Too good a photographic opportunity to miss, so I duly performed with my camera.

Our suspicions were also confirmed; The Moss was the only Deltic north of the border. We walked back to Waverley station after a climb up to Arthur's Seat overlooking this very fine city. Eventually the time drew near for 1E11's arrival and spot on cue 55018 arrived from Haymarket ready to takeover from a class 47.

We boarded the train, which was a bit of a wedge, but I managed to find the necessary seat, facing the direction of travel and milepost side. When we reached the WCML just south of Carstairs, The Moss then demonstrated what a Deltic could do with a heavy train over gradients more testing than usually encountered on the ECML. A satisfying run ensued and when Newcastle was reached we came to a stand next to 55013 'The Black Watch' on another London bound train. As I'd had a good dose of The Moss I decided to opt for 55013 for the run home, as did most other bashers. An arrival back at King's Cross just before 22:00 brought a very satisfying 24-hour period chasing Deltics to a close. A few weeks later whilst heading north behind 55011 'The Royal Northumberland Fusiliers' on (1S17) 09:00 King's Cross-Edinburgh I heard some 'normals' talking about a bridge that was supposed to have collapsed north of Darlington. Apparently they'd heard it on the news earlier that day. It eventually transpired that in fact it had been Penmanshiel tunnel north of Berwick that had collapsed bringing chaos to the ECML. Over the preceding months work had taken place on Stoke and Peascliffe tunnels so as to allow larger freight containers to use the line and the third and final tunnel to receive the attention was Penmanshiel. Out of the tragic event (I believe two workers lost their lives) was interesting news on the Deltic front. All overnight trains between London and Scotland would be diverted via Carlisle presenting many opportunities to travel behind a Deltic over Beattock. Most daytime trains would terminate at Berwick with buses to take passengers forward to Dunbar from where a shuttle service would operate to Edinburgh.

Early April saw me embark on an Eastern Rover, once again in pursuit of Deltics. By this time I was now one of the regulars in the chase for Deltic mileage and I was now fully conversant with diagrams and what trains may or may not produce a Deltic and also of course what the best moves usually were in order to maximise mileage. The first train I caught from King's Cross was (1N00) 09:30 (SuO) King's Cross-Newcastle which was headed by 55005 no less. A great way to start I thought on a non-stop run to Doncaster. However, it soon became apparent that my favourite Deltic was not in the best of health as it was struggling, apparently low on power. We were losing time and at one point we were climbing Stoke bank at just 11 mph! At Grantham we were put around the back to allow the following trains to pass us before we continued our journey north. We eventually arrived at Doncaster in an overall time of 238 minutes from King's Cross against the 134 minutes in the timetable! Needless to say 55005 was immediately removed from the train, so I baled out so as to see what was around to work forward. Initially I could see nothing, but then from under the road bridge north of the station I could see an absolutely immaculate yellow nose of a Deltic. It turned out to be 55012 'Crepello', fresh out of Doncaster Works after a 'Light' repair. In fact 55012 had emerged the previous night after rectification work having been in traffic for just a couple of days after her 'Light' repair. Curiously the reason she had to return to the Works was for a loss of power, the same reason she was now replacing 55005.

It was nearly two months since I had last had a dose of 55012, so I decided to take her through to Newcastle. However, once we were north of Darlington she too was in trouble and it was once again a loss of power that was the problem. On arrival at Newcastle she was despatched to Gateshead depot and not seen again that day. Other Deltics were on Gateshead, however, they were all receiving attention; 55014 – 'C' exam; 55019 – 'B' exam; 55022 – unknown. There was no sign of a Deltic working back south so the only thing open to me was to get back to Doncaster as soon as possible, so I boarded an HST to get me there. Once back at Doncaster I didn't have long to wait for a Deltic because 55002 'The King's own Yorkshire Light Infantry' pulled in with (1A18) 18:50 Leeds-King's Cross, which I promptly boarded and found a seat in the well filled train. I soon noticed a couple of lads with Scottish accents, about the same age as me, sitting opposite talking about Deltics.

We soon started a discussion on our return to King's Cross and we then spent most of the following week together searching for Deltics. They told me they came from Muir of Ord and Dingwall; to be honest I'd never heard of either place, well Deltics don't go there I thought, so there was no reason to know of these places!

We became firm friends over the following week and remain so to this day. We had some excellent runs behind Deltics during that week, such as an ailing 55002 on a Leeds-King's Cross train when it kept losing an engine. When it was running on both engines the driver was able to take it up to about 107 mph, which managed to off set the arrears caused by running on one engine only. We also made an overnight move to Hull behind 55003 just a couple of days after it had received white paint around its cab windows. When I first saw 'Meld' with this embellishment it looked very strange. I had been standing by the buffer stops at King's Cross and she was stabled by the entrance to Gasworks tunnel and from that distance my mind couldn't take in what I was seeing. Once I was closer it was easier to see what had been done to her. I think it looked quite good after getting over the initial shock of seeing a Deltic in what was basically a new livery variation. This had been probably my best period chasing Deltics, there were plenty of them in action, therefore offering plenty of variety, it was the Easter holidays so extra trains were running allowing Deltics to work them and of course the sun shone (but didn't it always back then?).

May 1979 was to be a big turning point in the lives of the Deltics; I suppose it was the beginning of the final chapter in their lives. To start with, Saturday 12th saw the last workings of many Anglo-Scottish trains that had been Deltic hauled for nearly 20 years. There was a good gathering of Deltic bashers at King's Cross on that morning, all there to travel on the last (1S17) 09:00 King's Cross-Edinburgh (or Berwick due to the Penmanshiel blockage) and fortunately for me 55 005 was turned out to work the train. The loco was even carrying a small headboard on the top lamp bracket to recognise the end of Deltic supremacy on the East Coast Main Line. From the following Monday the H.S.T.'s took over all but one daytime King's Cross-Leeds/Bradford/Newcastle/Scottish workings. The Deltics were relegated to work King's Cross-York/Hull trains calling at all stations between Peterborough and Doncaster. This involved the reallocation of Haymarket and Gateshead Deltics to York due to the severe reduction in workings available to them north of York. The new timetable did, however, see the introduction of Britain's fastest ever timed locomotive hauled train, (1D04) 17:05 King's Cross-Hull 'The Hull Executive', which was timed to travel the 138.6 miles from King's Cross to it's first stop at Retford in 91 minutes at an average speed of 91.38 mph! For that inaugural working I arrived at the Cross in plenty of time to see 55 003 'Meld' sitting at the sharp end with headboard in place. There was an air of anticipation about the train as Doncaster driver Joe Hodgson absolutely blasted out of the Cross in a fashion that I never witnessed repeated behind a Deltic. That sort of start was the sort of thing that dispels the long talked about nonsense of a Deltic being a slow starter. If the driver knew how much he could give a Deltic without overloading it then it was quite easy to beat the pants off most other types of loco. It was quite simply down to the skill of the driver. Unfortunately due to numerous speed restrictions in force at the time we were 14 minutes late at Retford, but we had attained a maximum speed of 114 mph including breasting Stoke Summit in excess of 100 mph, the first time I achieved that behind a Deltic. By the end of the week I had travelled on the train five times and on two occasions we were just over half a minute down on the schedule having suffered delays of several minutes en route. The Executive became a train that I would travel on many more times over the following 18 months or so and there were to be several more superb runs but perhaps none to equal the performances of Joe Hodgson in that first week.

The next couple of months was spent getting used to the new timetable and diagrams which was so different from what we had previously been used to. It became rare for me to go north of Doncaster as most of the moves took place south of there. During August I had my first two-week period of being out on the road continuously since the introduction of the new timetable. I soon found my way heading to Scotland on an overnight train behind 55 009 'Alycidon' being diverted via Carlisle due to the Penmanshiel diversion not yet open. There always seemed to be someone else about so I was rarely alone for long and on arrival at Edinburgh once again 'The Talisman' buffet was visited for breakfast and after a wash we would see what was about. One of the main sources of employment for a Deltic that found itself at Edinburgh at this time was for it to work one of the Dunbar shuttles. There were about three trains that would spend the day working between Edinburgh and Dunbar usually consisting of about 5 coaches and quite often Deltic-hauled. On this particular day two of the trains were worked by Deltics, 55 009 'Alycidon' and 55 008 'The Green Howards'. We spent most of the day travelling behind these two locos on the shuttle trains until the afternoon when another diagram would bring another Deltic into the frame. Whilst at Dunbar at around 16:30, we decided to allow 55 008 to return to Edinburgh while we waited for an empty train to arrive that would work back as a passenger train to Edinburgh. We decided to take a short walk so as to photograph the train approaching, I was not to be disappointed as the train approached behind a spotless 55 005, just out of Works after a 'Light' repair.

For me this was a big score, I could now travel behind my favourite Deltic back to Edinburgh and then it would form (1E26) 18:25 Edinburgh-York via Carlisle. A daytime run over Beattock was too good to miss. I said goodbye to my fellow bashers as they were going to remain with the shuttle trains before returning south overnight for maximum doss. My move would not give me a good night's sleep as I would be arriving at York at about 23:00 and it would still be a few hours before I could catch up with an overnight train for my doss. The run behind 55 005 over Beattock was most enjoyable, the descent was quite lively and I still have the coffee stains in my gradient profile book to prove it! The following night I was heading north once again on (1S66) 20:15 King's Cross-Edinburgh behind 55 011 'The Royal Northumberland Fusiliers' when it developed engine trouble. At Newark the secondman was seen to use the telephone, presumably to request a fresh engine at either Doncaster or York. I was travelling with three fellow Deltic bashers and we assumed that we would have to make alternative plans for a good night's doss behind a Deltic. On arrival at Doncaster there was no sign of a replacement loco, but on the platform we recognised a few more Deltic bashers who appeared to be in a bit of a state.

"It's going to be number two"; "It's going to be number two!" They were shouting. At this time 55 002 'The King's own Yorkshire Light Infantry' had been in Doncaster Works since 1st May and we were in the middle of August. So we were quite excited by this prospect, but where was number two? After what seemed an age, 55 011 had already been removed from the train, we could hear the sound of twin Napiers drifting in from the south and sure enough 55 002 appeared from behind our train on the through road and shunted onto the stock. We had scored, KOYLI had just been outshopped from Works and we were about to get a dose of it on it's first train. It's three and a half month stay in Doncaster had been primarily due to waiting replacement engines. We were finally ready to depart from Doncaster and I recall that myself and fellow basher Chris Short were hanging out of the first window as we pulled away. When the driver applied full power, the cobwebs were certainly blown out in the shape of an incredible amount of white smoke. As speed increased the exhaust continued to thicken and this continued until about Shaftholme Junction, 4 and a quarter miles to the north of Doncaster. At this point Chris and myself returned to our seat and as we slid open the door into the carriage our friends took one look at us and burst out laughing. Puzzled, we looked at each other and to our amazement we were both covered in what appeared like hundreds of black spots! Our faces were covered in oil! We soon washed ourselves and then settled down for the journey north. When I awoke, it was brilliant sunshine as we took the curve to avoid Carstairs, when I was told by my only companion, Paul Ancrum, that KOYLI was now only on one engine. It wasn't a serious problem as she was back in action a few days later. This was the final week of the Penmanshiel diversions as the new alignment was due to open as I finished my two-week period of Deltic bashing. This was a fantastic achievement to build a new stretch of railway and road and all the associated work and have the railway open in almost five months to the day of the tragedy. I sampled the new alignment on it's second day of operation with a trip to Edinburgh aboard (1S12) 05:50 King's Cross-Aberdeen behind 55 008 'The Green Howards'.

When in Edinburgh most Deltic bashers would congregate in 'The Coppers' for a sampling of their finest ales before embarking on an overnight journey south for more Deltic mileage. Part of the attraction of Deltic bashing was also the social side of things where it was possible to meet friends completely unarranged for an evening's drinking before sleeping it off behind a Deltic. This enabled people to become familiar with others from many different places such as London, Reading, Grantham, Newark, Selby, York, Darlington, Newcastle and various places around the country as like-minded enthusiasts flocked to the E.C.M.L. in search of Deltics. At around this time my name was changed from 'Mr Wembley' to 'Mr Hillingdon', due to moving house, I kept this name until the end of the Deltics lives on BR. One of my most amusing memories of travelling overnight with others in search of Deltics features Paul Gash. I had known Paul for sometime before I was able to understand a word of what he was saying, as his Geordie accent was so strong to someone like me from the London area. If travelling from Edinburgh with Paul on an overnight train to King's Cross, at Newcastle there would inevitably be a reason to stir from dossing. I vividly remember the sound of a tapping noise followed by the sound of a woman's voice. This would gradually get closer until it was possible to make out what was being said. There would be a tap on the window followed by the question, once you were awake of course, "Do you know Paul Gash"? Tap, tap, tap, "Do you know Paul Gash"? It was his mother and she used to go along the length of the train waking everybody and asking this question. Most people would just grunt until she found someone who knew him and would wake him. She would regularly appear with fresh clothes and provisions for him. My, my, he had her well trained!

We would frequent pubs at strategic locations in between Deltic hauled trains for a pint and perhaps a game of Space Invaders whilst listening to the jukebox. The music of the day was also part of the scene, I still hear certain songs to this day and they take me back to my Deltic bashing days on the ECML. At about this time E.L.O. were quite successful and they had a song called 'Last train to London' which was quite relevant, so this was adopted by some as a bit of an anthem in the summer of '79. I remember one Deltic Basher, Dave Sampson, was the spitting image of E.L.O. lead singer, Jeff Lynne and I believe that somebody asked Dave for his autograph on one occasion. During September 1979 I was travelling back to the Cross behind 55 007 'Pinza', when, as we were passing through the London suburbs the brakes came on hard. We were just north of New Southgate and after a while the guard announced that the locomotive had failed. I put my head out of the window and could clearly hear two Napiers, so it wasn't an engine problem. We sat there for almost an hour, when finally I could hear the sound of detonators exploding, it was our assisting engine arriving.

I listened but was unable to make out what was coming to our rescue due to my position down the train. I suspected it was a Class 31 but I had my suspicions that it may have been another Deltic due to the sound from the front but I couldn't be sure as 55007 still had both engines running. It wasn't until we arrived in King's Cross and I made my way along the platform that I could make out four plumes of exhaust heading up into the overall roof. I had scored with a pair! It turned out that the assisting engine had been 55019 'Royal Highland Fusilier' to give me my first experience of a pair of Deltics. A couple of weeks later I skived off work for the one and only time in search of Deltics. I was due at work at 09:00 on a Sunday but I had found out that all daytime trains were to be diverted via Cambridge, something I had not done before. So on the Saturday evening I rang in and made up some cock and bull story as to why I would be giving up a 10-hour shift at double time. That goes to show our desperate I was to get a Deltic via Cambridge.

I arrived at King's Cross on that Sunday morning to find 55014 'The Duke of Wellington's Regiment' at the head of (1N02) 08:40 King's Cross-Newcastle. I was most pleased as I had a soft spot for 'The Duke' and decided to go all the way to Newcastle for maximum mileage. We headed off out of the Cross and at Hitchin we stopped to pick up a pilotman and then swung a right onto the line through Royston and on to Cambridge. About one and three quarter hours later we were drawing to a stand in Peterborough after the diversion before continuing along the main line. We were entertained to some lively running from 'The Duke' and were even diverted on the approach to Doncaster at Decoy South Junction for a run through the freight yards and into the station. What happened on departure from Doncaster was out of this world and I'm glad that Pete Manning was with me, as the standard of running that followed would not have been believed without a witness. This train was booked non-stop to York; this was via Selby of course. Once 'The Duke' got up to 100 mph speed stayed above this mark with a steady 105 mph attained before the brakes were applied for the Selby restriction which was taken at a minimum speed of 36 mph, Selby was passed in 13 minutes and 7 seconds from Doncaster against the booked 14 minutes. Between Selby and Chaloners Whin Junction (a Tesco supermarket marks the junction today) 'The Duke' attained a maximum speed of 103 mph, again this was a most impressive performance, we took the 55 mph restriction at Chaloners Whin at a minimum of 52 mph before the driver got the power back on and took speed back up to 66 mph before coming to a stand in York in an overall time from Doncaster of 24 minutes and 59 seconds. This was a quite staggering piece of running. I have never heard of a time remotely like that produced by 'The Duke' on this occasion and it is only a few more minutes longer than that possible via the new line today with a Deltic. Within a few days I was lucky to experience yet another outstanding piece of Deltic performance, this time courtesy of my old friend, 55 005. Earlier in the day 55016 had failed on it's return to traffic, after a long lay off in Doncaster Works, when it only managed to get about a mile south of York with (1A08) 08:05 York-King's Cross. This resulted in the train arriving very late at King's Cross, which resulted in the return working running late as well.

I was waiting for this train, (1D02) 12:05 King's Cross-Hull, at Peterborough. It was usually closely followed by (1L42) 12:20 King's Cross-York, the Hull train stopped at all stations from Huntingdon to Doncaster, where as the York train only stopped at Peterborough and Doncaster. As I waited at Peterborough I was unaware of what had occurred earlier in the day to cause the late running. The Hull train was due into Peterborough at 13:07, but it wasn't until 13:30 when it pulled in behind 55 015 'Tulyar'. I knew 55 005 was at King's Cross and I had been hoping for that to have worked this train. I boarded 55015's train and immediately looked out of the far window back onto the Nene Bridge where almost straight away another Deltic was coming to a stand. I decided to get off the train and wait for this next train, (1L42) 12:20 King's Cross-York. The Hull train pulled away and this then allowed 55005 to arrive to my satisfaction with the York train. This was normally a tedious train to travel on due to it not being allowed to pass the Hull train, as it was the connecting service at Doncaster for Selby and York. But as 55005 was in charge that compensated for the expected tedium that lay ahead. As we pulled away from Peterborough, over 15 minutes late, we were given the slow line to add to our inevitable slow running. As we headed north on the slow line the 12:50 King's Cross-Harrogate H.S.T. passed us, this was followed a short while later by the 13:00 King's Cross-Edinburgh H.S.T. This was unusual as these two trains were supposed to be connecting services from the Hull and York trains. Of course I didn't know whether they had been allowed to pass the Hull train, which had taken the fast line out of Peterborough. At Little Bytham on the climb of Stoke Bank we were allowed back on to the fast line. I thought this was good as whatever had happened to the Hull train there would be a clear run ahead of us until we caught it up some distance to the north. York driver Charlie Tibbett took 55005 over Stoke Summit at 84 mph, a quite impressive performance from a stand at Little Bytham some seven and three quarter miles to the south. This allowed us to pay no attention to the 90 mph restriction from Stoke to Great Ponton, although we came off it at 99 mph. We then touched 105 mph on the descent to Grantham, passed at 103 mph, this was most pleasing to be heading north behind a Deltic at this sort of speed as Grantham was usually a stopping point or with this train we would normally pass here at a severely reduced speed due to the presence of the Hull train. As we stormed round the curve north of Grantham we passed a rake of air-conditioned coaches in the loop, I thought, no, it can't be. YES, it was 55015 with the Hull train, we were away! On we stormed as Charlie Tibbett gave number five her head and we thrashed on, 108 mph passing Barkston, 105 mph at Hougham and 107 mph through Newark. Speed dropped to 102 mph for the 100 mph restriction over the flat crossing north of Newark before regaining 108 mph at Bathley Lane. We continued with this sort of running until breasting Markham summit at 99 mph before attaining 107 mph on the following descent to Retford, which was passed at 103 mph. Soon afterwards we were travelling at 108 mph again before the brakes came on for the 80 mph restriction in force at Bawtry, which was taken at 84 mph. After this we touched 100 mph again before the brakes were applied again but this time for Doncaster. As we approached the station we were stopped very annoyingly outside the station, I went to the window to see what the reason might be, when there in the station ahead I could see the two H.S.T.'s that had passed us some 70 miles further south.

I thought that was a clear demonstration of how little time an H.S.T. could make up over a Deltic that had the bit firmly between it's teeth. On leaving the train at Doncaster I calculated that 55005 had averaged 104 mph from Great Ponton to a point just south of Bawtry, a distance of some 45 miles, a most impressive display. It was displays like this that made me appreciate logging Deltics, where as if I just sat back and enjoyed the ride I wouldn't really have been aware of what a good run it had been. Logging also allows me to remember many runs with Deltics, good and bad, which would otherwise have faded into obscurity.

A couple of weeks later I finally managed to catch up with 55 016 'Gordon Highlander' after it's long stay in Doncaster Works. I decided to take it to York and back, when I arrived at King's Cross to see it sitting at the head of (1L44) 16:05 to York. Many other people appeared at various locations to sample a dose of number sixteen and they were not to be disappointed, where as not only was it's performance of a high standard but it was making such an incredible sound. Around this time if you were standing on a station having just left a number sixteen-hauled train, you could hear it for many minutes after it had left. Also, if you were travelling behind it you could clearly hear it all the time, such was the volume of it's engines. There was also a rumour as well concerning 55 016, that it had been up rated to 3,500 hp, but this I believe was pure speculation.

At the end of November I had a week off work and my goal for this period was to get a Deltic to Aberdeen. At about this time Deltics to Aberdeen had become an almost daily event so I thought I might be in with a chance. The train to be on was (1S12) 05:50 King's Cross-Aberdeen as this was the best bet, it also offered the opportunity of having a 523 mile run, which would leave a Deltic with just a few bucket loads of fuel in the tanks if the gauge was anything to go by. After a day at the southern end of the ECML I thought the best way of being in position for 1S12 was to do an overnight to Doncaster and then back into the Cross on one of the earlier arrivals from the north. I therefore left the Cross behind 55 016 on (1L22) 23:00 King's Cross-Bradford which I took to Doncaster. From here I could cover (1A45) 22:55 Newcastle-King's Cross and (1E35) 20:20 Edinburgh-King's Cross, both trains regularly produced Deltics. When 1A45 arrived it had a nondescript class 47, bowled, but 1E35 shouldn't be too far behind. I looked to the north, awaiting the arrival of 1E35, when I noticed two white dots approaching. Initially it was too difficult to say what it was, but as it got closer I could see that the dots were too low to be a Deltic, bowled again. Yet another class 47 arrived, this now put my chances of a 523 mile run behind a Deltic in jeopardy. I had one more chance, (1E39) 22:30 Edinburgh-King's Cross, was due in at the Cross at 05:31. When an announcement was made at Doncaster stating that this train was running 45 minutes late I realised now there was little chance of achieving a 523 mile run. When it finally arrived behind another class 47 I decided to board it as the next southbound overnight arrived a few minutes behind it and that too was a class 47. So a bad time for southbound Deltics I thought as I headed south and thought about what to do next as I drifted off to sleep. When I awoke the train was just running into Peterborough just before 05:00, there was no chance of making King's Cross, so I decided to leave the train here and spend the next couple of hours festering in the waiting room on platform 4 to see what the new day might bring. After what seemed an age it was now time for the arrival of 1S12 and as I looked towards the Nene Bridge I could see a Deltic with white cabs approaching the platform. At last I was back in business and I decided to go as far as I could with this Deltic as 55 007 'Pinza' came to a halt alongside me. I boarded the first coach and got down to some much needed doss.

By the time York was reached I decided it was time to get out my stopwatch to see how 'Pinza' would perform over the legendary Racing stretch between York and Darlington. A most competent run followed and my mind now switched to thinking about what would happen at Edinburgh. Would there be a class 47 waiting to replace us, or another Deltic maybe, or even nothing at all. When we finally arrived at the Scottish capital I was off the train like a shot to see what indeed would happen. There were no other locos about, the crew left the cab of 55 007 and another crew boarded it. I asked the driver if it was going through, to which he replied in a broad Scottish accent, "Aye, it is sonny". Yes, that's it I thought with a Cheshire cat sized grin, I got back on the train for my first run with a Deltic to the Granite City courtesy of a fellow Londoner, 'Pinza'. About a week later I was standing at Peterborough when another monumental event took place. I was waiting for 1L43 14:05 King's Cross-York, when it pulled in behind 55 004 'Queen's Own Highlander', another loco that had been out of action, in number four's case it had been in Doncaster for 18 months, originally waiting for replacement engines before becoming cannibalised for spares. But here she was back in traffic, leaving just 'St. Paddy' and 'Nimbus' as long-term residents of Doncaster. Over the preceding months people would ask what was in Works, the reply would always start with, apart from 1, 4, 16 & 20. Those four locos had become pretty much permanent fixtures but finally things were looking good, or so we thought. Within a few weeks we found out that 1 & 20 were to be withdrawn. Although they had been out of action for so long we always hoped they would return, especially after the re-emergence of 4 & 16, but it was not to be. It still came as a bit of a shock to everyone and it really made us realise that the days of the Deltics were numbered. Not a happy way to end the year. During January 1980 I made my first runs in a sleeper behind a Deltic when during the course of a weekend I travelled twice on (1N00) 01:00 King's Cross-Newcastle, whose sleepers continued as part of (1S08) 07:05 Newcastle-Edinburgh. I travelled on this train regularly from this date onwards. Initially I think it cost £5 to Newcastle or £6 to Edinburgh for a berth that was good value for a good nights doss especially if you were out for the week.

At the end of February I was travelling north to Doncaster on (1D00) 08:05 King's Cross-Hull behind 55 003 'Meld' with the intention of returning on (1A13) 09:35 Hull-King's Cross. However, having watched 'Meld' head off disaster struck in the shape of a class 47 on the up train. This was bad news, we could either catch this south for a Deltic on a later down working or just wait at Doncaster. As there were three of us we decided to hang around at Doncaster.

Someone went off and made a phone call to see if he could establish what Deltics were about, when he returned he shouted the length of the subway on Doncaster station proclaiming that there was a pair on (1A35) 12:15 York-King's Cross! With this news we boarded the first H.S.T. to York and sure enough on arrival there indeed was a pair of Deltics on this train. The train engine was 55 008 'The Green Howards' and the pilot engine was 55 013 'The Black Watch' in immaculate condition after an Intermediate repair in Doncaster Works. The reason for this pairing was because the Doncaster Works test train was out of action so a service train was being used instead. 55 013 piloted the train as far as Peterborough where it was removed before returning to Doncaster Works for more attention.

A few days later I headed north behind 55 008 on (1S72) 22:30 King's Cross-Edinburgh, in the company of quite a few other Deltic bashers. On arrival at Edinburgh we made the usual visit to 'The Talisman' buffet for breakfast before seeing what was working. We were most pleased to see that Haymarket depot turned out 55 006 'The Fife & Forfar Yeomanry' to work (1A23) 08:50 Edinburgh-Aberdeen, which we promptly boarded. For me the highlight of the out and back run to Aberdeen was on the return journey, pulling out of Montrose. On the adverse gradient that crosses the Montrose Basin 55 006 was being severely tested on the apparently greasy rails but needless to say she triumphed, but the music that was provided was most satisfying. Towards the end of March I was planning another weekend visit to Scotland and on the Tuesday prior to my trip I was jokingly telling people that 55 005 would be working (1S12) 05:50 King's Cross-Aberdeen on the Saturday morning so I could take it to Edinburgh. However, by the Friday night number five was in fact in pole position to work that train as it was working south on (1A34) 19:56 York-King's Cross. When I arrived at the Cross off an overnight I made my way to the stock, which was always in long before the 05:50 departure time. Soon after 05:30 a familiar yellow nose backed on to the train and indeed it was 55 005, my favourite Deltic. I was very satisfied at the idea of a daytime King's Cross-Edinburgh run behind number five, as most runs to Edinburgh were done overnight since May 1979. A good run was had and once at Edinburgh I did a fill-in bash to Newcastle at back on a stopping train behind 55 021 'Argyll & Sutherland Highlander'. Once back at Edinburgh and having spent some time in the local hostelry we chose to observe the overnight trains to the Cross. The first train, (1E35) 20:40 to King's Cross failed to get a Deltic so it was back to the pub for a couple of hours. We came back to see (1E40) 19:25 Aberdeen-King's Cross and this train did get a Deltic from Edinburgh and suitably enough it was 55 005. This was a good night for me to be on this train as not only was it number five but we were to be diverted via Leamside, Knottingley and Lincoln offering some rare track and extra mileage.

One of my next trips to Edinburgh was to be during April at a weekend when overnight trains were being diverted via Carlisle. When this was happening you could guarantee to see many Deltic bashers out and sure enough it was with my old friend 'Muir of Ord' that we headed north behind 55 021 on (1S72) 22:30 King's Cross-Edinburgh. At Carlisle we both left our welcoming compartment and made our way to an open carriage for milepost side seats so as to log the run over Beattock. It was a very pleasant spring morning and an enjoyable run was had. As we approached Edinburgh through Prince's Street Gardens we put our heads out of the window to see all the other Deltic bashers who were on the footbridge that crossed the line at this point. They had travelled north behind 55 013 'The Black Watch' on (1S66) 21:00 King's Cross-Edinburgh and when we saw them all we were treated to the sight of our friend Barney Rubble, who was completely mad about 55 021, seeing his favourite Deltic coming in from Carlisle and not being on the train. We found this most amusing, needless to say he was none too pleased even though he must have had it via Carlisle many times he still didn't like to miss out, especially as we had earlier been diverted via Cambridge and Leamside as well.

At the beginning of May I had another two-week rover spent chasing the Deltics. A couple of days into the first week I found myself at King's Cross for the overnight trains after an evening in the local hostelry. I was a bit late back at the station and therefore I was unable to identify the Deltic on (1S70) 22:15 King's Cross-Aberdeen. At least it was a Deltic so that was a good sign, as it would increase my chances in the morning at Edinburgh. The next departure was (1S72) 22:30 to Edinburgh and as this produced 55 010 'The King's own Scottish Borderer' I decided to board the train, settle down for the night and enjoy a 393 mile run behind number ten. Arrival at Edinburgh was at about 06:00, so there was plenty of time for a wash and some breakfast before the morning departures. The first train to view was (1E08) 08:25 to Newcastle, which was a stopping train with six very grotty MK1's. It was not a train I liked to do too often and fortunately it produced a 'Peak', to the cries of, "Too many wheels"!

The next departure worth covering was (1A23) 08:50 to Aberdeen. If this worked it would be considered as a score but it was not to be, as it produced a class 47.

At about 09:15, I was standing on the concourse waiting to see what might appear for (1V93) 09:50 to Plymouth. This was most likely to produce a Deltic and was a good train from the point of view that it would offer a 410 mile round trip to York and also allow me to log a Deltic on a 12 or even 13 coach train on an interesting piece of the line. I then heard, above the hustle and bustle, the sound of twin Napiers but was unable to distinguish where it was coming from due to the overall roof of the station. I fully expected the loco to be 55 010, having forgotten about the previous night's 1S70, but a break in the railings allowed me to identify it as 55005, my machine, yes, I had scored big time! The ECML was, to a London based basher like me, always more interesting north of York. Sure, there wasn't so much high speed running, but the loco would be working harder and of course there was the 'Racing stretch' to look forward to. After coming to a stand in York in 32 minutes and 25 seconds from Darlington, there was time for a spot of lunch before the return to Edinburgh. This left York more or less on time and there was nothing special about the return but once again with my machine at the helm I was more than happy. Arrival back at Edinburgh was about six minutes late due to several severe signal checks north of Dunbar. The move now was to get something to eat and then cover (1E26) 16:30 Aberdeen-York, which a Deltic regularly worked if only from Edinburgh. On this evening 55 008 worked forward from Edinburgh, but with 55 004/5/16/21/22 all on Haymarket, I decided to reject number eight as 1E26 would not offer a good night's doss where as one of the overnight trains to King's Cross definitely would. The ideal train to head south on was (1E35) 20:20 Edinburgh-King's Cross as this was the only train that would guarantee a connection into the following morning's (1S12) 05:50 King's Cross-Aberdeen. Imagine the state I was in when those nice people at Haymarket turned out 55005 to work 1E35, I had scored again and all I was doing was the obvious move.

 I awoke in my compo the next morning and peered out of the window to discover we were at King's Cross with the station clock showing 04:30, Yuk. I now had to endure my most hated fester. King's Cross at that time of day among many dodgy individuals was not the most inviting of places, I can't imagine what it would be like today. At about 05:30, whilst waiting for the Deltic to appear for 1S12 I walked along the platform when, shock, horror, it was one great big hideous 'Duff', 'Banjo', 'Strummer' (we called the class 47's all these names) that was backing onto the train, I was heavily bowled! There would be nothing now until (1D00) 08:05 King's Cross-Hull, so I decided to continue the fester and get some breakfast when the buffet opened at 07:00. Once topped up with fodder, I was making my way along platform two to await the loco for 1D00 when out of Gasworks tunnel appeared none other than 'The Prince', I had scored again with number five.

 The only place I could go with my machine was Hull, so that's exactly what I did. Once there I had an hour to kill, so I thought as number five had run round fairly quickly I could repay the pleasure it had given me by setting to work and cleaning up the nameplate. 'The Prince of Wales's own Regiment of Yorkshire' wasn't the easiest nameplate to clean, apart from the obvious reason, the letters of the English regiments were much smaller than the Scottish ones and the racehorses, so therefore, much harder to get in between. I think they called this action between man and machine, bonding, or was it something completely different? We were soon on our way back to the Cross and once back I bade farewell to number five after about 30 hours of sheer pleasure. A couple of weeks later whilst heading north behind 55 022 'Royal Scots Grey' on (1D00) 08:05 King's Cross-Hull I met a friend we called Sylvester, he told me he was going to have a day at the lineside taking photographs and asked me to join him. We met up with Martin Hyman at Grantham and then all got into Sylvester's Hillman Imp and headed towards Little Bytham which is on the climb to Stoke Summit. I saw for the first time 55013 'The Black Watch' storm south in it's new blue coat of paint and silver embellishments that had been applied for it's proposed attendance at the 'Rainhill 150' cavalcade. It made a fine, eye-catching sight and I thought it looked quite good. Around this time David Essex was in a film called 'Silver Dream Racer' and the title song was called 'Silver Dream Machine'. Needless to say 55013 was nicknamed as the Silver Dream Machine from this point on. We saw about nine Deltics in five hours and we also had lunch in 'The Mallard' public house at Little Bytham.

On the last day of May I had one of my most amazing experiences involving a Deltic. With a group of friends we were heading south behind 55022 'Royal Scots Grey' on (1A31) 18:13 York-King's Cross. We decided to leave the train at Peterborough and await the arrival of (1A32) 17:43 Cleethorpes-King's Cross which should have been 55 010 'The King's own Scottish Borderer'. Sure enough, we didn't have to wait long before number ten arrived. About six of us boarded the train, which had second-class accommodation at the front, whilst the remaining people stood on the platform before heading back north to their homes. While the train stood in the station I was at the leading door window talking to a friend on the platform. I noticed the driver starting to wave, but couldn't make out what it was he meant. Another of my friends went to him to see what it was he wanted, my friend came towards me and told me the driver wanted to talk to me. I left the train and walked towards him not knowing what he could possibly want. When I got to him he said, "Are you going to London"? "Yes", I replied. "You can come and sit up front then if you like" the driver said. As quick as a flash I opened the sliding cab door and entered into the most amazing place on the planet, the cab of a Deltic. I settled into the secondman's seat, as this turn was driver only. We then started to pull away.

It was an amazing experience as we slowly rumbled out of the station, the sound from behind us was totally unlike it was from the outside, it seemed to have more of a whistle about it when power was applied and it also sounded as though there was a lot more going on in their rather than just the deep drone you hear from the platform end as a Deltic pulls away.

After a while I became familiar to my new surroundings and thought of all my previous exploits with number ten, which now culminated in this experience. As we forged our way south on full power the driver told me that when I saw a board with a 'W' on it that I could operate the horn. Was it bliss or what? Soon the driver applied the brakes for our Huntingdon stop where we had to turn off the main line and onto the platform road. We were soon on our way again and regaining the main line the driver applied full power, this then made number ten scream out, but soon our speed increased. I noticed that our speed seemed to increase all the time although from my position I was unable to see the speedometer. As we passed Biggleswade I thought I would take a speed using the stopwatch that was on my wristwatch. I realised we were travelling at 110 mph and the driver didn't touch the power handle from the moment he applied full power leaving Huntingdon until he shut off to brake for our Stevenage stop. Awesome.

As we sped on we passed Hatfield, on the platform were a couple of enthusiasts who took our photograph. As we passed them the driver blew the horn and waved to them. I thought he was obviously someone who enjoyed his job and appreciated people taking an interest in it. One thing I did notice sitting high up in a Deltic cab is that it made me feel like I was on top of the world, as everybody and everything seemed to be below me. A very grand feeling. All too soon we pulled slowly in to platform 7 at King's Cross, I thanked the driver very much for his kind invitation and as I stepped down onto the platform from the cab of the Deltic I felt I was floating. It had been a truly memorable experience. By this time nearly every free minute I had was spent out chasing Deltics on the ECML, photographing them and when on the trains logging their performance. Most of the time was spent between King's Cross and Doncaster with the occasional trip to Hull and York. However, during the middle of June 1980 I seized upon an opportunity for a minor deviation from the norm. There was a regular loco-hauled Leeds-King's Cross and return working which was necessary while an HST set was being used for training purposes. The trains were re-timed for loco-haulage and would quite often get a Deltic.

I had found out that on this particular day 55 009 'Alycidon' was diagrammed to work (1A14) 10:45 Leeds-King's Cross. The only problem was getting to Leeds for it. It was possible to take the 07:45 King's Cross-Bradford HST to Leeds or take (1D00) 08:05 King's Cross-Hull, Deltic hauled to Doncaster for the 08:50 King's Cross-Harrogate HST to Wakefield and take 1A14 from there as it was non-stop Wakefield-King's Cross. On this occasion I decided to take the latter option, 55 014 obliged on 1D00 before catching the following HST to Wakefield where on arrival 55 009 was already approaching. By this stage in the Deltics' lives it was nice to get a train that didn't stop at all stations between Huntingdon and Doncaster, so a non-stop run like this was a special treat and number nine didn't disappoint us with a maximum speed of 110 mph on the run to the Capital. The overall Deltic situation was now quite good compared to a couple of years earlier.

For example on the date of the above run with 55 009, 13th June 1980 only two Deltics were in Doncaster Works. 55 004 was undergoing a 'Light' repair and 55

017, which actually entered Works on that day for a power unit change, having failed on the previous night's (1S70) 22:15 King's Cross-Aberdeen. By August of 1980 there was talk again about the possible withdrawal of another Deltic. The word was that it would be between 55 003 'Meld' and 55 010 'The King's own Scottish Borderer'. The reason for this was that these were the next two locos due an Intermediate repair and the word was that one of them would get the repair and the other would be withdrawn at the end of the year. This was obviously not good news for Deltic followers, personally I was rather fond of these two machines so I tried to chase both of them that extra bit more. During the middle of the month I was fortunate to go to Cleethorpes with number ten. This was always a fairly common destination for Deltics during the last few years of their lives, but nonetheless always regarded as a bit of a score if you were in position to take a Deltic there.

It was by now quite noticeable the appalling state that number ten was in. It had lost a nameplate and the bodyside was riddled with holes, some of which were quite large. It really looked that this machine was playing out it's final months, especially later that day when it failed while working a King's Cross-Hull train. In contrast 55 003 was quite a reliable performer and on my return from Cleethorpes with 55 010 I was fortunate to find number three waiting to work 'The Hull Executive'. This was too good an opportunity to miss. However, due to a signal failure we left King's Cross 26 minutes late. This meant we were only five minutes in front of the following HST and we had lost our path amongst all the evening commuter trains. But 'Meld' was as reliable as ever and produced a scintillating piece of running with a top speed of 111 mph. It wasn't long before her fate was sealed and number ten got the call to Doncaster Works for the all important Intermediate repair, 'Meld' was doomed. Some people began to wonder if there was a hidden agenda after the first two withdrawals were both racehorses and now the third to go was also to be a Finsbury Park Deltic.

After the decision had been taken that 'Meld' was next in line for withdrawal she became a popular loco, as everybody seemed to chase her so as to pay their respects to an old friend who wasn't long for this world. Rumours began to spread when 'Meld' was ensconced inside Finsbury Park for attention from September 21st until October 24th, over a month out of action, but happily she returned for a week before another visit ended by a call to Doncaster Works for repairs before she embarked on her final stint of duty. By the middle of September it was time for me to spend another two-week session out on the road in the search for Deltics. I would usually try and travel on trains that I didn't usually travel on, such as the Edinburgh-Plymouth train and other Scottish based workings. When the May 1980 timetable was introduced there was a working that would see a Deltic work (1E10) 09:10 Dundee-King's Cross, although I don't believe a Deltic was ever diagrammed to work this train from Dundee. In practice the loco that took the empty stock to Dundee would invariably work all the way to King's Cross. If you arrived at

Edinburgh early enough on an overnight train from the south you would be able to see the empty working pass through the station and therefore you would know whether to go to Dundee for it if it was a Deltic. My first time of doing this I was rewarded with a run south from Dundee behind 55 011, which I took as far as York.

The following morning I was at King's Cross with my old friend Chris Short. We walked along the platform to board (1D00) 08:05 King's Cross-Hull behind his favourite Deltic, 55 018 'Ballymoss'. As we were admiring number eighteen, the driver signalled to us and invited us in for a ride. Bull's-eye. Twice inside three months I had been given a cab ride in a Deltic. This time, however, I had to stand, as this train was double-manned, so Chris and I stood behind the crew as we headed north out of King's Cross. The driver said we could stay in the cab as far as Peterborough just in case there was someone in authority knocking about. It was still a wonderful experience to have had a cab ride both ways between Peterborough and King's Cross. The following week I travelled behind 55 009 'Alycidon' on the Dundee-King's Cross working throughout and in the process I recorded my fastest ever speed behind a Deltic north of the border, 109 mph north of Dunbar. This two week rover ended in satisfying fashion when I travelled behind 55 003 'Meld' on 1E35 20:45 Edinburgh-King's Cross throughout, diverted via Knottingley and Lincoln.

I then had to endure one week back at work before I had yet another two week rover chasing Deltics! During the early part of my first week back on the road I once again covered the Dundee-King's Cross and was rewarded with 55 005 doing the honours. As an extra bonus the stock was marshalled the wrong way round so that second class accommodation was at the south end enabling me to sit right behind my machine throughout. The following Sunday a few daytime trains were to be diverted via Cambridge. From King's Cross I travelled behind 55015 'Tulyar' on (1N02) 08:40 to Newcastle via the main line to Peterborough to await the arrival of (1A01) 08:30 Hull-King's Cross. I knew that the loco in the diagram for this was once again 55 005 and sure enough 'The Prince' performed the honours for me on a daytime diversion via Cambridge. Later that week whilst enduring an unsuccessful overnight search for Deltics I found myself at Doncaster in the wee small hours. No Deltics worked north from King's Cross on this night so eventually I decided to head towards Doncaster for the southbound workings. There had been three Deltics in Scotland, so I was hoping to pick one of them up on it's way south. Unfortunately 55016 worked only as far as York, 55017 worked (1A45) 22:55 Newcastle-King's Cross, having worked south from Edinburgh earlier in the evening. This was an early southbound overnight and therefore I wasn't at Doncaster in time for it. Unfortunately the other Deltic was 55005, likewise I was not at Doncaster for this as 'The Prince' worked (1E35) 20:25 Edinburgh-King's Cross. Disaster, all I could hope for now was for York to re-engine something with a Deltic.

Fortunately though 55 007 'Pinza' had just been outshopped from Doncaster

Works after a 'Light' repair and she appeared at the station and was put in a bay road to await (1N12) 00:02 King's Cross-Newcastle. That was a relief otherwise the night, with little sleep would have been a complete disaster. On arrival at Newcastle, with no Deltics in Scotland there was only one way to go, south. I took the first HST south to York so as to be in position for (1A08) 08:05 York-King's Cross with 55006 at the helm. This was another successful two-week period spent chasing the Deltics, in fact I had been out and about with them for four weeks out of five having had two two-week rovers. By late 1980, 55003 'Meld' was a very sought after loco, due to it's believed impending demise. However, it seemed to spend a lot of time out of action at Finsbury Park and therefore it became quite elusive. Also around this time I suffered one of my very rare failures with a Deltic. The culprit was 55012 'Crepello' which expired at Huntingdon whilst working (1A34) 19:55 York-King's Cross. Not a good train to fail on, as it was due in the Cross at 22:56 which always meant a late night at the best of times, but when I had to get up for work at 05:50 it was definitely worse. We had to await the arrival of a Class 31 and finally arrived at King's Cross at about 00:15.

I only ever suffered four Deltic failures where I was left stranded in the middle of nowhere, which considering I had almost 2000 runs behind them is pretty impressive. During December 55002 was restored to two-tone green after receiving the final Intermediate repair on a Deltic and therefore a lot of us descended on the ECML so as to see and ride behind KOYLI on it's first train in this condition. After a ceremony at the NRM it worked (1A22) 14:10 York-King's Cross which I boarded at Doncaster. It had been over 15 years since I had seen a Deltic in this livery and to my untrained eye it didn't seem quite right. The lighter green didn't seem to be correct and neither did the grey paint around the cab windows. It also looked a bit odd with the plated over route indicator panel, but at least an effort had been made to try and make it look a little special. About three days before Christmas I had my final run behind 'Meld' and she was still performing admirably to the end. She was to be withdrawn just before the end of the year having left King's Cross for the last time on an additional train on Christmas Eve. I had seen her pass through Doncaster in the evening light and I paid my last farewell to a very popular machine. The withdrawal of 'Meld' was in a way more significant than the earlier withdrawals of 'St. Paddy' and 'Nimbus'. Where as they had been out of traffic for about 18 months 'Meld' was taken out of traffic and withdrawn almost immediately. With the dawn of 1981, I purchased for the first time a privilege season ticket valid between King's Cross and Doncaster for three months costing £110. This was a sound investment allowing me to travel at will without the need for a multitude of tickets and allowed me to save a lot of money as well. The first week of the New Year saw the final Deltic workings of 'The Hull Executive'. I travelled on the train all week and Finsbury Park once again turned out an immaculate 55015 and for the final runs 55007. They carried the headboard all week and rumour was that had she survived 'Meld' was to have had the honour of working the final train. A real shock for Deltic bashers came at the beginning of February when we learnt of the impending withdrawal of 55005 and 55006! Not my machine, surely? I thought it was a wind up initially, but it was the truth. The reason given was that these two were the next on the list for an Intermediate repair. 'Meld' had been withdrawn for this same reason so I suppose it was logical to carry this on. My final run behind 55005 was about a week before the end of her life from King's Cross to Doncaster and she performed admirably once again. Within a fortnight 'The Prince' could be seen languishing outside Doncaster Works with nameplates removed. It was a sorry sight to see my favourite Deltic awaiting the call to enter the Works for the final time. There were a lot of disgruntled Deltic bashers around at this time due to the withdrawal of these two Deltics.

They were both fit to carry on in service and the demise of 55006 sent some people absolutely livid. This particular Deltic had long been regarded as possibly the finest performer in the fleet and to this day, many enthusiasts still think she was. Later that month 55022 was bestowed with a headboard courtesy of the Deltic Preservation Society to celebrate her 20th anniversary since entering traffic. This was a bright note in a period of gloom when we were wondering which Deltic was to be next to be withdrawn. There always seemed to be crowds of people out chasing Deltics now and it was a far cry from a few years earlier when I used to leave King's Cross on a morning departure with the leading coach to myself and listen to the sound of twin Napiers performing just for me. At weekends it almost became unbearable with young enthusiasts shouting, screaming and running up and down the train. I suppose this was inevitable as the Deltics entered their final year.

The grapevine started sending messages out about which Deltic was next for the axe. It came as no surprise when 55 012 'Crepello' became the prime candidate. Its bodywork was in a deplorable condition and it seemed to spend long periods out of action. It was also the next one due for an intermediate repair. This was inevitably the reason that would send yet another racehorse to an early grave. During February and March I chased after 'Crepello' quite a bit, until descending Stoke bank behind her on (1A13) 09:33 Hull-King's Cross I attained the landmark of travelling 10,000 miles behind her. During her final months, she didn't perform as though she was about to be pensioned off, in fact quite the opposite. I had a couple of runs behind her where 114 mph was recorded. 'Crepello', named after arguably the finest racehorse in history according to the experts, was going out in style. At about this time I was making full use of my season ticket. For example if I was due to start work at 15:00, I would take (1D00) 08:05 King's Cross-Hull as far as Doncaster and return on (1A13) 09:33 Hull-King's Cross, arriving back in London soon after 13:00. If I was finishing work at 15:00 I would travel to the Cross for (1L44) 16:05 King's Cross-York and have several options before returning on (1A34) 19:55 York-King's Cross, arriving back at 22:56. If I was working nights, starting at 23:00, I would again be at the Cross for (1L44) at 16:05 but would be back in London on (1A31) 18:10 York-King's Cross, due in just after 21:00. Finally if I was rest day I would quite often be out the night before and catch an overnight train to Edinburgh for either an opportunity to go to Aberdeen or to travel on (1V93) 09:50 Edinburgh-Plymouth as far as York.

The general performance of the Deltics during the spring was consistently high. I achieved many personal records with them and recorded some very high speeds. There were several instances of the locos recording speeds of 120 mph and knowing the people that logged these speeds, I have absolutely no reason to doubt them. I used to keep track of my fastest start to stop times behind the fleet and many of these records were quite literally taken to the cleaners. It was an amazing 'Indian Summer' for the fleet as they were by now into their final months of service and they just seemed to get better and better. In May, I had what turned out to be my final two-week period out on the road chasing the Deltics. The fortnight started off behind 'Crepello', not knowing that in two weeks time she would be the next casualty. I was also fortunate enough to travel in a sleeper behind her that night as well. Travelling in sleepers became more and more popular because being out on the road without returning home for a week at a time would take its toll. So, armed with a holdall full of the bare minimum in the way of clean clothes and toiletries, we would set off in pursuit of our prey. By the time of their final demise I had ridden in a sleeper behind 15 different members of the class.

During the second week of my stint on the ECML I met up with 'Crepello' for what would be the final time. I was travelling south overnight behind 55004 on (1E35) 20:25 Edinburgh-King's Cross and as we pulled into York I was awoken by Paul Gash telling me that 55012 was just arriving on (1S72) 22:30 King's Cross-Edinburgh. So we baled out and crossed the platform to return to Edinburgh behind the ageing racehorse. At Edinburgh the next morning she was turned out to work (1A23) 08:55 Edinburgh-Aberdeen. It was to be her final northbound journey. I was most satisfied to get a dose of her to Aberdeen and back before I returned south to King's Cross behind 55016 'Gordon Highlander'. Paul Gash was sitting with the rest of us on (1E35) 20:25 Edinburgh-King's Cross but he disappeared shortly before departure leaving his bag to sample the delights of 55016 while he, we assumed, would follow on a later train. He was re-united with his bag the next day, having travelled south behind 55012 on (1E39) 22:30 Edinburgh-King's Cross — number twelve's final working.

The end of May brought about the demise of nearly all the King's Cross-Hull trains due to the delivery of another batch of H.S.T.'s. On the final Saturday I had been working the night shift but there was no way I was going to miss travelling on the train that had started many Deltic bashing days for me — (1D00) 08:05 King's Cross-Hull. I had also had 19 Deltics to Hull, the only one (apart from 'St. Paddy and 'Nimbus') to elude me thus far was 55013 'The Black Watch'. I arrived at the Cross at about 07:50 and met up with a group of friends. The Deltic was already on the front of the train and when I asked for its identify, I was told it was 55013! Just what the doctor ordered I thought!

The start of the new timetable was delayed until June 1, 1981. Initially things were not good. After 1S12 at 05:50 from King's Cross the next departure was at 09:40, this was basically the old 10:05 retimed and booked on the slow line before picking up pretty much it's old path. The 12:05 to York replaced the 12:05 and 12:20 departures and the 14:03 and 16:03 trains ran pretty much as before. The 18:05 to York now left at 17:40 and stopped at Biggleswade, then all stations to York! The 'up' trains suffered as well, with most timings being eased presumably to accommodate lesser power after the Deltics demise that was now known to be set for January 1982.

My first few runs with Deltics in this new timetable also showed a deterioration in their performance as well. Most runs were pedestrian compared to the previous few months but by the end of the month they started to perform to the best once more. With fewer diagrams, the 'moves' became less varied and I would usually arrive at the Cross and go to York and back with whatever turned up as opposed to travelling behind several different locos during an afternoon's bashing.

Fewer Deltic hauled trains meant that more and more newcomers were appearing on the scene and subsequently most trains were full of people trying to get Deltic haulage. This was starting to take the edge off chasing Deltics for me as more and more people continued to appear. At the beginning of August I went into semi-retirement from Deltic bashing, this was not brought about by the situation on the trains but by the fact that I had met my future wife.

The timing of her arrival on the scene for me was impeccable, as it allowed me to slowly drift away from Deltic bashing. I travelled on my final Deltic-hauled service train at the end of November when I did an out and back to York behind 55 007 'Pinza'. I was not out at all during December and I don't regret it one bit. I am glad that I wasn't there to see those 22 old friends passing away one by one. All that running on one engine only and being flogged to death? No, I remember them as the 'Kings' of the ECML. So it was to 2nd January 1982 when I travelled on 'The Deltic Scotsman Farewell'. I had a ticket in a party of all my old Deltic bashing friends so we could see the passing of an era together. The outward journey was of course entrusted to 'Tulyar' and how superb she looked on that bleak morning at the Cross and how appropriate it was that an old Finsbury Park stalwart should be given the honour of hauling the last Deltic-hauled train out of the Capital. She performed beautifully on the journey north, but oh, what a pathetic rake of coaches. They were so appalling that speed was limited to 90 mph. For the return journey there could be only one choice — D9000/55 022 'Royal Scots Grey'. During the preceding couple of months her reliability had been pretty poor to say the least but on that final day she was superb. Who can forget the way she accelerated away from the signal stop north of Stevenage? I recall that on that final southbound run that the pass through York was quite breathtaking. The amount of people that turned out to witness the end of a legend was incredible and from that moment on the atmosphere on the train seemed to change.

36 MEMOIRS OF AN OLD FOOL

We knew now that we were on the final leg of our hobby and our way of life. The arrival scenes at the Cross have been well documented and so I will leave them alone. But after 'RSG' had finally left the Cross, we adjourned to our favourite watering hole — 'The Malt & Hops'. We had a few drinks before saying goodbye to old friends with whom we had enjoyed some memorable experiences over the preceding years.

Some of those people remain good friends to this day but others such as 'Kippers', Mick Feeney and 'Harry Hall' to name just a few, I haven't seen since . Thank you Deltics and thank you fellow Deltic bashers, we had some great, never to be repeated times,but the memories of them all will stay with us forever.

Above: The Deltics made hundreds of works visits during their lives and I have tried to provide details of them all in this publication. This has been a mammoth task but I feel their inclusion makes this tribute to the ECML legends quite unique. But as I mentioned in my introduction, there are still discrepancies in certain areas, particularly with regard to the loss of the double windscreen wipers. However, the works visits form the major part of this book and one of the class, 55011 The Royal Northumberland Fusiliers is captured by the camera undergoing attention in the diesel repair shop at Doncaster Works on March 12th, 1978.
Picture: L. P. Gater

Above: The first member of the class to reach two million miles in traffic was D9010/55010 The King's Own Scottish Borderer which is seen here at York station with the 11.00 King's Cross-Edinburgh on Saturday, April 30, 1977. Picture: L. P. Gater.

Above: In their formative days...quite literally! The Deltics were delivered in two-tone green and un-named to Doncaster Works. Here D9014 is captured by Les Feasby in the works yard on October 8th, 1961. The loco had arrived from builders English Electric on September 29th. D9014 is awaiting trials that were undertaken later in the week. Picture: L. Feasby.

2 Fact Files

D9000/9000/55 022

ENGLISH ELECTRIC WORKS NO: 2905; VULCAN FOUNDRY NO: D557; DELIVERED: 28/02/1961; TO TRAFFIC: 09/03/1961; NAMED: 18/06/1962; LOCATION OF NAMING: Edinburgh Waverley; DUAL BRAKED: 03/11/1967; FULL YELLOW ENDS ADDED TO GREEN LIVERY: N/A; PAINTED INTO BLUE: 03/11/1967; E.T.H. FITTED: 30/10/1971; RENUMBERED: 10/04/1974; ROUTE INDICATOR REMOVAL: N/A; FINSBURY PARK STYLE WHITE CABS: N/A; ALLOCATION HISTORY: 28/02/1961-03/12/1967 - Haymarket; 03/12/1967-16/06/1968 - Finsbury Park; 16/06/1968-13/05/1979 Haymarket; 13/05/1979-02/01/1982 - York; LAST TRAIN: (1F50) 14:30 Edinburgh-King's Cross "Deltic Scotsman Farewell" - 02/01/1982; WITHDRAWN: 02/01/1982 - York; REASON FOR WITHDRAWAL: Rundown of class; DATE ARRIVED AT DONCASTER: 05/01/1982; DISPOSAL: Preserved by the Deltic 9000 Fund; RECORDED WORKS VISITS: Doncaster 120; St. Rollox 2; R.S.H. Darlington 1; Stratford D.R.S. 3; Total: 126

D9001/9001/55 001

ENGLISH ELECTRIC WORKS NO: 2906; VULCAN FOUNDRY NO: D558; DELIVERED: 16/01/1961; TO TRAFFIC: 23/02/1961; NAMED: 20/07/1961; LOCATION OF NAMING: Doncaster Works; DUAL BRAKED: 29/03/1968; FULL YELLOW ENDS ADDED TO GREEN LIVERY: 30/03/1967; PAINTED INTO BLUE: 26/07/1969; E.T.H. FITTED: 26/03/1971; RENUMBERED: 07/02/1974; ROUTE INDICATOR REMOVAL: 27/02/1977; FP STYLE WHITE CABS: N/A; ALLOCATION HISTORY: 23/02/1961-03/12/1967 Finsbury Park; 03/12/1967-16/06/1968 Haymarket; 16/06/1968-05/01/1980 Finsbury Park; LAST TRAIN: (1S16) 08:00 King's Cross-Edinburgh to Doncaster – 24/03/1978; WITHDRAWN: 05/01/1980 – Doncaster Works; REASON FOR WITHDRAWAL: Cannibalised - beyond economic repair, rundown of class; DATE ARRIVED AT DONCASTER: 24/03/1978; DISPOSAL: Cut up at Doncaster 02/1980; RECORDED WORKS VISITS: Doncaster 113; Vulcan Foundry 2; Total: 115.

D9002/9002/55 002

ENGLISH ELECTRIC WORKS No: 2907; VULCAN FOUNDRY No: D559; DELIVERED: 09/03/1961; TO TRAFFIC: by 22/03/1961; NAMED: 04/04/1963; LOCATION OF NAMING: York; DUAL BRAKED: 24/11/67; DATE FULL YELLOW ENDS ADDED TO GREEN LIVERY: N/A; PAINTED INTO BLUE: 18/10/1966; RE:PAINTED INTO GREEN: 11/12/1980; E.T.H. FITTED: 04/05/1971; RENUMBERED: 08/12/1973; ROUTE INDICATOR REMOVAL: 10/11/1976; FP STYLE WHITE CABS: N/A; ALLOCATION HISTORY: 09/03/1961-13/05/1979 - Gateshead; 13/05/1979-02/01/1982 - York; LAST TRAIN: (1E98) 12:05 Liverpool:York – 30/12/1981; WITHDRAWN: 02/01/1982 - York; REASON FOR WITHDRAWAL: Rundown of class; DATE ARRIVED AT DONCASTER: N/A; DISPOSAL: Preserved as part of the National collection in the National Railway Museum, York;
RECORDED WORKS VISITS: Doncaster 106; R.S.H. Darlington 1; Stratford D.R.S. 2;
Total: 109

D9003/9003/55 003

ENGLISH ELECTRIC WORKS No: 2908; VULCAN FOUNDRY No: D560; DELIVERED: 27/03/1961; TO TRAFFIC: Not recorded; NAMED: 12/07/1961; LOCATION OF NAMING: Doncaster Works; DUAL BRAKED: 14/02/1968; FULL YELLOW ENDS ADDED TO GREEN LIVERY: 25/05/1967; PAINTED INTO BLUE: 14/02/1968; E.T.H. FITTED:05/12/1970; DATE RENUMBERED: w/e 23/02/1974; ROUTE INDICATOR REMOVAL:14/01/1977; FP STYLE WHITE CABS: 07/04/1979 ALLOCATION HISTORY: 27/03/1961-03/12/1967 - Finsbury Park; 03/12/1967-16/06/1968 - Haymarket; 16/06/1968-30/12/1980 - Finsbury Park; LAST TRAIN: (1S27) 07:22 Plymouth:Edinburgh from York to Newcastle – 29/12/1980; WITHDRAWN: 30/12/1980- York; REASON FOR WITHDRAWAL: Overdue Intermediate repair, rundown of class; DATE ARRIVED AT DONCASTER: 31/12/1980; DISPOSAL: Cut up at Doncaster 03/1981; RECORDED WORKS VISITS: Doncaster 111; Vulcan Foundry 3; R.S.H. Darlington 2; Stratford D.R.S. 1; Total: 117.

D9004/9004/55 004

ENGLISH ELECTRIC WORKS No: 2909; VULCAN FOUNDRY No: D561 DELIVERED:18/05/1961; TO TRAFFIC: Not recorded; NAMED: 23/05/1964 LOCATION OF NAMING: Inverness; DUAL BRAKED: 12/01/1968 FULL YELLOW ENDS ADDED TO GREEN LIVERY: N/A; PAINTED INTO BLUE: 12/01/1968; E.T.H. FITTED: 27/08/1971; RENUMBERED: 01/05/1974; ROUTE INDICATOR REMOVAL: 19/03/1977; FP STYLE WHITE CABS: N/A; ALLOCATION HISTORY: 18/05/1961-13/05/1979 - Haymarket; 13/05/1979-01/11/1981 - York; LAST TRAIN: (1M76) 15:50 York-Liverpool – 28/10/1981; WITHDRAWN: 01/11/1981 - Stratford; REASON FOR WITHDRAWAL:To provide a good power unit for 55 008; DATE ARRIVED AT DONCASTER: 05/01/1982; DISPOSAL: Cut up at Doncaster 07/1983 RECORDED WORKS VISITS: Doncaster 123; Vulcan Foundry 1; Stratford D.R.S. 1; Total: 125.

D9005/9005/55 005

ENGLISH ELECTRIC WORKS No: 2910; VULCAN FOUNDRY No: D562; DELIVERED: 25/05/1961; TO TRAFFIC: Not recorded; NAMED: 08/10/1963; LOCATION OF NAMING: York; DUAL BRAKED: 25/04/1968; FULL YELLOW ENDS ADDED TO GREEN LIVERY:15/04/1967; PAINTED INTO BLUE: 21/08/1969; E.T.H. FITTED: 17/04/1971; DATE RENUMBERED: 25/01/1974; ROUTE INDICATOR REMOVAL: 21/10/1977; FP STYLE WHITE CABS: N/A; ALLOCATION HISTORY: 25/05/1961-13/05/1979 - Gateshead; 13/05/1979-03/02/1981 - York; LAST TRAIN: (1E24) 22:50 Shrewsbury:York from Leeds 29-30/01/1981; WITHDRAWN: 03/02/1981 - York
REASON FOR WITHDRAWAL: Due Intermediate repair, rundown of class DATE ARRIVED AT DONCASTER: 21/02/1981; DISPOSAL: Cut up at Doncaster 02/1983; RECORDED WORKS VISITS: Doncaster 116; R.S.H. Darlington 1; Total: 117

D9006/9006/55 006

ENGLISH ELECTRIC WORKS No: 2911; VULCAN FOUNDRY No: D563; DELIVERED: 29/06/1961; TO TRAFFIC: Not recorded; NAMED: 05/12/1964; LOCATION OF NAMING: Cupar; DUAL BRAKED: 11/04/1968; FULL YELLOW ENDS ADDED TO GREEN LIVERY: 07/04/1967 ; PAINTED INTO BLUE: 21/06/1969; E.T.H. FITTED: 05/03/1971; RENUMBERED: 06/03/1974; ROUTE INDICATOR REMOVAL: 28/06/1977; FP STYLE WHITE CABS: N/A; ALLOCATION HISTORY: 29/06/1961-13/05/1979 - Haymarket; 13/05/1979- 08/02/1981 - York; LAST TRAIN: (5E74) 19.00 Newcastle-York — 06/02/1981; WITHDRAWN: 08/02/1981- York; REASON FOR WITHDRAWAL: Due Intermediate repair, rundown of class; DATE ARRIVED AT DONCASTER: 09/02/1981; DISPOSAL: Cut up at Doncaster 07/1981; RECORDED WORKS VISITS: Doncaster 108; Total: 108

D9007/9007/55 007

ENGLISH ELECTRIC WORKS NO: 2912; VULCAN FOUNDRY NO. D564; DATE DELIVERED: 22/06/1961; DATE TO TRAFFIC: Not recorded; DATE NAMED: 22/06/1961; LOCATION OF NAMING: Doncaster Works; DATE DUAL BRAKED: 14/12/1968; DATE FULL YELLOW ENDS ADDED TO GREEN LIVERY: 12/01/1967; DATE PAINTED INTO BLUE: 24/10/1967; DATE E.T.H. FITTED: 18/12/1971; DATE RENUMBERED: w/e 16/02/1974; ROUTE INDICATOR REMOVAL: 29/04/1979; FP STYLE WHITE CABS: 03/08/1979: ALLOCATION HISTORY: 22/06/1961-31/05/1981 - Finsbury PARK; 31/05/1981- 31/12/1981 - York; LAST TRAIN : (1A08) 08:07 York-King's Cross failed at Doncaster, assisted forward by 47 146 - 30/12/1981; DATE WITHDRAWN: 31/12/1981 - York; REASON FOR WITHDRAWAL: Both engines defective, rundown of class; DATE ARRIVED AT DONCASTER: 04/01/1982; DISPOSAL: Cut up at Doncaster Works 08/1982; RECORDED WORKS VISITS: Doncaster 110; Vulcan Foundry 1; R.S.H. Darlington 2; Stratford D.R.S. 1; Total: 114

D9008/9008/55 008

ENGLISH ELECTRIC WORKS NO: 2913; VULCAN FOUNDRY NO: D565; DATE DELIVERED: 07/07/1961; DATE TO TRAFFIC: Not recorded; DATE NAMED: 30/09/1963; LOCATION OF NAMING: Darlington; DATE DUAL BRAKED: 1705/1968; DATE FULL YELLOW ENDS ADDED TO GREEN LIVERY: N/A; DATE PAINTED INTO BLUE: 01/07/1967; DATE E.T.H. FITTED: 02/10/1971; DATE RENUMBERED: 31/01/1974; ROUTE INDICATOR REMOVAL: N/A; FP STYLE WHITE CABS: N/A; ALLOCATION HISTORY: 07/07/1961-13/05/1979 - Gateshead; 13/05/1979-31/12/1981 - York; LAST TRAIN: 1E48 21:20 Aberdeen-King's Cross from Edinburgh 29-30/12/1981; DATE WITHDRAWN: 31/12/1981 - Finsbury Park; REASON FOR WITHDRAWAL: Rundown of class; DATE ARRIVED AT DONCASTER: 23/01/1982; DISPOSAL: Cut up at Doncaster Works 08/1982; No.2 end cab preserved; RECORDED WORKS VISITS: Doncaster 101; R.S.H. Darlington 3; Stratford D.R.S. 1; Total: 105

D9009/9009/55 009

ENGLISH ELECTRIC WORKS NO: 2914; VULCAN FOUNDRY NO: D566; DATE DELIVERED: 21/07/1961; DATE TO TRAFFIC: by 29/07/1961; DATE NAMED: 21/07/1961; LOCATION OF NAMING: Doncaster Works; DATE DUAL BRAKED: 14/06/1968; DATE FULL YELLOW ENDS ADDED TO GREEN LIVERY: 15/03/1967; DATE PAINTED INTO BLUE: 14/06/1968; DATE E.T.H. FITTED: 17/10/1970; DATE RENUMBERED: w/e 26/01/1974; ROUTE INDICATOR REMOVAL: 03/11/1978; FP STYLE WHITE CABS: 21/08/1979; ALLOCATION HISTORY: 21/07/1961-03/12/1967 - Finsbury Park; 03/12/1967-16/06/1968 - Haymarket; 16/06/1968-31/05/1981 Finsbury Park; 31/05/1981-02/01/1982 York; LAST TRAIN: 1A40 21:00 Newcastle-King's Cross - 30/12/1981; DATE WITHDRAWN: 02/01/1982 - York; REASON FOR WITHDRAWAL: Rundown of class; DATE ARRIVED AT DONCASTER: 05/01/1982; DISPOSAL: Preserved by The Deltic Preservation Society; RECORDED WORKS VISITS: Doncaster 124; R.S.H. Darlington 4; Stratford D.R.S. 1; Total: 129

D9010/9010/55010

ENGLISH ELECTRIC WORKS NO: 2915; VULCAN FOUNDRY NO: D567; DATE DELIVERED: 24/07/1961; DATE TO TRAFFIC: by 02/08/1961; DATE NAMED: 08/05/1965; LOCATION OF NAMING: Dumfries; DATE DUAL BRAKED: 01/02/1968; DATE FULL YELLOW ENDS ADDED TO GREEN LIVERY: 23/12/1966; DATE PAINTED INTO BLUE: 01/02/1968; DATE E.T.H. FITTED: 07/11/1970; DATE RENUMBERED: 16/06/1974; ROUTE INDICATOR REMOVAL: 17/12/1976; FP STYLE WHITE CABS: N/A; ALLOCATION HISTORY: 24/07/1961-13/05/1979 - Haymarket; 13/05/1979-24/12/1981 - York; LAST TRAIN: 1L22 23:00 King's Cross-Bradford failed at Corby Glen (assisted to Doncaster) - 23/12/1981; DATE WITHDRAWN: 24/12/1981 - Doncaster Works; REASON FOR WITHDRAWAL: Both engines defective, rundown of class; DATE ARRIVED AT DONCASTER: 24/12/1981; DISPOSAL: Cut up at Doncaster 05/1982; RECORDED WORKS VISITS: Doncaster 118; R.S.H. Darlington 1; Total: 119

D9011/9011/55011

ENGLISH ELECTRIC WORKS NO: 2916; VULCAN FOUNDRY NO: D568; DATE DELIVERED: 24/08/1961; DATE TO TRAFFIC: Not recorded; DATE NAMED: 28/05/1963; LOCATION OF NAMING: Newcastle; DATE DUAL BRAKED: 08/07/1968; DATE FULL YELLOW ENDS ADDED TO GREEN LIVERY: 11/05/1967; DATE PAINTED INTO BLUE: 08/07/1968; DATE E.T.H. FITTED: 06/08/1971; DATE RENUMBERED: w/e 16/02/1974; ROUTE INDICATOR REMOVAL: 22/05/1978; FP STYLE WHITE CABS: N/A; ALLOCATION HISTORY: 24/08/1961-13/05/1979 Gateshead; 13/05/1979-08/11/1981 York; LAST TRAIN: 1A45 22:55 Newcastle-King's Cross - 05/11/1981; DATE WITHDRAWN: 08/11/1981 - Stratford; REASON FOR WITHDRAWAL: To provide a good power unit for 55 022; DATE ARRIVED AT DONCASTER: 24/11/1981; DISPOSAL: Cut up at Doncaster - 12/1982; RECORDED WORKS VISITS: Doncaster 119; R.S.H. Darlington 1; Stratford D.R.S. 1; Total: 121

D9012/9012/55012

ENGLISH ELECTRIC WORKS NO: 2917; VULCAN FOUNDRY NO: D569; DATE DELIVERED: 04/09/1961; DATE TO TRAFFIC: 12/09/1961; DATE NAMED: 04/09/1961; LOCATION OF NAMING: Doncaster Works; DATE DUAL BRAKED: 20/03/1968; DATE FULL YELLOW ENDS ADDED TO GREEN LIVERY: 02/03/1967; DATE PAINTED INTO BLUE: 20/03/1968; DATE E.T.H. FITTED: 22/01/1971; DATE RENUMBERED: w/e 02/02/1974; ROUTE INDICATOR REMOVAL: 27/04/1977; FP STYLE WHITE CABS: 15/10/1979; ALLOCATION HISTORY: 04/09/1961-03/12/1967 - Finsbury Park; 03/12/1967-16/06/1968 - Haymarket; 16/06/1968-18/05/1981 - Finsbury Park; LAST TRAIN: 1E39 22:30 Edinburgh-King's Cross - 13/05/1981; DATE WITHDRAWN: 18/05/1981 - Finsbury Park; REASON FOR WITHDRAWAL: Overdue Intermediate repair, rundown of class; DATE ARRIVED AT DONCASTER: 15/06/1981; DISPOSAL: Cut up at Doncaster 09/1981; RECORDED WORKS VISITS: Doncaster 127; R.S.H. Darlington 1; Total 128

D9013/9013/55013

ENGLISH ELECTRIC WORKS NO: 2918; VULCAN FOUNDRY NO: D570; DATE DELIVERED: 14/09/1961; DATE TO TRAFFIC: Not recorded; DATE NAMED: 16/01/1963; LOCATION OF NAMING: Dundee West; DATE DUAL BRAKED: 18/12/1967; DATE FULL YELLOW ENDS ADDED TO GREEN LIVERY: 27/01/1967; DATE PAINTED INTO BLUE: 18/12/1967; DATE E.T.H. FITTED: 15/05/1971; DATE RENUMBERED: 28/02/1974; ROUTE INDICATOR REMOVAL: 12/12/1976; FP STYLE WHITE CABS: N/A; ALLOCATION HISTORY: 14/09/1961-25/02/1968 - Haymarket; 25/02/1968-16/06/1968 - Finsbury Park; 16/06/1968-13/05/1979 - Haymarket; 13/05/1979-20/12/1981 - York; LAST TRAIN: 1B26 07:23 Peterborough-King's Cross failed at Wood Green assisted forward by 31 292 - 16/12/1981; DATE WITHDRAWN: 20/12/1981 - Finsbury Park; REASON FOR WITHDRAWAL: Both power units defective, rundown of class; DATE ARRIVED AT DONCASTER: 23/01/1982; DISPOSAL: Cut up at Doncaster - 12/1982; RECORDED WORKS VISITS: Doncaster 130; R.S.H. Darlington 1; Total: 131

D9014/9014/55014

ENGLISH ELECTRIC WORKS NO: 2919; VULCAN FOUNDRY NO: D571; DATE DELIVERED: 29/09/1961; DATE TO TRAFFIC: 16/10/1961; DATE NAMED: 22/10/1963; LOCATION OF NAMING: Darlington; DATE DUAL BRAKED: 06/06/1968; DATE FULL YELLOW ENDS ADDED TO GREEN LIVERY: 09/06/1967; DATE PAINTED INTO BLUE: 18/11/1969; DATE E.T.H. FITTED: 23/07/1971; DATE RENUMBERED: 29/01/1974; ROUTE INDICATOR REMOVAL: 28/04/1978; FP STYLE WHITE CABS: N/A; ALLOCATION HISTORY: 29/09/1961-13/05/1979 - Gateshead; 13/05/1979-22/11/1981 York; LAST TRAIN: 1S14 08:10 Newcastle-Edinburgh failed at Cramlington assisted forward by 37 082 - 10/11/1981; DATE WITHDRAWN: 22/11/1981 - York; REASON FOR WITHDRAWAL: To provide spares, rundown of class; DATE ARRIVED AT DONCASTER: 05/12/1981 DISPOSAL: Cut up at Doncaster 02/1982: RECORDED WORKS VISITS: Doncaster 114; Vulcan Foundry 1; R.S.H. Darlington 1; Total: 116

D9015/9015/55015

ENGLISH ELECTRIC WORKS NO: 2920; VULCAN FOUNDRY NO: D572; DATE DELIVERED: 13/10/1961; DATE TO TRAFFIC: 23/10/1961; DATE NAMED: 13/10/1961; LOCATION OF NAMING: Doncaster Works; DATE DUAL BRAKED: 22/02/1968; DATE FULL YELLOW ENDS ADDED TO GREEN LIVERY: 02/02/1967; DATE PAINTED INTO BLUE: 02/05/1969 DATE E.T.H. FITTED: 13/02/1971 DATE RENUMBERED: w/e 02/02/1974; ROUTE INDICATOR REMOVAL: 29/06/1979; FP STYLE WHITE CABS: 12/07/1979; ALLOCATION HISTORY: 13/10/1961-31/05/1981 - Finsbury Park; 31/05/1981-02/01/1982 - York; LAST TRAIN: 1F50 08:30 King's Cross-Edinburgh 'Deltic Scotsman Farewell' - 02/01/1982; DATE WITHDRAWN: 02/01/1982 - York; REASON FOR WITHDRAWAL: Rundown of class; DATE ARRIVED AT DONCASTER: 05/01/1982 DISPOSAL; Preserved privately and later by The Deltic Preservation Society; RECORDED WORKS VISITS: Doncaster 125; R.S.H. Darlington 2; Stratford D.R.S. 1; Total: 128

D9016/9016/55016

ENGLISH ELECTRIC WORKS NO: 2921; VULCAN FOUNDRY NO: D573; DATE DELIVERED: 27/10/1961; DATE TO TRAFFIC: 06/11/1961; DATE NAMED: 28/07/1964; LOCATION OF NAMING: Aberdeen; DATE DUAL BRAKED: 07/10/1967; DATE FULL YELLOW ENDS ADDED TO GREEN LIVERY: N/A; DATE PAINTED INTO BLUE: 07/10/1967; DATE E.T.H. FITTED: 12/10/1971; DATE RENUMBERED: 16/03/1974; ROUTE INDICATOR REMOVAL: 27/04/1976; FP STYLE WHITE CABS: N/A; ALLOCATION HISTORY: 27/10/1961-03/12/1967 - Haymarket; 03/12/1967-16/06/1968 - Finsbury Park; 16/06/1968-13/05/1979 - Haymarket; 13/05/1979-30/12/1981 York; LAST TRAIN: 5L04 23:30 Hull-York - 23/12/1981; DATE WITHDRAWN: 30/12/1981 - York; REASON FOR WITHDRAWAL: Defective power unit and boiler, rundown of class; DATE ARRIVED AT DONCASTER: 05/01/1982 DISPOSAL: Preserved by the Deltic 9000 Fund; RECORDED WORKS VISITS: Doncaster 108; Total: 108

D9017/9017/55017

ENGLISH ELECTRIC WORKS NO: 2922; VULCAN FOUNDRY NO: D574; DATE DELIVERED: 10/11/1961; DATE TO TRAFFIC: Not recorded; DATE NAMED: 29/10/1963 LOCATION OF NAMING: Durham; DATE DUAL BRAKED: 08/05/1968; DATE FULL YELLOW ENDS ADDED TO GREEN LIVERY: 27/04/1967; DATE PAINTED INTO BLUE: 04/10/1969; DATE E.T.H. FITTED: 21/05/1971; DATE RENUMBERED: 03/02/1974; ROUTE INDICATOR REMOVAL: 19/01/1978; FP STYLE WHITE CABS: N/A; ALLOCATION HISTORY: 10/11/1961-13/05/1979 - Gateshead; 13/05/1979-31/12/1981 - York; LAST TRAIN: 1G26 18:58 Grantham-King's Cross failed at Knebworth assisted forward as 5G26 by 47 426 - 31/12/1981; DATE WITHDRAWN: 31/12/1981 - Finsbury Park; REASON FOR WITHDRAWAL: Rundown of class; DATE ARRIVED AT DONCASTER: 23/01/1982; DISPOSAL: Cut up at Doncaster Works 01/1983; RECORDED WORKS VISITS: Doncaster 101; R.S.H. Darlington 2; Total: 103

D9018/9018/55018

ENGLISH ELECTRIC WORKS NO: 2923; VULCAN FOUNDRY NO: D575; DATE DELIVERED: 24/11/1961; DATE TO TRAFFIC: 13/12/1961; DATE NAMED: 24/11/1961; LOCATION OF NAMING: Doncaster Works; DATE DUAL BRAKED: 07/03/1968; DATE FULL YELLOW ENDS ADDED TO GREEN LIVERY: 15/02/1967; DATE PAINTED INTO BLUE: 10/05/1969; DATE E.T.H. FITTED: 23/02/1971; DATE RENUMBERED: w/e 09/02/1974; ROUTE INDICATOR REMOVAL: 10/12/1977; FP STYLE WHITE CABS: 15/08/1979; ALLOCATION HISTORY: 24/11/1961-31/05/1981 - Finsbury Park; 31/05/1981-18/10/1981 - York; LAST TRAIN: 1D08 19:40 King's Cross-Hull to Doncaster - 12/10/1981; DATE WITHDRAWN: 18/10/1981 - York; REASON FOR WITHDRAWAL: To provide a power unit for 55 008, rundown of class; DATE ARRIVED AT DONCASTER: 24/11/1981; DISPOSAL: Cut up at Doncaster Works 01/1982; RECORDED WORKS VISITS: Doncaster 95; R.S.H. Darlington 1; Total: 96

D9019/9019/55019

ENGLISH ELECTRIC WORKS NO: 2924; VULCAN FOUNDRY NO: D576; DATE DELIVERED: 11/12/1961; DATE TO TRAFFIC: 19/12/1961 approx.; DATE NAMED: 11/09/1965; LOCATION OF NAMING: Glasgow Central; DATE DUAL BRAKED: 10/11/1967; DATE FULL YELLOW ENDS ADDED TO GREEN LIVERY: 15/03/1967; DATE PAINTED INTO BLUE: 10/11/1967 DATE E.T.H. FITTED: 24/04/1971; DATE RENUMBERED: 22/11/1973; ROUTE INDICATOR REMOVAL: 22/09/1976; FP STYLE WHITE CABS: N/A; ALLOCATION HISTORY: 11/12/1961-03/12/1967 Haymarket; 03/12/1967-16/06/1968 Finsbury Park; 16/06/1968-13/05/1979 - Haymarket 13/05/1979-31/12/1981 - York; LAST TRAIN: 1E26 16:30 Aberdeen-York from Edinburgh 31/12/1981; DATE WITHDRAWN: 31/12/1981 - York; REASON FOR WITHDRAWAL: Rundown of class DATE ARRIVED AT DONCASTER: 04/01/1982; DISPOSAL: Preserved by The Deltic Preservation Society; RECORDED WORKS VISITS: Doncaster 122; R.S.H. Darlington 1; Total: 123

D9020/9020/55020

ENGLISH ELECTRIC WORKS NO: 2925; VULCAN FOUNDRY NO: D577; DATE DELIVERED: 12/02/1962; DATE TO TRAFFIC: 21/02/1962; DATE NAMED: 12/02/1962; LOCATION OF NAMING: Doncaster Works; DATE DUAL BRAKED: 30/12/1967; DATE FULL YELLOW ENDS ADDED TO GREEN LIVERY: N/A; DATE PAINTED INTO BLUE: 30/12/1967; DATE E.T.H. FITTED: 08/04/1971; DATE RENUMBERED: 10/11/1973; ROUTE INDICATOR REMOVAL: N/A; FP STYLE WHITE CABS: N/A ALLOCATION HISTORY: 12/02/1962-05/01/1980 - Finsbury Park; LAST TRAIN: 4E05 19:15 Oxford-Newcastle from York 29-30/03/1978; DATE WITHDRAWN: 05/01/1980 - Doncaster Works; REASON FOR WITHDRAWAL: Cannibalised beyond economic repair, rundown of class; DATE ARRIVED AT DONCASTER: 25/04/1978; DISPOSAL: Cut up at Doncaster Works 01/1980; RECORDED WORKS VISITS: Doncaster 102; Total: 102

D9021/9021/55021

ENGLISH ELECTRIC WORKS NO: 2926; VULCAN FOUNDRY NO: D578; DATE DELIVERED: 16/03/1962; DATE TO TRAFFIC: 02/05/1962; DATE NAMED: 29/11/1963; LOCATION OF NAMING: Stirling; DATE DUAL BRAKED: 06/12/1967; DATE FULL YELLOW ENDS ADDED TO GREEN LIVERY: N/A; DATE PAINTED INTO BLUE: 06/12/1967; DATE E.T.H. FITTED: 19/09/1970; DATE RENUMBERED: w/e 02/01/1974; ROUTE INDICATOR REMOVAL: 19/01/1977; FP STYLE WHITE CABS: N/A; ALLOCATION HISTORY: 16/03/1962-29/11/1964 Haymarket; 29/11/1964-26/06/1965 Finsbury Park; 29/06/1965-13/05/1979 Haymarket; 13/05/1979-31/12/1981 York; LAST TRAIN: 1L40 09:40 King's Cross-York 31/12/1981; DATE WITHDRAWN: 31/12/1981 - York; REASON FOR WITHDRAWAL: Rundown of class; DATE ARRIVED AT DONCASTER: 04/01/1982; DISPOSAL: Cut up at Doncaster Works 09/1982. One cab preserved; RECORDED WORKS VISITS: Doncaster 96; Vulcan Foundry 1; Stratford D.R.S. 1; Total: 98

Above: The original Deltic with the garish chevrons so disliked by the Design Panel. new archive information reveals that English Electric thought there was little wrong with this prototype which now resides in the National Collection at York. Sadly for EE, the Design Panel and in particular, consultant designer Ted Wilkes, wanted changes made to the production models. The battle was a hard fought one behind the scenes and in the end EE managed to stave off the majority of the changes to the front end styling and wrap-around windows which the Panel had wanted. However, the garish livery and chevrons went and you will read here for the first time about how the first choice liveries for the Deltics were 'Flame Red' and 'Coronation Blue'. It is fascinating stuff.

4 Design and Livery — Archive Revelations

No book on the Deltics would be complete without referring to their outward design and livery. New information, now in the public domain, makes this possible and I have included this chapter to demonstrate that there is much new archive material still unknown about the class. A lot of what I am about to reveal will be new information to the most ardent Deltic locomotive fan. Much of it concerns the battle and what a fight it was too, over changes to the outward look of the production models from that of the prototype locomotive (now preserved in the National Collection at York along with production version D9002) produced by the English Electric Company (EE Co.) and tested by British Railways (BR).

The British Transport Commission (BTC) had appointed the Design Panel in September 1956. This Panel was set-up to advise on the best means of attaining a high standard of appearance and amenity in the design of their equipment. The Panel was concerned with equipment of all kinds which was used by passenger, customers and staff or that was prominently visible to them or to the general public. The BTC were anxious to make the most effective use of professional designers and consultants outside the transport industry as well as of its own staff designers and one of the principal objectives of the Panel was to assist them in that task.

Originally, the BTC Design Panel consisted of: Chairman - T. H. Summerson, a part-time member of the Commission and chairman of the Commission's North Eastern Area Board. To help the Panel to keep abreast of contemporary ideas in design, the Commission appointed two outside members prominently associated with the development of industrial design in Britain. These were W. J. Worboys (a Director of Imperial Chemical Industries Ltd and Chairman of the Council of Industrial Design) and Sir Gordon Russell (Director of the Council of Industrial Design). The other Panel members included three officers of the Commission: Major-General Lt. Wansbrough-Jones (Secretary-General); Mr. J. Ratter (Technical Adviser); and Mr. Christian Barman (Chief Publicity Officer); with Mr. E. W. Arkle (Chief Commercial, London Midland Region of British Railways) and Mr. E. C. Ottaway (Chief Supplies Officer, London Transport Executive), whose contribution to the design of London Transport road vehicles was well known. Williams was the Panel's Design Officer.

Barman was a past president of the Society of Industrial Artists and he was appointed Executive Member of the Panel. Like Ottaway, he was a member of the Faculty of Royal Designers for Industry. Barman was responsible for the administration of the Panel's activities and of special design services associated with it. The Modernisation Plan of Britain's railways called for the building of large numbers of locomotives, railway vehicles and electrical and other installations and the Commission asked the Panel to give priority to this part of their work. The new equipment was to be modern and highly efficient and the Commission intended that those qualities should be clearly reflected in form and appearance. If that could be achieved, the Commission felt sure that the result would be an increased sense of pride among the staff and a new confidence in the future of the service on the part of the public. It was however, the late George Williams, who was the real driving force behind the Panel. A great deal of its success and the way it shaped the future of British locomotive design, can now be fully attributed to his clever manipulation of those in power at the BTC and his skillful handling of consultant designers who he hand-picked to carry out various pilot scheme jobs. His tenacious attitude and drive provided the necessary spark to push through a host of innovations against some of the stiffest opposition the BTC hierarchy could muster. His role was to ensure that good design caught the public imagination and his role was to act as the conduit between locomotive builders, engineers and industrial designers such as Ted Wilkes, of Wilkes and Ashmore and Sir Misha Black of the Design Research Unit. However, Williams could only advise as the Design Panel had no executive status. Williams was appointed to the new post of Design Officer with the Panel in 1957. He was considered the perfect linchpin for a job that would have to try and knit together all the differing factions of a railway industry which required much new thinking in the period of transition between steam and diesel.

His background was impressive. He was originally trained as an engineer in the motor industry and then saw service in the Second World War in the Royal Navy where he designed acoustic and magnetic aircraft-laid weapons. Most interestingly though, Williams spent two years with Black's Design Research Unit before moving onto become Senior Industrial officer with the Council of Industrial Design. His next career switch saw him join British Railways. It was clear his two-year stint with Black had a marked effect on him as when he was given the task of creating a new look for Britain's diesels, it was to the Russian-born designer, among others, to whom he turned. Williams arrived after the formation of the Panel which of course had Barman as its Executive Member and T. H. Summerson as its chairman. Williams had full support from both men as they had already played a major role in getting the BTC to understand that the railways needed a design structure. His partnership with Barman, himself a keen enthusiast of transport design, was such a triumph that by the time Barman retired in 1962 and Williams was appointed Director of Industrial Design, the pair had defeated their critics and established a successful link between engineers, designers and locomotive manufacturers.

But with the Deltics, it was a case of 'some you win and some you lose. For a titanic battle unfolded behind the scenes as EE Co. put up stiff opposition to the Panel's proposed changes to their prototype design, which they clearly felt was perfect. One man in particular, S. C. Lyon, design chief at English Electric, provided a stream of objections, on both operational and production grounds, to the Panel's attempts to change the shape of the leading nose and over their preference for the use of curved glass windscreens. In the end Lyon won some of the battles and the Panel claimed victory in other areas. The nose shape was altered, the 'American style' chevrons and light on the prototype, were dispensed with but plans to use curved glass for the windscreens was dropped. Indeed, when EE Co. decided to change some of the smaller elements of Ted Wilkes' design without consultation, he wrote a stiff letter to Lyon washing his hands of the whole affair. He also told Williams, in no uncertain terms, that Lyon had finally got the locomotive he wanted. The Panel were unhappy too. They realised the Deltic's outward appearance could have been better but consoled themselves with the fact that the production versions were an improvement in looks on the 'ugly' prototype.

Then there was the livery battle. Wilkes had felt so put-out by English Electric's refusal to compromise on his design, that he turned his attention to the livery of the fleet. His first suggestion was that they were painted bright red. This idea was taken up by Williams who then suggested his own version - flame red with suitable lining. This I have supported with copies of letters in this book as the red colour has often been doubted by fans of the class and indeed author Brian Webb in his excellent book on the Deltics. Indeed, the first two Deltics, D9000 and D9001 were to be painted flame red and grey. This plan was passed by all the necessary parties including the various regional chairmen and the first two engines were all set to be outshopped in the respective liveries until BR's Sub-Commission intervened in August 1960. They rejected the two experiment liveries and recommended to the BTC that the Deltics were, instead, painted in 'Coronation Blue' - a variant of the 'Garter blue' in use on the 25kV AC electrics.

The Deltics would have got this livery too if the Sub-Commission had met a little earlier. For by the time they decreed 'Coronation Blue' for the Deltic colours, the first locomotive had already been earmarked for standard green based on Wilkes' two-tone green livery for the Hymek diesel-hydraulic locomotives. There were so many 'ifs and buts' regarding the choice of livery for the Deltics that I feel it is best if I begin the story with the Design Panel's fight to change the look of the prototype before moving on to the livery section. It is clear from official correspondence at the time, that the outward appearance of the prototype 'light blue' Deltic, did not impress T. H. Summerson, then Chairman of the Panel.

On January 24, 1958 he wrote to Christian Barman asking: "What steps, if any, are being taken to tidy up the appearance of the Deltics? As you know, a number are either on order or will be in the near future. The present design has unsatisfactory details, particularly in relation to the drivers' windows. Personally, I like their colour but am not impressed by their American sergeant's chevrons, which are thoroughly vulgar. A little vulgarity, yes, but not so much."

In June of 1958, steps were taken by George Williams to give the consultancy job to Wilkes and Ashmore for the Deltics then on order from the EE Co. A letter from Williams revealed that the Design Panel had also been given the job of collaborating with the EE Co. on the cab interior and control layouts. A month later Williams sent more correspondence to Wilkes and it was clear from this that they still had to convince EE Co. about their ideas for the final design.

Williams wrote: "A finished perspective drawing showing what improvements might be necessary, would be the best way of encouraging English Electric to listen to our later and more considered proposals. If necessary we might get Mr. Summerson to have a word with Sir George Nelson and a good drawing from you might provide us with just the ammunition we want."

Williams knew that it wasn't the best way to design a locomotive but had no other choice as he had to work with EE Co. on the project. He told Wilkes that the prototype could be seen at Euston at about 5.45pm most days and enclosed a recent picture of the locomotive with his letter. On July 23rd, Wilkes first introduced his livery ideas to the Design Panel. Here is the startling revelation that Wilkes first thought about red as the main livery for the locomotives.

In his notes on design recommendations for the Deltic, he stated: "We are recommending a paler tone of green for the band around the nose containing the route indicator box. We think that this band should be slightly less emphatic than the light grey top and bottom areas and if this is a bright colour such as red or yellow, it will over power everything else and throw the design out of balance. We think that whereas the complete locomotive in bright red might look very good, a large patch of bright red on a dark green background would only look garish."

Meanwhile the changes regarding the locomotive's nose, windows, driver's door, roof grilles and side lamps were still being discussed. This debate had now moved on to include letters between Summerson and Charles Cock of EE Co, at Marconi House in London's Strand. At a previous meeting it was agreed that the following changes would be made:

Nose - This was to be re-designed to incorporate new route indicator (subject to confirmation) and be lowered generally by 5-8 inches. The general shaping was to be reviewed and proportions of the grille on each side of the nose were to be modified. The shape of front cutaway over coupling was to be modified also.

Front Windows - The bottom sill was to be lowered to follow the dropped nose. The idea of curved glass was to be pursued.

Driver's Door - Window was to be omitted.

Roof Grilles - The grille immediately rear of the driver's door was to be modified to line up with the line of larger grilles.

Side Lamps - These were to be raised.

Matters moved on to November 19, 1958 when a meeting was held at EE Co. in Preston. Here S. Lyon, Mr. Hughes, and Mr. Stables from EE Preston, were joined by P. J. Martin from the company's Bradford office. The BTC representatives were George Williams and Ted Wilkes. The meeting had been arranged by the CME through the CM&EE's office at Doncaster to discuss the styling and external design of the 22 Deltics that were on order following BR's tests on the prototype.

English Electric had been justifiably proud of this locomotive and were reluctant to alter its design too much. Every time the Design Panel asked for changes, they were met with some opposition on either technical or operational grounds. But the design officer and consultant believed that with an expenditure of something like

£3million on these engines, the most careful consideration to detail was required. The Panel said the design of the prototype was 'ugly' and that even if the first delivery of the production batch was delayed three months by enforced changes to its look, then so be it. There then followed a healthy debate on the following items:

1) Ventilators - It was understood from an earlier meeting that these were likely to be removed from cantrail level and replaced by roof ventilation. It now appeared that this was by no means the case and they were to be retained in the same position. It was agreed that the small generator ventilator immediately aft of the cab door could be brought into line dimensionally with the main units. Mr. Lyon said he was reluctant to do this as the necessary extension would be ineffective as a ventilator. However, the point was agreed.

2) Door Window - It was explained to Mr. Lyon that the circular door windows were objected to on aesthetic grounds as they bore no relation whatsoever to the other rectangular components of the design. It was also explained that it had been agreed by the CME that it was not necessary to provide a window in the door. Lyon again reluctantly agreed to this saying that operational experience had proved it had been desirable the driver should be able to see any member of the crew who might be trying to enter the cab after the locomotive had started moving. However, it was remembered that the original objection to changing from a circular to a rectangular window was on structural grounds, but having dispensed with this argument it appeared that an operational one had arisen. But Lyon agreed to delete the window.

3) Screens - The design officer explained that the Panel and Mr. Summerson in particular, were insistent that the leading end of the locomotive should be developed in a style which reflected the most modern trends in transport design and for this reason it was desired to consider the possibility of using the type of wrap-around windscreen which, for practical and aesthetic reasons, was now common both on light and heavy road and rail vehicles throughout the world. Mr. Lyon's objection to this was on structural and operational grounds. He said that small boys had taken to throwing stones at locomotives and they had already had screens broken on the Deltic during its trial runs. He added that the replacement of the screen glasses could only be done at the end of a run of anything up to 300 miles and the stocking of curved glass was likely to be a difficulty. This was not the view shared by the Panel and a decision to continue with curved glass was made.

4) Leading Nose - It has already been decreed that the overall height of the nose could be reduced by anything between 5-8". Such a reduction was seriously recommended on aesthetic grounds as the overall dimensions of the prototype nose contributed very considerably to the generally poor visual effect of a design in which the high nose was reminiscent of pre-war American locomotives. Mr. Lyon argued that the overall height of this nose was to a large extent dictated by the headroom of 5'3 1/2" required for the toilet but agreed it might be possible to slightly flatten the top curve in cross section. He added though that the Deltic prototype had proved aerodynamically satisfactory.

5) Side Contour - The EE Co. had been informed that the lower bodysides must have a distinct turn-under in order to conform to BR loading gauge requirements. Mr. Wilkes would have preferred a sharp 'O-Gee' shape at this point in order to relieve the depth of the bodyside, but it was pointed out that although this was in fact the actual shape required by the loading gauge requirements, it was difficult to achieve structurally and that the BTC had now agreed to a simple curve at this point. Mr. Wilkes did not see how this curve could be satisfactorily lost at the leading end, which tapers towards the front making the turn-under impossible owing to the dimensions of the main underframe.

6) Bodyside Mountings - The EE Co. were anxious to keep these mouldings that were intended as stiffeners for the cladding. However, Mr. Lyon was convinced that the double moulding engine in the exaggerated 'V' could be replaced by a single wider applied moulding which could have a beneficial effect on the appearance and link-up with the other elements of the nose.

7) Route Indicator - Mr. Lyon was aware of the need for the indicators on the new design and agreed that this could form an important element from which the nose design might be developed.

A date of January 15, 1959 was laid down for Wilkes to get line drawings and a possible scale model to EE Co. By December 1958, Wilkes was in a position to take sketches of the windscreen design to the EE Co and by this time the lowering of the top level of the nose was not being insisted upon. Williams intervened in matters again on December 19 in a letter to designer Felix Samuely. Here he pointed out that at first the EE Co. were reluctant to change the design of their prototype because they felt, in their opinion, it was right.

However, the one battle that had still to be won by the Panel was the driver's windscreens. The Panel wanted to improve vision and appearance by re-designing the windows with a curved or wrap-around unit. This, claimed the Panel, would give an otherwise ugly locomotive at least some degree of character.

Williams wanted Samuely to attend a meeting on January 15 with them and the EE Co. so that they could meet any arguments against the window change that were put forward by the company. But slowly the Panel were winning the battle with English Electric's Mr. Lyon about certain changes.

By January 8, 1959 Christian Barman noted that Lyon had now agreed to remove the lining and frontal chevron pattern together with the headlight. But the Panel were still unhappy about other adornments and wanted them removed. Firstly, Barman said the excessively heavy frontal appearance, reminiscent of US and Canadian designs of the 1930s, needed attention. The lack of 'character' in the form of the nose and its great apparent height also needed further thought as did the lack of cohesion or consistency between various parts of the locomotive.

It is at this point timely to refer to the meetings held at Doncaster Works on January 2, and 7, 1959. Present at the first gathering were Mr. R. Hart-Davies and F. Horne of the CM&EE Dept, Doncaster, George Williams, Design Officer of the

BTC and E.G.M. Wilkes and Felix Samuely of the Design Consultants, Wilkes and Ashmore. The meeting had been arranged at the suggestion of the CME in order to consider with the CM&EE, the technical implications of the design proposals put forward by Wilkes and which they wanted to put before the EE. Co. at a later date. The effect of a redesign on construction, operation and maintenance was discussed at some length. The major item upon which no decision could be reached centred on the wide version wrap-round windscreen to the driver's cab. Chiefly the problem of maintenance and storage of replacement windows gave cause for concern. There was also the problem of random reflections disturbing the driver and this matter had to be looked into further.

The changes from the prototype version to the production models mainly concerned the shape of the nose. Doncaster's CM&EE department raised no objections to the redesign but added that the matter would need to be discussed with the EE Co. Overall though, Doncaster saw no reason why the contours for the nose, proposed by the consultant, could not be achieved.

The second meeting, held five days later, saw Mr. S. Lyon and P. J. Martin from EE Co. in attendance. Mr. Hart-Davies explained that at a previous meeting between the design officer and the EE Co. on November 19, 1958, it was agreed that the Design Panel would complete their proposals for the redesign of the Deltic by January 15. Mr. Wilkes then explained his redesign to those present and Mr. Lyon immediately said he was disturbed by the Panel's continued insistence on a wrap-around wide vision screen. He had been assured at previous meetings that Wilkes would concentrate on designing an engine with the same type of windscreens employed on the prototype.

However, Williams told the meeting that leading ends of new locomotives had to reflect the most modern trends in transport design and that he was pleased to see that Wilkes had produced a most striking improvement in the frontal wrap-around windscreen. Mr. Lyon was not convinced though and repeated his opposition to the wrap-around screen on operational grounds. It was then suggested by Mr. Hart-Davies and Williams that there maybe some way of alleviating the difficulties by having the glass mounted in a metal frame and then assembled to the superstructure, but Wilkes said he was confident that normal rubber glazing would take up any inaccuracies in the glass and metal which were likely to be experienced.

However, the meeting was unable to reach an agreement on this matter. Wilkes then went on to seek approval for a 6" ledge just above the solebar height near the driver's door and which would continue around the front of the locomotive. He said this would be invaluable in the cleaning and maintenance of the nose ends. The meeting welcomed this idea and added that the appearance of the whole nose had been very considerably improved. However, Lyon quickly voiced his opposition to the step idea. He felt it might encourage the crew to use it at places other than the extreme front and this could be dangerous to personnel. Williams countered his objections by saying that the driver would not be able to get on to the ledge near the door as the step did not protrude more than 1/2" at that point. However, Lyon added that changes to the nose form in the way suggested might well involve structural difficulties.

Neither Lyon nor Martin liked the idea of enclosing the horns in the position shown on top of the nose and preferred to see them on top of the cab roof. Lyon, it has to be stated, was clearly disturbed at the extent of the modifications to the original Deltic design and appeared to be very reluctant to contribute to the changes which the Design Panel and the Members of the BTC wished to see achieved.

Lyon was worried that it might involve considerable extra cost and the delay in delivery of the locomotives. A date for a further meeting, January 19, was set and Hart-Davies requested that Lyon returned with a full report into the effect of the changes in terms of cost and structure. A final decision on the locomotive's outward design was then to be taken at this meeting.

Indeed, this meeting was to be a major turning point in the evolution of the locomotive's final appearance and involved a number of heavyweights. E. S. Cox of the BTC chaired the meeting, which also included Christian Barman, George Williams, Ted Wilkes and Hart-Davies. English Electric's corner included S. C. Lyon, P. J. Martin and H. V. Stewart. J. F. Harrison of the BTC was also present.

There followed much discussion about the cab window treatment and the shape and styling of the nose end. It was revealed that curved glass would prevent adoption of the 'gold foil' system of windscreen demisting which was then being adopted as standard on diesels and electrics. The meeting was also told that to assure satisfactory fitting and replacement of the curved glasses, the corresponding cab framing members would require to be manufactured by pressed tools in order to ensure the necessary degree of accuracy. English Electric said this would cost an extra £1,250 per locomotive and a two-month delay in delivery.

Other uncertainties such as the effect of suction on the glass when two trains passed each other were also discussed and the following conclusions then reached: Firstly, because of the practical uncertainties in connection with a locomotive which, by agreement, was required to attain the highest possible availability, it was agreed that curved glass would not be used. However, it was also agreed that some modification to the front and side window arrangement was still acceptable if it could be done within a fortnight.

The nose shape agreed upon was that put forward by Wilkes on his original drawing and collaboration on the placing of the destination indicators and tail lights as well as the radius of the front top corner should be worked out between Wilkes and English Electric within a fortnight. English Electric, clearly happy that curved glass was now off the menu, said there would be no change to delivery date or price of the locomotives.

Just over two weeks later, on February 2, Wilkes sent Lyon drawings of the windscreen, cabside windows, driver's step, indicator box, lamps, horns, nameplates, grab rails, front mounting step and colour division. The Design Panel were forced to lick their wounds as they had not got exactly what they wanted either. At a meeting of the Panel on March 25, 1959, it was clear they were unhappy about the final look of what would be the production fleet of Deltics. However, they did agree that the locomotives would be an improvement on the prototype. They said: "It was agreed that while the appearance of the new locomotive was not all that could have been desired and that the aim of the Panel had been to combine better appearance with improved conditions particularly those concerning visibility for the driver, the design now to be produced would be an appreciable advance at least in appearance upon that of the present prototype locomotive."

The Panel had been forced to back down on insisting all their changes be carried out because English Electric were threatening a delay in delivery of the locomotives if they had to undertake them. This would have had repercussions for the Panel's future involvement on other locomotive projects. However, by July 1959, English Electric were still making alterations to Wilkes' design as they went along and without any consultation.

On July 8, Wilkes wrote to Lyon concerning their decision to lengthen the cab handrails and the introduction of recessed steps at the ends.

Wilkes complained: "With regard to the lengthening of the cab handrails, we think that your idea of fitting the rails within the footstep is the most satisfactory manner in terms of appearance. You mention that the proposed footstep across the ends has been removed on the grounds of being dangerous, and a small recessed step has been added. Obviously you have some reason for doing this although it is not clear to us why the latter is less dangerous than the former."

Lyon though had made other changes. The warning horns were too long to accommodate inside the nose compartment and had been re-positioned below the buffer beam, in accordance, generally, with the Type 2 diesels. The tail lamps were to be brought nearer to the longitudinal centre-line to make room for lamp irons. The flat plate footsteps were to be positioned on top of the buffers and the existing handrails on each side of the cab doors, which Wilkes referred to in his reply, were lengthened so that they could be reached from ballast level. Alternatively, handrails at the side of the footsteps were to be provided. This followed a suggestion from a member off EE's own staff. EE were also making the corners rounded to the cab door and side windows, this Wilkes agreed with. English Electric though also dispensed with the recessed area on the front of the nose for the train headboard. This incensed Wilkes. He wrote to Williams on August 12, 1959 in a clearly unhappy state of mind. He said: "I was so disgusted by the methodical deletion of every one of our recommendations that in my reply to Mr. Lyon, I made it fairly obvious that I was not interested in trying to compromise on the design any further. Mr. Lyon has got precisely the design he wants and as far as I am concerned I have no more recommendations to offer."

Having lost the battle to integrate some of their more radical design ideas and more than a little fed-up with the way English Electric and Mr. Lyon in particular, had changed much of his plans, Wilkes, at the suggestion of Williams, turned his attention to the livery of the locomotives instead. In correspondence with CME J. F. Harrison, it appeared he had no real preferences with regard to the livery of the Deltics and said standard green livery would suffice. But the placement of numbers and lining is something Harrison said, he would leave to the advice of the Design Panel. Wilkes first produced livery drawings on March 9, 1960. He put forward two schemes - the first showed standard loco green with a 3.5" lining and an orange coloured door to the cab.

The fuel tanks were to be loco green. Another suggestion was to have the lining in light grey and the doors in dark green body colour. The second scheme, a new one, was to have the body in standard green and a lower sill of lighter green. The cab superstructure was to be in aluminium with fuel tanks remaining loco green.

Neither scheme showed the placement or type of number. However, this is where the whole livery question became very interesting. Williams had shown Wilkes' sketches to the General Manager of the Eastern Region whose reply, said Williams, was unprintable. Williams said that he thought the best colour for visual warning and good appearance would be a strong flame red with suitable lining.

He was to ask Harrison if he could have a Brush locomotive painted up in such a colour for the visual warning tests.

The other colours suggested in Williams' letter were Desert Sand (later used on D1000 Western Enterprise of course); Aluminium and a pale green rather like the old railway 'improved green'. However, He had also had a suggestion for yellow ruled out by Harrison who disliked the colour used on the Brush type 2 locomotive in conjunction with visual warning tests.

Williams added that Eastern Region General Manager (Johnson) was not keen on the latter but Harrison rejected Williams' red proposal out of hand. He replied: "We would almost certainly be accused of emphasising our nationalised status by what would be in effect a form of Post Office red. I think that in this particular locomotive, the overall aesthetic value is of at least as great an importance as is that of visual warning."

So, in May 1960, Wilkes supplied more colours. 1) His original standard green; 2) Wilkes' recommended scheme if it was decided to retain loco green; 3) Wilkes' suggested scheme using bronze yellow; 4) Wilkes' favourite, a grey/aluminium livery based on a Ford colour; 5) Bright red; 6) Blue and 7) A slightly darker red intended to be similar to the Austin A40 red.

In the meantime though, Williams reported that the CME, Harrison, had since agreed to his original proposal that the Deltics be painted bright RED! This he mentioned in a memo dated July 27, 1960 and said that the idea was now going forward to the General Managers in order for permission to get the first locomotive to be so treated. He had also persuaded Harrison that a flashing light should be considered and EE Co. were to have one fitted to the Deltic. Wilkes was again disappointed by the choice of red. He felt the Deltics were too big to stand bright red and added it would not look good against maroon coaches. Wilkes said that if he ever got the chance to experiment again, he would favour a two-tone grey which he claimed would be a completely new look for the locomotive world and look very 'classy'. Events moved on further when Christian Barman revealed that he had obtained ER General Manager, Bill Johnson's permission to paint the first locomotive red. However, it was then suggested by the Panel's Secretary-General, General Wansborough-Jones that an alternative livery would also be a good idea.

Barman added that a medium-light grey colour was chosen so that the first two production engines would be painted in these liveries. The red paint shade 538 was to be used and BS.2660: 1955 No. 4-049 (grey) would form the alternative locomotive livery. Further support for D9000 to be painted red and D9001 in grey was gathered from the General Managers of the North Eastern and Scottish regions and Williams then wrote to F. Fancutt, assistant director of research (chemical) at Euston Square. He asked if the two colours would be acceptable and added the first locomotive was due for painting in red livery at any moment. Fancutt gave all the colours the thumbs up but trouble was on the horizon in the shape of the BTC.

On August 26, 1960 Williams reported to Wilkes that at a BR Sub-Commission meeting the previous day, the two colour schemes had been rejected and that there was now talk of using mid-blue or green. Indeed, on September 21, Barman produced a hand-written note to Williams saying: "It looks as though, with the Deltics, we shall be back on the green. What about getting Ted to do a Beyer Peacock type of two-colour livery, which has green predominantly?"

The Sub-Commission had been dead against the use of red and grey for the first two Deltics. This has indeed been evident from the minutes from their meeting, which read: "Standard Green had been chosen as the standard colour for all types of diesel and electric locomotives in a BTC meeting on April 26, 1955 (Minute 9/214a). However, this ruling also allowed for the consideration of limited exceptions. Their minute 12/138 of March 26, 1959 saw the Commission approve the Design Panel's recommendation that the livery of the new 25kV A.C. Electric locomotives should be a modified form of Garter Blue, with black for the underframe and bogies and red for the buffer beams.

"However, at their meeting on August 25, the Sub-Commission gave consideration to the two new experimental liveries of red and grey for the first two Deltics. After discussion, the Sub-Commission agreed to recommend that all the Deltics be painted in 'Coronation Blue', similar to the Garter Blue already in use for the 25kV electrics. This livery was to be submitted in preference to the red and grey suggestions."

On September 26 1960, Wilkes sent Williams a drawing of a Deltic as it would look in Garter Blue and black with a yellow 'warning of approach' band. However, the blue idea was dropped on October 12, 1960 when the secretary of the Sub-Commission withdrew the idea. Basically, the painting of the Deltics had progressed rapidly on the shop floor with standard green already in use on the first

62   Design & Livery — Archive Revelations

locomotive and this information had not been passed on to the Sub-Commission at the time they made their decision. The Secretary wrote: "It was ascertained that progress in painting the Deltic locomotives in the standard green livery approved by Commission Minute 9/214(a) of April 26, 1956, was much further forward than the Sub-Commission had understood at their meeting.

"In these circumstances the Chairman of the Railways Sub-Commission has consulted members of the Sub-Commission and the Chairman of the Eastern Area Board and it has been agreed to withdraw the recommendation to use a blue livery for the Deltics which will be painted in standard locomotive green. This decision does not affect the Sub-Commission's decision recorded under the same Note 2 of the meeting of 25th August, that the naming of the locomotives should be left to the discretion of the region to which they were allocated."

An idea by Williams to use the cast aluminium crest on the Deltics as worn by the AC Electrics and later by D1000 Western Enterprise was dispensed with because it would have put the Deltics outside the loading gauge. Another bid by Williams to use aluminium as the colour for the cab superstructure was rejected by Harrison in favour of light grey but the flashing headlight experiment was still on going. If successful he said, there would be no need for a warning panel on the front of the Deltics. The final livery colours chosen for the Deltics were: Body - standard locomotive green; Lower Colour Band (1' 9" wide) - Sherwood Green (No. 177 - 25321); Cab Superstructure - Light grey; Roof - Dark grey (BS2660 9-101); Fuel tanks - Locomotive green; Bogies: Black. So there you have it. The real inside story into the battle of the Deltics in terms of livery and design. Brian Webb's excellent book on the Deltics goes some way to telling this story but not in so much detail. The fact EE changed some of the details of Wilkes' design without informing him was the last straw as far as he was concerned. Other revelations concern the livery of course. In Brian Webb's book, he said rumours of both maroon (red) and Garter Blue for the Deltics were not supported by factual documents. Well, now they are, thanks to new files in the public domain. These spell out for the first time that flame red and indeed 'Coronation Blue', a version of Garter Blue, were chosen for the Deltics. Indeed, had painting of D9000 not already begun in standard green, then the class would have merged in 'Coronation Blue' as recommended by BR's Sub-Commission. D9000 itself was built with a high-power flashing headlight above the buffer beam but this did not last long. Indeed, in the space where the headlight was located on D9000, a recessed step was provided instead. All in all, these revelations will surprise and delight many Deltic fans and I am proud to have unearthed them. Just for historical purposes, EE Co. quoted £3,410,000 for 22 locomotives. this was accepted by the BTC on May 1, 1958. The stated delivery time being 30/3/60 for D9000 and two per month until the final engine was due for delivery on March 15, 1961. In the end the final locomotive, D9021 was not delivered until a year later, entering traffic on March 16, 1962. The delays were due to modifications required during construction of the 22 examples.

WILKES & ASHMORE

INDUSTRIAL DESIGNERS   5, THE CAUSEWAY, HORSHAM, SUSSEX.   Tel: Horsham 4467

George Williams, Esq.,   10th. May 1960
Design Officer,
British Transport Commission,
222, Marylebone Road,
London, N.W.1.

Dear George,

Deltic Colours

Enclosed are five new colour schemes for the new Deltic as follows:-

Scheme 1   Our original colour drawing in standard loco green - returned.

Scheme 2   (in your possession) Our recommended scheme if it is decided to retain the loco green.

Scheme 3   Our suggested scheme using Bronze Yellow.

Scheme 4   We like this scheme best of all. We decided it was a cooler, more engineering colour than the sand colour and it would look much better with the maroon coaches than the sand. The choice was Don's, based on a Ford colour.

Scheme 5   Bright red. We think that the locomotive is too big to take this bright colour, and not elegant enough. It looked good on the old steam locomotives because they were smaller, and had intricate detail with no large plain areas of colour.

Scheme 6   An interesting blue but there are certain objections to blue because it is already used by electric locos, Pullmans, and Glasgow.

Scheme 7   A slightly darker red intended to be similar to the Austin A40 red. Still not as good as schemes 3 or 4.

I think you had better look at these schemes before we do any more. The only other alternatives that might be in the running

---

Above: Ted Wilkes' original colour scheme letter to George Williams, Design Officer, with the British Transport Commission's Design Panel. It clearly reveals a number of livery ideas including one based on a dark red colour similar to the colour used on the Austin A40 car.

WILKES & ASHMORE

INDUSTRIAL DESIGNERS   5, THE CAUSEWAY, HORSHAM, SUSSEX. Tel: Horsham 4467

George Williams, Esq.,
Design Officer,
British Transport Commission,
222, Marylebone Road,
London, N.W.1.

30th. July 1960

Dear George,

<u>Deltic Livery</u>

    Thank you for your letter informing me of the acceptance of the bright red for the first of the Deltics.

    I am afraid that we were all a little disappointed at this end to hear that the colour chosen was the one that we consider the least satisfactory. As stated at the time, we feel that the locomotive is too big to stand bright red and it will not look at all good against maroon carriages.

    If ever we get the chance to experiment again, I would very much like to try the two-tone grey that we put forward. I think it will give a completely 'new look' for the locomotive world and look very 'classy' !

    I have chosen a new light green for the new Brush locomotive and it will be interesting to see the result. In this case, the choice is not connected with any B.R. requirements, but is a 'private enterprise' job, so please treat this as confidential.

<u>New Birmingham Locomotive</u>

    This looks quite interesting and I will report on it as soon as possible.

Yours sincerely,

Ted

E.G.M.Wilkes.

Williams had told Wilkes that the choice of livery for the first Deltic had been agreed by the various General Managers as 'Flame Red' with lining. Wilkes was clearly disappointed saying that he thought the Deltics were too big to stand red and that it would not look good against maroon coaches.

Personal

xxxxxxxxx Hunter 1272
Ext. 5460

9 August 1960

H. C. Johnson Esq.,
British Railways,
Eastern Region,
Liverpool Street Station,
London, E.C.2

Dear Bill

    I am very grateful to you for supporting our proposal to try out a new livery for the Deltic locomotive. I have had a word with the Secretary-General, and I am happy to say he is in full agreement with the choice of red for our first experiment.

    Since deliveries once they start will be at the rate of two a month, General Wansborough-Jones is anxious to reach a final decision quickly. In this connection he feels, and I am bound to agree, that it would be helpful if we could view an alternative colour at the same time. We have therefore prepared another scheme for a medium-light grey livery, the proposal being that of the first two Deltics one should be painted red and the other grey.

    I hope that this proposal will commend itself to you. We have a drawing here of the grey livery and I should be very pleased to come over and show it to you if you would like me to do so.

Ever Vincent
Christian

Christian Barman wrote to H. C. Johnson at the Eastern Region on August 9, 1960 thanking him for supporting the Panel's proposal to paint the first production Deltic in red and also informing him that the second one would be painted in a medium-light grey colour.

- Ext. 5213

Our Ref: 1a2-17

E.G.M. Wilkes Esq.,
Wilkes and Ashmore,
5 The Causeway,
HORSHAM, Sussex.

26th August 1960

Dear Ted,

Deltic Livery

Thank you for your letter of the 25th August and for the 4 prints giving details of the Deltic livery.

You will not be surprised to learn that at a Commission meeting yesterday, the two proposals were not liked and there is now some talk of using mid-blue or green.

We are looking into this to see what can be done.

Yours sincerely,

George Williams

All the plans for flame red and two-tone grey went out of the window when the livery proposals were discussed by the British Railways Sub-Commission in August 1960. They ditched the Panel's plans and instead wanted to paint the production Deltics in 'Coronation Blue'. In the end, standard two-tone green was used instead.

DESIGN & LIVERY — ARCHIVE REVELATIONS   67

Ted Wilkes had a battle royal with members of English Electric over the wrap-around style windows for the production Deltics. He also lost out on the 'step' he wanted around the front of the cab and along the side to the driver's door. The full details of this battle behind the scenes is unearthed for the first time in this book.
Above are two proposals from Wilkes for the Deltic look. The top one shows the wrap-around windows and integrated headboard recess, marker lights and train indicator panel. The bottom one shows the windows slightly altered.

How they eventually looked when new. Standard two-tone green, no step around the front of the cab and no integrated headcode panel. The train indicator panel was included in the final design but the wrap-around window idea was ditched. The horizontal grab rail on the front of the cab was also ditched in favour of a recessed footstep. D9006 in un-named fashion resides at Doncaster Works on July 9, 1961. Picture: L. Feasby.

68 Design & Livery — Archive Revelations

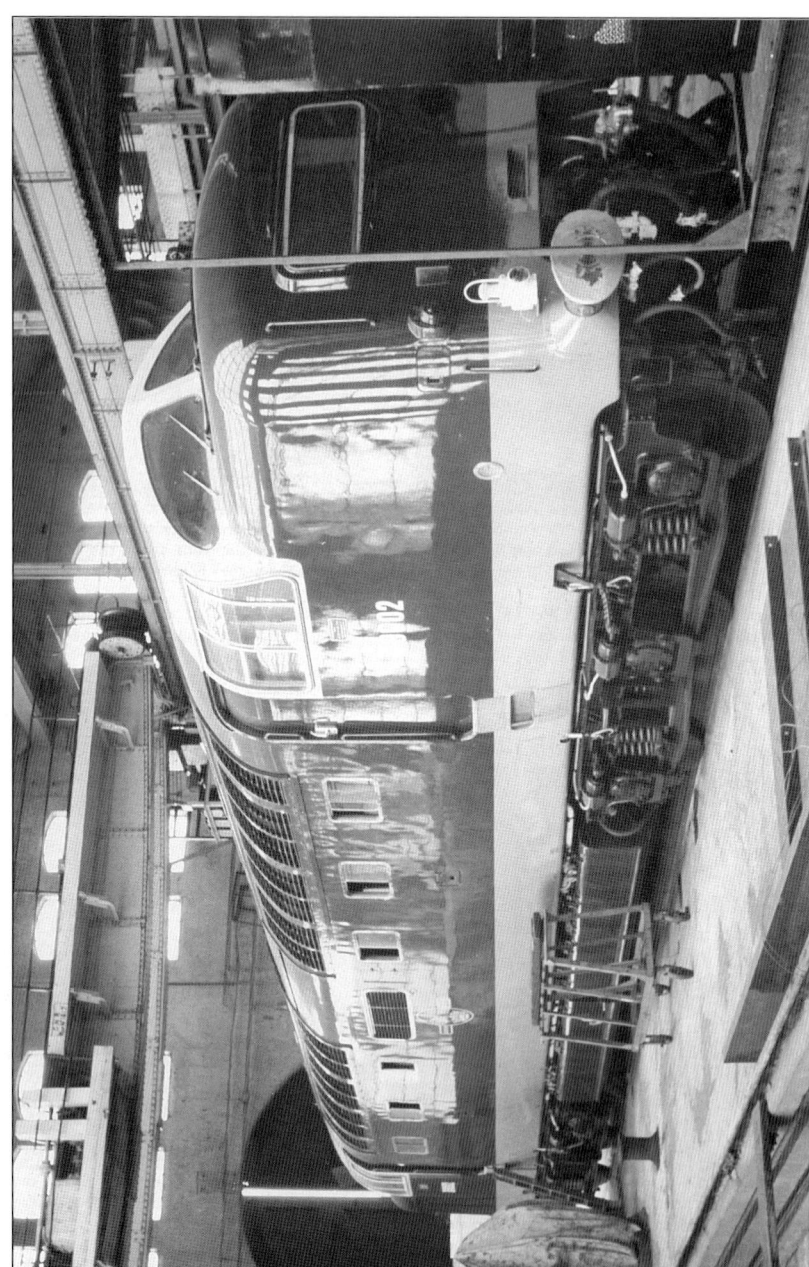

D9002 is seen inside Doncaster Works awaiting a return to English Electric for modifications to the bogies. The locomotive had been stopped on April 8, 1961 for structural problems with the bogies. The loco was already a year late to traffic at this point. Picture: L. Feasby

DESIGN & LIVERY — ARCHIVE REVELATIONS

It is June 10, 1979 and 55012 Crepello and 55020 Nimbus ponder their futures on the reception roads at Doncaster Works. The Deltics underwent thousands of works visits during their lives and these are detailed for the first time later on in this book. Picture: L. P. Gater

70 DESIGN & LIVERY — ARCHIVE REVELATIONS

55009 Alycidon is pictured at Doncaster depot on April 22, 1979. The locomotive was based at Finsbury Park but four days earlier it had undergone repairs at Doncaster Works. The loco's No.1 engine, 436, would not shut down and so the run solenoid was replaced. Picture: L. P. Gater

5 The Last Months Of the Deltics

1981 — A YEAR TO REMEMBER

The withdrawal of 55003 at the end of 1980 meant that the New Year dawned with 19 members of the Deltic fleet still in traffic. The first casualty of the year was not a locomotive but a train that seems to have become something of a legend since its demise, 'The Hull Executive'. Introduced in May 1979 with a booked time of 91 minutes to its first stop at Retford at an average speed in excess of 91 mph, this train captured the imagination of Deltic enthusiasts. By September of 1979 a stop at Newark had been added and by May 1980, four minutes additional running time had also been added, but all of this failed to detract from the appeal of 'The Exec.' Its final week of Deltic operation did not pass without Finsbury Park ensuring that both 55007 and 55015 were in immaculate condition to work the train. The new Deltic diagrams that came into force on January 5th showed no real change to what had gone before other than that the 'up' and 'down' 'Hull Executive' was no longer included as the HST had taken over.

Throughout January the Deltics went about their normal duties and also put in appearances at Aberdeen, Carstairs and Liverpool until the 29th when the first significant workings occurred. 55008 worked (1D00) 08:05 King's Cross-Hull and (1A18) 12:34 Hull-King's Cross. On the return working it is believed, although not confirmed, that 55008 was in trouble. On Doncaster depot was 55021, which was commandeered to assist 55008 to King's Cross. Nearly 240 miles away, in Edinburgh, 55011 was very unusually turned out to work (1O42) 16:00 Edinburgh-Glasgow Queen Street and (1O49) 17:00 Glasgow Queen Street-Edinburgh, complete with MKIII 'push-pull' set! On the return journey 55011 was dragged out of Queen Street still at the rear with 37111 leading and taken to the Cowlairs triangle so as to turn the train and allow 55011 to take it on to Edinburgh without the class 37. Early February saw the sad demise of 55005 and 55006 taking the fleet total down to 17, but with only 12 diagrams this was still, in theory at least, enough to cover them.

Deltics were still regular visitors to Aberdeen and to a lesser extent Liverpool throughout the month but it was Stratford depot that started to host Deltics on a more regular basis than had hitherto been the case. This was a relationship that would last until their final demise. The 12th saw 55004 expire at Babworth, north of Retford, whilst working (1L44) 16:05 King's Cross-York. Assistance came in the shape of Class 37, 37068. The 22nd saw 55021 require the assistance of Class 25, 25321 on (1L41) 10:05 King's Cross-York. March 3rd saw 55012 repeating 55011's Glasgow Queen Street expedition although with the 17:00 and 18:00 workings. On the 20th, 55004 was again in trouble, this time at Hitchin and assistance came in the shape of Class 31, 31113. This failure was due to a loss of power and I can confirm this as I was one of the victims on the train! On the 21st, 55004 was employed on (1A15) 10:30 Newcastle-King's Cross, a H.S.T. diagram, otherwise it was just Aberdeen and Liverpool that saw regular Deltic workings away from their more familiar haunts. April dawned with several visits made by the class to Carstairs. In the first six days of the month (1S70) 22:15 King's Cross-Aberdeen was Deltic hauled five times and on only one occasion did the engine that left King's Cross make it through to Edinburgh. As the month progressed the class made many visits to Aberdeen, often two locos would work into the Granite City in the same day as Haymarket sought employment for them. On the 21st, 55014 ran out of fuel at Lincoln whilst in charge of (1D01) the morning King's Cross-Cleethorpes working. It was replaced by Class 31s, 31180 and 31283 before running 'light' to Cleethorpes for the return working. On the 23rd, 55011 failed at Biggleswade with (1A08) 08:05 York-King's Cross.

The 24th was not a good day for the ECML due to an incident between Grantham and Doncaster. This resulted in some unusual workings for the Deltics. 55009 worked an additional service from Grantham to King's Cross, relieving 55019 at Peterborough. 55019 had worked the empty stock from London to Grantham before working the additional to Peterborough where 55009 took over. 55010 worked (1S12) 05:50 King's Cross-Aberdeen which was diverted via the 'Joint line' through Lincoln, this caused the train to be terminated at York due to the late running which was a consequence of the diversion.

Meanwhile, 55021 left York 'right time' with another (1S12) that started from the Yorkshire City and indeed 55021 worked through to Aberdeen. The following day saw 55002 on rail tour duty with 'The North Briton' from York to Edinburgh. Two days later, on the 27th, 55002 was covering for a non-available HST on (1A15) 10:30 Newcastle-King's Cross and (1N05) 15:35 King's Cross-Newcastle. The month of May dawned and on the 4th 55002 was once again on rail tour duty working the 'Deltic Fenman' to the Nene Valley Railway. Saturday 9th saw 55007 receive the assistance of Class 40, 40006 on (1A13) 09:33 Hull-King's Cross as the Deltic was suffering from a loss of power.

On Wednesday 13th 55012 worked overnight from Edinburgh to King's Cross. On arrival at Finsbury Park she was due a 'C' exam, however, instead of receiving the necessary attention 'Crepello' was withdrawn bringing the class down to 16 members. On the 19th, 55013 visited Liverpool, the first member of the class to do so since 26th March. The summer timetable was implemented on June 1st and saw some trains retimed and certain others had their timings eased. There were now 11 diagrams for the remaining Deltics as they entered their last summer.

The remaining members were kept quite active during June with 55008 being the star performer. On the 19th she was recorded at 120 mph descending Stoke bank and on the 30th she was covering for a HST on (1N01) 07:10 King's Cross-Newcastle and (1A35) 11:15 Newcastle-King's Cross. She was seen arriving at Newcastle on (1N01) just two minutes late!

The following day 55008 was used on (1F53) 08:20 Edinburgh-King's Cross — a special train conveying a high-speed track recording coach. Were the powers that be up to something with 55008? A couple of days later, at the beginning of July, 55019 was also recorded at 120 mph. Deltics continued to visit Aberdeen on a regular basis, otherwise July was a fairly quiet month for unusual workings except perhaps the 25th when 55016 visited Glasgow Queen Street. Of course Scarborough had become a regular haunt by now with a through working to King's Cross. August 2nd saw 55021 work from Edinburgh to Oban with a merrymaker and 55002 worked a similar train to Whitby from Newcastle. Three weeks later 55021 repeated its Scottish outing, otherwise the month passed with regular visits to all the now familiar haunts. September dawned with both 55008 and 55022 covering for HSTs, 55011 visiting Liverpool and 55019 visiting Aberdeen. The month also saw such happenings as on the 3rd when 55022 suffered collision damage at Finsbury Park, in an incident that is believed to have involved 55021. After this prang 55022 didn't work another train until 21st October. 55009 made the by now unusual visit to Bradford Exchange on the 6th. Four days later, 55007 assisted a failed 55010 from Hitchin to King's Cross and the 12th saw 55007 in rail tour action with the 'Deltic Anglian' while 55014 was at Old Oak Common for the open day. On 2nd October 55009 made a most unusual visit to North Berwick from Haymarket when it was sent to rescue a failed DMU. We were entering the final three months of Deltic operation that has already been well documented, so it is not my intention to repeat it here. Instead, here are a few highlights. The final rail tours commenced on the 17th with 55009 visiting Perth and Aberdeen whilst 55015 worked on the Southern region with the 'Wessex Deltic', 55018 was withdrawn on the 18th.

November dawned with the withdrawal of 55004. This loco. had spent a long time out of use in 1978 and 1979 and it's eventual return to traffic at the end of 1979 was a great bonus for Deltic fans. However, just under 2 years later it was withdrawn and the countdown to the end of the Deltics had begun. 55011 was also withdrawn a week later and on the 13th, 55017 was the final Deltic to be outshopped from Doncaster Works after the very last engine change carried out on the fleet at the 'plant'. The 20th saw the end for 55014 and it was now every Deltic for itself. December 1981, the last full month of Deltic operation on British Rail commenced with 12 members of the class left in traffic. Within a few days the survivors had visited Aberdeen, Carstairs, Carlisle, Dunfermline and Liverpool. The weather turned arctic cold and several failures occurred as a result of the severe conditions. The next withdrawal, that of 55013, occurred on the 22nd and within the following fortnight these once mighty 'Dragons' of the East Coast had been slain for good. Their awesome roar, a mesmeric symphony along the ECML to all those who loved the fleet, was now an echo of the past. Here I've produced another first for you all...the last months in action of the remaining Deltics.

ABBREVIATIONS: AB-Aberdeen (Ferryhill); BFD-Bradford; BG-Hull (Botanic Gardens) BH-Barrow Hill; DE-Dundee; DR-Doncaster; FP-Finsbury Park; GD-Gateshead; HA-Haymarket; HI-Hitchin; HO-Holbeck; HT(N)-Heaton; LIV-Liverpool; LN-Lincoln; NL-Neville Hill; NR-Norwich (Crown Point); NRM-National Railway Museum; OC-Old Oak Common; PB-Peterborough; SF-Stratford; TE-Thornaby (Tees); TY-Tyne Yard YK-York; 'ao'- air brakes only; 'eo' - electric heat only; 'oe' - on one engine only 'vo'- vacuum brakes only; H.W.T. - High Water Temperature; L.O.P. - Loss of Power.

D9000/9000/55022
Royal Scots Grey

JUNE 1981
Mon. 1: YK; Tues. 2: YK; Wed. 3: 1A08 08:07 York-King's Cross/FP/1L44 16:03 King's Cross-York/1A34 20:19 York-King's Cross; Thurs. 4: 1S12 05:50 King's Cross-Aberdeen to Edinburgh/HA/1E35 20:25 Edinburgh-King's Cross; Fri. 5: FP/1B03 17:10 King's Cross-Peterborough/0B02 Peterborough-Finsbury Park/FP/0L01 Finsbury Park-York; Sat. 6: YK Until Thurs. 11: YK/1A34 20:19 York-King's Cross; Fri. 12: 1S12 05:50 King's Cross-Aberdeen to York (55 004 forward)/YK Until Thurs. 18: YK; Fri. 19: 1A37 10:47 York-King's Cross/FP/1D08 19:40 King's Cross-Hull/1D26 23:40 Hull-Doncaster; Sat. 20: DR 'oe'/0L01 Doncaster-York/YK; Sun. 21: YK/0B02 York-Finsbury Park/FP; Mon. 22: 1N00 01:00 King's Cross-Newcastle/1S08 07:05 Newcastle-Edinburgh/1E10 09:10 Dundee-King's Cross from Edinburgh/FP; Tues. 23: 1L42 12:05 King's Cross-York/1A26 15:50 York-King's Cross/FP; Wed. 24: 1S12 05:50 King's Cross-Aberdeen/1E26 16:30 Aberdeen-Leeds/1E24 22:50 Shrewsbury-York from Leeds; Thurs. 25: 1M62 08:50 York-Liverpool/1E99 13:05 Liverpool-York/YK/0B02 York-Finsbury Park; Fri. 26: 1N12 00:05 King's Cross-Newcastle/GD/0L01 08:08 Gateshead-York/YK Until Tues. 30: YK

JULY
Wed. 1: 1E94 08:05 Liverpool-Newcastle from York/GD/1A40 21:00 Newcastle-King's Cross; Thurs. 2: FP 'oe'/5S70 Ferme Park-King's Cross; Fri. 3: 1N12 00:05 King's Cross-Newcastle/GD 'oe'/0L01 08:08 Gateshead-York/YK 'oe'/1N14 14:03 King's Cross-Newcastle from York (55 002 off)/GD 'oe'/0L01 Gateshead-York; Sat. 4: YK 'oe'; Sun. 5: YK 'oe'; Mon. 6: YK 'oe'/0D01 York-Doncaster/On DONCASTER WORKS "Unclassified repair" (No.2 engine, 426, replaced by 413) Until Thurs. 9:

Off DONCASTER WORKS/DR; Fri. 10: DR/1A13 09:36 Hull-King's Cross from Doncaster/FP/1D08 19:40 King's Cross-Hull/1D26 23:40 Hull-Doncaster; Sat. 11: 1D62 03:55 Doncaster-Hull/1A13 09:36 Hull-King's Cross/FP/1L45 18:05 King's Cross-York/YK; Sun. 12: YK/1A10 15:50 York-King's Cross/1S79 23:20 King's Cross-Aberdeen to Edinburgh; Mon. 13: 1V93 09:50 Edinburgh-Plymouth to York/1S27 07:36 Plymouth-Edinburgh from York to Newcastle (55 009 forward)/GD/0L01 Gateshead-York/YK; Tues. 14: YK/1A26 15:50 York-King's Cross/1S72 22:30 King's Cross-Edinburgh; Wed. 15: 1V93 09:50 Edinburgh-Plymouth to York/1S27 07:36 Plymouth-Edinburgh from York/1E39 22:25 Edinburgh-King's Cross to Newcastle; Thurs. 16: GD/1G10 Newcastle-York (Driver training)/1G10 York-Newcastle (Driver training)/GD/1N03 21:20 Newcastle-Darlington/0L01 Darlington-York; Fri. 17: YK 'B' exam Until Wed. 22:YK 'B' exam/0B02 York-Finsbury Park/FP; Thurs. 23: 1N12 00:05 King's Cross-Newcastle/GD/1G10 Newcastle-York (Driver training)/1G10 York-Newcastle (Driver training)/GD/1A40 21:00 Newcastle-King's Cross; Fri. 24: 5B26 05:24 King's Cross-Peterborough/1B26 07:23 Peterborough-King's Cross/FP/1N14 14:03 King's Cross-Newcastle to York/1A31 18:14 York-King's Cross/FP; Sat. 25: 1S84 08:35 King's Cross-Edinburgh/HA/1E35 20:45 Edinburgh-King's Cross; Sun. 26: FP; Mon. 27: FP/1L44 16:03 King's Cross-York/1A34 20:19 York-King's Cross; Tues. 28: 1S12 05:50 King's Cross-Aberdeen to Edinburgh/HA; Wed. 29: 5E10 06:40 Craigentinny-Dundee/1E10 09:10 Dundee-King's Cross to Newcastle/GD/1N03 21:20 Newcastle-Darlington/0L01 Darlington-York; Thurs. 30: YK; Fri. 31: 1A08 08:07 York-King's Cross/FP/1B04 16:06 King's Cross-Peterborough/ 0B02 Peterborough-Finsbury Park/FP/1S72 22:30 King's Cross-Edinburgh

AUGUST

Sat. 1: 1V93 09:50 Edinburgh-Plymouth to York/1S27 07:36 Plymouth-Edinburgh from York/1E35 20:45 Edinburgh-King's Cross to Newcastle/GD/1E48 21:20 Aberdeen-King's Cross from Newcastle; Sun. 2: FP/1S70 22:15 King's Cross-Aberdeen to Edinburgh; Mon. 3: HA/1E10 09:10 Dundee-King's Cross from Edinburgh/FP/1S70 22:15 King's Cross-Aberdeen to Edinburgh; Tues. 4: 5E10 06:40 Craigentinny-Dundee/1E10 09:10 Dundee-King's Cross/FP 'B' exam; Wed. 5: FP 'B' exam; Thurs. 6: 1S76 09:40 King's Cross-Edinburgh/HA/1E26 16:30 Aberdeen-Leeds from Edinburgh/1E24 22:50 Shrewsbury-York from Leeds; Fri. 7: YK/1A34 20:19 York-King's Cross; Sat. 8: 1S76 09:40 King's Cross-Edinburgh/HA/1E43 20:05 Aberdeen-King's Cross from Edinburgh; Sun. 9: FP/1L43 16:05 King's Cross-York/YK Mon. 10: 1A08 08:07 York-King's Cross/FP/1L44 16:03 King's Cross-York/1A34 20:19 York-King's Cross; Tues. 11: 1S12 05:50 King's Cross-Aberdeen to Edinburgh/HA/1E39 22:25 Edinburgh-King's Cross; Wed. 12: 1S76 09:40 King's Cross-Edinburgh to Newcastle (55 021 forward)/GD/1A40 21:00 Newcastle-King's Cross; Thurs. 13: 5B26 05:24 King's Cross-Peterborough/1B26 07:23 Peterborough-King's Cross/FP; Fri. 14: 1N00 01:00 King's Cross-Newcastle/1S08 07:05 Newcastle-Edinburgh/HA/ 1E84 13:25 Edinburgh-King's Cross/1S79 23:20 King's Cross-Aberdeen to Edinburgh; Sat. 15: 1E28 08:10 Glasgow Q.St.-Scarborough from Edinburgh/1S51 15:08 Scarborough-Glasgow Q.St. to Edinburgh/1E43 20:05 Aberdeen-King's Cross from Edinburgh; Sun. 16: FP; Mon. 17: 1N00 01:00 King's Cross-Newcastle/1S08 07:05 Newcastle-Edinburgh/HA/ 1E39 22:25 Edinburgh-King's Cross; Tues. 18: 1L42 12:05 King's Cross-York/1A26 15:50 York-King's Cross/1S77 23:55 King's Cross-Edinburgh; Wed. 19: 1V93 09:50 Edinburgh-Plymouth to York/1S27 07:36 Plymouth-Edinburgh from York/1E26 16:30 Aberdeen-Leeds from Edinburgh to York; Thurs. 20: YK 'B' exam; Fri. 21: YK 'B' exam; Sat. 22: 1N12 00:05 King's Cross-Newcastle from York (55 016 off)/GD; Sun. 23: GD/0L01 Gateshead-York/YK; Mon. 24: YK; Tues. 25: 1A08 08:07 York-King's Cross/FP/1L44 16:03 King's Cross-York/1A34 20:19 York-King's Cross; Wed. 26: 1S12 05:50 King's Cross-Aberdeen to Edinburgh/HA/1E35 20:25 Edinburgh-King's Cross; Thurs. 27: 1S76 09:40 King's Cross-Edinburgh/HA/1E39 22:25 Edinburgh-King's Cross; Fri. 28: 1L42 12:05 King's Cross-York/1A26 15:50 York-King's Cross/1S70 22:15 King's Cross-Aberdeen to Edinburgh; Sat. 29: 1V93 09:50 Edinburgh-Plymouth to York/1S27 07:36 Plymouth-Edinburgh from York/HA; Sun. 30: 1V93 11:25 Edinburgh-Plymouth to York/1S27 09:00 Plymouth-Edinburgh from York/1E43 20:35 Aberdeen-King's Cross from Edinburgh; Mon. 31: FP

SEPTEMBER

Tues. 1: 1N12 00:05 King's Cross-Newcastle/GD/1A15 10:30 Newcastle-King's Cross (vice HST)/ FP; Wed. 2: 1N00 01:00 King's Cross-Newcastle/1S08 07:05 Newcastle-Edinburgh/0Z69 Haymarket-Carstairs/1Z69 Carstairs-Edinburgh/1A38 14:55 Edinburgh-Aberdeen/1G20 18:23 Aberdeen-Edinburgh/1E43 20:35 Aberdeen-King's Cross from Edinburgh; Thurs. 3: FP (Collision damage – with 55 021); Fri. 4: FP/0D01 Finsbury Park-Doncaster/DR/0L01 Doncaster-York/YK Until; Thurs. 8: YK/0B02 York-Finsbury Park/FP/0C01 Finsbury Park-Stratford; Fri. 9: SF (Collision damage repairs and loco. repainted) Until Wed. 30: SF

OCTOBER

Thurs. 1: SF Until Mon. 12: SF; Tues. 13: SF/0B02 Stratford-Finsbury Park/FP; Wed. 14: FP (Derailed leaving depot for 1S76); Thurs. 15: FP Until Wed. 21: FP/1D08 19:40 King's Cross-Hull to Peterborough (failed)/0B02 Peterborough-Finsbury Park; Thurs. 22: FP/1L43 14:03 King's Cross-York/1A31 18:14 York-King's Cross/FP; Fri. 23: FP/1L44 16:03 King's Cross-York/1A34 20:19 York-King's Cross; Sat. 24: 1S12 05:50 King's Cross-Aberdeen to Newcastle/0L01 Newcastle-York/YK 'C' exam Until Sat. 31: YK 'C' exam

NOVEMBER

Sun. 1: YK; Mon. 2: YK; Tues. 3: YK; Wed. 4: 1M62 08:50 York-Liverpool/1E99 13:05 Liverpool-York (failed – double flashover and No.1 main generator catching fire - assisted from Manchester Vic. by 45 005)/YK 'oe' (awaiting decision); Thurs. 5: YK 'oe' ; Fri. 6: YK 'oe'/0B02 York-Finsbury Park/FP/0C01 Finsbury Park-Stratford/SF (No.1 engine, 421, replaced by 434) Until Wed. 11: SF; Thurs. 12: 0B02 Stratford-Finsbury Park/FP/1S70 22:15 King's Cross-Aberdeen to Newcastle; Fri. 13: GD/0L01 Gateshead-York/YK Until Thurs. 19: YK; Fri. 20: 1M62 08:50 York-Liverpool to Leeds (failed – No.1 engine fuel racks jamming)/0L01 Leeds-York/YK; Sat. 21: YK; Sun. 22: YK; Mon. 23: 1M62 08:50 York-Liverpool/1E99 13:05 Liverpool-York/YK; Tues. 24: YK; Wed. 25: YK; Thurs. 26: 1M62 08:50 York-Liverpool/1E99 13:05 Liverpool-York/YK; Fri. 27: YK; Sat. 28: 1Z38 08:12 York-Paddington "Deltic Venturer" rail tour/1Z38 16:15 Paddington-York "Deltic Venturer" rail tour/YK; Sun. 29: YK; Mon. 30: YK

DECEMBER

Tues. 1: YK; Wed. 2: YK; Thurs. 3: YK; Fri. 4: 1M62 08:50 York-Liverpool/1E99 13:05 Liverpool-York/YK Until Tues. 8: YK; Wed. 9: 1A08 08:07 York-King's Cross/FP/1L44 16:03 King's Cross-York/1A34 20:19 York-King's Cross; Thurs. 10: 1L41 09:40 King's Cross-York/1A22 14:15 York-King's Cross/1D08 19:40 King's Cross-Hull/5L04 23:30 Hull-York; Fri. 11: YK Until Wed. 16: YK; Thurs. 17: 1M62 08:50 York-Liverpool/1E99 13:05 Liverpool-York/YK Until Sun. 20: YK/1M69 09:45 Edinburgh-Liverpool from York/1E22 19:10 Liverpool-York; Mon. 21: YK Until Wed. 30: YK/1A26 15:50 York-King's Cross/FP; Thurs. 31: 1S12 05:50 King's Cross-Aberdeen to Edinburgh/HA

JANUARY 1982

Fri. 1: HA; Sat. 2: HA/1F50 14:30 Edinburgh-King's Cross "Deltic Scotsman Farewell" rail tour/FP/0L01 Finsbury Park-York – WITHDRAWN; Sun. 3: YK; Mon. 4: YK; Tues. 5: YK/9… York-Doncaster (with 55 009, 55 015 & 55 016 towed by 47 522)/ On DONCASTER WORKS Until **September 1983**; Thurs. 8: Off DONCASTER WORKS/7G30 09:30 Doncaster-Peterborough West Yard (towed by 31 102)/ Nene Valley Railway — Locomotive Preserved.

Class 55, 55009 Alycidon on the blocks at King's Cross with the (1A18) 12:34 Hull-King's Cross on Saturday April 24, 1981. the locomotive had worked up to Hull that morning with the (1D00) 08:05 King's Cross-Hull service. Picture: J. Davenport Collection

D9002/9002/55002
The King's Own Yorkshire Light Infantry

JUNE 1981
Mon. 1: HA/5G99 Craigentinny-Heaton/GD; Tues. 2: 1S14 08:10 Newcastle-Edinburgh/HA/1E35 20:25 Edinburgh-King's Cross; Wed. 3: 1D01 08:30 King's Cross-Cleethorpes/1A21 13:20 Cleethorpes-King's Cross/ 1S66 20:15 King's Cross-Edinburgh Thurs. 4: 5E10 06:40 Craigentinny-Dundee/1E10 09:10 Dundee-King's Cross to York/YK; Fri. 5: YK/0M00 07:30 York-Crewe/Crewe Works; Sat. 6: Crewe Works (Open day exhibit); Sun. 7: Crewe Works (Open day exhibit); Mon. 8: 0E00 Crewe Works-York/YK/0B02 York-Finsbury Park/FP/1S72 22:30 King's Cross-Edinburgh; Tues. 9: 1V93 09:50 Edinburgh-Plymouth to York/1S27 07:36 Plymouth-Edinburgh from York/HA; Wed. 10: 1V93 09:50 Edinburgh-Plymouth to York/1S27 07:36 Plymouth-Edinburgh from York/1E40 19:25 Aberdeen-King's Cross from Edinburgh; Thurs. 11: FP/1L42 12:05 King's Cross-York/1A26 15:50 York-King's Cross/FP; Fri. 12: 1N12 00:05 King's Cross-Newcastle/0L01 Newcastle-York/YK/1A31 18:14 York-King's Cross; Sat. 13: 1N00 01:00 King's Cross-Newcastle/1S08 07:05 Newcastle-Edinburgh/HA/ 1A38 14:55 Edinburgh-Aberdeen/1G20 18:30 Aberdeen-Edinburgh/HA; Sun. 14: 1V93 11:25 Edinburgh-Plymouth to York/1S27 11:25 Reading-Edinburgh from York/1E39 22:30 Edinburgh-King's Cross; Mon. 15: FP 'B' exam; Tues. 16: FP 'B' exam/1S60 20:00 King's Cross-Aberdeen to Edinburgh; Wed. 17: 5E10 06:40 Craigentinny-Dundee/1E10 09:10 Dundee-King's Cross/1S60 20:00 King's Cross-Aberdeen to Edinburgh; Thurs. 18: 1M04 07:18 Edinburgh-Carlisle/1S15 15:53 Carlisle-Edinburgh/1E42 23:15 Edinburgh-King's Cross; Fri. 19: FP; Sat. 20: 1N12 00:05 King's Cross-Newcastle/GD/1A39 10:50 Newcastle-King's Cross/ FP/1S66 21:00 King's Cross-Edinburgh to Newcastle; Sun. 21: GD/1A40 21:28 Newcastle-King's Cross; Mon. 22: 5B26 05:24 King's Cross-Peterborough/1B26 07:23 Peterborough-King's Cross/FP/1L45 17:40 King's Cross-York; Tues. 23: YK/1S27 07:36 Plymouth-Edinburgh from York/1E35 20:25 Edinburgh-King's Cross; Wed. 24: FP/1L43 14:03 King's Cross-York/1A31 18:14 York-King's Cross/FP; Thurs. 25: 1S12 05:50 King's Cross-Aberdeen to Edinburgh/HA/1E29 17:18 Edinburgh-Newcastle/1A45 22:55 Newcastle-King's Cross; Fri. 26: FP/1L42 12:05 King's Cross-York/YK Until Tues. 30: YK

JULY
Wed. 1: 1A08 08:07 York-King's Cross/FP/1L44 16:03 King's Cross-York/1A34 20:19 York-King's Cross; Thurs. 2: 1S12 05:50 King's Cross-Aberdeen to Edinburgh/HA/1E40 19:25 Aberdeen-King's Cross from Edinburgh; Fri. 3: FP/1N14 14:03 King's Cross-Newcastle to York (55 022 forward)/1A31 18:14 York-King's Cross/FP; Sat. 4: 1S12 05:50 King's Cross-Aberdeen to Edinburgh/HA/1E35 20:45 Edinburgh-King's Cross; Sun. 5: FP/1L43 16:05 King's Cross-York/YK; Mon. 6: 1A37 10:47 York-King's Cross/FP/1D08 19:40 King's Cross-Hull/0L01 Hull-York; Tues. 7: YK 'B' exam; Wed. 8: 0D01 York-Doncaster/1D62 03:55 Doncaster-Hull/1A13 09:36 Hull-King's Cross/FP/1L45 17:40 King's Cross-York; Thurs. 9: 1A08 08:07 York-King's Cross/1L43 14:03 King's Cross-York/1A31 18:14 York-King's Cross/FP; Fri. 10: FP/1L42 12:05 King's Cross-York/1A26 15:50 York-King's Cross/FP; Sat. 11: FP/1L42 12:05 King's Cross-York/1A26 15:50 York-King's Cross/FP; Sun. 12: FP/1L22 23:00 King's Cross-Bradford to Leeds; Mon. 13: 0L01 Leeds-York/YK; Tues. 14: 1A08 08:07 York-King's Cross/FP/1L44 16:03 King's Cross-York/1A34 20:19 York-King's Cross; Wed. 15: 1S12 05:50 King's Cross-Aberdeen to Edinburgh/HA/1E42 23:15 Edinburgh-King's Cross; Thurs. 16: FP/1L42 12:05 King's

Cross-York/1A26 15:50 York-King's Cross/FP; Fri. 17: 1N00 01:00 King's Cross-Newcastle/1S08 07:05 Newcastle-Edinburgh/HA/ 1A51 17:00 Edinburgh-Aberdeen/1E48 21:20 Aberdeen-King's Cross to Edinburgh; Sat. 18: 5E10 06:40 Craigentinny-Dundee/1E10 09:10 Dundee-King's Cross/FP/1S72 22:30 King's Cross-Edinburgh; Sun. 19: HA/1E42 23:15 Edinburgh-King's Cross; Mon. 20: 1L42: 12:05 King's Cross-York/1A26 15:50 York-King's Cross/FP; Tues. 21: 1N12 00:05 King's Cross-Newcastle/1A37 09:20 Newcastle-King's Cross to York (55 008 forward)/YK 'D' exam Until Mon. 27: YK 'D' exam; Tues. 28: YK/0B02 York-Finsbury Park/FP Wed. 29: 1S76 09:40 King's Cross-Edinburgh/HA/1E26 16:30 Aberdeen-Leeds from Edinburgh/1E24 22:50 Shrewsbury-York from Leeds; Thurs. 30: 1A37 10:47 York-King's Cross/FP/1D08 19:40 King's Cross-Hull to Doncaster/DR; Fri. 31: 1D62 03:55 Doncaster-Hull/1A13 09:36 Hull-King's Cross/1L44 16:03 King's Cross-York/1A34 20:19 York-King's Cross

AUGUST

Sat. 1: 1S12 05:50 King's Cross-Aberdeen to Newcastle/GD; Sun. 2: 1G10 09:30 Newcastle-Whitby/1G10 12:44 Whitby-Middlesbrough/1G10 15:10 Middlesbrough-Whitby/1G10 17:27 Whitby-Newcastle/GD/1A40 21:28 Newcastle-King's Cross to York; Mon. 3: YK; Tues. 4: YK; Wed. 5: 1M62 08:50 York-Liverpool/1E99 13:05 Liverpool-York/1A34 20:19 York-King's Cross; Thurs. 6: 1S12 05:50 King's Cross-Aberdeen to Edinburgh/HA/1E35 20:25 Edinburgh-King's Cross; Fri. 7: 1D01 08:30 King's Cross-Cleethorpes/1A21 13:20 Cleethorpes-King's Cross (failed at Cleethorpes but was not releasing - 31 143 forward)/0D01 Cleethorpes-Doncaster/0L01 Doncaster-York/YK; Sat. 8: 1A08 08:07 York-King's Cross/FP; Sun. 9: FP/1N11 22:45 King's Cross-Newcastle to York; Mon. 10: YK; Tues. 11: YK/0D01 York-Doncaster; Wed. 12: On DONCASTER WORKS "Unclassified repair" (No.2 engine, 406, replaced by 419) Until Tues. 18: Off DONCASTER WORKS/0B02 Doncaster-Finsbury Park/FP/1L22 23:00 King's Cross-Bradford to Leeds; Wed. 19: HO/0L01 Holbeck-York/0D01 York-Doncaster; Thurs. 20: On DONCASTER WORKS "Unclassified repair" (No. 2 engine, 419, replaced by 437) Until Fri. 28: Off DONCASTER WORKS/0B02 Doncaster-Finsbury Park; Sat. 29: 1N12 00:05 King's Cross - Newcastle/GD; Sun. 30: 1G30 Newcastle-Whitby/1G30 Whitby-Newcastle; Mon. 31 GD/1A40 21:00 Newcastle-King's Cross

SEPTEMBER

Tues. 1: 5B26 05:24 King's Cross-Peterborough/1B26 07:23 Peterborough-King's Cross/FP/1L45 17:40 King's Cross-York/YK; Wed. 2: YK; Thurs. 3: YK; Fri. 4: 0B02 York-Finsbury Park/1N92 15:05 King's Cross-Newcastle to York (failed)/YK Sat. 5: 0N60 York-Filey/1N60 08:54 Filey-Newcastle/1L24 13:10 Newcastle-Scarborough/0L01 Scarborough-York; Sun. 6: YK/1N12 00:05 King's Cross-Newcastle from York/GD/1A90 Newcastle-King's Cross; Mon. 7: 1N12 00:05 King's Cross-Newcastle to York (55 009 forward)/YK/5L01 York-Scarborough/0L01 Scarborough-York/0D01 York-Doncaster; Tues. 8: On DONCASTER WORKS "Unclassified repair" (No.1 engine, 407, replaced by 457) Until Fri. 11: Off DONCASTER WORKS/DR/0B06 Doncaster-Peterborough/PB; Sat. 12: 5A38 Peterborough-Skegness/2D61 09:54 Skegness-Grantham/1A38 11:05 Skegness-King's Cross from Grantham/FP/1S72 22:30 King's Cross-Edinburgh; Sun. 13: HA/1E42 23:15 Edinburgh-King's Cross; Mon. 14: FP/1L45 17:40 King's Cross-York; Tues. 15: YK 'B' exam; Wed. 16: 1A08 08:07 York-King's Cross/1L43 14:03 King's Cross-York/1A31 18:14 York-King's Cross; Thurs. 17: 1N00 01:00 King's Cross-Newcastle/1S08 07:05 Newcastle-Edinburgh/HA/ 1E43 20:35

Aberdeen-King's Cross from Edinburgh; Fri. 18: FP/1D03 13:05 King's Cross-Cleethorpes/1A32 17:45 Cleethorpes-King's Cross/1S77 23:55 King's Cross-Edinburgh; Sat. 19: HA/1E35 20:45 Edinburgh-King's Cross to Newcastle (coaches derailed at Manors); Sun. 20: GD/1A40 21:28 Newcastle-King's Cross; Mon. 21: 1S12 05:50 King's Cross-Aberdeen to Edinburgh/HA/1E29 17:18 Edinburgh-Newcastle/1A45 22:55 Newcastle-King's Cross; Tues. 22nd: 0B06 Finsbury Park-Peterborough/1B26 07:23 Peterborough-King's Cross/ FP/1S77 23:55 King's Cross-Edinburgh; Wed. 23: HA/1E39 22:25 Edinburgh-King's Cross; Thurs. 24: 1L42 12:05 King's Cross-York/1A26 15:50 York-King's Cross/1S70 22:15 King's Cross-Aberdeen to Edinburgh; Fri. 25: HA 'oe'/1C91 10:25 Edinburgh-Carstairs/1S37 07:37 Liverpool-Edinburgh from Carstairs/1E29 17:18 Edinburgh-Newcastle/1A45 22:55 Newcastle-King's Cross; Sat. 26: FP/1L22 23:00 King's Cross-Bradford to Leeds; Sun. 27: HO; Mon. 28: HO/0L01 Holbeck-York/YK; Tues. 29: YK/1S27 07:36 Plymouth-Edinburgh from York/1E39 22:25 Edinburgh-King's Cross; Wed. 30: 1L42 12:05 King's Cross-York/1A26 15:50 York-King's Cross/1S79 23:20 King's Cross-Aberdeen to Edinburgh

OCTOBER

Thurs. 1: HA/1E29 17:18 Edinburgh-Newcastle/1A40 21:00 Newcastle-King's Cross to York; Fri. 2: YK 'B' exam Until Fri. 9: YK; Sat. 10: 1Z73 Preston-Dundee from York to Edinburgh/HA/1Z73 Dundee-Preston from Edinburgh to York "Two Firths Express Rail tour"; Sun. 11: YK Until Thurs. 15: YK; Fri. 16: 1M62 08:50 York-Liverpool/1E74 14:05 Liverpool-Newcastle/GD; Sat. 17: 0L01 Gateshead-York/YK; Sun. 18: YK; Mon. 19: YK; Tues. 20: 1M62 08:50 York-Liverpool/1E99 13:05 Liverpool-York/YK Until Wed. 28: YK; Thurs. 29: 1M62 08:50 York-Liverpool/1E99 13:05 Liverpool-York; Fri. 30: YK/0B02 York-Finsbury Park/FP; Sat. 31: 1F52 10:10 King's Cross-Edinburgh/1F52 Edinburgh-Peterborough "Celtic Deltic Rail tour"/5F52 Peterborough-King's Cross

NOVEMBER

Sun. 1: FP/1L42 14:05 King's Cross-York/YK; Mon. 2: YK Until Fri. 6: YK/1A26 15:50 York-King's Cross/1S70 22:15 King's Cross-Aberdeen to Edinburgh; Sat. 7: 1F51 Edinburgh-King's Cross "Deltic Queen of Scots Rail tour"; Sun. 8: 1L41 10:05 King's Cross-York/1A10 15:50 York-King's Cross/1S70 22:15 King's Cross-Aberdeen to Edinburgh; Mon. 9: 1M04 07:18 Edinburgh-Carlisle/1S15 15:53 Carlisle-Edinburgh/1E39 22:25 Edinburgh-King's Cross; Tues. 10: FP/1L43 14:03 King's Cross-York/1A31 18:14 York-King's Cross/FP; Wed. 11: FP; Thurs. 12: FP/0L01 Finsbury Park-York (towed by 55 015)/YK Until Tues. 17: YK; Wed. 18: 1M62 08:50 York-Liverpool/1E99 13:05 Liverpool-York/YK; Thurs. 19: YK/1M76 15:50 York-Liverpool/1E59 18:05 Liverpool-York; Fri. 20: YK; Sat. 21: 1Z10 York-Inverkeithing 'Deltic Scotsman Railtour'/1Z10 17:05 Inverkeithing-Bradford to Edinburgh (55 013 forward) 'Deltic Scotsman Railtour'/HA/1E40 19:15 Aberdeen-King's Cross from Edinburgh; Sun. 22nd: FP 'oe'/1S72 22:40 King's Cross-Edinburgh ; Mon. 23: HA 'oe'/1E29 17:18 Edinburgh-Newcastle/1N03 21:20 Newcastle-Darlington; Tues. 24: 0L01 Darlington-York/YK 'oe'/0C01 York-Stratford (towing 55 014 & 40 058)/SF 'oe' (No.2 engine, 437, replaced by 442 or 449.); Wed. 25: SF; Thurs. 26: SF/0B02 Stratford-Finsbury Park/FP; Fri. 27: 1L41 09:40 King's Cross-York/1A22 14:15 York-King's Cross/FP 'oe' Until Mon. 30: FP 'oe'

DECEMBER

Tues. 1: FP/0C01 Finsbury Park-Stratford/SF 'oe' (No.1 engine, 457, replaced by 442 or 449) Until Fri. 4: SF/0B02 Stratford-Finsbury Park/FP; Sat. 5: FP; Sun. 6: FP/1S70 22:15 King's Cross-Aberdeen to Edinburgh; Mon. 7: HA/1E35 20:25 Edinburgh-King's Cross; Tues. 8: 1L41 09:40 King's Cross-York/1A22 14:15 York-King's Cross/FP; Wed. 9: 1N12 00:05 King's Cross-Newcastle/1M04 07:18 Edinburgh-Carlisle from Newcastle/1S15 15:53 Carlisle-Edinburgh/1E39 22:25 Edinburgh-King's Cross; Thurs. 10: FP; Fri. 11: FP; Sat. 12: 1B50 02:00 King's Cross-Peterborough/0G06 Peterborough-Norwich/1G06 Norwich-York/1G06 York-Norwich; Sun. 13: NR; Mon. 14: NR; Tues. 15: 0B01 Norwich-Peterborough/0B02 Peterborough-Finsbury Park/1S77 23:55 King's Cross-Edinburgh to Newcastle; Wed. 16: 1S14 08:10 Newcastle-Edinburgh/HA/1A38 14:55 Edinburgh-Aberdeen/1G20 18:23 Aberdeen-Edinburgh/1E43 20:35 Aberdeen-King's Cross from Edinburgh to York (failed - No.2 engine shutting down - 55 016 forward); Thurs. 17: YK; Fri. 18: YK; Sat. 19: YK/1Z25 05:10 Plymouth-Scarborough from York/1Z25 14:45 Scarborough-Plymouth to Doncaster "Napier North-Eastern Railtour"/0L01 Doncaster-York; Sun. 20: YK/1M70 15:40 York-Liverpool/1E50 21:15 Liverpool-York; Mon. 21: YK Until Tues. 29 YK; Wed. 30: 1M53 07:40 York-Liverpool (No.1 engine passing oil)/1E98 12:05 Liverpool-York/YK 'oe'/NRM 'oe'; Thurs. 31: NRM 'oe'

JANUARY 1982

Fri. 1: NRM 'oe'; Sat. 2: NRM 'oe' - WITHDRAWN

D9003/9003/55003
Meld

JANUARY 1981
Thurs. 1: DONCASTER WORKS Until
MARCH 1981
Mon. 9: DONCASTER WORKS (Cutting up commenced) Until
Thurs. 12: Locomotive cut up

D9004/9004/55004
Queens Own Highlander

JUNE 1981
Mon. 1: 1N00 01:00 King's Cross-Newcastle/1S08 07:05 Newcastle-Edinburgh/HA/ 1A38 14:55 Edinburgh-Aberdeen/1G20 18:23 Aberdeen-Edinburgh/1E42 23:15 Edinburgh-King's Cross; Tues. 2: FP/1L44 16:03 King's Cross-York/1A34 20:19 York-King's Cross; Wed. 3: 1S12 05:50 King's Cross-Aberdeen to Edinburgh/HA/1E35 20:25 Edinburgh-King's Cross; Thurs. 4: 1S76 09:40 King's Cross-Edinburgh/HA/1E40 19:25 Aberdeen-King's Cross from Edinburgh; Fri. 5: FP/1N14 14:03 King's Cross-Newcastle to York/1A31 18:14 York-King's Cross; Sat. 6: 1N00 01:00 King's Cross-Newcastle/1S08 07:05 Newcastle-Edinburgh/HA/ 1E39 22:15 Edinburgh-King's Cross; Sun. 7: FP/1L43 16:05 King's Cross-York/YK; Mon. 8: 1A08 08:07 York-King's Cross/FP/1L44 16:03 King's Cross-York/1A34 20:19 York-King's Cross; Tues. 9: 1S12 05:50 King's Cross-Aberdeen to Edinburgh/HA/1E35 20:25 Edinburgh-King's Cross; Wed. 10: 1S76 09:40 King's Cross-Edinburgh/HA/1E39 22:25 Edinburgh-King's Cross to York (55 010 forward); Thurs. 11: YK 'B' exam; Fri. 12: YK/1S12 05:50 King's Cross-Aberdeen from York (55 022 off) to Edinburgh/ HA/1E39 22:25 Edinburgh-King's Cross; Sat. 13: FP/1L43 14:03 King's Cross-York/YK/1S60 20:00 King's Cross-Aberdeen from York (55

015 off) to Edinburgh; Sun. 14: HA/1E07 12:15 Edinburgh-King's Cross (vice HST) to Newcastle (train terminated)/5E07 Newcastle-Edinburgh/HA/1E43 20:35 Aberdeen-King's Cross from Edinburgh; Mon. 15: 1D03 13:05 King's Cross-Cleethorpes/1A32 17:45 Cleethorpes-King's Cross/ 1S77 23:55 King's Cross-Edinburgh; Tues. 16: 1V93 09:50 Edinburgh-Plymouth to York/1S27 07:36 Plymouth-Edinburgh from York/1E39 22:25 Edinburgh-King's Cross; Wed. 17: FP; Thurs. 18: 1N12 00:05 King's Cross-Newcastle/GD/0B02 Gateshead-Finsbury Park/FP/ 1B03 17:10 King's Cross-Peterborough/0B02 Peterborough-Finsbury Park/ FP/1S72 22:30 King's Cross-Edinburgh; Fri. 19: 1V93 09:50 Edinburgh-Plymouth to York/1S27 07:36 Plymouth-Edinburgh from York/1E35 20:25 Edinburgh-King's Cross; Sat. 20: 1L42 12:05 King's Cross-York/1A26 15:50 York-King's Cross/1S72 22:30 King's Cross-Edinburgh; Sun. 21: HA/1E42 23:15 Edinburgh-King's Cross; Mon. 22: FP; Tues. 23: 1N12 00:05 King's Cross-Newcastle/GD/0L01 Gateshead-York/YK 'B' exam; Wed. 24: YK 'B' exam; Thurs. 25: 1M53 07:49 York-Liverpool/1E98 12:05 Liverpool-York/YK/1A34 20:19 York-King's Cross; Fri. 26: 1S12 05:50 King's Cross-Aberdeen to Edinburgh/HA/1E35 20:25 Edinburgh-King's Cross; Sat. 27: 1S76 09:40 King's Cross-Edinburgh/1S51 12:00 Scarborough-Glasgow Q.St. from Edinburgh/0G99 Glasgow Q.St.-Haymarket/HA/1E43 20:05 Aberdeen-King's Cross from Edinburgh; Sun. 28: FP/1L42 14:05 King's Cross-York/1A19 19:13 York-King's X/FP; Mon. 29: 1S12 05:50 King's X-Aberdeen to Edinburgh/HA/1E35 20:25 Edinburgh-King's X Tues. 30: 1S76 09:40 King's X-Edinburgh/HA/1E35 20:25 Edinburgh-King's X

JULY

Wed. 1: 1S76 09:40 King's Cross-Edinburgh/HA/1E39 22:25 Edinburgh-King's Cross; Thurs. 2: 1L42 12:05 King's Cross-York/1A26 15:50 York-King's Cross/FP; Fri. 3: 1S76 09:40 King's Cross-Edinburgh/HA/1E35 20:25 Edinburgh-King's Cross; Sat. 4: 1L42 12:05 King's Cross-York/1A26 15:50 York-King's Cross/FP; Sun. 5: 1L41 10:05 King's Cross-York/1A10 15:50 York-King's Cross/FP; Mon. 6: 1N00 01:00 King's Cross-Newcastle/1S08 07:05 Newcastle-Edinburgh/HA/ 1A38 14:55 Edinburgh-Aberdeen/1G20 18:23 Aberdeen-Edinburgh/1E43 20:35 Aberdeen-King's Cross from Edinburgh; Tues. 7: FP/1L43 14:03 King's Cross-York/1A31 18:14 York-King's Cross/FP; Wed. 8: 1S85 10:35 King's Cross-Edinburgh/HA/1E39 22:25 Edinburgh-King's Cross; Thurs. 9: FP/1S70 22:15 King's Cross-Aberdeen to Edinburgh; Fri. 10: 1V93 09:50 Edinburgh-Plymouth to York/1S27 07:36 Plymouth-Edinburgh from York/1E39 22:25 Edinburgh-King's Cross; Sat. 11: FP/1D08 19:40 King's Cross-Hull/0D01 Hull-Doncaster; Sun. 12: DR/0L01 Doncaster-York/YK 'B' exam; Mon. 13: YK 'B' exam; Tues. 14: YK 'B' exam; Wed. 15: YK/0B02 York-Finsbury Park/FP/1L44 16:03 King's Cross-York/YK; Thurs. 16: 1A08 08:07 York-King's Cross/FP/1S66 20:15 King's Cross-Edinburgh; Fri. 17: 5E10 06:40 Craigentinny-Dundee/1E10 09:10 Dundee-King's Cross/1S66 20:15 King's Cross-Edinburgh; Sat. 18: 1V93 09:50 Edinburgh-Plymouth to York/1S27 07:36 Plymouth-Edinburgh from York/1E35 20:45 Edinburgh-King's Cross; Sun. 19: 1N02 08:30 King's Cross-Newcastle to Peterborough/0B02 Peterborough-Finsbury Park/FP; Mon. 20: 0B05 Finsbury Park-Peterborough/1B18 07:50 Peterborough-King's Cross/ FP/1B03 17:10 King's Cross-Peterborough/0B02 Peterborough-Finsbury Park/FP/1S72 22:30 King's Cross-Edinburgh; Tues. 21: HA/1E35 20:25 Edinburgh-King's Cross; Wed. 22: 1D01 08:30 King's Cross-Cleethorpes/1A21 13:20 Cleethorpes-King's Cross/ FP/1S70 22:15 King's Cross-Aberdeen to Edinburgh; Thurs. 23: 1M04 07:18 Edinburgh-Carlisle/1S15 15:53 Carlisle-Edinburgh/1E39 22:25 Edinburgh-King's Cross;

Fri. 24: FP/1L44 16:03 King's Cross-York/1A34 20:19 York-King's Cross; Sat. 25: 1S12 05:50 King's Cross-Aberdeen to Edinburgh/1A38 14:55 Edinburgh-Aberdeen/1G20 18:30 Aberdeen-Edinburgh/1E43 20:05 Aberdeen-King's Cross from Edinburgh; Sun. 26: FP/1L43 16:05 King's Cross-York/YK 'D' exam Until Thurs. 30: YK 'D' exam/1A34 20:19 York-King's Cross; Fri. 31: 1S12 05:50 King's Cross-Aberdeen to Edinburgh/HA

AUGUST

Sat. 1: 1M04 07:18 Edinburgh-Carlisle/1S15 15:53 Carlisle-Newcastle/1E39 22:15 Edinburgh-King's Cross; Sun. 2: FP/1L42 14:05 King's Cross-York/1A19 19:13 York-King's Cross/FP; Mon. 3: 1S76 09:40 King's Cross-Edinburgh/HA/1E35 20:25 Edinburgh-King's Cross; Tues. 4: 1L42 12:05 King's Cross-York/1A26 15:50 York-King's Cross/1S70 22:15 King's Cross-Aberdeen to Edinburgh; Wed. 5: 5E10 06:40 Craigentinny-Dundee/1E10 09:10 Dundee-King's Cross/FP/1S70 22:15 King's Cross-Aberdeen to Edinburgh; Thurs. 6: 1V93 09:50 Edinburgh-Plymouth to York/1S27 07:36 Plymouth-Edinburgh from York/1E40 19:25 Aberdeen-King's Cross from Edinburgh; Fri. 7: FP/1N14 14:03 King's Cross-Newcastle/0L01 Newcastle-York/YK; Sat. 8: 0N60 York-Filey/1N60 08:54 Filey-Newcastle to Scarborough/1A37 08:47 Bridlington-King's Cross/1L44 16:03 King's Cross-York/1A34 20:19 York-King's Cross; Sun. 9: 1N02 08:30 King's Cross-Newcastle/1A21 14:57 Newcastle-King's Cross to York (55 021 forward)/YK; Mon. 10: 0B02 York-Finsbury Park/FP/0A21 Finsbury Park-Cleethorpes/1A21 13:20 Cleethorpes-King's Cross/FP; Tues. 11: 1N00 01:00 King's Cross-Newcastle/1S08 07:05 Newcastle-Edinburgh/HA/ 1E35 20:25 Edinburgh-King's Cross; Wed. 12: 1D01 08:30 King's Cross-Cleethorpes/1A21 13:20 Cleethorpes-King's Cross/1S66 20:15 King's Cross-Edinburgh; Thurs. 13: 5E10 06:40 Craigentinny-Dundee/1E10 09:10 Dundee-King's Cross/1S60 20:00 King's Cross-Aberdeen to Edinburgh; Fri. 14: 5E10 06:40 Craigentinny-Dundee/1E10 09:10 Dundee-King's Cross/FP/1S77 23:55 King's Cross-Edinburgh; Sat. 15: 1V93 09:50 Edinburgh-Plymouth to York/YK 'B' exam Until Tues. 18: YK 'B' exam; Wed. 19: 5A37 York-Scarborough/1A37 09:54 Scarborough-King's Cross/FP/1D08 19:40 King's Cross-Hull/0D01 23:35 Hull-Doncaster; Thurs. 20: 1D62 03:55 Doncaster-Hull/1A13 09:36 Hull-King's Cross/FP/1L45 17:40 King's Cross-York/YK; Fri. 21: YK/0B02 York-Finsbury Park/FP/1N14 14:03 King's Cross-Newcastle to York/1A31 18:14 York-King's Cross to Doncaster/DR; Sat. 22: 0B05 Doncaster-Peterborough/5A38 Peterborough-Skegness/1A38 11:05 Skegness-King's Cross/FP/1D08 19:40 King's Cross-Hull/0D01 23:35 Hull-Doncaster; Sun. 23: DR; Mon. 24: 1D62 03:55 Doncaster-Hull/1A13 09:36 Hull-King's Cross/1B21 17:17 King's Cross-Peterborough/0B02 Peterborough-Finsbury Park/FP/1N11 22:45 King's Cross-Newcastle; Tues. 25: 1S43 Newcastle-Edinburgh/5E43 Edinburgh-Heaton/5G06 Heaton-Sunderland/1G06 Sunderland-Darlington/1G06 Darlington-Sunderland/5G06 Sunderland-Heaton/GD; Wed. 26: 1S43 Newcastle-Edinburgh/5E43 Edinburgh-Heaton/1N03 21:20 Newcastle-Darlington/0L01 Darlington-York; Thurs. 27: YK; Fri. 28: 0D01 York-Doncaster/DR/0L01 Doncaster-York to Arksey/6G60 Arksey-York; Sat. 29: YK; Sun. 30: YK; Mon. 31: YK

SEPTEMBER

Tues. 1: YK; Wed. 2: YK/0D01 York-Doncaster Works (towed by 37 022) Thurs. 3: On DONCASTER WORKS "Unclassified repair" (No.2 engine, 439, replaced by 427) Until Fri. 11: Off DONCASTER WORKS/DR; Sat. 12: 1D62 03:55 Doncaster-Hull/1A13 09:36 Hull-King's Cross/1L44 16:03 King's Cross-York/1A34 20:19 York-King's Cross; Sun. 13: FP/1L22 23:00 King's Cross-Bradford to Leeds

Mon. 14: HO/0B02 Holbeck-Finsbury Park/FP/1L22 23:00 King's Cross-Bradford to Leeds; Tues. 15: HO/0B02 Holbeck-Finsbury Park/FP/1S70 22:15 King's Cross-Aberdeen to Edinburgh; Wed. 16: 1V93 09:50 Edinburgh-Plymouth to York/1S27 07:36 Plymouth-Edinburgh from York/1E40 19:25 Aberdeen-King's Cross from Edinburgh; Thurs. 17: FP/1L43 14:03 King's Cross-York/1A31 18:14 York-King's Cross/FP; Fri. 18: 1S12 05:50 King's Cross-Aberdeen to Edinburgh/HA/1E42 23:15 Edinburgh-King's Cross to Newcastle; Sat. 19: 1A39 10:50 Newcastle-King's Cross to York/YK Until Tues. 22: YK/1A34 20:19 York-King's Cross; Wed. 23: 1S12 05:50 King's Cross-Aberdeen to Newcastle/GD/1A40 21:00 Newcastle-King's Cross; Thurs. 24: 5B26 05:24 King's Cross-Peterborough/1B26 07:23 Peterborough-King's Cross/FP/1S72 22:30 King's Cross-Edinburgh to York (55 013 forward); Fri. 25: 1A37 10:47 York-King's Cross/FP/1D08 19:40 King's Cross-Hull/1D26 23:40 Hull-Doncaster; Sat. 26: 1D62 03:55 Doncaster-Hull/1A13 09:36 Hull-King's Cross/FP/1D08 19:40 King's Cross-Hull/0D01 23:35 Hull-Doncaster; Sun. 27: DR/0B02 Doncaster-Finsbury Park/FP; Mon. 28: 1L41 09:40 King's Cross-York/YK; Tues. 29: YK; Wed. 30: YK

OCTOBER

Thurs. 1: YK Until Wed. 14: YK/1A40 21:00 Newcastle-King's Cross from York; Thurs. 15: 5B26 05:24 King's Cross-Peterborough/1B26 07:23 Peterborough-King's Cross/FP/1L43 14:03 King's Cross-York/1A31 18:14 York-King's Cross/FP; Fri. 16: 1L41 09:40 King's Cross-York/1A22 14:15 York-King's Cross/FP/1S70 22:15 King's Cross-Aberdeen to Edinburgh; Sat. 17: 1V93 09:50 Edinburgh-Plymouth to York/1S27 07:36 Plymouth-Edinburgh from York/1E43 20:05 Aberdeen-King's Cross from Edinburgh; Sun. 18: FP/1S70 22:15 King's Cross-Aberdeen to Edinburgh; Mon. 19: 1V93 09:50 Edinburgh-Plymouth to York/1S27 07:36 Plymouth-Edinburgh from York/1E35 20:25 Edinburgh-King's Cross; Tues. 20: FP/1D08 19:40 King's Cross-Hull/5L04 23:30 Hull-York; Wed. 21: YK; Thurs. 22:YK/1A22 14:15 York-King's Cross/1D08 19:40 King's Cross-Hull/5L04 23:30 Hull-York; Fri. 23: 1A08 08:07 York-King's Cross/1N14 14:03 King's Cross-Newcastle to York/1A31 18:14 York-King's Cross/1S77 23:55 King's Cross-Edinburgh; Sat. 24: 1V93 09:50 Edinburgh-Plymouth to York/1S27 07:36 Plymouth-Edinburgh from York/1E39 22:15 Edinburgh-King's Cross; Sun. 25: FP; Mon. 26: 1N00 01:00 King's Cross-Newcastle/1S08 07:05 Newcastle-Edinburgh/HA/ 1E35 20:25 Edinburgh-King's Cross; Tues. 27: 1L41 09:40 King's Cross-York/1A22 14:15 York-King's Cross/1D08 19:40 King's Cross-Hull/5L04 23:30 Hull-York 'oe' (No.2 engine dephased); Wed. 28: 1M53 07:49 York-Liverpool 'oe'/1E98 12:05 Liverpool-York 'oe'/1M76 15:50 York-Liverpool 'oe'/LIV (No.1 engine H.W.T.); Thurs. 29: LIV/0Z00 Liverpool-York (towed by 31 405)/YK; Fri. 30: YK/0B02 York-Finsbury Park (towed with 47 019 & 47 411)/FP/0C01 Finsbury Park-Stratford (towed with 47 019 & 47 411); Sat. 31: SF (No.1 engine, 430, replaced by 432)

NOVEMBER

Sun. 1: SF – WITHDRAWN Until Sun. 22: SF; Mon. 23: 9G36 01:23 Stratford-York (towed by 31 324 to Lincoln and 31 281 forward) with 55 011 & 55018; Tues. 24: YK (For spares) Until Mon. 30: YK

D9005/9005/55005
The Prince of Wales's Own Regiment of Yorkshire

JANUARY 1981

Thurs. 1: 1A13 09:33 Hull-King's Cross/FP/1D04 17:05 King's Cross-Hull/0D01 Hull-Doncaster/1A41 21:20 Bradford-King's Cross from Doncaster; Fri. 2: 1L41 10:05 King's Cross-York/1A22 14:10 York-King's Cross/1S60 20:00 King's Cross-Aberdeen to Edinburgh; Sat. 3: 1V93 09:50 Edinburgh-Plymouth to York/1S27 07:22 Plymouth-Edinburgh from York/1E40 19:15 Aberdeen-King's Cross from Edinburgh; Sun. 4: FP/1N58 15:45 King's Cross-Newcastle/1A45 22:55 Newcastle-King's Cross; Mon. 5: 1D01 08:15 King's Cross-Cleethorpes/1A21 13:13 Cleethorpes-King's Cross/ FP/1S72 22:30 King's Cross-Edinburgh; Tues. 6: 1V93 09:50 Edinburgh-Plymouth to York/1S27 07:22 Plymouth-Edinburgh from York/1E48 21:20 Aberdeen-King's Cross from Edinburgh; Wed. 7: 1L41 10:05 King's Cross-York/1A22 14:10 York-King's Cross/FP/1S70 22:15 King's Cross-Aberdeen to Edinburgh; Thurs. 8: 1V93 09:50 Edinburgh-Plymouth to York/1S27 07:22 Plymouth-Edinburgh from York/HA 'ao'; Fri. 9: HA/1E26 16:30 Aberdeen-Leeds from Edinburgh/1E24 22:50 Shrewsbury-York from Leeds; Sat. 10: YK 'C' exam Until Wed. 14: YK 'C' exam; Thurs. 15: 1A08 08:05 York-King's Cross/FP/1L45 18:05 King's Cross-York/YK/1E35 20:25 Edinburgh-King's Cross from York (55 013 off); Fri. 16: 1D00 08:05 King's Cross-Hull/1A18 12:34 Hull-King's Cross/1L45 18:05 King's Cross-York; Sat. 17: YK/0D01 York-Doncaster/0L01 Doncaster-York/1S12 05:50 King's Cross-Aberdeen from York (55 006 off) to Edinburgh (55 014 forward)/HA/1E39 22:10 Edinburgh-King's Cross; Sun. 18: FP/1L42 14:05 King's Cross-York/1A19 19:10 York-King's Cross/FP; Mon. 19: 5B16 05:24 King's Cross-Peterborough/1B16 07:50 Peterborough-King's Cross/1L42 12:20 King's Cross-York/1A26 15:50 York-King's Cross/1S70 22:15 King's Cross-Aberdeen to Edinburgh; Tues. 20: 1A23 08:55 Edinburgh-Aberdeen/1G64 12:40 Aberdeen-Edinburgh/HA/1E39 22:30 Edinburgh-King's Cross; Wed. 21: FP/1L44 16:05 King's Cross-York/1A34 19:55 York-King's Cross; Thurs. 22: FP/1L42 12:20 King's Cross-York/YK; Fri. 23: 1A08 08:05 York-King's Cross/FP/1L44 16:05 King's Cross-York/1A34 19:55 York-King's Cross; Sat. 24: FP; Sun. 25: FP; Mon. 26: FP/1D03 13:05 King's Cross-Cleethorpes/1A32 17:43 Cleethorpes-King's Cross/FP; Tues. 27: 1D02 12:05 King's Cross-Hull/1A28 16:30 Hull-King's Cross/FP; Wed. 28: 1D00 08:05 King's Cross-Hull/1A18 12:34 Hull-King's Cross/FP/1S70 22:15 King's Cross-Aberdeen to Edinburgh; Thurs. 29: HA/1E26 16:30 Aberdeen-Leeds from Edinburgh/1E24 22:50 Shrewsbury-York from Leeds; Fri. 30: YK 'B' exam; Sat. 31: YK 'B' exam

FEBRUARY

Sun. 1: YK 'B' exam; Mon. 2: YK 'B' exam; Tues. 3: YK - WITHDRAWN Until Sun. 15: YK; Mon. 16: YK/York-Stratford (towed); Tues. 17: SF (No.1 bogie, 9000-27, replaced by 9000-49. No.2 bogie, 9000-28, replaced by 9000-50).; Wed. 18: SF; Thurs. 19: SF; Fri. 20: SF/Stratford-Doncaster Works (towed); Sat. 21: On DONCASTER WORKS Until **FEBRUARY 1983**: Locomotive cut up

D9006/9006/55006
The Fife and Forfar Yeomanry

JANUARY 1981
Thurs. 1: DONCASTER WORKS Until Fri. 16: Off DONCASTER WORKS/DR Sat. 17: DR/0B01 Doncaster-King's Cross/1S12 05:50 King's Cross-Aberdeen to York (55 005 forward)/YK 'oe' ; Sun. 18th: YK; Mon. 19: 1M63 11:49 York-Liverpool/1E88 16:05 Liverpool-Newcastle/1N03 21:30 Newcastle-Darlington/0L01 Darlington-York; Tues. 20: YK 'D' exam; Wed. 21: YK 'D' exam; Thurs. 22: 1A37 10:45 York-King's Cross/1B03 17:12 King's Cross-Peterborough/0B02 Peterborough-Finsbury Park/FP/1S79 23:15 King's Cross-Aberdeen to Peterborough (55 009 forward); Fri. 23: 0B02 Peterborough-Finsbury Park/FP/1D30 04:05 King's Cross-Doncaster/ 0L01 Doncaster-York/YK; Sat. 24: 1S12 05:50 King's Cross-Aberdeen from York to Edinburgh/HA/1E35 20:45 Edinburgh-King's Cross; Sun. 25: FP/1L45 15:05 King's Cross-York/5D44 York-Hull/0D01 Hull-Doncaster; Mon. 26: 1D62 03:55 Doncaster-Hull/1A13 09:33 Hull-King's Cross/FP/1L22 23:00 King's Cross-Bradford to Leeds; Tues. 27: 0L01 Leeds-York/YK/1A37 10:45 York-King's Cross/1B03 17:12 King's Cross-Peterborough/0B02 Peterborough-Finsbury Park/FP; Wed. 28: 5B16 05:24 King's Cross-Peterborough/1B16 07:50 Peterborough-King's Cross/FP/1D08 19:35 King's Cross-Hull/0D01 23:35 Hull-Doncaster; Thurs. 29: 1D62 03:55 Doncaster-Hull/1A13 09:33 Hull-King's Cross/FP/1L45 18:05 King's Cross-York/0B05 York-Peterborough/1E35 20:25 Edinburgh-King's Cross from Peterborough; Fri. 30: 1D00 08:05 King's Cross-Hull/1A18 12:34 Hull-King's Cross/FP/1S70 22:15 King's Cross-Aberdeen to Edinburgh; Sat. 31: HA/1E40 19:15 Aberdeen-King's Cross from Edinburgh to Peterborough

FEBRUARY
Sun. 1: 0B02 Peterborough-Finsbury Park/FP/1B36 18:20 King's Cross-Peterborough/0B02 Peterborough-Finsbury Park; Mon. 2: 1N00 01:00 King's Cross-Newcastle to York/YK; Tues. 3: YK; Wed. 4: 1A08 08:05 York-King's Cross/1L43 14:05 King's Cross-York/1A31 18:10 York-King's Cross/1S77 23:55 King's Cross-Edinburgh; Thurs. 5: HA/0E20 Haymarket-Gateshead/GD; Fri. 6: GD/5E74 19:00 Newcastle-York/YK; Sat. 7: YK; Sun. 8: YK —WITHDRAWN at 22:30; Mon. 9: YK/York-Doncaster Works (towed)/On DONCASTER WORKS; Tues. 10: DONCASTER WORKS Until **JULY 1981** Sun. 19: Cutting up completed

D9007/9007/55007
Pinza

JUNE 1981
Mon. 1: SF Until Tues. 16: SF/0B02 Stratford-Finsbury Park/FP; Wed. 17: 1S76 10:05 King's Cross-Edinburgh/HA/1E39 22:25 Edinburgh-King's Cross to Newcastle (Boiler fire); Thurs. 18: GD/0L01 Gateshead-York/YK; Fri. 19: YK Until Tues. 23: YK; Wed. 24: 1A08 08:07 York-King's Cross/FP/1D08 19:40 King's Cross-Hull/0D01 23:35 Hull-Doncaster; Thurs. 25: 1D62 03:55 Doncaster-Hull/1A13 09:36 Hull-King's Cross/FP/1L45 17:40 King's Cross-York; Fri. 26: 1A08 08:07 York-King's Cross/FP/1S70 22:15 King's Cross-Aberdeen to Edinburgh; Sat. 27: 1M04 07:18 Edinburgh-Carlisle/1S15 15:53 Carlisle-Edinburgh/1E40 19:15 Aberdeen-King's Cross from Edinburgh; Sun. 28: FP; Mon. 29: 1N12 00:05 King's Cross-Newcastle/0L01 Newcastle-York/YK/1S27 07:36 Plymouth-Edinburgh from York/1E48 21:20 Aberdeen-King's Cross from Edinburgh; Tues. 30: FP/1L43 14:03 King's Cross-York/1A31 18:14 York-King's Cross

JULY

Wed. 1: 1N00 01:00 King's Cross-Newcastle/1S08 07:05 Newcastle-Edinburgh/HA/ 1A38 14:55 Edinburgh-Aberdeen/1G20 18:23 Aberdeen-Edinburgh/1E48 21:20 Aberdeen-King's Cross from Edinburgh; Thurs. 2: FP/1S70 22:15 King's Cross-Aberdeen to Edinburgh; Fri. 3: 1V93 09:50 Edinburgh-Plymouth to York/1S27 07:36 Plymouth-Edinburgh from York/1E48 21:20 Aberdeen-King's Cross from Edinburgh; Sat. 4: FP/1D08 19:40 King's Cross-Hull/0D01 23:35 Hull-Doncaster; Sun. 5: DR; Mon. 6: 1D62 03:55 Doncaster-Hull/1A13 09:36 Hull-King's Cross/FP/1B03 17:10 King's Cross-Peterborough/0B02 Peterborough-Finsbury Park/FP/1S70 22:15 King's Cross-Aberdeen to Edinburgh; Tues. 7: 5E10 06:40 Craigentinny-Dundee/1E10 09:10 Dundee-King's Cross/FP 'B' exam; Wed. 8: FP 'B' exam/1L43 14:03 King's Cross-York to Doncaster (train terminated - signal failure)/1A31 18:14 York-King's Cross from Doncaster (train started at 18:52 ex Doncaster)/FP; Thurs. 9: 1S12 05:50 King's Cross-Aberdeen to Edinburgh/HA/1E39 22:25 Edinburgh-King's Cross; Fri. 10: FP/1S70 22:15 King's Cross-Aberdeen to Edinburgh; Sat. 11: 1V93 09:50 Edinburgh-Plymouth to York/1S27 07:36 Plymouth-Edinburgh from York/1E43 20:05 Aberdeen-King's Cross from Edinburgh; Sun. 12: FP/1L43 16:05 King's Cross-York/YK Mon. 13:1A37 10:47 York-King's Cross/FP/1D08 19:40 King's Cross-Hull/0D01 23:35 Hull-Doncaster; Tues. 14: 1D62 03:55 Doncaster-Hull/1A13 09:36 Hull-King's Cross/1L45 17:40 King's Cross-York/YK; Wed. 15: 1A08 08:07 York-King's Cross/1L43 14:03 King's Cross-York/1A31 18:14 York-King's Cross/FP; Thurs. 16: 1S12 05:50 King's Cross-Aberdeen to Edinburgh/HA/1E35 20:25 Edinburgh-King's Cross; Fri. 17: 1L42 12:05 King's Cross-York/1A26 15:50 York-King's Cross/FP; Sat. 18: 1S84 08:35 King's Cross-Edinburgh/HA/1E40 19:15 Aberdeen-King's Cross from Edinburgh; Sun. 19: FP; Mon. 20: FP/1S66 20:15 King's Cross-Edinburgh; Tues. 21:1M04 07:18 Edinburgh-Carlisle/1S15 15:53 Carlisle-Edinburgh/1E43 20:35 Aberdeen-King's Cross from Edinburgh to York (55 021 forward); Wed. 22: YK 'B' exam Until Fri. 31: YK 'B' exam

AUGUST

Sat. 1: YK 'B' exam Until Sun. 16: YK 'B' exam/1M70 15:40 York-Liverpool/1E50 21:15 Liverpool-York; Mon. 17: 1A08 08:07 York-King's Cross/1L45 17:40 King's Cross-York/YK; Tues. 18: YK/1A34 20:19 York-King's Cross; Wed. 19: 1S12 05:50 King's Cross-Aberdeen to Edinburgh/HA/1E35 20:25 Edinburgh-King's Cross; Thurs. 20: FP; Fri. 21: FP; Sat. 22: 1S76 09:40 King's Cross-Edinburgh to Peterborough/PB; Sun. 23: PB/1D00 11:05 King's Cross-Cleethorpes from Peterborough/1A17 17:44 Cleethorpes-King's Cross; Mon. 24: 1N00 01:00 King's Cross-Newcastle/1S08 07:05 Newcastle-Edinburgh/HA/ 1E29 17:18 Edinburgh-Newcastle/GD/0L01 Gateshead-York (with 55 011); Tues. 25: YK/5E56 York-King's Cross/1L22 23:00 King's Cross-Bradford to Leeds; Wed. 26: HO/0B06 Holbeck-Peterborough/PB; Thurs. 27: PB/0L01 Peterborough-York (towed by 40 074)/YK; Fri. 28: 1A37 10:47 York-King's Cross/FP/1D08 19:40 King's Cross-Hull/1D26 23:40 Hull-Doncaster; Sat. 29: 1D62 03:55 Doncaster-Hull/1A13 09:36 Hull-King's Cross/1L44 16:03 King's Cross-York/1A34 20:19 York-King's Cross; Sun. 30: 1L41 10:05 King's Cross-York/1A10 15:50 York-King's Cross/FP; Mon. 31: 1N00 01:00 King's Cross-Newcastle/1S08 07:05 Newcastle-Edinburgh/HA/ 1E29 17:18 Edinburgh-Newcastle/1A45 22:55 Newcastle-King's Cross

SEPTEMBER

Tues. 1: FP/1S60 20:00 King's Cross-Aberdeen to Edinburgh; Wed. 2: 5E10 06:40 Craigentinny-Dundee/1E10 09:10 Dundee-King's Cross/FP/1S79 23:20 King's Cross-Aberdeen to Edinburgh; Thurs. 3: 1V93 09:50

Edinburgh-Plymouth to York/1S27 07:36 Plymouth-Edinburgh from York/1E40 19:25 Aberdeen-King's Cross from Edinburgh Fri. 4: FP/1F14 14:05 King's Cross-Edinburgh (extended from Newcastle)/5F14 Edinburgh-Heaton/HTN/GD/1S60 20:00 King's Cross-Aberdeen from Newcastle; Sat. 5: 5E10 06:40 Craigentinny-Dundee/1E10 09:10 Dundee-King's Cross/1S66 21:00 King's Cross-Edinburgh to York; Sun. 6: YK 'D' exam Until Thurs. 10: YK 'D' exam/0B02 York-Finsbury Park to Hitchin/1A13 09:36 Hull-King's Cross from Hitchin (assisting 55 010)/FP; Fri. 11: FP; Sat. 12: 1Z31 09:28 Finsbury Park-Wansford "Deltic Anglian Rail tour"/1Z31 17:20 Wansford-King's Cross "Deltic Anglian Rail tour"/FP Until Tues. 15: FP/1L43 14:03 King's Cross-York/1A31 18:14 York-King's Cross; Wed. 16: 1N00 01:00 King's Cross-Newcastle/1S08 07:05 Newcastle-Edinburgh/HA/ 1F50 Aberdeen-Ipswich "Footex" from Edinburgh to Newcastle/GD/1A40 21:00 Newcastle-King's Cross; Thurs. 17: 5B26 05:24 King's Cross-Peterborough/1B26 07:23 Peterborough-King's Cross/FP/1D03 13:05 King's Cross-Cleethorpes/1A32 17:45 Cleethorpes-King's Cross; Fri. 18: 1N00 01:00 King's Cross-Newcastle/1S08 07:05 Newcastle-Edinburgh/HA/ 1F50 16:25 Edinburgh-Scarborough to York; Sat. 19: 0A37 York-Scarborough/1A37 09:50 Scarborough-King's Cross/FP/1D08 19:40 King's Cross-Hull/0D01 23:35 Hull-Doncaster; Sun. 20: DR; Mon. 21: 1D62 03:55 Doncaster-Hull/1A13 09:36 Hull-King's Cross/FP/1S60 20:00 King's Cross-Aberdeen to Edinburgh; Tues. 22: 1M04 07:18 Edinburgh-Carlisle/1S15 15:53 Carlisle-Edinburgh/1E40 19:25 Aberdeen-King's Cross from Edinburgh; Wed. 23: FP/1L43 14:03 King's Cross-York/1A31 18:14 York-King's Cross/FP; Thurs. 24: 1S12 05:50 King's Cross-Aberdeen to Edinburgh/HA/1E39 22:25 Edinburgh-King's Cross; Fri. 25: 1L42 12:05 King's Cross-York/1A26 15:50 York-King's Cross/1S70 22:15 King's Cross-Aberdeen to Edinburgh; Sat. 26: 1V93 09:50 Edinburgh-Plymouth to York/YK; Sun. 27: YK/1E35 20:25 Edinburgh-King's Cross from York to Doncaster; Mon. 28: 1D62 03:55 Doncaster-Hull/1A13 09:36 Hull-King's Cross/FP/1L45 17:40 King's Cross-York/YK; Tues. 29:YK/0B02 York-Finsbury Park/FP/1S60 20:00 King's Cross-Aberdeen to Newcastle; Wed. 30: GD/1S08 07:05 Newcastle-Edinburgh/HA/1E35 20:25 Edinburgh-King's Cross

OCTOBER

Thurs. 1: 1L41 09:40 King's Cross-York/YK 'B' exam; Fri. 2: YK 'B' exam/1A22 14:15 York-King's Cross/1S66 20:15 King's Cross-Edinburgh; Sat. 3: 1Z13 07:40 Edinburgh-Kyle of Lochalsh to Perth/1Z13 15:50 Kyle of Lochalsh-Edinburgh from Perth/HA; Sun. 4: 1V93 11:25 Edinburgh-Plymouth to York/YK; Mon. 5: 1M62 08:50 York-Liverpool/1E99 13:05 Liverpool-York/5A47 18:18 Clifton-Ferme Park/1S79 23:20 King's Cross-Aberdeen to Edinburgh; Tues. 6: 1V93 09:50 Edinburgh-Plymouth to York/YK; Wed. 7: 1A08 08:07 York-King's Cross/FP/1L44 16:03 King's Cross-York/1A34 20:19 York-King's Cross; Thurs. 8: 1L41 09:40 King's Cross-York/1A22 14:15 York-King's Cross/1S60 20:00 King's Cross-Aberdeen to Edinburgh; Fri. 9: 1M04 07:18 Edinburgh-Carlisle/1S15 15:53 Carlisle-Edinburgh/HA; Sat. 10: HA/0C01 Haymarket-Carstairs/1Z70 Coventry-Edinburgh from Carstairs/ 1E29 17:18 Edinburgh-Newcastle/GD; Sun. 11: GD/1A40 21:28 Newcastle-King's Cross; Mon. 12: 5B26 05:24 King's Cross-Peterborough/1B26 07:23 Peterborough-King's Cross/FP; Tues. 13: 1N00 01:00 King's Cross-Newcastle to York/YK/1A40 21:00 Newcastle-King's Cross from York; Wed. 14: 1L41 09:40 King's Cross-York/1A22 14:15 York-King's Cross/1D08 19:40 King's Cross-Hull/5L04 23:30 Hull-York; Thurs. 15: 1A08 08:07 York-King's Cross/FP 'oe' (No.2 engine fractured cylinder liner); Fri. 16: 1N12 00:05 King's Cross-Newcastle/GD 'oe'; Sat. 17: 1S14 08:10 Newcastle-Edinburgh/HA 'oe'/1E29 17:18

Edinburgh-Newcastle/ GD 'oe'; Sun. 18: GD 'oe'/1A40 21:28 Newcastle-King's Cross; Mon. 19: 5B26 05:24 King's Cross-Peterborough/1B26 07:23 Peterborough-King's Cross/FP 'oe'; Tues. 20: 1N12 00:05 King's Cross-Newcastle/GD/0L01 Gateshead-York/YK 'oe' Until Fri. 23: YK 'oe'/0C01 York-Stratford (towing 40 193)/SF (No.2 engine, 453, replaced by 423) Until Fri. 30: SF/0B02 Stratford-Finsbury Park/FP; Sat. 31:FP

NOVEMBER

Sun. 1: FP; Mon. 2: FP/1L43 14:03 King's Cross-York/1A31 18:14 York-King's Cross/1S77 23:55 King's Cross-Edinburgh; Tues. 3: HA/1E35 20:25 Edinburgh-King's Cross; Wed. 4: 1L41 09:40 King's Cross-York/1A22 14:15 York-King's Cross/1D08 19:40 King's Cross-Hull/5L04 23:30 Hull-York; Thurs. 5: 1A08 08:07 York-King's Cross/FP/1L44 16:03 King's Cross-York/1A34 20:19 York-King's Cross; Fri. 6: 1S12 05:50 King's Cross-Aberdeen/1E26 16:30 Aberdeen-York; Sat. 7: 1A08 08:07 York-King's Cross/1L43 14:03 King's Cross-York/1A31 18:14 York-King's Cross/FP; Sun. 8: FP/1S79 23:20 King's Cross-Aberdeen to Edinburgh; Mon. 9: HA/1E35 20:25 Edinburgh-King's Cross; Tues. 10: 1L41 09:40 King's Cross-York/1A22 14:15 York-King's Cross/1D08 19:40 King's Cross-Hull/5L04 23:30 Hull-York; Wed. 11: 1A08 08:07 York-King's Cross/FP/1L44 16:03 King's Cross-York/1A34 20:19 York-King's Cross; Thurs. 12: 1S12 05:50 King's Cross-Aberdeen to York/0B06 York Peterborough/0B02 Peterborough-Finsbury Park/1S72 22:30 King's Cross-Edinburgh; Fri. 13: HA/1E35 20:25 Edinburgh-King's Cross; Sat. 14: FP/1L43 14:03 King's Cross-York/1A31 18:14 York-King's Cross/FP 'eo'; Sun. 15: FP 'eo'/1L42 14:05 King's Cross-York/1A19 19:13 York-King's Cross/FP 'eo'; Mon. 16: 5B26 05:24 King's Cross-Peterborough/1B26 07:23 Peterborough-King's Cross/FP 'eo'/1S70 22:15 King's Cross-Aberdeen to Edinburgh; Tues. 17: 5G18

Craigentinny-Markinch/2G18 07:25 Markinch-Edinburgh/HA 'eo'/1A38 14:55 Edinburgh-Aberdeen/1G20 18:23 Aberdeen-Edinburgh/HA 'eo'/1E48 21:20 Aberdeen-King's Cross from Edinburgh; Wed. 18: FP 'eo' Until Tues. 24: FP; Wed. 25: 1L41 09:40 King's Cross-York/1A22 14:15 York-King's Cross/1D08 19:40 King's Cross-Hull/5L04 23:30 Hull-York; Thurs. 26: YK/1A26 15:50 York-King's Cross/1S77 23:55 King's Cross-Edinburgh; Fri. 27: HA/1E40 19:25 Aberdeen-King's Cross from Edinburgh; Sat. 28: FP/1S60 20:00 King's Cross-Aberdeen to Edinburgh; Sun. 29: HA/1E40 19:25 Aberdeen-King's Cross from Edinburgh; Mon. 30: FP/1S60 20:00 King's Cross-Aberdeen to Edinburgh

DECEMBER

Tues. 1: 5G18 Craigentinny-Markinch/2G18 07:25 Markinch-Edinburgh/HA/1S12 05:50 King's Cross-Aberdeen from Edinburgh/1E26 16:30 Aberdeen-York; Wed. 2: YK/1A26 15:50 York-King's Cross/1S70 22:15 King's Cross-Aberdeen to Edinburgh; Thurs. 3: 1M04 07:18 Edinburgh-Carlisle/1S15 15:53 Carlisle-Edinburgh/1E43 20:35 Aberdeen-King's Cross from Edinburgh; Fri. 4: FP/1N14 14:03 King's Cross-Newcastle to York/1A31 18:14 York-King's Cross/FP; Sat. 5: 1S12 05:50 King's Cross-Aberdeen to Newcastle (55 019 forward)/0L01 Newcastle-York/1M76 15:50 York-Liverpool/1E89 20:40 Liverpool-York; Sun. 6: YK Until Wed. 9: YK/1A26 15:50 York-King's Cross/1S70 22:15 King's Cross-Aberdeen to York (assisted from Grantham by 47 416); Thurs. 10: YK/1A08 08:07 York-King's Cross/FP/1S66 20:15 King's Cross-Edinburgh to Newcastle (failed); Fri. 11: GD; Sat. 12: 5F05 Heaton-Edinburgh/1E05 09:15 Edinburgh-King's Cross (vice HST) to Newcastle/GD/1M77 15:18 Newcastle-Liverpool/1E89 20:40 Liverpool-York; Sun. 13: YK/1S79 23:20 King's Cross-Aberdeen from York to Edinburgh; Mon. 14: HA/1E29 17:18 Edinburgh-Newcastle/GD;

Tues. 15: 1M58 08:15 Newcastle-Liverpool/0E00 Liverpool-York/1A26 15:50 York-King's Cross/1S79 23:20 King's Cross-Aberdeen to Newcastle (failed - brakes frozen); Wed. 16: GD; Thurs. 17: GD 'oe' (No.1 engine defective fuel pump); Fri. 18: GD 'oe'/0N04 Gateshead-Darlington/1N04 07:15 Darlington-Newcastle/GD 'oe'/1N03 21:20 Newcastle-Darlington; Sat. 19: 0L0 1 Darlington-York/YK 'oe'; Sun. 20: YK 'oe'; Mon. 21: YK/1A22 14:15 York-King's Cross/FP/1S77 23:55 King's Cross-Edinburgh to York (failed); Tues. 22: YK/1A08 08:07 York-King's Cross/FP/1L44 16:03 King's Cross-York/1A34 20:19 York-King's Cross; Wed. 23: 1S12 05:50 King's Cross-Aberdeen to Edinburgh/HA/1E40 19:25 Aberdeen-King's Cross from Edinburgh; Thurs. 24: FP; Until; Sun. 27: FP/1L42 14:05 King's Cross-York/1A19 19:13 York-King's Cross/FP; Mon. 28: 1L41 09:40 King's Cross-York/YK; Tues. 29: YK; Wed. 30: 1A08 08:07 York-King's Cross (assisted from Doncaster by 47 146)/FP (No.1 engine aerating. No.2 engine losing coolant); Thurs. 31: FP/0L01 Finsbury Park-York (towed by 31 121)/YK - WITHDRAWN

D9008/9008/55008
The Green Howards

JUNE 1981

Mon. 1: 1S12 05:50 King's Cross-Aberdeen to Edinburgh/HA/1E29 17:18 Edinburgh-Newcastle/1A45 22:55 Newcastle-King's Cross; Tues. 2: FP/1L43 14:03 King's Cross-York/1A31 18:14 York-King's Cross; Wed. 3: 1N00 01:00 King's Cross-Newcastle/1S08 07:05 Newcastle-Edinburgh/HA/ 1E29 17:18 Edinburgh-Newcastle/GD; Thurs. 4: GD Driver training/1G10/0B02 -Finsbury Park; Fri. 5: 1S76 09:40 King's Cross-Edinburgh/HA/1E26 16:30 Aberdeen-Leeds from Edinburgh/1E24 22:50 Shrewsbury-York from Leeds; Sat. 6: 1A08 08:07 York-King's Cross/1L43 14:03 King's Cross-York/1A31 18:14 York-King's Cross/FP; Sun. 7: 1N02 08:30 King's Cross-Newcastle/1A21 14:57 Newcastle-King's Cross to York/YK; Mon. 8:0A13 York-Hull/1A13 09:36 Hull-King's Cross/FP/1D08 19:40 King's Cross-Hull/BG; Tues. 9: 1A13 09:36 Hull-King's Cross/1L44 16:03 King's Cross-York/1A34 20:19 York-King's Cross; Wed. 10:1S12 05:50 King's Cross-Aberdeen/1E26 16:30 Aberdeen-Leeds/1E24 22:50 Shrewsbury-York from Leeds; Thurs. 11: 5A37 York-Durham/1A37 09:30 Durham-King's Cross/FP/1D08 19:40 King's Cross-Hull/0D01 23:35 Hull-Doncaster; Fri. 12:DR/0A13 Doncaster-Hull/1A13 09:36 Hull-King's Cross/FP/1D08 19:40 King's Cross-Hull/0D01 23:35 Hull-Doncaster; Sat. 13: DR/0A13 Doncaster-Hull/1A13 09:36 Hull-King's Cross/FP/1L45 18:05 King's Cross-York/YK; Sun. 14: YK; Mon. 15: YK; Tues. 16: 1A08 08:07 York-King's Cross/FP/1L44 16:03 King's Cross-York/1A34 20:19 York-King's Cross; Wed. 17: 1S12 05:50 King's Cross-Aberdeen to Edinburgh/HA/1E26 16:30 Aberdeen-Leeds from Edinburgh/1E24 22:50 Shrewsbury-York from Leeds; Thurs. 18: 1A08 08:07 York-King's Cross/FP/1L44 16:03 King's Cross-York/YK; Fri. 19: YK/0A31 York-Neville Hill/5A31 Neville Hill-York/1A31 18:14 York-King's Cross/FP; Sat. 20: 1S12 05:50 King's Cross-Aberdeen to Edinburgh/HA/1E40 19:15 Aberdeen-King's Cross from Edinburgh to Newcastle; Sun. 21: GD/1A45 22:55 Newcastle-King's Cross; Mon. 22: FP/1L44 16:03 King's Cross-York/1A34 20:19 York-King's Cross; Tues. 23: 1N16 10:45 King's Cross-Newcastle (vice HST/1A29 16:40 Newcastle-King's Cross (vice HST)/1S70 22:15 King's Cross-Aberdeen to Edinburgh; Wed. 24: 1M04 07:18 Edinburgh-Carlisle/1S15 15:53 Carlisle-Edinburgh/HA; Thurs. 25: 5E10 06:40 Craigentinny-Dundee/1E10 09:10 Dundee-King's Cross/FP/1S70 22:15 King's Cross-Aberdeen to Edinburgh; Fri. 26: 1M04 07:18 Edinburgh-Carlisle/1S15 15:53 Carlisle-Edinburgh/1E43 20:35 Aberdeen-King's Cross from Edinburgh; Sat. 27: 1L42 12:05 King's Cross-York/1A26 15:50 York-King's

Cross/1S70 22:15 King's Cross-Aberdeen to Edinburgh; Sun. 28: HA/1E48 21:20 Aberdeen-King's Cross from Edinburgh; Mon. 29: FP/1L43 14:03 King's Cross-York/1A31 18:14 York-King's Cross/FP; Tues. 30: 1N01 07:10 King's Cross-Newcastle (vice HST)/1A35 11:15 Newcastle-King's Cross (vice HST)/FP/1S70 22:15 King's Cross-Aberdeen to Edinburgh

JULY

Wed. 1: 1F53 08:20 Edinburgh-King's Cross (High Speed Track Recording Coach)/ 1L45 17:40 King's Cross-York/YK; Thurs. 2: YK 'B' exam; Fri. 3: 1A08 08:07 York-King's Cross/FP/1L44 16:03 King's Cross-York/1A34 20:19 York-King's Cross; Sat. 4: 1S76 09:40 King's Cross-Edinburgh/HA/1E43 20:05 Aberdeen-King's Cross from Edinburgh; Sun. 5: FP 'eo'; Mon. 6: 1S12 05:50 King's Cross-Aberdeen/1E26 16:30 Aberdeen-Leeds/1E24 22:50 Shrewsbury-York from Leeds; Tues. 7: 1A08 08:07 York-King's Cross/FP/1S70 22:15 King's Cross-Aberdeen to Edinburgh; Wed. 8: 5E10 06:40 Craigentinny-Dundee/1E10 09:10 Dundee-King's Cross/FP Until Mon. 13: FP/1S70 22:15 King's Cross-Aberdeen to Edinburgh; Tues. 14: 1V93 09:50 Edinburgh-Plymouth to York/1S27 07:36 Plymouth-Edinburgh from York/1E48 21:20 Aberdeen-King's Cross from Edinburgh; Wed. 15: FP/1D08 19:40 King's Cross-Hull/BG; Thurs. 16: 1A13 09:36 Hull-King's Cross/FP/1L45 17:40 King's Cross-York/YK; Fri. 17: 1A08 08:07 York-King's Cross/FP; Sat. 18: FP 'eo'/1L44 16:03 King's Cross-York/1A34 20:19 York-King's Cross; Sun. 19: 1L41 10:05 King's Cross-York/1A10 15:50 York-King's Cross/FP; Mon. 20: 1S12 05:50 King's Cross-Aberdeen/1E26 16:30 Aberdeen-Leeds to York; Tues. 21: 1A37 10:47 York-King's Cross/FP/1L45 17:40 King's Cross-York/YK; Wed. 22: 1A08 08:07 York-King's Cross/FP/1L44 16:03 King's Cross-York/1A34 20:19 York-King's Cross; Thurs. 23: 1S12 05:50 King's Cross-Aberdeen/1E26 16:30 Aberdeen-Leeds/1E24 22:50 Shrewsbury-York from Leeds; Fri. 24: YK 'B' exam; Sat. 25: 1A08 08:07 York-King's Cross/1L43 14:03 King's Cross-York/1A31 18:14 York-King's Cross/FP; Sun. 26: 1N02 08:30 King's Cross-Newcastle/GD/1N03 21:20 Newcastle-Darlington/ 0L01 Darlington-York; Mon. 27: 1A37 10:47 York-King's Cross/FP; Tues. 28: FP/1L42 12:05 King's Cross-York/1A26 15:50 York-King's Cross/FP; Wed. 29: 1N00 01:00 King's Cross-Newcastle/1S08 07:05 Newcastle-Edinburgh/HA/ 1E39 22:25 Edinburgh-King's Cross; Thurs. 30: 1L42 12:05 King's Cross-York/1A26 15:50 York-King's Cross; Fri. 31: 1N12 00:05 King's Cross-Newcastle/0L01 Newcastle-York/YK/1A31 18:14 York-King's Cross

AUGUST

Sat. 1: 1N00 01:00 King's Cross-Newcastle/1S08 07:05 Newcastle-Edinburgh/HA/ 1E84 13:20 Edinburgh-King's Cross; Sun. 2: FP/1L43 16:05 King's Cross-York/YK 'D' exam Until Fri. 7: YK 'D' exam/0B02 York-Finsbury Park/FP/1L44 16:03 King's Cross-York/YK; Sat. 8: YK/1S27 07:36 Plymouth-Edinburgh from York/1E40 19:15 Aberdeen-King's Cross from Edinburgh; Sun. 9: FP/1L42 14:05 King's Cross-York/1A19 19:13 York-King's Cross/FP; Mon. 10: 1S12 05:50 King's Cross-Aberdeen/1E26 16:30 Aberdeen-Leeds to York; Tues. 11: 1A37 10:47 York-King's Cross/FP/1D08 19:40 King's Cross-Hull/0D01 23:35 Hull-Doncaster; Wed. 12:1D62 03:55 Doncaster-Hull/1A13 09:36 Hull-King's Cross/FP/1L45 17:40 King's Cross-York/YK; Thurs. 13: 1A08 08:07 York-King's Cross/FP/1L44 16:03 King's Cross-York/1A34 20:19 York-King's Cross; Fri. 14: 1S76 09:40 King's Cross-Edinburgh/HA/1E35 20:25 Edinburgh-King's Cross; Sat. 15: FP/1L44 16:03 King's Cross-York/1A34 20:19 York-King's Cross; Sun. 16: 1L41 10:05 King's Cross-York/1A10 15:50 York-King's Cross/1S72 22:40 King's Cross-Edinburgh; Mon. 17: 1V93 09:50 Edinburgh-Plymouth to York/1S27 07:36 Plymouth-Edinburgh from York/1E42 23:15 Edinburgh-King's Cross;

Tues. 18: FP/1B03 17:10 King's Cross-Peterborough/0B02 Peterborough-Finsbury Park/FP/1S79 23:20 King's Cross-Aberdeen to Edinburgh; Wed. 19: HA/1E48 21:20 Aberdeen-King's Cross from Edinburgh; Thurs. 20: FP/1L44 16:03 King's Cross-York/1A34 20:19 York-King's Cross; Fri. 21: 1S12 05:50 King's Cross-Aberdeen/1E26 16:30 Aberdeen-Leeds/5L08 Leeds-York; Sat. 22: YK; Sun. 23: 1A06 11:50 York-King's Cross/FP/1S70 22:15 King's Cross-Aberdeen to Edinburgh; Mon. 24: HA/1S12 05:50 King's Cross-Aberdeen from Edinburgh/1E26 16:30 Aberdeen-Leeds to York; Tues. 25: YK; Wed. 26: 5A37 York-Durham/1A37 09:30 Durham-King's Cross/FP/1D08 19:40 King's Cross-Hull/0D01 23:35 Hull-Doncaster; Thurs. 27: 1D62 03:55 Doncaster-Hull/1A13 09:36 Hull-King's Cross/FP/1L45 17:40 King's Cross-York/YK; Fri. 28: 1A08 08:07 York-King's Cross/FP/1L44 16:03 King's Cross-York/1A34 20:19 York-King's Cross; Sat. 29: 1S12 05:50 King's Cross-Aberdeen to Edinburgh/HA/1E39 22:15 Edinburgh-King's Cross; Sun. 30: FP/1L42 14:05 King's Cross-York/YK; Mon. 31: 1A37 10:47 York-King's Cross/FP/1D08 19:40 King's Cross-Hull/0D01 23:35 Hull-Doncaster

SEPTEMBER

Tues. 1: 1D62 03:55 Doncaster-Hull/1A13 09:36 Hull-King's Cross/1N05 15:35 King's Cross-Newcastle (vice HST)/1A45 22:55 Newcastle-King's Cross; Wed. 2: 1L42 12:05 King's Cross-York/1A26 15:50 York-King's Cross/1S77 23:55 King's Cross-Edinburgh; Thurs. 3: HA; Fri. 4: 5E10 06:40 Craigentinny-Dundee/1E10 09:10 Dundee-King's Cross to York/ YK; Sat. 5: 1A08 08:07 York-King's Cross/FP/1D08 19:40 King's Cross-Hull/0D01 23:35 Hull-Doncaster; Sun. 6: DR; Mon. 7: 1D62 03:55 Doncaster-Hull/1A13 09:36 Hull-King's Cross/FP/1L45 17:40 King's Cross-York/YK; Tues. 8: 1A08 08:07 York-King's Cross/FP/1L44 16:03 King's Cross-York/1A34 20:19 York-King's Cross; Wed. 9: 1S12 05:50 King's Cross-Aberdeen/1E26 16:30 Aberdeen-Leeds to York; Thurs. 10: 1A37 10:47 York-King's Cross/FP/1S66 20:15 King's Cross-Edinburgh; Fri. 11: 5E10 06:40 Craigentinny-Dundee/1E10 09:10 Dundee-King's Cross/FP/1S70 22:15 King's Cross-Aberdeen to Newcastle; Sat. 12: GD 'oe'/1S14 08:10 Newcastle-Edinburgh/HA/1E29 17:18 Edinburgh-Newcastle/GD; Sun. 13: GD/0L01 Gateshead-York/YK 'B' exam; Mon. 14: YK 'eo' 'B' exam; Tues. 15: 1A08 08:07 York-King's Cross/FP/1L44 16:03 King's Cross-York/1A34 20:19 York-King's Cross; Wed. 16: 1S12 05:50 King's Cross-Aberdeen to Edinburgh/HA/1A51 17:02 Edinburgh-Aberdeen/1E48 21:20 Aberdeen-King's Cross to Hitchin (failed, out of fuel); Thurs. 17: HI/0B02 Hitchin-Finsbury Park/FP/1S70 22:15 King's Cross-Aberdeen to Edinburgh; Fri. 18: HA/2L52 16:23 Edinburgh-Dundee/DE/7K79 20:10 Dundee West-Millerhill (conveyed in train)/6E68 23:30 Millerhill-Tyne Yard (conveyed in train)/TY Until Mon. 21: TY/8L81 Tyne Yard-Dringhouses (conveyed in train)/YK Until Wed. 30: YK

OCTOBER

Thurs. 1: YK Until Mon. 5: YK/1A22 14:15 York-King's Cross/1D08 19:40 King's Cross-Hull/5L04 23:30 Hull-York; Tues. 6: YK/1A22 14:15 York-King's Cross/FP/1S70 22:15 King's Cross-Aberdeen to Edinburgh; Wed. 7: 1V93 09:50 Edinburgh-Plymouth to York/1S27 07:36 Plymouth-Edinburgh from York/1E48 21:20 Aberdeen-King's Cross from Edinburgh; Thurs. 8: FP/1S70 22:15 King's Cross-Aberdeen to Newcastle (failed - No.1 engine auxiliary generator drive sheared); Fri. 9: GD 'oe'/0L01 Gateshead-York/YK 'oe' Until Wed. 14: YK 'oe'/1M62 08:50 York-Liverpool/1E99 13:05 Liverpool-York/0B02 York-Finsbury Park/FP 'oe'; Thurs. 15: FP 'oe'/1D08 19:40 King's Cross-Hull/5L04 23:30 Hull-York; Fri. 16: YK 'oe'/0L01 14:20 York-Neville Hill/5A31 15:54 Neville Hill-York/1N14 14:03 King's Cross-Newcastle from York (55 010 off) (via Leamside)/1A45 22:55 Newcastle-King's Cross;

Sat. 17:FP 'oe'; Sun. 18: 1N12 00:05 King's Cross-Newcastle to Peterborough/PB 'oe'; Mon. 19: PB 'oe'/0B02 Peterborough-Finsbury Park/FP 'oe'/1D08 19:40 King's Cross-Hull/5L04 23:30 Hull-York; Tues. 20: YK 'oe'/1M26 13:50 York-Liverpool/1E59 18:05 Liverpool-York/YK 'oe'; Wed. 21: YK 'oe'/1M62 08:50 York-Liverpool/1E99 13:05 Liverpool-York/YK 'oe' Until Thurs. 29: YK 'oe'/0B02 York-Peterborough/PB/0B02 Peterborough-Finsbury Park/FP 'oe'; Fri. 30: 1N00 01:00 King's Cross-Newcastle to York/YK 'oe'; Sat. 31: YK 'oe'/1A31 18:14 York-King's Cross/FP 'oe'

NOVEMBER

Sun. 1: FP 'oe'/0C01 Finsbury Park-Stratford/SF 'oe' (No.1 engine, 432, replaced by 430) Until Thurs. 12: SF/0B02 Stratford-Finsbury Park/FP/1L44 16:03 King's Cross-York/YK; Fri. 13: 1A08 08:07 York-King's Cross/FP/1L44 16:03 King's Cross-York/1A34 20:19 York-King's Cross; Sat. 14: FP; Sun. 15: 1N12 00:05 King's Cross-Newcastle/GD/1E48 21:20 Aberdeen-King's Cross from Newcastle; Mon. 16: FP 'eo'/1L44 16:03 King's Cross-York/1A34 20:19 York-King's Cross; Tues. 17: 1S12 05:50 King's Cross-Aberdeen to Newcastle/0L01 Newcastle-York/YK/ 1A22 14:15 York-King's Cross/1D08 19:40 King's Cross-Hull/5L04 23:30 Hull-York; Wed. 18: YK/1A26 15:50 York-King's Cross/1S77 23:55 King's Cross-Edinburgh; Thurs. 19: HA/1E35 20:25 Edinburgh-King's Cross; Fri. 20: 1L41 09:40 King's Cross-York/1A22 14:15 York-King's Cross/1D08 19:40 King's Cross-Hull/5L04 23:30 Hull-York; Sat. 21: YK; Sun. 22: YK/1A19 19:13 York-King's Cross; Mon. 23: 1N00 01:00 King's Cross-Newcastle/1S08 07:05 Newcastle-Edinburgh/HA/ 1E35 20:25 Edinburgh-King's Cross; Tues. 24: 1S12 05:50 King's Cross-Aberdeen (assisted from Peterborough by 46 046 - low fuel) to Doncaster/0B02 Doncaster-Finsbury Park/FP/1L43 14:03 King's Cross-York/1A31 18:14 York-King's Cross/1S77 23:55 King's Cross-Edinburgh; Wed. 25: HA/1E29 17:18 Edinburgh-Newcastle/1A45 22:55 Newcastle-King's Cross; Thurs. 26: 5B26 05:24 King's Cross-Peterborough/1B26 07:23 Peterborough-King's Cross/FP/1S66 20:15 King's Cross-Edinburgh; Fri. 27: 1M04 07:18 Edinburgh-Carlisle/1S15 15:53 Carlisle-Edinburgh/1E42 23:15 Edinburgh-King's Cross; Sat. 28: FP/1L44 16:03 King's Cross-York/YK 'C' exam; Sun. 29: YK 'C' exam Mon. 30: YK 'C' exam

DECEMBER

Tues. 1: YK 'C' exam 'eo' (Boiler isolated - burst element tubes); Wed. 2: 1A08 08:07 York-King's Cross/FP/1L44 16:03 King's Cross-York/1A34 20:19 York-King's Cross; Thurs. 3: 1S12 05:50 King's Cross-Aberdeen/1E26 16:30 Aberdeen-York; Fri. 4: 1A08 08:07 York-King's Cross/FP/1L44 16:03 King's Cross-York/YK 'eo'/ 0D01 York-Doncaster/1S66 20:15 King's Cross-Edinburgh from Doncaster; Sat. 5: HA 'eo'; Sun. 6: HA 'eo'/1E48 21:20 Aberdeen-King's Cross from Edinburgh; Mon. 7: FP 'eo'/1L43 14:03 King's Cross-York/1A31 18:14 York-King's Cross/FP 'eo'; Tues. 8: 1S12 05:50 King's Cross-Aberdeen to Edinburgh/HA 'eo'/1A38 14:55 Edinburgh-Aberdeen/1G20 18:23 Aberdeen-Edinburgh/1E48 21:20 Aberdeen-King's Cross from Edinburgh; Wed. 9: FP 'eo'; Thurs. 10: 1S12 05:50 King's Cross-Aberdeen to Edinburgh/HA 'eo'/1E48 21:20 Aberdeen-King's Cross from Edinburgh; Fri. 11: FP 'eo'/1S70 22:15 King's Cross-Aberdeen to Edinburgh; Sat. 12: 5E13 Edinburgh-Montrose/1E13 Montrose-King's Cross (vice 10:25 Aberdeen HST) to Edinburgh/HA 'eo'; Sun. 13: HA 'eo'; Mon. 14: HA 'eo'/1E26 16:30 Aberdeen-York from Edinburgh Tues. 15: 1A08 08:07 York-King's Cross/FP/1L44 16:03 King's Cross-York/1A34 20:19 York-King's Cross; Wed. 16: 1S12 05:50 King's Cross-Aberdeen/1E26 16:30 Aberdeen-York; Thurs. 17: 1A08 08:07 York-King's Cross to Peterborough (failed - frozen brakes & train terminated)/PB/ 5G08 Peterborough-King's Cross/FP 'eo'/1S70 22:15

King's Cross-Aberdeen to Edinburgh; Fri. 18: HA 'eo'; Sat. 19: HA 'eo'/1A38 14:55 Edinburgh-Aberdeen/1G20 18:30 Aberdeen-Edinburgh/ HA 'eo'; Sun. 20: HA 'eo'/1Z98 Edinburgh-Carstairs/0G00 Carstairs-Haymarket/HA 'eo'/1E48 21:20 Aberdeen-King's Cross from Edinburgh; Mon. 21: FP 'eo'/1S70 22:15 King's Cross-Aberdeen to Edinburgh; Tues. 22: HA 'eo'; Wed. 23: 5F52 Craigentinny-Dundee/1E52 09:10 Dundee-King's Cross/FP 'eo'/1S70 22:15 King's Cross-Aberdeen to Edinburgh Thurs. 24: HA 'eo'/1O54 18:00 Edinburgh-Glasgow Q.St./1O61 19:30 Glasgow Q.St.-Edinburgh/HA 'eo' Until Sun. 27: HA 'eo'/5E27 21:34 Craigentinny-Ferme Park; Mon. 28: FP 'eo'/1S70 22:15 King's Cross-Aberdeen to Edinburgh; Tues. 29: 1C86 09:07 Edinburgh-Carstairs/1G44 11:23 Carstairs-Edinburgh/1A38 14:55 Edinburgh-Aberdeen/1G20 18:23 Aberdeen-Edinburgh/1E48 21:20 Aberdeen-King's Cross from Edinburgh Wed. 30: FP 'eo'; Thurs. 31: FP 'eo'/(Failed - flat batteries - for 1L43 14:03 King's Cross-York) WITHDRAWN

D9009/9009/55009 Alycidon

JUNE 1981

Mon. 1: 1A08 08:07 York-King's Cross/FP/1L44 16:03 King's Cross-York/1A34 20:19 York-King's Cross; Tues. 2: 1S76 09:40 King's Cross-Edinburgh/HA/1E26 16:30 Aberdeen-Leeds from Edinburgh/1E24 22:50 Shrewsbury-York from Leeds; Wed. 3: 1A37 10:47 York-King's Cross/1L45 17:40 King's Cross-York/YK; Thurs. 4: YK; Fri. 5: 1A37 10:47 York-King's Cross/FP/1D08 19:40 King's Cross-Hull/1D26 23:40 Hull-Doncaster; Sat. 6: 1D62 03:55 Doncaster-Hull/1A13 09:36 Hull-King's Cross/1L44 16:03 King's Cross-York/1A34 20:19 York-King's Cross; Sun. 7: 1L41 10:05 King's Cross-York/1A10 15:50 York-King's Cross/1S72 22:40 King's Cross-Edinburgh; Mon. 8: 1V93 09:50 Edinburgh-Plymouth to York/1S27 07:36 Plymouth-Edinburgh from York/1E42 23:15 Edinburgh-King's Cross; Tues. 9: FP; Wed. 10: 1D01 08:30 King's Cross-Cleethorpes/1A21 13:20 Cleethorpes-King's Cross/ 1S66 20:15 King's Cross-Edinburgh; Thurs. 11: 1V93 09:50 Edinburgh-Plymouth to York/1S27 07:36 Plymouth-Edinburgh from York/1E39 22:25 Edinburgh-King's Cross; Fri. 12: 1L42 12:05 King's Cross-York/YK 'B' exam; Sat. 13: 1A08 08:07 York-King's Cross/FP/1S77 23:55 King's Cross-Edinburgh; Sun. 14: HA (failed for 1E39 - 'eo'); Mon. 15: 5E10 06:40 Craigentinny-Dundee/1E10 09:10 Dundee-King's Cross/FP/1S70 22:15 King's Cross-Aberdeen to Edinburgh; Tues. 16: 1M04 07:18 Edinburgh-Carlisle/1S15 15:53 Carlisle-Edinburgh/1E40 19:25 Aberdeen-King's Cross from Edinburgh; Wed. 17: FP; Thurs. 18: 1L42 12:05 King's Cross-York/1A26 15:50 York-King's Cross/FP; Fri. 19: 1S12 05:50 King's Cross-Aberdeen/1E26 16:30 Aberdeen-Leeds/1E24 22:50 Shrewsbury-York from Leeds; Sat. 20: YK/0A13 York-Hull/BG/1A13 09:36 Hull-King's Cross/FP/1L45 18:05 King's Cross-York/YK; Sun. 21: 1A06 11:50 York-King's Cross/FP; Mon. 22: 1L42 12:05 King's Cross-York/1A26 15:50 York-King's Cross/FP Tues. 23: 1S12 05:50 King's Cross-Aberdeen to Edinburgh/HA/1E29 17:18 Edinburgh-Newcastle/1A45 22:55 Newcastle-King's Cross; Wed. 24: FP; Thurs. 25: FP/1L43 14:03 King's Cross-York/1A31 18:14 York-King's Cross; Fri. 26: 1N00 01:00 King's Cross-Newcastle/1S08 07:05 Newcastle-Edinburgh/1E10 09:10 Dundee-King's Cross from Edinburgh/FP; Sat. 27: 1N12 00:05 King's Cross-Newcastle/GD/1A39 10:50 Newcastle-King's Cross/ FP/1S60 20:00 King's Cross-Aberdeen to Edinburgh; Sun. 28: 1V93 11:25 Edinburgh-Plymouth to York/1S27 09:00 Plymouth-Edinburgh from York/1E43 20:05 Aberdeen-King's Cross from Edinburgh; Mon. 29: 1L42 12:05 King's Cross-York/YK 'oe'; Tues. 30: YK/0D01 York-Doncaster Works/On DCR WORKS "Unclassified repair" (No.1 engine, 436, replaced by 417)

JULY

Wed. 1: DONCASTER WORKS; Thurs. 2: DONCASTER WORKS; Fri. 3: Off DONCASTER WORKS/0L01 Doncaster Works-York (towing 55 011)/YK 'B' exam Until Tues. 7: YK 'B' exam; Wed. 8: 1A08 08:07 York-King's Cross/FP/1L44 16:03 King's Cross-York/1A34 20:19 York-King's Cross; Thurs. 9: 1S76 09:40 King's Cross-Edinburgh/HA/1E40 19:25 Aberdeen-King's Cross from Edinburgh; Fri. 10: FP/1L44 16:03 King's Cross-York/1A34 20:19 York-King's Cross; Sat. 11: 1S76 09:40 King's Cross-Edinburgh/HA; Sun. 12: HA/1E39 22:30 Edinburgh-King's Cross to Newcastle Mon. 13: GD/1S27 07:36 Plymouth-Edinburgh from Newcastle (55 022 off)/1E39 22:25 Edinburgh-King's Cross; Tues. 14: FP/1L43 14:03 King's Cross-York/1A31 18:14 York-King's Cross; Wed. 15: 1N00 01:00 King's Cross-Newcastle/GD/1A40 21:00 Newcastle-King's Cross; Thurs. 16: 5B26 05:24 King's Cross-Peterborough/1B26 07:23 Peterborough-King's Cross/FP/1S60 20:00 King's Cross-Aberdeen to Newcastle; Fri. 17: GD/1V98 16:17 Newcastle-Cardiff to York/1A31 18:14 York-King's Cross/FP; Sat. 18: FP 'eo'/1L11 11:25 King's Cross-Scarborough/1A31 17:05 Scarborough-King's Cross to York (55 017 forward)/YK; Sun. 19: 1A06 11:50 York-King's Cross/FP/1S70 22:15 King's Cross-Aberdeen to Edinburgh; Mon. 20: 1M04 07:18 Edinburgh-Carlisle/1S15 15:53 Carlisle-Edinburgh/1E48 21:20 Aberdeen-King's Cross from Edinburgh; Tues. 21: 1D03 13:05 King's Cross-Cleethorpes/1A32 17:45 Cleethorpes-King's Cross/ FP; Wed. 22: FP; Thurs. 23: FP/1L44 16:03 King's Cross-York/1A34 20:19 York-King's Cross; Fri. 24: 1S76 09:40 King's Cross-Edinburgh/HA/1E43 20:35 Aberdeen-King's Cross from Edinburgh to Doncaster; Sat. 25: DR/0L01 Doncaster-York/YK; Sun. 26: 1A06 11:50 York-King's Cross/FP/1S70 22:15 King's Cross-Aberdeen to Edinburgh; Mon. 27: 5E10 06:40 Craigentinny-Dundee/1E10 09:10 Dundee-King's Cross/FP; Tues. 28: 1S76 09:40 King's Cross-Edinburgh to York (55 010 forward)/YK 'B' exam Until; Fri. 31: YK 'B' exam

AUGUST

Sat. 1: YK 'B' exam Until Tues. 4: YK 'B' exam; Wed. 5: 5A37 York-Newcastle/GD/0L01 Gateshead-York/YK; Thurs. 6: 1A37 10:47 York-King's Cross/1L44 16:03 King's Cross-York/YK; Fri. 7: 1A08 08:07 York-King's Cross/FP; Sat. 8: 1S12 05:50 King's Cross-Aberdeen to Edinburgh/HA/1E26 16:30 Aberdeen-Leeds to York from Edinburgh; Sun. 9: YK/0B02 York-Finsbury Park/FP; Mon. 10: FP/0C01 Finsbury Park-Stratford/SF (No.1 boiler water tank holed) Until Wed. 19: SF/0B02 Stratford-Finsbury Park/FP; Thurs. 20: 1S76 09:40 King's Cross-Edinburgh/HA/1E26 16:30 Aberdeen-Leeds from Edinburgh (55 011 off); Fri. 21: 5L08 Leeds-York/YK/1M63 11:49 York-Liverpool/1E88 16:05 Liverpool-Newcastle/0L01 Newcastle-York/YK; Sat. 22: 1A08 08:07 York-King's Cross/FP/1L44 16:03 King's Cross-York/1A34 20:19 York-King's Cross; Sun. 23: 1L41 10:05 King's Cross-York/1S27 09:00 Plymouth-Edinburgh from York/ 1E48 21:20 Aberdeen-King's Cross from Edinburgh; Mon. 24: FP/1L45 17:40 King's Cross-York/YK; Tues. 25: 5A37 York-Newcastle/1A37 09:20 Newcastle-King's Cross/1L45 17:40 King's Cross-York/YK 'D' exam Until Fri. 28: YK 'D' exam; Sat. 29: 5M61 York-Scarborough/1N60 08:54 Filey-Newcastle from Scarborough   (55 013 off)/GD/1A40 21:00 Newcastle-King's Cross to York; Sun. 30: YK/1A19 19:13 York-King's Cross; Mon. 31: 1S76 09:40 King's Cross-Edinburgh/HA/1E39 22:25 Edinburgh-King's Cross to Newcastle

SEPTEMBER

Tues. 1: GD/0L01 Gateshead-York/YK; Wed. 2: 1M62 08:50 York-Liverpool/1E99 13:05 Liverpool-York/0B02 York-Finsbury Park/FP; Thurs. 3: 1N12 00:05 King's Cross-Newcastle to York/YK/0B02 York-Finsbury Park/ FP/1S79 23:15 King's Cross-Aberdeen to

Edinburgh; Fri. 4: HA 'oe'/1E29 17:18 Edinburgh-Newcastle/1A45 22:55 Newcastle-King's Cross; Sat. 5: FP 'oe'/1L22 23:15 King's Cross-Bradford; Sun. 6: BFD/Bradford-Holbeck/HO 'oe'; Mon. 7: 1D57 00:50 Leeds-Doncaster/0L01 Doncaster to York/YK 'oe'/1N12 00:05 King's Cross-Newcastle from York (55 002 off)/1S14 08:10 Newcastle-Edinburgh/HA 'oe'/1E29 17:18 Edinburgh-Newcastle/GD 'oe'; Tues. 8: 1S14 08:10 Newcastle-Edinburgh/HA 'oe'/1E29 17:18 Edinburgh-Newcastle/ 1A45 22:55 Newcastle-King's Cross; Wed. 9:1D01 08:30 King's Cross-Cleethorpes/1A21 13:20 Cleethorpes-King's Cross/ FP 'oe'; Thurs. 10: 1N12 00:05 King's Cross-Newcastle/GD 'oe'/1A40 21:00 Newcastle-King's Cross; Fri. 11: 5B26 05:24 King's X-Peterborough/1B26 07:23 Peterborough-King's Cross/FP 'oe'; Sat. 12: 1N12 00:05 King's Cross-Newcastle/GD 'oe'/1A39 10:50 Newcastle-King's Cross/FP 'oe'/1L22 23:15 King's Cross-Bradford; Sun. 13: 0L50 Bradford-Holbeck/HO 'oe'; Mon. 14: 1D57 00:50 Leeds-Doncaster/On DONCASTER WORKS "Unclassified repair" (No.2 engine, 444, replaced by 419) Until Fri. 18: Off DONCASTER WORKS/DR; Sat. 19: 0B02 Doncaster-Finsbury Park/FP/1S12 05:50 King's Cross-Aberdeen to Edinburgh/HA/1M79 15:20 Edinburgh-Liverpool to York/YK; Sun. 20: 1A06 11:50 York-King's Cross/FP/1S70 22:15 King's Cross-Aberdeen to Edinburgh; Mon. 21: 1M04 07:18 Edinburgh-Carlisle/1S15 15:53 Carlisle-Edinburgh/1E39 22:25 Edinburgh-King's Cross; Tues. 22: 1L42 12:05 King's Cross-York/1A26 15:50 York-King's Cross/FP; Wed. 23: 1L41 09:40 King's Cross-York/1A22 14:15 York-King's Cross/FP/1S70 22:15 King's Cross-Aberdeen to Edinburgh; Thurs. 24: 1V93 09:50 Edinburgh-Plymouth to York/YK 'B' exam; Until Tues. 29: YK 'B' exam/0B02 York-Finsbury Park/FP/1S70 22:15 King's Cross-Aberdeen to Edinburgh; Wed. 30: 1M04 07:18 Edinburgh-Carlisle/1S15 15:53 Carlisle-Edinburgh/1E48 21:20 Aberdeen-King's Cross from Edinburgh

OCTOBER

Thurs. 1: FP/1L43 14:03 King's Cross-York/1A31 18:14 York-King's Cross; Fri. 2: 1N00 01:00 King's Cross-Newcastle/1S08 07:05 Newcastle-Edinburgh/HA/ 0G92 Haymarket-North Berwick/2G92 11:05 North Berwick-Edinburgh (towing failed DMU)/HA/1E35 20:25 Edinburgh-King's Cross; Sat. 3: FP/1L43 14:03 King's Cross-York/1A31 18:14 York-King's Cross/FP 'oe'; Sun. 4: FP 'oe'; Mon. 5: 1N12 00:05 King's Cross-Newcastle/1S14 08:10 Newcastle-Edinburgh/HA 'oe'/1E29 17:18 Edinburgh-Newcastle/1A45 22:55 Newcastle-King's Cross; Tues. 6: FP/1D08 19:40 King's Cross-Hull/5L04 23:30 Hull-York; Wed. 7: YK; Thurs. 8: 1A08 08:07 York-King's Cross/FP/1D08 19:40 King's Cross-Hull/5L04 23:30 Hull-York; Fri. 9: YK Until Fri. 16: YK/1S60 20:00 King's Cross-Aberdeen from York to Newcastle; Sat. 17: 1F52 06:45 Newcastle-Inverness to Perth/0F52 Perth-Aberdeen/1F52 Inverness-Newcastle from Aberdeen; Sun. 18: 1M73 11:21 Newcastle-Liverpool to York/YK Until Wed. 21: YK; Thurs. 22: 1A08 08:07 York-King's Cross/FP/1L44 16:03 King's Cross-York/YK; Fri. 23: YK Until Sat. 31: YK

NOVEMBER

Sun. 1: YK Until Wed. 11: YK; Thurs. 12: 1M62 08:50 York-Liverpool/1E99 13:05 Liverpool-York/YK; Fri. 13: YK/1A26 15:50 York-King's Cross/FP; Sat. 14: 1Z37 09:20 King's Cross-Carlisle/1Z37 Carlisle-King's Cross "Deltic Cumbrian" Rail tour; Sun. 15: FP; Mon. 16: 1N12 00:05 King's Cross-Newcastle/1S14 08:10 Newcastle-Edinburgh/HA/ 1E35 20:25 Edinburgh-King's Cross; Tues. 17: 1L41 09:40 King's Cross-York/YK/1A26 15:50 York-King's Cross/1S70 22:15 King's Cross-Aberdeen to Edinburgh; Wed. 18: 1F50 07:00 Edinburgh-King's Cross/FP/1S66 20:15 King's Cross-Edinburgh to York; Thurs. 19: YK Until Tues. 24: YK; Wed. 25: 1M62 08:50 York-Liverpool/1E99

13:05 Liverpool-York/YK; Thurs. 26: YK; Fri. 27: YK/0L50 York-Neville Hill/5A31 15:54 Neville Hill-York/0N20 York-Gateshead; Sat. 28: 1Z11 Newcastle-Edinburgh/HA/1Z11 Edinburgh-Newcastle/1A40 21:00 Newcastle-King's Cross; Sun. 29: 1L41 10:05 King's Cross-York/YK; Mon. 30: YK

DECEMBER
Tues. 1: YK; Wed. 2: YK; Thurs. 3: 1M62 08:50 York-Liverpool/1E99 13:05 Liverpool-York/YK; Fri. 4: YK Until Wed. 9: YK; Thurs. 10: 1M62 08:50 York-Liverpool/1E99 13:05 Liverpool-York/0B02 York-Finsbury Park/FP/1S79 23:20 King's Cross-Aberdeen to Edinburgh; Fri. 11: HA (failed for 2L36 11:25 Edinburgh-Dundee with boiler failure)/1A38 14:55 Edinburgh-Aberdeen/1G20 18:23 Aberdeen-Edinburgh/HA; Sat. 12: 1Z55 09:42 Edinburgh-Aberdeen/1Z55 15:43 Aberdeen-Edinburgh "Grampian Deltic" Rail tour/1E35 20:45 Edinburgh-King's Cross; Sun. 13: FP/1S70 22:15 King's Cross-Aberdeen to Edinburgh; Mon. 14: HA/1E13 10:25 Aberdeen-King's Cross (vice HST) from Edinburgh to York/ 0E74 York-Tollerton/1E74 14:05 Liverpool-Newcastle from Tollerton (assisting failed 47 444)/GD/1S60 20:00 King's Cross-Aberdeen from Newcastle to Edinburgh; Tues. 15: 1M04 07:18 Edinburgh-Carlisle/1S15 15:53 Carlisle-Edinburgh/1E39 22:25 Edinburgh-King's Cross; Wed. 16: FP/1L44 16:03 King's Cross-York/1A34 20:19 York-King's Cross; Thurs. 17: 1S12 05:50 King's Cross-Aberdeen to Edinburgh/HA/1E35 20:25 Edinburgh-King's Cross to Doncaster (failed - brake cylinder gauges frozen - 55 021 forward); Fri. 18: DR/0B02 Doncaster-Finsbury Park/FP; Sat. 19: 1G10 08:20 King's Cross-Norwich/1G10 13:00 Norwich-Liverpool Street "Deltic Broadsman" Rail tour/SF; Sun. 20: SF; Mon. 21: SF/0B02 Stratford-Finsbury Park/FP/1L43 14:03 King's Cross-York/YK; Tues. 22: YK; Wed. 23: YK; Thurs. 24: 1M62 08:50 York-Liverpool/1E99 13:05 Liverpool-York/YK; Fri. 25: YK; Sat. 26: YK; Sun. 27: YK/1M69 09:45 Edinburgh-Liverpool from

York/1E22 19:10 Liverpool-York/ YK/1E43 20:35 Aberdeen-King's Cross from York; Mon. 28: FP/1L44 16:03 King's Cross-York/1A34 20:19 York-King's Cross; Tues. 29: 1G06 King's Cross-York/1G06 York-King's Cross "Deltic Executive" Rail tour/ 1S79 23:20 King's Cross-Aberdeen to Edinburgh; Wed. 30: 1M04 07:18 Edinburgh-Carlisle to Newcastle (failed - boiler failure)/GD/1A40 21:00 Newcastle-King's Cross; Thurs. 31: FP

JANUARY 1982
Fri. 1: FP/0B06 Finsbury Park-Peterborough/PB; Sat. 2: PB/0G50 08:05 Peterborough-Newcastle/0G50 Newcastle-Peterborough/ 0G50 Peterborough-York/YK WITHDRAWN

D9010/9010/55010
The King's Own Scottish Borderer

JUNE 1981
Mon. 1: FP/1L45 17:40 King's Cross-York to Peterborough/0B02 Peterborough-Finsbury Park/FP; Tues. 2: 1D01 08:30 King's Cross-Cleethorpes/1A21 13:20 Cleethorpes-King's Cross/ 1S66 20:15 King's Cross-Edinburgh; Wed. 3: 1M04 07:18 Edinburgh-Carlisle/1S15 15:53 Carlisle-Edinburgh/1E42 23:15 Edinburgh-King's Cross; Thurs. 4: 1L42 12:05 King's Cross-York/1A26 15:50 York-King's Cross/1S72 22:30 King's Cross-Edinburgh; Fri. 5; 1V93 09:50 Edinburgh-Plymouth to York/YK 'C' exam Until Wed. 10: YK 'C' exam/1E39 22:25 Edinburgh-King's Cross from York (55 004 off); Thurs. 11: FP/1L43 14:03 King's Cross-York/1A31 18:14 York-King's Cross; Fri. 12: 1N00 01:00 King's Cross-Newcastle/1S08 07:05 Newcastle-Edinburgh/HA/ 1E40 19:25 Aberdeen-King's Cross from Edinburgh; Sat. 13: FP/1L44 16:03 King's Cross-York/1A34 20:19 York-King's Cross; Sun. 14: 1L41 10:05 King's Cross-

York/1A10 15:50 York-King's Cross/FP; Mon. 15: 1S12 05:50 King's Cross-Aberdeen/1E26 16:30 Aberdeen-Leeds/1E24 22:50 Shrewsbury-York from Leeds; Tues. 16: 1A37 10:47 York-King's Cross/1L45 17:40 King's Cross-York/YK/1A45 22:55 Newcastle-King's Cross from York (55 021 off); Wed. 17: 1L42 12:05 King's Cross-York/1A26 15:50 York-King's Cross/1S77 23:55 King's Cross-Edinburgh; Thurs. 18: 1V93 09:50 Edinburgh-Plymouth to York/1S27 07:36 Plymouth-Edinburgh from York/1E39 22:25 Edinburgh-King's Cross; Fri. 19: FP/1L45 17:40 King's Cross-York/YK; Sat. 20: 1A08 08:07 York-King's Cross/FP; Sun. 21: 1L41 10:05 King's Cross-York/1A10 15:50 York-King's Cross/FP; Mon. 22: 1S76 09:40 King's Cross-Edinburgh/HA/1E35 20:25 Edinburgh-King's Cross; Tues. 23: FP/1L44 16:03 King's Cross-York/1A34 20:19 York-King's Cross; Wed. 24: 1L42 12:05 King's Cross-York/1A26 15:50 York-King's Cross/FP; Thurs. 25: 1N12 00:05 King's Cross-Newcastle/1S14 08:10 Newcastle-Edinburgh/HA/ 1E42 23:15 Edinburgh-King's Cross; Fri. 26: FP/1L44 16:03 King's Cross-York/1A34 20:19 York-King's Cross; Sat. 27: 1S12 05:50 King's Cross-Aberdeen to Edinburgh/HA/1E35 20:45 Edinburgh-King's Cross; Sun. 28: FP/1L43 16:05 King's Cross-York/YK 'B' exam; Mon. 29: YK 'B' exam/1A37 10:47 York-King's Cross/FP/1D08 19:40 King's Cross-Hull/ 0D01 23:35 Hull-Doncaster; Tues. 30: 1D62 03:55 Doncaster-Hull/1A13 09:36 Hull-King's Cross/1L45 17:40 King's Cross-York/YK 'B' exam

JULY

Wed. 1: 1A37 10:47 York-King's Cross/FP/1D08 19:40 King's Cross-Hull/0D01 23:35 Hull-Doncaster; Thurs. 2: 1D62 03:55 Doncaster-Hull/1A13 09:36 Hull-King's Cross/1L45 17:40 King's Cross-York/1S66 20:15 King's Cross-Edinburgh from York (55 016 off); Fri. 3: 5E10 06:40 Craigentinny-Dundee/1E10 09:10 Dundee-King's Cross/1D08 19:40 King's Cross-Hull/1D26 23:40 Hull-Doncaster; Sat. 4: 1D62 03:55 Doncaster-Hull/1A13 09:36 Hull-King's Cross/FP/1S70 22:15 King's Cross-Aberdeen to Edinburgh; Sun. 5: 1V93 11:25 Edinburgh-Plymouth to York/1S27 09:00 Plymouth-Edinburgh from York/1E43 20:05 Aberdeen-King's Cross from Edinburgh; Mon. 6: FP/1L43 14:03 King's Cross-York/1A31 18:14 York-King's Cross/FP; Tues. 7: 1S76 09:40 King's Cross-Edinburgh/HA/1E35 20:25 Edinburgh-King's Cross; Wed. 8:1L42 12:05 King's Cross-York/1A26 15:50 York-King's Cross/FP; Thurs. 9: 1N00 01:00 King's Cross-Newcastle/1S08 07:05 Newcastle-Edinburgh/HA/ 1S76 09:40 King's Cross-Edinburgh extended to Aberdeen from Edinburgh (55 009 off)/AB/5Z21 Aberdeen-Craigentinny/HA; Fri. 10: 5E10 06:40 Craigentinny-Dundee/1E10 09:10 Dundee-King's Cross/FP Until Mon. 13: FP/1L43 14:03 King's Cross-York/1A31 18:14 York-King's Cross/FP; Tues. 14: 1N00 01:00 King's Cross-Newcastle/1S08 07:05 Newcastle-Edinburgh/HA/ 1E29 17:18 Edinburgh-Newcastle/1A45 22:55 Newcastle-King's Cross; Wed. 15: 1S76 09:40 King's Cross-Edinburgh/HA/1E35 20:25 Edinburgh-King's Cross; Thurs. 16: 1S76 09:40 King's X-Edinburgh/HA/1E39 22:25 Edinburgh-King's X; Fri. 17: FP/1L45 17:40 King's X-York/YK; Sat. 18: YK 'B' exam Until Fri. 24: YK 'B' exam; Sat. 25: York-Scarborough/1S98 14:35 Scarborough-Glasgow to Edinburgh/HA/1E39 22:15 Edinburgh-King's Cross; Sun. 26; FP/1S72 22:40 King's Cross-Edinburgh; Mon. 27: 1V93 09:50 Edinburgh-Plymouth to Newcastle/GD/1N03 21:20 Newcastle-Darlington/0L01 Darlington-York; Tues. 28: YK/1S76 09:40 King's Cross-Edinburgh from York (55 009 off)/HA/1E35 20:25 Edinburgh-King's Cross; Wed. 29: 1L42 12:05 King's Cross-York/1A26 15:50 York-King's Cross/FP; Thurs. 30: 1N12 00:05 King's Cross-Newcastle/1S14 08:10 Newcastle-Edinburgh/HA/ 1E39 22:25 Edinburgh-King's Cross; Fri. 31: 1L42 12:05 King's Cross-York/1A26 15:50 York-King's Cross/FP

AUGUST

Sat. 1: 1N12 00:05 King's Cross-Newcastle/GD/1A39 10:50 Newcastle-King's Cross/ 1L44 16:03 King's Cross-York; Sun. 2: 1A06 11:50 York-King's Cross/FP; Mon. 3: FP/1L43 14:03 King's Cross-York/YK; Tues. 4: YK; Wed. 5: 1A08 08:07 York-King's Cross/FP/1L44 16:03 King's Cross-York/YK; Thurs. 6: YK; Fri. 7: 1A37 10:47 York-King's Cross/FP/1D08 19:40 King's Cross-Hull/BG; Sat. 8: 1A13 09:36 Hull-King's Cross/FP/1L45 18:05 King's Cross-York/YK; Sun. 9: 1A06 11:50 York-King's Cross/FP/1S70 22:15 King's Cross-Aberdeen to Edinburgh; Mon. 10: 5E10 06:40 Craigentinny-Dundee/1E10 09:10 Dundee-King's Cross/1S66 20:15 King's Cross-Edinburgh; Tues. 11: 5E10 06:40 Craigentinny-Dundee/1E10 09:10 Dundee-King's Cross/FP; Wed. 12: 1N00 01:00 King's Cross-Newcastle/1S08 07:05 Newcastle-Edinburgh/HA/ 1A38 14:55 Edinburgh-Aberdeen/1G20 18:23 Aberdeen-Edinburgh/1E42 23:15 Edinburgh-King's Cross to York; Thurs. 13: YK 'C' exam Until Mon. 17: YK 'C' exam/0D01 York-Doncaster Works (towed by 31 293); Tues. 18: On DONCASTER WORKS "Unclassified repair" (No.1 engine, 427, replaced by 438) Until Thurs. 27: Off DONCASTER WORKS/0L01 Doncaster Works-York/YK 'C' exam ; Fri. 28: YK 'C' exam; Sat. 29: 1A08 08:07 York-King's Cross/FP; Sun. 30: 1N02 08:30 King's Cross-Newcastle/1A21 14:57 Newcastle-King's Cross/FP; Mon. 31: 1S12 05:50 King's Cross-Aberdeen to Edinburgh/HA/1E35 20:25 Edinburgh-King's Cross

SEPTEMBER

Tues. 1: FP/1L43 14:03 King's Cross-York/YK; Wed. 2: 1A08 08:07 York-King's Cross/FP/1L44 16:03 King's Cross-York/1A34 20:19 York-King's Cross; Thurs. 3: 1D01 08:30 King's Cross-Cleethorpes/1A21 13:20 Cleethorpes-King's Cross/ 1S66 20:15 King's Cross-Edinburgh; Fri. 4: 1M04 07:18 Edinburgh-Carlisle/1S15 15:53 Carlisle-Edinburgh/5E91 Edinburgh-Heaton/GD; Sat. 5: 1A39 10:50 Newcastle-King's Cross/1L45 18:05 King's Cross-York/YK Until Tues. 8: YK; Wed. 9: 0D01 York-Doncaster/1D62 03:55 Doncaster-Hull/1A13 09:36 Hull-King's Cross/FP/1D08 19:40 King's Cross-Hull/0D01 23:35 Hull-Doncaster; Thurs. 10: 1D62 03:55 Doncaster-Hull/1A13 09:36 Hull-King's Cross (assisted from Hitchin by 55 007)/FP; Fri. 11: 1N00 01:00 King's Cross-Newcastle/1S08 07:05 Newcastle-Edinburgh/HA/ 1E35 20:25 Edinburgh-King's Cross; Sat. 12: 1L42 12:05 King's Cross-York/1A26 15:50 York-King's Cross/1S70 22:15 King's Cross-Aberdeen to Edinburgh; Sun. 13: HA/1E40 19:25 Aberdeen-King's Cross from Edinburgh; Mon. 14: FP/1L43 14:03 King's Cross-York/1A31 18:14 York-King's Cross; Tues. 15: 1N00 01:00 King's Cross-Newcastle/1S08 07:05 Newcastle-Edinburgh/1E10 09:10 Dundee-King's Cross from Edinburgh/FP; Wed. 16: FP 'B' exam; Thurs. 17: 1S12 05:50 King's Cross-Aberdeen to Edinburgh/HA/1E35 20:25 Edinburgh-King's Cross; Fri. 18: 1S76 09:40 King's Cross-Edinburgh/HA/1E39 22:25 Edinburgh-King's Cross; Sat. 19: 1L42 12:05 King's Cross-York/1A26 15:50 York-King's Cross/1S70 22:15 King's Cross-Aberdeen to Edinburgh; Sun. 20: HA/1E39 22:30 Edinburgh-King's Cross to Peterborough; Mon. 21: 5B42 Peterborough-Ferme Park/FP/1B03 17:10 King's Cross-Peterborough/ 0B02 Peterborough-Finsbury Park/FP; Tues. 22: 1N12 00:05 King's Cross-Newcastle/0L01 Newcastle-York/0B06 York-Peterborough/0B02 Peterborough-Finsbury Park; Wed. 23: 1N12 00:05 King's Cross-Newcastle/0L01 Newcastle-York/YK Until Mon. 28: YK/0D01 York-Doncaster Works/On DONCASTER WORKS "Unclassified repair"; Tues. 29: DONCASTER WORKS; Wed. 30: DONCASTER WORKS

OCTOBER

Thurs. 1: Off DONCASTER WORKS/DR/0B06 Doncaster-Peterborough/PB; Fri. 2: 1B18 07:50 Peterborough-King's Cross/1L42 12:05 King's Cross-York/1A26 15:50 York-King's Cross/1S79 23:20 King's Cross-Aberdeen to Edinburgh; Sat. 3: 1V93 09:50 Edinburgh-Plymouth to York/1S27 07:36 Plymouth-Edinburgh from York/1E40 19:15 Aberdeen-King's Cross from Edinburgh; Sun. 4; FP/1L43 16:05 King's Cross-York/YK; Mon. 5: 1A08 08:07 York-King's Cross/FP/1L44 16:03 King's Cross-York/YK; Tues. 6: 1A08 08:07 York-King's Cross/FP/1L44 16:03 King's Cross-York/1A34 20:19 York-King's Cross; Wed. 7: 1S12 05:50 King's Cross-Aberdeen to Newcastle/0L01 Newcastle-York/1A26 15:50 York-King's Cross/YK; Thurs. 8:1N12 00:05 King's Cross-Newcastle to Doncaster/0B02 Doncaster-Finsbury Park/FP/1L43 14:03 King's Cross-York/1A31 18:14 York-King's Cross; Fri. 9: 1N12 00:05 King's Cross-Newcastle/GD/1S12 05:50 King's Cross-Aberdeen from Newcastle to Edinburgh/HA/1E29 17:18 Edinburgh-Newcastle/1A45 22:55 Newcastle-King's Cross; Sat. 10: FP/1L46 23:00 King's Cross-York; Sun. 11: YK; Mon. 12:YK/1A26 15:50 York-King's Cross/1S79 23:20 King's Cross-Aberdeen to Edinburgh; Tues. 13: 1V93 09:50 Edinburgh-Plymouth to York/1S27 07:36 Plymouth-Edinburgh from York/1E35 20:25 Edinburgh-King's Cross; Wed. 14: FP/1L43 14:03 King's Cross-York/1A31 18:14 York-King's Cross/FP; Thurs. 15: 1S12 05:50 King's Cross-Aberdeen to Edinburgh/HA/1E35 20:25 Edinburgh-King's Cross; Fri. 16: FP/1N14 14:03 King's Cross-Newcastle to York (55 008 forward)/1A31 18:14 York-King's Cross/1S77 23:55 King's Cross-Edinburgh; Sat. 17: HA/1E40 19:15 Aberdeen-King's Cross from Edinburgh; Sun. 18: FP; Mon. 19: 1N00 01:00 King's Cross-Newcastle/1S08 07:05 Newcastle-Edinburgh/HA/ 1E29 17:18 Edinburgh-Newcastle/1A45 22:55 Newcastle-King's Cross; Tues. 20: FP/1L44 16:03 King's Cross-York/1A34 20:19 York-King's Cross; Wed. 21: 1L41 09:40 King's Cross-York/1A22 14:15 York-King's Cross/FP/1S79 23:20 King's Cross-Aberdeen to Edinburgh; Thurs. 22: 1V93 09:50 Edinburgh-Plymouth to York/1S27 07:36 Plymouth-Edinburgh from York/1E39 22:25 Edinburgh-King's Cross; Fri. 23: FP Until Mon. 26: FP/1L43 14:03 King's Cross-York/1A31 18:14 York-King's Cross; Tues. 27: 1N00 01:00 King's Cross-Newcastle/1S08 07:05 Newcastle-Edinburgh/HA/ 1E35 20:25 Edinburgh-King's Cross; Wed. 28: 1L41 09:40 King's Cross-York/1A22 14:15 York-King's Cross/1D08 19:40 King's Cross-Hull/5L04 23:30 Hull-York; Thurs. 29: YK; Fri. 30: 1A08 08:07 York-King's Cross/FP/1L44 16:03 King's Cross-York/1A34 19:55 York-King's Cross; Sat. 31: 1S12 05:50 King's Cross-Aberdeen to Newcastle/0L01 Newcastle-York/1A26 15:50 York-King's Cross (failed at Belle Isle - brake defect - propelled to King's Cross by 55 011)/FP

NOVEMBER

Sun. 1: FP; Mon. 2: 1L41 09:40 King's Cross-York/1A22 14:15 York-King's Cross/1D08 19:40 King's Cross-Hull/5L04 23:30 Hull-York; Tues. 3: YK/0B02 York-Finsbury Park/FP/1S72 22:30 King's Cross-Edinburgh; Wed. 4: HA/1E35 20:25 Edinburgh-King's Cross; Thurs. 5: FP/1L43 14:03 King's Cross-York/1A31 18:14 York-King's Cross/1S77 23:55 King's Cross-Edinburgh; Fri. 6: HA/1E35 20:25 Edinburgh-King's Cross; Sat. 7: FP/1S72 22:30 King's Cross-Edinburgh; Sun. 8: HA/1E35 20:25 Edinburgh-King's Cross; Mon. 9: FP/1L43 14:03 King's Cross-York/1A31 18:14 York-King's Cross; Tues. 10: 1N00 01:00 King's Cross-Newcastle/1S08 07:05 Newcastle-Edinburgh/HA/ 1E29 17:18 Edinburgh-Newcastle/1A45 22:55 Newcastle-King's Cross; Wed. 11: 1L41 09:40 King's Cross-York/1A22 14:15 York-King's Cross/FP/1S70 22:15 King's Cross-Aberdeen to Edinburgh; Thurs. 12: 1M04 07:18 Edinburgh-Carlisle/1S15 15:53 Carlisle-

Edinburgh/1E39 22:25 Edinburgh-King's Cross; Fri. 13: FP/1N14 14:03 King's Cross-Newcastle to York/1A31 18:14 York-King's Cross/1S77 23:55 King's Cross-Edinburgh; Sat. 14: HA/1E48 21:20 Aberdeen-King's Cross from Edinburgh to Drem (failed); Sun. 15: 0G99 Drem-Haymarket/HA; Mon. 16: HA; Tues. 17: HA/0E00 Haymarket-York (towed by 40 033)/YK Until Fri. 20: YK; Sat. 21: 1A08 08:07 York-King's Cross/1L43 14:03 King's Cross-York/1A31 18:14 York-King's Cross/FP; Sun. 22: FP/1S79 23:20 King's Cross-Aberdeen to Edinburgh; Mon. 23: 1C86 09:07 Edinburgh-Carstairs/1S37 07:37 Liverpool-Edinburgh from Carstairs/1A38 14:55 Edinburgh-Aberdeen/1G20 18:23 Aberdeen-Edinburgh/ 1E48 21:20 Aberdeen-King's Cross from Edinburgh; Tues. 24: FP/1B21 17:17 King's Cross-Peterborough/0B02 Peterborough-Finsbury Park/FP/1S72 22:30 King's Cross-Edinburgh; Wed. 25: 1C83 08:08 Edinburgh-Carstairs/1G44 11:23 Carstairs-Edinburgh/1A38 14:55 Edinburgh-Aberdeen/1G20 18:23 Aberdeen-E'burgh/1E43 20:35 Aberdeen-King's Cross from Edinburgh; Thurs. 26: FP/1S60 20:00 King's Cross-Aberdeen to Edinburgh; Fri. 27: 5G18 Craigentinny-Markinch/2G18 07:25 Markinch-Edinburgh/1C91 10:25 Edinburgh-Carstairs/1S37 07:37 Liverpool-Edinburgh from Carstairs/1A38 14:55 Edinburgh-Aberdeen/1G20 18:23 Aberdeen-Edinburgh/1E43 20:35 Aberdeen-King's Cross from Edinburgh; Sat. 28: FP/1L46 23:00 King's Cross-York to Doncaster/1E40 19:15 Aberdeen-King's Cross from Doncaster; Sun. 29: FP; Mon. 30: 1N12 00:05 King's Cross-Newcastle/0L01 Newcastle-York/YK/1A31 18:14 York-King's Cross/1S77 23:55 King's Cross-Edinburgh

DECEMBER

Tues. 1: HA/0E00 Haymarket-Gateshead/GD/0L01 Gateshead-York/YK/1A26 15:50 York-King's Cross; Wed. 2: FP; Thurs. 3: 1N00 01:00 King's Cross-Newcastle/1S08 07:05 Newcastle-Edinburgh/HA/ 1E35 20:25 Edinburgh-King's Cross; Fri. 4: 1L41 09:40 King's Cross-York/1A22 14:15 York-King's Cross/1D08 19:40 King's Cross-Hull/5L04 23:30 Hull-York; Sat. 5: YK/1A26 15:50 York-King's Cross/FP; Sun. 6:FP/1S60 20:00 King's Cross-Aberdeen to Edinburgh; Mon. 7: 1M04 07:18 Edinburgh-Carlisle/1S15 15:53 Carlisle-Edinburgh/HA 'oe'/1E43 20:35 Aberdeen-King's Cross from Edinburgh to Doncaster; Tues. 8: DR/0L01 Doncaster-York/YK; Wed. 9: YK 'B' exam/0B06 York-P'borough/0B02 Peterborough-Finsbury Park to Hitchin/1S60 20:00 King's Cross-Aberdeen from Hitchin (assisting failed 47 417 to Peterborough) to Edinburgh; Thurs. 10: HA/1E29 17:18 Edinburgh-Newcastle (failed at Heaton - assisted by 40 068)/ GD; Fri. 11: 1S08 07:05 Newcastle-Edinburgh/HA/1E29 17:18 Edinburgh-Newcastle/ 1A45 22:55 Newcastle-King's Cross to Doncaster (failed - No.2 engine aerating); Sat. 12: 0L01 Doncaster-York/YK 'oe'; Sun. 13: YK 'oe'/1M70 15:40 York-Liverpool/1E50 21:15 Liverpool-York; Mon. 14: 1M62 08:50 York-Liverpool/1E99 13:05 Liverpool-York/YK 'oe'; Until; Thurs. 17: YK 'oe'/1M41 22:08 York-Shrewsbury to Stockport/1E24 22:50 Shrewsbury-York from Stockport to Leeds; Fri. 18: HO 'oe'/1E00 07:05 Liverpool-York from Leeds/YK 'oe'/1A26 15:50 York-King's Cross/1S79 23:20 King's Cross-Aberdeen to Newcastle; Sat. 19: 1M73 11:21 Newcastle-Liverpool to York/YK 'oe'; Sun. 20: YK 'oe'; Mon. 21: YK 'oe'/0B01 York-King's Cross to P'borough (failed - No.1 engine silencer passing oil)/PB 'oe'; Tues. 22: PB 'oe'/0D01 P'borough-Doncaster (towed by 55 016)/DR 'oe'; Wed. 23: DR 'oe'/0B02 Doncaster-Fins. Park (with 55 016)/FP 'oe'/1L22 23:00 King's Cross-Bradford to DCR (failed at Corby Glen fractured lubricating oil pipe on No.1 eng - propelled by 47 458 on 1S77 to Grantham - assisted from Grantham to Doncaster by 37 137); Thurs. 24: DR/DR-DR Works (towed by 55 019)/DCR WORKS - WITHDRAWN.

Last Months of the Deltics — 1981

Haymarket-based class 55, 55022 Royal Scots Grey, is captured attacking Gamston Bank, south of Retford, with the inaugural run of the up "Silver Jubilee" (15.00 Edinburgh-King's Cross) on June 8, 1977. Picture: L. P. Gater

102 LAST MONTHS OF THE DELTICS — 1981

Now preserved in the National Collection, Class 55, 55002 "The King's Own Yorkshire Light Infantry" heads the last up 'Yorkshire Pullman' through Doncaster on Friday, May 5, 1978. Picture: L. P. Gater.

D9011/9011/55011
The Royal Northumberland Fusiliers

JUNE 1981

Mon. 1: YK 'B' exam; Tues. 2: 1A08 08:07 York-King's Cross/FP/1D08 19:40 King's Cross-Hull/0D01 23:35 Hull-Doncaster; Wed. 3: 1D62 03:55 Doncaster-Hull/1A13 09:36 Hull-King's Cross/FP/1D08 19:40 King's Cross-Hull/0D01 23:35 Hull-Doncaster; Thurs. 4: 1D62 03:55 Doncaster-Hull/1A13 09:36 Hull-King's Cross (train terminated at Welwyn Garden City due to activation of a hot axle box detector)/5A13 Welwyn Garden City-King's Cross/FP/1L45 17:40 King's Cross-York/YK; Fri. 5: YK/1S27 07:36 Plymouth-Edinburgh from York/1E39 22:25 Edinburgh-King's Cross; Sat. 6: FP; Sun. 7: FP; Mon. 8: 1S76 09:40 King's Cross-Edinburgh/HA/1E39 22:25 Edinburgh-King's Cross; Tues. 9: FP/1L43 14:03 King's Cross-York/1A31 18:14 York-King's Cross; Wed. 10: 1N00 01:00 King's Cross-Newcastle/1S08 07:05 Newcastle-Edinburgh/HA/ 1E35 20:25 Edinburgh-King's Cross; Thurs. 11: 1D01 08:30 King's Cross-Cleethorpes/1A21 13:20 Cleethorpes-King's Cross/ 1S66 20:15 King's Cross-Edinburgh; Fri. 12: 5E10 06:40 Craigentinny-Dundee/1E10 09:10 Dundee-King's Cross/FP/1S79 23:20 King's Cross-Aberdeen to Edinburgh; Sat. 13: HA/1E10 09:10 Dundee-King's Cross from Edinburgh/FP; Sun. 14: FP; Mon. 15: FP; Tues. 16: 1S12 05:50 King's Cross-Aberdeen to York/YK; Wed. 17: 1A37 10:47 York-King's Cross/FP/1D08 19:40 King's Cross-Hull/0D01 23:35 Hull-Doncaster; Thurs. 18: 1D62 03:55 Doncaster-Hull/1A13 09:36 Hull-King's Cross/FP; Fri. 19: 1N12 00:05 King's Cross-Newcastle/0L01 Newcastle-York/YK/0B02 York-Finsbury Park/FP/1S79 23:20 King's Cross-Aberdeen to Edinburgh; Sat. 20: 1V93 09:50 Edinburgh-Plymouth to York/1S27 07:36 Plymouth-Edinburgh from York/1E43 20:05 Aberdeen-King's Cross from Edinburgh; Sun. 21: FP/1L43 16:05 King's Cross-York/YK 'D' exam Until Thurs. 25: YK 'D' exam/0N10 York-Thornaby/TE 'Tyre Turning' (Tyres too thin to turn); Fri. 26: TE/0L01 Thornaby-York/YK; Until Tues. 30: YK/0D01 York-Doncaster/On DONCASTER WORKS "Unclassified repair" (No.1 bogie, 9000-39, replaced by 9000-46. No.2 bogie, 9000-40, replaced by 9000-42).

JULY

Wed. 1: DONCASTER WORKS; Thurs. 2: DONCASTER WORKS; Fri. 3: Off DONCASTER WORKS/0L01 Doncaster Works-York (towed by 55 009)/ YK 'D' exam Until; Sun. 12: YK 'D' exam/1A21 14:57 Newcastle-King's Cross from York/FP; Mon. 13: 1S76 09:40 King's Cross-Edinburgh/HA/1E35 20:25 Edinburgh-King's Cross; Tues. 14: 1L42 12:05 King's Cross-York/YK/0D01 York-Doncaster/DR; Wed. 15: 1D62 03:55 Doncaster-Hull/1A13 09:36 Hull-King's Cross/1L45 17:40 King's Cross-York/YK; Thurs. 16: 1A37 10:47 York-King's Cross/FP/1D08 19:40 King's Cross-Hull/0D01 23:35 Hull-Doncaster; Fri. 17: 1D62 03:55 Doncaster-Hull/1A13 09:36 Hull-King's Cross/1B04 16:12 King's Cross-Peterborough/5B04 Peterborough-Ferme Park/FP; Sat. 18: 1N00 01:00 King's Cross-Newcastle/1S08 07:05 Newcastle-Edinburgh/1E78 11:45 Edinburgh-Newcastle/GD/1A40 21:00 Newcastle-King's Cross; Sun. 19: FP; Mon. 20: 1N12 00:05 King's Cross-Newcastle/GD/1A40 21:00 Newcastle-King's Cross; Tues. 21: 5B26 05:24 King's Cross-Peterborough/1B26 07:23 Peterborough-King's Cross/1L42 12:05 King's Cross-York/1A26 15:50 York-King's Cross/1S77 23:55 King's Cross-Edinburgh; Wed. 22: 1V93 09:50 Edinburgh-Plymouth to York/1S27 07:36 Plymouth-Edinburgh from York/1E40 19:25 Aberdeen-King's Cross from Edinburgh; Thurs. 23: FP/1L43 14:03 King's Cross-York to Askern (loco. on fire)/0L01

Askern-York/ YK Until Sun. 26: YK/0B02 York-Finsbury Park/FP; Mon. 27:1N12 00:05 King's Cross-Newcastle to Peterborough/0D01 Peterborough-Doncaster/DR/0L01 Doncaster-York/YK Until Thurs. 30: YK/0D01 York-Doncaster Works (towed by 55 013)/On DONCASTER WORKS "Unclassified repair" (No.1 engine, 449, replaced by 434); Fri. 31: DONCASTER WORKS

AUGUST

Sat. 1: DONCASTER WORKS Until Thurs. 6: Off DONCASTER WORKS; Fri. 7: 0B02 Doncaster Works-Finsbury Park/FP/1S66 20:15 King's Cross-Edinburgh to Doncaster/DR; Sat. 8: DR/0L01 Doncaster-York/YK; Sun. 9: YK; Mon. 10: YK/0B02 York-Finsbury Park/FP/1S79 23:20 King's Cross-Aberdeen to Doncaster; Tues. 11: 0L01 Doncaster-York/YK 'B' exam; Wed. 12: YK 'B' exam; Thurs. 13: 1A37 10:47 York-King's Cross/FP/1D08 19:40 King's Cross-Hull/0D01 23:35 Hull-Doncaster; Fri. 14: 1D62 03:55 Doncaster-Hull/1A13 09:36 Hull-King's Cross/FP/1L45 17:40 King's Cross-York/YK; Sat. 15: 0N60 York-Filey/1N60 08:54 Filey-Newcastle to Scarborough/1A37 08:47 Bridlington-King's Cross from Scarborough/FP/1D08 19:40 King's Cross-Hull/ 0D01 23:35 Hull-Doncaster Sun. 16: DR; Mon. 17: 1D62 03:55 Doncaster-Hull/1A13 09:36 Hull-King's Cross/1L44 16:03 King's Cross-York/YK; Tues. 18: 1A37 10:47 York-King's Cross/1L44 16:03 King's Cross-York/YK; Wed. 19: 1A08 08:07 York-King's Cross/FP/1L44 16:03 King's Cross-York/1A34 20:19 York-King's Cross; Thurs. 20: 1S12 05:50 King's Cross-Aberdeen/1E26 16:30 Aberdeen-Leeds to Edinburgh (55 009 forward)/1E39 22:25 Edinburgh-King's Cross; Fri. 21: 1L42 12:05 King's Cross-York/1A26 15:50 York-King's Cross/1S77 23:55 King's Cross-Edinburgh; Sat. 22: HA; Sun. 23: 1V93 11:25 Edinburgh-Plymouth to Newcastle/GD; Mon. 24: GD/0L01 Gateshead-York (with 55 007)/YK Until Mon. 31: YK

SEPTEMBER

Tues. 1: 1M62 08:50 York-Liverpool/1E99 13:05 Liverpool-York/YK; Wed. 2: 5A37 York-Scarborough/1A37 09:54 Scarborough-King's Cross/FP/1D08 19:40 King's Cross-Hull/0D01 23:35 Hull-Doncaster; Thurs. 3: 1D62 03:55 Doncaster-Hull/1A13 09:36 Hull-King's Cross/1L45 17:40 King's Cross-York/YK; Fri. 4: 1A08 08:07 York-King's Cross/FP/1L44 16:03 King's Cross-York/1A34 19:55 York-King's Cross; Sat. 5: 1S12 05:50 King's Cross-Aberdeen to Edinburgh/HA/1E39 22:15 Edinburgh-King's Cross; Sun. 6: FP/1L42 14:05 King's Cross-York/1A19 19:13 York-King's Cross/FP; Mon. 7: 1S12 05:50 King's Cross-Aberdeen/1E26 16:30 Aberdeen-Leeds to York; Tues. 8: YK 'B' exam Until Wed. 23: YK 'B' exam; Thurs. 24: 1A08 08:07 York-King's Cross/FP/1D08 19:40 King's Cross-Hull/0D01 23:35 Hull-Doncaster; Fri. 25: 1D62 03:55 Doncaster-Hull/1A13 09:36 Hull-King's Cross/1L45 17:40 King's Cross-York/YK; Sat. 26: 1A08 08:07 York-King's Cross/FP; Sun. 27: FP; Mon. 28: 1N00 01:00 King's Cross-Newcastle to York/YK/1A08 08:07 York-King's Cross/FP/1L44 16:03 King's Cross-York/1A34 20:19 York-King's Cross; Tues. 29: FP; Wed. 30: FP/1D03 13:05 King's Cross-Cleethorpes/1A32 17:45 Cleethorpes-King's Cross/FP

OCTOBER

Thurs. 1: 1N00 01:00 King's Cross-Newcastle/1S08 07:05 Newcastle-Edinburgh/HA/ 2C20 17:30 Edinburgh-Cardenden/5G00 Cardenden-Craigentinny/HA 'oe'/ 1E39 22:25 Edinburgh-King's Cross; Fri. 2: FP 'oe'/1D03 13:05 King's Cross-Cleethorpes/1A32 17:45 Cleethorpes-King's Cross/1S77 23:55 King's Cross-Edinburgh; Sat. 3: HA 'oe'/1E29 17:18 Edinburgh-Newcastle/GD 'oe'; Sun. 4: GD 'oe'/1A40 21:28 Newcastle-King's Cross; Mon. 5: 5B26 05:24 King's Cross-Peterborough/1B26 07:23 Peterborough-King's Cross/FP 'oe'; Tues. 6: 1N12 00:05 King's Cross-Newcastle/0L01

Newcastle-York/YK 'oe'/0B02 York-Finsbury Park/FP 'oe'; Wed. 7: 1N00 01:00 King's Cross-Newcastle/1S08 07:05 Newcastle-Edinburgh/HA 'oe'/1E29 17:18 Edinburgh-Newcastle/1E42 23:15 Edinburgh-King's Cross from Newcastle; Thurs. 8: FP 'oe'/1L22 23:00 King's Cross-Bradford; Fri. 9: 0L50 Bradford-Holbeck/HO 'oe'/0L01 Holbeck-York/YK 'oe'/1A26 15:50 York-King's Cross/1L22 23:00 King's Cross-Bradford; Sat. 10: 0L50 Bradford-Holbeck/HO 'oe'/0L01 Holbeck-York/YK 'oe'; Sun. 11: YK 'oe'; Mon. 12: YK 'oe'; Tues. 13: 1M62 08:50 York-Liverpool/1E99 13:05 Liverpool-York/YK 'oe'/0B02 York-Finsbury Park/FP 'oe'/1S79 23:20 King's Cross-Aberdeen to Edinburgh; Wed. 14: 1V93 09:50 Edinburgh-Plymouth to York/1S27 07:36 Plymouth-Edinburgh from York/1E39 22:25 Edinburgh-King's Cross; Thurs. 15: FP 'oe'; Fri. 16: FP 'oe'/1S72 22:30 King's Cross-Edinburgh to York; Sat. 17: YK 'oe'; Sun. 18: YK 'oe'; Mon. 19: YK 'oe'/0B02 York-Finsbury Park/FP 'oe'/1S72 22:30 King's Cross-Edinburgh; Tues. 20; HA 'oe'/1E29 17:18 Edinburgh-Newcastle/1A45 22:55 Newcastle-King's Cross; Wed. 21: FP 'oe'; Thurs. 22; FP 'oe'; Fri. 23: 1N12 00:05 King's Cross-Newcastle/1S14 08:10 Newcastle-Edinburgh/HA 'oe'/1E29 17:18 Edinburgh-Newcastle/1A45 22:55 Newcastle-King's Cross; Sat. 24: FP 'oe'; Sun. 25: 1N12 00:05 King's Cross-Newcastle/GD 'oe'/1N03 21:20 Newcastle-Darlington/0L01 Darlington-York; Mon. 26: 1M62 08:50 York-Liverpool/1E99 13:05 Liverpool-York/YK 'oe'; Tues. 27: 1M62 08:50 York-Liverpool/1E99 13:05 Liverpool-York/1M76 15:50 York-Liverpool/1E89 20:40 Liverpool-York; Wed. 28: 1M62 08:50 York-Liverpool/1E99 13:05 Liverpool-York/1M77 15:18 Newcastle-Liverpool from York/1E89 20:40 Liverpool-York; Thurs. 29: YK 'oe'; Fri. 30: YK 'oe'/1N14 14:03 King's Cross-Newcastle from York (55 014 off)/GD 'oe'/ 1A45 22:55 Newcastle-King's Cross; Sat. 31: FP 'oe'/1A26 15:50 York-King's Cross from Belle Isle (propelling - 55 010 failed)

NOVEMBER

Sun. 1: 1N12 00:05 King's Cross-Newcastle/GD 'oe'/1N03 21:20 Newcastle-Darlington/0L01 Darlington-York; Mon. 2: YK 'oe'; Tues. 3: YK 'oe'; Wed. 4: YK 'oe'/0B02 York-Finsbury Park/FP 'oe'/1S72 22:30 King's Cross-Edinburgh Thurs. 5: HA 'oe'/1E29 17:18 Edinburgh-Newcastle/1A45 22:55 Newcastle-King's Cross; Fri. 6: FP 'oe'/0C01 Finsbury Park-Stratford/SF 'oe' (No.1 engine, 434, replaced by 421); Sat. 7: SF 'oe'; Sun. 8: SF - WITHDRAWN

D9012/9012/55012 Crepello

JANUARY 1981

Thurs. 1: FP; Fri. 2: 1L42 12:20 King's Cross-York/1A26 15:50 York-King's Cross/1S70 22:15 King's Cross-Aberdeen to Newcastle; Sat. 3: GD; Sun. 4: GD/1A62 15:20 Newcastle-King's Cross/FP; Mon. 5: 1S12 05:50 King's Cross-Aberdeen to Edinburgh/HA/1E26 16:30 Aberdeen-Leeds from Edinburgh/1E24 22:50 Shrewsbury-York from Leeds; Tues. 6: 1A08 08:05 York-King's Cross/1L12 14:50 King's Cross-Leeds/HO; Wed. 7: 1A14 10:45 Leeds-King's Cross/1L12 14:50 King's Cross-Leeds/HO; Thurs. 8: 1A14 10:45 Leeds-King's Cross/FP 'B' exam Until Mon. 12: FP 'B' exam/1S60 20:00 King's Cross-Aberdeen from Holloway to Edinburgh; Tues. 13: 1A23 08:55 Edinburgh-Aberdeen/1G64 12:40 Aberdeen-Edinburgh/HA/1E35 20:25 Edinburgh-King's Cross; Wed. 14: 1D00 08:05 King's Cross-Hull/1A18 12:34 Hull-King's Cross/1D08 19:35 King's Cross-Hull/0D01 23:35 Hull-Doncaster; Thurs. 15: 1D62 03:55 Doncaster-Hull/1A13 09:33 Hull-King's Cross/FP/1S60 20:00 King's Cross-Aberdeen to Edinburgh; Fri. 16: 1E08 07:30 Edinburgh-Newcastle/GD/1S15 17:35 Newcastle-Edinburgh/ 1E39 22:30 Edinburgh-King's Cross; Sat. 17: 1L42 12:20 King's Cross-

York/1A26 15:50 York-King's Cross/1S72 22:30 King's Cross-Edinburgh; Sun. 18: HA/1E35 20:25 Edinburgh-King's Cross; Mon. 19: 1D00 08:05 King's Cross-Hull/1A18 12:34 Hull-King's Cross/1D08 19:35 King's Cross-Hull/0D01 23:35 Hull-Doncaster; Tues. 20: 1D62 03:55 Doncaster-Hull/1A13 09:33 Hull-King's Cross/1L44 16:05 King's Cross-York/1A34 19:55 York-King's Cross; Wed. 21: 1D01 08:15 King's Cross-Cleethorpes/1A21 13:13 Cleethorpes-King's Cross/ FP; Thurs. 22: 1S12 05:50 King's Cross-Aberdeen to Edinburgh/HA/1E48 21:25 Aberdeen-King's Cross from Edinburgh; Fri. 23: 1L42 12:20 King's Cross-York/1A26 15:50 York-King's Cross/FP 'B' exam Until Sat. 31: FP 'B' exam

FEBRUARY

Sun. 1: FP 'B' exam; Mon. 2: 1D00 08:05 King's Cross-Hull/1A18 12:34 Hull-King's Cross/1D08 19:35 King's Cross-Hull/0D01 23:35 Hull-Doncaster; Tues. 3: 1D62 03:55 Doncaster-Hull/1A13 09:33 Hull-King's Cross/FP/1L45 18:05 King's Cross-York/0B05 York-Peterborough; Wed. 4: 1B16 07:50 Peterborough-King's Cross/FP; Thurs. 5: FP/1L44 16:05 King's Cross-York/1A34 19:55 York-King's Cross; Fri. 6: 1S12 05:50 King's Cross-Aberdeen to Edinburgh (55 007 forward)/HA/1E26 16:30 Aberdeen-Leeds from Edinburgh (55 007 off)/1E24 22:50 Shrewsbury-York from Leeds; Sat. 7: YK/1A31 18:13 York-King's Cross/FP Until Tues. 10: FP; Wed. 11: 1L42 12:20 King's Cross-York/1A26 15:50 York-King's Cross/FP 'C' exam Until Mon. 23: FP 'C' exam/1D08 19:35 King's Cross-Hull/0D01 23:35 Hull-Doncaster; Tues. 24: 1D62 03:55 Doncaster-Hull/1A13 09:33 Hull-King's Cross/1L44 16:05 King's Cross-York/1A34 19:55 York-King's Cross; Wed. 25: 1S12 05:50 King's Cross-Aberdeen to Edinburgh/HA/1A51 17:00 Edinburgh-Aberdeen/1E48 21:25 Aberdeen-King's Cross; Thurs. 26: 1D02 12:05 King's Cross-Hull/1A28 16:30 Hull-King's Cross/FP; Fri. 27: FP/1L45 18:05 King's Cross-York/YK; Sat. 28: 1A08 08:05 York-King's Cross/FP

MARCH

Sun. 1: FP/1L45 15:05 King's Cross-York/5D44 York-Hull/BG; Mon. 2: 1A13 09:33 Hull-King's Cross/1L44 16:05 King's Cross-York/1A34 19:55 York-King's Cross; Tues. 3: 1S12 05:50 King's Cross-Aberdeen to Edinburgh/HA/1O50 17:00 Edinburgh-Glasgow Q. St./1O53 18:00 Glasgow Q. St.-Edinburgh/1E40 19:25 Aberdeen-King's Cross from Edinburgh; Wed. 4: FP/1D08 19:35 King's Cross-Hull/0D01 23:35 Hull-Doncaster; Thurs. 5: 1D62 03:55 Doncaster-Hull/1A13 09:33 Hull-King's Cross/1L44 16:05 King's Cross-York/1A34 19:55 York-King's Cross; Fri. 6: 1D00 08:05 King's Cross-Hull/1A18 12:34 Hull-King's Cross/FP/1S60 20:00 King's Cross-Aberdeen to Edinburgh; Sat. 7: 1E08 07:30 Edinburgh-Newcastle/GD/1S15 17:35 Newcastle-Edinburgh/ 1E43 20:05 Aberdeen-King's Cross from Edinburgh; Sun. 8: FP/1L42 14:05 King's Cross-York/1A19 19:10 York-King's Cross/FP; Mon. 9: 1D00 08:05 King's Cross-Hull/1A18 12:34 Hull-King's Cross/FP 'B' exam; Tues. 10: FP 'B' exam; Wed. 11: FP 'B' exam; Thurs. 12: 1N00 01:00 King's Cross-Newcastle/1S08 07:05 Newcastle-Edinburgh/HA/ 1E35 20:25 Edinburgh-King's Cross; Fri. 13: FP; Sat. 14: 1D00 08:05 King's Cross-Hull/1A18 12:34 Hull-King's Cross/FP; Sun. 15: FP/1S79 23:15 King's Cross-Aberdeen to Edinburgh; Mon. 16: 1V93 09:50 Edinburgh-Plymouth to York/1S27 07:22 Plymouth-Edinburgh from York/1E40 19:25 Aberdeen-King's Cross from Edinburgh; Tues. 17: FP; Wed. 18: 1D02 12:05 King's Cross-Hull/1A28 16:30 Hull-King's Cross/1S77 23:55 King's Cross-Edinburgh; Thurs. 19: 1V93 09:50 Edinburgh-Plymouth to York/1S27 07:22 Plymouth-Edinburgh from York/1E35 20:25 Edinburgh-King's Cross; Fri. 20: 1D02 12:05 King's Cross-Hull/1A28 16:30 Hull-King's Cross/1S79 23:15 King's Cross-Aberdeen to Edinburgh; Sat. 21: HA/1E40 19:15 Aberdeen-King's Cross from Edinburgh; Sun. 22: FP/1S79 23:15 King's Cross-Aberdeen to Edinburgh; Mon. 23: HA/1E42 23:15 Edinburgh-King's Cross; Tues. 24: 1D02

12:05 King's Cross-Hull/1A28 16:30 Hull-King's Cross/1S77 23:55 King's Cross-Edinburgh; Wed. 25: 1A23 08:55 Edinburgh-Aberdeen/1G64 12:40 Aberdeen-Edinburgh/HA/1E39 22:30 Edinburgh-King's Cross; Thurs. 26: 1L41 10:05 King's Cross-York/1A22 14:10 York-King's Cross/FP 'B' exam Until Mon. 30: FP 'B' exam/1L45 18:05 King's Cross-York/0B05 York-Peterborough; Tues. 31: 1N12 00:05 King's Cross-Newcastle from Peterborough/GD/1A40 20:30 Newcastle-King's Cross

APRIL
Wed. 1: 5B16 05:24 King's Cross-Peterborough/1B16 07:50 Peterborough-King's Cross/FP/1S66 20:15 King's Cross-Edinburgh; Thurs. 2: 1E08 07:30 Edinburgh-Newcastle/GD/0D01 Gateshead-Doncaster/DR/1S70 22:15 King's Cross-Aberdeen from Doncaster (55 004 off) to Edinburgh; Fri. 3: 1V93 09:50 Edinburgh-Plymouth to York/1S27 07:22 Plymouth-Edinburgh from York/1E48 21:25 Aberdeen-King's Cross from Doncaster; Sat. 4: 1D02 12:05 King's Cross-Hull/1A28 16:30 Hull-King's Cross/FP; Sun. 5: 1D02 12:05 King's Cross-Hull/1A13 16:50 Hull-King's Cross/FP; Mon. 6: 1N00 01:00 King's Cross-Newcastle/1S08 07:05 Newcastle-Edinburgh/HA/ 1E35 20:25 Edinburgh-King's Cross; Tues. 7: 1D01 08:15 King's Cross-Cleethorpes/1A21 13:13 Cleethorpes-King's Cross/ FP; Wed. 8: 1S12 05:50 King's Cross-Aberdeen to Edinburgh (55 007 forward)/HA/1E29 17:07 Edinburgh-Newcastle/1A45 22:55 Newcastle-King's Cross; Thurs. 9: 1D02 12:05 King's Cross-Hull/1A28 16:30 Hull-King's Cross/1L22 23:00 King's Cross-Bradford to Leeds; Fri. 10: 0L01 Leeds-York/YK/1N43 14:05 King's Cross-Newcastle from York/0L01 Newcastle-York/YK; Sat. 11: YK/0D01 York-Doncaster (towing 37 194)/DR; Sun. 12: DR; Mon. 13: On DONCASTER WORKS "Unclassified repair" (No.1 engine, 413, replaced by 419) Until Fri. 24: Off DONCASTER

WORKS/DR/5A28 Doncaster-King's Cross (1A28 terminated at Doncaster); Sat. 25: 1N00 01:00 King's Cross-Newcastle/1S08 07:05 Newcastle-Edinburgh/HA/ 1E35 20:45 Edinburgh-King's Cross; Sun. 26: FP/1L13 15:05 King's Cross-York/5D44 York-Hull/BG; Mon. 27: 1A13 09:33 Hull-King's Cross/1L44 16:05 King's Cross-York/1A34 19:55 York-King's Cross; Tues. 28: FP; Wed. 29: FP/0C01 Finsbury Park-Stratford/SF; Thurs. 30: SF

MAY
Fri. 1: SF/0B02 Stratford-Finsbury Park/FP/1L41 10:05 King's Cross-York/YK 'B' exam; Sat. 2: 1A08 08:05 York-King's Cross/1L43 14:05 King's Cross-York/YK; Sun. 3: YK; Mon. 4: YK/1A34 19:55 York-King's Cross; Tues. 5: 1D00 08:05 King's Cross-Hull/1A18 12:34 Hull-King's Cross/FP; Wed. 6: 1N00 01:00 King's Cross-Newcastle/1S08 07:05 Newcastle-Edinburgh/HA/ 1E35 20:25 Edinburgh-King's Cross; Thurs. 7: 1L41 10:05 King's Cross-York/YK/1S66 20:15 King's Cross-Edinburgh from York; Fri. 8: 1V93 09:50 Edinburgh-Plymouth to York/YK; Sat. 9: 1A37 10:45 York-King's Cross/1L44 16:05 King's Cross-York/YK; Sun. 10: 1A06 11:43 York-King's Cross/FP; Mon. 11: 1S12 05:50 King's Cross-Aberdeen/1E26 16:30 Aberdeen-Leeds/1E24 22:50 Shrewsbury-York from Leeds; Tues. 12: 1A37 10:45 York-King's Cross/FP/1S72 22:30 King's Cross-Edinburgh; Wed. 13: 1A23 08:55 Edinburgh-Aberdeen/1G64 12:40 Aberdeen-Edinburgh/HA/1E39 22:30 Edinburgh-King's Cross; Thurs. 14: FP 'C' exam Until Sun. 17: FP 'C' exam; Mon. 18: FP - WITHDRAWN

D9013/9013/55013
The Black Watch

JUNE 1981
Mon. 1: 1N12 00:05 King's Cross-Newcastle/1S14 08:10 Newcastle-Edinburgh/HA/ 1E35 20:25 Edinburgh-King's Cross; Tues. 2: 1L42 12:05 King's Cross-York/1A26 15:50 York-King's Cross/1S72 22:30 King's Cross-Edinburgh; Wed. 3: 1E10 09:10 Dundee-King's Cross from Edinburgh/FP/1S72 22:30 King's Cross-Edinburgh; Thurs. 4: 1V93 09:50 Edinburgh-Plymouth to York/1S27 07:36 Plymouth-Edinburgh from York/1E43 20:35 Aberdeen-King's Cross from Edinburgh; Fri. 5: 1L42 12:05 King's Cross-York/1A26 15:50 York-King's Cross/FP; Sat. 6: 1N12 00:05 King's Cross-Newcastle/GD/1A39 10:50 Newcastle-King's Cross/ 1L45 18:05 King's Cross-York/YK; Sun. 7: 1A06 11:50 York-King's Cross to Peterborough/PB/1S79 23:20 King's Cross-Aberdeen from Peterborough to Edinburgh; Mon. 8: HA/1E29 17:18 Edinburgh-Newcastle/1A45 22:55 Newcastle-King's Cross; Tues. 9: 5B26 05:24 King's Cross-Peterborough/1B26 07:23 Peterborough-King's Cross/1L42 12:05 King's Cross-York/1A26 15:50 York-King's Cross/FP; Wed. 10: 1N12 00:05 King's Cross-Newcastle/0L01 Newcastle-York/YK/0D01 York-Doncaster/1A31 18:14 York-King's Cross from Doncaster; Thurs. 11: 1N00 01:00 King's Cross-Newcastle/0L01 Newcastle-York/YK 'B' exam; Fri. 12: YK/1A26 15:50 York-King's Cross/FP; Sat. 13: 1N12 00:05 King's Cross-Newcastle/1S14 08:10 Newcastle-Edinburgh/HA/ 1E35 20:45 Edinburgh-King's Cross; Sun. 14: FP/1S70 22:15 King's Cross-Aberdeen to Edinburgh; Mon. 15: 1V93 09:50 Edinburgh-Plymouth to York/1S27 07:36 Plymouth-Edinburgh from York/1E39 22:25 Edinburgh-King's Cross; Tues. 16: FP; Wed. 17: 1N12 00:05 King's Cross-Newcastle/0L01 Newcastle-York/YK; Thurs. 18: YK; Fri. 19: 1A08 08:07 York-King's Cross/FP/1L44 16:03 King's Cross-York/1A34 20:19 York-King's Cross; Sat. 20: 1S76 09:40 King's Cross-Edinburgh/HA; Sun. 21: 1V93 11:25 Edinburgh-Plymouth to York/1S27 09:00 Plymouth-Edinburgh from York/1E43 20:35 Aberdeen-King's Cross from Edinburgh; Mon. 22: FP/1D08 19:40 King's Cross-Hull/0D01 23:35 Hull-Doncaster; Tues. 23: 1D62 03:55 Doncaster-Hull/1A13 09:36 Hull-King's Cross/FP/1B21 17:17 King's Cross-Peterborough/0B02 Peterborough-Finsbury Park/FP/1S72 22:30 King's Cross-Edinburgh; Wed. 24: 1V93 09:50 Edinburgh-Plymouth to York/1S27 07:36 Plymouth-Edinburgh from York/1E39 22:25 Edinburgh-King's Cross; Thurs. 25: FP 'B' exam Until Tues. 30: FP 'B' exam

JULY
Wed. 1: FP 'B' exam/1S60 20:00 King's Cross-Aberdeen to Edinburgh; Thurs. 2: 5E10 06:40 Craigentinny-Dundee/1E10 09:10 Dundee-King's Cross/FP; Fri. 3: 1N00 01:00 King's Cross-Newcastle/1S08 07:05 Newcastle-Edinburgh/HA/ 1E39 22:25 Edinburgh-King's Cross; Sat. 4: FP/1L43 14:03 King's Cross-York/1A31 18:14 York-King's Cross/FP; Sun. 5: FP; Mon. 6: FP; Tues. 7: 1L01 04:05 King's Cross-Leeds/0L01 Leeds-York/YK; Wed. 8: YK/0D01 York-Doncaster (towed by 55 017)/On DONCASTER WORKS "Unclassified repair" Until Tues. 14: Off DONCASTER WORKS/DR/1S77 23:55 King's Cross-Edinburgh from Doncaster; Wed. 15: HA/1A38 14:55 Edinburgh-Aberdeen/1G20 18:23 Aberdeen-Edinburgh/1E43 20:35 Aberdeen-King's Cross from Edinburgh; Thurs. 16: FP/1L43 14:03 King's Cross-York/1A31 18:14 York-King's Cross/FP; Fri. 17: 1S76 09:40 King's Cross-Edinburgh/HA/1E42 23:15 Edinburgh-King's Cross; Sat. 18: FP/1S70 22:15 King's Cross-Aberdeen to Edinburgh; Sun. 19: 1V93 11:25 Edinburgh-Plymouth to York/1S27 09:00 Plymouth-Edinburgh from York/1E43 20:35 Aberdeen-King's Cross from Edinburgh; Mon. 20: FP/1S60 20:00 King's Cross-Aberdeen to

Edinburgh; Tues. 21: 5E10 06:40 Craigentinny-Dundee/1E10 09:10 Dundee-King's Cross/FP; Wed. 22: 1N12 00:05 King's Cross-Newcastle/5A37 Heaton-Durham/1A37 09:30 Durham-King's Cross/FP/1D08 19:40 King's Cross-Hull/0D01 23:35 Hull-Doncaster; Thurs. 23: 1D62 03:55 Doncaster-Hull/1A13 09:36 Hull-King's Cross/FP/1L45 17:40 King's Cross-York/YK 'C' exam Until Sun. 26: YK 'C' exam/1A21 14:57 Newcastle-King's Cross from York/FP/1S77 23:55 King's Cross-Edinburgh; Mon. 27: HA/1E29 17:18 Edinburgh-Newcastle/1A45 22:55 Newcastle-King's Cross; Tues. 28: FP/0L01 Finsbury Park-York/YK; Wed. 29: YK; Thurs. 30: YK/0D01 York-Doncaster (towing 55 011)/DR "Tyre Turning"; Fri. 31: DR "Tyre Turning"

AUGUST

Sat. 1: DR/0L01 Doncaster-York/YK/1A34 20:19 York-King's Cross; Sun. 2: 1N02 08:30 King's Cross-Newcastle/GD/1A45 22:55 Newcastle-King's Cross; Mon. 3: FP/1L44 16:03 King's Cross-York/1A34 20:19 York-King's Cross; Tues. 4: 1S12 05:50 King's Cross-Aberdeen to Edinburgh/HA/1A51 17:00 Edinburgh-Aberdeen/1E48 21:20 Aberdeen-King's Cross; Wed. 5: 1L42 12:05 King's Cross-York/1A26 15:50 York-King's Cross/FP; Thurs. 6: FP/1S70 22:15 King's Cross-Aberdeen to Edinburgh; Fri. 7: 1V93 09:50 Edinburgh-Plymouth to York/1S27 07:36 Plymouth-Edinburgh from York/1E48 21:20 Aberdeen-King's Cross from Edinburgh; Sat. 8: FP; Sun. 9: FP; Mon. 10: FP/1S60 20:00 King's Cross-Aberdeen to York; Tues. 11: YK/1S27 07:36 Plymouth-Edinburgh from York/1E48 21:20 Aberdeen-King's Cross from Edinburgh; Wed. 12: FP/1D08 19:40 King's Cross-Hull/0D01 23:35 Hull-Doncaster; Thurs. 13: On DONCASTER WORKS "Unclassified repair"; Fri. 14: Off DONCASTER WORKS/DR; Sat. 15: 1D62 03:55 Doncaster-Hull/1A13 09:36 Hull-King's Cross/FP/1L45 18:05 King's Cross-York/YK; Sun. 16: 1A06 11:50 York-King's Cross/FP; Mon. 17: 1S12 05:50 King's Cross-Aberdeen/1E26 16:30

Aberdeen-Leeds to Edinburgh/1E43 20:35 Aberdeen-King's Cross from Edinburgh to York; Tues. 18: YK 'B' exam Until Tues. 25: YK 'B' exam; Wed. 26: 1A08 08:07 York-King's Cross/FP/1L44 16:03 King's Cross-York/1A34 20:19 York-King's Cross; Thurs. 27: 1S12 05:50 King's Cross-Aberdeen to Edinburgh/HA/1E35 20:25 Edinburgh-King's Cross to York; Fri. 28: YK; Sat. 29: 0N60 York-Scarborough/5N60 Scarborough-Filey/1N60 08:54 Filey-Newcastle to Scarborough (55 009 forward)/1A37 08:47 Bridlington-King's Cross from Scarborough/FP/1L45 18:05 King's Cross-York/YK; Sun. 30: 1A06 11:50 York-King's Cross/FP/1S79 23:20 King's Cross-Aberdeen to Edinburgh; Mon. 31:1V93 09:50 Edinburgh-Plymouth to York/1S27 07:36 Plymouth-Edinburgh from York/1E40 19:25 Aberdeen-King's Cross from Edinburgh

SEPTEMBER

Tues. 1: FP/1L44 16:03 King's Cross-York/1A34 20:19 York-King's Cross; Wed. 2: 1S12 05:50 King's Cross-Aberdeen to Edinburgh/HA/1E35 20:25 Edinburgh-King's Cross; Thurs. 3: 1S76 09:40 King's Cross-Edinburgh/HA/1E35 20:25 Edinburgh-King's Cross; Fri. 4: 1S76 09:40 King's Cross-Edinburgh/HA/1E40 19:25 Aberdeen-King's Cross from Edinburgh; Sat. 5: 1L42 12:05 King's Cross-York/1A26 15:50 York-King's Cross/1S72 22:30 King's Cross-Edinburgh; Sun. 6: HA/1E39 22:30 Edinburgh-King's Cross; Mon. 7: FP/1S70 22:15 King's Cross-Aberdeen to Edinburgh; Tues. 8: 0S72 Edinburgh-Dunbar/1S72 22:30 King's Cross-Edinburgh from Dunbar/ 1M04 07:18 Edinburgh-Carlisle/1S15 15:53 Carlisle-Edinburgh/1E39 22:25 Edinburgh-King's Cross; Wed. 9: FP/1L45 17:40 King's Cross-York/YK; Thurs. 10: YK; Fri. 11: 1A08 08:07 York-King's Cross/5Bxx King's Cross-Hornsey (towing failed E.M.U.)/FP/1L44 16:03 King's Cross-York/1A34 20:19 York-King's Cross; Sat. 12: 1S12 05:50 King's Cross-Aberdeen to Edinburgh/HA/1E35 20:45

Edinburgh-King's Cross; Sun. 13: FP/1L43 16:05 King's Cross-York/YK Until Wed. 16: YK; Thurs. 17: 0D01 York-Doncaster/1D62 03:55 Doncaster-Hull/1A13 09:36 Hull-King's Cross/FP/1L45 17:40 King's Cross-York; Fri. 18: 1A08 08:07 York-King's Cross/FP/1B21 17:17 King's Cross-Peterborough/ 5B21 Peterborough-Ferme Park/FP/1S79 23:20 King's Cross-Aberdeen to Edinburgh; Sat. 19: 1Z83 Edinburgh-Carstairs/1G89 Carstairs-Edinburgh/HA/1E40 19:15 Aberdeen-King's Cross from Edinburgh; Sun. 20: FP; Mon. 21: 1N12 00:05 King's Cross-Newcastle/0L01 Newcastle-York/1A37 10:47 York-King's Cross/1L45 17:40 King's Cross-York/YK; Tues. 22: 1A37 10:47 York-King's Cross/FP/1S66 20:15 King's Cross-Edinburgh; Wed. 23: 1V93 09:50 Edinburgh-Plymouth to York/1S27 07:36 Plymouth-Edinburgh from York/1E35 20:25 Edinburgh-King's Cross; Thurs. 24: 1L41 09:40 King's Cross-York/1A22 14:15 York-King's Cross/1S60 20:00 King's Cross-Aberdeen to York/1S72 22:30 King's Cross-Edinburgh from York (55 004 off); Fri. 25: 1V93 09:50 Edinburgh-Plymouth to York/1S27 07:36 Plymouth-Edinburgh from York/1E35 20:25 Edinburgh-King's Cross; Sat. 26: FP/1L45 18:05 King's Cross-York/YK; Sun. 27: 1A06 11:50 York-King's Cross/FP/1S79 23:20 King's Cross-Aberdeen to Edinburgh; Mon. 28: 1V93 09:50 Edinburgh-Plymouth to York/1S27 07:36 Plymouth-Edinburgh from York to Newcastle/GD/1N03 21:20 Newcastle-Darlington/0L01 Darlington-York; Tues. 29: YK 'B' exam/1A31 18:14 York-King's Cross/FP; Wed. 30: 1S12 05:50 King's Cross-Aberdeen to Edinburgh/HA/1E40 19:25 Aberdeen-King's Cross from Edinburgh

OCTOBER

Thurs. 1: FP/1L44 16:03 King's Cross-York/1A34 20:19 York-King's Cross; Fri. 2:FP 'oe'/5B26 05:24 King's Cross-Peterborough/1B26 07:23 Peterborough-King's Cross/FP 'oe'; Sat. 3: 1N12 00:05 King's Cross-Newcastle to Doncaster/DR/5L40 06:15 Ferme Park-York (Clifton) from Doncaster/YK/ 5A47 18:18 York (Clifton)-Ferme Park; Sun. 4th FP 'oe'; Mon. 5: FP 'oe'/1L22 23:00 King's Cross-Bradford to Leeds; Tues. 6: 0L01 Leeds-York/YK; Wed. 7: YK/0B02 York-Finsbury Park/FP/1L43 14:03 King's Cross-York/1A31 18:14 York-King's Cross/FP; Thurs. 8: 1B50 02:00 King's Cross-Peterborough/PB/1B13 07:00 Peterborough-King's Cross/FP/1S77 23:55 King's Cross-Edinburgh; Fri. 9: 1V93 09:50 Edinburgh-Plymouth to York/1S27 07:36 Plymouth-Edinburgh from York/1E39 22:15 Edinburgh-King's Cross to Newcastle; Sat. 10: 1S14 08:10 Newcastle-Edinburgh/HA/1A38 14:55 Edinburgh-Aberdeen/1G20 18:30 Aberdeen-Edinburgh/1E40 19:15 Aberdeen-King's Cross from Edinburgh; Sun. 11: FP/1S60 20:00 King's Cross-Aberdeen to Edinburgh; Mon. 12: 5G18 Craigentinny-Markinch/2G18 07:25 Markinch-Edinburgh/HA/1E35 20:25 Edinburgh-King's Cross; Tues. 13: FP/1D08 19:40 King's Cross-Hull/5L04 23:30 Hull-York; Wed. 14: YK Thurs. 15: YK/1A26 15:50 York-King's Cross/1S70 22:15 King's Cross-Aberdeen to Edinburgh; Fri. 16: 1V93 09:50 Edinburgh-Plymouth to York/1S27 07:36 Plymouth-Edinburgh from York/1E42 23:15 Edinburgh-King's Cross; Sat. 17: FP/1L43 14:03 King's Cross-York/1A31 18:14 York-King's Cross/FP; Sun. 18: 1L41 10:05 King's Cross-York/1A10 15:50 York-King's Cross/FP; Mon. 19: 1L41 09:40 King's Cross-York/1A22 14:15 York-King's Cross/FP/1S70 22:15 King's Cross-Aberdeen to Edinburgh; Tues. 20: 1M04 07:18 Edinburgh-Carlisle/1S15 15:53 Carlisle-Edinburgh/1E43 20:35 Aberdeen-King's Cross from Edinburgh; Wed. 21: FP/1L44 16:03 King's Cross-York/1A34 20:19 York-King's Cross; Thurs. 22: 1S12 05:50 King's Cross-Aberdeen to Newcastle/0L01 Newcastle-York/1A26 15:50 York-King's Cross/FP; Fri. 23: 1S12 05:50 King's Cross-Aberdeen to Newcastle/0L01 Newcastle-York/1A26 15:50 York-King's Cross/1S70 22:15 King's Cross-Aberdeen to Edinburgh; Sat. 24: HA/1E35

20:45 Edinburgh-King's Cross; Sun. 25: FP; Mon. 26: 1N12 00:05 King's Cross-Newcastle/1S14 08:10 Newcastle-Edinburgh/HA/ 1E39 22:25 Edinburgh-King's Cross; Tues. 27: FP; Wed. 28: 1N00 01:00 King's Cross-Newcastle/1S08 07:05 Newcastle-Edinburgh/HA/ 1E35 20:25 Edinburgh-King's Cross; Thurs. 29: FP/1S66 20:15 King's Cross-Edinburgh; Fri. 30: 1M04 07:18 Edinburgh-Carlisle/1S15 15:53 Carlisle-Edinburgh/1E43 20:35 Aberdeen-King's Cross from Edinburgh; Sat. 31: FP/1S72 22:30 King's Cross-Edinburgh

NOVEMBER

Sun. 1: HA/1E40 19:25 Aberdeen-King's Cross from Edinburgh; Mon. 2: FP; Tues. 3: FP; Wed. 4: FP/1L43 14:03 King's Cross-York/1A31 18:14 York-King's Cross/FP; Thurs. 5: 1S12 05:50 King's Cross-Aberdeen to Newcastle/0L01 Newcastle-York/1A26 15:50 York-King's Cross/1S79 23:20 King's Cross-Aberdeen to Edinburgh; Fri. 6: HA/1E29 17:18 Edinburgh-Newcastle/1A45 22:55 Newcastle-King's Cross; Sat. 7: FP/1L44 16:03 King's Cross-York/YK; Sun. 8: YK; Mon. 9: YK/1A22 14:15 York-King's Cross/1D08 19:40 King's Cross-Hull/5L04 23:30 Hull-York; Tues. 10: 1A08 08:07 York-King's Cross/FP/1S77 23:55 King's Cross-Edinburgh; Wed. 11: HA/1E35 20:25 Edinburgh-King's Cross to York; Thurs. 12: YK/1A26 15:50 York-King's Cross/FP; Fri. 13: 1N12 00:05 King's Cross-Newcastle/1S14 08:10 Newcastle-King's Cross/HA/ 1E39 22:25 Edinburgh-King's Cross; Sat. 14: FP/1S60 20:00 King's Cross-Aberdeen to Edinburgh; Sun. 15: HA/1E39 22:30 Edinburgh-King's Cross; Mon. 16: FP/1S66 20:15 King's Cross-Edinburgh; Tues. 17: 1M04 07:18 Edinburgh-Carlisle/1S15 15:53 Carlisle-Edinburgh/1E40 19:25 Aberdeen-King's Cross from Edinburgh; Wed. 18: FP/1L44 16:03 King's Cross-York/1A34 20:19 York-King's Cross; Thurs. 19: 1S12 05:50 King's Cross-Aberdeen to Edinburgh/HA/1E39 22:25 Edinburgh-King's Cross; Fri. 20: FP/1L43 14:03 King's Cross-

York/1A31 18:14 York-King's Cross; Sat. 21: 1N12 00:05 King's Cross-Newcastle/1S14 08:10 Newcastle-Edinburgh/1Z10 17:05 Inverkeithing-Bradford from Edinburgh (55 002 off) "Deltic Scotsman" Rail tour/1Z10 21:33 Bradford-York; Sun. 22: YK 'B' exam; Mon. 23: YK 'B' exam; Tues. 24: 1A08 08:07 York-King's Cross/FP/1L44 16:03 King's Cross-York/1A34 20:19 York-King's Cross; Wed. 25: 1S12 05:50 King's Cross-Aberdeen/1E26 16:30 Aberdeen-York; Thurs. 26: 1A08 08:07 York-King's Cross/FP/1S79 23:20 King's Cross-Aberdeen to Edinburgh; Fri. 27: HA/1E29 17:18 Edinburgh-Newcastle/1A45 22:55 Newcastle-King's Cross; Sat. 28: FP/1S66 21:00 King's Cross-Edinburgh; Sun. 29: HA/1E39 22:30 Edinburgh-King's Cross; Mon. 30: FP/1S66 20:15 King's Cross-Edinburgh

DECEMBER

Tues. 1: 1M04 07:18 Edinburgh-Carlisle/1S15 15:53 Carlisle-Edinburgh/1E40 19:25 Aberdeen-King's Cross from Edinburgh; Wed. 2: FP/1S77 23:55 King's Cross-Edinburgh ('oe' from Doncaster); Thurs. 3: 1C91 10:25 Edinburgh-Carstairs/1G44 11:23 Carstairs-Edinburgh/HA 'oe'/ 1E29 17:18 Edinburgh-Newcastle/GD 'oe'/1S60 20:00 King's Cross-Aberdeen from Newcastle to Edinburgh; Fri. 4: HA 'oe'/1E29 17:18 Edinburgh-Newcastle/1A45 22:55 Newcastle-King's Cross; Sat. 5: FP 'oe'; Sun. 6: 1N12 00:05 King's Cross-Newcastle/GD 'oe'/1A40 21:28 Newcastle-King's Cross to York (failed); Mon. 7: YK; Tues. 8: YK; Wed. 9: YK/1A31 18:14 York-King's Cross/1S77 23:55 King's Cross-Edinburgh; Thurs. 10: HA/1E35 20:25 Edinburgh-King's Cross; Fri. 11: FP/1N14 14:03 King's Cross-Newcastle/GD/1E40 19:25 Aberdeen-King's Cross from Newcastle; Sat. 12: FP; Sun. 13: 1L41 10:05 King's Cross-York/1A10 15:50 York-King's Cross/1S77 23:55 King's Cross-Edinburgh; Mon. 14: HA/1E35 20:25 Edinburgh-King's Cross; Tues. 15: 1L41 09:40 King's Cross-York/1A22 14:15 York-King's Cross/FP (No.2 engine coolant leak) 'oe'; Wed. 16: 5B26 05:24 King's Cross-Peterborough/1B26 07:23 Peterborough-King's Cross (failed at Wood Green - No.1 engine fractured liner - assisted forward by 31 292)/FP 'oe' Until Sun. 20: FP - WITHDRAWN

D9014/9014/55014
The Duke of Wellington's Regiment

JUNE 1981

Mon. 1: 1M04 07:18 Edinburgh-Carlisle to Newcastle/GD/1S15 15:53 Carlisle-Edinburgh from Newcastle/1E43 20:35 Aberdeen-King's Cross from Edinburgh; Tues. 2: FP/1S60 20:00 King's Cross-Aberdeen to Edinburgh/HA/1S79 23:15 King's Cross-Aberdeen from Edinburgh; Wed. 3: AB/1G64 12:40 Aberdeen-Edinburgh/HA/1E39 22:25 Edinburgh-King's Cross; Thurs. 4: FP/1L43 14:03 King's Cross-York/1A31 18:14 York-King's Cross; Fri. 5: 1N00 01:00 King's Cross-Newcastle/1S08 07:05 Newcastle-Edinburgh/1E10 09:10 Dundee-King's Cross from Edinburgh/FP/1S72 22:30 King's Cross-Edinburgh; Sat. 6: 1V93 09:50 Edinburgh-Plymouth to York/1S27 07:36 Plymouth-Edinburgh from York/1E40 19:15 Aberdeen-King's Cross from Edinburgh; Sun. 7: FP/1L42 14:05 King's Cross-York/1A19 19:13 York-King's Cross; Mon. 8: 1N00 01:00 King's Cross-Newcastle/1S08 07:05 Newcastle-Edinburgh/HA/ 1E26 16:30 Aberdeen-Leeds from Edinburgh; Tues. 9: 0L01 Leeds-York/YK/York-King's Cross/1L45 17:40 King's Cross-York/YK; Wed. 10: YK; Thurs. 11: YK/1S76 09:40 King's Cross-Edinburgh from York/HA/1E35 20:25 Edinburgh-King's Cross; Fri. 12: FP/1N14 14:03 King's Cross-Newcastle to Doncaster/DR/0L01 Doncaster-York/YK; Sat. 13: 0N60 York-Filey/1N60 08:54 Filey-Newcastle to Scarborough/1A37 08:47 Bridlington-King's Cross from Scarborough to York (55 015 forward)/YK; Sun. 14: YK Mon. 15: YK/0D01 York-Doncaster

(towing 55 012); Tues. 16: On DONCASTER WORKS "Unclassified repair" (No.2 engine, 538, replaced by 457); Wed. 17: DONCASTER WORKS; Thurs. 18: Off DONCASTER WORKS/DR; Fri. 19: 1D62 03:55 Doncaster-Hull/1A13 09:36 Hull-King's Cross/FP/1S77 23:55 King's Cross-Edinburgh; Sat. 20: HA/1E26 16:30 Aberdeen-Leeds from Edinburgh; Sun. 21: 5E26 Leeds-York/YK; Mon. 22: YK/0L50 York-Neville Hill/1A70 09:17 Leeds-King's Cross/FP; Tues. 23: FP/1S66 20:15 King's Cross-Edinburgh; Wed. 24: 5E10 06:40 Craigentinny-Dundee/1E10 09:10 Dundee-King's Cross/FP/1S70 22:15 King's Cross-Aberdeen to Edinburgh; Thurs. 25: 1M04 07:18 Edinburgh-Carlisle/1S15 15:53 Carlisle-Edinburgh/1E40 19:25 Aberdeen-King's Cross from Edinburgh; Fri. 26: FP/1D08 19:40 King's Cross-Hull/1D26 23:40 Hull-Doncaster; Sat. 27: 1D62 03:55 Doncaster-Hull/1A13 09:36 Hull-King's Cross/1L44 16:03 King's Cross-York/1A34 20:19 York-King's Cross; Sun. 28: 1L41 10:05 King's Cross-York/1A10 15:50 York-King's Cross/FP; Mon. 29: 1N00 01:00 King's Cross-Newcastle to York/YK; Tues. 30: 1A37 10:47 York-King's Cross/FP/1D08 19:40 King's Cross-Hull/0D01 23:35 Hull-Doncaster

JULY

Wed. 1: 1D62 03:55 Doncaster-Hull/1A13 09:36 Hull-King's Cross/FP; Thurs. 2: 1N12 00:05 King's Cross-Newcastle/0L01 Newcastle-York/1A37 10:47 York-King's Cross/FP/1D08 19:40 King's Cross-Hull/0D01 23:35 Hull-Doncaster; Fri. 3: 1D62 03:55 Doncaster-Hull/1A13 09:36 Hull-King's Cross/FP/1L45 17:40 King's Cross-York/YK 'B' exam; Sat. 4: YK 'B' exam; Sun. 5: YK 'B' exam/0B02 York-Finsbury Park/FP/1S60 20:00 King's Cross-Aberdeen to Edinburgh; Mon. 6: 1V93 09:50 Edinburgh-Plymouth to York/1S27 07:36 Plymouth-Edinburgh from York to Newcastle/GD/1A40 21:00 Newcastle-King's Cross; Tues. 7: 5B26 05:24 King's Cross-Peterborough/1B26 07:23 Peterborough-King's Cross/FP; Wed. 8: 1N12 00:05 King's Cross-

D9014 — THE LAST MONTHS OF THE DELTICS — 1981

Newcastle/GD/1A40 21:00 Newcastle-King's Cross; Thurs. 9: 5B26 05:24 King's Cross-Peterborough/1B26 07:23 Peterborough-King's Cross/FP; Fri. 10: 1N12 00:05 King's Cross-Newcastle/GD/0L01 Gateshead-York/YK Until Mon. 13: YK/0D01 York-Doncaster/On DONCASTER WORKS "Unclassified repair" (No.2 engine, 457, replaced by 455); Tues. 14: DONCASTER WORKS; Wed. 15: Off DONCASTER WORKS/DR; Thurs. 16: DR/0B02 Doncaster-Finsbury Park/FP/1S70 22:15 King's Cross-Aberdeen to Edinburgh; Fri. 17: 1V93 09:50 Edinburgh-Plymouth to York/1S27 07:36 Plymouth-Edinburgh from York to Newcastle/GD/1A40 21:00 Newcastle-King's Cross; Sat. 18: FP/1L42 12:05 King's Cross-York/1Z68 York-Edinburgh "Hadrian Flyer" Rail tour/HA/0E20 Haymarket-Gateshead/1E43 20:05 Aberdeen-King's Cross from Newcastle; Sun. 19: FP/1S77 23:55 King's Cross-Edinburgh; Mon. 20: 1V93 09:50 Edinburgh-Plymouth to Newcastle/GD/0L01 Gateshead-York/YK; Tues. 21: YK 'vo'/0B02 York-Finsbury Park/FP 'vo'/1L22 23:00 King's Cross-Bradford to Leeds; Wed. 22: HO 'vo'/0B02 Holbeck-Finsbury Park/FP 'vo'/1L22 23:00 King's Cross-Bradford to Leeds; Thurs. 23: 0L01 Leeds-York/YK 'vo'; Fri. 24: 1A37 10:47 York-King's Cross/1L45 17:40 King's Cross-York/YK; Sat. 25: YK/0N60 York-Filey/1N60 08:54 Filey-Newcastle to Scarborough/1A37 08:47 Bridlington-King's Cross from Scarborough/1L44 16:03 King's Cross-York/1A34 20:19 York-King's Cross; Sun. 26: 1L41 10:05 King's Cross-York/1A10 15:50 York-King's Cross/1S79 23:20 King's Cross-Aberdeen to Edinburgh; Mon. 27: 1A28 11:00 Edinburgh-Aberdeen/1G80 14:40 Aberdeen-Edinburgh/HA/1E39 22:25 Edinburgh-King's Cross; Tues. 28:FP/1L43 14:03 King's Cross-York/YK 'B' exam; Wed. 29: YK 'B' exam; Thurs. 30: 1A08 08:07 York-King's Cross/FP/1L44 16:03 King's Cross-York/YK; Fri. 31: 1A37 10:47 York-King's Cross/1L45 17:40 King's Cross-York/YK

AUGUST

Sat. 1: YK Until Tues. 4: YK/1E43 20:35 Aberdeen-King's Cross from York; Wed. 5: FP; Thurs. 6: 1N12 00:05 King's Cross-Newcastle/GD/0L01 Gateshead-York/YK; Fri. 7: YK/0D01 York-Doncaster/On DONCASTER WORKS "Unclassified repair" Until Tues. 11: Off DONCASTER WORKS; Wed. 12: 0B02 Doncaster-Finsbury Park/FP/1S72 22:30 King's Cross-Edinburgh; Thurs. 13: 1V93 09:50 Edinburgh-Plymouth to York/1S27 07:36 Plymouth-Edinburgh from York/1E39 22:25 Edinburgh-King's Cross; Fri. 14: FP/1D03 13:05 King's Cross-Cleethorpes/1A32 17:45 Cleethorpes-King's Cross/FP; Sat. 15: 1N12 00:05 King's Cross-Newcastle/GD/1A39 10:50 Newcastle-King's Cross/ FP/1S60 20:00 King's Cross-Aberdeen to Edinburgh; Sun. 16: 1V93 11:25 Edinburgh-Plymouth to York/1S27 11:25 Reading-Edinburgh from York/1E43 20:35 Aberdeen-King's Cross from Edinburgh; Mon. 17: FP/1L43 14:03 King's Cross-York/1A31 18:14 York-King's Cross; Tues. 18: 1N00 01:00 King's Cross-Newcastle/1S08 07:05 Newcastle-Edinburgh/HA/ 1E29 17:18 Edinburgh-Newcastle/1A45 22:55 Newcastle-King's Cross; Wed. 19: FP/1L45 17:40 King's Cross-York/YK 'D' exam Until Wed. 26: YK 'D' exam/0B02 York-Finsbury Park/FP/0C01 Finsbury Park-Stratford/SF; Thurs. 27: SF; Fri. 28: SF/0B02 Stratford-Finsbury Park/FP/1S66 20:15 King's Cross-Edinburgh; Sat. 29: 1E28 08:10 Glasgow Q. St.-Scarborough from Edinburgh to York/1S51 15:08 Scarborough-Glasgow Q. St. from York to Edinburgh/1E43 20:05 Aberdeen-King's Cross from Edinburgh; Sun. 30: FP/1L43 16:05 King's Cross-York/YK; Mon. 31: 1A08 08:07 York-King's Cross/FP/1L44 16:03 King's Cross-York/1A34 20:19 York-King's Cross

SEPTEMBER

Tues. 1: 1S76 09:40 King's Cross-Edinburgh/HA/1E35 20:25 Edinburgh-King's Cross; Wed. 2: 1S76 09:40 King's Cross-

Edinburgh/HA/1E40 19:25 Aberdeen-King's Cross from Edinburgh; Thurs. 3: FP/1L43 14:03 King's Cross-York/1A31 18:14 York-King's Cross; Fri. 4: 1N00 01:00 King's Cross-Newcastle/1S08 07:05 Newcastle-Edinburgh/HA/ 1A38 14:55 Edinburgh-Aberdeen/1G20 18:23 Aberdeen-Edinburgh/1E42 23:15 Edinburgh-King's Cross; Sat. 5: FP/1L44 16:03 King's Cross-York/1A34 20:19 York-King's Cross; Sun. 6: 1N02 08:30 King's Cross-Newcastle/1A21 14:57 Newcastle-King's Cross to York/YK; Mon. 7: 1A08 08:07 York-King's Cross/FP/1D08 19:40 King's Cross-Hull/0D01 23:35 Hull-Doncaster; Tues. 8: 1D62 03:55 Doncaster-Hull/5A13 Hull-York (1A13 cancelled)/YK/1A31 18:14 York-King's Cross; Wed. 9: 1N00 01:00 King's Cross-Newcastle/1S08 07:05 Newcastle-Edinburgh/HA/ 1E35 20:25 Edinburgh-King's Cross to York; Thurs. 10: 1A08 08:07 York-King's Cross/FP/1L44 16:03 King's Cross-York/YK; Fri. 11: YK; Sat. 12: YK/5A47 18:18 York (Clifton)-Ferme Park/FP; Sun. 13: 1N12 00:05 King's Cross-Newcastle/GD/1A40 21:28 Newcastle-King's Cross; Mon. 14: FP 'oe'; Tues. 15: 1N12 00:05 King's Cross-Newcastle/1S14 08:10 Newcastle-Edinburgh/HA 'oe'/1E29 17:18 Edinburgh-Newcastle/1A45 22:55 Newcastle-King's Cross; Wed. 16: 1S76 09:40 King's Cross-Edinburgh to York (55 017 forward)/YK 'oe'/0B02 York-Finsbury Park/FP 'oe'; Thurs. 17: 1N12 00:05 King's Cross-Newcastle/GD 'oe'/0L01 Gateshead-York/YK 'oe'/ 0B02 York-Finsbury Park/FP 'oe'; Fri. 18: 1N12 00:05 King's Cross-Newcastle/GD 'oe'/0L01 Gateshead-York/YK 'oe'/ 1N14 14:03 King's Cross-Newcastle from York/GD 'oe'/1A40 21:00 Newcastle-King's Cross; Sat. 19: FP 'oe'/0V00 Finsbury Park-Old Oak Common/OC 'oe' "Open day exhibit"; Sun. 20: OC 'oe' "Open day exhibit"/0E00 Old Oak Common-Finsbury Park/FP 'oe'; Mon. 21: 1D01 08:30 King's Cross-Cleethorpes/1A21 13:20 Cleethorpes-King's Cross/ 1D08 19:40 King's Cross-Hull/0D01 23:35 Hull-Doncaster;

Tues. 22: 1D62 03:55 Doncaster-Hull/0L01 Hull-York/YK 'oe'/0B02 York-Finsbury Park/FP 'oe'/1D08 19:40 King's Cross-Hull/0D01 23:35 Hull-Doncaster; Wed. 23: On DONCASTER WORKS "Unclassified repair" (No.2 engine, 455, replaced by 449) Until Mon. 28: Off DONCASTER WORKS; Tues. 29: 0B02 Doncaster-Finsbury Park/FP/1D08 19:40 King's Cross-Hull/0D01 23:35 Hull-Doncaster; Wed. 30: 1D62 03:55 Doncaster-Hull/1A13 09:36 Hull-King's Cross/FP/1L45 17:40 King's Cross-York/YK

OCTOBER

Thurs. 1: 1A08 08:07 York-King's Cross/FP/1S66 20:15 King's Cross-Edinburgh; Fri. 2: 1V93 09:50 Edinburgh-Plymouth to York/1S27 07:36 Plymouth-Edinburgh from York/1E39 22:25 Edinburgh-King's Cross; Sat. 3: FP/1L42 12:05 King's Cross-York/1A26 15:50 York-King's Cross/1S72 22:30 King's Cross-Edinburgh; Sun. 4: HA/1E42 23:15 Edinburgh-King's Cross; Mon. 5: 1L41 09:40 King's Cross-York/YK; Tues. 6:YK/1A26 15:50 York-King's Cross/1S77 23:55 King's Cross-Edinburgh; Wed. 7: HA/1A38 14:55 Edinburgh-Aberdeen/1G20 18:23 Aberdeen-Edinburgh/1E43 20:35 Aberdeen-King's Cross from Edinburgh; Thurs. 8: FP/1L44 16:03 King's Cross-York/1A34 20:19 York-King's Cross; Fri. 9: 1N00 01:00 King's Cross-Newcastle/1S08 07:05 Newcastle-Edinburgh/HA/ 1E35 20:25 Edinburgh-King's Cross; Sat. 10: FP/1L43 14:03 King's Cross-York/1A31 18:14 York-King's Cross/FP; Sun. 11: 1L41 10:05 King's Cross-York/1A10 15:50 York-King's Cross/1S70 22:15 King's Cross-Aberdeen to Edinburgh; Mon. 12: 1V93 09:50 Edinburgh-Plymouth to York/1S27 07:36 Plymouth-Edinburgh from York/1E40 19:25 Aberdeen-King's Cross from Edinburgh; Tues. 13: FP/1S66 20:15 King's Cross-Edinburgh to York; Wed. 14: YK/1A26 15:50 York-King's Cross/1S70 22:15 King's Cross-Aberdeen to Edinburgh; Thurs. 15: 1V93 09:50 Edinburgh-Plymouth to York/1S27 07:36 Plymouth-Edinburgh from York/1E42 23:15 Edinburgh-

King's Cross; Fri. 16: FP; Sat. 17: 1N12 00:05 King's Cross-Newcastle/GD/0L01 Gateshead-York/YK; Sun. 18: YK; Mon. 19: 1A08 08:07 York-King's Cross/FP/1L44 16:03 King's Cross-York/1A34 20:19 York-King's Cross; Tues. 20: 1S12 05:50 King's Cross-Aberdeen to Newcastle/GD/0L01 Gateshead-York/YK/1A26 15:50 York-King's Cross/1S77 23:55 King's Cross-Edinburgh; Wed. 21: 1V93 09:50 Edinburgh-Plymouth to York/1S27 07:36 Plymouth-Edinburgh from York/1E35 20:25 Edinburgh-King's Cross; Thurs. 22: FP 'B' exam Until Fri. 30: FP 'B' exam/1N14 14:03 King's Cross-Newcastle to York (55 011 forward)/1A31 18:14 York-King's Cross/1S77 23:55 King's Cross-Edinburgh to York; Sat. 31: 1A08 08:07 York-King's Cross/FP/1L44 16:03 King's Cross-York/YK

NOVEMBER
Sun. 1: YK/1A19 19:13 York-King's Cross/FP; Mon. 2: 1S12 05:50 King's Cross-Aberdeen to Edinburgh/HA/1E48 21:20 Aberdeen-King's Cross from Edinburgh; Tues. 3: FP/1L44 16:03 King's Cross-York/1A34 20:19 York-King's Cross; Wed. 4: 1S12 05:50 King's Cross-Aberdeen/1E26 16:30 Aberdeen-York; Thurs. 5: YK; Fri. 6: YK/1S60 20:00 King's Cross-Aberdeen from York to Newcastle; Sat. 7: GD; Sun. 8: GD; Mon. 9: GD; Tues. 10: 1S14 08:10 Newcastle-Edinburgh (failed at Cramlington - Loss of power (No.1 traction motor defective, No.2 traction motor water contamination) - assisted forward by 37 082)/HA; Wed. 11: HA/0E00 Haymarket-Gateshead (towed by 47 710)/GD/0L01 Gateshead-York (towed)/YK Until Sun. 22nd YK - WITHDRAWN

D9015/9015/55015
Tulyar

JUNE 1981

Mon. 1:FP/1S79 23:20 King's Cross-Aberdeen to Edinburgh; Tues. 2: HA; Wed. 3: HA/0E00 Haymarket-Gateshead/GD/0L01 Gateshead-York/YK Until Sat. 6: YK/0B02 York-Finsbury Park/FP/1S72 22:30 King's Cross-Edinburgh; Sun. 7: HA/1E39 22:25 Edinburgh-King's Cross; Mon. 8: 1L42 12:05 King's Cross-York/YK; Tues. 9: YK; Wed. 10: 1M62 08:50 York-Liverpool/1E99 13:05 Liverpool-York/1M76 15:50 York-Liverpool/1E89 20:40 Liverpool-York; Thurs. 11: 1A08 08:07 York-King's Cross/FP/1L45 17:40 King's Cross-York/YK; Fri. 12: YK; Sat. 13: YK/1A37 08:47 Bridlington-King's Cross from York (55 014 off)/FP/1S60 20:00 King's Cross-Aberdeen to York (55 004 forward); Sun. 14: 1M71 07:45 York-Liverpool/1E99 12:40 Liverpool-Newcastle/GD/1A45 22:55 Newcastle-King's Cross; Mon. 15: 1L42 12:05 King's Cross-York/1A26 15:50 York-King's Cross/FP; Tues. 16: 1N12 00:05 King's Cross-Newcastle/GD/0L01 Gateshead-York/YK; Wed. 17: YK/0B02 York-Finsbury Park/FP/1L45 17:40 King's Cross-York/YK Thurs. 18: 1A37 10:47 York-King's Cross/FP/1D08 19:40 King's Cross-Hull/0D01 23:35 Hull-Doncaster; Fri. 19: 0B05 Doncaster-Peterborough/PB/0D01 Peterborough-Doncaster/DR/0L01 Doncaster-York/YK; Sat. 20: 0N60 York-Filey/1N60 08:54 Filey-Newcastle to Scarborough/1A37 08:47 Bridlington-King's Cross from Scarborough/FP; Sun. 21: 1N12 00:05 King's Cross-Newcastle/GD/1N03 21:30 Newcastle-Darlington/ 0L01 Darlington-York; Mon. 22: YK 'oe'; Tues. 23: 1A08 08:07 York-King's Cross/FP; Wed. 24: 1L00 01:10 King's Cross-Leeds/5N02 05:35 Neville Hill-Heaton/HT/0L01 Heaton-York/YK ; Thurs. 25: YK/1E32 07:44 Cardiff-Newcastle from York/GD/1A40 21:00 Newcastle-King's Cross; Fri. 26: FP/1B04 16:06 King's Cross-Peterborough/5B04 Peterborough-Ferme Park/1S60 20:00 King's Cross-Aberdeen to Edinburgh; Sat. 27: 5E10 06:40 Craigentinny-Dundee/1E10 09:10 Dundee-King's Cross/FP/1S72 22:30 King's Cross-Edinburgh Sun. 28th HA/1E42 23:15 Edinburgh-King's Cross; Mon. 29: FP; Tues. 30: 1D01 08:30

116   THE LAST MONTHS OF THE DELTICS — 1981 — D9015

King's Cross-Cleethorpes/1A21 13:20 Cleethorpes-King's Cross/ 1S66 20:15 King's Cross-Edinburgh

JULY

Wed. 1: 5E10 06:40 Craigentinny-Dundee/1E10 09:10 Dundee-King's Cross/1S66 20:15 King's Cross-Edinburgh; Thurs. 2: 1V93 09:50 Edinburgh-Plymouth to York/YK 'D' exam; Fri. 3: YK 'D' exam; Sat. 4: 0N60 York-Filey/1N60 08:54 Filey-Newcastle to Scarborough/1A37 08:47 Bridlington-King's Cross from Scarborough/FP/1S72 22:30 King's Cross-Edinburgh; Sun. 5: HA/1E35 20:25 Edinburgh-King's Cross; Mon. 6: FP 'eo'; Tues. 7: FP 'eo'/1L44 16:03 King's Cross-York/1A34 20:19 York-King's Cross; Wed. 8: 1S12 05:50 King's Cross-Aberdeen/1E26 16:30 Aberdeen-Leeds/1E24 22:50 Shrewsbury-York from Leeds; Thurs. 9: YK; Fri. 10: 1A37 10:47 York-King's Cross/1L45 17:40 King's Cross-York/YK 'B' exam; Sat. 11: YK 'B' exam/0N60 York-Filey/1N60 08:54 Filey-Newcastle to Scarborough/ 1S97 Scarborough-Edinburgh/1E26 16:30 Aberdeen-Leeds from Edinburgh; Sun. 12: 5E26 Leeds-York/YK/1A06 11:50 York-King's Cross/FP/1S70 22:15 King's Cross-Aberdeen to Edinburgh; Mon. 13: 1M04 07:18 Edinburgh-Carlisle/1S15 15:53 Carlisle-Edinburgh/1E48 21:20 Aberdeen-King's Cross from Edinburgh; Tues. 14: FP/1S70 22:15 King's Cross-Aberdeen to Edinburgh; Wed. 15: 5E10 06:40 Craigentinny-Dundee/1E10 09:10 Dundee-King's Cross/FP/1S70 22:15 King's Cross-Aberdeen to Edinburgh; Thurs. 16: 1V93 09:50 Edinburgh-Plymouth to York/1S27 07:36 Plymouth-Edinburgh from York/1E48 21:20 Aberdeen-King's Cross from Edinburgh; Fri. 17: FP/1L44 16:03 King's Cross-York/1A34 20:19 York-King's Cross; Sat. 18: 1S76 09:40 King's Cross-Edinburgh/HA/1E26 16:30 Aberdeen-Leeds from Edinburgh; Sun. 19: 5E26 Leeds-York/YK 'B' exam; Mon. 20: YK 'B' exam; Tues. 21: YK 'B' exam/1A40

21:00 Newcastle-King's Cross from York; Wed. 22: 5B26 05:24 King's Cross-Peterborough/1B26 07:23 Peterborough-King's Cross/1L43 14:03 King's Cross-York/1A31 18:14 York-King's Cross; Thurs. 23: 1N00 01:00 King's Cross-Newcastle/1S08 07:05 Newcastle-Edinburgh/HA/ 1A38 14:55 Edinburgh-Aberdeen/1G20 18:23 Aberdeen-Edinburgh/1E48 21:20 Aberdeen-King's Cross from Edinburgh; Fri. 24: FP/1D08 19:40 King's Cross-Hull/1D26 23:40 Hull-Doncaster; Sat. 25: 1D62 03:55 Doncaster-Hull/1A13 09:36 Hull-King's Cross/FP/1D08 19:40 King's Cross-Hull/0D01 23:35 Hull-Doncaster; Sun. 26: DR; Mon. 27: 1D62 03:55 Doncaster-Hull/1A13 09:36 Hull-King's Cross/FP/1L45 17:40 King's Cross-York/YK/1S70 22:15 King's Cross-Aberdeen from York to Edinburgh; Tues. 28: 5E10 06:40 Craigentinny-Dundee/1E10 09:10 Dundee-King's Cross/FP; Wed. 29: 1N12 00:05 King's Cross-Newcastle/1S14 08:10 Newcastle-Edinburgh/HA/ 1E40 19:25 Aberdeen-King's Cross from Edinburgh; Thurs. 30: FP/1L43 14:03 King's Cross-York/1A31 18:14 York-King's Cross; Fri. 31: 1N00 01:00 King's Cross-Newcastle/1S08 07:05 Newcastle-Edinburgh/HA/ 1E29 17:18 Edinburgh-Newcastle/1A45 22:55 Newcastle-King's Cross

AUGUST

Sat. 1: FP/1L22 23:00 King's Cross-Bradford to Leeds; Sun. 2: 0L01 Leeds-York/YK; Mon. 3: YK/1A31 18:14 York-King's Cross; Tues. 4: 1N00 01:00 King's Cross-Newcastle/1S08 07:05 Newcastle-Edinburgh/HA/ 1E35 20:25 Edinburgh-King's Cross; Wed. 5:1S76 09:40 King's Cross-Edinburgh/HA/1E39 22:25 Edinburgh-King's Cross; Thurs. 6: FP 'B' exam; Fri. 7: FP 'B' exam/1S79 23:20 King's Cross-Aberdeen to Edinburgh; Sat. 8: 1E10 09:10 Dundee-King's Cross from Edinburgh/1D08 19:40 King's Cross-Hull/0D01 23:35 Hull-Doncaster; Sun. 9: DR; Mon. 10: 1D62 03:55 Doncaster-Hull/1A13 09:36 Hull-King's Cross/FP/1L45

17:40 King's Cross-York/YK; Tues. 11: 1A08 08:07 York-King's Cross/FP/1L44 16:03 King's Cross-York to Doncaster (Train terminated)/1A34 20:19 York-King's Cross from Doncaster; Wed. 12: 1S12 05:50 King's Cross-Aberdeen/1E26 16:30 Aberdeen-Leeds/1E24 22:50 Shrewsbury-York from Leeds; Thurs. 13: YK/0B02 York-Finsbury Park/FP/1L45 17:40 King's Cross-York/YK; Fri. 14: YK/1A34 20:19 York-King's Cross; Sat. 15: 1S12 05:50 King's Cross-Aberdeen to Edinburgh/HA/1E35 20:45 Edinburgh-King's Cross to Newcastle/1E48 21:20 Aberdeen-King's Cross from Newcastle; Sun. 16: FP/1S70 22:15 King's Cross-Aberdeen to Edinburgh; Mon. 17: 5E10 06:40 Craigentinny-Dundee/1E10 09:10 Dundee-King's Cross/1S66 20:15 King's Cross-Edinburgh; Tues. 18: 1V93 09:50 Edinburgh-Plymouth to York/1S27 07:36 Plymouth-Edinburgh from York/1E39 22:25 Edinburgh-King's Cross Wed. 19: FP/1L43 14:03 King's Cross-York/YK; Thurs. 20: YK; Fri. 21: 1A37 10:47 York-King's Cross/FP/1L22 23:00 King's Cross-Bradford to Leeds; Sat. 22: FP Until Tues. 25: FP/1D08 19:40 King's Cross-Hull to Peterborough/PB/0D01 Peterborough-Doncaster; Wed. 26: On DONCASTER WORKS "Unclassified repair" (No.1 engine, 447, replaced by 538) Until Mon. 31: Off DONCASTER WORKS/DR

SEPTEMBER

Tues. 1: DR/0B02 Doncaster-Finsbury Park/FP/1L42 12:05 King's Cross-York/1A26 15:50 York-King's Cross/FP; Wed. 2: 1N12 00:05 King's Cross-Newcastle/GD/0L01 Gateshead-York/YK 'B' exam; Thurs. 3: YK 'B' exam; Fri. 4: 1A37 10:47 York-King's Cross/FP/1D08 19:40 King's Cross-Hull/1D26 23:40 Hull-Doncaster; Sat. 5: 1D62 03:55 Doncaster-Hull/1A13 09:36 Hull-King's Cross/FP/1S60 20:00 King's Cross-Aberdeen to Edinburgh; Sun. 6: HA/1E35 20:25 Edinburgh-King's Cross; Mon. 7: 1L42 12:05 King's Cross-York/1A26 15:50 York-King's Cross/FP; Tues. 8: 1N12 00:05

King's Cross-Newcastle/5G03 Heaton-York/1S27 07:36 Plymouth-Edinburgh from York/1E35 20:25 Edinburgh-King's Cross; Wed. 9: 1S76 09:40 King's Cross-Edinburgh/HA/1E39 22:25 Edinburgh-King's Cross to Newcastle; Thurs. 10: GD/0L01 Gateshead-York/YK/0B02 York-Finsbury Park/FP/1D08 19:40 King's Cross-Hull/0D01 23:35 Hull-Doncaster; Fri. 11: 1D62 03:55 Doncaster-Hull/1A13 09:36 Hull-King's Cross/FP/1L45 17:40 King's Cross-York/YK; Sat. 12: 1A08 08:07 York-King's Cross/1L43 14:03 King's Cross-York/1A31 18:14 York-King's Cross/FP Until Tues. 15: FP/1L42 12:05 King's Cross-York/1A26 15:50 York-King's Cross/FP; Wed. 16: FP/1S70 22:15 King's Cross-Aberdeen to Edinburgh; Thurs. 17: 5E10 06:40 Craigentinny-Dundee/1E10 09:10 Dundee-King's Cross/FP/1S77 23:55 King's Cross-Edinburgh; Fri. 18: 1E10 09:10 Dundee-King's Cross from Edinburgh/1S66 20:15 King's Cross-Edinburgh; Sat. 19: 5E10 06:40 Craigentinny-Dundee/1E10 09:10 Dundee-King's Cross/1S60 20:00 King's Cross-Aberdeen to Edinburgh; Sun. 20: 1V93 11:25 Edinburgh-Plymouth to York/YK 'C' exam Until Wed. 23: YK 'C' exam/0D01 York-Doncaster/DR 'Tyre Turning' Until Tues. 29: DR/0B02 Doncaster-Finsbury Park/FP/0C01 Finsbury Park-Stratford/SF Wed. 30th SF 'Tyre Turning'

OCTOBER

Thurs. 1: SF/0B02 Stratford-Finsbury Park/FP/1S60 20:00 King's Cross-Aberdeen to Edinburgh; Fri. 2: 1M04 07:18 Edinburgh-Carlisle/1S15 15:53 Carlisle-Edinburgh to Grantshouse (flooding)/1S15 Grantshouse-Newcastle/GD; Sat. 3: 1S08 07:05 Newcastle-Edinburgh/HA/1E43 20:05 Aberdeen-King's Cross from Edinburgh to Newcastle; Sun. 4: GD 'B' exam; Mon. 5: GD 'B' exam/1A40 21:00 Newcastle-King's Cross; Tues. 6: 5B26 05:24 King's Cross-Peterborough/1B26 07:23 Peterborough-King's Cross/FP Until Tues. 13: FP/1L44 16:03 King's Cross-York/1A34 20:19 York-King's Cross; Wed. 14: FP;

118 THE LAST MONTHS OF THE DELTICS — 1981 — D9015/6

Thurs. 15: FP; Fri. 16: FP; Sat. 17: 1Z47 09:15 Finsbury Park-Bournemouth "Wessex Deltic" rail tour/1Z47 Bournemouth-Finsbury Park "Wessex Deltic" rail tour/FP Sun. 18: FP/1L42 14:05 King's Cross-York/YK Until Wed. 21: YK; Thurs. 22: 1M62 08:50 York-Liverpool/1E99 13:05 Liverpool-York/1M76 15:50 York-Liverpool/1E89 20:40 Liverpool-York; Fri. 23: YK/0L50 York-Neville Hill/NL; Sat. 24: 5F50 Neville Hill-York/1F50 09:30 York-Aberdeen "Deltic Salute" rail tour/1F50 Aberdeen-York "Deltic Salute" rail tour/5F50 York-Neville Hill; Sun. 25: 0L01 Neville Hill-York/YK Until Sat. 31: YK

NOVEMBER

Sun. 1: YK; Mon. 2: YK; Tues. 3: YK; Wed. 4: 1A08 08:07 York-King's Cross/1L44 16:03 King's Cross-York/YK; Thurs. 5: YK; Fri. 6: YK/0B02 York-Finsbury Park/FP; Sat. 7: 1F51 King's Cross-Edinburgh "Deltic Queen of Scots" rail tour/HA/1E39 22:15 Edinburgh-King's Cross; Sun. 8: FP Until Thurs. 12: FP/0L01 Finsbury Park-York (towing 55 002)/YK Until Tues. 17: YK; Wed. 18: 1A08 08:07 York-King's Cross/FP; Thurs. 19: FP/1S66 20:15 King's Cross-Edinburgh; Fri. 20: 1M04 07:18 Edinburgh-Carlisle/1S15 15:53 Carlisle-Edinburgh/1E39 22:25 Edinburgh-King's Cross; Sat. 21: FP Until Mon. 30: FP/1L43 14:03 King's Cross-York/YK

DECEMBER

Tues. 1: 1A08 08:07 York-King's Cross/FP/1D08 19:40 King's Cross-Hull/5L04 23:30 Hull-York; Wed. 2: 1M62 08:50 York-Liverpool/1E99 13:05 Liverpool-York/1M76 15:50 York-Liverpool/1E89 20:40 Liverpool-York; Thurs. 3: YK; Fri. 4: YK/0B02 York-Finsbury Park/FP; Sat. 5: 1B50 02:00 King's Cross-Peterborough/PB/1Z35 Peterborough-Carlisle "Hadrian Flyer" rail tour/1Z35 Carlisle-Peterborough "Hadrian Flyer" rail tour; Sun. 6: PB/0B02 Peterborough-Finsbury Park/FP/1S77 23:55 King's Cross-Edinburgh;

Mon. 7: HA/1E29 17:18 Edinburgh-Newcastle/1A45 22:55 Newcastle-King's Cross; Tues. 8: FP/1L43 14:03 King's Cross-York/1A31 18:14 York-King's Cross/1S77 23:55 King's Cross-Edinburgh; Wed. 9: HA/1E29 17:18 Edinburgh-Newcastle/1A45 22:55 Newcastle-King's Cross; Thurs. 10: FP/1S60 20:00 King's Cross-Aberdeen to Edinburgh/1S70 22:15 King's Cross-Aberdeen from Edinburgh to Leuchars (failed - No.2 engine on fire); Fri. 11: 0G00 Leuchars-Haymarket/HA Until Tues. 15: HA/0E00 Haymarket-York (towed by 47 522)/YK Until Tues. 22: YK; Wed. 23: 1M62 08:50 York-Liverpool/1E99 13:05 Liverpool-York/YK Until Sun. 27: YK/1M70 15:40 York-Liverpool/1E50 21:15 Liverpool-York Mon. 28: YK Until Thurs. 31: YK/1A26 15:50 York-King's Cross/FP

JANUARY 1982

Fri. 1: FP; Sat. 2: 1F50 08:30 King's Cross-Edinburgh "Deltic Scotsman Farewell" rail tour/HA/ 0F50 Haymarket-Gateshead/GD/0F50 Gateshead-York/YK - WITHDRAWN

D9016/9016/55016 Gordon Highlander

JUNE 1981

Mon. 1: 1A13 09:36 Hull-King's Cross/FP/1S66 20:15 King's Cross-Edinburgh; Tues. 2: 1M04 07:18 Edinburgh-Carlisle/1S15 15:53 Carlisle-Edinburgh/1E.. Edinburgh-King's Cross; Wed. 3: 1L42 12:05 King's Cross-York/YK/1A31 18:14 York-King's Cross; Thurs. 4: 1N00 01:00 King's Cross-Newcastle/1S08 07:05 Newcastle-Edinburgh/HA/ Edinburgh-Carstairs/Carstairs-Edinburgh/1E39 22:25 Edinburgh-King's Cross; Fri. 5: FP/1L44 16:03 King's Cross-York/YK 'B' exam Until Mon. 8: YK 'B' exam; Tues. 9: 1A37 10:47 York-King's Cross/1B03 17:12 King's Cross-Peterborough/0B02 Peterborough-Finsbury

Park/FP/1S70 22:15 King's Cross-Aberdeen to Edinburgh; Wed. 10: 1M04 07:18 Edinburgh-Carlisle/1S15 15:53 Carlisle-Edinburgh/HA; Thurs. 11: 5E10 06:40 Craigentinny-Dundee/1E10 09:10 Dundee-King's Cross/FP/1S70 22:15 King's Cross-Aberdeen to Edinburgh; Fri. 12: 1M04 07:18 Edinburgh-Carlisle/1S15 15:53 Carlisle-Edinburgh/1E43 20:35 Aberdeen-King's Cross from Edinburgh; Sat. 13: 1L11 11:25 King's Cross-Scarborough/1A31 17:05 Scarborough-King's Cross; Sun. 14: 1N12 00:05 King's Cross-Newcastle/GD/1A40 21:28 Newcastle-King's Cross; Mon. 15: 5B26 05:24 King's Cross-Peterborough/1B26 07:23 Peterborough-King's Cross/FP/1L44 16:03 King's Cross-York/1A34 20:19 York-King's Cross; Tues. 16: 1L01 04:05 King's Cross-Leeds/0L01 Leeds York/YK 'D' exam; Wed. 17: YK 'D' exam; Thurs. 18: YK 'D' exam/0D01 York-Doncaster/DR 'Tyre Turning'; Fri. 19: DR 'Tyre Turning'; Sat. 20: DR/0B02 Doncaster-Finsbury Park/FP/1L43 14:03 King's Cross-York/YK; Sun. 21: YK/1A19 19:13 York-King's Cross; Mon. 22: 1S12 05:50 King's Cross-Aberdeen to Edinburgh/HA/1A51 17:02 Edinburgh-Aberdeen/AB/1E48 21:20 Aberdeen-King's Cross; Tues. 23: FP/1L45 17:40 King's X-York/YK; Wed. 24: 1A37 10:47 York-King's X/1B21 17:17 King's X-Peter'boro/0B02 Peterborough-Finsbury Park/FP/1S72 22:30 King's X-Edinburgh; Thurs. 25: 1V93 09:50 Edinburgh-Plymouth to York/1S27 07:36 Plymouth-Edinburgh from York/1E39 22:25 Edinburgh-King's X; Fri. 26: FP/1S66 20:15 King's X-Edinburgh; Sat. 27: 1E70 07:44 Edinburgh-King's X/FP/1D08 19:40 King's X-Hull/0D01 23:35 Hull-Doncaster; Sun. 28: DR; Mon. 29: 1D62 03:55 Doncaster-Hull/1A13 09:36 Hull-King's Cross/FP; Tues. 30: FP

JULY

Wed. 1: FP; Thurs. 2: FP/1S66 20:15 King's Cross-Edinburgh to York (55 010 forward); Fri. 3: YK/0B02 York-Finsbury Park/FP/1S72 22:30 King's Cross-Edinburgh; Sat. 4: 1V93 09:50 Edinburgh-Plymouth to York/1S27 07:36 Plymouth-Edinburgh from York/1E40 19:15 Aberdeen-King's Cross from Edinburgh; Sun. 5: FP; Mon. 6: FP/1L44 16:03 King's Cross-York/1A34 20:19 York-King's Cross; Tues. 7: FP/1L42 12:05 King's Cross-York/1A26 15:50 York-King's Cross/FP; Wed. 8: 1N00 01:00 King's Cross-Newcastle/1S08 07:05 Newcastle-Edinburgh/HA/ 1E35 20:25 Edinburgh-King's Cross; Thurs. 9: FP; Fri. 10: 1S76 09:40 King's Cross-Edinburgh/HA/1E35 20:25 Edinburgh-King's Cross; Sat. 11: FP/1L43 14:03 King's Cross-York/1A31 18:14 York-King's Cross/FP; Sun. 12: 1N03 11:45 King's Cross-Newcastle (vice HST)/1A15 16:45 Newcastle-King's Cross (vice HST)/FP; Mon. 13: FP/1L42 12:05 King's Cross-York/1A26 15:50 York-King's Cross/FP; Tues. 14: 1N12 00:05 King's Cross Newcastle/GD/0L01 Gateshead-York/YK/0B02 York-Finsbury Park; Wed. 15: 5B26 05:24 King's Cross-Peterborough/PB/0L01 Peterborough-York/YK/ 1A34 20:19 York-King's Cross; Thurs. 16: FP/1L44 16:03 King's Cross-York/1A34 20:19 York-King's Cross; Fri. 17: 1S12 05:50 King's Cross-Aberdeen to Edinburgh/HA/1E39 22:25 Edinburgh-King's Cross; Sat. 18: FP/1D08 19:40 King's Cross-Hull/0D01 23:35 Hull-Doncaster; Sun. 19: DR; Mon. 20: 1D62 03:55 Doncaster-Hull/1A13 09:36 Hull-King's Cross/FP/1L45 17:40 King's Cross-York/YK; Tues. 21: 1A08 08:07 York-King's Cross/1L43 14:03 King's Cross-York/1A31 18:14 York-King's Cross/FP; Wed. 22: 1S76 09:40 King's Cross-Edinburgh/HA/1E42 23:15 Edinburgh-King's Cross; Thurs. 23: 1L42 12:05 King's Cross-York/1A26 15:50 York-King's Cross/FP; Fri. 24: 1S12 05:50 King's Cross-Aberdeen/1E26 16:30 Aberdeen-Leeds/1E24 22:50 Shrewsbury-York from Leeds; Sat. 25: YK/1S97 12:00 Scarborough-Glasgow Q.St. from York/0G99 Glasgow Q.St.-Haymarket/HA/1E40 19:15 Aberdeen-King's Cross from Edinburgh; Sun. 26: FP/1L42 14:05 King's Cross-York/1A19 19:13 York-King's

Cross/FP; Mon. 27: 1S12 05:50 King's Cross-Aberdeen to Edinburgh/HA/1E35 20:25 Edinburgh-King's Cross; Tues. 28: FP/1L45 17:40 King's Cross-York/YK; Wed. 29: 1A08 08:07 York-King's Cross/FP/1L44 16:03 King's Cross-York/1A34 20:19 York-King's Cross; Thurs. 30: 1S12 05:50 King's Cross-Aberdeen/1E26 16:30 Aberdeen-Leeds Fri. 31: 0L01 Leeds-York/YK 'B' exam

AUGUST

Sat. 1: 1A08 08:07 York-King's Cross/1L43 14:03 King's Cross-York/1A31 18:14 York-King's Cross/FP; Sun. 2: 1L41 10:05 King's Cross-York/1A10 15:50 York-King's Cross/FP; Mon. 3: 1N00 01:00 King's Cross-Newcastle/1S08 07:05 Newcastle-Edinburgh/HA/ 1S12 05:50 King's Cross-Aberdeen from Edinburgh (55 017 off)/1E26 16:30 Aberdeen-Leeds to Edinburgh/1E40 19:25 Aberdeen-King's Cross from Edinburgh; Tues. 4: FP/1N04 13:35 King's Cross-Newcastle (vice HST)/GD/1A40 21:00 Newcastle-King's Cross; Wed. 5: 5B26 05:24 King's Cross-Peterborough/1B26 07:23 Peterborough-King's Cross/FP/1L43 14:03 King's Cross-York/1A31 18:14 York-King's Cross/FP; Thurs. 6: 1N00 01:00 King's Cross-Newcastle/1S08 07:05 Newcastle-Edinburgh/HA/ 1E39 22:25 Edinburgh-King's Cross; Fri. 7: 1L42 12:05 King's Cross-York/1A26 15:50 York-King's Cross/1S70 22:15 King's Cross-Aberdeen to Edinburgh Sat. 8: 1V93 09:50 Edinburgh-Plymouth to York/YK/1A31 18:14 York-King's Cross/ FP; Sun. 9: 1L41 10:05 King's Cross-York/YK; Mon. 10: 1A37 10:47 York-King's Cross/FP/1D08 19:40 King's Cross-Hull/0D01 23:35 Hull-Doncaster; Tues. 11: 1D62 03:55 Doncaster-Hull/1A13 09:36 Hull-King's Cross/FP/1L45 17:40 King's Cross-York (terminated at Doncaster)/5L45 Doncaster York/YK; Wed. 12: YK/0B05 York-Peterborough/PB; Thurs. 13: PB/0B02 Peterborough-Finsbury Park/FP 'B' exam Until Wed. 19: FP 'B' exam/1S66 20:15 King's Cross-Edinburgh; Thurs. 20: 5E10 06:40 Craigentinny-Dundee/1E10 09:10 Dundee-King's Cross to Newcastle/GD/1A40 21:00 Newcastle-King's Cross; Fri. 21: 5B26 05:24 King's Cross-Peterborough/1B26 07:23 Peterborough-King's Cross/FP; Sat. 22: 1N12 00:05 King's Cross-Newcastle to York/YK Until Wed. 26: YK/0D01 York-Doncaster/On DONCASTER WORKS "Unclassified repair" (No.1 engine, 424, replaced by 406. Collision damage repairs.) Until Mon. 31: DONCASTER WORKS

SEPTEMBER

Tues. 1: DONCASTER WORKS Until Mon. 7: Off DONCASTER WORKS/DR/0B02 Doncaster-Finsbury Park/FP; Tues. 8: 1S12 05:50 King's Cross-Aberdeen to Edinburgh/HA/1S85/5E85/HA/1E42 23:15 Edinburgh-King's Cross; Wed. 9:1L42 12:05 King's Cross-York/1A26 15:50 York-King's Cross/1S70 22:15 King's Cross-Aberdeen to Edinburgh; Thurs. 10: 1M04 07:18 Edinburgh-Carlisle/1S15 15:53 Carlisle-Edinburgh/1E40 19:25 Aberdeen-King's Cross from Edinburgh to Newcastle; Fri. 11: GD/0L01 Gateshead-York/YK/1A37 10:47 York-King's Cross to Peterborough/PB/0L01Peterborough-York/YK; Sat. 12: YK/0A37 York-Scarborough/1A37 08:47 Bridlington-King's Cross from Scarborough/FP/1D08 19:40 King's Cross-Hull/0D01 23:35 Hull-Doncaster; Sun. 13: DR; Mon. 14: 1D62 03:55 Doncaster-Hull/1A13 09:36 Hull-King's Cross/1L44 16:03 King's Cross-York/1A34 20:19 York-King's Cross; Tues. 15: FP/1S66 20:15 King's Cross-Edinburgh; Wed. 16: 5E10 06:40 Craigentinny-Dundee/1E10 09:10 Dundee-King's Cross/1D08 19:40 King's Cross-Hull/0D01 23:35 Hull-Doncaster; Thurs. 17: DR/0L01 Doncaster-York/YK 'C' exam Fri. 18: 1A37 10:47 York-King's Cross/FP/1S72 22:30 King's Cross-Edinburgh; Sat. 19: HA/1E39 22:15 Edinburgh-King's Cross; Sun. 20: FP/1L43 16:05 King's Cross-York/YK; Mon. 21: YK/1S27 07:36 Plymouth-Edinburgh from York/1E35 20:25 Edinburgh-King's Cross; Tues. 22: 1L41 09:40 King's

D9016 — THE LAST MONTHS OF THE DELTICS — 1981

Cross-York/1A22 14:15 York-King's Cross/FP/1S79 23:20 King's Cross-Aberdeen to Edinburgh; Wed. 23: HA/1E40 19:25 Aberdeen-King's Cross from Edinburgh; Thurs. 24: FP/1L43 14:03 King's Cross-York/1A31 18:14 York-King's Cross/FP; Fri. 25: 1N00 01:00 King's Cross-Newcastle/1S08 07:05 Newcastle-Edinburgh/HA/ 1A38 14:55 Edinburgh-Aberdeen/1G20 18:23 Aberdeen-Edinburgh/1E42 23:15 Edinburgh-King's Cross; Sat. 26: 1L42 12:05 King's Cross-York/1A26 15:50 York-King's Cross/1S72 22:30 King's Cross-Edinburgh; Sun. 27: HA/1M73 17:00 Edinburgh-Liverpool to Newcastle/GD/1A45 22:55 Newcastle-King's Cross; Mon. 28: 1L42 12:05 King's Cross-York/1A26 15:50 York-King's Cross/FP; Tues. 29: 1N00 01:00 King's Cross-Newcastle/1S08 07:05 Newcastle-Edinburgh/HA/ 1E29 17:18 Edinburgh-Newcastle/1A45 22:55 Newcastle-King's Cross; Wed. 30: 1L41 09:40 King's Cross-York/1A22 14:15 York-King's Cross/FP/1S70 22:15 King's Cross-Aberdeen to Edinburgh

OCTOBER

Thurs. 1: 1V93 09:50 Edinburgh-Plymouth to York/1S27 07:36 Plymouth-Edinburgh from York/1E42 23:15 Edinburgh-King's Cross; Fri. 2: FP/1N14 14:03 King's Cross-Newcastle/GD/1A45 22:55 Newcastle-King's Cross; Sat. 3: FP/1L45 18:05 King's Cross-York/YK; Sun. 4: YK 'B' exam; Mon. 5: YK 'B' exam/1A34 20:19 York-King's Cross; Tues. 6: 1S12 05:50 King's Cross-Aberdeen to Newcastle/0L01 Newcastle-York/YK/ 1S27 07:36 Plymouth-Edinburgh from York/1E42 23:15 Edinburgh-King's Cross; Wed. 7: FP/1S79 23:20 King's Cross-Aberdeen to Edinburgh; Thurs. 8: 1C86 09:07 Edinburgh-Carstairs/1G44 11:23 Carstairs-Edinburgh/1A38 14:55 Edinburgh-Aberdeen/1G20 18:23 Aberdeen-Edinburgh/1E42 23:15 Edinburgh-King's Cross; Fri. 9: FP/1S70 22:15 King's Cross-Aberdeen to Edinburgh; Sat. 10: 1V93 09:50 Edinburgh-Plymouth to York/1S27 07:36

Plymouth-Edinburgh from York/1E39 22:15 Edinburgh-King's Cross; Sun. 11: FP/1L42 14:05 King's Cross-York/1A19 19:13 York-King's Cross/FP (No.2 engine radiator fan cardan shaft adrift and camshaft damaged) Until Mon. 19: FP 'oe'; Tues. 20: 1N00 01:00 King's Cross-Newcastle/1S08 07:05 Newcastle-Edinburgh/HA 'oe'/ 1E35 20:25 Edinburgh-King's Cross to Newcastle/GD 'oe'; Wed. 21: 1S14 08:10 Newcastle-Edinburgh/HA 'oe'/1E29 17:18 Edinburgh-Newcastle/ 1A45 22:55 Newcastle-King's Cross; Thurs. 22: 5B26 05:24 King's Cross-Peterborough/1B26 07:23 Peterborough-King's Cross/FP 'oe'; Fri. 23:1N00 01:00 King's Cross-Newcastle/1S08 07:05 Newcastle-Edinburgh/HA 'oe'; Sat. 24: HA 'oe'/1E29 17:18 Edinburgh-Newcastle/GD 'oe'; Sun. 25: GD 'oe'/1A40 21:28 Newcastle-King's Cross; Mon. 26: 5B26 05:24 King's Cross-Peterborough/1B26 07:23 Peterborough-King's Cross/FP 'oe'/1S77 23:55 King's Cross-Edinburgh; Tues. 27: HA 'oe'/1E39 22:25 Edinburgh-King's Cross; Wed. 28: FP 'oe'; Thurs. 29: 1N00 01:00 King's Cross-Newcastle/1S08 07:05 Newcastle-Edinburgh/HA 'oe'/1C92 13:25 Edinburgh-Carstairs/1G83 17:15 Carstairs-Edinburgh/1E39 22:25 Edinburgh-King's Cross; Fri. 30: FP 'oe'/1S72 22:30 King's Cross-Edinburgh; Sat. 31: HA 'oe'/1E26 16:30 Aberdeen-York from Edinburgh

NOVEMBER

Sun. 1: YK 'oe' 'B' exam; Mon. 2: YK 'B' exam; Tues. 3: 1A08 08:07 York-King's Cross/1L43 14:03 King's Cross-York/1A31 18:14 York-King's Cross Wed. 4: 1N12 00:05 King's Cross-Newcastle/GD/1N03 21:20 Newcastle-Darlington/ 0L01 Darlington-York; Thurs. 5: YK Until Mon. 9: YK/1A26 15:50 York-King's Cross/1S70 22:15 King's Cross-Aberdeen to Edinburgh; Tues. 10: 1C86 09:07 Edinburgh-Carstairs/1G44 11:23 Carstairs-Edinburgh/1A38 14:55 Edinburgh-Aberdeen/1G20 18:23 Aberdeen-

Edinburgh/1E48 21:20 Aberdeen-King's Cross from Edinburgh; Wed. 11: FP/1L43 14:03 King's Cross-York/1A31 18:14 York-King's Cross/FP; Thurs. 12: 5B26 05:24 King's Cross-Peterborough/1B26 07:23 Peterborough-King's Cross/FP/1L43 14:03 King's Cross-York/1A31 18:14 York-King's Cross/FP; Fri. 13: 1L41 09:40 King's Cross-York/1A22 14:15 York-King's Cross/1D08 19:40 King's Cross-Hull/5L04 23:30 Hull-York; Sat. 14: 1A08 08:07 York-King's Cross/FP/1L44 16:03 King's Cross-York/YK/1E35 20:45 Edinburgh-King's Cross from York; Sun. 15: FP; Mon. 16: 1N00 01:00 King's Cross-Newcastle/1S08 07:05 Newcastle-Edinburgh/HA/ 1E29 17:18 Edinburgh-Newcastle/1A45 22:55 Newcastle-King's Cross; Tues. 17: FP/1L43 14:03 King's Cross-York/1A31 18:14 York-King's Cross/1S77 23:55 King's Cross-Edinburgh; Wed. 18: HA/1E35 20:25 Edinburgh-King's Cross; Thurs. 19: 1L41 09:40 King's Cross-York/1A22 14:15 York-King's Cross/1D08 19:40 King's Cross-Hull/5L04 23:30 Hull-York; Fri. 20: YK; Sat. 21: YK/0L01 York-Neville Hill/5G08 Neville Hill-York/1G08 07:43 York-King's Cross/FP/1L44 16:03 King's Cross-York/YK; Sun. 22: YK; Mon. 23: 1A08 08:07 York-King's Cross/FP/1L44 16:03 King's Cross-York/1A34 20:19 York-King's Cross; Tues. 24: FP; Wed. 25: FP; Thurs. 26: FP/1L44 16:03 King's Cross-York/1A34 20:19 York-King's Cross; Fri. 27: 1S12 05:50 King's Cross-Aberdeen to Edinburgh/HA/1E35 20:25 Edinburgh-King's Cross; Sat. 28: 1Z40 08:34 Finsbury Park-Exeter "Deltic Devonian" rail tour/1Z40 Exeter-Liverpool Street "Deltic Devonian" rail tour/0C01 Liverpool Street-Stratford/SF; Sun. 29: SF; Mon. 30: SF/0B02 Stratford-Finsbury Park/FP/1S72 22:30 King's Cross-Edinburgh

DECEMBER

Tues. 1: 1C86 09:07 Edinburgh-Carstairs/1G44 11:23 Carstairs-Edinburgh/1A38 14:55 Edinburgh-Aberdeen/1G20 18:23 Aberdeen-Edinburgh/HA; Wed. 2: 1M04 07:18 Edinburgh-Carlisle/1S15 15:53 Carlisle-Edinburgh/1E39 22:25 Edinburgh-King's X; Thurs. 3: FP/1L43 14:03 King's X-York/1A31 18:14 York-King's X/1S77 23:55 King's X-Edinburgh; Fri. 4: HA/1E35 20:25 Edinburgh-King's X; Sat. 5: FP; Sun. 6: 1L41 10:05 King's X-York/1A10 15:50 York-King's X/FP; Mon. 7: FP; Tues. 8: FP/1B21 17:17 King's X-Peterborough/0B02 Peterborough-Finsbury Park/FP/1S72 22:30 King's X-Edinburgh; Wed. 9: HA/1E35 20:25 Edinburgh-King's X; Thurs. 10: FP/1L44 16:03 King's X-York/1A34 20:19 York-King's X; Fri. 11: FP/1L44 16:03 King's X-York/1A34 20:19 York-King's X; Sat. 12: FP/1L43 14:03 King's X-York/1A31 18:14 York-King's X/FP; Sun. 13: FP/1L42 14:05 King's X-York/1A19 19:13 York-King's X/FP; Mon. 14: 1S12 05:50 King's X-Aberdeen to Edinburgh/HA 'eo'/1E48 21:20 Aberdeen-King's X from Edinburgh to York (failed); Tues. 15: YK 'eo' 'B' exam; Wed. 16: YK 'eo' 'B' exam/1E43 20:35 Aberdeen-King's X from York (55 002 off) to Doncaster (failed at Daw Lane - A.W.S. horn defect, compressors defective and boiler defect - assisted to Doncaster by 08 115); Thurs. 17: DR/1A34 20:19 York-King's X from Doncaster; Fri. 18: 1S12 05:50 King's X-Aberdeen to Edinburgh/HA 'eo'/1E26 16:30 Aberdeen-York from Edinburgh; Sat. 19: 1A08 08:07 York-King's X/FP 'eo'/1L44 16:03 King's X-York/YK 'eo'; Sun. 20: YK 'eo'; Mon. 21: 1A08 08:07 York-King's X to Peterborough (failed - No.1 engine collector drum fire)/PB 'eo'; Tues. 22: PB 'eo'/0D00 Peterborough-Doncaster (towing 55 010)/DR 'eo'; Wed. 23:DR 'eo'/0B02 Doncaster-Finsbury Park (and 55 010)/FP 'eo'/1D08 19:40 King's X-Hull/5L04 23:30 Hull-York; Thurs. 24: YK 'eo' 'oe' (Build up of oil in No.1 engine collector drum) Until Wed. 30: YK 'eo' 'oe' - WITHDRAWN

D9017/9017/55017
The Durham Light Infantry

JUNE 1981

Mon. 1:DR/0L01 Doncaster-York/YK; Tues. 2: YK; Wed. 3: YK; Thurs. 4: 1A08 08:07 York-King's Cross/FP/1L44 16:03 King's Cross-York/1A34 20:19 York-King's Cross; Fri. 5: 1S12 05:50 King's Cross-Aberdeen to Edinburgh/HA/1E35 20:25 Edinburgh-King's Cross; Sat. 6: 1L42 12:05 King's Cross-York/1A26 15:50 York-King's Cross/1S70 22:15 King's Cross-Aberdeen to Edinburgh; Sun. 7: 1V93 11:25 Edinburgh-Plymouth to York/1S27 11:25 Reading-Edinburgh from York/1E48 21:20 Aberdeen-King's Cross from Edinburgh; Mon. 8: FP/1L43 14:03 King's Cross-York/1A31 18:14 York-King's Cross/FP Until Thurs. 11: FP; Fri. 12: 5B26 05:24 King's Cross-Peterborough/1B26 07:23 Peterborough-King's Cross/1L04 09:50 King's Cross-Leeds (vice HST)/5G05 Leeds-Ferme Park/1S66 20:15 King's Cross-Edinburgh; Sat. 13: 1V93 09:50 Edinburgh-Plymouth to York/1S27 07:30 Plymouth-Edinburgh from York/1E43 20:05 Aberdeen-King's Cross from Edinburgh; Sun. 14: FP/1L43 16:05 King's Cross-York/YK; Mon. 15: 1A37 10:47 York-King's Cross/1L45 17:40 King's Cross-York/YK 'B' exam; Tues. 16: YK 'B' exam/0B01 York-King's Cross; Wed. 17: 5B26 05:24 King's Cross-Peterborough/1B26 07:23 Peterborough-King's Cross/FP/1L43 14:03 King's Cross-York/1A31 18:14 York-King's Cross; Thurs. 18: 1N00 01:00 King's Cross-Newcastle/1S08 07:05 Newcastle-Edinburgh/HA/ 1E35 20:25 Edinburgh-King's Cross; Fri. 19: 1S76 09.40 King's Cross-Edinburgh ext. to Dundee/5Z21 Dundee-Craigentinny/HA/3E50 23:49 Edinburgh-Peterborough; Sat. 20: 5E50 Peterborough-Ferme Park/0L01 Ferme Park-York; Sun. 21: YK; Mon. 22: YK; Tues. 23: 1A37 10:47 York-King's Cross/FP/1D08 19:40 King's Cross-Hull/0D01 23:35 Hull-Doncaster; Wed. 24: 1D62 03:55 Doncaster-Hull/1A13 09:36 Hull-King's Cross/FP/1L45 17:40 King's Cross-York/YK Thurs. 25: 1A37 10:47 York-King's Cross/FP/1D08 19:40 King's Cross-Hull/0D01 23:35 Hull-Doncaster; Fri. 26: 1D62 03:55 Doncaster-Hull/1A13 09:36 Hull-King's Cross/FP/1L45 17:40 King's Cross-York/YK; Sat. 27: 1A08 08:07 York-King's Cross/1L43 14:03 King's Cross-York/1A31 17:05 Scarborough-King's Cross from York/FP; Sun. 28: 1N02 08:30 King's Cross-Newcastle/1A21 14:57 Newcastle-King's Cross to York/YK; Mon. 29: YK/1A26 15:50 York-King's Cross/FP; Tues. 30: 1N12 00:05 King's Cross-Newcastle/0L01 08:08 Newcastle-York/YK/1S27 07:30 Plymouth-Edinburgh from York to Newcastle/GD/1A45 22:55 Newcastle-King's Cross

JULY

Wed. 1: 1L42 12:05 King's Cross-York/1A26 15:50 York-King's Cross/1S70 22:15 King's Cross-Aberdeen to Edinburgh; Thurs. 2: 1M04 07:18 Edinburgh-Carlisle to Newcastle/GD/1A40 21:00 Newcastle-King's Cross; Fri. 3: 5B26 05:24 King's Cross-Peterborough/1B26 07:23 Peterborough-King's Cross/1S91 12:35 King's Cross-Edinburgh to Newcastle/0L01 Newcastle-York; Sat. 4: 1A08 08:07 York-King's Cross/FP/1L45 18:05 King's Cross-York/YK 'B' exam; Sun. 5: YK 'B' exam; Mon. 6: YK 'B' exam/1S77 23:55 King's Cross-Edinburgh from York to Newcastle; Tues. 7: GD/0L01 Gateshead-York; Wed. 8: 0D01 York-Doncaster (towing 55 013)/On/Off DONCASTER WORKS "Unclassified repair"/0L01 Doncaster - York/YK; Thurs. 9: 1A37 10:47 York-King's Cross/FP; Fri. 10: FP; Sat. 11: 1N00 01:00 King's Cross-Newcastle/1S08 07:05 Newcastle-Edinburgh/1E52 11:55 Edinburgh-King's Cross/FP/1S72 22:30 King's Cross-Edinburgh; Sun. 12: HA/1E35 20:25 Edinburgh-King's Cross to Peterborough; Mon. 13: 1B26 07:23 Peterborough-King's Cross/FP/1L44 16:03 King's Cross-York/

124 LAST MONTHS OF THE DELTICS — 1981 — D9017

1A34 20:19 York-King's Cross; Tues. 14: 1S85 11:xx King's Cross-Aberdeen to Edinburgh/HA/1E35 20:25 Edinburgh-King's Cross; Wed. 15: 1D01 08:30 King's Cross-Cleethorpes/1A21 13:20 Cleethorpes-King's Cross/ FP; Thurs. 16: 1N00 01:00 King's Cross-Newcastle/1S08 07:05 Newcastle-Edinburgh/HA/ 1E29 17:18 Edinburgh-Newcastle/1A45 22:55 Newcastle-King's Cross; Fri. 17: FP/1N14 14:03 King's Cross-Newcastle/GD/1A45 22:55 Newcastle-King's Cross; Sat. 18: FP/1L43 14:03 King's Cross-York/1A31 17:05 Scarborough-King's Cross from York (55 009 off)/FP; Sun. 19: FP/1L42 14:05 King's Cross-York/1A19 19:13 York-King's Cross/FP; Mon. 20: 1S76 09.40 King's Cross-Edinburgh/HA/1E35 20:25 Edinburgh-King's Cross; Tues. 21: 1S76 09.40 King's Cross-Edinburgh/HA/1E39 22:25 Edinburgh-King's Cross; Wed. 22: FP/1S66 20:15 King's Cross-Edinburgh; Thurs. 23: 5E10 06:40 Craigentinny-Dundee/1E10 09:10 Dundee-King's Cross to York/ YK 'C' exam Until Mon. 27: YK 'C' exam; Tues. 28: 1A08 08:07 York-King's Cross/FP/1L44 16:03 King's Cross-York/1A34 20:19 York-King's Cross; Wed. 29: 1S12 05:50 King's Cross-Aberdeen to Edinburgh/HA/1E29 17:18 Edinburgh-Newcastle/GD; Thurs. 30: 0L01 Gateshead-York/YK/0B01 York-King's Cross/1L45 17:40 King's Cross-York/YK; Fri. 31: YK/0B02 York-Finsbury Park/FP//1D08 19:40 King's Cross-Hull/0D01 23:35 Hull-Doncaster

AUGUST

Sat. 1: 1D62 03:55 Doncaster-Hull/1A13 09:36 Hull-King's Cross/1L45 18:05 King's Cross-York/YK; Sun. 2: YK/1A21 14:57 Newcastle-King's Cross from York/FP; Mon. 3: 1S12 05:50 King's Cross-Aberdeen to Edinburgh (55 016 forward)/1A38 14:55 Edinburgh-Aberdeen/1G20 18:23 Aberdeen-Edinburgh/1E42 23:15 Edinburgh-King's Cross; Tues. 4: FP/1L43 14:03 King's Cross-York/1A31 18:14 York-King's Cross; Wed. 5: 1N00 01:00 King's Cross-Newcastle/1S08 07:05 Newcastle-Edinburgh/HA/ 1E26 16:30 Aberdeen-Leeds from Edinburgh/1E24 22:50 Shrewsbury-York from Leeds; Thurs. 6: 0N10 York-Thornaby/TE 'Tyre turning'; Fri. 7: 0L01 Thornaby-York/YK; Sat. 8: YK; Sun. 9: 1G06 York-Scarborough/1G06 Scarborough-King's Cross/FP; Mon. 10: 1N00 01:00 King's Cross-Newcastle/1S08 07:05 Newcastle-Edinburgh/HA/ 1E40 19:25 Aberdeen-King's Cross from Edinburgh; Tues. 11: FP/1L43 14:03 King's Cross-York/1L52 York-Leeds/0L01 Leeds-York; Wed. 12: 1A08 08:07 York-King's Cross/1L42 12:05 King's Cross-York/1A26 15:50 York-King's Cross/FP; Thurs. 13: 1N12 00:05 King's Cross-Newcastle/1S14 08:10 Newcastle-Edinburgh/HA/ 1E35 20:25 Edinburgh-King's Cross; Fri. 14: 1L42 12:05 King's Cross-York/1A26 15:50 York-King's Cross/1S70 22:15 King's Cross-Aberdeen to Edinburgh; Sat. 15: 5E10 06:40 Craigentinny-Dundee/1E10 09:10 Dundee-King's Cross/FP; Sun. 16: 1N02 08:30 King's Cross-Newcastle/1A21 14:57 Newcastle-King's Cross to York/YK 'B' exam; Mon. 17: YK 'B' exam; Tues. 18: YK 'B' exam/1E43 20:35 Aberdeen-King's Cross from York; Wed. 19: 1L42 12:05 King's Cross-York/1A26 15:50 York-King's Cross/1S77 23:55 King's Cross-Edinburgh; Thurs. 20: 1V93 09:50 Edinburgh-Plymouth to York/1S27 07:30 Plymouth-Edinburgh from York/1E35 20:25 Edinburgh-King's Cross; Fri. 21: 1S76 09.40 King's Cross-Edinburgh/HA/1E39 22:25 Edinburgh-King's Cross; Sat. 22: 1L42 12:05 King's Cross-York/1A26 15:50 York-King's Cross/1S72 22:30 King's Cross-Edinburgh; Sun. 23: HA/1E39 22:30 Edinburgh-King's Cross; Mon. 24: FP/1L43 14:03 King's Cross-York/1A31 18:14 York-King's Cross/FP; Tues. 25: 1S12 05:50 King's Cross-Aberdeen/AB/1E48 21:20 Aberdeen-King's Cross; Wed. 26: 1L42 12:05 King's Cross-York/1A26 15:50 York-King's Cross/1S79 23:20 King's Cross-Aberdeen to Edinburgh Thurs. 27: 1V93 09:50 Edinburgh-Plymouth to York/1S27 07:30 Plymouth-Edinburgh from

York/1E42 23:15 Edinburgh-King's Cross; Fri. 28: 1S76 09.40 King's Cross-Edinburgh/HA; Sat. 29: 5E10 06:40 Craigentinny-Dundee/1E10 09:10 Dundee-King's Cross to York/ YK; Sun. 30: YK; Mon. 31: YK

SEPTEMBER

Tues. 1: 5A37 York-(Durham)/1A37 09:30 Durham-King's Cross/1D08 19:40 King's Cross-Hull/0D01 23:35 Hull-Doncaster; Wed. 2: 1D62 03:55 Doncaster-Hull/1A13 09:36 Hull-King's Cross/FP/1L45 17:40 King's Cross-York/YK; Thurs. 3: 1A08 08:07 York-King's Cross/FP/1L44 16:03 King's Cross-York/1A34 20:19 York-King's Cross; Fri. 4: 1S12 05:50 King's Cross-Aberdeen to Edinburgh/HA/1E35 20:25 Edinburgh-King's Cross; Sat. 5: 1S84 11:03 King's Cross-Edinburgh/HA/1E43 20:05 Aberdeen-King's Cross from Edinburgh; Sun. 6: FP/1S60 20:00 King's Cross-Aberdeen to Edinburgh; Mon. 7: 2L25 06:25 Edinburgh-Dundee/1E10 09:10 Dundee-King's Cross/1S60 20:00 King's Cross-Aberdeen to Edinburgh; Tues. 8: 5E10 06:40 Craigentinny-Dundee/1E10 09:10 Dundee-King's Cross/1S60 20:00 King's Cross-Aberdeen to Edinburgh; Wed. 9: 2L25 06:25 Edinburgh-Dundee/1E10 09:10 Dundee-King's Cross/1S66 20:15 King's Cross-Edinburgh; Thurs. 10: 5E10 06:40 Craigentinny-Dundee/1E10 09:10 Dundee-King's Cross/FP; Fri. 11: 1N12 00:05 King's Cross-Newcastle/1S14 08:10 Newcastle-Edinburgh/HA/ 1E40 19:25 Aberdeen-King's Cross from Edinburgh; Sat. 12: FP; Sun. 13: 1N02 08:30 King's Cross-Newcastle/1A21 14:57 Newcastle-King's Cross/FP; Mon. 14: 1N00 01:00 King's Cross-Newcastle/1S08 07:05 Newcastle-Edinburgh/1E10 09:10 Dundee-King's Cross from Edinburgh/FP/1S77 23:55 King's Cross-Edinburgh; Tues. 15: 1V93 09:50 Edinburgh-Plymouth to York/YK 'B' exam; Wed. 16: YK 'B' exam/1S76 09.40 King's Cross-Edinburgh from York (55 014 off)/HA/ 1E35 20:25 Edinburgh-King's Cross; Thurs. 17: 1S76 09.40 King's Cross-Edinburgh/HA/1E39 22:25 Edinburgh-King's Cross; Fri. 18: FP/1S70 22:15 King's Cross-Aberdeen to Edinburgh; Sat. 19: 1V93 09:50 Edinburgh-Plymouth to York/1S27 07:30 Plymouth-Edinburgh from York/1E43 20:05 Aberdeen-King's Cross from Edinburgh; Sun. 20: FP/1L42 14:05 King's Cross-York/1A19 19:13 York-King's Cross; Mon. 21: 1N00 01:00 King's Cross-Newcastle/1S08 07:05 Newcastle-Edinburgh/1E10 09:10 Dundee-King's Cross from Edinburgh/1S66 20:15 King's Cross-Edinburgh; Tues. 22: HA/1E35 20:25 Edinburgh-King's Cross; Wed. 23: 1L42 12:05 King's Cross-York/1A26 15:50 York-King's Cross/1S79 23:20 King's Cross-Aberdeen to Edinburgh; Thurs. 24: HA/1E40 19:25 Aberdeen-King's Cross from Edinburgh; Fri. 25: FP/1N14 14:03 King's Cross-Newcastle to York/1A31 18:14 York-King's Cross; Sat. 26: 1N00 01:00 King's Cross-Newcastle/1S08 07:05 Newcastle-Edinburgh/HA/ 1E43 20:05 Aberdeen-King's Cross from Edinburgh; Sun. 27: FP/1L43 16:05 King's Cross-York/YK 'D' exam Until Wed. 30: YK 'D' exam/1A45 22:55 Newcastle-King's Cross from York (55 019 off)

OCTOBER

Thurs. 1: 1L42 12:05 King's Cross-York/1A26 15:50 York-King's Cross/FP; Fri. 2: 1N12 00:05 King's Cross-Newcastle/GD/1A40 21:00 Newcastle-King's Cross to York; Sat. 3: 1A08 08:07 York-King's Cross/FP/1S60 20:00 King's Cross-Aberdeen to Edinburgh; Sun. 4: HA/1E40 19:25 Aberdeen-King's Cross from Edinburgh; Mon. 5: FP/1L43 14:03 King's Cross-York/1A31 18:14 York-King's Cross; Tues. 6: 1N00 01:00 King's Cross-Newcastle/1S08 07:05 Newcastle-Edinburgh/HA/ 1E40 19:25 Aberdeen-King's Cross from Edinburgh; Wed. 7: FP; Thurs. 8: 1N00 01:00 King's Cross-Newcastle/1S08 07:05 Newcastle-Edinburgh/HA/ 1C94 17:35 Edinburgh-Carstairs/1G12 19:31 Carstairs-Edinburgh/1E35 20:25 Edinburgh-King's Cross; Fri. 9: FP/1N14 14:03 King's Cross-Newcastle to York/1A31 18:14 York-King's Cross; Sat. 10: 1N12 00:05 King's Cross-

126 LAST MONTHS OF THE DELTICS — 1981 — D9017

Newcastle/0L01 Newcastle-York/YK; Sun. 11: YK; Mon. 12: 1A08 08:07 York-King's Cross/FP/1L44 16:03 King's Cross-York/1A34 20:19 York-King's Cross; Tues. 13: 1S12 05:50 King's Cross-Aberdeen to Edinburgh/HA/1E29 17:18 Edinburgh-Newcastle/1A45 22:55 Newcastle-King's Cross; Wed. 14: 5B26 05:24 King's Cross-Peterborough/1B26 07:23 Peterborough-King's Cross/FP/1S66 20:15 King's Cross-Edinburgh; Thurs. 15: HA; Fri. 16: HA/1E29 17:18 Edinburgh-Newcastle/1N03 21:20 Newcastle-Darlington/0L01 Darlington-York; Sat. 17: YK; Sun. 18: YK/1A19 19:13 York-King's Cross/FP; Mon. 19: FP/1L43 14:03 King's Cross-York/1A31 18:14 York-King's Cross/1S77 23:55 King's Cross-Edinburgh; Tues. 20: 1V93 09:50 Edinburgh-Plymouth to York/1S27 07:30 Plymouth-Edinburgh from York/1E39 22:25 Edinburgh-King's Cross; Wed. 21: FP/1L43 14:03 King's Cross-York/YK; Thurs. 22: YK/1A34 20:19 York-King's Cross; Fri. 23: FP; Sat. 24: FP/1L43 14:03 King's Cross-York/1A31 18:14 York-King's Cross/FP; Sun. 25: 1L41 10:05 King's Cross-York/1A10 15:50 York-King's Cross/1S72 22:40 King's Cross-Edinburgh; Mon. 26: 1V93 09:50 Edinburgh-Plymouth to York/1S27 07:30 Plymouth-Edinburgh from York/1E43 20:35 Aberdeen-King's Cross from Edinburgh; Tues. 27: FP/1L44 16:03 King's Cross-York/1A34 20:19 York-King's Cross; Wed. 28: 1S12 05:50 King's Cross-Aberdeen to Newcastle/0L01 Newcastle-York/0B02 York-Finsbury Park/1L22 23:00 King's Cross-Bradford; Thurs. 29: 0L50 Bradford-Holbeck/0L01 Holbeck-York/1A22 14:15 York-King's Cross/ 1D08 19:40 King's Cross-Hull/5L04 23:30 Hull-York; Fri. 30: YK 'oe' (No.1 eng. dephased);Sat. 31: YK 'oe'

NOVEMBER

Sun. 1: YK 'oe'; Mon. 2: YK 'oe'; Tues. 3: YK/1N12 00:05 King's Cross-Newcastle from York/GD/1A40 21:00 Newcastle-King's Cross Wed. 4: 5B26 05:24 King's Cross-Peterborough/1B26 07:23 Peterborough-King's Cross/FP 'oe'/1S66 20:15 King's Cross-Edinburgh ; Thurs. 5: 1M04 07:18 Edinburgh-Carlisle/1S15 15:53 Carlisle-Edinburgh/1E39 22:25 Edinburgh-King's Cross ; Fri. 6: FP 'oe'; Sat. 7: 1N12 00:05 King's Cross-Newcastle/GD 'oe'; Sun. 8: GD 'oe'; Mon. 9: GD 'oe'/1A40 21:00 Newcastle-King's Cross to York ; Tues. 10: YK/1A26 15:50 York-King's Cross/1S70 22:15 King's Cross-Aberdeen to Peterborough (55 019 fwd)/1A40 21:00 Newcastle-King's Cross from Peterborough; Wed. 11: 5B26 05:24 King's Cross-Peterborough/1B26 07:23 Peterborough-King's Cross/FP 'oe'; Thurs. 12: 1N12 00:05 King's Cross-Newcastle/GD 'oe'/0D01 Gateshead-Doncaster; Fri. 13: On DCR WORKS "Unclassified repair" (No.1 engine, 443, replaced by 424.) Until Tues. 17: Off DCR WORKS; Wed. 18: 0B02 Doncaster-Finsbury Park/1S60 20:00 King's Cross-Aberdeen to York (failed); Thurs. 19: YK; Fri. 20: YK; Sat. 21: 0B02 York-Finsbury Park/FP/1G08 19:35 King's Cross-York/5G08 York-Neville Hill/0L01 Neville Hill-York; Sun. 22: YK/0B02 York-Peterborough; Mon. 23: 1B18 07:50 Peterborough-King's Cross/FP/1B21 17:17 King's Cross-Peterborough/0B02 Peterborough-Finsbury Park/1S72 22:30 King's Cross-Edinburgh; Tues. 24: HA/1E35 20:25 Edinburgh-King's Cross; Wed. 25: FP/1L43 14:03 King's Cross-York/1A31 18:14 York-King's Cross/FP 'eo' (Boiler water tank holed and flexible on main steam pipe missing); Thurs. 26: 1S12 05:50 King's Cross-Aberdeen to Newcastle/0L01 Newcastle-York/1A22 14:15 York-King's Cross/1D08 19:40 King's Cross-Hull/5L04 23:30 Hull-York ; Fri. 27: 1A08 08:07 York-King's Cross/FP 'eo'/1L44 16:03 King's Cross-York/1A34 20:19 York-King's Cross ; Sat. 28: 1S12 05:50 King's Cross-Aberdeen to Edinburgh/HA 'eo'; Sun. 29: HA 'eo'/1E48 21:20 Aberdeen-King's Cross from Edinburgh; Mon. 30:   FP 'eo'/1L44 16:03 King's Cross-York/1A34 20:19 York-King's Cross

DECEMBER

Tues. 1: 1L41 09:40 King's Cross-York/1A22 14:15 York-King's Cross/FP 'eo'/1S70 22:15 King's Cross-Aberdeen to Edinburgh ; Wed. 2: HA 'eo'/5V44 12:35 Edinburgh-Polmadie/5G00 Polmadie-Edinburgh/1E48 21:20 Aberdeen-King's Cross from Edinburgh; Thurs. 3: FP 'eo'/1L44 16:03 King's Cross-York/YK 'eo'; Fri. 4: YK 'eo'; Sat. 5: 1A08 08:07 York-King's Cross/FP 'eo'/1L44 16:03 King's Cross-York/YK 'eo'; Sun. 6: YK 'eo'/1A19 19:13 York-King's Cross ; Mon. 7: 1S12 05:50 King's Cross-Aberdeen to Newcastle/0L01 Newcastle-York/1A22 14:15 York-King's Cross/1D08 19:40 King's Cross-Hull/5L04 23:30 Hull-York ; Tues. 8: 1A08 08:07 York-King's Cross/FP 'eo'/1L44 16:03 King's Cross-York/1A34 20:19 York-King's Cross ; Wed. 9: 1S12 05:50 King's Cross-Aberdeen to Edinburgh/0G00 Edinburgh-Carstairs/ 1A55 14:05 Birmingham-Aberdeen from Carstairs to Edinburgh/1E48 21:20 Aberdeen-King's Cross from Edinburgh; Thurs. 10: FP 'eo'/1L43 14:03 King's Cross-York/1A31 18:14 York-King's Cross/FP 'eo'; Fri. 11: FP 'eo'; Sat. 12: 1S12 05:50 King's Cross-Aberdeen to Edinburgh/1A38 14:55 Edinburgh-Aberdeen/1G20 18:30 Aberdeen-Edinburgh/HA 'eo'; Sun. 13: HA 'eo'/1E48 21:20 Aberdeen-King's Cross from Edinburgh; Mon. 14: FP 'eo'/1S70 22:15 King's Cross-Aberdeen to Edinburgh ; Tues. 15: 5Z20 07:35 Edinburgh-Aberdeen (MKIII Sleepers)/0G99 Aberdeen-Haymarket/HA 'eo'/1C95 18:53 Edinburgh-Carstairs/0G99 Carstairs-Haymarket/HA 'eo'/1E48 21:20 Aberdeen-King's Cross from Edinburgh; Wed. 16: FP 'eo'/1S70 22:15 King's Cross-Aberdeen to Edinburgh ; Thurs. 17: 1C86 09:07 Edinburgh-Carstairs/1G44 11:23 Carstairs-Edinburgh/HA 'eo'/1E26 16:30 Aberdeen-York; Fri. 18: 1A08 08:07 York-King's Cross/FP 'eo'/1S70 22:15 King's Cross-Aberdeen to Edinburgh; Sat. 19: 1C90 07:14 Edinburgh-Carstairs/Carstairs-Edinburgh/1E61 09:00 Aberdeen-King's Cross from Edinburgh/FP 'eo'; Sun. 20: FP 'eo'/1L42 14:05 King's Cross-York/YK 'eo'; Mon. 21: 5B26 York-Peterborough/1B26 07:23 Peterborough-King's Cross/FP 'eo'/ 1L44 16:03 King's Cross-York/1A34 20:19 York-King's Cross ; Tues. 22: 1S12 05:50 King's Cross-Aberdeen/1E26 16:30 Aberdeen-York; Wed. 23: 1A08 08:07 York-King's Cross/FP 'eo'/1L44 16:03 King's Cross-York/1A34 20:19 York-King's Cross; Thurs. 24: 1S12 05:50 King's Cross-Aberdeen/1E26 16:30 Aberdeen-York; Fri. 25: YK 'eo' Until Mon. 28: YK 'eo'; Tues. 29: 1A08 08:07 York-King's Cross/FP 'eo'/1L44 16:03 King's Cross-York/1A34 20:19 York-King's Cross; Wed. 30: 1S12 05:50 King's Cross-Aberdeen to Edinburgh/HA 'eo'/1E48 21:20 Aberdeen-King's Cross from Edinburgh; Thurs. 31: FP 'eo'/1L44 16:03 King's Cross-York to Grantham - train terminated due to a broken rail/1G26 18:58 Grantham-King's Cross to Knebworth (failed - Wheel Slip Relay No.5 sticking)/5G26 Knebworth-King's Cross (towed by 47 426)/FP 'eo' - WITHDRAWN

D9018/9018/55018 Ballymoss

APRIL 1981

Wed. 1: 1D00 08:05 King's Cross-Hull/1A18 12:34 Hull-King's Cross/FP; Thurs. 2: 1D00 08:05 King's Cross-Hull/1A18 12:34 Hull-King's Cross/1L45 18:05 King's Cross-York/0B05 York-Peterborough to Doncaster/1A40 20:30 Newcastle-King's Cross from Doncaster; Fri. 3: 1D00 08:05 King's Cross-Hull/1A18 12:34 Hull-King's Cross/FP/1D08 19:35 King's Cross-Hull/0D01 23:35 Hull-Doncaster/1S70 22:15 King's Cross-Aberdeen from Doncaster (55 004 off) to Edinburgh; Sat. 4: HA/1E29 17:07 Edinburgh-Newcastle/1A40 21:00 Newcastle-King's Cross; Sun. 5: FP 'B' exam Until Fri. 10: FP 'B' exam/1L44 16:05 King's Cross-York/1A34 19:55 York-King's Cross; Sat. 11: 1N00 01:00 King's Cross-Newcastle/1S08

128 LAST MONTHS OF THE DELTICS — 1981 — D9018

07:05 Newcastle-Edinburgh/HA/ 1S12 05:50 King's Cross-Aberdeen from Edinburgh (55 022 off)/1E26 16:30 Aberdeen-Leeds; Sun. 12: 5E26 Leeds-York/YK; Mon. 13: YK/0L50 York-Holbeck/HO/1A14 10:45 Leeds-King's Cross/1L12 14:50 King's Cross-Leeds/0L01 Leeds-York/YK; Tues. 14: 1A08 08:05 York-King's Cross/FP/1L44 16:05 King's Cross-York/1A34 19:55 York-King's Cross; Wed. 15: 1D00 08:05 King's Cross-Hull/1A18 12:34 Hull-King's Cross/FP/1D08 19:35 King's Cross-Hull/0D01 23:35 Hull-Doncaster; Thurs. 16: 1D62 03:55 Doncaster-Hull/5L08 Hull-York/YK; Fri. 17: YK/1E52 11:55 Edinburgh-King's Cross from York (55 010 off)/FP/1S72 22:30 King's Cross-Edinburgh; Sat. 18: HA/1E35 20:45 Edinburgh-King's Cross; Sun. 19: FP/1B31 22:00 King's Cross-Peterborough/PB/1S77 23:55 King's Cross-Edinburgh from Peterborough (55 019 off); Mon. 20: 1E52 11:55 Edinburgh-King's Cross/FP; Tues. 21: 1D00 08:05 King's Cross-Hull/1A18 12:34 Hull-King's Cross/FP Wed. 22: FP/1D08 19:35 King's Cross-Hull to Doncaster/DR; Thurs. 23: DR/0D.. Doncaster-Hull/BG/0L01 Hull-York/YK Until Mon. 27: YK/0D01 York-Doncaster; Tues. 28: On DONCASTER WORKS "Unclassified repair" (No.2 engine, 446, replaced by 423); Wed. 29: DONCASTER WORKS; Thurs. 30: DONCASTER WORKS

MAY

Fri. 1: DONCASTER WORKS Until Fri. 8: Off DONCASTER WORKS/DR/0L01 Doncaster-York/YK/1A31 18:10 York-King's Cross/FP; Sat. 9: 1D02 12:05 King's Cross-Hull/1A28 16:30 Hull-King's Cross/FP 'B' exam Until Wed. 13: FP 'B' exam/1L43 14:05 King's Cross-York/1A31 18:10 York-King's Cross; Thurs. 14: 1N00 01:00 King's Cross-Newcastle/1S08 07:05 Newcastle-Edinburgh/HA/ 1E29 17:07 Edinburgh-Newcastle/1A45 22:55 Newcastle-King's Cross; Fri. 15: 1L41 10:05 King's Cross-York/YK/1A31 18:10 York-King's Cross/FP; Sat. 16: 1D00 08:05 King's Cross-Hull/1A18 12:34 Hull-King's Cross/FP; Sun. 17: FP/1S79 23:15 King's Cross-Aberdeen to Edinburgh; Mon. 18: 1V93 09:50 Edinburgh-Plymouth to York/1S27 07:22 Plymouth-Edinburgh from York/1E35 20:25 Edinburgh-King's Cross; Tues. 19: 1D00 08:05 King's Cross-Hull/1A18 12:34 Hull-King's Cross/FP/1D08 19:35 King's Cross-Hull/0D01 23:35 Hull-Doncaster; Wed. 20: 1D62 03:55 Doncaster-Hull/1A13 09:33 Hull-King's Cross/1L44 16:05 King's Cross-York/1A34 19:55 York-King's Cross; Thurs. 21: 1D00 08:05 King's Cross-Hull/1A18 12:34 Hull-King's Cross/1L45 18:05 King's Cross-York/0B05 York-Peterborough; Fri. 22: 1B05 08:36 Peterborough-King's Cross/FP/1S79 23:15 King's Cross-Aberdeen to Newcastle; Sat. 23: GD/1A37 09:20 Newcastle-King's Cross/FP; Sun. 24: FP/1L43 16:05 King's Cross-York/YK Mon. 25: 1A08 08:05 York-King's Cross (assisted by a Class 31 from Doncaster due to a speedo defect)/FP 'B' exam Until Sat. 30: FP 'B' exam; Sun. 31: 1N12 00:05 King's Cross-Newcastle/GD/1A40 21:28 Newcastle-King's Cross

JUNE

Mon. 1: 5B26 05:24 King's Cross-Peterborough/1B26 07:23 Peterborough-King's Cross/FP/1L43 14:03 King's Cross-York/1A31 18:14 York-King's Cross; Tues. 2: 1N00 01:00 King's Cross-Newcastle/1S08 07:05 Newcastle-Edinburgh/HA/ 1A38 14:55 Edinburgh-Aberdeen/1G20 18:23 Aberdeen-Edinburgh/1E40 19:25 Aberdeen-King's Cross from Edinburgh; Wed. 3: FP/1L43 14:03

King's Cross-York/YK; Thurs. 4: 1A37 10:47 York-King's Cross/FP/1D08 19:40 King's Cross-Hull/0D01 23:35 Hull-Doncaster; Fri. 5: 1D62 03:55 Doncaster-Hull/1A13 09:36 Hull-King's Cross/FP/1S66 20:15 King's Cross-Edinburgh; Sat. 6: 5E10 06:40 Craigentinny-Dundee/1E10 09:10 Dundee-King's Cross/FP; Sun. 7: FP/1L22 23:00 King's Cross-Bradford to Leeds; Mon. 8: 0L01 Leeds-York/YK; Tues. 9: 1A08 08:07 York-King's Cross/FP/1D08 19:40 King's Cross-Hull/0D01 23:35 Hull-Doncaster; Wed. 10: 1D62 03:55 Doncaster-Hull/1A13 09:36 Hull-King's Cross/FP/1L45 17:40 King's Cross-York/YK; Thurs. 11: YK; Fri. 12: 1A08 08:07 York-King's Cross/FP/1L44 16:03 King's Cross-York/1A34 20:19 York-King's Cross; Sat. 13: 1S12 05:50 King's Cross-Aberdeen to Edinburgh/HA/1E40 19:15 Aberdeen-King's Cross from Edinburgh; Sun. 14: FP/1L42 14:05 King's Cross-York/1A19 19:13 York-King's Cross; Mon. 15: 1N00 01:00 King's Cross-Newcastle/1S08 07:05 Newcastle-Edinburgh/HA/ 1E35 20:25 Edinburgh-King's Cross; Tues. 16: FP/1L43 14:03 King's Cross-York/1A31 18:14 York-King's Cross; Wed. 17: 1N00 01:00 King's Cross-Newcastle/1S08 07:05 Newcastle-Edinburgh/HA/ 1E35 20:25 Edinburgh-King's Cross; Thurs. 18: 1S76 09:40 King's Cross-Edinburgh/HA/1E40 19:25 Aberdeen-King's Cross from Edinburgh; Fri. 19: 1L42 12:05 King's Cross-York/1A26 15:50 York-King's Cross/FP; Sat. 20: 1N00 01:00 King's Cross-Newcastle/1S08 07:05 Newcastle-Edinburgh/HA/ 1E35 20:45 Edinburgh-King's Cross; Sun. 21: FP; Mon. 22: FP/1L43 14:03 King's Cross-York/1A31 18:14 York-King's Cross/FP; Tues. 23: FP/1L43 14:03 King's Cross-York/1A31 18:14 York-King's Cross; Wed. 24: 1N00 01:00 King's Cross-Newcastle/1S08 07:05 Newcastle-Edinburgh/HA/ 1E35 20:25 Edinburgh-King's Cross; Thurs. 25: 1L42 12:05 King's Cross-York/1A26 15:50 York-King's Cross/1S79 23:20 King's Cross-Aberdeen to Edinburgh; Fri. 26: 1V93 09:50 Edinburgh-Plymouth to York/1S27 07:36 Plymouth-Edinburgh from York/1E40 19:25 Aberdeen-King's Cross from Edinburgh; Sat. 27: FP/1L45 18:05 King's Cross-York/YK 'B' exam Until Tues. 30: YK 'B' exam

JULY

Wed. 1: YK/0B02 York-Finsbury Park/FP/1D01 08:30 King's Cross-Cleethorpes/1A21 13:20 Cleethorpes-King's Cross/FP/1S79 23:20 King's Cross-Aberdeen to Edinburgh; Thurs. 2: HA/1E35 20:25 Edinburgh-King's Cross; Fri. 3: FP/1B03 17:12 King's Cross-Peterborough/0B02 Peterborough-Finsbury Park/FP; Sat. 4: 1N12 00:05 King's Cross-Newcastle/GD/1A39 10:50 Newcastle-King's Cross to York/YK 'oe'; Sun. 5: 1A06 11:50 York-King's Cross to Holgate Junction (failed)/YK; Mon. 6: 1A08 08:07 York-King's Cross/FP; Tues. 7: 1N00 01:00 King's Cross-Newcastle/GD/0L01 Gateshead-York/1A37 10:47 York-King's Cross/1L45 17:40 King's Cross-York/YK; Wed. 8: 1A37 10:47 York-King's Cross/FP/1D08 19:40 King's Cross-Hull/0D01 23:35 Hull-Doncaster; Thurs. 9: 1D62 03:55 Doncaster-Hull/1A13 09:36 Hull-King's Cross to Doncaster/0L01 Doncaster-York/YK Until; Wed. 22: YK; Thurs. 23: 1A37 10:47 York-King's Cross/FP/1D08 19:40 King's Cross-Hull/0D01 23:35 Hull-Doncaster; Fri. 24: 1D62 03:55 Doncaster-Hull/1A13 09:36 Hull-King's Cross/FP; Sat. 25: 1S76 09:40 King's Cross-Edinburgh to Peterborough/PB/0B02 Peterborough-Finsbury Park/FP Until Thurs. 30: FP/1S66 20:15 King's Cross-Edinburgh; Fri. 31: 1V93 09:50 Edinburgh-Plymouth to York/1S27 07:36 Plymouth-Edinburgh from York/1E39 22:25 Edinburgh-King's Cross

AUGUST

Sat. 1: 1L42 12:05 King's Cross-York/1A26 15:50 York-King's Cross/FP; Sun. 2: 1N12 00:05 King's Cross-Newcastle/GD/1A40 21:28 Newcastle-King's Cross; Mon. 3:5B26 05:24 King's Cross-Peterborough/1B26 07:23 Peterborough-King's Cross/1L42 12:05 King's

Cross-York/1A26 15:50 York-King's Cross/1S79 23:20 King's Cross-Aberdeen to Edinburgh; Tues. 4: 1V93 09:50 Edinburgh-Plymouth to York/YK 'B' exam; Wed. 5: YK 'B' exam; Thurs. 6: YK 'B' exam/1A26 15:50 York-King's Cross/1S60 20:00 King's Cross-Aberdeen to Newcastle; Fri. 7: 1S14 08:10 Newcastle-Edinburgh/1F11 12:15 Edinburgh-Newcastle/5F11 Newcastle-Edinburgh/HA/1E35 20:25 Edinburgh-King's Cross; Sat. 8: 1L42 12:05 King's Cross-York/1A26 15:50 York-King's Cross/1S72 22:30 King's Cross-Edinburgh; Sun. 9: HA/1E42 23:15 Edinburgh-King's Cross; Mon. 10: 1L42 12:05 King's Cross-York/1A26 15:50 York-King's Cross/1S70 22:15 King's Cross-Aberdeen to Edinburgh; Tues. 11: 1V93 09:50 Edinburgh-Plymouth to York/YK/0B02 York-Finsbury Park/FP/ 1S79 23:20 King's Cross-Aberdeen to Edinburgh; Wed. 12: HA/1E17 15:15 Edinburgh-King's Cross (vice HST) to Newcastle/5F00 Newcastle-Edinburgh/HA/1E43 20:35 Aberdeen-King's Cross from Edinburgh; Thurs. 13: FP/1L43 14:03 King's Cross-York (piloting 31 411)/YK Until Thurs. 20: YK; Fri. 21: 1A08 08:07 York-King's Cross/FP/1S72 22:30 King's Cross-Edinburgh; Sat. 22: 1V93 09:50 Edinburgh-Plymouth to York/1S27 07:36 Plymouth-Edinburgh from York/1E35 20:45 Edinburgh-King's Cross; Sun. 23: FP/1L43 16:05 King's Cross-York/YK; Mon. 24: 1A08 08:07 York-King's Cross/FP; Tues. 25: FP; Wed. 26: FP/1L23 20:50 King's Cross-Leeds (vice HST)/HO; Thurs. 27: HO/0L01 Holbeck-York/YK Until Mon. 31: YK

SEPTEMBER

Tues. 1: YK; Wed. 2: YK/1A31 18:14 York-King's Cross/FP; Thurs. 3: 1S12 05:50 King's Cross-Aberdeen to Edinburgh/HA/1E29 17:18 Edinburgh-Newcastle/1A45 22:55 Newcastle-King's Cross; Fri. 4: 1L42 12:05 King's Cross-York/1A26 15:50 York-King's Cross/1S70 22:15 King's Cross-Aberdeen to Edinburgh; Sat. 5: 1V93 09:50 Edinburgh-Plymouth to York/1S27 07:36 Plymouth-Edinburgh from York/1E40 19:15 Aberdeen-King's Cross from Edinburgh to Belford (failed - assisted to Newcastle by 47 428 on 1Z41 23:40 Edinburgh-Gloucester); Sun. 6: GD/0L01 Gateshead-York/YK; Mon. 7: YK; Tues. 8: 1A37 10:47 York-King's Cross/FP Until Thurs. 17: FP/1L42 12:05 King's Cross-York/1A26 15:50 York-King's Cross/1S79 23:20 King's Cross-Aberdeen to Edinburgh; Fri. 18: 1V93 09:50 Edinburgh-Plymouth to Newcastle/GD/0L01 Gateshead-York/YK Until Mon. 21: YK; Tues. 22: 1A08 08:07 York-King's Cross/1L43 14:03 King's Cross-York/1A31 18:14 York-King's Cross; Wed. 23: 1N00 01:00 King's Cross-Newcastle/1S08 07:05 Newcastle-Edinburgh/HA/ 1E29 17:18 Edinburgh-Newcastle/1A45 22:55 Newcastle-King's Cross; Thurs. 24: FP/1L44 16:03 King's Cross-York/1A34 20:19 York-King's Cross; Fri. 25: FP/1S66 20:15 King's Cross-Edinburgh to York; Sat. 26: 0A37 York-Scarborough/1A37 08:47 Bridlington-King's Cross from Scarborough/FP/1S60 20:00 King's Cross-Aberdeen to Edinburgh; Sun. 27: 1V93 11:25 Edinburgh-Plymouth to York/1S27 09:00 Plymouth-Edinburgh from York/1E43 20:35 Aberdeen-King's Cross from Edinburgh; Mon. 28: FP/1L43 14:03 King's Cross-York/1A31 18:14 York-King's Cross/FP; Tues. 29: 1L42 12:05 King's Cross-York/1A26 15:50 York-King's Cross/1S77 23:55 King's Cross-Edinburgh; Wed. 30: 1V93 09:50 Edinburgh-Plymouth to York/1S27 07:36 Plymouth-Edinburgh from York/1E39 22:25 Edinburgh-King's Cross

OCTOBER

Thurs. 1: FP/1L45 17:40 King's Cross-York/YK 'D' exam (Boiler condemned on 05/10/81) Until Tues. 6: YK 'eo' 'D' exam; Wed. 7: YK 'eo'/0B06 York-Peterborough/PB 'eo'/0B02 Peterborough-Finsbury Park/ FP 'eo'/1S70 22:15 King's Cross-Aberdeen to Edinburgh; Thurs. 8: 1V93 09:50 Edinburgh-Plymouth to York/1S27 07:36 Plymouth-Edinburgh from York/1E48 21:20 Aberdeen-

King's Cross from Edinburgh; Fri. 9: FP 'eo'/1L44 16:03 King's Cross-York/1A34 20:19 York-King's Cross; Sat. 10: 1S12 05:50 King's Cross-Aberdeen to Edinburgh/HA 'eo'; Sun. 11: 1V93 11:25 Edinburgh-Plymouth to York/1S27 11:25 Reading-Edinburgh from York/1E48 21:20 Aberdeen-King's Cross from Edinburgh; Mon. 12: FP 'eo' 'oe' (No.1 engine aerating)/1D08 19:40 King's Cross-Hull to Doncaster/0L01 Doncaster-York/ YK 'eo' 'oe' Until Sun. 18: YK 'eo' 'oe' - WITHDRAWN

D9019/9019/55019
Royal Highland Fusilier

JULY 1981
Wed. 1: 1S12 05:50 King's Cross-Aberdeen/1E26 16:30 Aberdeen-Leeds/1E24 22:50 Shrewsbury-York from Leeds; Thurs. 2: 1A08 08:07 York-King's Cross/FP/1L44 16:03 King's Cross-York/1A34 20:19 York-King's Cross; Fri. 3: 1S12 05:50 King's Cross-Aberdeen to Edinburgh/HA/1E29 17:18 Edinburgh-Newcastle/1A45 22:55 Newcastle-King's Cross; Sat. 4: FP/1L44 16:03 King's Cross-York/1A34 20:19 York-King's Cross; Sun. 5: FP/1L42 14:05 King's Cross-York/1A19 19:13 York-King's Cross/FP; Mon. 6: FP; Tues. 7: FP/1D08 19:40 King's Cross-Hull/0D01 23:35 Hull-Doncaster; Wed. 8: 0L01 Doncaster-York/YK/0B02 York-Finsbury Park/FP/1S72 22:30 King's Cross-Edinburgh; Thurs. 9: 1V93 09:50 Edinburgh-Plymouth to York/1S27 07:36 Plymouth-Edinburgh from York/1E35 20:25 Edinburgh-King's Cross; Fri. 10: FP/1B03 17:10 King's Cross-Peterborough/0B02 Peterborough-Finsbury Park/FP/1S60 20:00 King's Cross-Aberdeen to Newcastle; Sat. 11: 1A39 10:50 Newcastle-King's Cross/FP/1S60 20:00 King's Cross-Aberdeen to Edinburgh; Sun. 12: 1V93 11:25 Edinburgh-Plymouth to York/1S27 09:00 Plymouth-Edinburgh from York/1E43 20:35 Aberdeen-King's Cross from Edinburgh Mon. 13: FP/1S66 20:15 King's Cross-Edinburgh; Tues. 14: 1M04 07:18 Edinburgh-Carlisle/1S15 15:53 Carlisle-Edinburgh/1E39 22:25 Edinburgh-King's Cross; Wed. 15: 1L42 12:05 King's Cross-York/1A26 15:50 York-King's Cross/FP; Thurs. 16: 1N12 00:05 King's Cross-Newcastle/GD/0L01 08:08 Gateshead-York/YK 'B' exam; Fri. 17: 1A37 10:47 York-King's Cross/FP/1D08 19:40 King's Cross-Hull/1D26 23:40 Hull-Doncaster; Sat. 18: 1D62 03:55 Doncaster-Hull/1A13 09:36 Hull-King's Cross/FP; Sun. 19: 1N12 00:05 King's Cross-Newcastle/GD/1A40 21:28 Newcastle-King's Cross; Mon. 20: 5B26 05:24 King's Cross-Peterborough/1B26 07:23 Peterborough-King's Cross/FP/1L43 14:03 King's Cross-York/1A31 18:14 York-King's Cross; Tues. 21: 1N00 01:00 King's Cross-Newcastle/1S08 07:05 Newcastle-Edinburgh/1V93 09:50 Edinburgh-Plymouth to Newcastle/GD/0L01 Gateshead-York/YK; Wed. 22: YK/0D01 York-Doncaster; Thurs. 23: On DONCASTER WORKS "Unclassified repair" (No.1 engine, 448, replaced by 458) Until Fri. 31: DONCASTER WORKS

AUGUST
Sat. 1: DONCASTER WORKS Until Thurs. 6: Off DONCASTER WORKS; Fri. 7: DR/0B02 Doncaster-Finsbury Park/FP/1B.. 16:25 King's Cross-Peterborough/0B02 Peterborough-Finsbury Park/FP/1S60 20:00 King's Cross-Aberdeen to Newcastle; Sat. 8: 1S14 08:10 Newcastle-Edinburgh/HA/1E35 20:45 Edinburgh-King's Cross to Newcastle; Sun. 9: GD/1A40 21:28 Newcastle-King's Cross; Mon. 10: 5B26 05:24 King's Cross-Peterborough/1B26 07:23 Peterborough-King's Cross/FP/1N14 14:03 King's Cross-Newcastle/5N14 Newcastle-York/YK 'oe' Until Mon. 17: YK 'oe'/0D01 York-Doncaster/On DONCASTER WORKS "Unclassified repair" (No.1 engine, 458, replaced by 451) Until; Thurs. 20: Off DONCASTER WORKS; Fri. 21: DR/0B02 Doncaster-Finsbury Park/FP/1L45 17:40 King's Cross-York/YK; Sat. 22: 0N60 York-Filey/1N60 08:54 Filey-Newcastle

to Scarborough/1A37 08:47 Bridlington-King's Cross from Scarborough/FP/1S60 20:00 King's Cross-Aberdeen to Edinburgh; Sun. 23: HA/1E35 20:25 Edinburgh-King's Cross; Mon. 24: 1L42 12:05 King's Cross-York/1A26 15:50 York-King's Cross/1S79 23:20 King's Cross-Aberdeen to Edinburgh; Tues. 25: 1V93 09:50 Edinburgh-Plymouth to York/1S27 07:36 Plymouth-Edinburgh from York/1E40 19:25 Aberdeen-King's Cross from Edinburgh; Wed. 26: FP/1L43 14:03 King's Cross-York/1A31 18:14 York-King's Cross/FP; Thurs. 27: 1D01 08:30 King's Cross-Cleethorpes/1A21 13:20 Cleethorpes-King's Cross/ FP; Fri. 28: 1N12 00:05 King's Cross-Newcastle/1A60 Newcastle-King's Cross/1L45 17:40 King's Cross-York/YK; Sat. 29: YK/1A92 York-King's Cross/FP/1S70 22:15 King's Cross-Aberdeen to Edinburgh; Sun. 30: HA/1E42 23:15 Edinburgh-King's Cross; Mon. 31: 1L42 12:05 King's Cross-York/1A26 15:50 York-King's Cross/FP

SEPTEMBER

Tues. 1: 1S12 05:50 King's Cross-Aberdeen to Edinburgh/1A38 14:55 Aberdeen-Edinburgh; Aberdeen/1G20 18:23 Aberdeen-Edinburgh/1E48 21:20 Aberdeen-King's Cross from Edinburgh; Wed. 2: FP; Thurs. 3: 1N00 01:00 King's Cross-Newcastle/1S08 07:05 Newcastle-Edinburgh/1E10 09:10 Dundee-King's Cross from Edinburgh/1F50 King's Cross-Edinburgh; Fri. 4: 1V93 09:50 Edinburgh-Plymouth to York/YK; Sat. 5: YK; Sun. 6: 1A06 11:50 York-King's Cross/FP/1S70 22:15 King's Cross-Aberdeen to Edinburgh; Mon. 7:1M04 07:18 Edinburgh-Carlisle/1S15 15:53 Carlisle-Edinburgh/1E39 22:25 Edinburgh-King's Cross; Tues. 8: FP; Wed. 9: FP/1L43 14:03 King's Cross-York/1A31 18:14 York-King's Cross; Thurs. 10: 1N00 01:00 King's Cross-Newcastle/1S08 07:05 Newcastle-Edinburgh/HA/ 2G.. 17:15 North Berwick-Edinburgh from Craigentinny (assisting failed DMU)/1E35 20:25 Edinburgh-King's Cross; Fri. 11: 1L42 12:05 King's Cross-York/1A26 15:50 York-King's

Cross/1S77 23:55 King's Cross-Edinburgh; Sat. 12: 1V93 09:50 Edinburgh-Plymouth to York/1S27 07:30 Plymouth-Edinburgh from York/HA; Sun. 13: 1V93 11:25 Edinburgh-Plymouth to York/YK; Mon. 14: YK; Tues. 15: YK/1S27 07:30 Plymouth-Edinburgh from York/1E48 21:20 Aberdeen-King's Cross from Edinburgh; Wed. 16: FP/1L44 16:03 King's Cross-York/1A34 20:19 York-King's Cross; Thurs. 17: FP; Fri. 18: FP/1L45 17:40 King's Cross-York/YK; Sat. 19: 1A08 08:07 York-King's Cross/1L43 14:03 King's Cross-York/1A31 18:14 York-King's Cross/FP; Sun. 20: 1L41 10:05 King's Cross-York/1A10 15:50 York-King's Cross/1S79 23:20 King's Cross-Aberdeen to Edinburgh; Mon. 21: 1V93 09:50 Edinburgh-Plymouth to York/YK/1A31 18:14 York-King's Cross; Tues. 22: 1N00 01:00 King's Cross-Newcastle/1S08 07:05 Newcastle-Edinburgh/HA/ 1A38 14:55 Edinburgh-Aberdeen/1G20 18:23 Aberdeen-Edinburgh/1E48 21:20 Aberdeen-King's Cross from Edinburgh; Wed. 23: FP/1S66 20:15 King's Cross-Edinburgh to Newcastle; Thurs. 24: 1S14 08:10 Newcastle-Edinburgh/HA; Fri. 25: HA/1E39 22:25 Edinburgh-King's Cross Sat. 26: FP/1L43 14:03 King's Cross-York/1A31 18:14 York-King's Cross/1S77 23:55 King's Cross-Edinburgh to York; Sun. 27: YK/0B02 York-Finsbury Park/FP/1S70 22:15 King's Cross-Aberdeen to Edinburgh; Mon. 28: 1M04 07:18 Edinburgh-Carlisle/1S15 15:53 Carlisle-Edinburgh/1E39 22:25 Edinburgh-King's Cross; Tues. 29: FP; Wed. 30: 1N12 00:05 King's Cross-Newcastle/1S14 08:10 Newcastle-Edinburgh/HA/ 1E29 17:18 Edinburgh-Newcastle/1A45 22:55 Newcastle-King's Cross to York (55 017 forward)

OCTOBER

Thurs. 1: YK 'C' exam; Fri. 2: YK 'C' exam Sat. 3: YK/0J01 York-Barrow Hill/BH "Open Day exhibit"; Sun. 4: BH "Open Day exhibit"; Mon. 5: BH/0L01 Barrow Hill-York/YK; Tues. 6: YK/0D01 York-Doncaster; Wed. 7: DCR WORKS "Unclassified repair" (No.2 eng. 428, replaced by 407) Until Sat. 31: DCR WORKS

NOVEMBER

Sun. 1: DONCASTER WORKS Until Mon. 9: Off DONCASTER WORKS; Tues. 10: DR/0B06 Doncaster-Peterborough to Ponton/6C30 13:55 Tyneside Central Freight Depot-Dagenham Dock from Ponton to Peterborough (assisting)/PB/ 1S70 22:15 King's Cross-Aberdeen from Peterborough (55 017 off) to Edinburgh; Wed. 11: 1M04 07:18 Edinburgh-Carlisle/1S15 15:53 Carlisle-Edinburgh to Newcastle/ GD; Thurs. 12: GD/0L01 Gateshead-York/YK; Fri. 13: YK/0B06 York-Peterborough/0B02 Peterborough-Finsbury Park/FP; Sat. 14: 1S12 05:50 King's Cross-Aberdeen to York (assisted by 31 175 from Peterborough)/YK; Sun. 15: YK; Mon. 16: YK; Tues. 17: 1A08 08:07 York-King's Cross/FP/1L44 16:03 King's Cross-York/1A34 20:19 York-King's Cross; Wed. 18: 1L41 09:40 King's Cross-York/1A22 14:15 York-King's Cross/1D08 19:40 King's Cross-Hull/5L04 23:30 Hull-York/1E42 23:15 Edinburgh-King's Cross from York; Thurs. 19: FP/1L43 14:03 King's Cross-York/1A31 18:14 York-King's Cross/1S77 23:55 King's Cross-Edinburgh; Fri. 20: HA/1E35 20:25 Edinburgh-King's Cross; Sat. 21: FP; Sun. 22: FP/1S70 22:15 King's Cross-Aberdeen to Edinburgh; Mon. 23: 1M04 07:18 Edinburgh-Carlisle/1S15 15:53 Carlisle-Edinburgh/1E43 20:35 Aberdeen-King's Cross from Edinburgh; Tues. 24: FP/1S60 20:00 King's Cross-Aberdeen to Edinburgh;Wed. 25: HA/1E35 20:25 Edinburgh-King's Cross; Thurs. 26: FP/1L43 14:03 King's Cross-York/1A31 18:14 York-King's Cross/FP; Fri. 27: FP/1N14 14:03 King's Cross-Newcastle/GD/1S60 20:00 King's Cross-Aberdeen from Newcastle to Edinburgh; Sat. 28: 1M04 07:18 Edinburgh-Carlisle/1S15 15:53 Carlisle-Edinburgh/1E43 20:05 Aberdeen-King's Cross from Edinburgh; Sun. 29: FP/1L42 14:05 King's Cross-York/1A19 19:13 York-King's Cross Mon. 30: 1N00 01:00 King's Cross-Newcastle/1S08 07:05 Newcastle-Edinburgh/HA/ 0C00 Haymarket-Carstairs/0G99 Carstairs-Haymarket (towing Class 47)/HA/ 1E35 20:25 Edinburgh-King's Cross

DECEMBER

Tues. 1: FP Until Fri. 4: FP; Sat. 5: 1N12 00:05 King's Cross-Newcastle/GD/1S12 05:50 King's Cross-Aberdeen from Newcastle (55 007 off) to Edinburgh/HA/1E35 20:45 Edinburgh-King's Cross; Sun. 6: FP/1S72 22:40 King's Cross-Edinburgh; Mon. 7: HA/1E40 19:25 Aberdeen-King's Cross from Edinburgh; Tues. 8: FP/1S66 20:15 King's Cross-Edinburgh; Wed. 9: 1C86 09:07 Edinburgh-Carstairs (failed at Carstairs)/0G99 Carstairs-Haymarket/HA; Thurs. 10: 1C91 10:25 Edinburgh-Carstairs/1G44 11:23 Carstairs-Edinburgh/1A38 14:55 Edinburgh-Aberdeen/1G20 18:23 Aberdeen-Edinburgh/1E39 22:25 Edinburgh-King's Cross (failed at Scremerston - assisted to Newcastle by 37 149); Fri. 11: GD/1A40 21:00 Newcastle-King's Cross; Sat. 12: FP/1S60 20:00 King's Cross-Aberdeen to Peterborough (failed - No.1 engine oil radiator leaking due to a burst element)/PB 'oe'; Sun. 13: PB 'oe'; Mon. 14: PB 'oe'; Tues. 15: 1B26 07:23 Peterborough-King's Cross/FP 'oe'; Wed. 16: 1N12 00:05 King's Cross-Newcastle (failed at Aycliffe - loss of air - assisted to Newcastle by 45 076)/GD 'oe'/1A40 21:00 Newcastle-King's Cross to Doncaster (failed - defective compressor governor); Thurs. 17: DR 'oe'/0B01 Doncaster-King's Cross/KX 'oe'; Fri. 18: KX 'oe'; Sat. 19: KX 'oe'; Sun. 20: FP 'oe' Mon. 21: FP 'oe'; Tues. 22: FP 'oe'/1L22 23:00 King's Cross-Bradford to Leeds; Wed. 23: HO 'oe'/0D01 Holbeck-Doncaster/DR 'oe' Thurs. 24: DR 'oe'/0L01 Doncaster-York/YK 'oe'/1A31 18:14 York-King's Cross to Doncaster (failed)/DR 'oe'/Doncaster-Doncaster Works (towing 55 010)/DR 'oe' Until Tues. 29: DR 'oe'; Wed. 30: 0B00 Doncaster-Grantham (with 46 009)/0B02 Grantham-Finsbury Park/FP 'oe'/1L43 14:03

Last Months of the Deltics — 1981 — D9019

King's Cross-York/0B02 York-Finsbury Park/FP 'oe'; Thurs. 31: 1N12 00:05 King's Cross-Newcastle/1S14 08:10 Newcastle-Edinburgh/HA 'oe'/1E26 16:30 Aberdeen-York from Edinburgh/YK 'oe' - WITHDRAWN

This section is continued on page 151...

Below (top): Deltic Class 55, 55004 Queen's Own Highlander reposed on Haymarket shed on August 18, 1976. 55004 is pictured without her regimental crest in blue livery but turn to page 150 for a shot of the locomotive carrying the crest in two-tone green.

A Deltic in green livery with BR double arrows under the numbers and yellow front end! D9010 The King's Own Scottish Borderer sports the unusual combination in this undated view from Phil Caley's collection.

6 Deltic Pictorial

Outshopped from Doncaster Works after overhaul, Class 55, 55007 Pinza passes through York on the return to the Works with an acceptance trial run on November 20, 1976. The loco had been in Doncaster Works since November 8th, and was eventually released back into traffic two days after this picture was taken. During her time in the works for a light classified overhaul, 55007 underwent the following attention: No.1 engine, 419 and No.2 engine, 442, were given light repairs and refitted. No.1 bogie, 9000-47 was replaced by 9000-37 and No.2 bogie, 9000-22, replaced by 9000-38. The boiler, 1494/J2950, was given an unclassified repair. The body was given a light repair and the locomotive weighed 104t 16cwt. Picture: L.P. Gater.

136 DELTIC PICTORIAL

An East Coast Main Line without wires...a marvellous memory. Here Class 55, 55006 The Fife & Forfar Yeomanry is captured at the end of a down express at Doncaster on July 25, 1976. Picture: L.P. Gater

DELTIC PICTORIAL 137

Careful...a superb, but undated shot, of a still un-named D9019 undergoing an engine change at Doncaster Works. D9019 was eventually named Royal Highland Fusilier, but as official records show, the locomotive should have been named 'Cameron Highlander'. Picture courtesy: NRM 162/97

Class 55, 55011 The Royal Northumberland Fusiliers undergoing overhaul inside the paint shop at Doncaster Works on May 7, 1978. Thanks to official works records, the locomotive was nearing the end of her final Intermediate overhaul. 55011 had entered the works on January 9th and was finally released on May 22. Work carried out included: No.1 engine, 433, replaced by 416. No.2 engine, 445, replaced by 458, due for General repair. No.1 bogie, 9000-24, replaced by 9000-7. No.2 bogie, 9000-48, replaced by 9000-8. Boiler, 1491/J2947, replaced by 1489/J2945. Route indicator panels were plated over and the loco weighed at 105t 3cwt. Picture: L.P. Gater.

DELTIC PICTORIAL 139

A new look for the Deltics...the first of the class to have the route indicators plated over. Class 55, 55016 Gordon Highlander in the process of being outshopped at Doncaster Works on April 11, 1976. The locomotive had lost its regimental crests prior to entering works on July 5, 1975. However, when she finally emerged on April 27 the following year, they had been replaced as can be seen in this view. 55016 had been in the works for a Heavy General repair, a first for the class, and work done included: No.1 engine, 539, replaced by 421. No.2 engine, 538, replaced by 458. No.1 bogie, 9000-1, replaced by 9000-7. No.2 bogie, 9000-2, replaced by 9000-8. Boiler, 1494/J2950, replaced by 5095/J3246. The regimental crests were replaced and route indicator panels plated over. Picture: L.P. Gater.

Deltic Class 55, 55022 Royal Scots Grey hides in the paint shop at Doncaster Works on March 27, 1977. The locomotive had been on works since March 14 and was eventually released three days after this picture was taken by Len Gater. Work carried out included: No.1 engine, 429, replaced by 420, due to high spectrographic analysis. No.2 engine, 416, replaced by 407, due to fuel dilution problems. No.1 bogie, 9000-31, replaced by 9000-3. No.2 bogie, 9000-32, replaced by 9000-4. Boiler, 5096/J3247, was given an unclassified repair.

DELTIC PICTORIAL **141**

Rough riding had forced 55012 Crepello into Doncaster Works on July 23, 1977. As a result of a five-day visit, several dampers were reported defective and removed and sent for testing. Both bogies were rectified. The locomotive was weighed at 103t 13cwt and released back into traffic on July 28. This picture of the front end styles of Crepello and Class 50, 50010, was taken by Len Gater on July 24.

How the Deltics used to look. An immaculate 9020 Nimbus powers the up "Flying Scotsman" (10.00 from Edinburgh under clear signals at Hornsey on June 16. 1972. The locomotive sports numbers behind cab doors and BR emblems on cabsides, as dictated under BR's corporate image styling for diesels painted blue. 9020 had been released from Doncaster after an unclassified repair lasting two days on June 8th. Both boiler water tanks were fractured and No.1 exhaust drum tank was badly split along with 'B' bank exhaust inlet bellows . No.1 exhaust drum was replaced and all other repairs were carried out. Picture: G. Gillham

DELTIC PICTORIAL 143

Class 55, 55003 Meld awaits departure from York with the 09.00 King's Cross to Newcastle service on January 16, 1978. Picture: L. P. Gater.

The two-tone green livery suited the Deltics in the early years although the revelations regarding Flame Red and Coronation Blue in this book will doubtless open up the debate once again. Here an un-named D9016 (Gordon Highlander) resides at Haymarket depot in Scotland on August 3, 1963. Picture: A. G. Ellis.

Another un-named Deltic, D9014 (The Duke of Wellington's Regiment) rests at Haymarket on July 18, 1963. The locomotive had been released off Doncaster Works two days earlier after having No.1 bogie, 1009, replaced by 1023. No.2 bogie, 1010 was replaced by 1024. Picture: A. G. Ellis.

DELTIC PICTORIAL   **145**

Doncaster Plant yard on July 25, 1976 held 55007 Pinza (nearest camera) and 55010 The King's Own Scottish Borderer. Picture: L. P. Gater.

There are not many pictures which show D9013 The Black Watch carrying her regimental crest...but here is one such photograph. D9013 has gained the yellow front end panel in this shot taken on April 28, 1963 at Haymarket depot in Scotland. The loco had been named at Dundee on January 16. Picture A. G. Ellis.

An un-named D9010 (The King's Own Scottish Borderer) heads the up "Flying Scotsman" at Grantshouse on August 18, 1964. The 'Winged Thistle' was used as the headboard for this train. Originally, Deltic designer Ted Wilkes included a recessed headboard space on the front end. It was ditched by EE Co. Picture: A. G. Ellis.

D9015 Tulyar poses in immaculate condition at London's King's Cross station on August 2, 1962. The locomotive had been in traffic for less than a year at this point in her career. Picture: A. G. Ellis.

55007 Pinza stretches its legs at Gamston, south of Retford, with the 09.04 King's Cross to Leeds working on March 24, 1979. Picture: L.P. Gater.

55012 Crepello is still in immaculate condition externally some two months after her final intermediate overhaul at Doncaster Works in April 1977. During a stay of just over four months, Doncaster carried out the following work on the locomotive: No.1 engine, 455, replaced by 416. No.2 engine, 451, replaced by 538. No.1 bogie, 9000-29 and No. 2 bogie 9000-10, were given standard repairs. Boiler, 5087/J3238, was handed a standard repair. Experiment DL/543 — "Electrically operated windscreen washer pump" — was fitted and the body was given an Intermediate repair. The loco's route indicators were plated over. The loco weighed 104t 11cwt and is captured with the 16.00 Edinburgh-King's Cross at York on June 8, 1977. Picture: J. Davenport Collection.

Immaculate Class 55, 55003 Meld approaches Retford with the outward SLOA "Northumbrian Limited" railtour on April 7, 1979. This was the locomotive's first working with white-painted cab window surrounds courtesy of Finsbury Park depot. Picture: L. P. Gater.

55015 Tulyar ticks over noisily at King's Cross on the misty evening of January 18, 1978, shortly before departing with the 18.04 to Bradford. Picture. G. Gillham

55005 The Prince Of Wales's Own Regiment of Yorkshire runs light engine at King's Cross on June 25, 1974. Picture: C. L. Caddy

150   DELTIC PICTORIAL

A fine shot of D9004 Queens Own Highlander complete with regimental crest on Haymarket shed in Scotland on August 16, 1964. The crests themselves did not always remain with the nameplates and are now collector's items in themselves. Picture: A. G. Ellis.

55012 Crepello leaves King's Cross with a typical burst of exhaust from her Napier engines. The locomotive was pictured by Colin Caddy on June 27, 1976.

Continued from page 134...

D9021/9021/55021
Argyll & Sutherland Highlander

JULY 1981

Wed. 1:1V93 09:50 Edinburgh-Plymouth to York/1S27 07:36 Plymouth-Edinburgh from York/1E40 19:25 Aberdeen-King's Cross from Edinburgh; Thurs. 2: FP/1L43 14:03 King's Cross-York/1A31 18:14 York-King's Cross/FP; Fri. 3: FP/1L42 12:05 King's Cross-York/1A26 15:50 York-King's Cross/FP; Sat. 4: 1N00 01:00 King's Cross-Newcastle/1S08 07:05 Newcastle-Edinburgh/1E78 11:50 Edinburgh-King's Cross; Sun. 5: 1N02 08:30 King's Cross-Newcastle/1A21 14:57 Newcastle-King's Cross/FP; Mon. 6: 1S76 09:40 King's Cross-Edinburgh to York/YK 'B' exam Until Fri. 10: YK 'B' exam/0C01 York-Stratford (with 56 023)/SF; Sat. 11: SF "Open Day exhibit"; Sun. 12:SF/0B02 Stratford-Finsbury Park/FP; Mon. 13: FP/0L01 Finsbury Park-York/YK/0D01 York-Doncaster/On DONCASTER WORKS "Unclassified repair" (No.1 engine, 437, replaced by 425); Tues. 14: DONCASTER WORKS; Wed. 15: Off DONCASTER WORKS; Thurs. 16: DR/0B02 Doncaster-Finsbury Park/FP; Fri. 17: 1N12 00:05 King's Cross-Newcastle/GD/0N20 Gateshead-Tweedmouth/ 9N20 Tweedmouth-Gateshead (towing 03 107)/GD; Sat. 18: GD 'oe'/0L01 Gateshead-York/YK 'oe' Until Tues. 21: YK/1E43 20:35 Aberdeen-King's Cross from York (55 007 off); Wed. 22: 1L42 12:05 King's Cross-York/1A26 15:50 York-King's Cross/1S79 23:20 King's Cross-Aberdeen to Edinburgh; Thurs. 23: 1V93 09:50 Edinburgh-Plymouth to York/1S27 07:36 Plymouth-Edinburgh from York/1E42 23:15 Edinburgh-King's Cross; Fri. 24: 1L42 12:05 King's Cross-York/1A26 15:50 York-King's Cross/FP; Sat. 25: 1N12 00:05 King's Cross-Newcastle/GD/1A39 10:50 Newcastle-King's Cross/ 1L45 18:05 King's Cross-York/YK; Sun. 26: YK; Mon. 27: 1A08 08:07 York-King's Cross/1L43 14:03 King's Cross-York/1A31 18:14 York-King's Cross; Tues. 28: 1N00 01:00 King's Cross-Newcastle/1S08 07:05 Newcastle-Edinburgh/HA/ 1A38 14:55 Edinburgh-Aberdeen/1G20 18:23 Aberdeen-Edinburgh/1E39 22:25 Edinburgh-King's Cross; Wed. 29: FP/1L43 14:03 King's Cross-York/1A31 18:14 York-King's Cross; Thurs. 30: 1N00 01:00 King's Cross-Newcastle/1S08 07:05 Newcastle-Edinburgh/HA/ 1S76 09:40 King's Cross-Dundee from Edinburgh/5Z21 Dundee-Craigentinny/HA; Fri. 31: 5E10 06:40 Craigentinny-Dundee/1E10 09:10 Dundee-King's Cross/1S60 20:00 King's Cross-Aberdeen to Edinburgh

AUGUST

Sat. 1: 1C91 10:25 Edinburgh-Carstairs/1G60 14:06 Carstairs-Edinburgh/HA; Sun. 2: 1Z19 09:15 Edinburgh-Oban/1Z19 15:00 Oban-Edinburgh/1E39 22:30 Edinburgh-King's Cross; Mon. 3: FP/0L01 Finsbury Park-York/YK 'B' exam Until Fri. 7: YK 'B' exam/1A31 18:14 York-King's Cross; Sat. 8: 1N00 01:00 King's Cross-Newcastle/1S08 07:05 Newcastle-Edinburgh/1E78 11:50 Edinburgh-King's Cross to Newcastle/GD/1A40 21:00 Newcastle-King's Cross; Sun. 9: 1G06 King's Cross-Scarborough to York (55 017 forward)/YK/1A21 14:57 Newcastle-King's Cross from York (55 004 off)/FP/1S79 23:20 King's Cross-Aberdeen to Edinburgh; Mon. 10: 1V93 09:50 Edinburgh-Plymouth to York/1S27 07:36 Plymouth-Edinburgh from York/1E39 22:25 Edinburgh-King's Cross; Tues. 11: 1L42 12:05 King's Cross-York/1A26 15:50 York-King's Cross/1S70 22:15 King's Cross-Aberdeen to Newcastle; Wed. 12: GD/1S76 09:40 King's Cross-Edinburgh from Newcastle (55 022 off)/HA/ 1E39 22:25 Edinburgh-King's Cross; Thurs. 13: 1L42 12:05 King's Cross-York/1A26 15:50 York-King's Cross/1S77 23:55 King's Cross-Edinburgh; Fri. 14: 1V93 09:50 Edinburgh-Plymouth to York/1S27 07:36

Plymouth-Edinburgh from York/1E39 22:25 Edinburgh-King's Cross; Sat. 15: FP; Sun. 16: FP/1L43 16:05 King's Cross-York/YK; Mon. 17: YK/1A34 20:19 York-King's Cross; Tues. 18: 1S12 05:50 King's Cross-Aberdeen to Edinburgh/HA/1E35 20:25 Edinburgh-King's Cross; Wed. 19: 1S76 09:40 King's Cross-Edinburgh/HA/1E39 22:25 Edinburgh-King's Cross; Thurs. 20: 1L42 12:05 King's Cross-York/1A26 15:50 York-King's Cross/1S77 23:55 King's Cross-Edinburgh; Fri. 21: 1V93 09:50 Edinburgh-Plymouth to York/1S27 07:36 Plymouth-Edinburgh from York/HA; Sat. 22: HA; Sun. 23: 1Z19 09:15 Edinburgh-Oban/1Z19 15:00 Oban-Edinburgh/1E40 19:25 Aberdeen-King's Cross from Edinburgh; Mon. 24: FP/1L44 16:03 King's Cross-York/1A34 20:19 York-King's Cross; Tues. 25: 1S76 09:40 King's Cross-Edinburgh/HA/1E35 20:25 Edinburgh-King's Cross; Wed. 26: 1S76 09:40 King's Cross-Edinburgh/HA/1E26 16:30 Aberdeen-Leeds from Edinburgh to York; Thurs. 27: YK 'D' exam; Fri. 28: YK 'D' exam; Sat. 29: YK 'D' exam/0B02 York-Finsbury Park/FP/1S60 20:00 King's Cross-Aberdeen to Edinburgh; Sun. 30: HA/1E48 21:20 Aberdeen-King's Cross from Edinburgh; Mon. 31: FP/1L43 14:03 King's Cross-York/1A31 18:14 York-King's Cross/FP

SEPTEMBER

Tues. 1: 1N00 01:00 King's Cross-Newcastle/1S08 07:05 Newcastle-Edinburgh/HA/ 1E29 17:18 Edinburgh-Newcastle/GD/1S66 20:15 King's Cross-Edinburgh from Newcastle; Wed. 2: 1V93 09:50 Edinburgh-Plymouth to York/1S27 07:36 Plymouth-Edinburgh from York/1E42 23:15 Edinburgh-King's Cross; Thurs. 3: 1L42 12:05 King's Cross-York/1A26 15:50 York-King's Cross/1S70 22:15 King's Cross-Aberdeen to Edinburgh; Fri. 4: 1C83 08:08 Edinburgh-Carstairs/1S37 07:37 Liverpool-Edinburgh from Carstairs/HA/1E39 22:25 Edinburgh-King's Cross; Sat. 5: FP/1L43 14:03 King's Cross-York/1A31 18:14 York-King's Cross/FP; Sun. 6: 1L41 10:05 King's Cross-York/1A10 15:50 York-King's Cross/FP; Mon. 7: 1S76 09:40 King's Cross-Dundee/5Z21 Dundee-Craigentinny/HA/1E42 23:15 Edinburgh-King's Cross; Tues. 8: 1L42 12:05 King's Cross-York/1A26 15:50 York-King's Cross/1S70 22:15 King's Cross-Aberdeen to Edinburgh; Wed. 9: 1M04 07:18 Edinburgh-Carlisle/1S15 15:53 Carlisle-Edinburgh/1E40 19:25 Aberdeen-King's Cross from Edinburgh; Thurs. 10: 1L42 12:05 King's Cross-York/1A26 15:50 York-King's Cross/1S79 23:20 King's Cross-Aberdeen to Edinburgh; Fri. 11: 1V93 09:50 Edinburgh-Plymouth to York/1S27 07:36 Plymouth-Edinburgh from York/1E39 22:25 Edinburgh-King's Cross; Sat. 12: FP/1L45 18:05 King's Cross-York/YK 'B' exam; Sun. 13: YK 'B' exam; Mon. 14: YK 'B' exam; Tues. 15: 5A37 York-Scarborough/1A37 09:54 Scarborough-King's Cross/FP/1D08 19:40 King's Cross-Hull/0D01 23:35 Hull-Doncaster; Wed. 16: 1D62 03:55 Doncaster-Hull/1A13 09:36 Hull-King's Cross/FP/1L45 17:40 King's Cross-York/YK; Thurs. 17: 1A08 08:07 York-King's Cross/FP/1L44 16:03 King's Cross-York/1A34 20:19 York-King's Cross; Fri. 18: 1D01 08:30 King's Cross-Cleethorpes/1A21 13:20 Cleethorpes-King's Cross/ 1D08 19:40 King's Cross-Hull/0D01 23:35 Hull-Doncaster; Sat. 19: 1D62 03:55 Doncaster-Hull/1A13 09:36 Hull-King's Cross/1L44 16:03 King's Cross-York/1A34 20:19 York-King's Cross; Sun. 20: 1N02 08:30 King's Cross-Newcastle/GD/1N03 21:30 Newcastle-Darlington/ 1A45 22:55 Newcastle-King's Cross from Darlington; Mon. 21: 1L41 09:40 King's Cross-York/YK/0B02 York-Finsbury Park/FP/1S70 22:15 King's Cross-Aberdeen to Edinburgh; Tues. 22: 1V93 09:50 Edinburgh-Plymouth to York/1S27 07:36 Plymouth-Edinburgh from York/1E39 22:25 Edinburgh-King's Cross; Wed. 23: FP/1L44 16:03 King's Cross-York/1A34 20:19 York-King's Cross; Thurs. 24: 1N00 01:00 King's Cross-Newcastle to York/YK; Fri. 25: 1A08 08:07 York-King's Cross/FP/1B04 16:06 King's Cross-Peterborough/ 5B04 Peterborough-Ferme

Park/FP/1S60 20:00 King's Cross-Aberdeen to Newcastle/1E43 20:35 Aberdeen-King's Cross from Newcastle; Sat. 26: FP/1L44 16:03 King's Cross-York/1A34 20:19 York-King's Cross; Sun. 27: 1L41 10:05 King's Cross-York/1A10 15:50 York-King's Cross/1S72 22:40 King's Cross-Edinburgh to York; Mon. 28: YK/1A22 14:15 York-King's Cross to Selby/0L01 Selby-York/YK; Tues. 29: YK 'B' exam; Wed. 30: 1M62 08:50 York-Liverpool/1E99 13:05 Liverpool-York/YK/0B02 York-Finsbury Park/FP

OCTOBER

Thurs. 1: 1N12 00:05 King's Cross-Newcastle/1S14 08:10 Newcastle-Edinburgh/HA 'oe'/1E35 20:25 Edinburgh-King's Cross; Fri. 2: 1D01 08:30 King's Cross-Cleethorpes/1A21 13:20 Cleethorpes-King's Cross/ FP 'oc'/1L22 23:00 King's Cross-Bradford; Sat. 3: 0L50 Bradford-Holbeck/HO 'oe'/1A70 08:30 Leeds-King's Cross/FP 'oe'/1L22 23:00 King's Cross-Bradford to Leeds; Sun. 4: HO 'oe'/0L01 Holbeck-York/YK 'oe'; Mon. 5: YK 'oe'/0D01 York-Doncaster/On DONCASTER WORKS "Unclassified repair" (No.1 engine, 425, replaced by 439) Until Thurs. 15: Off DONCASTER WORKS; Fri. 16: 0B06 Doncaster-Peterborough/0B02 Peterborough-Finsbury Park/FP/1D08 19:40 King's Cross-Hull/5L04 23:30 Hull-York; Sat. 17: YK/1Z42 Plymouth-Scarborough from York "Minsterman" Rail tour/1Z42 Scarborough-Plymouth to York "Minsterman" Rail tour/YK; Sun. 18: YK/0B02 York-Finsbury Park/FP/1S79 23:20 King's Cross-Aberdeen to Edinburgh; Mon. 19: HA/1E39 22:25 Edinburgh-King's Cross; Tues. 20: FP/1S70 22:15 King's Cross-Aberdeen to Edinburgh; Wed. 21: 1M04 07:18 Edinburgh-Carlisle/1S15 15:53 Carlisle-Edinburgh/1E39 22:25 Edinburgh-King's Cross; Thurs. 22: FP/1S70 22:15 King's Cross-Aberdeen to Edinburgh; Fri. 23: 1V93 09:50 Edinburgh-Plymouth to York/1S27 07:36 Plymouth-Edinburgh from York/1E35 20:25 Edinburgh-

King's Cross; Sat. 24: 1Z30 08:45 King's Cross-Blackpool to Leeds/0D01 Leeds-Doncaster/DR/ 9Z11 21:35 Crofton-Gascoigne Wood to Doncaster/1Z30 Blackpool-King's Cross from Doncaster; Sun. 25: FP/1S77 23:55 King's Cross-Edinburgh; Mon. 26: HA/1E29 17:18 Edinburgh-Newcastle/1A45 22:55 Newcastle-King's Cross; Tues. 27: FP/1L43 14:03 King's Cross-York/YK/1M41 22:08 York-Shrewsbury to Stockport/1E24 22:50 Shrewsbury-York from Stockport; Wed. 28: YK/1A26 15:50 York-King's Cross/FP; Thurs. 29: 1N12 00:05 King's Cross Newcastle/GD/0L01 Gateshead-York/YK/1A26 15:50 York-King's Cross/1S70 22:15 King's Cross-Aberdeen to Edinburgh; Fri. 30: 1V93 09:50 Edinburgh-Plymouth to York/1S27 07:36 Plymouth-Edinburgh from York/1E42 23:15 Edinburgh-King's Cross; Sat. 31: FP

NOVEMBER

Sun. 1: FP/1S70 22:15 King's Cross-Aberdeen to Edinburgh; Mon. 2:1M04 07:18 Edinburgh-Carlisle/1S15 15:53 Carlisle-Edinburgh/1E39 22:25 Edinburgh-King's Cross to Newcastle; Tues. 3: GD/1A45 22:55 Newcastle-King's Cross; Wed. 4: FP; Thurs. 5: 1N00 01:00 King's Cross-Newcastle/1S08 07:05 Newcastle-Edinburgh/HA/ 1E35 20:25 Edinburgh-King's Cross; Fri. 6: FP/1N14 14:03 King's Cross-Newcastle to York/1A31 18:14 York-King's Cross/1S77 23:55 King's Cross-Edinburgh; Sat. 7: HA/1E29 17:18 Edinburgh-Newcastle/GD; Sun. 8: GD/0L01 Gateshead-York/YK/1A19 19:13 York-King's Cross; Mon. 9: 1N00 01:00 King's Cross-Newcastle/1S08 07:05 Newcastle-Edinburgh/HA/ 1E29 17:18 Edinburgh-Newcastle/1A45 22:55 Newcastle-King's Cross; Tues. 10: FP 'oe'/1L44 16:03 King's Cross-York/1A34 20:19 York-King's Cross; Wed. 11: 1S12 05:50 King's Cross-Aberdeen to Newcastle/0L01 Newcastle-York/YK/ 1A22 14:15 York-King's Cross/FP/1S77 23:55 King's Cross-Edinburgh; Thurs. 12: HA/1S12 05:50 King's Cross-Aberdeen from

154 LAST MONTHS OF THE DELTICS — 1981 — D9021

Edinburgh/1E26 16:30 Aberdeen-York; Fri. 13: YK 'C' exam; Sat. 14: YK 'C' exam/1A26 15:50 York-King's Cross/FP; Sun. 15: 1L41 10:05 King's Cross-York/YK; Mon. 16: 1A08 08:07 York-King's Cross/1L43 14:03 King's Cross-York/1A31 18:14 York-King's Cross/1S77 23:55 King's Cross-Edinburgh; Tues. 17: HA/1E35 20:25 Edinburgh-King's Cross; Wed. 18: FP/1L43 14:03 King's Cross-York/1A31 18:14 York-King's Cross; Thurs. 19: 1N00 01:00 King's Cross-Newcastle/1S08 07:05 Newcastle-Edinburgh/HA/ 1E29 17:18 Edinburgh-Newcastle/1A45 22:55 Newcastle-King's Cross; Fri. 20: FP/1L44 16:03 King's Cross-York/1A34 20:19 York-King's Cross; Sat. 21: 1N00 01:00 King's Cross-Newcastle/1S08 07:05 Newcastle-Edinburgh/HA/ 1F11 12:15 Edinburgh-Newcastle/5F11 Newcastle-Craigentinny/1E35 20:45 Edinburgh-King's Cross; Sun. 22: FP/1S77 23:55 King's Cross-Edinburgh; Mon. 23: 1F55 Edinburgh-Glasgow Central/0G99 Glasgow Central-Haymarket/HA/ 1E39 22:25 Edinburgh-King's Cross; Tues. 24: 1L41 09:40 King's Cross-York/1A22 14:15 York-King's Cross/1D08 19:40 King's Cross-Hull/5L04 23:30 Hull-York; Wed. 25: YK/0Z00 York-Thirsk/0Z00 Thirsk-York/YK/1A26 15:50 York-King's Cross/ 1S79 23:20 King's Cross-Aberdeen to Edinburgh; Thurs. 26: HA/1E29 17:18 Edinburgh-Newcastle/1A45 22:55 Newcastle-King's Cross; Fri. 27: FP/1D08 19:40 King's Cross-Hull/5L04 23:30 Hull-York; Sat. 28: YK 'B' exam; Sun. 29: YK 'B' exam/1A10 15:50 York-King's Cross (on fire at King's Cross)/FP; Mon. 30: FP

DECEMBER

Tues. 1: FP; Wed. 2: FP 'oe'; Thurs. 3: 1N12 00:05 King's Cross-Newcastle/0L01 Newcastle-York/YK 'oe'; Fri. 4: YK/1A34 20:19 York-King's Cross; Sat. 5: FP/1L43 14:03 King's Cross-York/YK; Sun. 6: YK; Mon. 7: 1A08 08:07 York-King's Cross/FP/1L44 16:03 King's Cross-York/1A34 20:19 York-King's Cross; Tues. 8: 0B05 Finsbury Park-Peterborough/1B18 07:50

Peterborough-King's Cross/ FP/1S60 20:00 King's Cross-Aberdeen to York (failed - No.2 engine aerating); Wed. 9: YK/0Z00 York-Thirsk/0Z00 Thirsk-York/YK 'oe' Thurs. 10: YK 'oe'/0C01 York-Stratford (towed)/SF 'oe'/0B02 Stratford-Finsbury Park/FP 'oe'/0L01 Finsbury Park-York/YK 'oe' Until Mon. 14: YK 'oe'; Tues. 15: YK 'oe'/0B06 York-Peterborough/0B01 Peterborough-King's Cross/1L22 23:00 King's Cross-Bradford; Wed. 16: 0L50 Bradford-Holbeck/HO 'oe'/0B02 Holbeck-Finsbury Park/FP 'oe'/1L22 23:00 King's Cross-Bradford; Thurs. 17: 0L50 Bradford-Holbeck/HO 'oe'/1A41 21:20 Bradford-King's Cross from Leeds (failed at Wakefield - exhaust manifold defect - assisted to Doncaster by 25 083)/DR 'oe'/1E35 20:25 Edinburgh-King's Cross from Doncaster (55 009 off); Fri. 18: FP 'oe' Until Wed. 23: FP 'oe'; Thurs. 24: 1N12 00:05 King's Cross-Newcastle/GD 'oe'; Fri. 25: GD 'oe'; Sat. 26: GD 'oe'; Sun. 27: 1F50 00:50 Newcastle-York/YK 'oe'/0N20 York-Gateshead/GD 'oe'/1S60 20:00 King's Cross-Aberdeen from Newcastle to Edinburgh; Mon. 28: HA 'oe'/1E52 09:10 Dundee-King's Cross from Edinburgh/FP 'oe'; Tues. 29: 1N00 01:00 King's Cross-Newcastle/1S08 07:05 Newcastle-Edinburgh/1E52 09:10 Dundee-King's Cross from Edinburgh/FP 'oe'; Wed. 30: 1N12 00:05 King's Cross-Newcastle/1S14 08:10 Newcastle-Edinburgh/HA 'oe'/1E35 20:25 Edinburgh-King's Cross; Thurs. 31: 1L41 09:40 King's Cross-York/YK 'oe' - WITHDRAWN

7 Deltic Highlights

D9000/9000/55022

DECEMBER 1960
Fri. 2: At Vulcan Foundry - First test. Four-hour continuous full load test
FEBRUARY 1961
Tues. 28: 'Light' Vulcan Foundry-Doncaster (suffers minor collision damage at Doncaster - "Acceptance trials"/Enters traffic allocated to 64B Haymarket
MARCH
Fri. 10: 0D01 Finsbury Park-Doncaster (testing of "flashing light" in Hadley Wood area)
Wed. 15th Doncaster-New Southgate 'Test train'/New Southgate-Doncaster 'Test train'
Wed. 22nd Doncaster-Haymarket "Light" (for crew training - based at Leith due to Haymarket depot still being rebuilt)
APRIL
Fri. 14: Edinburgh-Newcastle "Light" (crew training)
MAY
Fri. 12: Leith Central (crew training)
JUNE 1962
Mon. 18: Naming ceremony at Edinburgh - Loco. named, "Royal Scots Grey"
DECEMBER 1967
Sun. 3: Loco reallocated to 34G Finsbury Park
JUNE 1968
Sun. 16: Loco reallocated to 64B Haymarket
OCTOBER 1968
Mon. 21: 1A46 17:00 King's Cross-Newcastle "The Tees-Tyne Pullman" (failed - loco on fire)
NOVEMBER 1971
Tues. 16: 20:01 Peterborough-Crewe (parcels) to Derby; Wed. 17: Bristol-Peterborough (parcels) from Derby
NOVEMBER 1972
Thurs. 16: Peterborough-Leicester (parcels)
NOVEMBER 1973
Sun. 25: Dipped rail-joint tests between Wamphray and Lockerbie with 86 019/Lockerbie-Haymarket (towing prototype H.S.T. and two MKIII carriages.)

D9001/9001/55001

JANUARY 1961
Mon. 16: 'Light' Newton-le-Willows-Doncaster Works for "Acceptance trials"
Tues. 17th 'Light' Doncaster Works-Stratford (for exhibition); Wed. 18: 'Light' Stratford-Doncaster Works - "Acceptance trials""
Until Tues. 31: DONCASTER WORKS
FEBRUARY 1961
Wed. 1: DONCASTER WORKS
Until Thurs. 23: Off DONCASTER WORKS/Enters traffic allocated to 34G Finsbury Park/Doncaster-Peterborough (trial run, load 14)
MARCH
Wed. 15: 09:55 King's Cross-Doncaster (test train)/Doncaster-King's Cross (test train); Tues. 21: 1Z25 06:54 King's Cross-Newcastle (test train)/GD; Wed. 22: 11:32 Newcastle-King's Cross (test train - failed at King's Cross)
APRIL
Thurs. 6: On VULCAN FOUNDRY for "Modifications" Until Fri. 21.
JUNE
Sun. 4: 08:20 King's Cross-Edinburgh (via Lincoln - first known Deltic at Lincoln)
JULY
Wed. 19: On DONCASTER WORKS "Unclassified repair" (Nameplates fitted - "St. Paddy")
AUGUST
Tues. 1: VULCAN FOUNDRY Until Tues. 22
NOVEMBER 1962
Tues. 23: Hornsey-Doncaster (High speed braking trials) Until Tues. 30: Hornsey-Doncaster (High speed braking trials)
MAY 1963
Wed. 1: Hornsey-Doncaster (High speed braking trials); Mon. 6: Hornsey-Doncaster (High speed braking trials) Until Wed. 15: Hornsey-Doncaster (High speed braking trials)
APRIL 1965
Thurs. 15: 1A30 14:00 King's Cross-Edinburgh "Heart of Midlothian" to Welwyn Garden City (failed - assisted by D5062)

156 DELTIC HIGHLIGHTS

D9001/9001/55001 (continued)...
JUNE 1965
Sat. 5: Passing Newark on 'up' goods train
JUNE 1967
Sat. 24: One million miles recorded since new (at week-ending)
DECEMBER 1967
Sun. 3: Loco. reallocated to 64B Haymarket
JUNE 1968
Sun. 16: Loco reallocated to 34G Finsbury Park

D9002/9002/55002
MARCH 1961
Thurs. 9: 'Light' Vulcan Foundry-Doncaster for "Acceptance trials"/Enters traffic allocated to 52A Gateshead; Wed. 22: GD (Crew training); Wed. 29: Leeds-Newcastle (via Harrogate & Ripon) (test train)/GD
APRIL
Sat. 8:Newcastle-Carlisle (parcels)
MAY
Mon. 8:17:50 Newcastle-York (Class 'C' freight)
APRIL 1963
Thurs. 4: Naming ceremony at York performed by General Sir Roger Bower (Colonel of 'KOYLI' 1960-1965) Loco. named - "The King's Own Yorkshire Light Infantry"/1A16 10:00 King's Cross-Edinburgh "The Flying Scotsman" from York ; Tues. 23: Hornsey-Doncaster/Doncaster-Hornsey (High Speed braking trials) Until Tues. 30: Hornsey-Doncaster/Doncaster-Hornsey (High Speed braking trials)
MAY
Wed. 1:Hornsey-Doncaster/Doncaster-Hornsey (High Speed braking trials) Until Tues. 7: Hornsey-Doncaster/Doncaster-Hornsey (High Speed braking trials); Fri. 10: Hornsey-Doncaster/Doncaster-Hornsey (High Speed braking trials) Until Wed. 15: Hornsey-Doncaster/Doncaster-Hornsey (High Speed braking trials); Sun. 16: 11:00 Edinburgh-King's Cross (via Waverley Route)/22:15 King's Cross-Aberdeen to Edinburgh

D9002/9002/55002 (continued)...
OCTOBER 1966
18: First Deltic outshopped in blue livery from Doncaster Works.
JANUARY 1969
Sat. 4: 1Z11 Newcastle-Edinburgh (via Waverley Route) ('The Waverley' Rail tour)/ 1Z11 Edinburgh-Newcastle 'The Waverley' Rail tour)

D9003/9003/55003
MARCH 1961
Mon. 27: 'Light' Vulcan Foundry-Doncaster for "Acceptance trials"/Enters traffic allocated to 34G Finsbury Park
MAY
Thurs. 11: On display at Marylebone in connection with 'Golden Jubilee of the Institution of Locomotive Engineers' exhibition Until Sun. 14.
JUNE
Tues. 20: King's Cross-Doncaster (test train)/Doncaster-King's Cross (test train)
JULY
Mon. 10: On DONCASTER WORKS "Unclassified repair" (Nameplates fitted - "Meld"); Tues. 18: 1Z25 King's Cross-Leeds (High Speed test run)/1Z25 Leeds-King's Cross (High Speed test run)
JULY 1965
Wed. 21: Noted passing Newark on 'up' Goods train.
NOVEMBER 1966
Mon. 7: 'Up' parcels
SEPTEMBER 1967
Thurs. 14: Water scoop test runs at Wiske Moor troughs. Up runs, 300 & 190 gallons at 100mph. Down runs, 250 & 190 gallons at 90 mph.
DECEMBER 1967
Sun. 3: Loco reallocated to 64B Haymarket
JUNE 1968
Sat. 8: Edinburgh-Dundee (parcels); Sun. 16: Loco. reallocated to 34G Finsbury Park
Tues. 18: 3Z29 King's Cross-Edinburgh (pigeon special)

DELTIC HIGHLIGHTS

D9003/9003/55003 (continued)...
DECEMBER 1969
Wed. 31: 08:50 Hull-King's Cross from Doncaster (piloting 1660)
MAY 1972
Sun. 28: 11:00 Edinburgh-King's Cross (coaches derailed at Chathill)
SEPTEMBER 1974
Sun. 1: Immingham 'Open Day' exhibit
OCTOBER 1975
Sun. 12: Paddington-Cardiff 'Rail tour'/Cardiff-Paddington 'Rail tour'

D9004/9004/55004
MAY 1961
Thurs. 18: 'Light' Vulcan Foundry-Doncaster for "Acceptance trials"/Enters traffic allocated to 64B Haymarket
AUGUST 1963
Thurs. 22: 09:20 King's Cross-Leeds "The White Rose" to Peterborough (assisted from Hitchin by a class 31)/0B02 Peterborough-Finsbury Park
MAY 1964
Sat. 23: Naming ceremony at Inverness - Loco named "Queen's Own Highlander"
MARCH 1967
Sat. 4: King's Cross-Leeds "White Rose Pullman" (Last one); Sun. 5: 22:30 King's Cross-Edinburgh - coaches derailed at Conington South; Sat. 25: 1A35 10:00 Edinburgh-King's Cross "The Flying Scotsman" (assisting failed D9019)
JANUARY 1968
During the month working air brake trials - 11:35 Haymarket West-Dundee/ Dundee-Haymarket West/17:40 Haymarket West-Dundee/Dundee-Haymarket West
FEBRUARY 1968
Sat. 3: Edinburgh-Aberdeen (air brake trials)
JUNE
Sat. 8: "Light" Haymarket-Carlisle/21:27 Manchester-Aberdeen (news) from Carlisle
MAY 1970
Fri. 8: 4E47 13:46 Aberdeen-King's Cross (fish)

D9004/9004/55004 (continued)...
JUNE 1970
Wed. 3: 16:40 Stockton-Gushetfaulds (freightliner) from Edinburgh; Thurs. 4: 01:30 Gushetfaulds-Stockton (freightliner)
NOVEMBER 1972
Mon. 20: 1A29 16:28 Doncaster-King's Cross (with 'Peak' 164)
JUNE 1973
Sat. 9: IS "Open Day exhibit"; Sun. 10: IS "Open Day exhibit"/Inverness-Euston "Royal Highlander" (piloting) to Perth
JANUARY 1976
Fri. 16: 0E13 Newcastle-Dudley/1E13 12:40 Edinburgh-King's Cross from Dudley (47 462 failed)

D9005/9005/55005
MAY 1961
Thurs. 25: 'Light' Vulcan Foundry-Doncaster for "Acceptance trials"/Enters traffic allocated to 52A Gateshead
OCTOBER 1963
Tues. 8: Naming ceremony at York - Loco. named "The Prince of Wales's Own Regiment of Yorkshire"
AUGUST 1972
Fri. 4: 17:37 Cambridge-King's Cross
SEPTEMBER 1972
Sun. 3: BH "Open Day exhibit"
SEPTEMBER 1974
Fri. 27: 1A16 Harrogate-King's Cross "The Yorkshire Pullman" (with 45 011)
JANUARY 1975
Mon. 6: 1A11 08:30 Newcastle-King's Cross (assisted from Peterborough by 31 128)

D9006/9006/55006
JUNE 1961
Thurs. 29: 'Light' Vulcan Foundry-Doncaster for "Acceptance trials"/Enters traffic allocated to 64B Haymarket
FEBRUARY 1962
Thurs. 15: 11:35 King's Cross-Edinburgh (failed at Innerwick - out of fuel - assisted forward by A3 60089)

158   DELTIC HIGHLIGHTS

D9006/9006/55006 (continued)...
MAY 1963
Sun. 12: 10:50 Edinburgh-King's Cross (assisted from south of Peterborough by D5064)
SEPTEMBER 1964
Thurs. 17: Derailed at Bradford (whilst bringing stock for up "White Rose" out of a siding)
DECEMBER
Sat. 5: Naming ceremony at Cupar- Loco. named "The Fife & Forfar Yeomanry"
JANUARY 1973
Wed. 17: 4E47 Aberdeen-King's Cross (fish)
MARCH 1976
Sat. 27: Mileage since new recorded as 2,534,563
APRIL
Wed. 14: 1S67 17:00 King's Cross-Edinburgh (piloted by 45 027 - noted at Darlington)

D9007/9007/55007
JUNE 1961
Thurs. 22: 'Light' Vulcan Foundry-Doncaster for "Acceptance trials"/Enters traffic allocated to 34G Finsbury Park (Nameplates fitted - "Pinza")
MAY 1968
Sat. 25: Edinburgh-Darlington from Newcastle (special charter - 4472 failed)
JANUARY 1969
Sun. 5: Leeds-Edinburgh (via Waverley Route) R.C.T.S. rail tour
APRIL 1970
Sat. 4: 1E01 08:00 Edinburgh-King's Cross (on fire near Newark)
SEPTEMBER 1972
Fri. 8: 23:15 King's Cross-Newcastle (struck cattle on the line at Kimblesworth); Fri. 22: 1A29 16:25 Doncaster-King's Cross (piloting 1569)
JANUARY 1975
Sun. 12: To Western Region for dipped rail joint testing between Didcot and Swindon
AUGUST 1975
Fri. 15: 1S67 17:00 King's Cross-Edinburgh (assisted from Abbeyhill Junction by a class 25)

D9008/9008/55008
JULY 1961
Fri. 7: 'Light' Vulcan Foundry-Doncaster for "Acceptance trials"/Enters traffic allocated to 52A Gateshead; Sat. 29: Ayr-Newcastle from Carlisle (Driver training)
SEPTEMBER 1963
Sat. 28: R.S.H. DARLINGTON WORKS (Nameplates fitted); Mon. 30: Naming ceremony at Darlington performed by Brigadier G. W. Eden. Loco named - "The Green Howards"
MAY 1966
Thurs. 28: Perth-King's Cross "Car Carrier" from Edinburgh (D9004 off)

D9009/9009/55009
JULY 1961
Fri. 21: 'Light' Vulcan Foundry-Doncaster for "Acceptance trials"/Enters traffic allocated to 34G Finsbury Park (Nameplates fitted - "Alycidon"); Sat. 29: Newcastle-Carlisle (parcels)
APRIL 1965
Thurs. 29: 4E01 01:59 Millerhill-King's Cross goods
MARCH 1967
Thurs. 23: 1A33 Newcastle-King's Cross from Doncaster (piloting D188)
DECEMBER 1967
Sun. 3: Loco reallocated to 64B Haymarket; Fri. 8: 1A46 17:00 King's Cross-Newcastle "Tees-Tyne Pullman" (On fire at St. Neots)
JUNE 1968
Sun. 16: Reallocated to 34G Finsbury Park
SEPTEMBER 1972
Thurs. 28: FP (Numeric route indicator at No.1 end replaced with two white dots)
JANUARY 1974
Sat. 26: Officially shown as renumbered to 55 009
MARCH
Fri. 22: 1A16 09:52 Harrogate-King's Cross "The Yorkshire Pullman" (with 47457)
APRIL
Sat. 20: 1N21 Doncaster-Newcastle/1D21 Newcastle-Doncaster (with 31 419)

D9010/9010/55010

JULY 1961
Fri. 21:'Light' Vulcan Foundry-Doncaster; Mon. 24: "Acceptance trials"/Enters traffic allocated to 64B Haymarket
DECEMBER 1965
Fri. 3: 1V67 18:40 York-Swindon to Sheffield Victoria/'Light' Sheffield Victoria-Doncaster
NOVEMBER 1967
Sun. 5: 1X20 Edinburgh-King's Cross (Conveying President Suyan of Turkey - Royal Saloons and L.M.R. sleeping cars)
JULY 1968
Sun. 28: Suffers cab fire
SEPTEMBER 1972
Sun. 10: TE "Open day"
JANUARY 1973
Tues. 16: First member of class to attain 2,000,000 miles since new
MAY 1973
Sat. 12: St. Rollox Works "Open day"

D9011/9011/55011

AUGUST 1961
Thurs. 24: 'Light' Vulcan Foundry-Doncaster for "Acceptance trials"/Enters traffic allocated to 52A Gateshead
MAY 1963
Mon. 20: On R.S.H. DARLINGTON WORKS "Unclassified repair" (Nameplates fitted.); Tues. 28: Naming ceremony at Newcastle. Loco. named - "The Royal Northumberland Fusiliers"/12:35 Newcastle-King's Cross "The Northumbrian"
MARCH 1968
Tues. 12: 1A21 Newcastle-King's Cross (on fire at Conington)
MAY 1969
Wed. 7: 1S60 19:40 King's Cross-Aberdeen (train derailed at Morpeth due to excessive speed - fatalities)
DECEMBER 1973
Sun. 9: 1S32 12:00 King's Cross-Aberdeen (assisted by 1509 from Doncaster)
FEBRUARY 1974
Sat. 16: Officially shown renumbered to 55 011

D9012/9012/55012

SEPTEMBER 1961
Mon. 4: 'Light' Vulcan Foundry-Doncaster for "Acceptance trials"/Enters traffic allocated to 34G Finsbury Park (Nameplates fitted - "Crepello")
DECEMBER 1961
Fri. 15: 09:55 Newcastle-Holloway e.c.s. (Collided with derailed 21:50 New England-King's Cross freight at Wood Walton)
FEBRUARY 1963
Tues. 12: 1N03 King's Cross-Leeds "The West Riding"/12:55 Leeds-King's Cross (with Dynamometer Car for Boiler tests); Wed. 13: 1N03 King's Cross-Leeds "The West Riding"/12:55 Leeds-King's Cross (with Dynamometer Car for Boiler tests); Thurs. 14: 1N03 King's Cross-Leeds "The West Riding"/12:55 Leeds-King's Cross (with Dynamometer Car for Boiler tests)
APRIL 1966
Mon. 4: 1Z10 09:56 King's Cross-Doncaster/1Z10 13:56 Doncaster-King's Cross (Press demonstration runs)
DECEMBER 1966
Thurs. 1: 4O92 ('Up' cement empties, noted at Grantham)
DECEMBER 1967
Sun. 3: Reallocated to 64B Haymarket
JUNE 1968
Sun. 16: Reallocated to 34G Finsbury Park
MAY 1970
Sun. 17: 1Z20 Leeds-Diss/0Z20 Diss-Norwich/0Z20 Norwich-Diss/1Z20 16:28 Diss-Leeds ("The East Anglian" R.C.T.S. rail tour) Tues. 26th 1S17 10:00 King's Cross-Edinburgh to Newcastle (assisted from Peterborough by 5605)
FEBRUARY 1974
Sat. 2: Officially shown renumbered to 55 012
DECEMBER 1976
Mon. 20: On DONCASTER WORKS "Intermediate repair - headcode panels plated over".

D9013/9013/55013
SEPTEMBER 1961
Thurs. 14: 'Light' Vulcan Foundry-Doncaster for "Acceptance trials"/Enters traffic allocated to 64B Haymarket
JANUARY 1963
Wed. 16: Naming ceremony at Dundee West. Loco. named - "The Black Watch"/"Light" Dundee-Edinburgh/16:00 Edinburgh-King's Cross
FEBRUARY 1964
Tues. 25: 4E01 Millerhill-King's Cross Goods
FEBRUARY 1968
Sun. 25: Reallocated to 34G Finsbury Park
JUNE 1968
Sun. 16: Reallocated to 64B Haymarket
SEPTEMBER 1972
Fri. 1: 6E39 Leith-Haverton Hill (tankers) to Newcastle
JUNE 1975
Sat. 7: 1Z14 Dundee-Crewe from Haymarket (60009 failed) to Edinburgh
OCTOBER 1975
Mon. 6: 1A02 06:45 Hull-King's Cross "The Hull Pullman" (assisted from Peterborough by 25 099); Tues. 7: 1A04 07:20 Bradford-King's Cross (assisted from Doncaster by 31 250)
MARCH 1976
Wed. 24: 1S32 12:00 King's Cross-Aberdeen (with 55 003 - noted at Newark)
DECEMBER 1976
Sat. 11: 1N21 08:40 Doncaster-Tyne Yard/1D21 12:57 Tyne Yard-Doncaster

D9014/9014/55014
SEPTEMBER 1961
Fri. 29: 'Light' Vulcan Foundry-Doncaster for "Acceptance trials"/Enters traffic allocated to 52A Gateshead
OCTOBER 1963
Tues. 22: Naming ceremony at Darlington performed by Major-General K.G. Exham
APRIL 1966
Tues. 19:4S04 King's Cross-Millerhill goods
SEPTEMBER 1967
Wed. 13:Water scoop test - Wiske Moor troughs

D9014/9014/55014 (continued)...
AUGUST 1970
Mon. 31: 1E05 10:00 Edinburgh-King's Cross "The Flying Scotsman" (assisted from Darlington by 6871)
FEBRUARY 1971
Mon. 8: 20:20 King's Cross-Edinburgh to Doncaster (failed at Newark - assisted by 1560)
SEPTEMBER 1973
Wed. 5: 1L33 17:05 King's Cross-Leeds (assisted from Peterborough by 5642)
JANUARY 1974
Tues. 29: GD (Renumbered to 55 014)
FEBRUARY 1974
Sat. 2: Officially shown renumbered to 55014

D9015/9015/55015
OCTOBER 1961
Fri. 13:"Light' Vulcan Foundry-Doncaster for "Acceptance trials"/Enters traffic allocated to 34G Finsbury Park (Nameplates fitted - "Tulyar"); Mon. 23: Light Doncaster Works-Finsbury Park; Fri. 27: 07:20 King's Cross-Sheffield Victoria "The Master Cutler" (failed at Marshmoor - assisted forward by D5696)
NOVEMBER 1976
Sat. 20: 1A15 09:20 Newcastle-King's Cross (assisted from York by 47 187)

D9016/9016/55016
OCTOBER 1961
Fri. 27: 'Light' Vulcan Foundry-Doncaster for "Acceptance trials"/Enters traffic allocated to 64B Haymarket
JULY 1963
Sat. 20: 12:00 King's Cross-Glasgow Q.St. "Queen of Scots Pullman" (piloted by D274 from Leeds-Newcastle)
JULY 1964
Tues. 28: Naming ceremony at Aberdeen - Loco named "Gordon Highlander"
AUGUST
Tues. 11: 08:00 King's Cross-Edinburgh "The Talisman" (failed - assisted by D5605)/ FP
OCTOBER
Thurs. 8: Derailed at King's Cross (for 17:37 King's Cross-Harrogate)

DELTIC HIGHLIGHTS

D9016/9016/55016 (continued)...
MAY 1967
Wed. 10: 1A24 11:00 Newcastle-King's Cross to York (failed - assisted by D1986)/ 'Light' York-Doncaster
NOVEMBER
Sun. 5: 11:34 Newcastle-Edinburgh (failed near Dunbar - assisted by D1836)
DECEMBER
Sun. 3: Reallocated to 34G Finsbury Park
MAY 1968
Fri. 10: King's Cross-Harrogate "The Yorkshire Pullman" (piloted by D1574)
JUNE
Sun. 16: Reallocated to 64B Haymarket
Sat. 22nd 21:27 Manchester-Aberdeen (Newspapers) from Carlisle
JULY 1975
Sat. 5;DONCASTER WORKS "Heavy General repair- headcode panels plated over"
SEPTEMBER 1976
Fri. 17: 1S42 16:00 King's Cross-Edinburgh "The Talisman" (failed at Darlington - assisted to Newcastle by 45 010)
OCTOBER 1976
Wed. 27: 1E11 08:50 Aberdeen-King's Cross from Edinburgh to Cockburnspath (failed - No.2 main generator exploded)/0G99 Cockburnspath-Haymarket (towed by 40 152)

D9017/9017/55017
NOVEMBER 1961
Thurs. 9: 'Light' Vulcan Foundry-Doncaster; Fri. 10: "Acceptance trials"/Enters traffic allocated to 52A Gateshead
OCTOBER 1963
Fri. 25: On R.S.H. DARLINGTON WORKS "Unclassified repair" (Nameplates fitted)
Until Tues. 29: Off R.S.H. DARLINGTON WORKS/Naming ceremony at Durham - Loco named "The Durham Light Infantry"
DECEMBER 1970
Mon. 28: 1E25 16:00 Edinburgh-King's Cross "The Talisman" (failed at Browney - 1519 forward)

D9017/9017/55017 (continued)...
JUNE 1972
Sat. 17: Newcastle (On display); Sun. 18: Newcastle (On display)
FEBRUARY 1974
Sun. 3: GD - renumbered to 55 017; Sat. 9: Officially shown as renumbered to 55 017
JULY 1975
Sat. 19: 1A22 10:47 Newcastle-King's Cross (piloting a class 31)
SEPTEMBER 1976
Fri. 17: 1S42 16:00 King's Cross-Edinburgh "The Talisman" (failed north of Darlington - assisted by 45 010)

D9018/9018/55018
NOVEMBER 1961
Fri. 24: 'Light' Vulcan Foundry-Doncaster for "Acceptance trials"/Enters traffic allocated to 34G Finsbury Park. Nameplates fitted - "Ballymoss"
JUNE 1963
Tues. 4:1A16 10:00 King's Cross-Edinburgh "The Flying Scotsman" to Grantham (failed - on fire)
JUNE 1964
Wed. 17: 08:00 Edinburgh-King's Cross to Darlington (assisted from Durham by 67628)
SEPTEMBER 1969
Fri. 26: Noted passing Newark towing 3 car DMU
JANUARY 1976
Mon. 19: 1S72 22:30 King's Cross-Edinburgh (assisted by 40 077 from Dunbar - out of fuel)
OCTOBER
Sat. 16: 1F53 Doncaster-Edinburgh (piloted by 40 077 from Newcastle)

D9019/9019/55019
DECEMBER 1961
Mon. 11:'Light' Vulcan Foundry-Doncaster for "Acceptance trials"/Enters traffic allocated to 64B Haymarket
SEPTEMBER 1965
Sat. 11: Naming ceremony at Glasgow Central - Loco named "Royal Highland Fusilier";
MARCH 1967
Thurs. 23: "Royal Train" from Newcastle; Sat. 25: 1A35 10:00 Edinburgh-King's Cross "The Flying Scotsman" (failed - noted piloted by D9004 passing Newark)
DECEMBER
Sun. 3: Reallocated to 34G Finsbury Park
JUNE 1968
Sun. 16: Reallocated to 64B Haymarket
APRIL 1969
Tues. 15:Perth-Inverness "The Highland Mail" (piloting D5338)/'Troop train'
AUGUST
Mon. 4: 18:55 King's Cross-Aberdeen F.L.T.
NOVEMBER 1973
Thurs. 22: Officially shown as renumbered to 55 019

D9020/9020/55020
FEBRUARY 1962
Mon. 12: 'Light' Vulcan Foundry-Doncaster for "Acceptance trials"/Enters traffic allocated to 34G Finsbury Park. Nameplates fitted - "Nimbus"
FEBRUARY 1964
Tues. 4: 4E01 Millerhill-King's Cross goods
DECEMBER 1966
Sat. 31: 03:15 Millerhill-Hawick (class 6 goods)
JUNE 1969
Tues. 17:1A01 07:25 Lincoln-King's Cross/At King's Cross platform 15 with 3 MK11a's for publicity photos in connection with "See a friend this weekend" campaign
NOVEMBER 1973
Sat. 10: Officially shown renumbered to 55 020
JANUARY 1974
Sat. 12:Derailed at Newcastle

D9021/9021/55021
MARCH 1962
Fri. 16: 'Light' Vulcan Foundry-Doncaster for "Acceptance trials"; Sat. 31: Vulcan Foundry (At the end of the month loco used on high speed trials (with no brushes on traction motors) between Manchester-Crewe, towed by an electric loco, in connection with rail end stress tests)
MAY 1962
Wed. 2:'Light' Vulcan Foundry-Doncaster for "Acceptance trials"/"Light" Doncaster Works-Haymarket (Enters traffic allocated to 64B Haymarket); Thurs. 3: 1A4714:00 Edinburgh-King's Cross "The Heart of Midlothian"; Fri. 4: 1A23 08:00 Edinburgh-King's Cross "The Talisman" to Berwick (failed - assisted to Newcastle by 60072)
JUNE 1963
Wed. 5: 20:05 Edinburgh-King's Cross (plus three extra vehicles for Princess Marina)
NOVEMBER 1964
Sun. 29: Reallocated to 34G Finsbury Park
JUNE 1965
Sat. 26: Reallocated to 64B Haymarket
APRIL 1966
Tues. 19: 09:56 King's Cross-Doncaster (High speed Press demonstration run)/13:56 Doncaster-King's Cross (High speed Press demonstration run)
MARCH 1967
Fri. 10: 03:15 Millerhill-Hawick (class six goods)
AUGUST 1968
Mon. 5: 1A29 Perth-Holloway "Motorail"
OCTOBER
Mon. 7: "1st Euro-Scot Freightliner"
DECEMBER
Thurs. 12: Edinburgh-Perth/09:45 Perth-Euston (due to pick up the "Save the Argylls" petition from Stirling)/HA
JANUARY 1971
Thurs. 21: 1X01 Larbert-Stirling "Royal Train" (conveying H.M. Queen Elizabeth 2 visiting the regiment of the Argyll & Sutherland Highlanders)

DELTIC HIGHLIGHTS   **163**

D9021/9021/55021 (continued)...
SEPTEMBER 1971
Thurs. 16: 1E05 10:00 Edinburgh-King's Cross "The Flying Scotsman" (failed at Biggleswade - assisted by 1554)

SEPTEMBER 1972
Sat. 16: ED "Open day"; Sun. 17th ED "Open day"; Mon. 18: 4E47 Aberdeen-King's Cross (fish) to Newcastle
JANUARY 1974
Wed. 2: Officially shown renumbered to 55021

Below: 55005 The Prince of Wales's Own Regiment of Yorkshire awaits departure from Platform 15 at York with the return working of the 150th Anniversary 'Mail by Rail' train on November 11, 1980. Picture: L. P. Gater

164 DELTIC HIGHLIGHTS

Haymarket Class 55, 55016 Gordon Highlander heads the up "Flying Scotsman" at York on April 30, 1977. The Deltic passes ex-LMS Class 5, 5305 which is pausing at the station to take the Humberside Locomotive Preservation Group's return steam special (1G10) forward to Scarborough. Picture: L. P. Gater.

DELTIC HIGHLIGHTS 165

King's Cross and an un-named D9004 (Queens Own Highlander) departs from the termini with a down express. The London station is unrecognisable from this 1960s view which is full of the heady atmosphere of the old British Railways that is now sadly missed by most enthusiasts. Picture: P. Caley Collection.

166 DELTIC HIGHLIGHTS

55002 The King's Own Yorkshire Light Infantry pauses at Retford on its first revenue earning duty following repainting into two-tone green and a formal dedication ceremony at NRM York on December 12, 1980. The locomotive is at the head of the 14.10 York to King's Cross. Picture: L. P. Gater.

8 Deltic Names

In the author's opinion the names bestowed upon the 22 'Deltics' were quite superb. The Finsbury Park based locomotives continued an East Coast tradition of naming locomotives after famous 'racehorses'. Those names instantly created an impression of a creature that might be slightly aloof, sometimes temperamental and sometimes quite stunning in their performance. This could be a description of a 'Deltic' or a racehorse. The Scottish regiments for the most part have names that are typically from north of the border. For an Englishman, some of those very Scottish sounding names hold almost an air of mystery around them. Who could fail to be impressed by 'Argyll & Sutherland Highlander' as a name? You would also be left in no doubt as to where the name was from, it oozes Scotland. The English regiments could not really equal their Scottish counterparts charismatic sounding names. Perhaps this is why the 'Deltics' named after the English regiments were always less popular than the 'racehorse' and Scottish regiment named locomotives. I have always been slightly intrigued to know a bit more about the racehorses and regiments that the Deltics were named after, so I decided to look into the subject a little more and I have produced a very brief history of those very familiar names but from a different angle...

D9000 ROYAL SCOTS GREY

The Royal Scots Greys (Second Dragoons) were raised in 1678 as three independent troops of Scots Dragoons and formed as The Royal Regiment of Scots Dragoons in 1681. In 1694 they were mounted on grey horses and by 1702 they were using unofficial titles such as 'Grey Dragoons' and 'Scots Regiment of White Horses'. In 1707 they were renamed Royal North British Dragoons and the term 'Scots Greys' was in common use. In 1921 they became The Royal Scots Greys (Second Dragoons). During the 20th Century they took part in the following conflicts. 1899-1902 South Africa. The Regiment took part in the last cavalry charge of the British Army at the Relief of Kimberley. WW1. The grey horses were dyed chestnut to prevent the Regiment from being identified. WW2. The Royal Scots Greys were the last operational regular Regiment to be horsed cavalry in the British Army. The last mounted parade was held in March 1941; from then on they converted to M3 Stuart, M3 Grant and Sherman tanks. The Regiment also took part in the Gulf War in 1991. A few years ago I visited the Regimental museum in Edinburgh castle and saw the famous eagle on display. This eagle is of course familiar to 'Deltic' enthusiasts as it can be seen on the locomotive's bodysides. However, the eagle in the museum is kept in a dark case and is floodlit which makes it look quite stunning. The origins of the eagle is that during the 'Battle of Waterloo' the French carried the eagle at the top of their flagpole and when The Royal Scots Greys defeated the French they kept their eagle as a souvenir. Nowadays the Regiment is called The Royal Scots Dragoon Guards (Carabiniers and Greys) after amalgamation in 1971 with the 3rd Carabiniers (Prince of Wales's

168   DELTIC NAMES

Dragoon Guards). So versatile are the Regiment that in 1972 they even had a number 1 hit in the pop charts! Who remembers Amazing Grace? Well, that was by The pipes and drums of The Royal Scots Dragoon Guards.

D9001 ST. PADDY
St. Paddy, a bay stallion, was the third of the Deltic racehorses to be owned by Sir Victor Sassoon and the most recent of all the eight. He was foaled in 1957 by Aureole and out of Edie Kelly. In 1960 St. Paddy won the Derby, St. Leger, 2000 Guineas, Eclipse Stakes and the Hardwick Stakes, an impressive record indeed. Included in St. Paddy's pedigree is Gainsborough, himself a classic winner in 1918, he can be traced back in six of the Deltic racehorses (not Pinza or Nimbus) and is in the bloodline of most of today's thoroughbred racehorses. St. Paddy sired Connaught, the 1970 Eclipse Stakes winner. Whilst two other noteworthy classic winning thoroughbreds from St. Paddy's bloodline are; Dunfermline (1977 Oaks and St. Leger), Pebbles (1984 100 Guineas and 1985 Eclipse Stakes). Dunfermline is also a descendant of Ballymoss and Pebbles from the bloodline of Crepello. St. Paddy enjoyed a long retirement at Newmarket and died in 1984, aged 27.

D9002 THE KING'S OWN YORKSHIRE LIGHT INFANTRY
Raised in 1755 by Colonel Robert Napier (an excellent connection with the Deltics!) was the 53rd Regiment of Foot, who in 1757 became the 51st Regiment of Foot. In 1881 the 51st (2nd Yorkshire – West Riding) The King's Light Infantry, as they had by then become, merged with the 105th (Madras Light Infantry) Regiment. In 1887 they became The King's Own (Yorkshire Light Infantry) and in 1921 the brackets were removed to give the Deltic associated name. Over the years, indeed centuries even, they have been involved in conflicts such as Waterloo, WW1 in Le Cateau, Marne, Messines, Ypres, Somme and Italy. During WWII they were in action in Norway, North West Europe and Burma. In 1968 they merged with The Somerset and Cornwall Light Infantry, The King's Shropshire Light Infantry and The Durham Light Infantry and since then have been known as The Light Infantry. They have a Regimental museum in Doncaster where I believe one of the original Deltic nameplates is on display. Perhaps it may be worth a visit.

D9003 MELD
Meld was the only filly of the eight Deltic racehorses and was in fact sired in 1952 by Alycidon. She was owned by Lady Zia Wernher and in 1955 won the Oaks, St. Leger, 1000 Guineas and the Coronation Stakes.

The only classic winning racehorse I have managed to find, having been foaled by Meld, is Charlottown, which won the 1966 Derby. The last reports of Meld were in 1979 when the Deltic Preservation Society reported she was enjoying her retirement and living in Ayrshire, then aged 27.

D9004 QUEEN'S OWN HIGHLANDER

The Queen's Own Highlanders were formed in 1961 from the amalgamation of The Seaforth Highlanders and The Queen's Own Cameron Highlanders. In 1994 they merged with no less a Regiment than The Gordon Highlanders to become The Highlanders (Seaforth, Gordon and Camerons). Their origins can be traced back to about 1800 and around that time they would have been known as 72nd, 78th and 79th Scottish Highland Infantry. It would appear that they were heavily involved in both World Wars and prior to that they were involved in conflicts at Waterloo, Central India, Egypt and in South Africa. The only conflict that they were involved in that I am aware of whilst carrying the familiar name was during the Gulf War of 1991. They have a Regimental museum at Fort George, Ardersier in Inverness-shire.

D9005 THE PRINCE OF WALES'S OWN REGIMENT OF YORKSHIRE

The Prince of Wales's Own Regiment of Yorkshire (PWO) was formed on 25th April 1958 (ten years to the day before the locomotive was outshopped from Doncaster after dual braking). They were formed by the amalgamation of two old and famous Regiments, The West Yorkshire Regiment (The Prince of Wales's Own) being the 14th Regiment of Foot and the East Yorkshire Regiment (The Duke of York's Own) being the 15th Regiment of foot. Since the amalgamation the Regiment has served in Germany, Aden, Britain, Northern Ireland and Bosnia. In May 1985 Her Royal Highness the Duchess of Kent was appointed Colonel-in-Chief. They have a Regimental museum in York.

D9006 THE FIFE & FORFAR YEOMANRY

The Fife & Forfar Yeomanry over the years have had numerous name changes, in fact they only carried the familiar Deltic name from 1947 until 1956. It would appear they were raised in 1797 as the Kirkcaldy Troop before becoming Fife Yeomanry Cavalry in 1803. They were disbanded in 1828 but were formed again in 1831 but once again disbanded in 1838. The Forfarshire Yeomanry were formed in 1846, a name that brings together the components to make up the name we are familiar with. Another twelve variations in name followed before as previously mentioned they became The Fife & Forfar Yeomanry. They had in fact almost been named thus since 1939 but it was only the word "The" that was missing from the title. In 1956 they amalgamated with The Scottish Horse to become The Fife & Forfar Yeomanry/Scottish Horse. In 1992 they became 'The Scottish Yeomanry' making up 'C' Squadron being known as 'C' (Fife & Forfar Yeomanry/Scottish Horse) Squadron. In 1999 'The Scottish Yeomanry' was disbanded but 'C' Squadron were re-designated into 'The Queen's Own Yeomanry'.

D9007 PINZA
Pinza, like Crepello, was owned by Sir Victor Sassoon and was foaled in 1950, he won the Derby in 1953 ridden by Sir Gordon Richards. Pinza's legacy has given rise to some classic winners, namely; Teenoso (1983 Derby and 1984 King George & Queen Elizabeth Stakes) and Troy (1979 Derby and King George & Queen Elizabeth Stakes), Pinza being grandsire in both pedigrees on the dam side. Pinza also sired Pindari, a horse owned by Her Majesty the Queen, which finished 3rd in the 1959 St. Leger. Names such as Pin Stripe, Pin Prick and Pinza Again are also likely to be linked to the Deltic favourite.

D9008 THE GREEN HOWARDS
The Green Howards were formed in 1688 and designated 19th Regiment of Foot. The Regiment received the nickname The Green Howards in 1744 to avoid confusion on the battlefield when two Regiments were named after their Colonel – Howard's Regiment. As one Regiment wore green facings on their scarlet uniforms they were called The Green Howards, the nickname became official in 1920. The Green Howards raised 24 Battalions in World War 1 and 13 in World War II and fought in all the major theatres of war. Since 1945 the Regiment has seen active service in Malaya, Cyprus, Northern Ireland and Bosnia. They have a Regimental museum in Richmond, North Yorkshire.

D9009 ALYCIDON
Alycidon was owned by the 17th Earl of Derby and won the Ascot Gold Cup, Goodwood Cup, Corporation Stakes and Doncaster Cup in 1949. There used to be an "Alycidon Stakes" run at Goodwood during July, no doubt in honour of the 1949 Goodwood Cup winner. It is interesting to note the amount of interbreeding within Alycidon's pedigree, with one filly, Canterbury Pilgrim, appearing on three occasions. Alycidon would himself go on to sire racehorses of which Meld was one. Also included in Alycidon's descendents are Charlottown (1966 Derby), Lupe (1970 Oaks) and Troy (1979 Derby and King George & Queen Elizabeth Stakes). Also of note is that Pinza shows up as great grandsire on the dam line.

D9010 THE KING'S OWN SCOTTISH BORDERER
The King's Own Scottish Borderers were formed by Royal Warrant on 18th March 1689. In just 2 hours, over 800 men were sworn to protect the Scottish capital, once established they became known as the Edinburgh Regiment of Foot.
They have been involved in such conflicts as The Napoleonic Wars, India and Pakistan, both World Wars, Korea and Malaya, Aden and Radfan and the Gulf War. They have a Regimental museum in Berwick-upon-Tweed.

D9011 THE ROYAL NORTHUMBERLAND FUSILIERS
The Regiment was raised in 1674 as The Irish Regiment for Dutch service and until 1751 were also known by the names of Colonels. In 1751 they became the 5th Regiment of Foot and in 1782 the 5th (the Northumberland) Regiment of Foot. In 1881 they became The Northumberland Fusiliers and in 1935 The Royal Northumberland Fusiliers. In 1968 they were amalgamated with The Royal Warwickshire Fusiliers, The Royal Fusiliers (City of London Regiment) and The Lancashire Fusiliers to form 1st Battalion, The Royal Regiment of Fusiliers. Their Battle Honours stretch back to St. Lucia 1778 and through both World Wars.

D9012 CREPELLO
Crepello was owned by Sir Victor Sassoon and won the classic races; Derby and 2000 Guineas in 1957, beating Ballymoss into second place by a large margin in the Derby. Crepello went on to sire many foals and is in the bloodline of many classic-winning thoroughbreds. In 1967 Busted won the Eclipse Stakes and in 1973 'Mysterious' won the Oaks and 1000 Guineas, both being sired by Crepello. Further down the pedigree Crepello was grandsire to; Altesse Royale (1971 Oaks and 1000 Guineas), Ginerva (1972 Oaks), Bustino (1974 St. Leger and 1975 Coronation Cup) and Opace (1984 Irish St. Leger). Both Bustino and Opace were by Busted. Crepello's impressive lineage continues into a fourth generation with Pebbles (1984 1000 Guineas and 1985 Eclipse Stakes) and Celeric (1997 Gold Cup). In fact the T.V. pundit John McCririck once claimed Crepello to be the finest racehorse of all time.

D9013 THE BLACK WATCH
In the wake of the 1715 Scottish rebellion, companies of trustworthy Highlanders were raised from local clans. They became known as The Black Watch for the watch they kept on the Highlands and from their dark government tartan. In 1739 King George II authorised the companies be formed into a regiment of foot "the men to be natives of that country and none other to be taken". The Regiment's first conflict occurred in Flanders in 1745, where the French dubbed them 'Highland Furies'. In 1751 the Regiment was numbered the 42nd, the Gallant Forty Two. Seven years later the title 'Royal' was granted and it became the 42nd Royal Highland Regiment. The Regiment saw further action in the Americas and later in the Napoleonic Wars including Waterloo. In the 1860's Queen Victoria authorised the addition of the name 'The Black Watch' to the official title of the 42nd Royal Highlanders, a title that has become known throughout the world. The Regiment had 11 battalions fighting in World War 1 in France and Flanders, Macedonia, Mesopotamia and Palestine. In World War II the Regiment was present at Dunkirk and fought at Crete, Tobruk, El Alamein, Sicily, Normandy, Ardennes and Burma. There is a Regimental museum in Perth.

D9014 THE DUKE OF WELLINGTON'S REGIMENT
The Regiment is a direct descendant of two old Regiments of foot, the 33rd, raised in 1702 and the 76th, raised in 1787. In 1881 these two Regiments were amalgamated to form The Duke of Wellington's Regiment and is now only one of a handful that have not been disbanded or amalgamated since that time. Arthur Wellesley, later the Duke of Wellington, joined the 33rd in 1793 and subsequently commanded it in the Netherlands, India and at the Battle of Waterloo. Owing to his particularly close connections with the Regiment they were awarded the title of "The Duke of Wellington's Regiment" on 18th June 1853, the first anniversary of Waterloo following his death. Since then they have served in such places as The Crimea, India and they took part in both World Wars.

D9015 TULYAR
Tulyar was another of the Deltic racehorses with an impressive pedigree, having among his predecessors Nearco and Gainsborough. Tulyar was owned by the Aga Khan and in 1952 won the Derby, St. Leger and Eclipse Stakes. Tulyar was honoured with the "Tulyar Stakes" a race that used to be run at Lingfield. The winning horse of the 1991 Derby and King George VII & Queen Elizabeth Stakes was Generous, which has Tulyar on the dam line. What is possibly more interesting is that a descendant of Tulyar is none other than the Lord Lucan of the equine world, Shergar, winner of the 1981 Derby and King George VII & Queen Elizabeth Stakes. This was the horse allegedly taken for ransom by the I.R.A. in the early 1980's and never seen again.

D9016 GORDON HIGHLANDER
The Gordon Highlanders were raised by the 4th Duke of Gordon, by command of a Royal Warrant issued on 10th February 1794. Over a history of 200 years the Gordons were to earn for themselves a reputation as a Regiment second to none. Indeed Winston Churchill described them as "The finest Regiment in the World". They have seen action in The Napoleonic Wars, Afghanistan in 1879, India, Suez and both World Wars. On 17th September 1994 they were finally amalgamated with The Queen's Own Highlanders after much protesting. Arguably the finest Regiment that ever was fell victim to British reliance on NATO and UN joint action, but the spirit of the Regiment lives on in the men who serve the new Highland Regiment.

D9017 THE DURHAM LIGHT INFANTRY
The army reorganisation of 1881 saw the 68th and 106th become 1st and 2nd Battalions The Durham Light Infantry and Militia Battalions renamed 3rd and 4th Battalions The Durham Light Infantry. Interestingly in 1884 their depot was moved from Sunderland to Newcastle and they then shared with The Royal Northumberland Fusiliers. They have also been involved in most of the major conflicts such as India, South Africa and both World Wars. In 1968 they merged

with The Somerset and Cornwall Light Infantry, The King's Shropshire Light Infantry and The King's Own Yorkshire Light Infantry and since then they have been known as The Light Infantry.

D9018 BALLYMOSS
Ballymoss was foaled in 1954 by Mossborough and out of Indian Call. In 1957 he won the St. Leger and the Irish Derby and was beaten into second place that year by Crepello in the English Derby. The following year saw Ballymoss triumphant in the Eclipse Stakes and in the French Prix de L'Arc de Triumphe. Owned by Mr. S. McShain Ballymoss would become one of the leading broadmare sires in England and sire 177 dams with 1032 foals, of which 630 were runners – 341 winners, 91 of which were 2 year old winners. Amongst his pedigree is Nearco (also in the blood line of Nimbus) another broadmare sire which would give rise to Northern Dancer, himself a classic winning racehorse and the predecessor of many of today's leading thoroughbreds. The Ballymoss legend would live on in such racehorses as Royal Palace (1967 Derby and 2000 Guineas and 1968 Eclipse Stakes), Teenoso (1983 Derby and 1984 King George & Queen Elizabeth Stakes), Dunfermline (1977 Oaks and St. Leger), Lev Moss (1969 Gold Cup) and Le Moss (1979 and 1980 Gold Cup). Both Lev Moss and Le Moss were foaled by Feemoss a Dam by Ballymoss.

D9019 ROYAL HIGHLAND FUSILIER
The Royal Highland Fusiliers were formed on 20th January 1959 by the amalgamation of the Royal Scots Fusiliers and the Highland Light Infantry. These two famous Regiments were formerly three - The 21st Fusiliers, the 71st Highlanders (Light Infantry) and the 74th Highlanders. Their combined history covers that of the British Army itself. During fifteen reigns, from King Charles II to Queen Elizabeth II, there are few battlefields of importance on which they have not been present, either together or separately.

D9020 NIMBUS
Nimbus was foaled in 1946, out of Kong and by the leading broadmare sire Nearco. Nearco can be traced in almost all of the leading blood stock lines, including that of a recent leading Broadmare sire, Northern Dancer. Northern Dancer has led to such horses as, The Minstral, Mill Reef, Nijinsky and Arkle. Owned by Mrs H. A. Glenister, Nimbus won the Derby and 2000 Guineas in 1949. Nimbus is the only thoroughbred racehorse that I have been unable to trace any classic-winning descendants. The last report of Nimbus was that he had gone to Japan and not heard of again in this country.

D9021 ARGYLL & SUTHERLAND HIGHLANDER
The 91st Argyllshire Highlanders were raised in 1794 and saw service in South Africa, Waterloo and India. In 1799 the 93rd Sutherland Highlanders were raised

and they saw service in New Orleans, Crimea including Balaklava, where they earned the nickname of the Thin Red Line and in India. In 1881 the two Regiments amalgamated to form The Argyll & Sutherland Highlanders (Princess Louise's). After amalgamation battalions of the Regiment served in South Africa (Zululand), Boer War, India and the Far East and both World Wars. Since World War II the 1st Battalion has served in Palestine, Korea, British Guiana, Berlin, Suez, Cyprus, Malaya and Singapore, Borneo, Aden, Germany, Falkland Islands and Northern Ireland. They have a Regimental museum in Stirling Castle.

THE AMAZING CASE OF THE DELTIC IMPOSTER

This story begins back in November 1960 in Buchanan Street, Glasgow - home at the time of the Scottish Region. The Deltics were at this stage in the throes of construction at the Vulcan Foundry and the first of their ilk - D9000 was eagerly awaited by all and sundry.

The contract for the building of the Deltics between British Rail and English Electric had been sealed in March 1958. Due to manufacturing difficulties, the delivery dates were altered during 1960 and as the year neared its end the first of the mighty East Coast beasts was still some three months away from making its debut from the factory.

However, while English Electric frantically tried to avoid a claim for damages from the British Transport Commission for late delivery, a claim that never materialised, discussions were beginning to get under way about the names these flagship diesels would carry.

During these initial meetings it quickly became apparent that there would be some difference of opinion as to whether racehorses or indeed regiments would win the day - the Eastern Area Board favouring racehorses and the Scottish equivalent preferring regiments which had an association with the East Coast main line.

This difference first reared its head during the aforementioned meeting when minute 60/275 titled 'Naming of Main Line Diesel Locomotives' broached the subject of Deltic namings. The first Deltic was, according to a note accompanying the minute, to be delivered in February 1961 and all 22 by October of the same year - a timetable that didn't go exactly according to plan with the last one, D9021, being put into service on March 16th, 1962.

However, the first point of interest is the fact that at that meeting the board were informed that it WASN'T possible to name the fleet of locomotives after regiments and that the Eastern Area Board had elected to use racehorse names. Therefore, in the circumstances, the Scottish Region would name their Deltics after characters in history and literature and the chairman asked for suitable suggestions. So it was clear from this that the ER were determined to get their way with the racehorses although it was, at this juncture, unclear as to why the ScR could not name their locos after regiments.

Instead, the hunt began for suitable names but before they could come up with anything like 'Robert The Bruce' or 'Bonnie Prince Charlie', the picture began to change somewhat. Early the following month, Jock Brebner, the BTC's Public Relations Advisor, wrote to the all the regional general managers about the naming of diesels, with a note to the ScR that the BTC chairman, Sir Brian Robertson, 'still did not understand why it was not possible to name Deltics after Regiments'. That simple comment seemed to do the trick. For the advent of the new year saw a distinct change in the ScR's view of the Deltic namings. By this time, they knew which members of the fleet they would be getting.

Locomotives D9000, D9004, D9006, D9010 and D9013 were confirmed by mid-January while three more locos, the numbers of which had yet to be allocated, were also due to head for Scotland. They had finally agreed to push for regimental names, the only problem now was to decide which ones. This will lead us on to one of the most fascinating stories of the diesel. For one preserved locomotive could well have been known by a completely different name had events taken another route.

With the first Deltic just a month away from being put into traffic, The ScR's assistant general manager G. W. Stewart wrote back to Brebner saying that regimental names would be bestowed on their eight machines. The first draft list put together by the ScR allocated the following names to the eight locos: D9000 - Royal Scots Grey. This was a name held by steam locomotive 46101 and the ScR added that the name would be transferred from the London Midland Region as long as General Manager David Blee was in agreement. D9004 - Queen's Own Highlander - a new name never before carried by a locomotive. D9006 - The Fife and Forfar Yeomanry - this too was a new name for a locomotive. D9010 - The King's Own Scottish Borderer - this would involve taking the name of ScR steam loco 46104. D9013 - The Black Watch - this name was already in use on ScR steam loco 46102 and would simply be transferred.

The remaining three Deltics had not yet been allocated numbers but interestingly they had already got their names. And it was here that the one surprise emerges. For the names picked to adorn these three were Gordon Highlander, Cameron Highlander and Argyll & Sutherland Highlander. Out of these, the latter two were to be transferred from ScR steamers 46105 and 46107 respectively while Gordon Highlander's name was carried by LMR example 46106 and would be transferred with David Blee's permission again. But it is at this point in the tale that the name of Cameron Highlander crops up for the first time.

Brebner replied that none of the names conflicted with any chosen by the other five regions and he noted that the ScR general manager James Ness was in touch with Blee concerning D9000 and Gordon Highlander. The BTC also notified the War Office of the plans at this point. Eric Merrill, Chief Public relations Officer, confirmed the selections of the ScR and he duly recommended that the respective Colonels get in touch with the ScR to make arrangements for naming ceremonies.

176 DELTIC NAMES

His letter was received at Berkeley Square in London by Lieutenant Colonel Sir Jeffrey Darell, Bt, MC, of the Coldstream Guards. It was at this stage in the proceedings that the Cameron Highlander began to lose its battle to join the ranks of the most powerful diesel locomotives in the world. But before I deal with Darell's intervention on behalf of the War Office, the North Eastern Region, who were allocated six of the 22 Deltics, had also chosen to use regimental names. But unlike the ScR, all their chosen regiments ended up on their allotted locos. Yet the correspondence that flew back and forth between the War Office, Marylebone Road and the ScR concerning that regions choice of regiments was about to go into overdrive.

Darell wrote back to Merrill pointing out two vital changes to the make up of two of the regiments chosen in the ScR list of Deltic names. Before he would ask the regiments to get in touch with the ScR general manager, he wanted to clarify the position with the BTC. Firstly, the Queen's Own Highlanders was a new regiment which had been formed by the amalgamation of the Cameron Highlanders and the Seaforth Highlander and Darell suggested that it would perhaps be better to name steam loco 46105 Queen's Own Highlanders. Secondly, The Fife and Forfar Yeomanry had been amalgamated and was then called The Fife and Forfar Yeomanry/Scottish Horse.

Darell suggested that this name was no doubt too long and put forward the solution of choosing another regiment instead - naming the Royal Highland Fusilier or The Cameronians as possible replacements. Merrill quickly got in touch with Ness in Glasgow to pass on Darell's points but also adding a few of his own. The chief one of these was the view that he thought the Queen's Own Highlanders regiment would prefer to see their name on a new Deltic diesel than to have it replace The Cameron Highlander on a steam loco which would eventually go out of service. Merrill also pointed out that The Cameronian name suggested by Darell as a possible replacement for the Fife and Forfar Yeomanry/Scottish Horse was already carried on two locos - a former LNER Pacific and Royal Scot. Significantly, he added, they had no Royal Highland Fusilier. By now D9000's appearance into service was imminent.

Royal Scots Grey had been accepted as a name without any problems, but the ScR were becoming increasingly exasperated with the War Office. G. W. Stewart, Ness's assistant, made this clear in his reply to Merrill some 11 days before D9000 was put into traffic. He made it clear that the War Office should be made aware that the Deltics were to run on East Coast Anglo/Scottish services and that the region had tried to choose regimental names, which, as far as possible, had an association with the route.

That link was mainly through regimental recruitment areas and he went on to pour cold water on the War Office's suggestions. Stewart declared that there had obviously been some misunderstanding about the naming of D9004 The Queen's Own Highlander and the Cameron Highlanders. For he went on to point out that their naming proposals clearly showed that the newly amalgamated regiment of the Queen's Own would be bestowed on D9004 and that the Cameron Highlander, then held by steam loco 46105, would be perpetuated on one of the Deltics whose number had not yet been allocated. Furthermore, he said that it was their intention to name D9006 The Fife and Forfar Yeomanry without the appendage of the Scottish Horse as steam loco 46129 currently held the name Scottish Horse. Also, Stewart added that the name Royal Highland Fusilier was considered but rejected for the reason that it did not have an association with the route.

Stewart could not see why there should be any doubt about their naming proposals and left it to Merrill to pass on his observations to Darell at the War Office. This he duly did but Darell was away when the letter reached the War Office leaving Colonel F. A. Milnes to accept the suggestions and to inform the BTC that he would ask the respective regiments to get in touch with Mr. Ness in Glasgow. However, as the Deltics rolled off the production line and into main line action, D9019 - the loco selected for the name of Cameron Highlander - would not follow until the end of the year.

In between, the name disappeared from the plans of the ScR to be replaced by the War Office's suggested Royal Highland Fusilier. The locomotive came so close to being born as the Cameron Highlander but the mystery as to why the plates were never cast is a relatively easy one to solve in the end. It was obviously clear from the correspondence between the War Office and the ScR that Cameron Highlander was not a popular choice. In the end the name simply ceased to exist because the regiment ceased to exist in its own right. The difference of opinion over the two names swung back in the War Office's favour when it became clear to everyone that the regiment had become incorporated under the banner of the Queen's Own Highlanders - a name already destined for D9004. Therefore, Cameron Highlanders was in fact redundant as a regiment in its own right and therefore as a contender for the bodyside of a Deltic. To have allowed the name to stand would presumably have been like naming a loco twice with what would be the same regiment. After all, the Seaforth Highlanders was never even considered and they merged into the Queen's Own along with the Cameronians. Yet it took them almost four years to affix the name of the Royal Highland Fusilier to D9019's bodyside. She was the last Deltic to be named and in view of the battle to decide upon which one she would carry, it is perhaps not surprising. Yet even if it was apparent that the name of Cameron Highlander was no longer viable, why did the ScR eventually go for the Royal Highland Fusilier when clearly it did not fit the criteria of having an association with the route in terms of being a regimental recruitment area?

The answer may well lie in correspondence between the War Office and the BTC chairman Sir Brian Robertson as far back as June 1960. The ScR clearly felt that a regiment had to have an association with the route, but the BTC threw this point out when the War Office suggested it in a four-point plan for transferring locomotive names from steam to diesels at the start of the decade. The BTC had

178 DELTIC NAMES

asked the War Office to contact all the colonels of regiments which had steam locomotives bearing their name to ascertain whether or not they wanted to switch the name from the steam loco to a diesel. Whitehall's General Sir Hugh Stockwell, GCB, KBE, DSO, Adjutant General to the Forces, wrote back to Sir Brian Robertson with the news that most of the colonels were in general agreement with the proposal to transfer the names. However, he made it clear that they had raised four key points during the survey: a) That the old nameplates should be presented to the Regiment or Corps. To this the BTC agreed readily. b) That the Regiments should liaise closely with the BTC regarding naming ceremonies. This the BTC rejected, preferring them to deal with region concerned instead. c) That as in the past, 'Regimental' locos should draw troop trains on special occasions. This the BTC agreed to where possible but it was going to be unlikely that the top flight East Coast Deltics would be included. d) And this is the key one...that locos should operate in or through the Regimental Recruiting areas. The BTC rejected this.

This effectively paved the way for the Royal Highland Fusilier to adorn the flank of D9019 five years later when the ScR finally lost the argument over names with recruiting area links. However, that argument may not be entirely true. For the Royal Highland Fusilier was also a relatively new regiment - one born out of the amalgamation of the Highland Light Infantry, City of Glasgow Regiment and the Royal Scots Fusiliers - their barracks being located at Maryhill in the city. Therefore, the recruiting area would have had links with the Scottish Region - possibly the reasoning behind the fact that when she was eventually named on September 11th, 1965, the ceremony was carried out at Glasgow Central. That then is the fascinating and intriguing story behind the Cameron Highlander - the Deltic that never was.

The design of the nameplates themselves was left to the Design Panel and they put the work out to Sir Misha Black's Design Research Unit in London. Black had come up with the style of plates for the Warship and Western Class, Diesel-Hydraulics for the Western Region. These were based on a steel backplate, aluminium border with colour infill. In 1959, his designs were given the all clear to be used as the template for other regions by BTC, Chief Mechanical Engineer, J. F. Harrison.

The first correspondence regarding the design of the Deltic plates came in January 1961 when H. A. Short, North Eastern Region, General Manager, wrote to Christian Barman at Marylebone Road concerning the design of the nameplate for 'The Royal Northumberland Fusiliers'. He followed this with a further letter concerning a plate for 'The Prince of Wales's Own Regiment of Yorkshire'.

On February 9, 1961, the BTC Design Officer George Williams contacted Black at the DRU saying: "We have been approached by the General Manager, North Eastern Region for assistance in the design of nameplates for two diesel locomotives working in that Region. The Chief Mechanical Engineer here has agreed that the style of lettering and nameplates which you devised for the Western

Region locomotives are suitable for standard use and we should like you to produce layouts using the same form for the North Eastern diesels."

In the meantime however, M. G. Burrows, CM&EE of the NER, put forward his designs for the two plates in question. These differed with one design having three rows of letters and the other with two rows. While Burrows waited for a reaction, Harrison told Williams that the Eastern Region required plates for the following locomotives: D9001 St. Paddy; D9003 Meld; and D9007 Pinza. These, he said, should be cleared through the Design Panel for the sake of uniformity with the plates already in hand for the NER. Enter Kenneth Lamble of the DRU. On March 14, 1961 he wrote to Jack Bloomfield at the BTC enclosing full scale lettering layouts for the two regimental plates of the NER. Lamble said that in order to incorporate the regimental badge centrally about the plate, it had been necessary to move the BR badge to each end of the locomotive above the number. Ten days later Lamble sent Bloomfield more drawings for the racehorse plates required by the ER.

Burrows thought he had spotted a flaw in the Swindon drawings. On April 20th, 1961, he wrote to Williams saying: "On comparing the lettering of the nameplates which accompanied your letter of March 27, I find that the width of the letters shown on the two drawings do not agree and if the nameplates are manufactured using letters as shown on the Swindon drawing, they will be considerably longer than those shown on the two drawings supplied by you."

However, Williams replied by saying that the Swindon drawings were merely to give Burrows an indication of the style and manufacture of the plates and method used by the Western Region for fixing them. The lettering style was altered slightly to accommodate the length of the names and the go ahead was given for the manufacture of patterns for the plates concerned. On November 16, 1961, Burrows told Williams that a further four locomotives had been selected for names and these were 'The Durham Light Infantry'; 'The Green Howards'; "The King's Own Yorkshire Light Infantry' and 'The Duke of Wellington's Regiment'.

Burrows asked for approval of these plates in the same style as the 'The Prince of Wales's Own Regiment of Yorkshire' and 'The Royal Northumberland Fusiliers'. However, Williams replied: "I have examined these and consider that they could be improved so far as letter spacing is concerned and I am preparing new drawings and will despatch them to you as soon as possible."

He then contacted Black and asked for him to draw up new layouts with improved spacing as he claimed the NER's design was too 'inaccurate'.

Black went away to come up with a more tighter spacing and once this was achieved the plates were cast. Not many Deltic enthusiasts are aware of Black's heavy involvement in the locomotive names. But after being given a free hand to design the WR diesel-hydraulic plates, it was clear the Design Panel wanted to keep the look of the plates as close to one style as possible. But it should be remembered that the Panel, and Black in turn, were responsible for the look of most aspects that affected the aesthetic appearance of locomotives in the 1955 modernisation plan.

9 Deltics On Works

In the early years of the Deltic locomotives, the records that were kept in relation to major components carried were not entirely accurate. Therefore, in some instances it is possible that some visits to major Works have not been recorded. It is also apparent that in some cases the major components have either been inaccurately recorded or not recorded at all. However, through extensive research and cross checking it has in most cases been possible to establish exactly which components individual locomotives carried. Unfortunately there are still some instances of uncertainty as to which components were carried, particularly with regard to D9005/9005/55 005, where little early information exists.

D9000/9000/55 022 Royal Scots Grey

Loco Works	On Works	Off Works	Class of repair
Doncaster	28/02/61	09/03/61	Acceptance trials

New locomotive fitted with the following known components; No.1 engine, (Unknown). No.2 engine, (Unknown) – It is, however, believed that engine 413 was fitted. No.1 bogie, 1001. No.2 bogie, 1002. Boiler, 1494/J2950. Minor collision damage repairs.

Doncaster	22/06/61	Not recorded	Not recorded

Engine, 413, removed. (It is not recorded which engine replaced 413, however, the next mention of engines refers to No.1 engine as, 456 and No.2 engine as 457. Whether they were fitted on this visit is unknown.

Doncaster	09/08/61	11/08/61	Unclassified

Nos. 1 & 2 exhaust collector tanks fractured. These were both replaced.

R.S.H. Darlington	Not recorded	07/03/62	Not recorded

No.1 engine, 456, replaced by 427. No.2 engine, 457, replaced by unrecorded engine.

Doncaster	07/03/62	10/03/62	General

No.1 bogie, 1001, replaced by 1049. No.2 bogie, 1002, replaced by 1050. Boiler, 1494/J2950 was overhauled. The body had a six monthly exam and at No.2 end a new driver's side demister window was fitted.

Doncaster	27/04/62	27/04/62	Unclassified

Derailment damage at No.1 end. No.1 bogie, 1049, replaced by 1005. No.2 bogie, 1050, replaced by 1006.

St. Rollox	01/06/62	02/06/62	Unclassified

Bosses and holes for nameplates were drilled and stripped.

St. Rollox	14/06/62	16/06/62	Unclassified

Royal Scots Grey nameplates fitted.

Doncaster	26/09/62	28/09/62	Light

Flashover damage to all traction motors and 'Vee' ringsto re-tape. No. 1 bogie 1005, replaced by 1007. No.2 bogie, 1006, replaced by 1008. Both replacement bogies had been modified with stiffening plates. The body was given a six monthly exam. All traction equipment accessories including control cubicles and cable runs were overhauled. The following modifications were carried out – Exhaust pipe bellows fitted; Drawgear mod; Driver's brake valve mod. The locomotive's mileage is recorded as 184,000 miles since new.

Doncaster	19/12/62	11/01/63	General

No.1 engine, 427, replaced by 441 due to a suspected fractured cylinder liner. No.2 engine, unknown, replaced by 449. No.1 bogie, 1007, replaced by 1045. No.2 bogie, 1008, replaced by 1046. Boiler, 1494/J2950, replaced by 5087/J3238. The body was given an annual repair. The following modifications were carried out – Radiator fan grills; Lubricating oil and water sampling cocks; Bracket to compressor outlet pipe; Additional exhaust pipe filter; Exhaust tank drain pipes fitted to both power units. The locomotive mileage is recorded as 213,990 miles since new.

Doncaster	18/01/63	23/01/63	Unclassified

No.2 engine, 449, had 'B' side coolant radiator replaced. The coolant pipe test cock boss was welded.

Doncaster	14/07/63	15/07/63	Unclassified

No.2 exhauster was replaced and No.2 engine, 449, had a new primary fan shaft fitted.

D9000/9000/55 022 Royal Scots Grey (continued)

Loco Works	On Works	Off Works	Class of repair
Doncaster	29/07/63	03/08/63	Light

No.1 bogie, 1045, replaced by 1025. No.2 bogie, 1046, replaced by 1018. Boiler, 5087/J3238, replaced by 5098/J3249. No.1 engine, 441, had a secondary fan shaft fitted. The following modifications were carried out – Air supply and caustic injection to boiler feed water; Brake hanger rubbing bracket gussets.

Doncaster	02/10/63	05/10/63	Unclassified

Traction motor flashover damage. No.1 bogie, 1025, replaced by 1011. No.2 bogie, 1018, replaced by 1012.

Doncaster	15/10/63	16/10/63	Unclassified

No.1 engine, 441, replaced by 442 due to unknown defect.

Doncaster	13/11/63	14/11/63	Unclassified

Completion of boiler modifications. Fuel tanks were overhauled and lagged. Water treatment tank filler and overflow pipes were re-routed.

Doncaster	28/11/63	17/12/63	General

No.1 engine, 442, replaced by 430. No.2 engine, 449, replaced by 413. No.1 bogie, 1011, replaced by 1041. No.2 bogie, 1012, replaced by 1042. Boiler, 5098/J3249, replaced by 1486/J2942. The body was given a General repair. The coolant header tank overflow modification was carried out.

Doncaster	01/06/64	05/06/64	Light

No.1 bogie, 1041, replaced by 1005. No.2 bogie, 1042, replaced by 1006.

Doncaster	02/10/64	03/10/64	Unclassified

Defect to No.2 main generator. A load check was carried out. No.1 bogie, 1005, and No.2 bogie, 1006 received light attention.

Doncaster	05/10/64	06/10/64	Unclassified

No.2 engine, 430, replaced by 441. No.1 bogie, 1005, and No.2 bogie, 1006 were given "Light" repairs.

Doncaster	31/10/64	31/10/64	Unclassified

No.1 engine, 413, had the fan clutch repaired and gearbox examined. Boiler, 1486/J2942, had a new tube fitted.

Doncaster	12/11/64	15/11/64	Unclassified

No.2 engine, 441, replaced by 419 due to a suspected defective liner seal. No.1 bogie, 1005, and No.2 bogie, 1006 received light attention.

Doncaster	17/11/64	17/11/64	Unclassified

Bogies to be removed for inspection, locomotive derailed at Leeds City on 15/11/64. Bogie "crabbing" very badly after locomotive re-railed. No.1 bogie, 1005, replaced by 1003, No.2 bogie, 1006, replaced by 1004. All traction motors were replaced.

Doncaster	26/01/65	14/02/65	General

No.1 engine, 413, replaced by 444. No.2 engine, 419, replaced by 445. No.1 bogie, 1003, replaced by 1035. No.2 bogie, 1004, replaced by 1036. Boiler, 1486/J2942, replaced by 1494/J2950. The body was given a General repair and bodyside fractures were grooved and welded. All traction motors were replaced and modifications were carried out to exhauster access door.

Doncaster	15/04/65	15/04/65	Unclassified

Derailment damage. No.1 bogie, 1035, replaced by 1037. No.2 bogie, 1036, replaced by 1038. All traction motors were replaced.

Doncaster	27/05/65	29/05/65	Light

No.1 bogie, 1037, replaced by 1013. No.2 bogie, 1038, replaced by 1028. Boiler, 1494/J2950, was acid washed, tubes cleaned out and mountings overhauled. The body was given an Unclassified repair including repairs to fractures underneath the generator at both ends. The primary fan shaft was renewed. All traction motors were replaced.

Doncaster	25/09/65	28/09/65	Modification

New bogies fitted. No.1 bogie, 1013, replaced by 9000-25. No.2 bogie, 1028, replaced by 9000-26. Boiler, 1494/J2950, replaced by 1490/J2946. All traction motors were changed and the brakework overhauled.

Doncaster	15/10/65	15/10/65	Unclassified

Adjustments to boiler, 1490/J2946. One new battery cell was fitted.

182 DELTICS ON WORKS

D9000/9000/55 022 Royal Scots Grey (continued)

Loco Works	On Works	Off Works	Class of repair
Doncaster	30/10/65	30/10/65	Unclassified

Adjustments carried out to boiler, 1490/J2946.

Doncaster	03/11/65	17/11/65	General

No specific defect. No.1 engine, 444 and No.2 engine, 445, were given Unclassified repairs. No.1 bogie, 9000-25, and No.2 bogie, 9000-26, were given Light repairs. Boiler, 1490/J2946, replaced by 1495/J2951. The body was given a General repair. The following modifications were carried out – Protection bars to EP valves; Fire alarm bell. Oil resisting compound to sand filler ducts and modifications to footstep plate.

Doncaster	12/01/66	14/01/66	Unclassified

No.1 engine, 444, to be examined for water leaks. No.2 bogie, 9000-26 had No.5 wheel set changed.

Doncaster	09/03/66	09/03/66	Unclassified

Burst tubes on boiler, 1495/J2951. No.2 end secondary fan shaft was replaced and defective boiler tubes were repaired.

Doncaster	24/03/66	30/03/66	Light

No.1 engine, 444, had intermittent faults and was given an Unclassified repair. No.2 engine, 445, had 'failed' and was given an Unclassified repair. No.1 bogie, 9000-25, replaced by 9000-31, No.2 bogie, 9000-26, replaced by 9000-32. Boiler, 1495/J2951 was given an Unclassified repair. The body was given an Unclassified repair; all radiators and a defective exhaust silencer were replaced.

Doncaster	05/05/66	05/05/66	Unclassified

Flat batteries were recharged.

Doncaster	31/05/66	05/06/66	Unclassified

No.1 engine, 444, replaced by 417. No.2 engine, 445, replaced by 430. No.1 lubricating oil radiators were changed, as was No.2 primary gearbox.

Doncaster	08/07/66	11/07/66	Unclassified

No.2 bogie, 9000-32, suspension tube bearing to be examined, not being greased on No.4 axle. The axle was changed, as was No.1 coolant fan.

Doncaster	21/09/66	23/09/66	Unclassified

Defective axles. All axles were ultrasonically tested and Nos. 4, 5 & 6 tyres were turned.

Doncaster	01/11/66	02/11/66	Unclassified

No.2 engine, 430, exhaust silencer tank in roof split approximately 14 inches. Unable to weld without preheating. Both exhaust silencers were replaced.

Doncaster	08/12/66	15/01/67	General

No.1 engine, 417, replaced by 445. No.2 engine, 430, replaced by 457. No.1 bogie, 9000-31 and No.2 bogie, 9000-32 were given Unclassified repairs. Boiler, 1495/J2951, replaced by 4093 (this boiler was never recorded as being carried by any other Deltic, assuming that the quoted serial number is correct). The body was given a General repair, which included repairs to bodywork behind No.2 right hand door.

Doncaster	20/03/67	22/03/67	Unclassified

No.2 engine, 457, replaced by 426 due to con rod adrift. Repairs were carried out to No.1 roof section and lubricating oil radiators were changed.

Doncaster	04/04/67	07/04/67	Unclassified

Derailment damage. No.1 bogie, 9000-31, No.3 wheel left hand side flange badly cut. Excessive side play on Nos.3 & 1 axle boxes, left hand brake cylinder pipe flattened. Vacuum train pipe damaged at No.1 end. Bogie rubbing pad knocked off right side leading wheel at No.1 end and bogie-rubbing pad damaged left side trailing wheel at No.1 end. All wheelsets on both bogies were changed and derailment damage repaired.

Doncaster	02/08/67	04/08/67	Unclassified

Boiler, 4093, replaced by 5087/J3238.

Doncaster	15/08/67	18/08/67	Unclassified

Brushes renewed on both main generators. No.1 bogie, 9000-31, handbrake chain to adjust, No.2 right hand side rubber sand pipe holed. No.2 bogie, 9000-32, handbrake chain to adjust, No.4 traction motor seal missing. Exhauster stand secured and load regulator cover clip renewed at No.1 end. Both bogies were given Unclassified repairs including the changing of all wheel sets.

D9000/9000/55 022 Royal Scots Grey (continued)

Loco Works	On Works	Off Works	Class of repair
Doncaster	25/09/67	03/11/67	General

*No.1 engine, 445, replaced by 453. No.2 engine, 426, replaced by 411. No.1 bogie, 9000-31 and No.2 bogie, 9000-32 were given General repairs and refitted. Boiler, 5087/J3238, replaced by 5098/J3249. The body was given a General repair and repainted into **blue livery with full yellow nose ends**. The locomotive was fitted for dual braking.*

Doncaster	19/11/67	19/11/67	Modification

Modification to dual brake pipe work.

Doncaster	17/12/67	18/12/67	Modification

Compressor stand modified.

Doncaster	13/02/68	16/02/68	Unclassified

No.1 engine, 453, replaced by 418 on C.M.& E.E.'s instruction. No.2 engine, 411, replaced by 409 on C.M.& E.E.'s instruction.

Doncaster	22/03/68	29/03/68	Light

No.1 engine, 418, replaced by 412 due to a suspected cracked cylinder liner. No.2 engine, 409, was given an Unclassified repair. No.1 bogie, 9000-31, replaced by 9000-27. No.2 bogie, 9000-32, replaced by 9000-28. Boiler, 5098/J3249, replaced by 1495/J2951. The body was given an Unclassified repair.

Doncaster	01/05/68	03/05/68	Unclassified

No.1 engine, 412, replaced by 416. No.1 main generator breaking brushes, commutator undercut 1/8th inch – distance between segments 1/16th inch plus.

Doncaster	17/06/68	19/06/68	Unclassified

No.2 engine, 409, replaced by 418 due to 'AB' No.3 cylinder and piston defective. Crankcase cover broken by connecting rod.

Doncaster	18/07/68	23/07/68	Unclassified

No.2 engine, 418, replaced by 415 due to con rod through crankcase. No.1 engine, 416, hunting when power applied. Load regulator sluggish. Lubricating oil tank cleaned out and radiators changed.

Doncaster	05/09/68	13/09/68	Unclassified

No.1 engine, 416, replaced by 450. Lubricating oil tank and radiators were removed, flushed out and refitted.

Doncaster	23/10/68	03/12/68	Intermediate

All cables in ducting behind right hand door from engine room at No.1 end badly burnt. Casualty occurred on 1A46 on 21/10/68. No.1 engine, 450 and No.2 engine, 415 were given Unclassified repairs. No.1 bogie, 9000-27, replaced by 9000-37. No.2 bogie, 9000-28, replaced by 9000-38. Boiler, 1495/J2951, replaced by 1497/J2953. The body was given an Intermediate repair.

Doncaster	24/02/69	24/02/69	Unclassified

Repairs were carried out to bodyside damage which was filled and part painted and louvres were repaired. No.1 bogie, 9000-37, repairs were carried out to a damaged footstep. No.2 bogie, 9000-38, a damaged footstep and brake cylinders were changed.

Doncaster	06/03/69	07/03/69	Unclassified

No.2 engine, 415, exhaust drum fractured.

Doncaster	23/04/69	24/04/69	Unclassified

No.2 engine, 415, replaced by 431 due to sump full of coolant, suspect fractured liner.

Doncaster	21/07/69	26/07/69	Light

No.1 engine, 450, replaced by 449. No.2 engine, 431, replaced by 415. No.1 bogie, 9000-37, replaced by 9000-5. No.2 bogie, 9000-38, replaced by 9000-6. Boiler, 1497/J2953 was given an Unclassified repair.

Doncaster	30/12/69	07/01/70	Unclassified

No.1 cab heater circuit breaker and panel burnt. No.1 traction motor blower was changed and all associated ducting was repaired. The cab heater circuit breaker was changed and burnt wiring was renewed.

Doncaster	08/01/70	16/01/70	Unclassified

No.1 engine, 449, replaced by 453. No.2 engine, 415, replaced by 450. All traction motors were changed.

184 DELTICS ON WORKS

D9000/9000/55 022 Royal Scots Grey (continued)

Loco Works	On Works	Off Works	Class of repair
Doncaster	16/03/70	10/04/70	Intermediate

No.1 engine, 453, was given a Light repair and refitted. No.2 engine, 450, replaced by 457. No.1 bogie, 9000-5 and No.2 bogie, 9000-6, were given General repairs and refitted. Boiler, 1497/J2953, replaced by 5092/J3243. The body was given an Intermediate repair and modified water tanks for extra capacity were fitted.

Doncaster	10/04/70	13/04/70	Rectification

Flashover damage to both main generators and both bogies. This was rectified.

Doncaster	31/05/70	03/06/70	Unclassified

Excessive overheating on cables running between No.1 & No.2 cab A.V.R.'s and No.2 A.V.R. throwing solder. This was rectified.

Stratford DRS	23/07/70	27/07/70	Depot

Collision damage to body and both bogies. This was repaired.

Doncaster	28/10/70	31/10/70	Unclassified

No.1 main generator flashover. No.2 engine, 457, replaced by, 435, due to suspect cracked liner. At both ends, coolant pipes in the roof were leaking. No.1 boiler water tank was removed, repaired and refitted, oil leaks were rectified and flashover damage repaired.

Doncaster	17/11/70	24/12/70	Light

No.1 engine, 453, replaced by 406, due to aerating and coolant level switch defective. No.2 engine, 435, was given an Unclassified repair, fitted to 9020 for traffic, removed and then refitted to No.2 end. No.1 bogie, 9000-5, replaced by 9000-43. No.2 bogie, 9000-6, replaced by 9000-44. Boiler, 5092/J3243, was given a General repair. The body was given a Light repair.

Doncaster	23/01/71	27/01/71	Unclassified

No.2 engine, 435, replaced by 412, due to cylinder liner leaks – gas in coolant.

Doncaster	28/04/71	30/10/71	Intermediate

No.1 engine, 406, replaced by 435. No.2 engine, 412, replaced by 420. No.1 bogie, 9000-43, replaced by 9000-39. No.2 bogie, 9000-44, replaced by 9000-40. Boiler, 5092/J3243, replaced by 1486/J2942. The body was given an Intermediate repair. The loco fitted with E.T.H. equipment.

Doncaster	03/12/71	07/12/71	Unclassified

No.2 engine, 420, replaced by 458.

Doncaster	19/04/72	20/04/72	Unclassified

No.1 engine, 435, sill plate leaking oil onto No.3 traction motor. No.3 traction motor interpole to earth. No.3 traction motor was replaced. Both bogies had brakework repaired.

Doncaster	11/05/72	12/05/72	Unclassified

No.3 traction motor replaced due to suspect open circuit.

Doncaster	23/05/72	24/05/72	Unclassified

No.4 traction motor replaced due to wheel slip problems.

Doncaster	25/07/72	27/07/72	Unclassified

No.1 engine, 435, replaced by 416 due to throwing coolant.

Doncaster	14/08/72	18/08/72	Light

No.1 engine, 416, replaced by 433, due to coolant in engine sump. No.2 engine, 458, replaced by 444. No.1 bogie, 9000-39, replaced by 9000-31. No.2 bogie, 9000-40, replaced by 9000-32. Boiler, 1486/J2942, was given an Unclassified repair. The body was given a Light repair.

Doncaster	01/12/72	05/12/72	Unclassified

No.2 engine, 444, replaced by 416, due to being dephased – 'AB' crankshaft out of phase with 'BC'. No.1 end right hand footsteps repaired.

Doncaster	02/03/73	06/03/73	Unclassified

No.2 engine, 416, replaced by 455, due to 'CA' crankcase holed at No.3 position. No.2 end lubricating oil tanks and radiators were removed, cleaned and refitted.

Doncaster	22/03/73	28/03/73	Unclassified

No.1 engine, 433, scavenge blower repaired. No.1 main generator replaced. No.1 traction motor replaced and coolant header tank repaired.

Doncaster	16/07/73	15/08/73	Intermediate

No.1 engine, 433, replaced by 418. No.2 engine, 455, replaced by 426. No.1 bogie, 9000-31 and No.2 bogie, 9000-32 were given standard repairs. Boiler, 1486/J2942, replaced by 5086/J3237. The body was given an Intermediate repair.

D9000/9000/55 022 Royal Scots Grey (continued)

Loco Works	On Works	Off Works	Class of repair
Doncaster	17/08/73	18/08/73	Rectification

No.1 engine, 418 and No.2 engine, 426 both received rectification work.

Doncaster	19/10/73	24/10/73	Unclassified

No.1 main generator interpole burnt. No.2 main generator and all traction motors flashed over.

Doncaster	09/11/73	10/11/73	Unclassified

No.1 engine, 418, replaced by 404, due to throwing coolant, suspect fractured liner.

Doncaster	21/01/74	21/01/74	Modification

Earth fault relay modification.

Doncaster	18/03/74	26/03/74	Unclassified

No.1 engine, 404, replaced by 417, due to 'A5' conrod through crankcase.

Doncaster	09/04/74	10/04/74	Unclassified

No.2 engine, 426, throwing oil and heavy breathing; No fault found.

Doncaster	30/07/74	28/08/74	Light

No.1 engine, 417, replaced by 438, due to smoking from 'BC' breather, suspect fractured piston. No.2 engine, 426, replaced by 415. No.1 bogie, 9000-31, replaced by 9000-9. No.2 bogie, 9000-32, replaced by 9000-42. Boiler, 5086/J3237 was given an Unclassified repair.

Doncaster	28/08/74	02/09/74	Rectification

No.2 main generator flashover damage repaired.

Doncaster	30/10/74	01/11/74	Unclassified

No.1 engine, 438, replaced by 447, due to conrod through crankcase. No.1 end lubricating oil tanks and radiators removed, cleaned and refitted.

Doncaster	11/12/74	13/12/74	Unclassified

No.2 engine, 415, replaced by 448, due to 'C3' conrod broken and sump holed. No.2 end lubricating oil tanks and radiators removed, repaired and refitted.

Doncaster	06/01/75	12/01/75	Unclassified

Both main generators replaced due to compounding and overloading. Locomotive load bank tested for E.T.H. faults.

Doncaster	24/01/75	29/01/75	Unclassified

No.1 engine, 447, replaced by 455, due to aerating – suspect fractured liner. No.2 engine, 448, reports of high water temperature. No.2 end coolant radiators changed. Locomotive load tested and graphed.

Doncaster	24/04/75	20/08/75	Unclassified

No.1 engine, 455, replaced by 430. No.2 engine, 448, replaced by 414, due to exhaust coming from air inlet side of engine. No.1 boiler water tank was repaired and locomotive load tested and graphed. Coolant checks done, all coolant radiators changed.

Doncaster	25/11/75	26/02/76	Intermediate

No.1 engine, 430, replaced by 452. No.2 engine, 414, replaced by 454. No.1 bogie, 9000-9, replaced by 9000-31. No.2 bogie, 9000-42, replaced by 9000-32. Boiler, 5086/J3237, replaced by 5096/J3247. No.2 end blower brush gear burnt out.

Doncaster	16/06/76	25/06/76	Unclassified

No.1 main generator commutator damaged due to flashover. No.2 main generator and all traction motors also flashed over. Both main generators were replaced. All traction motor flashover damage repaired as was No.2 traction motor nose suspension pad.

Doncaster	19/07/76	21/07/76	Unclassified

No.2 engine, 454, replaced by 417, due to being dephased.

Doncaster	10/08/76	13/08/76	Unclassified

No.1 engine, 452, replaced by 448, due to heavy oil leaks from phasing gear.

Doncaster	15/09/76	20/09/76	Unclassified

No.2 engine, 417, replaced by 434, due to 'AC' crankcase fractured at No.1 end by end cover. A boiler water tank was replaced and No.2 primary crankshaft was repaired.

Doncaster	21/11/76	24/11/76	Unclassified

No.1 engine, 448, had Martinair unit and governor replaced. No.1 bogie, 9000-31 -horn guides secured. No.1 roof section was repaired, as was boiler steam valve.

186 DELTICS ON WORKS

D9000/9000/55 022 Royal Scots Grey (continued)

Loco Works	On Works	Off Works	Class of repair
Doncaster	20/01/77	22/01/77	Unclassified

No.1 engine, 448, replaced by 429.

Doncaster	26/02/77	01/03/77	Unclassified

No.2 engine, 434, replaced by 416, due to Dowty pump drive shaft bearing collapsed in phasing gear case.

Doncaster	14/03/77	30/03/77	Light

No.1 engine, 429, replaced by 420, due to high spectrographic analysis. No.2 engine, 416, replaced by 407, due to fuel dilution problems. No.1 bogie, 9000-31, replaced by 9000-3. No.2 bogie, 9000-32, replaced by 9000-4. Boiler, 5096/J3247, was given an Unclassified repair.

Doncaster	29/04/77	03/05/77	Unclassified

No.2 engine, 407, replaced by 539, due to crankcase holed in four places. No.1 end right hand body footstep secured and No.1 traction motor blower casing replaced.

Doncaster	27/05/77	31/05/77	Unclassified

Flashover damage on both main generators repaired. All traction motors replaced.

Doncaster	03/10/77	07/10/77	Unclassified

No.2 engine, 539, replaced by 421, due to unusual noises and throwing oil. Bogie centre pivots secured and No.4 traction motor was repaired.

Doncaster	09/12/77	16/12/77	Unclassified

Both main generators replaced due to bad flashover damage. All traction motors had flashover damage repaired.

Doncaster	16/01/78	20/01/78	Unclassified

No.2 engine, 421, replaced by 407, due to aerating badly. No.1 end load regulator had oil leaks rectified.

Doncaster	08/02/78	10/02/78	Unclassified

No.2 engine, 407, replaced by 408, due to aerating. Load regulator oil leaks were repaired.

Doncaster	25/02/78	01/03/78	Unclassified

Flashover damage on both control cubicles and both main generators. Traction motor blower ducting was cleared out. Both main generators were replaced, as were all traction motors.

Doncaster	29/03/78	24/04/78	Unclassified

No.1 engine, 420, replaced by 430, due to aerating.

Doncaster	12/05/78	18/05/78	Unclassified

No.1 engine, 430, replaced by 419, due to crankcase holed. No.1 bogie, 9000-3, had 'R9' horn liner secured. No.1 primary shaft replaced and leaks on both load regulators were rectified.

Doncaster	02/06/78	13/06/78	Unclassified

No.2 engine, 408, replaced by 421, due to 'CA' crankcase holed and No.4 conrod fractured. Nos.1 & 2 traction motors were replaced. No.2 lubricating oil tank and radiator were cleaned out.

Doncaster	02/10/78	03/10/78	Unclassified

No.2 engine, 419, had exciter gearbox and engine hour recorder changed. No.1 driving flange bearing for crankshaft changed due to excessive wear. No.2 primary shaft was repaired.

Doncaster	19/10/78	25/10/78	Unclassified

No.1 engine, 419, replaced by 452, due to aerating. No.2 primary gearbox and No.3 radiator fan changed.

Doncaster	06/01/79	15/03/79	Unclassified

No.1 engine, 452, replaced by 442. No.2 engine, 421, replaced by 446. Boiler roof and stack fractures repaired.

Doncaster	29/03/79	04/04/79	Unclassified

No.1 engine, 442, replaced by 437. No.1 main generator field windings and interpoles to earth.

Doncaster	16/07/79	22/09/79	Intermediate

No.1 engine, 437, replaced by 409, due to a fractured liner. No.2 engine, 446, replaced by 430, due to pistons life expired. No.1 bogie, 9000-3 and No.2 bogie, 9000-4, were given standard repairs and refitted. Boiler, 5096/J3247, replaced by 1495/J2951.

Doncaster	15/02/80	18/02/80	Unclassified

No.1 engine, 409, replaced by 425, due to being dephased.

Doncaster	19/03/80	22/03/80	Unclassified

No.1 engine, 425, had governor and racks reset and the unit was graphed. No.2 engine, 430, replaced by 409, due to aerating, a suspect fractured liner.

D9000/9000/55 022 Royal Scots Grey (continued)

Loco Works	On Works	Off Works	Class of repair
Doncaster	10/05/80	14/05/80	Unclassified

No.2 engine, 409, replaced by 413, due to 'AB' crankcase damper and cover holed.

Doncaster	10/07/80	25/07/80	Unclassified

No.2 engine, 413, had governor changed. No.1 bogie, 9000-3 and No.2 bogie, 9000-4, had replacement swing links and springs fitted due to rough riding.

Doncaster	01/08/80	05/08/80	Unclassified

No.2 engine, 413, replaced by 427, due to a fractured liner.

Doncaster	15/08/80	19/08/80	Unclassified

No.2 engine, 427, replaced by 443, due to aerating.

Doncaster	03/09/80	05/09/80	Unclassified

No.2 engine, 443, replaced by 426, due to 'AB' crankshaft damper housing shattered.

Doncaster	17/12/80	19/12/80	Unclassified

No.1 engine, 425, replaced by 418, due to aerating.

Doncaster	03/02/81	09/02/81	Unclassified

No.1 engine, 418, replaced by 421, due to a fractured liner.

Doncaster	06/07/81	09/07/81	Unclassified

No.2 engine, 426, replaced by 413, due to coolant in lubricating oil. Lubricating oil tank and radiator flushed out. No.1 primary shaft replaced.

Stratford DRS	09/09/81	12/10/81	Depot

Collision damage at No.2 end, buffer knocked off. This was repaired.

Stratford DRS	06/11/81	11/11/81	Depot

No.1 engine, 421, replaced by 434, due to breathing heavy. Both main generators flashed over.

Doncaster	05/01/82	08/09/83	-

Locomotive arrived on Works after withdrawal on 02/01/82 with the following main components fitted; No.1 engine, 434. No.2 engine, 413. No.1 bogie, 9000-3. No.2 bogie, 9000-4. Boiler, 1495/J2951. Locomotive for scrap, but eventually sold for preservation.

D9001/9001/55 001 St. Paddy

Loco Works	On Works	Off Works	Class of repair
Doncaster	16/01/61	17/01/61	Acceptance trials

New locomotive fitted with the following major components; No.1 engine, 404. No.2 engine, 410. No.1 bogie, 1003. No.2 bogie, 1004. Boiler, 1495/J2951. Released for exhibition purposes at Stratford.

Doncaster	18/01/61	23/02/61	Acceptance trials

Continuation of Acceptance trials.

Doncaster	23/03/61	29/03/61	Modification

Modification of compressor housing. The locomotive mileage is recorded as 5,134 miles since new.

Vulcan Foundry	06/04/61	21/04/61	Modification

Bogie modification. The locomotive mileage was recorded as 6,059 miles since new.

Doncaster	19/07/61	20/07/61	Unclassified

St. Paddy nameplates fitted.

Vulcan Foundry	31/07/61	22/08/61	Unclassified

Remedial work to traction motor support brackets.

Doncaster	20/11/61	13/12/61	General

No.1 engine, 404, replaced by 451. No.2 engine, 410, replaced by 426. No.1 bogie, 1003, replaced by 1045. No.2 bogie, 1004, replaced by 1046. The body was given an annual repair. All four radiator fan gearboxes were replaced by modified units. All four cab doors were draughtproofed.

Doncaster	09/01/62	11/01/62	Unclassified

All brake blocks were renewed, No.1 sand pipes and water scoop snouts were repaired. Experimental asbestos gaiters were fitted to engine side of air intakes on both power units.

D9001/9001/55 001 St. Paddy (continued)

Loco Works	On Works	Off Works	Class of repair
Doncaster	27/02/62	27/02/62	Not recorded

No information recorded.

Doncaster	13/03/62	16/03/62	Unclassified

Derailment damage incurred on 13/03/62. The vacuum train pipe was damaged above the framing on the right hand side, the left hand rail guard was broken and the right hand one bent on No.1 bogie, 1045. Trailing sand pipes and water scoop nose were damaged and a buffer pad was missing from the right hand trailing end of No.2 bogie, 1046, which also had a brake pin working out on the left hand side middle wheel. All necessary repairs were carried out including the removal, welding and refitting of No.1 water tank.

Doncaster	23/05/62	24/05/62	Light

No.1 bogie, 1045, replaced by 1017. No.2 bogie, 1046, replaced by 1018. The body was given a six-month exam. The steam pipe from the train pipe for the cab gauge was repaired. The locomotive mileage was recorded as 129,020 miles since new.

Doncaster	13/06/62	15/06/62	Unclassified

No.1 engine, 451 and No.2 engine, 426, were load tested by E.E.Co. representatives. No.1 bogie, 1017, replaced by 1037. No.2 bogie, 1018, replaced by 1038. Seven repaired wire bogie restraining slings were fitted. No.2 'A' side coolant radiator was removed, repaired and refitted. A new suspension unit sleeve was fitted to No.5 wheelset. New Timken roller bearings were fitted to all suspension unit sleeves.

Doncaster	09/07/62	11/07/62	Unclassified

No.1 engine, 451, replaced by 445, due to 'B4' cylinder liner cracked. No.2 engine, 426, had a new crankcase top cover joint 'AB' fitted.

Doncaster	31/08/62	03/09/62	Unclassified

No.2 engine, 426, replaced by 413, due to 'B' crankshaft broken. Modified flexible exhaust pipes were fitted to both power units.

Doncaster	10/11/62	10/11/62	Unclassified

No.1 bogie, 1037, right hand corner cracked. Flexible vacuum pipe casting from train pipe removed, train pipe blanked off. Boiler high and low flame relay wanted – defective relay removed. Bogie frames were welded and the boiler motor was exchanged. The locomotive mileage was recorded as 206,020 miles since new.

Doncaster	03/12/62	04/12/62	Unclassified

No.1 bogie, 1037, replaced by 1002. No.2 bogie, 1038, replaced by 1049. The Drawgear modification was carried out.

Doncaster	08/03/63	08/03/63	Unclassified

Leaking boiler tubes. Boiler, 1495/J2951, was overhauled. The locomotive mileage was recorded as 267,400 miles since new.

Doncaster	13/03/63	14/03/63	Unclassified

Bogie change due to fractures. No.1 bogie, 1002, replaced by 1031. No.2 bogie, 1049, replaced by 1032.

Doncaster	01/04/63	20/04/63	General

No.1 engine, 445, replaced by 455. No.2 engine, 413, replaced by 452. No.1 bogie, 1031, replaced by 1047. No.2 bogie, 1032, replaced by 1048. Boiler, 1495/J2951, replaced by 5089/J3240. The body was given an annual repair. The locomotive was equipped for Dynamometer trials. The following modifications were carried out – Boiler air ducting and water treatment injection; Soundproofing; Control cubicle sealing; Sampling cocks; A.W.S. positioning; Fuel tank elbows; Lubricating oil strainer gauge; Exhaust drum drain pipes. The locomotive mileage was recorded as 279,000 miles since new.

Doncaster	18/05/63	20/05/63	Unclassified

Boiler tubes leaking 4th from left second row, 5th from left bottom row firebox end. Boiler, 5089/J3240 was overhauled, six new tubes were fitted, one re-expanded and welded. The locomotive mileage was recorded as 283,010 miles since new.

Doncaster	13/08/63	13/08/63	Unclassified

Axlebox horn liners loose, No.6 horn to be checked, cracked at front. No.1 bogie, 1047, replaced by 1045. No.2 bogie, 1048, replaced by 1046. The locomotive mileage was recorded as 334,018 since new.

DELTICS ON WORKS   189

D9001/9001/55 001 St. Paddy (continued)

Loco Works	On Works	Off Works	Class of repair
Doncaster	29/08/63	29/08/63	Unclassified

Boiler tube fractures. Tubes were tested and welded. The locomotive mileage was recorded as 343,700 miles since new.

| Doncaster | 18/09/63 | 21/09/63 | Light |

No.1 bogie, 1045, replaced by 1023. No.2 bogie, 1046, replaced by 1024. The body was given a six monthly exam.

| Doncaster | 11/11/63 | 14/11/63 | Unclassified |

Completion of boiler modifications. The fuel tanks were fibreglass coated. A fracture in No.2 water tank was repaired. The water treatment tank filler and overflow pipes were re-routed.

| Doncaster | 07/01/64 | 07/01/64 | Unclassified |

A reconditioned boiler burner motor was fitted.

| Doncaster | 08/02/64 | 11/02/64 | Unclassified |

No.1 bogie, 1023, headstock rivets loose. Nos. 1 & 6 traction motor headstocks were re-riveted and a fracture in a transom was welded. Both primary radiator fan shafts were renewed.

| Doncaster | 17/03/64 | 12/04/64 | General |

No. 1 engine, 455, replaced by 449. No. 2 engine, 452, replaced by 453. No.1 bogie, 1023, replaced by 1001. No.2 bogie, 1024, replaced by 1050. Boiler, 5089/J3240, replaced by 1491/J2947. The body was given a General repair that included the welding of bodyside fractures. The following modifications were carried out – Header overflow tank; Nose-end hatch for access to exhausters; Anti-frost precautions – Lagging of pipes, train heating valve, toilet header tank drain; Bogie transom; Speedometer clocks; Boiler fuses.

| Doncaster | 25/08/64 | 26/08/64 | Unclassified |

Derailment damage, suspect Nos. 4 & 6 axles bent. No.1 bogie, 1001, replaced by 1007. No. 2 bogie, 1050, replaced by 1008. The cab sides were repaired and sand ejector was renewed. A stabilising sling bracket was welded, bogie rubbing pads and warning horns were repaired. All traction motors were replaced. The following modifications were carried out – Boiler fuses; Boiler pump resistance; Speedometer (No.1 end); Exhauster cutout valve.

| Doncaster | 24/09/64 | 26/09/64 | Unclassified |

No. 1 main generator commutator to be trued.

| Doncaster | 06/11/64 | 10/11/64 | Light |

No.1 bogie, 1007, replaced by 1041. No.2 bogie, 1008, replaced by 1042. All traction motors were replaced.

| Doncaster | 20/03/65 | 22/03/65 | Unclassified |

Boiler, 1491/J2947, had a replacement burner motor fitted.

| Doncaster | 25/03/65 | 04/04/65 | General |

No. 1 engine, 449 and No. 2 engine, 453, were given a six monthly repair. No. 1 bogie, 1041, replaced by 1001. No. 2 bogie, 1042, replaced by 1050. Boiler, 1491/J2947, replaced by 1486/J2942. The body was given a General repair that also involved renewing No. 1 end boiler water tank.

| Doncaster | 08/07/65 | 10/07/65 | Unclassified |

No.1 engine, 449, replaced by 422, due to a cylinder liner seal defective.

| Doncaster | 21/07/65 | 22/07/65 | Unclassified |

Boiler, 1486/J2942, wiring burnt, 'NUWAY' parts to renew and leaking boiler tube. The 'NUWAY' burner was repaired and the leaking boiler tube was re-welded.

| Doncaster | 19/09/65 | 23/09/65 | Unclassified |

Fuel tank and boiler water tank damaged. No.1 left hand fuel tank was repaired. No.1 bogie, 1001, replaced by 9000-23. No.2 bogie, 1050, replaced by 9000-24. Boiler, 1486/J2942, had it's burner motor changed. All traction motors were replaced and brakegear was overhauled.

| Doncaster | 27/10/65 | 02/11/65 | Light |

No.2 engine, 453, replaced by 427. No.1 bogie, 9000-23 and No.2 bogie, 9000-24, were both given a Light repair. Boiler, 1486/J2942, was acid descaled. The following modifications were carried out – Protection bars for EP valves; Fire alarm bell gong.

DELTICS ON WORKS

D9001/9001/55 001 St. Paddy (continued)

Loco Works	On Works	Off Works	Class of repair
Doncaster	30/12/65	02/01/66	Unclassified

Boiler, 1486/J2942, replaced by 5090/J3241, due to split tubes.

| Doncaster | 20/01/66 | 20/01/66 | Unclassified |

Boiler mounting front brackets on floor broken. These were welded. The locomotive mileage was recorded as 767,910 miles since new.

| Doncaster | 01/02/66 | 02/02/66 | Unclassified |

No.1 engine, 422, replaced by 423, due to 'CA' flexible shaft broken.

| Doncaster | 20/03/66 | 02/04/66 | General |

No.1 engine, 423 and No.2 engine, 427, were given Unclassified repairs. No.1 bogie, 9000-23, replaced by 9000-3. No.2 bogie, 9000-24, replaced by 9000-4. Boiler, 5090/J3241, replaced by 1492/J2948. The body was given a General repair. The locomotive mileage was recorded as 974,840 miles since new.

| Doncaster | 02/06/66 | 03/06/66 | Unclassified |

No.1 engine, 423, replaced by 404. Boiler, 1492/J2948, right, back mounting fractured on 'B' side, this was repaired.

| Doncaster | 06/07/66 | 11/07/66 | Unclassified |

No.2 engine, 427, replaced by 422, due to water pump drive defective and under speed quill shaft to renew. No.1 primary fan shaft was renewed and the locomotive was lifted for access to fractured axles on No.1 bogie, 9000-3.

| Doncaster | 15/09/66 | 16/09/66 | Unclassified |

Six-mm fracture on No.6 axle gear side. The locomotive mileage was recorded as 1,049,880 miles since new.

| Doncaster | 26/09/66 | 26/09/66 | Unclassified |

Boiler floor fractured adjacent to carrier mounting. The floor decking was welded underneath boiler feet.

| Doncaster | 27/09/66 | 28/09/66 | Unclassified |

No.2 engine, 422, replaced by 421, due to coolant in sump. No.1 main generator was replaced. The locomotive mileage was recorded as 1,050,480 miles since new.

| Doncaster | 20/10/66 | 25/10/66 | Unclassified |

Boiler mounting legs broken at brackets adjacent to No.1 engine at the fillet welds, cracks extending into parent metal. Boiler, 1492/J2948, replaced by 5088/J3239. The boiler mounting brackets and fractures were welded. No.2 main generator right hand side terminal bar was renewed and thimbles resweated.

| Doncaster | 27/10/66 | 28/10/66 | Rectification |

Boiler, 5088/J3239, had the burner motor changed.

| Doncaster | 31/10/66 | 31/10/66 | Rectification |

Boiler, 5088/J3239, had the fuel pump changed. The locomotive mileage was recorded as 1,051,510 miles since new.

| Doncaster | 14/11/66 | 17/11/66 | Light |

No.1 engine, 404 and No.2 engine, 421, were given Unclassified repairs. No.1 bogie, 9000-3, replaced by 9000-45. No.2 bogie, 9000-4, replaced by 9000-46. Boiler, 5088/J3239, was given an Unclassified repair. The body was given an Unclassified repair.

| Doncaster | 28/12/66 | 29/12/66 | Unclassified |

Flashover damage was repaired and brush boxes cleaned up on both main generators. The locomotive mileage was recorded as 1,074,060 miles since new.

| Doncaster | 11/01/67 | 14/01/67 | Unclassified |

No.1 engine, 404, replaced by 442, due to a fractured liner. A split in No.2 coolant header tank was repaired. No.2 main generator was cleaned. Nos.4 & 6 wheelsets were changed due to fractured axles.

D9001/9001/55 001 St. Paddy (continued)

Loco Works	On Works	Off Works	Class of repair
Doncaster	02/03/67	30/03/67	General

No.1 engine, 442, replaced by 414. No.2 engine, 421, replaced by 429. No.1 bogie, 9000-45, replaced by 9000-47. No.2 bogie, 9000-46, replaced by 9000-48. Boiler, 5088/J3239 was given an Unclassified repair. The body was given a General repair and full yellow nose ends applied. The locomotive mileage was recorded as 1,097,240 miles since new.

Loco Works	On Works	Off Works	Class of repair
Doncaster	27/07/67	02/08/67	Unclassified

No.1 main generator commutator oval, No.1 deadman's valve to renew, parts missing, No.5 axle brake safety stay missing. Both exhaust silencers were replaced, as was No.1 main generator.

Doncaster	17/10/67	21/10/67	Light

No.1 bogie, 9000-47, replaced by 9000-5. No.2 bogie, 9000-48, replaced by 9000-6. Boiler, 5088/J3239 was given an Unclassified repair. Boiler water scoop piston seals were leaking, scoop taking 15 seconds to lift. Both control cubicles were overhauled and main generators were cleaned out. A note states ' I. R. Wells advises that the defect to the scoop is a depot repair'.

Doncaster	05/12/67	06/12/67	Unclassified

No.1 engine, 414, replaced by 410, due to 'AB' crankshaft case burst due to fractured No.5 cylinder con rod.

Doncaster	26/02/68	29/03/68	General

No.1 engine, 410, replaced by 438. No.2 engine, 429, replaced by 408. No.1 bogie, 9000-5, replaced by 9000-29. No.2 bogie, 9000-6, replaced by 9000-30. Boiler, 5088/J3239, replaced by 1486/J2942. The body was given a General repair and the locomotive was fitted for dual braking.

Doncaster	13/09/68	17/09/68	Unclassified

No.1 bogie, 9000-29, No.2 traction motor insulation reading low, motor throwing solder and suspected armature band breaking up. No.2 bogie, 9000-30, No.6 traction motor insulation reading very low. Flashover damage on both main generators was repaired and Nos. 2 & 6 traction motors were replaced.

Doncaster	18/11/68	22/11/68	Light

No.1 engine, 438 and No.2 engine, 408 were given Unclassified repairs. No.1 bogie, 9000-29, replaced by 9000-27. No.2 bogie, 9000-30, replaced by 9000-28. Boiler, 1486/J2942 was given an Unclassified repair. No.2 main generator was replaced.

Doncaster	25/04/69	29/04/69	Unclassified

No.2 engine, 408, replaced by 439, due to con rod through crankcase side.

Doncaster	16/05/69	16/05/69	Unclassified

No.2 bogie, 9000-28, No.6 traction motor earth defect. No.6 traction motor was replaced.

Doncaster	02/07/69	26/07/69	Intermediate

*No.1 engine, 438, replaced by 454, due to being time expired. No.2 engine, 439, replaced by 428. No.1 bogie, 9000-27, replaced by 9000-3. No.2 bogie, 9000-28, replaced by 9000-4. Boiler, 1486/J2942, replaced by 1494/J2950. The body was given an Intermediate repair and repainted into **blue livery with full yellow nose ends**.*

Doncaster	01/08/69	05/08/69	Rectification

Flashover damage to both main generators. Slight flashover damage to all traction motors on No.1 bogie, 9000-3. On No.2 bogie, 9000-4, Nos. 4 & 5 traction motors had slight flashover damage whilst No.6 traction motor needed one brush box renewing. All flashover damage was repaired.

Doncaster	17/10/69	17/10/69	Unclassified

Repairs were carried out to interior lighting cables.

D9001/9001/55 001 St. Paddy (continued)

Loco Works	On Works	Off Works	Class of repair
Doncaster	04/12/69	06/12/69	Unclassified

No.2 bogie, 9000-4, axle suspension tube bearings seized and retaining plate set screws sheared. No.4 wheelset and traction motor were changed.

| Doncaster | 13/12/69 | 18/12/69 | Unclassified |

Burnt cabling. Suspect cable damaged in bodyside trunking. Repeated trouble with heaters and lights not working. Burnt wiring in control cubicles in both cabs and all necessary wiring in trunking was repaired. A.V.R.'s and traction motor blower motors were checked.

| Doncaster | 01/03/70 | 11/03/70 | Light |

No.1 engine, 454 and No.2 engine, 428 were given Light repairs and refitted. No.1 bogie, 9000-3, replaced by 9000-25. No.2 bogie, 9000-4, replaced by 9000-26. Boiler, 1494/J2950 was given an Unclassified repair. The body was given a Light repair and modified boiler water tanks for extra capacity were fitted.

| Doncaster | 20/07/70 | 21/07/70 | Unclassified |

No.2 engine, 428, replaced by 414, due to a fractured liner, water in sump.

| Doncaster | 19/08/70 | 19/08/70 | Unclassified |

No.1 engine, 454, replaced by 436, due to running very rough, breathing badly and thick black exhaust. Also coolant level switch wiring reversed in cubicle.

| Doncaster | 24/10/70 | 25/10/70 | Unclassified |

No.2 engine, 414, replaced by 450, due to a fractured liner.

| Doncaster | 05/11/70 | 07/11/70 | Unclassified |

No.1 engine, 436, replaced by 424, due to an internal coolant leak.

| Doncaster | 01/12/70 | 26/03/71 | Intermediate |

No.1 engine, 424, replaced by 418. No.2 engine, 450, was given an Unclassified repair and refitted. No.1 bogie, 9000-25, replaced by 9000-5. No.2 bogie, 9000-26, replaced by 9000-6. Boiler, 1494/J2950, replaced by 1493/J2949. The body was given an Intermediate repair. The locomotive was fitted with E.T.H. equipment.

| Doncaster | 29/03/71 | 29/03/71 | Rectification |

Locomotive low in power and field weakening not taking place. The locomotive was trialed and faults rectified.

| Doncaster | 24/04/71 | 25/04/71 | Unclassified |

Bad leak in No.1 boiler water tank. This was replaced.

| Doncaster | 02/06/71 | 03/06/71 | Unclassified |

No.2 engine, 450, replaced by 538, due to breathing heavy and unusual noises when running.

| Doncaster | 02/08/71 | 05/08/71 | Unclassified |

No.1 engine, 418, replaced by 413, due to excessive water in lubricating oil. Oil tanks and radiators were changed.

| Doncaster | 14/08/71 | 18/08/71 | Unclassified |

No.2 traction motor severely flashed over. The traction motor was replaced.

| Doncaster | 06/12/71 | 07/12/71 | Unclassified |

No.1 bogie, 9000-5, bogie spring pin working out, fastening stud sheared. No.1 bogie, 9000-5 and No.2 bogie, 9000-6, both had spring hanger top pin securing plate studs adrift. All necessary repairs were carried out.

| Doncaster | 07/01/72 | 15/01/72 | Light |

No.1 engine, 413, was given a Light repair and refitted. No.2 engine, 538, was given an Intermediate repair and refitted. No.1 bogie, 9000-5, replaced by 9000-35. No.2 bogie, 9000-6, replaced by 9000-36. Boiler, 1493/J2949, was given an Unclassified repair. The body was given a Light repair.

| Doncaster | 27/03/72 | 30/03/72 | Unclassified |

No.1 engine, 413, replaced by 437, due to a defective liner seal. No.1 end wheel wear compensator down to earth. No.1 end radiators and lubricating oil tank were removed, cleaned and refitted.

| Doncaster | 06/05/72 | 12/05/72 | Unclassified |

No.1 engine, 437, replaced by 451, due to persistent high water temperature, No.1 end coolant radiators were changed. No.2 engine, 538, was given an Intermediate repair and refitted due to being dephased.

D9001/9001/55 001 St. Paddy (continued)

Loco Works	On Works	Off Works	Class of repair
Doncaster	10/08/72	11/08/72	Unclassified

No.1 engine, 451, 'AB' crankcase suspect fractured. No.2 engine, 538, persistent high water temperature. No.2 end coolant radiators were changed and crankcase fractures on No.1 engine, 451, were repaired.

Doncaster	06/09/72	05/10/72	Unclassified

No.1 engine, 451, replaced by 424. No.2 engine, 538, replaced by 416, due to driver reported 'knocking' noise. No.2 main generator armature banding burst.

Doncaster	15/11/72	17/11/72	Unclassified

Minor collision damage to body and bogies. No.1 engine, 424, had a missing overspeed trip replaced and the collision damage was repaired.

Doncaster	27/11/72	21/12/72	Intermediate

No.1 engine, 424, replaced by 451. No.2 engine, 416, replaced by 538. No.1 bogie, 9000-35, replaced by 9000-25. No.2 bogie, 9000-36, replaced by 9000-26. Boiler, 1493/J2949, replaced by 1488/J2944. The body was given an Intermediate repair.

Doncaster	08/01/73	10/01/73	Unclassified

No.2 engine, 538, replaced by 444, due to 3A 'C' bank injector and plug blown out. No.2 right hand fuel tank leaking. No.2 load regulator leaking oil. All repairs were carried out.

Doncaster	02/02/73	07/02/73	Unclassified

No.2 engine, 444, replaced by 417. No.2 main generator was replaced.

Doncaster	02/05/73	05/05/73	Unclassified

Flashover damage on both main generators and all traction motors. This was repaired.

Doncaster	07/05/73	08/05/73	Unclassified

No.2 engine, 417, governor to change.

Doncaster	22/06/73	03/07/73	Unclassified

Flashover damage to both main generators. No.2 boiler water tank fractured. Both main generators were replaced.

Doncaster	29/09/73	15/10/73	Light

No.1 engine, 451, replaced by 539. No.2 engine, 417, replaced by 438. No.1 bogie, 9000-25, replaced by 9000-11. No.2 bogie, 9000-26, replaced by 9000-12. Boiler, 1488/J2944 was given an Unclassified repair. The body was given a Light repair.

Doncaster	16/10/73	18/10/73	Rectification

Loss of power. This was rectified.

Doncaster	16/11/73	19/11/73	Unclassified

No.2 engine, 438, replaced by 440, due to suspect dephased.

Doncaster	24/01/74	24/01/74	Modification

Earth fault relay modification.

Doncaster	04/09/74	05/09/74	Unclassified

Leaking water tanks which were removed, repaired and refitted.

Doncaster	20/09/74	23/09/74	Unclassified

No.2 engine, 440, replaced by 427, due to suspected aerating.

Doncaster	25/09/74	05/11/74	Intermediate

No.1 engine, 539, replaced by 441, due to 'AB' crankcase fractured at free end of casing. No.2 engine, 427, replaced by 424. No.1 bogie, 9000-11, replaced by 9000-27. No.2 bogie, 9000-12, replaced by 9000-28. Boiler, 1488/J2944, replaced by 5089/J3240. Boiler water tanks leaking badly. The body was given an Intermediate repair.

Doncaster	22/01/75	24/01/75	Rectification

No.2 engine, 424, replaced by 410, due to 'A' side crankcase fractured.

Doncaster	02/05/75	19/05/75	Unclassified

No.1 engine, 441, replaced by 445, due to a fractured liner. No.1 end lubricating oil tank and radiators, removed, cleaned and refitted. No.1 end coolant radiators were changed.

Doncaster	30/06/75	02/07/75	Unclassified

No.3 wheelset, left hand side out of alignment. Wheelset changed.

Doncaster	25/07/75	29/07/75	Unclassified

No.1 main generator flashed over and interpoles to earth. No.2 main generator overhauled. All flashover damage repaired on both bogies and traction motors. No.1 main generator changed.

D9001/9001/55 001 St. Paddy (continued)

Loco Works	On Works	Off Works	Class of repair
Doncaster	03/10/75	08/10/75	Unclassified

No.1 bogie, 9000-27, replaced by 9000-15. No.2 bogie, 9000-28, replaced by 9000-16. No.1 traction motor pinion gear worn.

Doncaster	14/10/75	17/11/75	Light

No.1 engine, 445, replaced by 435, due to aerating. No.2 engine, 410, replaced by 441, due to breathing badly. No bogie or boiler details were recorded, however, none of these were changed. Locomotive weighed at 105t 1cwt.

Doncaster	17/03/76	19/03/76	Unclassified

No.2 engine, 441, replaced by 405, due to breathing heavy. No.1 boiler water tank holed.

Doncaster	29/03/76	31/03/76	Unclassified

No.2 engine, 405, replaced by 423, due to being dephased.

Doncaster	12/04/76	14/05/76	Unclassified

No.1 engine, 435, replaced by 410. No.2 engine, 423, replaced by 439, due to crankcase holed. No.2 end lubricating oil tank and radiator removed, cleaned and refitted.

Doncaster	23/06/76	30/06/76	Unclassified

No.1 main generator brush box copper collector ring burnt. No.1 main generator changed.

Doncaster	28/08/76	28/08/76	Unclassified

Boiler mounting foot adjacent to No.1 engine 'A' bank mounting block broken. Floor fractured about 18" long adjacent to No.1 engine 'C' bank. Locomotive restricted "No boiler" – All defects repaired.

Doncaster	21/10/76	26/10/76	Unclassified

No.1 main generator insulation value low. Boiler mounting foot adjacent to No.1 engine 'A' bank fractured. Floor fractured adjacent to boiler foot No.1 engine 'C' bank. Boiler water tank holed. No.2 primary crankshaft broken. Overspeed governor casing broken, governor linkage bent, all on No.2 engine. All defects repaired.

Doncaster	26/11/76	27/02/77	Intermediate

No.1 engine, 410, replaced by 443. No.2 engine, 439, replaced by 433. No.1 bogie, 9000-15, replaced by 9000-47. No.2 bogie, 9000-16, replaced by 9000-22. Boiler, 5089/J3240, had a standard repair and refitted. Route indicator panels were plated over. The body was given an Intermediate repair. Locomotive weighed at 104t.

Doncaster	22/03/77	23/03/77	Unclassified

No.1 engine, 443, replaced by 422, due to being dephased.

Doncaster	05/05/77	09/05/77	Unclassified

No.2 engine, 433, bottom crankcase joint blown out. 'AC' cover joint blown out adjacent to front engine mounting foot on 'A' side of engine. Also pressure test of fuel pipe from tank to transfer pump. This was found to be blocked and airlocked. No.2 engine, 433, 'AC' crankcase joint renewed.

Doncaster	14/05/77	24/05/77	Unclassified

No.1 engine, 422, bad oil leak at joint connection of 'AC' crankcase to phasing gearcase. No.2 engine, 433, repeatedly failing with fuel starvation. The fuel tank, pipework and filters were removed and refitted after examination. No.1 engine, 422, had phasing case replaced.

Doncaster	23/07/77	27/07/77	Unclassified

Both boiler water tanks leaking. No.1 end load regulator oil leak. All defects repaired.

Doncaster	20/11/77	21/03/78	Unclassified

Bogie centre pivot studs to renew. No.1 bogie, 9000-47 had segments on the bolster secured and No.2 & 3 traction motors repaired. No.2 bogie, 9000-22, had No.5 traction motor nose suspension plate and Nos.4 & 5 traction motor bellows repaired. Segments on the bolster also secured, as were 'L5' and 'R10' horn liners. No.1 engine, 422, replaced by 430. No.2 engine, 433, replaced by 438.

Doncaster	24/03/78	-	-

No.2 engine, 438, conrod through crankcase. No.2 radiator fan primary shaft splines worn. No.1 engine, 430, removed. No.2 engine, 438, removed. The locomotive arrived with the following other main components fitted; No.1 bogie, 9000-47. No.2 bogie, 9000-22. Boiler, 5089/J3240. The locomotive was eventually withdrawn on 05/01/80 while still on Works.

D9002/9002/55 002 The King's Own Yorkshire Light Infantry

Loco Works	On Works	Off Works	Class of repair
Doncaster	09/03/61	Not recorded	Acceptance trials

New locomotive fitted with the following main components; No.1 engine, 408. No.2 engine, 407. No.1 bogie, 1005. No.2 bogie, 1006. Boiler, 1487/J2943.

Doncaster	13/09/61	21/09/61	Unclassified

Collision and derailment damage to No.1 end. The nose superstructure at the left hand side was damaged and the left buffer had the face torn partly off. The air horn, footsteps, lifeguards, sand pipes and blower louvres all needed to be repaired. Air-cooling pipe to the voltage regulator was fractured. The bogie had all wheels derailed and had to be drawn from the other locomotive. No.1 left hand side cab superstructure was repaired. No.1 bogie, 1005, was examined and three new pairs of wheels were fitted. New footsteps, buffer, sand pipe and sand chute were fitted. Air horn and voltage regulator cooling pipe were repaired, as were lifeguards and horn guard. The locomotive mileage was recorded as 25,640 miles since new.

R.S.H. Darlington	25/10/61	28/02/62	Unclassified

No.1 engine, 408, replaced by 446, due to 'BC' crankshaft quill shaft broken or disconnected. No.2 engine, 407, replaced by 417.

Doncaster	28/02/62	01/03/62	General

No.1 bogie, 1005, replaced by 1011. No.2 bogie, 1006, replaced by 1012. Boiler, 1487/J2943, was overhauled. The body was given an annual repair. A new right hand front cab demister glass was fitted.

Doncaster	30/09/62	05/10/62	Light

No.1 bogie, 1011, replaced by 1019. No.2 bogie, 1012, replaced by 1020. Boiler, 1487/J2943, was overhauled. The body was given a six-monthly exam.

Doncaster	31/10/62	06/11/62	Unclassified

No.2 engine, 417, replaced by 431, due to a broken piston. Boiler, 1487/J2943, was overhauled. Nos.3 & 4 radiator fan grills were modified.

Doncaster	04/01/63	08/01/63	Unclassified

No.1 power unit drum tank split and No.1 bogie inside spring plank out of position at right side. No.1 power unit exhaust collector drum was removed, welded and refitted. No.1 bogie, 1019, trailing transom beam was reseated on swing link. Locomotive mileage recorded as 159,000.

Doncaster	27/02/63	14/03/63	General

No.1 engine, 446, replaced by 438. No.1 bogie, 1019, replaced by 1029. No.2 bogie, 1020, replaced by 1030. Boiler, 1487/J2943, replaced by 5091/J3242. The following modifications were carried out – A.W.S. positioning; Soundproofing; Cubicle sealing; Air ducts; Sampling cocks; Exhaust drain pipe; Fan guards; Water contents gauge; Sand traps and pipes.

Doncaster	08/05/63	09/05/63	Unclassified

Traction motor flashover damage. No.1 bogie, 1029, replaced by 1041. No.2 bogie, 1030, replaced by 1042.

Doncaster	16/06/63	17/06/63	Unclassified

Leaking boiler tubes. A boiler tube exam was carried out.

Doncaster	06/08/63	20/08/63	Light

No.2 engine, 431, replaced by 423. No.1 bogie, 1041, replaced by 1015. No.2 bogie, 1042, replaced by 1016.

Doncaster	22/08/63	23/08/63	Unclassified

No.1 engine, 438, replaced by 458. Boiler, 5091/J3242, replaced by 5087/J3238. The following modifications were carried out – Caustic injection to boiler water treatment; Rubbing bracket strengthening mod on bogies.

Doncaster	27/12/63	23/01/64	General

No.1 bogie, 1015, replaced by 1017. No.2 bogie, 1016, replaced by 1026. Boiler, 5087/J3238, replaced by 5093/J3244. The following modifications were carried out – Header tank overflow tank fitted; Generator bearer feet strengtheners fitted; Speedometer clocks.

Doncaster	24/03/64	26/03/64	Unclassified

Six boiler tubes leaking in centre at return box end. The boiler was acid washed, leaking tubes were welded and the caustic metering pump was repaired.

D9002/9002/55 002 The King's Own Yorkshire Light Infantry (continued)

Loco Works	On Works	Off Works	Class of repair
Doncaster	25/05/64	30/05/64	Light

No.1 bogie, 1017, replaced by 1025. No.2 bogie, 1026, replaced by 1018. The following modifications were carried out – Anti-frost precautions – Lagging of pipes; Auto drain valve; Steam heater valve.

Doncaster	31/05/64	01/06/64	Unclassified

No.3 traction motor was changed.

Doncaster	20/06/64	26/06/64	Unclassified

No.2 engine, 423, replaced by 429, due to No.5 'C' exhaust piston broken.

Doncaster	28/09/64	29/09/64	Unclassified

No.2 bogie, 1018, transom on right hand side fractured. No.1 bogie, 1025, had a headstock fracture welded and No.2 bogie had the fracture in the transom repaired.

Doncaster	12/10/64	12/11/64	General

No.1 engine, 458, replaced by 426. No.2 engine, 429, replaced by 438. No.1 bogie, 1025, replaced by 1049. No.2 bogie, 1018, replaced by 1002. Boiler, 5093/J3244, replaced by 5092/J3243. The body was given a General repair including the repair of bodyside superstructure fractures.

Doncaster	16/02/65	18/02/65	Unclassified

No.1 engine, 426, replaced by 437, due to 'C3' liner suspect cracked.

Doncaster	12/04/65	15/04/65	Light

No.1 engine, 437, replaced by 458. No.2 engine, 438, had an injector change. No.1 bogie, 1049, replaced by 1019. No.2 bogie, 1002, replaced by 1020. Boiler, 5092/J3243, was acid washed. The body was given an Unclassified repair. All traction motors were replaced and the tyres were turned. The following modifications were carried out – Spiders to transom; Transom radius; Centre gussets; Cold pins in headstock; Horn liners; Steel plate to brake hanger rubbing bracket; Nose suspension.

Doncaster	27/08/65	30/08/65	Unclassified

No.1 bogie, 1019, back cross stay fractured. The headstock was chipped and welded. Boiler, 5092/J3243, replaced by 5096/J3247.

Doncaster	26/09/65	23/10/65	General

No.1 engine, 458, replaced by 419. No.2 engine, 438, replaced by 430. No.1 bogie, 1019, replaced by 9000-33. No.2 bogie, 1020, replaced by 9000-34. Boiler, 5096/J3247, was given an Unclassified repair. The body was given a Gen. repair. The following mods were carried out – Protection bar for EP valves; Fire alarm bell; Fitting of jointing paste between sandbox filler flanges.

Doncaster	27/01/66	29/01/66	Unclassified

No.1 power unit silencer fractured. The split silencer was repaired and the safety valve on the Boiler was changed.

Doncaster	01/03/66	06/03/66	Light

No.1 engine, 419 and No.2 engine, 430, were given Unclassified repairs. No.1 bogie, 9000-33, replaced by 9000-29. No.2 bogie, 9000-34, replaced by 9000-30. Boiler, 5096/J3247, was given an Unclassified repair. The body was given an Unclassified repair.

Doncaster	23/03/66	24/03/66	Unclassified

No.2 engine, 430, replaced by 408.

Doncaster	13/05/66	15/05/66	Unclassified

Nos.3 & 4 traction motors to be examined. Despite this, the repairs are recorded as an Unclassified repair to No.1 traction motor and repairs to a fractured axle.

Doncaster	21/09/66	18/10/66	General

*No.1 engine, 419, replaced by 539. No.2 engine, 408, replaced by 433. No.1 bogie, 9000-29, replaced by 9000-9. No.2 bogie, 9000-30, replaced by 9000-10. Boiler, 5096/J3247, replaced by 1488/J2944. The body was given a General repair and repainted into **blue livery with full yellow nose ends.***

Doncaster	15/02/67	18/02/67	Light

No.1 engine, 539 and No.2 engine, 433, were given Unclassified repairs. No.1 bogie, 9000-9, replaced by 9000-21. No.2 bogie, 9000-10, replaced by 9000-22. Boiler, 1488/J2944, was given an Unclassified repair. The body was given an Unclassified repair.

Doncaster	04/07/67	05/07/67	Unclassified

No.1 engine, 539, replaced by 446.

D9002/9002/55 002 The King's Own Yorkshire Light Infantry (continued)

Loco Works	On Works	Off Works	Class of repair
Doncaster	09/08/67	11/08/67	Unclassified

No.2 engine, 433, replaced by 434, due to a suspected fractured liner. Boiler low water, Mobrey Niphon plug defective. A Boiler tube was repaired.

Doncaster	23/10/67	24/11/67	General

No.1 engine, 446, replaced by 432. No.2 engine, 434, replaced by 447. No.1 bogie, 9000-21, replaced by 9000-43. No.2 bogie, 9000-22, replaced by 9000-44. Boiler, 1488/J2944, replaced by 1492/J2948. The body was given a General repair. The locomotive was fitted for dual braking.

Doncaster	30/01/68	01/02/68	Unclassified

No.2 engine, 447, replaced by 427, due to 'water in engine'.

Doncaster	29/04/68	03/05/68	Light

No.1 engine, 432 and No.2 engine, 427, were given Unclassified repairs. No.1 bogie, 9000-43, replaced by 9000-13. No.2 bogie, 9000-44, replaced by 9000-14. Boiler, 1492/J2948 was given an Unclassified repair. The body was given an Unclassified repair.

Doncaster	30/09/68	02/10/68	Unclassified

No.1 engine, 432, replaced by 440. Flashover damage on No.2 main generator was cleaned up.

Doncaster	15/11/68	15/11/68	Unclassified

No.2 fan drive shaft and fan gearbox were changed. Flashover damage on both main generators was cleaned up.

Doncaster	02/12/68	23/12/68	General

No.1 engine, 440, replaced by 406. No.2 engine, 427, replaced by 435. No.1 bogie, 9000-13 and No.2 bogie, 9000-14, were given General repairs. Boiler, 1492/J2948, replaced by 5089/J3240. The body was given a General repair

Doncaster	22/04/69	23/04/69	Unclassified

No.1 power unit exhaust silencer was changed.

Doncaster	22/08/69	30/08/69	Light

No.1 engine, 406 and No.2 engine, 435, were given Unclassified repairs. No.1 bogie, 9000-13, replaced by 9000-1. No.2 bogie, 9000-14, replaced by 9000-2. Boiler, 5089/J3240, was given an Unclassified repair. The body was given an Unclassified repair. Water tank capacity modification carried out.

Doncaster	31/12/69	02/01/70	Unclassified

No.2 engine, 435, replaced by 452, due to a suspected fractured liner. No.1 main generator blower motor taken for 9000. Boiler safety valve taken for 9014. No.2 traction motor blower motor was removed and an overhauled replacement fitted. No.2 end lubricating oil radiators and tank were removed, cleaned and refitted. All missing items were replaced.

Doncaster	06/02/70	10/02/70	Unclassified

No.1 engine, 406, replaced by 443, due to coolant in sump.

Doncaster	05/03/70	11/03/70	Unclassified

Persistent flashover problems. The wheel slip relay was checked and oil leaks in both load regulators repaired. Traction motor ductings were also repaired and flashover damage cleaned up. Nos. 2 & 5 traction motors were replaced.

Doncaster	Not recorded	09/05/70	Intermediate

No.1 engine, 443 and No.2 engine 452, were given Light repairs and refitted. No.1 bogie, 9000-1, replaced by 9000-37. No.2 bogie, 9000-2, replaced by 9000-38. Boiler, J5091/J3240, replaced by 5091/J3242. The body was given an Intermediate repair.

Doncaster	26/06/70	28/06/70	Unclassified

No.1 engine, 443, replaced by 419, due to not rotating when generator turns over on starting.

Doncaster	31/10/70	01/11/70	Unclassified

No. 2 engine, 452, replaced by 404, due to fractured liners.

Doncaster	28/11/70	29/11/70	Unclassified

No.2 engine, 404, replaced by 433, due to high crankcase pressure.

198 DELTICS ON WORKS

D9002/9002/55 002 The King's Own Yorkshire Light Infantry (continued)

Loco Works	On Works	Off Works	Class of repair
Doncaster	29/01/71	04/05/71	Light

All traction motors and both main generators flashed over. No.1 engine, 419, replaced by 454. No.2 engine, 433, replaced by 414. No.1 bogie, 9000-37, replaced by 9000-17. No.2 bogie, 9000-38, replaced by 9000-18. Boiler, 5091/J3242 was given an Unclassified repair. The body was given a Light repair. The locomotive was fitted with E.T.H. equipment.

Doncaster	17/07/71	22/07/71	Unclassified

No.2 main generator to earth. No.2 main generator was replaced.

Doncaster	22/10/71	23/10/71	Unclassified

No.1 engine, 454, continually cutting out due to fuel starvation. This was rectified.

Doncaster	12/11/71	13/11/71	Unclassified

No.2 bogie, 9000-18, sheared studs on cross beam. These were replaced and No.5 traction motor gearcase oil was changed. Nos. 4 & 5 traction motor safety stays were also repaired.

Doncaster	09/03/72	22/04/72	Intermediate

No.1 engine, 454, replaced by 434. No.2 engine, 414, replaced by 454 (after removal from No.1 end and a General repair) due to breathing heavy. No.1 bogie, 9000-17 and No.2 bogie, 9000-18, were given General repairs and refitted. Boiler, 5091/J3242, replaced by 5093/J3244. The body was given an Intermediate repair.

Doncaster	24/04/72	26/04/72	Rectification

Rectification work to the body was carried out.

Doncaster	03/05/72	07/05/72	Unclassified

No.1 engine, 434, replaced by 437, due to throwing oil.

Doncaster	25/05/72	03/06/72	Unclassified

No.1 engine, 437, drive to main generator defective. 437 was given an Intermediate repair.

Doncaster	27/07/72	27/07/72	Unclassified

No.1 engine, 437, 'C' bank fuel pump camshaft assembly base joint leaking. The fuel pump cam box gasket was renewed. No.1 bogie, 9000-17, had a lifeguard changed, brake blocks renewed and brakework washed up. No.2 bogie, 9000-18 - brake blocks changed and brakework washed up.

Doncaster	01/09/72	02/09/72	Unclassified

No.1 engine, 437, injector adaptor seals leaking. The adaptor seals were changed.

Doncaster	31/10/72	01/11/72	Unclassified

No.1 engine, 437, replaced by 432. No.1 end lubricating oil tank and radiators were changed.

Doncaster	01/11/72	05/11/72	Unclassified

No.1 end upper structure suspected collision damage. Sand traps removed to give clearance on No.1 bogie, 9000-17, due to them being continually knocked off. No.1 engine, 432, had an internal coolant leak. All necessary repairs were carried out.

Doncaster	04/12/72	06/12/72	Unclassified

No.1 engine, 432, replaced by 424, due to being dephased.

Doncaster	15/01/73	17/01/73	Unclassified

No.1 engine, 424, replaced by 415, due to breathing heavy. No.2 engine, 454, replaced by 408, due to breathing heavy.

Doncaster	23/01/73	24/01/73	Unclassified

No.1 engine, 415, auxiliary generator drive defective. This was repaired.

Doncaster	26/01/73	30/01/73	Unclassified

No.1 engine, 415, replaced by 432, for phasing gear examination.

Doncaster	05/02/73	09/02/73	Unclassified

No.1 engine, 432, replaced by 415, due to being dephased. No.2 boiler water tank seam split. Both load regulators leaking oil. All repairs were carried out.

Doncaster	20/02/73	01/03/73	Light

No.1 engine, 415, replaced by 418, due to breathing heavy. No.2 engine, 408, replaced by 435. No.1 bogie, 9000-17, replaced by 9000-5. No.2 bogie, 9000-18, replaced by 9000-6. Boiler, 5093/J3244, was given an Unclassified repair. The body was given a Light repair.

Doncaster	02/03/73	05/03/73	Rectification

No.1 traction motor to be changed.

D9002/9002/55 002 The King's Own Yorkshire Light Infantry (continued)

Loco Works	On Works	Off Works	Class of repair
Doncaster	12/07/73	14/07/73	Unclassified

No.1 engine, 418, replaced by 411, due to aerating, suspected fractured liner.

Doncaster	25/07/73	27/07/73	Unclassified

No.2 engine, 435, replaced by 414, due to 'A' bank crankshaft damper through crankcase.

Doncaster	09/11/73	08/12/73	Intermediate

No.1 engine, 411, replaced by 416. No.2 engine, 414, replaced by 438. No.1 bogie, 9000-5, replaced by 9000-35. No.2 bogie, 9000-6, replaced by 9000-36. Boiler, 5093/J3244, replaced by 5098/J3249. The body was given an Intermediate repair.

Doncaster	10/12/73	11/12/73	Rectification

Flashover damage to No.1 main generator. This was rectified.

Doncaster	13/12/73	14/12/73	Unclassified

No.1 engine, 416, replaced by 448.

Doncaster	28/01/74	28/01/74	Modification

Earth fault relay modification.

Doncaster	25/06/74	12/07/74	Unclassified

No.2 engine, 438, replaced by 455, due to drive to main generator sheared. The boiler water tanks were repaired. E.T.H. and temperature probe modifications were fitted.

Doncaster	05/09/74	08/09/74	Unclassified

No.1 engine, 448, replaced by 456, due to aluminium particles in primary filter.

Doncaster	12/12/74	31/12/74	Light

No.1 engine, 456, replaced by 538. No.2 engine, 455, replaced by 443. No.1 bogie, 9000-35, replaced by 9000-24. No.2 bogie, 9000-36, replaced by 9000-48. Boiler, 5098/J3249, was given an Unclassified repair.

Doncaster	08/02/75	11/02/75	Unclassified

No.1 engine, 538, replaced by 415, due to breathing heavy and high spectrographic analysis. No.2 boiler water tank fractured. Flexible steam pipe to fit.

Doncaster	19/08/75	20/08/75	Unclassified

No.1 engine, 415, replaced by 405, due to 'BC' big end stud broken, one stud stretched and crankcase tie bolt broken. No.2 primary crankshaft and No.2 boiler water tank changed.

Doncaster	15/09/75	18/09/75	Unclassified

No.2 engine, 443, replaced by 429, due to breathing heavy.

Doncaster	24/10/75	29/10/75	Unclassified

No.2 engine, 429, replaced by 410, due to crankcase tie bolt broken.

Doncaster	05/11/75	05/11/75	Rectification

No.2 engine, 410, 'A2' injector studs broken. This was rectified.

Doncaster	03/12/75	07/12/75	Unclassified

No.2 engine, 410, replaced by 428. Boiler, 5098/J3249, replaced by 5088/J3239.

Doncaster	16/03/76	10/11/76	Heavy General

No.1 engine, 405, replaced by 441. No.2 engine, 428, replaced by 445. No.1 bogie, 9000-24, replaced by 9000-5. No.2 bogie, 9000-48, replaced by 9000-6. Boiler, 5088/J3239, replaced by 1487/J2943. Route indicator panels were plated over.

Doncaster	04/01/77	06/01/77	Unclassified

No.1 engine, 441, replaced by 451, due to crankcase holed. No.1 lubricating oil tank and radiator removed, cleaned and refitted.

Doncaster	15/03/77	17/03/77	Unclassified

No.1 engine, 451, replaced by 434, due to being dephased.

Doncaster	16/05/77	20/05/77	Unclassified

No.1 engine, 434, replaced by 446, due to breathing heavy and low oil pressure. No.2 engine, 445, replaced by 414, due to scavenger blower defective. No.2 radiator fan gearbox was exchanged, as were the batteries.

Doncaster	23/05/77	25/05/77	Unclassified

No.2 traction motor throwing solder. Nos. 2 & 5 traction motors isolated. No.2 motor replaced.

Doncaster	07/07/77	12/07/77	Unclassified

No.2 engine, 414, replaced by 454, due to main drive sheared.

Doncaster	01/11/77	08/11/77	Unclassified

No.1 engine, 446, replaced by 436.

D9002/9002/55 002 The King's Own Yorkshire Light Infantry (continued)

Loco Works	On Works	Off Works	Class of repair
Doncaster	22/11/77	25/11/77	Unclassified

No.3 traction motor throwing solder and insulation reading zero. No.3 traction motor replaced and No.2 traction motor junction box and cables were renewed. Locomotive weighed at 102t 13cwt.

Doncaster	13/01/78	18/01/78	Unclassified

No.1 main generator armature to earth. Generator was replaced. Wire 'E4' in conduit under No.1 engine to earth. This was renewed.

Doncaster	14/06/78	16/08/78	Light

No.1 engine, 436, replaced by 410. No.2 engine, 454, replaced by 445, due to special gudgeon pin housing examination required. No.1 bogie, 9000-5, replaced by 9000-33. No.2 bogie, 9000-6, replaced by 9000-34. Boiler, 1487/J2943, was given an Unclassified repair. Locomotive weighed at 103t 1cwt.

Doncaster	22/09/78	25/09/78	Unclassified

No.2 engine, 445, replaced by 539, due to a fractured liner. No.2 nose end door catch to repair.

Doncaster	11/11/78	14/11/78	Unclassified

No.2 engine, 539, replaced by 437, due to crankcase holed due to damper coming adrift. Nos. 1 & 2 primary crankshafts to renew. No.2 traction motor blower was changed.

Doncaster	28/12/78	08/01/79	Unclassified

No.1 engine, 410, replaced by 414, due to aerating. No.2 load regulator contacts to renew, regulator to be reset using a radius tool. Roof to body drain pipe flexibles to renew where necessary. Reported E.T.H. cutting out, sequence checks to be made from both cabs and generator voltage relay setting to be checked against both main generators. No.2 engine, 437, reported continually cutting out. No.1 bogie, 9000-33, 'L3' swing link adrift. 'R3' brake cylinder air pipe to renew. The E.T.H. checks were done and voltage relay adjusted. No.2 lubricating oil bypass valve was renewed. Repairs to No.2 engine, 437 and No.1 bogie, 9000-33, were carried out.

Doncaster	01/02/79	06/02/79	Unclassified

No.2 engine, 437, replaced by 421, due to aerating badly. No.1 load regulator tips to renew as necessary.

Doncaster	21/03/79	27/03/79	Unclassified

No.1 engine, 414, hose fractured near to phasing case. No.2 engine, 421, Martinair and overspeed unit to change and coolant leaks to rectify. All repairs were carried out.

Doncaster	01/05/79	16/08/79	Unclassified

No.1 engine, 414, replaced by 452, due to a fractured cylinder liner. No.2 engine, 421, replaced by 415, due to fuel dilution and high iron content. No.2 bogie, 9000-34, Nos. 4 & 6 traction motor nose pads fractured. No.1 end 'A' side engine room doorframe to renew. No.2 end driver's side windscreen leaking water. All repairs were carried out.

Doncaster	30/01/80	11/02/80	Unclassified

Collision damage repairs. No.1 buffer beam out of alignment on right hand side and back 2". Buffer beam bent causing bogie to strike E.T.H. socket. Second man's sliding window and frame required. No.2 load regulator badly burnt. All damage was repaired.

Doncaster	18/02/80	21/02/80	Unclassified

No.2 engine, 415, replaced by 449, due to a suspected fractured liner. The boiler roof was removed and refitted for repairs to boiler stack.

Doncaster	16/06/80	18/06/80	Unclassified

No.2 engine, 449, replaced by 404, due to a suspected fractured liner. Marked for depot attention was No.2 end train jumper cable insulation to be taped, as was No.1 generator field coils, 'Vee' ring insulators to be cleaned and brushes to be changed. No.1 bogie, 9000-33, required 'L1' horn liner to be secured. No.2 bogie, 9000-34, had 'R12' horn liner to secure. All horn liners secured.

Doncaster	05/08/80	15/08/80	Unclassified

No.1 engine, 452, replaced by 448, due to a suspect leaking cylinder liner. Also fuel hose robbed. Marked for depot attention was No.2 primary shaft fan excessive play. Horn liners had become detached on both bogies; these were repaired. Locomotive weighed at 103t 11cwt.

Doncaster	01/09/80	03/09/80	Unclassified

No.1 engine, 448, replaced by 447, due to being dephased. Engine room floors to clean.

D9002/9002/55 002 The King's Own Yorkshire Light Infantry (continued)

Loco Works	On Works	Off Works	Class of repair
Doncaster	14/10/80	11/12/80	Intermediate

*No.1 engine, 447, replaced by 407. No.2 engine, 404, replaced by 445. No.1 bogie, 9000-33, replaced by 9000-17. No.2 bogie, 9000-34, replaced by 9000-18. Boiler, 1487/J2943, replaced by 5092/J3243. The locomotive was repainted into original **two-tone green livery with full yellow ends** in readiness for eventual preservation at the National Railway Museum, York. Locomotive weighed at 103t 3cwt.*

Doncaster	18/12/80	18/12/80	Rectification

No.2 engine, 445, will not run. The Dowty oil pump was changed, racks reset and engine hour recorder changed.

Doncaster	03/02/81	10/02/81	Unclassified

No.2 engine, 445, replaced by 406, due to scavenge blower shaft sheared.

Doncaster	12/08/81	18/08/81	Unclassified

No.2 engine, 406, replaced by 419, due to being dephased. Both primary gearbox keys were loose. Depot to rectify.

Doncaster	20/08/81	28/08/81	Unclassified

No.2 engine, 419, replaced by 437, due to exciter drive smashing generator fan housing.

Doncaster	08/09/81	11/09/81	Unclassified

No.1 engine, 407, replaced by 457, due to a suspected fractured liner.

Stratford D.R.S.	24/11/81	26/11/81	Depot

No.2 engine, 437, replaced by 442 or 449, due to broken con. rod through 'B' & 'C' banks.

Stratford D.R.S.	01/12/81	03/12/81	Depot

No.1 engine, 457, replaced by 442 or 449, due to main generator down to earth.

D9003/9003/55 003 Meld

Loco Works	On Works	Off Works	Class of repair
Doncaster	27/03/61	Not recorded	Acceptance trials

New locomotive fitted with following components – No.1 engine, 415. No.2 engine, 414. No.1 bogie, 1007. No.2 bogie, 1008. Boiler, 1488/J2944.

Vulcan Foundry	07/04/61	27/04/61	Modifications

Modifications to bogies.

Doncaster	10/07/61	12/07/61	Unclassified

A boiler water tank was replaced and a superstructure fracture near a cab window was repaired. Meld nameplates fitted.

Vulcan Foundry	05/08/61	18/08/61	Unclassified

No.1 bogie, 1007, fractured headstock repaired. No.2 traction motor nose piece fractured at weld. This was repaired. The locomotive mileage was recorded as 21,000 miles.

Vulcan Foundry	25/10/61	02/11/61	Unclassified

No.1 engine, 415, replaced by 420. The locomotive mileage was recorded as 49,500 miles.

Doncaster	06/11/61	10/11/61	Light

Collision damage. No.1 end leading right hand side panelling split. Support brackets fractured and twisted. The bogie equalising beam was overhauled. Boiler, 1488/J2944 was defective and was made operable. The body had three monthly MP11 exams carried out and superstructure skin repairs. The locomotive mileage was recorded as 58,000 miles.

R.S.H. Darlington	07/12/61	22/12/61	Unclassified

No.2 engine, 414, replaced by 404, due to broken piston rings. Flashover damage on all traction motors and both main generators was repaired. The locomotive mileage was recorded as 62,360 miles.

R.S.H. Darlington	22/05/62	02/06/62	Unclassified

Bad flats on No.2 bogie, 1008, No.4 wheelset. The locomotive mileage was recorded as 119,440 miles.

D9003/9003/55 003 Meld (continued)

Loco Works	On Works	Off Works	Class of repair
Doncaster	02/06/62	05/06/62	Light

No.1 bogie, 1007, replaced by 1045. No.2 bogie, 1008, replaced by 1046. Boiler, 1488/J2944 was overhauled.

Doncaster	08/08/62	09/08/62	Unclassified

No.2 engine, 404, replaced by 430. The flexible exhaust pipes modification was fitted.

Doncaster	09/11/62	12/11/62	Unclassified

All traction motors and both main generators flashed over. No.1 bogie, 1045, left hand corner fractured. All traction motors were replaced.

Doncaster	05/12/62	14/12/62	General

No.1 engine, 420, replaced by 443. No.2 engine, 430, replaced by 448. No.1 bogie, 1045, replaced by 1031. No.2 bogie, 1046, replaced by 1032. Boiler, 1488/J2944, replaced by 5094/J3245. The body was given an annual repair.

Doncaster	12/03/63	13/03/63	Unclassified

No.1 bogie, 1031, replaced by 1009, due to transom cracks. No.2 bogie, 1032, replaced by 1010, due to transom cracks. The locomotive mileage is recorded as 261,700 miles.

Doncaster	01/04/63	04/04/63	Unclassified

Cracks in transoms of No.1 bogie, 1009 and No.2 bogie 1010. Cracks in main transom adjacent to No.4 traction motor suspension bracket. Footplates over grills on radiator cooling fans to be correctly fitted. Both bogies were chipped and welded. Exhaust drain extension modification was fitted. The locomotive mileage was recorded as 273,530 miles.

Doncaster	21/05/63	31/05/63	Light

No.1 bogie, 1009, replaced by 1035. No.2 bogie, 1010, replaced by 1036. The body was given a six monthly exam. The following modifications were carried out – Air supply ducting; Caustic injection to boiler; Automatic blow down to boiler fitted; Exhaust drain modification blanked off.

Doncaster	21/09/63	22/09/63	Unclassified

No.2 water tank split. The water tank was overhauled and a defective water contents gauge was replaced. The locomotive mileage was recorded as 364,220 miles.

Doncaster	04/10/63	09/10/63	Unclassified

No.1 bogie, 1035, replaced by 1025. No.2 bogie, 1036, replaced by 1018. No.2 traction motor armature down to earth. The locomotive mileage was recorded as 373,240 miles.

Doncaster	12/10/63	15/10/63	Unclassified

No.2 engine, 448, replaced by 426, due to a suspect fractured liner. No.1 engine, 443, had injector seats modified. The locomotive mileage was recorded as 374,320 miles.

Doncaster	19/11/63	03/12/63	General

No.1 engine, 443, replaced by 422. No.2 engine, 426, replaced by 447. No.1 bogie, 1025, replaced by 1009. No.2 bogie, 1018, replaced by 1010. Boiler, 5094/J3245, replaced by 1494/J2950. The body was given an annual repair. The following modifications were carried out – Soundproofing; Draughtsealing; Header tank overflow tank; Speedometer instruments. The locomotive mileage was recorded as 389,360 miles.

Doncaster	13/02/64	13/02/64	Unclassified

No.1 end bufferbeam and right hand buffer badly damaged. Vacuum pipe bracket on bufferbeam bent and fractured. No.1 end bufferbeam and vacuum pipes were repaired and a replacement right hand buffer was fitted.

Doncaster	09/06/64	12/06/64	Unclassified

No.1 bogie, 1009, replaced by 1017. No.2 bogie, 1010, replaced by 1026.

Doncaster	02/01/65	23/01/65	General

No.1 engine, 422, replaced by 423. No.2 engine, 447, replaced by 433. No.1 bogie, 1017, replaced by 1009. No.2 bogie, 1026, replaced by 1010. Boiler, 1494/J2950, replaced by 1487/J2943. The body was given a General repair. The following modification was carried out – Exhauster access doors.

Doncaster	06/03/65	06/03/65	Unclassified

No.1 end lubricating oil elements were renewed.

D9003/9003/55 003 Meld (continued)

Loco Works	On Works	Off Works	Class of repair
Doncaster	10/05/65	13/05/65	Light

No.1 bogie, 1009, replaced by 1015. No.2 bogie, 1010, replaced by 1016. Boiler, 1487/J2943, was acid washed and tubes were cleaned out. No.2 radiator fan gearbox was replaced. The following modifications were carried out – Spiders; Transom gussets; Cold pins in headstocks; Horn liners; Steel plate to brake hanger rubbing brackets; Nose suspension.

Doncaster	31/07/65	03/08/65	Unclassified

All coolant radiators were replaced. The boiler had a new "NU-WAY" burner fitted, the water pump was replaced and a restrictor valve was fitted.

Doncaster	04/08/65	08/08/65	Unclassified

All coolant radiators were replaced.

Doncaster	17/08/65	18/08/65	Unclassified

Batteries were replaced.

Doncaster	11/09/65	14/09/65	Unclassified

No.1 engine, 423, replaced by 439, due to water pump drive shaft broken. No.1 primary fan shaft was replaced. The burner motor on the boiler was also replaced.

Doncaster	06/11/65	06/11/65	Unclassified

No.4 axlebox horn block fractured. The fractures were welded.

Doncaster	10/12/65	23/12/65	General

No.1 engine, 439, replaced by 442. No.2 engine, 433, replaced by 417. No.1 bogie, 1015, replaced by 9000-1. No.2 bogie, 1016, replaced by 9000-2. Boiler, 1487/J2943, replaced by 1490/J2946. The body was given a General repair. The following modifications were fitted – Protection bar for EP valves; Hand pump and cock levers; Fire alarm bell; Cab footstep stiffening plates; Oil resisting compound to sand chutes.

Doncaster	22/01/66	24/01/66	Unclassified

Boiler tubes split and a split approximately two feet long in side panel of body. Both buffers were replaced at No.1 end, No.2 fan shaft was replaced and six defective boiler tubes were replaced.

Doncaster	15/04/66	17/04/66	Unclassified

No.2 header tank split. This was repaired.

Doncaster	23/04/66	29/04/66	Light

No.1 engine, 442, was given an Unclassified repair. No.2 engine, 417, was given an Unclassified repair but failed on test and was replaced by 414. No.1 bogie, 9000-1, replaced by 9000-9. No.2 bogie, 9000-2, replaced by 9000-10. Boiler, 1490/J2946, was given an Unclassified repair. The body was given an Unclassified repair.

Doncaster	09/05/66	10/05/66	Unclassified

Hole in main steam pipe above No.2 bogie caused by pipe rubbing on mainframe. The main steam pipe was repaired.

Doncaster	12/07/66	13/07/66	Unclassified

Three boiler tubes leaking. These were repaired.

Doncaster	08/09/66	09/09/66	Unclassified

No.1 bogie, 9000-9, replaced by 9000-25, due to No.2 axle flawed at gear end. No.2 bogie, 9000-10, replaced by 9000-26, due to No.5 axle flawed at the non-gear end.

Doncaster	23/09/66	27/09/66	Unclassified

No.2 engine, 414, replaced by 440, due to failure of No.6 'AB' bank piston.

Doncaster	24/10/66	26/10/66	Unclassified

No.1 end left leading equalising beam manganese liner fractured and worked out. This was renewed.

Doncaster	02/11/66	03/11/66	Unclassified

Four boiler tubes leaking in lower tube area at refractory end. Three tubes were renewed, several were re-expanded and the boiler was hydraulically tested to 75 psi.

Doncaster	16/11/66	22/11/66	Unclassified

No.1 engine, 442, replaced by 449, due to breathing badly. Both exhaust silencers were replaced. No.2 main and auxiliary generators were replaced.

Doncaster	28/11/66	28/11/66	Unclassified

No.1 coolant header tank was replaced.

D9003/9003/55 003 Meld (continued)

Loco Works	On Works	Off Works	Class of repair
Doncaster	07/12/66	23/12/66	General

No.1 main generator interpole burnt out and arc horn burnt off. No.1 engine, 449, was given an Unclassified repair. No.2 engine, 440, replaced by 425. No.1 bogie, 9000-25, replaced by 9000-23. No.2 bogie, 9000-26, replaced by 9000-24. Boiler, 1490/J2946, replaced by 1494/J2950. The body was given a General repair. The locomotive mileage was recorded as 887,090 miles.

Doncaster	17/04/67	18/04/67	Unclassified

Water scoop to be fitted and repairs to tank fairing. A compressor governor, the water scoop and the steam pipe over No.1 fuel tank were replaced.

Doncaster	16/05/67	25/05/67	Light

No.1 engine, 449, replaced by 404. No.2 engine, 425, was given an Unclassified repair. No.1 bogie, 9000-23, replaced by 9000-3. No.2 bogie, 9000-24, replaced by 9000-4. Boiler, 1494/J2950, was given an Unclassified repair. The body was given an Unclassified repair. Full yellow nose ends were applied.

Doncaster	23/06/67	24/06/67	Unclassified

No.2 engine, 425, primary gearbox defective. This was replaced.

Doncaster	21/10/67	23/10/67	Unclassified

No.2 main generator to earth. A cut out switch was repaired and flashover damage to both main generators was cleaned up. Slight flashover damage to Nos.1, 2, 3 & 4 traction motors was also cleaned up.

Doncaster	14/12/67	17/12/67	Unclassified

No.2 engine, 425, replaced by 409, due to No.2 main generator armature down to earth. No.1 main generator had flashover damage repaired.

Doncaster	09/01/68	14/02/68	General

No.1 engine, 404, replaced by 538. No.2 engine, 409, replaced by 444. No.1 bogie, 9000-3, replaced by 9000-33. No.2 bogie, 9000-4, replaced by 9000-34. Boiler, 1494/J2950, replaced by 5094/J3245. The body was given a General repair and repainted into **blue livery with full yellow nose ends**. *The locomotive was fitted for dual braking.*

Doncaster	20/02/68	22/02/68	Unclassified

No.1 end 'M8' valve blowing through when isolated and both main generators flashed over. All flashover damage was cleaned up.

Doncaster	26/02/68	28/02/68	Unclassified

No.1 engine, 538, replaced by 415, due to suspect piston seized, excessive swarf in oil strainer. Main fuel adaptors at 'A5' injector and blanking adaptor badly damaged.

Doncaster	22/03/68	22/03/68	Unclassified

All traction motors and both main generators flashed over. All damage was repaired.

Doncaster	04/06/68	04/06/68	Unclassified

No.1 bogie, 9000-33, No.1 axle suspected fracture. The axle was examined and no fault was found. A broken stud in No.1 swing link pin locking plate was repaired.

Doncaster	16/07/68	19/07/68	Light

No.1 engine, 415, replaced by 424. No.2 engine, 444, was given an Unclassified repair. No.1 bogie, 9000-33, replaced by 9000-43. No.2 bogie, 9000-34, replaced by 9000-44. Boiler, 5094/J3245, was given an Unclassified repair. The body was given an Unclassified repair.

Doncaster	30/12/68	31/12/68	Unclassified

No.2 engine, 444, replaced by 449, due to No.2 main generator down to earth. All traction motors were to be checked for flashover damage. No.1 main generator had flashover damage repaired.

Doncaster	24/01/69	24/01/69	Unclassified

No.2 engine 449, replaced by 428, due to a piston through crankcase on 'B' bank.

Doncaster	10/02/69	10/02/69	Unclassified

No.2 engine, 428, lubricating oil in coolant, suspect liner defect. A sample of coolant was taken and the coolant topped up.

Doncaster	25/02/69	27/03/69	General

No.1 engine, 424, replaced by 405. No.2 engine, 428, replaced by 447. No.1 bogie, 9000-43, replaced by 9000-41. No.2 bogie, 9000-44, replaced by 9000-42. Boiler, 5094/J3245, replaced by 1496/J2952. The body was given a General repair.

D9003/9003/55 003 Meld (continued)

Loco Works	On Works	Off Works	Class of repair
Doncaster	01/04/69	02/04/69	Rectification

No.1 engine, 405 cutting out. No.5 traction motor armature overheated, throwing solder and armature open circuit. The overspeed trip mechanism on No.1 engine, 405, was replaced. All traction motors on No.2 bogie, 9000-42, were examined and no fault was found.

Doncaster	08/04/69	10/04/69	Rectification

No.1 bogie, 9000-41, replaced by 9000-43, due to all traction motors with slight flashover damage. No.2 bogie, 9000-42, replaced by 9000-44, due to No.4 traction motor burnt out and slight flashover damage on No.5 traction motor.

Doncaster	19/08/69	20/08/69	Unclassified

No.1 bogie, 9000-43, No.2 traction motor armature pinion adrift, suspect key sheared and all traction motors slight flashover damage. No.2 bogie, 9000-44, No.5 traction motor contactor overload, all traction motors slight flashover damage. Nos. 2, 5 & 6 traction motors were replaced and all others were cleaned up.

Doncaster	22/08/69	23/08/69	Rectification

All traction motors flashed over and AWS defective. No.1 main generator had all brush boxes and commutator cleaned of flashover damage, as did No.2 main generator. All traction motors were also cleaned of flashover damage.

Doncaster	26/08/69	02/09/69	Unclassified

No.1 main generator slight flashover damage, No.2 main generator more severe flashover damage and one insulation pot to change. No.1 bogie, 9000-43, No.3 traction motor brush box cable disconnected. No.2 bogie, 9000-44, No.5 traction motor flashover. No.1 main generator was replaced. Flashover damage on No.2 main generator was repaired and insulators and brush boxes were changed. Flashover damage on traction motors was repaired.

Doncaster	09/12/69	18/12/69	Light

No.1 engine, 405 and No.2 engine, 447 were both given Unclassified repairs. No.1 bogie, 9000-43, replaced by 9000-11. No.2 bogie, 9000-44, replaced by 9000-12. Boiler, 1496/J2952, was given an Unclassified repair. The boiler was given an Unclassified repair and the water tank capacity modification was carried out.

Doncaster	23/12/69	31/12/69	Unclassified

No.2 engine, 447, replaced by 434, due to No.2 main generator defective.

Doncaster	15/04/70	18/04/70	Unclassified

Boiler back tube plate leaking at weld. This was re-welded. Damage to vacuum train pipe on No.2 bufferbeam was also repaired.

Doncaster	08/07/70	10/07/70	Unclassified

No.1 engine, 405, replaced by 439, due to being dephased.

Doncaster	16/09/70	05/12/70	Intermediate

No.1 engine, 439, replaced by 411. No.2 engine, 434, replaced by 418. No.1 bogie, 9000-11 and No.2 bogie, 9000-12, were given General repairs. Boiler, 1496/J2952, replaced by 1492/J2948. The body was given an Intermediate repair. The locomotive was fitted with E.T.H. equipment.

Doncaster	13/12/70	15/12/70	Rectification

A fractured coolant header tank was repaired.

Doncaster	07/01/71	10/01/71	Unclassified

E.T.H. voltage low, No.1 A.V.R. defective, No.1 engine, 411, governor power arm loose and No.2 engine, 418, under powered. Governors on both engines were replaced.

Doncaster	15/01/71	24/01/71	Unclassified

No.2 engine, 418, replaced by 413, due to breathing heavy and coolant in sump.

Doncaster	09/02/71	14/02/71	Unclassified

Intermittent earth fault when using E.T.H. This was rectified. No.6 wheelset and traction motor were replaced.

Doncaster	16/03/71	19/03/71	Unclassified

No.2 engine, 413, replaced by 424, due to aerating. No.1 main generator earth leakage when E.T.H. working. This was rectified. Both main generators had flashover damage repaired. No.1 bogie, 9000-11, left hand side guard iron missing. No.2 bogie, 9000-12, left hand side guard iron fractured. Bogie repairs were carried out.

D9003/9003/55 003 Meld (continued)

Loco Works	On Works	Off Works	Class of repair
Doncaster	13/05/71	15/05/71	Unclassified

No.2 engine, 424, replaced by 446, due to coolant pressurising. Oil pressure switches and gauges were re-positioned.

| Doncaster | 19/05/71 | 03/06/71 | Unclassified |

No.1 engine, 411, replaced by 434. No.2 engine, 446, replaced by 417, due to injector hole blanking plug 'C3' liner blown out, thread stripped and liner moved. No.2 lubricating oil tank and radiators were cleaned.

| Doncaster | 08/11/71 | 13/11/71 | Light |

No.1 engine, 434 and No.2 engine, 417, were given Light repairs. No.1 bogie, 9000-11, replaced by 9000-7. No.2 bogie, 9000-12, replaced by 9000-8. Boiler, 1492/J2948, was given an Unclassified repair. The body was given a Light repair.

| Doncaster | 06/12/71 | 08/12/71 | Unclassified |

No.1 engine, 434, replaced by 420, due to being dephased.

| Doncaster | 19/05/72 | 20/05/72 | Unclassified |

Boiler water tank split and holed. Both boiler water tanks were repaired.

| Doncaster | 18/07/72 | 21/07/72 | Unclassified |

No.1 engine, 420, replaced by 443, due to liner seal leaking. No.1 lubricating oil tank and radiators were cleaned.

| Doncaster | 21/08/72 | 20/10/72 | Intermediate |

No.1 engine, 443, replaced by 406. No.2 engine, 417, replaced by 458. No.1 bogie, 9000-7, replaced by 9000-29. No.2 bogie, 9000-8, replaced by 9000-10. Boiler, 1492/J2948, replaced by 5090/J3241. The body was given an Intermediate repair.

| Doncaster | 02/02/73 | 08/02/73 | Unclassified |

No.2 engine, 458, replaced by 538, due to piston adrift.

| Doncaster | 04/05/73 | 09/05/73 | Unclassified |

No.1 engine, 406, replaced by 539, due to crankcase fractured, damper adrift. No.2 boiler water tank had a fracture repaired.

| Doncaster | 28/07/73 | 07/08/73 | Light |

No.1 engine, 539, replaced by 436, due to header tank fractured. No.2 engine, 538, was given a Light repair. No.1 bogie, 9000-29, replaced by 9000-9. No.2 bogie, 9000-10, replaced by 9000-42. Boiler, 5090/J3241, was given an Unclassified repair. The body was given a Light repair.

| Doncaster | 03/09/73 | 04/09/73 | Unclassified |

Both A.V.R.'s to change and boiler flooring fractured. Both boiler water tanks were repaired and the boiler floor plates were repaired.

| Doncaster | 21/01/74 | 24/01/74 | Unclassified |

No.2 main generator was replaced due to field coils down to earth.

| Doncaster | 20/02/74 | 21/02/74 | Unclassified |

No.1 bogie, 9000-9, had No.2 traction motor nose suspension set screw fitted and centre segment secured. No.2 bogie, 9000-42, had the same attention to No.5 traction motor and swing link pins secured.

| Doncaster | 25/02/74 | 26/02/74 | Rectification |

No.2 bogie, 9000-42, had an axlebox beam liner renewed.

| Doncaster | 01/05/74 | 02/08/74 | Intermediate |

No.1 engine, 436, replaced by 452. No.2 engine, 538, replaced by 458, due to breathing heavy and throwing oil. No.1 bogie, 9000-9, replaced by 9000-13. No.2 bogie, 9000-42, replaced by 9000-14. Boiler, 5090/J3241, replaced by 5091/J3242. The body was given an Intermediate repair.

| Doncaster | 19/08/74 | 20/08/74 | Rectification |

No.1 engine, 452, silencer drain blocked. Six inch fracture in floor adjacent to water suction pipe non-return valve. Both cab doors at No.2 end will not fasten. All repairs were carried out.

| Doncaster | Not recorded | 31/08/74 | Not recorded |

Boiler, 5091/J3242, replaced by 1495/J2951.

| Doncaster | 03/09/74 | 03/09/74 | Rectification |

No.1 engine, 452, had 'B5' injector pocket and injector replaced.

D9003/9003/55 003 Meld (continued)

Loco Works	On Works	Off Works	Class of repair
Doncaster	03/10/74	06/10/74	Unclassified

No.1 engine, 452, replaced by 407, due to high copper content in oil. Oil tank and radiators were replaced.

Doncaster	22/10/74	25/10/74	Unclassified

No.2 engine, 458, replaced by 454, due to aerating, suspected fractured liner.

Doncaster	22/02/75	23/02/75	Unclassified

No.1 boiler water tank fractured. This was repaired.

Doncaster	Not recorded	03/07/75	Unclassified

No.2 engine, 454, replaced by 434.

Doncaster	31/07/75	20/08/75	Light

No.1 engine, 407, replaced by 412. No.2 engine, 434, replaced by 447. No.1 bogie, 9000-13, replaced by 9000-19. No.2 bogie, 9000-14, replaced by 9000-20. Boiler, 1495/J2951, was given an Unclassified repair. The locomotive was weighed at 103t 7cwt.

Doncaster	12/12/75	17/12/75	Unclassified

No.2 engine, 447, replaced by 414, due to 'CA' crankcase holed. No.1 traction motor was replaced.

Doncaster	26/04/76	28/04/76	Unclassified

No.2 engine, 414, replaced by 455, due to 'B6' conrod broken and crankcase damaged. The lubricating oil tank was drained and examined for debris. Nos.1 & 2 primary shaft splines showing excessive backlash. Speedometer plug and socket were renewed.

Doncaster	30/06/76	08/07/76	Unclassified

Both main generators flashed over. No.1 main generator insulation reading zero. Both main generators were replaced. Both bogies had bolsters removed and refitted after flashover damage repairs to traction motors.

Doncaster	21/07/76	21/07/76	Unclassified

No.1 engine, 412, replaced by 451, due to 'A' bank crankcase holed. Traction motor flashover damage repaired as was bogie brake gear.

Doncaster	11/09/76	15/09/76	Unclassified

No.3 traction motor commutator inside brush track oval. No.2 main generator had flashover damage repaired. No.3 traction motor was replaced. All other traction motors had flashover damage repaired.

Doncaster	18/10/76	14/01/77	Intermediate

No.1 engine, 451, replaced by 436. No.2 engine, 455, replaced by 412. No.1 bogie, 9000-19, replaced by 9000-49. No.2 bogie, 9000-20, replaced by 9000-50. Boiler, 1495/J2951, replaced by 5088/J3239. Route indicator panels were plated over. The locomotive was weighed at 103t 6cwt.

Doncaster	12/02/77	17/02/77	Rectification

No.1 engine, 436, with fuel dilution problems. 'A2' & 'C5' fuel pumps were changed.

Doncaster	21/06/77	25/06/77	Unclassified

No.1 engine, 436, replaced by 457, due to main generator drive suspect sheared. Locomotive lighting was inoperative and a water tank was leaking. These defects were rectified.

Stratford D.R.S.	16/08/77	17/08/77	Depot

No.1 bogie, 9000-49, had No.3 wheelset replaced.

Doncaster	26/09/77	11/10/77	Unclassified

No.1 bogie, 9000-49, pivot support casting to be examined. No.1 pivot casting had been completely adrift and had been temporarily secured. No.1 traction motor bellow to renew. No.1 end vacuum pipe to renew. E.T.H. cables to repair on No.1 end bufferbeam. Air pipe by pivot on body to repair. All these repairs were carried out. The locomotive was weighed at 104t 8cwt.

Doncaster	19/01/78	23/02/78	Unclassified

No.1 engine, 457, replaced by 410. No.2 engine, 412, replaced by 409, due to breathing heavy.

Doncaster	11/03/78	21/03/78	Rectification

No.1 engine, 410, fuel dilution of lubricating oil. No.1 bogie, 9000-49, No.3 right hand side brake pull rod safety bracket to fit. No.2 bogie, 9000-50, brake adjustment needed and No.2 boiler water tank leaking. All repairs were carried out.

Doncaster	30/03/78	30/04/78	Unclassified

No.2 engine, 409, replaced by 412, due to 'CA' crankcase fractured. No.2 lubricating oil tank cleaned out.

208 DELTICS ON WORKS

D9003/9003/55 003 Meld (continued)

Loco Works	On Works	Off Works	Class of repair
Doncaster	02/06/78	08/06/78	Rectification

No.1 engine, 410, continued fuel dilution of lubricating oil. This was rectified.

| Doncaster | 11/07/78 | 13/07/78 | Unclassified |

No.1 engine, 410, replaced by 413, due to fuel dilution. No.2 engine, 412, had primary shaft coupling loose on exciter gearbox. This was repaired. Nos.1 & 6 traction motors were replaced. No.2 load regulator tips were renewed and reset.

| Doncaster | 16/08/78 | 09/12/78 | Unclassified |

No.1 engine, 413, replaced by 446, due to primary shaft drive flange defective. No.2 engine, 412, replaced by 406. No.1 bogie, 9000-49, had all brake blocks renewed. No.2 bogie, 9000-50, had same and 'R2' lifeguard renewed and No.1 footsteps to weld on secondman's side. No.2 end primary shaft gearbox to repair. No.1 main generator to be cleaned up due to foreign body rubbing on commutator. No.2 compressor was overhauled.

| Doncaster | 17/01/79 | 24/02/79 | Light |

No.1 engine, 446, replaced by 410. No.2 engine, 406, replaced by 443, due to aerating. No.1 bogie, 9000-49, replaced by 9000-47. No.2 bogie, 9000-50, replaced by 9000-22. Boiler, 5088/J3239, was given an Unclassified repair. Boiler water pump to change and suction side to pressure test. The locomotive was weighed at 104t 17cwt.

| Doncaster | 27/06/79 | 30/06/79 | Unclassified |

No.2 engine, 443, replaced by 416, due to piston failure. Chip trap full of metal.

| Doncaster | 04/07/79 | 10/07/79 | Rectification |

No.2 engine, 416, surging and cutting out. This was rectified.

| Doncaster | 31/12/79 | 04/01/80 | Unclassified |

No.1 engine, 410, replaced by 422, due to a fractured liner. No.1 bogie, 9000-47, had No.3 traction motor nose pad loose. 'R2' & 'L2' swing link pin set screws loose. No.2 bogie, 9000-22, had No.6 traction motor nose pad loose. All defects repaired.

| Doncaster | 07/03/80 | 10/03/80 | Unclassified |

No.2 engine, 416, replaced by 424, due to aerating. No.2 header tank to renew, suspect hole in internal pipe, coolant running back through take up pipe. No.2 main generator commutator badly grooved. No.1 secondary fan fault to trace and repair. No.1 main generator contaminated by oil. All defects were rectified.

| Doncaster | 07/11/80 | 12/11/80 | Unclassified |

No.2 engine, 424, replaced by 415, due to a fractured liner. Nos. 3 & 6 traction motor nose pads loose. This was rectified.

| Doncaster | 31/12/80 | - | - |

Nil. The locomotive arrived after withdrawal with the following main components fitted. No.1 engine, 422. No.2 engine, 415, primary fan shaft damaged. No.1 bogie, 9000-47. No.2 bogie, 9000-22. Boiler, 5088/J3239.

D9003 Meld at speed near Grantham on July 29, 1963. The locomotive was withdrawn at the end of 1980. Her last working in traffic was the 07:22 Plymouth to Edinburgh from York to Newcastle on 29/12/1980.

D9004/9004/55 004 Queen's Own Highlander

Loco Works	On Works	Off Works	Class of repair
Doncaster	18/05/61	Not recorded	Acceptance trials

New locomotive fitted with the following main components; No.1 engine, 416. No.2 engine, 417. No.1 bogie, 1009. No.2 bogie, 1010. Boiler, 5090/J3241.

Vulcan Foundry	01/08/61	Not recorded	Unclassified

No.1 traction motor nose distance piece fractured at weld.

Doncaster	24/10/61	03/11/61	Light

No.1 engine, 416, replaced by 449. No.2 engine, 417, replaced by 441, due to 'C3' cylinder liner cracked. Repairs were carried out to bogie spring equalising beams and footsteps. Boiler, 5090/J3241, was overhauled. The body was given a six monthly exam. The locomotive mileage was recorded as 65,750 miles.

Doncaster	17/05/62	18/05/62	Light

No.1 bogie, 1009, replaced by 1019. No.2 bogie, 1010, replaced by 1020. Boiler, 5090/J3241, was overhauled. The body was given a six monthly exam.

Doncaster	06/06/62	07/06/62	Unclassified

No.1 bogie, 1019 and No.2 bogie, 1020, were removed for examination by E.E. Co. staff and refitted.

Doncaster	04/07/62	06/07/62	Unclassified

No.2 traction motor down to earth. This was replaced.

Doncaster	27/07/62	28/07/62	Unclassified

Flashover damage on all traction motors and both main generators. No.1 bogie, 1019, replaced by 1017. No.2 bogie, 1020, replaced by 1018. Boiler, 5090/J3241, was overhauled. The locomotive mileage was recorded as 171,400 miles.

Doncaster	14/09/62	14/09/62	Unclassified

No.1 bogie, 1017, No.2 axle horn cracked driver's side at No.1 end. This was welded. The locomotive mileage was recorded as 195,200 miles.

Doncaster	12/10/62	19/10/62	General

No.1 engine, 449, replaced by 422. No.2 engine, 441, replaced by 419. No.1 bogie, 1017, replaced by 1043. No.2 bogie, 1018, replaced by 1044. Boiler, 5090/J3241, replaced by 1490/J2946. The body was given an annual repair. Modifications were carried out to bogies, drawgear and vacuum brake valve. All cab doors were fitted with new handles and locks. The locomotive mileage was recorded as 207,000 miles.

Doncaster	13/02/63	15/02/63	Unclassified

Boiler, 1490/J2946, was overhauled. No.2 end right hand buffer was replaced.

Doncaster	03/04/63	08/04/63	Light

No.1 bogie, 1043, replaced by 1035. No.2 bogie, 1044, replaced by 1036. Boiler, 1490/J2946, was overhauled. The body was given a six monthly exam. An exhaust collector drum was replaced.

Doncaster	09/05/63	10/05/63	Unclassified

Derailment damage. AWS receiver broken and bracket bent, cable damaged. Fuel tank holed, steps broken, drawbar at No.1 end bent and coupling to be renewed. All guard irons bent, sand pipes broken at No.2 end. Toilet pipe (waste) broken and buffer at No.2 end left hand side to be examined. Bogies to be examined for alignment and spring centres to be examined. No.5 traction motor bellows to be refitted. Slight deflection on Nos.3 & 4 wheelsets. The following replacement items were fitted; No.1 right hand buffer, No.2 left hand fuel tank, toilet pipe, screw coupling guard. The following items were repaired; No.1 end vacuum pipe elbow and bracket, No.1 end left hand warning horn, No.1 end left hand bogie wheel restraining pad. A new primary fan shaft was fitted to No.2 engine, 419. Modified exhaust collector tanks were also fitted. No.1 bogie, 1035, replaced by 1005. No.2 bogie, 1036, replaced by 1006.

Doncaster	05/09/63	06/09/63	Unclassified

No.1 engine, 422, replaced by 442, due to 'C' bank No.5 cylinder exhaust seal defective. Bogie brake hanger side brackets were fitted with safety chains. The locomotive mileage was recorded as 83,540 miles since general repair.

D9004/9004/55 004 Queen's Own Highlander (continued)

Loco Works	On Works	Off Works	Class of repair
Doncaster	11/10/63	01/11/63	General

No.1 engine, 442, replaced by 418. No.2 engine, 419, replaced by 404, due to aerating, suspect cracked liner. No.1 bogie, 1005, replaced by 1035. No.2 bogie, 1006, replaced by 1036. Boiler, 1490/J2946, replaced by 1487/J2943. All roof lubricating and coolant hoses were renewed and water tanks were overhauled. The following modifications were carried out – Caustic injection to boiler; Coolant header tank expansion tank fitted.

| Doncaster | 04/02/64 | 04/02/64 | Unclassified |

No.4 traction motor armature down to earth. The traction motor was replaced.

| Doncaster | 20/02/64 | 20/02/64 | Unclassified |

No.1 oil radiator 'B' side leaking badly. This was replaced.

| Doncaster | 10/04/64 | 26/04/64 | Light |

No.1 bogie, 1035, replaced by 1007. No.2 bogie, 1036, replaced by 1008. No.2 primary fan shaft was replaced.

| Doncaster | 14/06/64 | 14/06/64 | Unclassified |

No.2 main generator 'B' side main cable burnt out at cut out switch. No.2 main generator was repaired, cable lugs renewed, tips and bridges replaced where necessary.

| Doncaster | 21/06/64 | 22/06/64 | Unclassified |

Nos.1, 2 & 3 axles slightly bent after derailment. No.1 bogie, 1007, replaced by 1041. No.2 bogie, 1008, replaced by 1042.

| Doncaster | 14/09/64 | 16/09/64 | Unclassified |

No.1 bogie, 1041 and No.2 bogie, 1042, were given Light repairs. Exhausters and stand were removed, welded and refitted.

| Doncaster | 17/09/64 | 17/09/64 | Unclassified |

Burnt out battery charging circuit at cable clip under No.2 voltage regulator hinged frame. Compressor load regulator wiring was renewed.

| Doncaster | 24/09/64 | 25/09/64 | Unclassified |

No.4 axle suspected to be bent after derailment. Bogie rubbing brackets and pads were repaired and a headstock fracture on No.1 bogie was welded. No.4 wheelset was replaced. The exhauster cut out valve modification was fitted.

| Doncaster | 09/10/64 | 09/10/64 | Unclassified |

No.1 bogie, 1041, replaced by 1028. No.2 bogie, 1042, replaced by 1029.

| Doncaster | 04/12/64 | 09/01/65 | General |

No.1 engine, 418 and No.2 engine, 404, were given six monthly overhauls. No.1 bogie, 1028, replaced by 1023. No.2 bogie, 1029, replaced by 1024. Boiler, 1487/J2943, replaced by 1490/J2946. The body was given a General repair.

| Doncaster | 27/01/65 | 28/01/65 | Unclassified |

No.1 engine, 418, replaced by 447, due to 'C' bank piston defective.

| Doncaster | 25/02/65 | 27/02/65 | Unclassified |

No.1 engine, 447, replaced by 456. No.1 bogie, 1023, had a broken anchor pin replaced.

| Doncaster | 26/04/65 | 07/05/65 | Light |

No.1 engine, 456, replaced by 443. No.2 engine, 404, replaced by 429. No.1 bogie, 1023, replaced by 1007. No.2 bogie, 1024, replaced by 1008. Boiler, 1490/J2946, was acid washed and had tubes cleaned out. The body was given an Unclassified repair. The following modifications were carried out — Spiders; Transom radius; Centre gussets; Cold pins in headstocks; Horn liners; Steel plate to brake hanger rubbing brackets; Nose suspension.

| Doncaster | 13/05/65 | 13/05/65 | Unclassified |

No.2 traction motor defective, commutator 'Vee' ring insulation badly burned. The traction motor was replaced.

| Doncaster | 12/08/65 | 14/08/65 | Unclassified |

No.1 engine, 443, replaced by 440, due to 'CA' flexible drive shaft fractured. No.1 bogie, 1007, replaced by 9000-15. No.2 bogie, 1008, replaced by 9000-16.

| Doncaster | 31/08/65 | 02/09/65 | Unclassified |

Boiler, 1490/J2946, replaced by 5088/J3239.

| Doncaster | 07/09/65 | 08/09/65 | Unclassified |

Derailed on Gateshead depot. Bogies not running to correct alignment. Waterscoop mouthpieces to be renewed.

D9004/9004/55 004 Queen's Own Highlander (continued)

Loco Works	On Works	Off Works	Class of repair
Doncaster	25/09/65	28/09/65	Unclassified

No.1 engine, 440, replaced by 438.

Doncaster	05/11/65	09/11/65	Unclassified

No.1 engine, 438, replaced by 436, due to water pump drive sheared.

Doncaster	02/01/66	23/01/66	General

No.1 engine, 436 and No.2 engine, 429, were repaired and refitted. No.1 bogie, 9000-15 and No.2 bogie, 9000-16, were repaired and refitted. Boiler, 5088/J3239, was repaired and refitted. The body was given a General repair. The following modifications were carried out – Protection bars for EP valves; Cab footstep stiffening plates; Oil resisting compound to sandbox filler ducts.

Doncaster	29/01/66	31/01/66	Unclassified

No.2 engine, 429, replaced by 455.

Doncaster	04/04/66	07/04/66	Light

No.1 engine, 436 and No.2 engine, 455, were given Unclassified repairs. No.1 bogie, 9000-15, replaced by 9000-25. No.2 bogie, 9000-16, replaced by 9000-26. Boiler, 5088/J3239, was given an Unclassified repair. The body was given an Unclassified repair.

Doncaster	06/05/66	10/05/66	Doncaster

Nos.1 & 6 axles fractured. These were rectified.

Doncaster	23/06/66	25/06/66	Doncaster

Boiler, 5088/J3239, replaced by 1497/J2953.

Doncaster	08/08/66	11/08/66	Unclassified

No.1 engine, 436, replaced by 437, due to 'AC' bank No.5 piston fractured.

Doncaster	08/09/66	13/09/66	Unclassified

No.1 engine, 437, replaced by 449, due to liner seal leaking. No.1 bogie, 900025, replaced by 900035. No.2 bogie, 9000-26, replaced by 9000-36.

Doncaster	30/09/66	30/09/66	Unclassified

No.3 traction motor overload was adjusted and main generators were examined for reported flashover damage but no repairs were needed.

Doncaster	17/11/66	08/12/66	General

No.1 engine, 449, replaced by 443. No.2 engine, 455, replaced by 410. No.1 bogie, 9000-35, replaced by 9000-3. No.2 bogie, 9000-36, replaced by 9000-4. Boiler, 1497/J2953, was given an Unclassified repair. The body was given a General repair.

Doncaster	15/12/66	20/12/66	Unclassified

No.2 main generator flashed over and field coils burnt. No.1 main generator was cleaned, two insulators and five arc horns were fitted. No.2 main generator commutator and insulators were cleaned and one arc horn was fitted. Extensive flashover damage to both bogies was repaired.

Doncaster	21/12/66	22/12/66	Unclassified

No.1 traction motor blower mounting broken, trunking and fan severely damaged. No.1 traction motor blower was replaced and repairs were carried out to blower air ducting, which was cleared of foreign matter.

Doncaster	09/01/67	11/01/67	Unclassified

No.2 engine, 410, replaced by 453.

Doncaster	07/02/67	08/02/67	Unclassified

No.1 engine, 443, replaced by 420, due to aerating, suspected fractured liner. No.1 exhaust silencer was replaced.

Doncaster	12/04/67	19/04/67	Light

No.1 engine, 420 and No.2 engine, 453, had injectors changed. No.1 bogie, 9000-3, replaced by 9000-35. No.2 bogie, 9000-4, replaced by 9000-36. Boiler, 1497/J2953, replaced by 5096/J3247. Flashover damage on both main generators was cleaned up.

Doncaster	13/09/67	14/09/67	Unclassified

No.2 engine, 453, replaced by 436, due to 'BC' bank quill shaft defective.

Doncaster	01/12/67	12/01/68	General

*No.1 engine, 420 and No.2 engine, 436, were given Unclassified repairs. No.1 bogie, 9000-35, replaced by 9000-39. No.2 bogie, 9000-36, replaced by 9000-40. Boiler, 5096/J3247, replaced by 5097/J3248. The body was given a General repair and repainted into **blue livery with full yellow nose ends**. The locomotive was fitted for dual braking.*

D9004/9004/55 004 Queen's Own Highlander (continued)

Loco Works	On Works	Off Works	Class of repair
Doncaster	11/03/68	13/03/68	Unclassified

Repairs to collision damage. No.2 end buffers to be renewed and realigned, both load regulators had oil leaks, No.1 end buffer cowls to be secured and No.2 engine, 436, exhaust collector drum to be repaired. Repairs to collision damage on the body were carried out, as were all other repairs.

Doncaster	14/03/68	15/03/68	Unclassified

Flashover damage to both main generators and all traction motors. No.2 engine, 436, coolant hose on right hand side free end leaking and an electrical control fault causing loss of power. All defects were rectified.

Doncaster	27/03/68	28/03/68	Unclassified

Flashover damage to both main generators and slight flashover damage to all traction motors. All damage was cleaned up.

Doncaster	26/04/68	30/04/68	Unclassified

No.2 engine, 436, replaced by 441, due to a broken con rod on 'B5' cylinder.

Doncaster	27/05/68	31/05/68	Light

No.1 engine, 420, replaced by 414. No.2 engine, 441, replaced by 539. No.1 bogie, 9000-29, replaced by 9000-15. No.2 bogie, 9000-40, replaced by 9000-16. Boiler, 5097/J3248, was given an unclassified repair. The body was given an unclassified repair.

Doncaster	21/01/69	21/02/69	General

Cables burnt at No.1 end. This was rectified. No.1 engine, 414, replaced by 430. No.2 engine, 539, replaced by 446. No.1 bogie, 9000-15, replaced by 9000-7. No.2 bogie, 9000-16, replaced by 9000-8. Boiler, 5097/J3248, replaced by 1489/J2945. The body was given a General repair.

Doncaster	29/07/69	30/07/69	Unclassified

No.1 engine, 430, had injectors and filters replaced. No.2 engine, 446, replaced by 431.

Doncaster	25/08/69	26/08/69	Unclassified

No.2 engine, 431, replaced by 443. Lubricating oil elements and tank were cleaned.

Doncaster	09/09/69	11/09/69	Unclassified

No.1 engine, 430, exhaust drum split and engine 'hunting' on load. A fracture in the exhaust drum tank was repaired.

Doncaster	12/09/69	12/09/69	Unclassified

No.1 engine, 430, asbestos lagging around exhaust collector drum smoking badly. No.2 engine, 443, cutting out. All defects were rectified.

Doncaster	11/11/69	24/11/69	Light

No.1 engine, 430 and No.2 engine, 443, were given unclassified repairs. No.1 bogie, 9000-7, replaced by 9000-29. No.2 bogie, 9000-8, replaced by 9000-10. Boiler, 1489/J2945, was given an Unclassified repair. The body was given an Unclassified repair. The boiler water tank modification was fitted.

Doncaster	25/11/69	26/11/69	Rectification

Wheel slip and load regulator faults were rectified.

Doncaster	29/11/69	30/11/69	Rectification

Flashover damage on No.2 main generator was rectified.

Doncaster	05/12/69	05/12/69	Unclassified

No.1 engine, 430 and No.2 engine, 443, 'excessive smoke'. No.1 left hand cab door sticking. Both engines were checked and rectified.

Doncaster	08/01/70	12/01/70	Unclassified

No.1 engine, 430, replaced by 447, due to being dephased. All traction motors were examined and cleaned out.

Doncaster	23/01/70	24/01/70	Unclassified

No.2 engine, 443, replaced by 449, due to being dephased. Fire in exhaust drum and pumping back into inlet air manifold.

Doncaster	16/02/70	20/02/70	Unclassified

No.2 traction motor bearing spacers adrift. All traction motors replaced. Both main generators had all brushes checked and replaced as necessary. 'S1' and 'S2' contactors were replaced.

D9004/9004/55 004 Queen's Own Highlander (continued)

Loco Works	On Works	Off Works	Class of repair
Doncaster	09/04/70	09/04/70	Unclassified

No.1 auxiliary generator drive shaft seal was replaced.

| Doncaster | 09/05/70 | 10/05/70 | Unclassified |

No.1 engine, 447, replaced by 456.

| Doncaster | 30/05/70 | 31/05/70 | Unclassified |

Battery cells collapsing (overcharging) and battery charging cables burnt both ends. Wiring was renewed where necessary.

| Doncaster | 05/06/70 | 06/06/70 | Unclassified |

Boiler water tank fractured. This was replaced.

| Doncaster | 03/08/70 | 21/08/70 | Intermediate |

No.1 engine, 456, was given an Unclassified repair. No.2 engine, 449, replaced by 539. No.1 bogie, 9000-29, replaced by 9000-23. No.2 bogie, 9000-10, replaced by 9000-30. Boiler, 1489/J2945, replaced by 1491/J2947. The body was given an Intermediate repair.

| Doncaster | 01/09/70 | 05/09/70 | Unclassified |

No.2 engine, 539, replaced by 430, due to fractured liner and con rod disintegrated.

| Doncaster | 25/11/70 | 27/11/70 | Unclassified |

No.1 engine, 456, replaced by 451, due to breathing badly.

| Doncaster | 11/12/70 | 13/12/70 | Unclassified |

No.1 boiler water tank fractured at weld. This was repaired.

| Doncaster | 13/01/71 | 13/01/71 | Unclassified |

No.1 engine, 451, 'B5' injector adaptor broken off. A replacement adaptor was fitted and bodyside lights wiring defect rectified.

| Doncaster | 03/02/71 | 04/02/71 | Unclassified |

Boiler steam pipe front flange to rejoint and 12" fracture at back end of boiler water tank. This was repaired and the heater pipeline joint renewed.

| Doncaster | 18/03/71 | 25/03/71 | Unclassified |

Both main generators earth faults. Both were changed. No.1 engine, 451 and No.2 engine, 430, had injectors replaced.

| Doncaster | 13/04/71 | 27/08/71 | Light |

No.1 engine, 451, replaced by 458, due to a fractured liner. No.2 engine, 430, replaced by 439. No.1 bogie, 9000-23, replaced by 9000-24. No.2 bogie, 9000-30, replaced by 9000-48. Boiler, 1491/J2947, was given an Unclassified repair. The body was given a Light repair. The locomotive was fitted with E.T.H. equipment.

| Doncaster | 04/12/71 | 29/01/72 | Unclassified |

No.1 engine, 458, replaced by 451. No.2 engine, 439, replaced by 446, due to coolant in sump, suspected fractured liner. Fractures in both boiler water tanks were repaired, as was No.2 primary cardan shaft. All lubricating oil tanks were cleaned.

| Doncaster | 17/03/72 | 19/03/72 | Unclassified |

No.2 engine, 446, replaced by 428, due to a fractured liner. No.2 end radiators and lubricating oil tank were cleaned.

| Doncaster | 27/03/72 | 15/04/72 | Unclassified |

No.1 engine, 451, replaced by 441, due to piston and con rod through crankcase. No.2 engine, 428, replaced by 405.

| Doncaster | 20/04/72 | 25/04/72 | Unclassified |

No.5 traction motor throwing solder. This traction motor was replaced and both bogies had swing link pin studs renewed.

| Doncaster | 10/05/72 | 17/05/72 | Unclassified |

No.2 engine, 405, replaced by 414, due to aerating.

| Doncaster | 05/07/72 | 14/07/72 | Unclassified |

No.1 engine, 441, replaced by 436, due to liner seal defective.

| Doncaster | 16/08/72 | 18/08/72 | Unclassified |

No.1 engine, 436, replaced by 458, due to breathing heavy.

| Doncaster | 18/08/72 | 19/08/72 | Unclassified |

No.2 engine, 414, had the governor replaced.

214   DELTICS ON WORKS

D9004/9004/55 004 Queen's Own Highlander (continued)

Loco Works	On Works	Off Works	Class of repair
Doncaster	25/08/72	30/08/72	Unclassified

No.1 engine, 458, replaced by 438, due to liner seal defective. No.2 engine, 414, replaced by 423. No.1 end lubricating oil tank and radiators were replaced. Both bogies had swing link pin studs and pin housing fractures repaired.

Doncaster	31/08/72	31/08/72	Unclassified

No.1 engine, 438, exhaust collector drum defective. This was repaired.

Doncaster	25/09/72	11/11/72	Intermediate

No.1 engine, 438, replaced by 439, due to liner seals defective. No.2 engine, 423, replaced by 449. No.1 bogie, 9000-24, replaced by 9000-33. No.2 bogie, 9000-48, replaced by 9000-34. Boiler, 1491/J2947, replaced by 5089/J3240. The body was given an Intermediate repair.

Doncaster	22/01/73	23/01/73	Unclassified

No.1 engine, 439, replaced by 427. No.1 main generator had flashover damage repaired.

Doncaster	30/01/73	02/02/73	Unclassified

No.1 engine, 427, replaced by 452, due to being dephased. No.2 main generator was repaired.

Doncaster	16/03/73	17/03/73	Unclassified

No.1 engine, 452, auxiliary drive and flexible couplings sheared, exciter drive smashed and top of generator casing also smashed. Fan gearbox casing holed and plug damaged. The secondary gearbox on 452 was replaced and the auxiliary drive shaft repaired.

Doncaster	25/04/73	30/04/73	Doncaster

No.1 engine, 452, replaced by 443, due to aerating. Footsteps on both bogies were renewed.

Doncaster	16/08/73	29/08/73	Light

No.1 engine, 443, replaced by 425. No.2 engine, 449, replaced by 441, due to auxiliary generator phasing gear drive sheared at phasing gear end. No.1 bogie, 9000-33, replaced by 9000-27. No.2 bogie. 9000-34, replaced by 9000-28. Boiler, 5089/J3240, was given an Unclassified repair. The body was given a Light repair.

Doncaster	29/01/74	29/01/74	Modification

Earth fault relay modification was carried out.

Doncaster	22/02/74	05/03/74	Doncaster

No.2 engine, 441, suspected dephased. It was given an Intermediate repair.

Doncaster	19/04/74	24/04/74	Doncaster

Boiler water tank split. This was repaired.

Doncaster	24/04/74	01/05/74	Modification

E.T.H. and coolant modification.

Doncaster	24/05/74	04/06/74	Unclassified

No.1 engine, 425, dephased. It was given an Intermediate repair. No.2 engine, 441, auxiliary drive gearbox bearing collapsed. It was given an Unclassified repair.

Doncaster	10/09/74	12/10/74	Intermediate

No.1 engine, 425, replaced by 426. No.2 engine, 441, replaced by 538. No.1 bogie, 9000-27, replaced by 9000-31. No.2 bogie, 9000-28, replaced by 9000-32. Boiler, 5089/J3240, replaced by 5090/J3241. No.2 main generator drive defective. This was repaired. The body was given an Intermediate repair.

Doncaster	04/12/74	05/12/74	Unclassified

No.2 engine, 538, replaced by 412, due to aerating.

Doncaster	29/01/75	31/01/75	Unclassified

No.2 engine, 412, replaced by 424, due to con rod through crankcase. No.2 boiler water tank was repaired.

Doncaster	17/02/75	19/02/75	Unclassified

No.2 main generator armature banding burst. No.1 main generator was given a three-month repair. No.2 main generator was replaced. No.1 bogie, 900031, No.1 traction motor nose suspension pad was welded. No.2 bogie, 900032, No.6 traction motor was changed and flashover damage was cleaned up. No.2 boiler water tank was repaired.

Doncaster	02/05/75	15/05/75	Unclassified

No.2 right hand side axle bearing hot. No.2 wheelset was replaced.

Doncaster	19/05/75	17/06/75	Unclassified

No.1 engine, 426, replaced by 406. No.2 engine, 424, replaced by 441, due to a suspected fractured liner.

D9004/9004/55 004 Queen's Own Highlander (continued)

Loco Works	On Works	Off Works	Class of repair
Doncaster	09/09/75	10/09/75	Unclassified

No.1 engine, 406, replaced by 451, due to being dephased. Repairs to swing link pin and studs.

| Doncaster | 08/11/75 | 28/11/75 | Light |

No.1 engine, 451, replaced by 454. No.2 engine, 441, replaced by 416. No.1 bogie, 9000-31, replaced by 9000-3. No.2 bogie, 9000-32, replaced by 9000-4. Boiler, 5090/J3241, was given an Unclassified repair. The body was given a Light repair. The locomotive was weighed at 105t 2cwt.

| Doncaster | 01/12/75 | 01/12/75 | Unclassified |

Boiler, 5090/J3241, burner motor will not run. Boiler motor contactor coil replaced. No.1 engine, 454, reportedly breathing heavy. Checked on load bank and no defect was found.

| Doncaster | 06/02/76 | 13/02/76 | Unclassified |

No.1 engine, 454, replaced by 426, due to being dephased. No.2 engine, 416, replaced by 436.

| Doncaster | 17/05/76 | 19/05/76 | Unclassified |

No.2 engine, 436, replaced by 428, due to aerating. No.2 boiler water tank had a leak repaired.

| Doncaster | 22/05/76 | 25/05/76 | Unclassified |

No.5 traction motor to earth and all other motors to examine. No.5 motor replaced.

| Doncaster | 04/08/76 | 11/08/76 | Unclassified |

Heavy flashover damage on No.1 main generator, slight flashover damage on No.2 main generator and all traction motors. No.1 main generator was replaced, No.2 main generator was overhauled and No.1 traction motor was replaced. All other traction motors had flashover damage cleaned up.

| Doncaster | 14/09/76 | 17/09/76 | Unclassified |

No.2 main generator low insulation, persistent flashovers. No.1 fan drive clutch was repaired. No.2 load regulator was replaced. No.1 main generator was given a three monthly overhaul and had coolant leaks rectified. No.2 main generator was replaced and all traction motors had flashover damage repaired.

| Doncaster | 15/12/76 | 19/03/77 | Intermediate |

No.1 engine, 426, replaced by 415. No.2 engine, 428, replaced by 448. No.1 bogie, 9000-3, replaced by 9000-15. No.2 bogie, 9000-4, replaced by 9000-16. Boiler, 5090/J3241, was given a standard repair. The body was given an Intermediate repair. Route indicator panels were plated over. The locomotive was weighed at 102t 6cwt.

| Doncaster | 28/04/77 | 02/05/77 | Unclassified |

All traction motors with flashover damage and both main generators flashed over. All repairs were carried out and No.1 traction motor nose suspension wear plate was repaired. The locomotive was weighed at 104t 16cwt.

| Doncaster | 17/08/77 | 21/08/77 | Unclassified |

Low megger readings on Nos.2 & 5 traction motors. No.2 end boiler water tank was repaired. Nos.1 & 2 primary fan shafts were repaired. No.2 traction motor was replaced. The locomotive was weighed at 103t 9cwt.

| Doncaster | 14/11/77 | 16/11/77 | Unclassified |

No.1 traction motor to earth. Bogie centre pivots, studs and nuts to renew. No.1 traction motor was replaced.

| Doncaster | 24/11/77 | 25/11/77 | Unclassified |

No.4 traction motor outer brush track scored badly. The locomotive had suffered three flashovers in as many days. No.4 traction motor was replaced. The locomotive was weighed at 102t 10cwt.

| Doncaster | 27/04/78 | 29/11/79 | Unclassified |

No.1 engine, 415, suspect fractured liner and No.2 engine, 448, aerating and header tank leaking. The locomotive was then cannibalised. Refit components that have been cannibalised. Clean bodywork exterior. Carry out brake tests and replace any defective item. Clean electrical equipment in cubicle and check electrical sequence on test. Check commutation on all auxiliary machines. On bogies, carry out brake tests paying special attention to brake cyls and double check valves. Examine traction motors. Check boiler for frost damage and carry out cyclic tests. On completion of repair the locomotive is to be given a trial 'light' run. All repairs carried out. No.1 engine, 415, replaced by 417. No.2 engine, 448, replaced by 423. No.1 bogie, 9000-15 and No.2 bogie, 9000-16, were given Unclassified repairs. Boiler, 5090/J3241, was given an Unclassified repair. The locomotive was weighed at 105t 5cwt.

D9004/9004/55 004 Queen's Own Highlander (continued)

Loco Works	On Works	Off Works	Class of repair
Doncaster	28/12/79	02/01/80	Unclassified

No.2 engine, 423, splines worn on auxiliary output shaft for radiator fans. This was repaired.

Doncaster	24/03/80	27/03/80	Unclassified

Rough riding. Bogie control gear worn. No.1 bogie, 9000-15, replaced by 9000-19. No.2 bogie, 9000-16, replaced by 9000-20. No.1 radiator fan gearbox defective. Severe oil leak from No.2 load regulator. Engine room to clean. All defects were rectified. The locomotive was weighed at 105t 8cwt.

Doncaster	03/06/80	28/06/80	Light

No.1 engine, 417, was given a Light repair. No.2 engine, 423, replaced by 439. No.1 bogie, 9000-19, replaced by 9000-25. No.2 bogie, 9000-20, replaced by 9000-26. Boiler, 5090/J3241, was given an Unclassified repair. The locomotive was weighed at 104t 16cwt.

Doncaster	10/03/81	19/03/81	Unclassified

No.1 engine, 417, replaced by 430, due to being dephased. No.2 bogie, 9000-26, No.4 wheelset replaced and various horn liners were secured. The locomotive was weighed at 102t 19cwt.

Doncaster	03/09/81	11/09/81	Unclassified

No.2 engine, 439, replaced by 427, due to a fractured liner.

Stratford D.R.S.	31/10/81	23/11/81	-

No.1 engine, 430, replaced by 432. This replacement was carried out to allow 55 008 to return to traffic.

Doncaster	05/01/82	-	-

The locomotive arrived after withdrawal with the following main components fitted. No.1 engine, 432, auxiliary drive sheared. No.2 engine, 427, dephased. No.1 bogie, 9000-25. No.2 bogie, 9000-26. Boiler, 5090/J3241.

55004 stands at King's Cross in June 1977 as the nose of 55021 Argyll and Sutherland Highlander creeps alongside. 55004's last train was the (1M76) 15:50 York-Liverpool on 28/10/1981. The locomotive was withdrawn on November 1, 1981 at Stratford in order to provide a good power unit for 55 008. Picture: R. E. Tiller.

D9005/9005/55 005 The Prince Of Wales's Own Regiment Of Yorkshire

Loco Works	On Works	Off Works	Class of repair
Doncaster	25/05/61	Not recorded	Acceptance trials

New locomotive fitted with the following known components; No.1 bogie, 1011. No.2 bogie, 1012.

| Doncaster | 26/06/61 | 29/06/61 | Not recorded |

No details recorded.

| Doncaster | 24/01/62 | 26/01/62 | Light |

No.2 engine replaced by 410. No.1 bogie, 1011, replaced by 1003. No.2 bogie, 1012, replaced by 1004.

| Doncaster | 30/05/62 | 31/05/62 | General |

No.1 bogie, 1003, replaced by 1009. No.2 bogie, 1004, replaced by 1010.

| Doncaster | 23/08/62 | 24/08/62 | Unclassified |

No.1 bogie, 1009, replaced by 1023. No.2 bogie, 1010, replaced by 1024.

| Doncaster | 03/11/62 | 07/11/62 | Light |

No.1 bogie, 1023, replaced by 1029. No.2 bogie, 1024, replaced by 1030.

| Doncaster | 20/11/62 | 27/11/62 | Unclassified |

No details recorded.

| Doncaster | 08/02/63 | 23/02/63 | General |

No.2 engine, 410, replaced. No.1 bogie, 1029, replaced by 1027. No.2 bogie, 1030, replaced by 1028.

| Doncaster | 22/07/63 | 22/07/63 | Unclassified |

Blower fan repairs.

| Doncaster | 31/07/63 | 09/08/63 | Light |

No.1 bogie, 1027, replaced by 1031. No.2 bogie, 1028, replaced by 1032. Traction motors and boiler overhauled.

| R.S.H. Darlington | 27/09/63 | 05/10/63 | Unclassified |

'The Prince of Wales's Own Regiment of Yorkshire' Nameplates fitted.

| Doncaster | 14/11/63 | 14/11/63 | Unclassified |

Anchor link bolt repairs.

| Doncaster | 06/01/64 | 07/01/64 | Unclassified |

No.1 bogie, 1031, replaced by 1033. No.2 bogie, 1032, replaced by 1034.

| Doncaster | 16/01/64 | 16/01/64 | Unclassified |

Load regulator contacts were cleaned.

| Doncaster | 12/02/64 | 04/03/64 | General |

No.2 engine replaced by 409. No.1 bogie, 1033, replaced by 1031. No.2 bogie, 1034, replaced by 1032.

| Doncaster | 12/11/64 | 20/11/64 | Light |

No.1 bogie, 1031, replaced by 1047. No.2 bogie, 1032, replaced by 1048.

| Doncaster | 06/01/65 | 07/01/65 | Unclassified |

Boiler water tank holed. No.1 boiler water tank was replaced.

| Doncaster | 27/02/65 | 18/03/65 | General |

No.1 engine, 456, replaced by 447. No.2 engine, 409, replaced by 451. No.1 bogie, 1047, replaced by 1031. No.2 bogie, 1048, replaced by 1032. Boiler, 1492/J2948, replaced by 1493/J2949. The body was given a General repair and the Drawgear slide block was reinforced.

| Doncaster | 31/07/65 | 02/08/65 | Unclassified |

No.1 bogie, 1031, replaced by 9000-11. No.2 bogie, 1032, replaced by 9000-12. The brakework was overhauled. A new "NUWAY" burner was fitted to the boiler.

| Doncaster | 19/09/65 | 25/09/65 | Light |

No.1 engine, 447, replaced by 416. No.1 bogie, 9000-11 and No.2 bogie, 9000-12 were given a Light repair. All coolant radiators were changed. The following modifications were carried out — Fire alarm bell; Protection bar for EP valves.

| Doncaster | 30/11/65 | 01/12/65 | Unclassified |

Seven boiler tubes leaking at No.1 end. These were renewed and the boiler washed out.

| Doncaster | 14/02/66 | 27/02/66 | General |

No.1 engine, 416 was given an Unclassified repair. No.2 engine, 451, replaced by 412. No.1 bogie, 9000-11, replaced by 9000-7. No.2 bogie, 9000-12, replaced by 9000-8. Boiler, 1493/J2949, replaced by 5091/J3242. The body was given a General repair.

218 Deltics On Works

D9005/9005/55 005 The Prince Of Wales's Own Regiment Of Yorkshire (continued)

Loco Works	On Works	Off Works	Class of repair
Doncaster	02/03/66	09/03/66	Unclassified

Wiring harness in No.1 end to renew, burnt out to M1, M2 and M3 auxiliary contacts. Burnt cables were replaced, No.2 traction motor brush gear was overhauled and Nos.1 & 2 main generators and all traction motors were cleaned.

Doncaster	13/05/66	14/05/66	Unclassified

No.6 axle fractured. This was changed.

Doncaster	20/07/66	21/07/66	Unclassified

No.1 engine, 416, replaced by 432, due to water pump flexible drive defective.

Doncaster	10/09/66	12/09/66	Unclassified

Repairs to No.2 engine, 412.

Doncaster	17/12/66	22/12/66	Light

No.1 engine, 432 and No.2 engine, 412 were given Unclassified repairs. No.1 bogie, 9000-7, replaced by 9000-29. No.2 bogie, 9000-8, replaced by 9000-30. Boiler, 5091/J3242 was given an Unclassified repair. The body was given a General repair.

Doncaster	20/01/67	26/01/67	Unclassified

No.2 engine, 412, replaced by 406, due to a heavy water leak.

Doncaster	01/02/67	01/02/67	Unclassified

No.1 engine, 432, high water temperature. The coolant thermostat was changed.

Doncaster	01/03/67	03/03/67	Unclassified

No.2 engine, 406, replaced by 424, due to 'CA' crankcase oil leak, suspect fractured. The lubricating oil radiators at No.2 end were changed.

Doncaster	30/03/67	15/04/67	General

No.1 engine, 432, replaced by 538. No.2 engine, 424, replaced by 431. No.1 bogie, 9000-29, replaced by 9000-41. No.2 bogie, 9000-30, replaced by 9000-42. Boiler, 5091/J3242, replaced by 5092/J3243. The body was given a General repair and full yellow nose ends applied.

Doncaster	21/08/67	22/08/67	Unclassified

No.1 engine, 538, replaced by 412, due to an oil leak, damaged sump.

Doncaster	13/11/67	18/11/67	Light

No.1 engine, 412 and No.2 engine, 431 had injectors changed, main generator cleaned, brush gear overhauled and auxiliary generator cleaned. No.1 bogie, 9000-41, replaced by 9000-21. No.2 bogie, 9000-42, replaced by 9000-22. Boiler, 5092/J3243 was given an Unclassified repair. The body was given an Unclassified repair.

Doncaster	01/02/68	02/02/68	Unclassified

No.1 exhaust silencer split. The silencer was replaced.

Doncaster	01/03/68	04/03/68	Unclassified

No.2 engine, 431, replaced by 458, due to an internal leak. No.1 bogie, 9000-21, No.1 traction motor cable left hand side to realign. No.2 bogie, 9000-22, No.4 traction motor nose suspension bracket retaining plate set screws broken. Engine room floor plates and surrounds to be cleaned of lubricating oil, coolant water etc. A fuel oil priming pump had been robbed by depot for 9021. All necessary work was carried out.

Doncaster	18/03/68	25/04/68	General

No.1 engine, 412, replaced by 446. No.2 engine, 458, replaced by 451. No.1 bogie, 9000-21 and No.2 bogie, 9000-22, were given General repairs and refitted. Boiler, 5092/J3243, replaced by 5088/J3239. The body was given a General repair. The locomotive was fitted for dual braking.

Doncaster	27/09/68	03/10/68	Unclassified

No.1 engine, 446, replaced by 457. No.2 engine, 451, was given an Unclassified repair. No.1 main generator, 3 brush boxes flashed and burnt and 3 arc horns burnt. No.2 main generator brush box insulator to renew, 3 brush boxes burnt, 2 arc horns and Vee ring burnt. All traction motors flashed over and the lubricating oil pipe on No.2 engine, 451, robbed by depot for 9008. All flashover damage was repaired.

Doncaster	21/10/68	23/10/68	Unclassified

All traction motors and both main generators flashed over. No.2 engine, 451, had new bellows fitted and the flashover damage was repaired.

D9005/9005/55 005 The Prince Of Wales's Own Regiment Of Yorkshire (continued)

Loco Works	On Works	Off Works	Class of repair
Doncaster	02/12/68	07/12/68	Light

No.1 engine, 457, replaced by 448. No.2 engine, 451, was given an Unclassified repair. No.1 bogie, 9000-21, replaced by 9000-23. No.2 bogie, 9000-22, replaced by 9000-24. Boiler, 5088/J3239, was given an Unclassified repair. The body was given an Unclassified repair.

Doncaster	31/01/69	01/02/69	Unclassified

No.2 engine, 451, replaced by 539, due to crankcase fractured.

Doncaster	26/03/69	27/03/69	Unclassified

No.2 engine, 539, auxiliary drive coupling to be refitted, No.1 bogie, 9000-23, all traction motors to be examined. No.2 bogie, 9000-24, Nos.4 & 5 traction motors insulation reading very low, No.6 traction motor to be examined. No.1 bogie, 9000-23, replaced by 9000-17. No.2 bogie, 9000-24, replaced by 9000-18. No.2 load regulator valve was fitted, footstep panels re-riveted. The sun visor in No.2 cab was changed and an oil leak on No.1 load regulator was rectified.

Doncaster	09/05/69	09/05/69	Unclassified

No.2 engine, 539, bad fuel leak from 'A' bank side between engine and generator at back of air manifold block. 'Locomotive is a fire risk'. Nos. 2 & 5 injectors on 'B' bank of 539 were changed.

Doncaster	02/06/69	05/06/69	Unclassified

No.1 engine, 448, replaced by 418, due to internal coolant leak. No.1 end load regulator leaking oil. No.1 end oil radiators were changed and No.1 oil tank flushed out.

Doncaster	27/06/69	03/07/69	Unclassified

No.1 engine, 418, 'CA' crankshaft end bearing leaking oil very badly. An overhauled replacement phasing case was fitted.

Doncaster	29/07/69	21/08/69	Intermediate

*No.1 engine, 418, replaced by 448. No.2 engine, 539, replaced by 416. No.1 bogie, 9000-17, replaced by 9000-37. No.2 bogie, 9000-18, replaced by 9000-38. Boiler, 5088/J3239, replaced by 5086/J3237. The boiler water tank modification was fitted. The body was given an Intermediate repair and repainted into **blue livery with full yellow nose ends**.*

Doncaster	03/09/69	04/09/69	Unclassified

No.1 main generator flashed over, No.1 bogie, 9000-37, all traction motors flashed over and No.2 bogie, 9000-38, No.4 traction motor throwing insulation from risers, No.5 traction motor flashed over and No.6 traction motor throwing solder. All flashover damage was cleaned up and No.6 traction motor was replaced.

Doncaster	30/12/69	31/12/69	Unclassified

No.2 engine, 416, replaced by 439, due to crankcase fractured, con rod disintegrated. No.2 end lubricating oil radiators and tanks were removed, cleaned and refitted. The locomotive was load tested and graphed.

Doncaster	16/01/70	17/01/70	Unclassified

No.2 engine, 439, replaced by 449, due to aerating badly. No.2 lubricating oil tank and radiators were flushed out.

Doncaster	19/01/70	20/01/70	Unclassified

No.2 engine, 449, replaced by 415.

Doncaster	23/02/70	26/02/70	Unclassified

No.2 engine, 415, replaced by 409, due to having seized, hole in 'C' bank. Lubricating oil tank and radiators were removed, cleaned and refitted. A fractured silencer and boiler water tank were also repaired.

Doncaster	11/03/70	13/03/70	Unclassified

No.4 traction motor down to earth. No.4 traction motor was replaced.

Doncaster	13/04/70	18/04/70	Light

No.1 engine, 448 and No.2 engine, 409, were given Light repairs and refitted. No.1 bogie, 9000-37, replaced by 9000-45. No.2 bogie, 9000-38, replaced by 9000-46. Boiler, 5086/J3237, was given an Unclassified repair. The body was given a Light repair.

Doncaster	28/08/70	01/09/70	Unclassified

No.2 engine, 409, replaced by 412, due to a seized piston and a hole in crankcase. No.2 end lubricating oil tank and radiators were removed for flushing and refitted. A fracture in No.1 boiler water tank was repaired.

D9005/9005/55 005 The Prince Of Wales's Own Regiment Of Yorkshire (continued)

Loco Works	On Works	Off Works	Class of repair
Doncaster	04/09/70	09/09/70	Unclassified

No.1 engine, 448, replaced by 405, due to a fractured liner.

| Doncaster | 22/09/70 | 25/09/70 | Unclassified |

Both main generators repeated flashover damage, arc horns burnt. Both main generators had flashover damage repaired. Field divert settings were examined and reset. No.2 collector drum was replaced due to a fracture. All traction motors were replaced.

| Doncaster | 15/12/70 | 18/12/70 | Unclassified |

No.1 exhauster drum tank fire. Water poured down exhaust. No.1 engine, 405, was given an Unclassified repair. No.1 boiler water tank had a fracture repaired.

| Doncaster | 24/01/71 | 17/04/71 | Intermediate |

No.1 engine, 405, replaced by 419. No.2 engine, 412, replaced by 425. No.1 bogie, 9000-45, replaced by 9000-37. No.2 bogie, 9000-46, replaced by 9000-38. Boiler, 5086/J3237, replaced by 5094/J3245. The body given an Intermediate repair. The locomotive fitted with E.T.H. equipment.

| Doncaster | 07/05/71 | 12/05/71 | Unclassified |

No.2 engine, 425, replaced by 405, due to liner seals leaking, coolant in sump. No.1 engine, 419, had fan clutch shoes changed. No.1 boiler water tank was changed.

| Doncaster | 24/05/71 | 25/05/71 | Unclassified |

No.2 engine, 405, replaced by 421. Lubricating oil tanks and radiators were removed, cleaned and refitted.

| Doncaster | 02/07/71 | 02/07/71 | Unclassified |

Exhauster support frame right hand leg broken at bottom. This was repaired.

| Doncaster | 07/09/71 | 07/09/71 | Unclassified |

No.2 engine, 421, replaced by 452, due to coolant system pressurising.

| Doncaster | 26/11/71 | 27/11/71 | Unclassified |

No.1 engine, 419, 'B2' injector pocket leaking coolant. 'B2' injector adaptor changed.

| Doncaster | 01/02/72 | 08/02/72 | Unclassified |

Both main generators flashed over and No.2 boiler water tank fractured. Both main generators were replaced. No.2 boiler water tank was removed, repaired and refitted.

| Doncaster | 16/02/72 | 26/02/72 | Light |

No.1 engine, 419, replaced by 436, due to a coolant leak. No.2 engine, 452, was given a Light repair. No.1 bogie, 9000-37, replaced by 9000-5. No.2 bogie, 9000-38, replaced by 9000-6. Boiler, 5094/J3245, was given an Unclassified repair. The body was given a Light repair.

| Doncaster | 28/02/72 | 02/03/72 | Rectification |

Rectification work was carried out on the body.

| Doncaster | 21/04/72 | 25/04/72 | Unclassified |

No.1 main generator commutator bars unevenly worn. No.1 main generator was replaced. The governor on No.1 engine, 436, was replaced.

| Doncaster | 14/06/72 | 15/06/72 | Unclassified |

No.2 engine, 452, replaced by 434, due to crankcase holed and con rod broken. Lubricating oil tank and radiator elements were cleaned and a fuel leak from the equalising pipe between main fuel tanks was rectified.

| Doncaster | 20/06/72 | 22/06/72 | Unclassified |

No.2 engine, 434, replaced by 426, due to a timing defect.

| Doncaster | 06/07/72 | 17/07/72 | Unclassified |

No.1 engine, 436, replaced by 427, due to being dephased and coolant header tank leaking. No.2 engine, 426, replaced by 408. No.1 primary fan and primary fan gearbox were replaced. No.1 coolant header tank and radiators were repaired.

| Doncaster | 17/07/72 | 18/07/72 | Unclassified |

Fuel tanks were removed and refitted to facilitate repairs to a leaking steam pipe.

| Doncaster | 04/09/72 | 08/09/72 | Unclassified |

No.1 engine, 427, replaced by 451, due to 'C' bank liner seal leaking. Lubricating oil tank and radiators were changed.

| Doncaster | 13/11/72 | 16/11/72 | Unclassified |

No.1 engine, 451, replaced by 407, due to piston through crankcase. Lubricating oil tank and radiators were cleaned.

D9005/9005/55 005 The Prince Of Wales's Own Regiment Of Yorkshire (continued)

Loco Works	On Works	Off Works	Class of repair
Doncaster	07/12/72	08/12/72	Unclassified

No.1 engine, 407, replaced by 444, due to crankcase holed. No.1 end lubricating oil tank and radiators were removed, cleaned and refitted.

| Doncaster | 11/12/72 | 11/12/72 | Unclassified |

No.1 engine, 444, shutting down. A coolant flow switch was changed.

| Doncaster | 29/12/72 | 26/01/73 | Intermediate |

No.1 engine, 444, replaced by 436. No.2 engine, 408, replaced by 440. No.1 bogie, 9000-5, replaced by 9000-21, due to excessive lateral movement. No.2 bogie, 9000-6, replaced by 9000-41. Boiler, 5094/J3245, replaced by 1489/J2945. The body was given an Intermediate repair.

| Doncaster | 02/05/73 | 04/05/73 | Unclassified |

No.2 engine, 440, replaced by 431, due to a fractured liner. A water tank fracture was repaired.

| Doncaster | 20/06/73 | 26/06/73 | Unclassified |

No.1 main generator armature banding burst. No.1 main generator was replaced.

| Doncaster | 12/07/73 | 14/07/73 | Unclassified |

No.1 engine, 436, replaced by 409, due to a fractured liner.

| Doncaster | 14/08/73 | 16/08/73 | Unclassified |

No.1 engine, 409, replaced by 420, due to a fractured liner. No.2 bogie, 9000-41, had bolster and bearer pad repaired. Side bearer restraining brackets on both sides were renewed.

| Doncaster | 12/09/73 | 14/09/73 | Unclassified |

No.1 engine, 420, replaced by 453, due to being dephased.

| Doncaster | 20/11/73 | 30/11/73 | Light |

No.1 eng. 453, replaced by 451. No.2 engine, 431, was given a Light repair. No.1 bogie, 9000-21, replaced by 9000-25. No.2 bogie, 9000-41, replaced by 9000-26. Boiler, 1489/J2945, was given an Unclassified repair. No.1 boiler water tank had a leak repaired. The body was given a Light repair.

| Doncaster | 02/01/74 | 04/01/74 | Unclassified |

No.2 engine, 431, replaced by 432, due to being dephased.

| Doncaster | 28/01/74 | 28/01/74 | Modification |

Earth fault relay modification. This was carried out.

| Doncaster | 29/01/74 | 01/02/74 | Unclassified |

No.2 engine, 432, replaced by 411, due to pumping coolant into recover tank — liner fractured.

| Doncaster | 02/04/74 | 04/04/74 | Unclassified |

No.1 engine, 451, replaced by 432, due to being dephased.

| Doncaster | 03/06/74 | 09/06/74 | Unclassified |

No.2 engine, 411, underspeed gear in phasing gearcase splines sheared. E.T.H. and temperature probe modifications were carried out and 411 was given an Intermediate repair and refitted.

| Doncaster | 30/07/74 | 07/08/74 | Unclassified |

No.1 engine, 432, replaced by 417. No.2 engine, 411, replaced by 412, due to breathing heavy, high water temperature and alloy particles in chip tray. No.2 bogie, 9000-26, had 'R1' swing link studs renewed.

| Doncaster | 07/11/74 | 10/12/74 | Intermediate |

Collision and flashover damage. No.1 engine, 417, replaced by 458. No.2 engine, 412, replaced by 428. No.1 bogie, 9000-25 and No.2 bogie, 9000-26, were given standard repairs and refitted. Boiler, 1489/J2945, replaced by 1488/J2944. The locomotive was taken out of service on 06/11/74 with both main generators flashed over. This had occurred five times since 18/10/74. The body was given an Intermediate repair and had slight damage repaired.

| Doncaster | 14/02/75 | 15/02/75 | Unclassified |

No.4 traction motor burst. No.2 boiler water tank fractured. All traction motors to be changed. No.1 bogie, 9000-25 and No.2 bogie, 9000-26, had various brake cotters to reset. 'R4' sand trap to fit. 'R1' footstep to secure. No.2 boiler water tank was repaired. Only No.4 traction motor was changed.

| Doncaster | 25/02/75 | 26/02/75 | Unclassified |

No.2 engine, 428, replaced by 422, due to 'BC' crankcase fractured. The locomotive was load tested and graphed.

D9005/9005/55 005 The Prince Of Wales's Own Regiment Of Yorkshire (continued)

Loco Works	On Works	Off Works	Class of repair
Doncaster	19/03/75	21/03/75	Unclassified

No.1 engine, 458, replaced by 431, due to high copper content in lubricating oil and coolant thermostat defective. Lubricating oil reservoirs and oil tank were cleaned out at No.1 end. No.2 end boiler water tank was removed, repaired and refitted.

Doncaster	11/10/75	13/10/75	Unclassified

No.2 boiler water tank leaking very badly. This was repaired.

Doncaster	22/10/75	23/10/75	Unclassified

No.2 engine, 422, replaced by 413, due to heavy breathing. Various defects on No.1 bogie, 9000-25 and No.2 bogie, 9000-26. 'L2' and 'L4' equalising beam blocks to secure, various brake block cotters to adjust. No.4 traction motor suspension bracket set screw to renew. No.3 traction motor safety stay to repair. No.1 load regulator leaking. All repairs were carried out.

Doncaster	01/12/75	02/12/75	Unclassified

No.1 engine, 431, replaced by 538.

Doncaster	30/12/75	08/01/76	Unclassified

No.2 engine, 413, replaced by 424.

Doncaster	24/01/76	28/01/76	Modification

Cab louvre experiment fitted.

Doncaster	29/01/76	12/02/76	Light

No.1 engine, 538, was given a Light repair and refitted. No.2 engine, 424, had injectors changed and was refitted. No.1 bogie, 9000-25, replaced by 900011. No.2 bogie, 9000-26, replaced by 9000-12. Boiler, 1488/J2944, was given an Unclassified repair. The locomotive was weighed at 102t 17cwt.

Doncaster	16/02/76	17/02/76	Unclassified

No.2 auxiliary generator no output. This was replaced.

Doncaster	05/08/76	10/08/76	Unclassified

No.1 engine, 538, replaced by 438. No.2 engine, 424, replaced by 444. Cab window frames secured and boiler water tank repaired.

Doncaster	11/12/76	15/12/76	Unclassified

Boiler, 1488/J2944, replaced by 1495/J2951, due to being burnt out and badly distorted. Boiler room floor plates and No.1 boiler water tank were repaired. No.2 main generator received repairs.

Doncaster	05/01/77	07/01/77	Unclassified

No.1 engine, 438, replaced by 454, due to crankcase fractured on right hand side above exhaust manifold near old weld.

Doncaster	31/03/77	21/10/77	Intermediate

No.1 engine, 454, replaced by 404, due to being dephased. No.2 engine, 444, replaced by 405. No.1 bogie, 9000-11, replaced by 9000-27. No.2 bogie, 9000-12, replaced by 9000-28. Boiler, 1495/J2951, was given an Unclassified repair. No.2 right hand side fuel tank leaking. This was repaired. Route indicator panels were plated over. The locomotive was weighed at 104t.

Doncaster	24/10/77	26/10/77	Rectification

No details recorded.

Doncaster	31/10/77	08/11/77	Rectification

Wheelslip at 80 mph. Control circuit breaker tripping intermittently. Auxiliary earth fault. Intermittent low power. Batteries were exchanged. An earth fault on cab heaters was rectified. No.2 main generator was grooved in centre of commutator. This was rectified. No.1 bogie, 9000-27, had footsteps secured.

Doncaster	08/12/77	18/12/77	Unclassified

No.2 cab heaters not working. No.2 cab hotplate not working. Control circuit breaker tripping. Burnt wiring was repaired.

Doncaster	08/03/78	10/03/78	Unclassified

No.2 engine, 405, replaced by 427, due to crankcase fractured. It's governor had also been robbed for 55 002. No.1 engine, 404, was down on power. The locomotive had also had repeated bookings for rough riding. No.2 radiator fan clutch fitted, as was No.1 E.T.H. jumper. On No.1 bogie, 9000-27, 'R1' horn liner was secured. On No.2 bogie, 9000-28, 'L2' footstep was secured.

D9005/9005/55 005 The Prince Of Wales's Own Regiment Of Yorkshire (continued)

Loco Works	On Works	Off Works	Class of repair
Doncaster	04/05/78	07/05/78	Unclassified

Earth faults on No.1 traction motor field coils. No.2 bogie, 9000-28, had 'L5' horn stay secured, No.4 gearcase side pull rod safety bracket to fit, 'R2' lifeguard to renew, set screw to fit in No.6 traction motor bracket and set screw to fit in wheel wear compensation box. No.1 traction motor was changed and No.3 brake rod safety stay was fitted. No.4 brake rod safety stay was also fitted.

Doncaster	12/07/78	20/07/78	Unclassified

No.1 engine, 404, replaced by 422, due to coolant aerated under load. No.2 engine, 427, radiator fan clutch slipping badly. 427 received a gudgeon pin housing examination. Defective lighting. All defects were rectified.

Doncaster	22/08/78	25/08/78	Unclassified

On No.1 engine, 422, the auxiliary generator shaft coupling bolts were loose and there was some flashover damage on the main generator, this was repaired. No.2 engine, 427, replaced by 409, due to being dephased. No.2 load regulator tips were renewed and reset.

Doncaster	12/09/78	15/09/78	Unclassified

No.1 engine, 422, replaced by 448, due to a fractured liner. Coolant coming out of header tank overflow pipe. All windscreen wipers were also defective. These were repaired.

Doncaster	04/12/78	08/12/78	Unclassified

No.1 engine, 448, replaced by 424, due to a fractured liner. No.1 primary cardan shaft to be renewed. No.2 load regulator oil leak to clean and rectify. No.1 bogie, 9000-27, had No.2 traction motor nose suspension pad loose. All defects were rectified.

Doncaster	05/07/79	08/08/79	Light

No.1 engine, 424, replaced by 444, due to time expired. No.2 engine, 409, replaced by 428, due to pistons time expired. No.1 bogie, 9000-27 and No.2 bogie, 9000-28, were given standard repairs and refitted. Boiler, 1495/J2951, replaced by 5091/J3242. The loco was weighed at 105t 10cwt.

Doncaster	24/01/80	29/01/80	Unclassified

No.1 engine, 444, replaced by 453, due to being dephased, suspect 'BC' crank quillshaft broken. On No.1 bogie, 9000-27, No.3 traction motor nose pad was loose. On No.2 bogie, 9000-28, No.6 traction motor had a similar defect, these were both repaired.

Doncaster	09/05/80	13/05/80	Unclassified

No.2 engine, 428, fan/auxiliary drive output shaft splines worn. The exciter gearbox was changed. The locomotive was weighed at 105t 10cwt.

Doncaster	11/07/80	16/07/80	Unclassified

No.1 engine, 453, replaced by 458, due to high spectrographic analysis.

Doncaster	23/09/80	25/09/80	Unclassified

No.2 engine, 428, replaced by 434, due to scavenge blower drive sheared.

Doncaster	17/11/80	18/11/80	Unclassified

The locomotive had been in collision with a herd of cows on the line near Egmanton, but was subsequently sent to Stratford D.R.S. for cleaning.

Stratford D.R.S.	17/02/81	20/02/81	-

No.1 bogie, 9000-27, replaced by 9000-49. No.2 bogie, 9000-28, replaced by 9000-50. This change was carried out to return 55 021 to traffic.

Doncaster	21/02/81	-	-

The locomotive arrived after withdrawal with the following main components fitted; No.1 engine, 458, required secondary fan shaft to be fitted. No.2 engine, 434. No.1 bogie, 9000-49. No.2 bogie, 9000-50. Boiler, 5091/J3242.

* * *

D9006/9006/55 006 The Fife & Forfar Yeomanry

Loco Works	On Works	Off Works	Class of repair
Doncaster	29/06/61	Not recorded	Acceptance trials

New locomotive fitted with the following main components; No.1 engine, 419. No.2 engine, 418. No.1 bogie, 1013. No.2 bogie, 1014. Boiler, 1489/J2945.

| Doncaster | 29/03/62 | 30/03/62 | Light |

No.2 engine, 418, replaced by 422. No.1 bogie, 1013, replaced by 1027. No.2 bogie, 1014, replaced by 1028. No.2 water tank was welded and micro pumps changed on both engines.

| Doncaster | 06/08/62 | 15/08/62 | General |

No.1 engine, 419, replaced by 406. No.2 engine, 422, replaced by 425. No.1 bogie, 1027, replaced by 1013. No.2 bogie, 1028, replaced by 1014. Boiler, 1489/J2945, replaced by 1497/J2953. The flexible exhaust pipe modification was carried out. The body was given an annual repair. The locomotive mileage was recorded as 162,000 miles.

| Doncaster | 13/09/62 | 13/09/62 | Unclassified |

Bogie fractures. No.1 bogie, 1013 and No.2 bogie, 1014 were chipped and welded.

| Doncaster | 12/02/63 | 14/02/63 | Light |

No.1 bogie, 1013, replaced by 1039. No.2 bogie, 1014, replaced by 1040. Boiler, 1497/J2953 was overhauled. The body was given a six monthly exam. New primary fan shafts were fitted to both engines. No.1 exhaust collector tank inspection lid and exhaust flexible pipe were fitted with new joints. A buffer was replaced at No.2 end. The following modifications were carried out — Additional exhaust pipe filter; Additional compressor outlet pipe bracket; Drivers vacuum brake valve.

| Doncaster | 04/05/63 | 05/05/63 | Unclassified |

Derailment damage to No.2 bogie, 1040. Fractured vacuum pipe elbows were replaced, the air pipes to the warning horns were repaired, bogie rubbing plates straightened and a crack welded under brake hanger bracket on No.2 bogie. Flashover damage to traction motors repaired.

| Doncaster | 19/05/63 | 06/06/63 | General |

No.1 engine, 406, replaced by 405. No.2 engine, 425, replaced by 421. No.1 bogie, 1039, replaced by 1017. No.2 bogie, 1040, replaced by 1026. Boiler, 1497/J2953, replaced by 5086/J3237. The body was given an annual repair. The following modifications were carried out — Soundproofing; Radiator grills; Exhaust drum tanks; Lubricating oil filters; Air supply and caustic injection to boiler feed water.

| Doncaster | 26/07/63 | 30/07/63 | Unclassified |

No.2 wheelset was replaced.

| Doncaster | 13/08/63 | 13/08/63 | Unclassified |

Fuel tank holed on side due to action of 'Liquor 8' leaking from inlet pipe of dosing tank. No.1 right hand fuel tank was welded and covered with fibreglass. No.2 main water tank was replaced. Temporary brake hanger modification was fitted to bracket on bogies.

| Doncaster | 24/10/63 | 26/10/63 | Modification |

Boiler modifications were carried out and Automatic blowdown fitted.

| Doncaster | 18/12/63 | 21/12/63 | Light |

No.1 bogie, 1017, replaced by 1025. No.2 bogie, 1026, replaced by 1018. Boiler, 5086/J3237 was overhauled as were the water tanks. The body was given a six monthly examination.

| Doncaster | 31/01/64 | 01/02/64 | Unclassified |

No.1 bogie, 1025, replaced by 1019. No.2 bogie, 1018, replaced by 1020.

| Doncaster | 02/04/64 | 02/04/64 | Unclassified |

No.1 bogie, 1019, replaced by 1045, due to rough riding, spring plank biased to right hand side. No.1 bogie transom also had a fracture at the top and No.1 axlebox right hand side held in horn. No.2 bogie, 1020, replaced by 1018.

| Doncaster | 09/05/64 | 02/06/64 | General |

No.1 engine, 405, replaced by 427. No.2 bogie, 421, replaced by 436. No.1 bogie, 1045, was given a General repair. No.2 bogie, 1018, replaced by 1046. Boiler, 5086/J3237, replaced by 5096/J3247. The body was given a General repair.

D9006/9006/55 006 The Fife & Forfar Yeomanry (continued)

Loco Works	On Works	Off Works	Class of repair
Doncaster	27/07/64	31/07/64	Unclassified

No.1 nose end damaged, No.1 blower motor disintegrated, trunking to be examined for blower blades. No.1 nose end roof door was repaired, as was No.1 end traction motor blower air ducting. No.1 voltage regulator was changed. No.1 engine, 427, had MP11 exams carried out. No.1 bogie, 1045 and No.2 bogie, 1046 were given Unclassified repairs. Boiler, 5096/J3247, was given an MP11 exam.

Doncaster	19/09/64	21/09/64	Unclassified

Locomotive was derailed at Bradford Exchange on 17/09/64. Will require complete examination of bogies, particularly No.2. No.6 traction motor wheel left hand flange sharp with indentation approximately 3" long on flange, requires reprofiling. No.1 traction motor wheel right hand flange sharp, also to be reprofiled. No.4 traction motor wheel centres out of alignment, suspect axle slightly bent. Locomotive fit to travel to Works at reduced speed. No.1 engine, 427, was given an MP11 exam. No.1 bogie, 1045, replaced by 1027. No.2 bogie, 1046, replaced by 1030. Boiler, 5096/J3247, was given an MP11 exam.

Doncaster	15/01/65	19/01/65	Light

No.1 engine, 427, was given an MP11 exam. No.1 bogie, 1027, replaced by 1043, due to leading transom fractured. No.2 bogie, 1030, replaced by 1044, for examination for fractures. Boiler, 5096/J3247, was given an MP11 exam.

Doncaster	26/03/65	27/03/65	Unclassified

No.2 engine, 436, replaced by 428, due to 'A5' liner fractured.

Doncaster	15/05/65	16/05/65	Unclassified

No.2 engine, 428, replaced by 452, due to water pump drive sheared.

Doncaster	31/05/65	18/06/65	General

No.1 engine, 427, replaced by 426. No.2 engine, 452, replaced by 412. No.1 bogie, 1043 and No.2 bogie, 1044, were given General repairs and refitted. Boiler, 5096/J3247, replaced by 1497/J2953. The body was given a General repair.

Doncaster	29/07/65	01/08/65	Unclassified

No.2 engine, 412, replaced by 435, due to suspect blower drive disengaged. Exhaust gases being emitted from air intake filters.

Doncaster	24/08/65	29/08/65	Unclassified

Derailment and collision damage. Water tank cladding damaged, scoop to be examined. No.1 end right hand side lamp bracket to repair. Left hand side bodywork holed. Nameplate damaged. Speedometer equipment, gauges, generator and wheel wear components taken for D9018. Both bogies to be examined for derailment damage. Collision damage on the body was repaired including No.1 left hand side superstructure and left hand side nameplate. No.1 bogie, 1043, replaced by 900019. No.2 bogie, 1044, replaced by 900020. Boiler, 1497/J2953, was given an Unclassified repair.

Doncaster	02/10/65	05/10/65	Unclassified

No.2 engine, 435, replaced by 413, due to sump full of water.

Doncaster	29/12/65	04/01/66	Light

No.1 engine, 426, was given an Unclassified repair. No.2 engine, 413, was given an Unclassified repair due to a heavy oil leak. No.1 bogie, 900019, was given an Unclassified repair and No.1 axle changed. No.2 bogie, 900020, was given an Unclassified repair. Boiler, 1497/J2953, was given an Unclassified repair due to being inoperative. Cab footstep stiffening modification was carried out. The body was given an Unclassified repair.

Doncaster	04/02/66	04/02/66	Unclassified

Exhaust bellows were replaced.

Doncaster	25/02/66	26/02/66	Unclassified

No.1 engine, 426, replaced by 432.

Doncaster	15/03/66	15/03/66	Unclassified

No.1 engine, 432, replaced by 437, due to 'B' bank inlet manifold leaking water, suspect liner seals.

Doncaster	08/05/66	21/05/66	General

No.1 engine, 437 and No.2 engine, 413, were given General repairs. No.1 bogie, 9000-19, replaced by 9000-41. No.2 bogie, 9000-20, replaced by 9000-42. Boiler, 1497/J2953, replaced by 5093/J3244. The body was given a General repair.

D9006/9006/55 006 The Fife & Forfar Yeomanry (continued)

Loco Works	On Works	Off Works	Class of repair
Doncaster	07/06/66	07/06/66	Unclassified

A fuel leak was rectified on No.1 end left hand fuel tank and two brush boxes were changed on each of Nos.3 & 5 traction motors. No.1 main generator had insulators cleaned and painted. No.2 main generator had flashover damage cleaned up.

Doncaster	20/07/66	21/07/66	Unclassified

No.1 engine, 437, replaced by 427, due to water pump drive shaft sheared.

Doncaster	26/07/66	27/07/66	Unclassified

No.1 engine, 427, replaced by 451.

Doncaster	13/10/66	18/10/66	Unclassified

No.1 engine, 451, received repairs. No.1 main generator was cleaned and had one new insulator fitted. No.2 main generator was also cleaned and had twelve new brushes fitted. Both auxiliary generators were replaced.

Doncaster	04/01/67	05/01/67	Unclassified

A boiler water tank and exhaust bellows were replaced and both main and auxiliary generators were cleaned.

Doncaster	13//03/67	07/04/67	General

No.1 engine, 451, replaced by 416. No.2 engine, 413, replaced by 441. No.1 bogie, 9000-41, replaced by 9000-45. No.2 bogie, 9000-42, replaced by 9000-46. Boiler, 5093/J3244, replaced by 1487/J2943. The body given a General repair and full yellow nose ends were applied.

Doncaster	27/07/67	28/07/67	Unclassified

Both main generators had flashover damage repaired and Nos.3 & 4 traction motors were replaced.

Doncaster	02/11/67	11/11/67	Light

Traction motor suspension tubes defective. No.1 engine, 416 and No.2 engine, 441, given Unclassified repairs. No.1 bogie, 9000-45, replaced by 9000-17. No.2 bogie, 9000-46, replaced by 9000-18. Boiler, 1487/J2943 given an Unclassified repair. The body given an Unclassified repair.

Doncaster	08/03/68	11/04/68	General

No.1 engine, 416, replaced by 410. No.2 engine, 441, replaced by 429. No.1 bogie, 9000-17, replaced by 9000-1. No.2 bogie, 9000-18, replaced by 9000-2. Boiler, 1487/J2943, replaced by 1490/J2946. The body was given a General repair and the locomotive was fitted for dual braking.

Doncaster	07/06/68	10/06/68	Unclassified

No.2 engine, 429, replaced by 441.

Doncaster	01/11/68	08/11/68	Light

No.1 engine, 410, replaced by 413, due to a fractured quill shaft. No.2 engine, 441, replaced by 418. No.1 bogie, 9000-1, replaced by 9000-3. No.2 bogie, 9000-2, replaced by 9000-4. Boiler, 1490/J2946, was given an Unclassified repair. The body was given an Unclassified repair.

Doncaster	02/04/69	02/04/69	Unclassified

No.2 engine, 418, to be load tested per C.M. & E.E.'s instructions.

Doncaster	10/04/69	11/04/69	Unclassified

No.2 engine, 418, was tested for a reported defect. The coolant level switch was changed and governor top secured.

Doncaster	08/05/69	09/05/69	Unclassified

Examination of bogies due to rough riding.

Doncaster	03/06/69	21/06/69	Intermediate

*No.1 engine, 413, replaced by 444. No.2 engine, 418, replaced by 414. No.1 bogie, 9000-3, replaced by 9000-45. No.2 bogie, 9000-4, replaced by 9000-46. Boiler, 1490/J2946, replaced by 5096/J3247. The body given an Intermediate repair and repainted into **blue livery with full yellow nose ends**.*

Doncaster	30/09/69	07/10/69	Unclassified

Persistent wheel slip indications, field divert resistances to check. Both main generators with flashover damage. All traction motors to be checked for flashover damage. Wheel slip relays were recalibrated, load regulators and resistance values checked. Sequence checked for correct operation of field diverts' relays. No.2 main generator was replaced. Flashover damage to all traction motors was repaired. The locomotive was load tested.

D9006/9006/55 006 The Fife & Forfar Yeomanry (continued)

Loco Works	On Works	Off Works	Class of repair
Doncaster	16/12/69	29/01/70	Unclassified

Fire damage. Burnt wiring in control cubicle and battery charge cables renewed. No.1 primary and No.2 secondary cardan shafts repaired. Traction motors on both bogies were changed.

Doncaster	23/03/70	06/04/70	Light

No.1 engine, 444 and No.2 engine, 414, were given light repairs and refitted. No.1 bogie, 9000-45, replaced by 9000-3. No.2 bogie, 9000-46, replaced by 9000-4. Boiler, 5096/J3247, was given a Light repair. The body was given a Light repair.

Doncaster	03/06/70	05/06/70	Unclassified

Flashover damage to both main generators and all traction motors. No.4 traction motor was changed and all other flashover damage repaired.

Doncaster	10/07/70	11/07/70	Unclassified

No.2 engine, 414, replaced by 443, due to scavenge blower failure.

Doncaster	21/07/70	24/07/70	Unclassified

No.2 main generator bearing hot. No.2 engine, 443, replaced by 437.

Doncaster	11/08/70	14/08/70	Unclassified

No.1 engine, 444, replaced by 443, due to gas in coolant system, suspect fractured liner. No.1 boiler water tank was replaced.

Doncaster	24/10/70	25/10/70	Unclassified

No.2 engine, 437, replaced by 451, due to a fractured liner.

Doncaster	02/11/70	05/03/71	Intermediate

No.1 engine, 443, replaced by 441, due to sump full of coolant. No.2 engine, 451, replaced by 539. No.1 bogie, 9000-3, replaced by 9000-25. No.2 bogie, 9000-4, replaced by 9000-26. Boiler, 5096/J3247, replaced by 1489/J2945. The body was given an Intermediate repair. The locomotive was fitted with E.T.H. equipment.

Doncaster	09/03/71	10/03/71	Rectification

Adjustments were carried out to field divert circuitry.

Doncaster	16/03/71	16/03/71	Rectification

Field divert faults were rectified.

Doncaster	18/03/71	21/03/71	Rectification

Adjustments were carried out to field divert circuitry.

Doncaster	28/04/71	28/04/71	Unclassified

E.T.H. overload relay was adjusted.

Doncaster	31/08/71	04/09/71	Unclassified

No.1 engine, 441, replaced by 448, due to a piston through crankcase. No.1 boiler water tank was changed, as was No.2 right hand bodyside window. Miscellaneous repairs were carried out to brakegear and traction motors on both bogies.

Doncaster	15/12/71	17/12/71	Unclassified

No.2 engine, 539, replaced by 434, due to knocking badly.

Doncaster	13/01/72	22/01/72	Light

No.1 engine, 448, was given a Light repair and refitted. No.2 engine, 434, replaced by 407, due to breathing heavy. No.1 bogie, 9000-25, replaced by 9000-21. No.2 bogie, 9000-26, replaced by 9000-41. Boiler, 1489/J2945, was given an Unclassified repair. The body was given a Light repair.

Doncaster	24/01/72	25/01/72	Rectification

Air, vacuum and electrical faults. These were rectified.

Doncaster	02/04/72	07/04/72	Unclassified

No.1 engine, 448, replaced by 446, due to throwing oil.

Doncaster	21/09/72	23/09/72	Unclassified

No.1 main generator flashed over and armature windings adrift. No.1 fan gearbox was replaced, as was No.1 main generator.

Doncaster	17/10/72	20/10/72	Unclassified

No.1 engine, 446, replaced by 411, due to fractured liners. Lubricating oil tanks were removed, cleaned and refitted.

Doncaster	07/11/72	08/12/72	Intermediate

No.1 engine, 411, replaced by 538. No.2 engine, 407, replaced by 446. No.1 bogie, 9000-21, replaced by 9000-11. No.2 bogie, 9000-41, replaced by 9000-12. Boiler, 1489/J2945, replaced by 5097/J3248.

D9006/9006/55 006 The Fife & Forfar Yeomanry (continued)

Loco Works	On Works	Off Works	Class of repair
Doncaster	08/12/72	12/12/72	Unclassified

No.1 main generator defective. No.1 engine, 538, replaced by 437.

| Doncaster | 25/01/73 | 26/01/73 | Unclassified |

No.2 boiler water tank fractured. This was repaired.

| Doncaster | 27/02/73 | 01/03/73 | Unclassified |

No.2 boiler water tank fractured. This was repaired.

| Doncaster | 02/08/73 | 03/08/73 | Unclassified |

No.1 engine, 437, replaced by 433, due to aerating. No.2 boiler water tank had a fracture repaired.

| Doncaster | 17/09/73 | 05/10/73 | Light |

No.1 engine, 433, replaced by 407. No.2 engine, 446, replaced by 408. No.1 bogie, 9000-11, replaced by 9000-7. No.2 bogie, 9000-12, replaced by 9000-8. Boiler, 5097/J3248, was given an Unclassified repair.

| Doncaster | 25/01/74 | 25/01/74 | Modification |

Earth fault relay modification.

| Doncaster | 19/03/74 | 27/03/74 | Unclassified |

No.1 engine, 407, replaced by 447. No.2 engine, 408, replaced by 419, due to a suspected fractured liner. No.2 boiler water tank had fractures repaired. No.2 end oil radiators were changed.

| Doncaster | 17/05/74 | 28/05/74 | Unclassified |

No.2 engine, 419, high water temperature. No.2 end radiators were changed.

| Doncaster | 15/10/74 | 26/11/74 | Intermediate |

No.1 engine, 447, replaced by 433. No.2 engine, 419, replaced by 418. No.1 bogie, 9000-7 and No.2 bogie, 9000-8, were given standard repairs and refitted. Boiler, 5097/J3248, replaced by 1492/J2948. Oil pipework in the roof was chafed and holed. The body was given an Intermediate repair.

| Doncaster | 08/01/75 | 11/01/75 | Unclassified |

No.1 engine, 433, replaced by 421, due to crankcase holed. No.1 end lubricating oil tank and radiators, removed, cleaned and refitted.

| Doncaster | 10/02/75 | 13/02/75 | Unclassified |

No.2 engine, 418, replaced by 425, due to coolant leaks.

| Doncaster | 18/03/75 | 21/03/75 | Unclassified |

Flashover damage on all traction motors and No.1 main generator. No.1 engine, 421, had coolant leaks rectified. No.1 main generator was replaced. Flashover damage on No.2 main generator and all traction motors, with the exception of No.3, was repaired. No.3 traction motor was replaced.

| Doncaster | 15/08/75 | 18/08/75 | Unclassified |

No.3 traction motor to renew and No.4 traction motor isolated. On No.1 bogie, 9000-7, Nos.2 & 3 traction motors were replaced and flashover damage cleaned up on No.1 traction motor. No.2 bogie, 9000-8, had all flashover damage cleaned up.

| Doncaster | 15/10/75 | 19/10/75 | Unclassified |

No.2 engine, 425, replaced by 444, due to No.6 'BC' crankshaft con rod and piston adrift, crankcase cover fractured.

| Doncaster | 01/11/75 | 02/11/75 | Unclassified |

No.1 engine, 421, replaced by 424, due to being dephased.

| Doncaster | 15/11/75 | 16/11/75 | Rectification |

No.2 engine, 424, aerating. Injector pockets were changed.

| Doncaster | 03/12/75 | 18/12/75 | Light |

No.1 engine, 424, replaced by 437. No.1 bogie, 9000-7, replaced by 9000-27. No.2 bogie, 9000-8, replaced by 9000-28. Boiler, 1492/J2948, was given an Unclassified repair. The locomotive was weighed at 104t 11cwt.

| Doncaster | 16/01/76 | 21/01/76 | Unclassified |

No.1 engine, 437, replaced by 404, due to 'BC' crankcase damper cover fractured and damper bolts broken.

| Doncaster | 05/07/76 | 08/07/76 | Unclassified |

No.1 engine, 404, exhaust collector drum fractured, as was No.1 boiler water tank. These repairs were carried out.

D9006/9006/55 006 The Fife & Forfar Yeomanry (continued)

Loco Works	On Works	Off Works	Class of repair
Doncaster	15/07/76	20/07/76	Unclassified

No.2 engine, 444, replaced by 458, due to high spectrographic analysis. A boiler water tank was repaired.

| Doncaster | 18/09/76 | 22/09/76 | Unclassified |

No.1 engine, 404, replaced by 454, due to breathing heavy and particles of metal in oil strainer.

| Doncaster | 24/09/76 | 26/09/76 | Unclassified |

No.2 engine, 458, replaced by 427, due to 'B1' con rod through crankcase. No.2 lubricating oil tank and radiators were removed for cleaning.

| Doncaster | 22/12/76 | 23/12/76 | Unclassified |

No.1 engine, 454, replaced by 426, due to being dephased.

| Doncaster | 05/02/77 | 25/02/77 | Unclassified |

No.1 engine, 426, replaced by 439, due to breathing heavy. No.2 engine, 427, replaced by 422, due to breathing heavy. No.1 boiler water tank was repaired, as was No.2 primary cardan shaft.

| Doncaster | 21/03/77 | 28/06/77 | Intermediate |

No.1 engine, 439, replaced by 455. No.2 engine, 422, replaced by 408. No.1 bogie, 9000-27, replaced by 9000-23. No.2 bogie, 9000-28, replaced by 9000-30. Boiler, 1492/J2948, replaced by J2905. Experiment DL/543 "Electrically operated windscreen washer pump" was fitted. The route indicator panels were plated over. The locomotive was weighed at 102t 17cwt.

| Doncaster | 28/08/77 | 01/09/77 | Unclassified |

No.2 engine, 408, replaced by 430, due to 'C' bank crankcase door joint blown out. Fracture in phasing gearcase underneath. The windscreen wipers, overspeed unit and governor of 408, had been robbed for 55 021. No.1 cab windscreen wipers were replaced.

| Doncaster | 06/09/77 | 11/09/77 | Unclassified |

No.2 engine, 430, replaced by 434, due to being dephased. No.2 boiler water tank had a leak repaired.

| Doncaster | 30/09/77 | 07/10/77 | Unclassified |

No.1 engine, 455, replaced by 425, due to breathing heavy. The locomotive was lifted and bogie centre pivot studs were secured.

| Doncaster | 08/12/77 | 12/12/77 | Unclassified |

No.1 engine, 425, exhaust silencer fractured in several places. Large exhaust bellows had been robbed for 55 015. No.2 boiler water tank was leaking. All defects were repaired.

| Doncaster | 01/02/78 | 03/02/78 | Unclassified |

No.1 engine, 425, replaced by 432, due to suspected fractured liner. Nos.1 & 2 primary cardan shaft splines badly worn. These were renewed.

| Doncaster | 20/06/78 | 23/06/78 | Unclassified |

No.1 engine, 432, had a coolant leak repaired. No.2 engine, 434, replaced by 442, due to being required for General repair. No.2 boiler water tank holed, No.1 fan drive clutch shoes to renew and No.1 load regulator had an oil leak. All defects were repaired.

| Doncaster | 20/08/78 | 29/08/78 | Unclassified |

No.1 engine, 432, had a fan clutch drive defect repaired. No.2 engine, 442, replaced by 438, due to 'AB' crankcase end cover fractured. No.1 bogie, 9000-23, had brake gear in poor condition. No.3 traction motor nose suspension pad was broken. No.2 bogie, 9000-30, also had brake gear in poor condition and all traction motors due overhaul. No.1 load regulator had an oil leak and No.1 end cab linoleum was damaged. The brakework on both bogies was overhauled. All traction motors were overhauled and refitted except for No.2, which was replaced. The loco weighed at 105t 3cwt.

| Doncaster | 12/10/78 | 16/10/78 | Unclassified |

No.1 engine, 432, removed for a gudgeon pin housing examination and refitted with a replacement exhauster drum. No.2 engine, 438, had an exciter gear cardan shaft flange drive defect repaired.

| Doncaster | 02/11/78 | 06/11/78 | Unclassified |

No.1 engine 432, replaced by 439 due to a fractured liner. No. 1 end coolant radiators were replaced and No. 1 load regulator had an oil leak rectified

| Doncaster | 09/11/78 | 15/11/78 | Unclassified |

Flashover damage on both main generators and all traction motors. No.1 main generator was replaced and No.2 main generator was overhauled and refitted. All traction motors except No.5 were repaired and refitted. No.5 traction motor was replaced. The locomotive was weighed at 105t 9cwt.

D9006/9006/55 006 The Fife & Forfar Yeomanry (continued)

Loco Works	On Works	Off Works	Class of repair
Doncaster	14/02/79	15/02/79	Unclassified

No.1 engine, 439, with a fractured liner. After tests on the load bank no defect was found.

Doncaster	03/04/79	13/04/79	Unclassified

No.2 engine, 438, replaced by 406, due to throwing oil, collector drum to clean out and lagging to renew. Nos.1 & 2 primary shafts were renewed, No.2 silencer tank fractures were repaired and No.2 coolant radiator and thermostat were changed.

Doncaster	18/05/79	21/06/79	Light

No.1 engine, 439, replaced by 447. No.2 engine, 406, replaced by 412. No.1 bogie, 9000-23, replaced by 9000-13. No.2 bogie, 9000-30, replaced by 9000-14. Boiler, J2905, was given an Unclassified repair. The locomotive was weighed at 105t 14cwt.

Doncaster	04/12/79	12/12/79	Unclassified

No.1 engine, 447, exhaust collector drum fractured and No.2 engine, 412, fire damage. No.1 primary fan gearbox was changed. No.1 engine's collector drum was repaired. No.2 engine's exhauster drum was repaired. No.1 bogie, 9000-13 and No.2 bogie, 9000-14, were fitted with experimental swing link bushes and those at No.3 position on No.1 bogie and No.6 position on No.2 bogie were examined. The burner motor on the boiler was missing and was replaced.

Doncaster	17/12/79	19/12/79	Unclassified

No.1 engine, 447, dephased. Examination showed no defect. No.1 fan drive gearbox was replaced due to a collapsed bearing caused by lack of oil. The burner motor on the boiler was also replaced.

Doncaster	15/01/80	18/01/80	Unclassified

No.1 engine, 447, replaced by 448, due to 'A6' injector adaptor threads damaged in liner. Engine governor robbed, overspeed shutdown mechanism robbed. No.2 engine, 412, had engine coolant flow switch metalistic bolts required.

Doncaster	11/04/80	16/04/80	Unclassified

No.1 engine, 448, replaced by 457, due to being dephased. No.2 engine, 412, replaced by 441, due to requiring renewal of 'B' bank expansion piece and examination of engine mountings.

Doncaster	04/06/80	07/06/80	Unclassified

No.1 engine, 457, replaced by 420, due to being dephased. Nos.1 & 2 load regulators leaking badly and engine room floors to clean.

Doncaster	30/12/80	16/01/81	Unclassified

Fire damage on exhaust systems of both engines. All fire bottles blown, both cab hand extinguishers used, engine room to clean. No.1 engine, 420, replaced by 415, due to coolant hoses burnt. No.2 engine, 441, was given an Unclassified repair.

Doncaster	09/02/81	-	-

The locomotive arrived after withdrawal with the following main components fitted. No.1 engine, 415. No.2 engine, 441. No.1 bogie, 9000-13. No.2 bogie, 9000-14. Boiler, J2905.

* * *

D9007/9007/55 007 Pinza

Loco Works	On Works	Off Works	Class of repair
Doncaster	22/06/61	Not recorded	Acceptance trials

New locomotive fitted with the following main components. No.1 engine, 422. No.2 engine, 421. No.1 bogie, 1015. No.2 bogie, 1016. Boiler, 1492/J2948. 'Pinza' nameplates fitted.

Vulcan Foundry	30/08/61	06/09/61	Not recorded

Modifications to bogies.

R.S.H. Darlington	03/01/62	18/01/62	Not recorded

No.1 engine, 422, replaced by 408, due to exhaust drum split. No.2 engine, 421, replaced by 414, due to blower bearing suspect.

R.S.H. Darlington	26/02/62	14/03/62	Not recorded

No.1 engine, 408 and No.2 engine, 414, received attention.

Doncaster	14/03/62	15/03/62	General

The exhaust butterfly valve locking handle on No.2 engine, 414, was repaired. No.1 bogie, 1015, replaced by 1047. No.2 bogie, 1016, replaced by 1048. Boiler, 1492/J2948, was overhauled. No.1 water tank had fractures welded. The body was given an annual repair.

Doncaster	17/04/62	17/04/62	Unclassified

No.4 traction motor armature down to earth and No.1 nose end to repair. No.4 traction motor was replaced. The locomotive mileage was recorded as 91,810 miles.

Doncaster	13/09/62	13/09/62	Unclassified

Traction motor flashover and No.2 axle horn cracked at No.1 end left side. Electric contacts were cleaned, new carbon brushes fitted and bogie fractures were chipped and welded.

Doncaster	17/09/62	18/09/62	Unclassified

All traction motors flashed over. No.1 bogie, 1047, replaced by 1027. No.2 bogie, 1048, replaced by 1028. Boiler, 1492/J2948, was overhauled. The following modifications were carried out — Radiator fan grills; Train heating pressure gauge pipe; Drawgear nuts and rubber washers. The locomotive mileage was recorded as 159,700 miles.

Doncaster	10/11/62	10/11/62	Unclassified

No.2 bogie, 1028, headstock fractured and right hand windscreen cracked at No.2 end. The bogie frame fractures were welded and the windscreen was replaced. The locomotive mileage was recorded as 188,110 miles.

Doncaster	21/01/63	04/02/63	General

No.1 engine, 408, replaced by 417. No.2 bogie, 414, replaced by 434. No.1 bogie, 1027, replaced by 1035. No.2 bogie, 1028, replaced by 1036. Boiler, 1492/J2948, replaced by 1494/J2950. The body was given an annual repair. The following modifications were carried out Radiator fan grill; Air compressor outlet pipe additional bracket; Oil tank filler filters; Exhaust collector tank drain; Anti wheel slip equipment fitted; Soundproofing part fitted.

Doncaster	12/03/63	12/03/63	Unclassified

No.1 bogie, 1035, replaced by 1023, due to fractures. No.2 bogie, 1036, replaced by 1024, due to fractures.

Doncaster	29/05/63	30/05/63	Unclassified

No.1 bogie, 1023, replaced by 1003, due to fractured transoms and horn liners loose. No.2 bogie, 1024, replaced by 1004, due to fractured transoms and horn liners loose. The locomotive mileage was recorded as 284,540 miles.

Doncaster	18/06/63	19/06/63	Unclassified

No.5 traction motor field open circuit. No.5 traction motor was replaced. The locomotive mileage was recorded as 294,830 miles.

Doncaster	13/08/63	15/08/63	Light

No.1 bogie, 1003, replaced by 1013, due to left hand side second transom fractured. No.2 bogie, 1004, replaced by 1014. Bogie brake block carrier guide stiffeners were fitted. The body was given a six-monthly exam. The locomotive mileage was recorded as 326,800 miles.

Doncaster	31/10/63	08/11/63	Unclassified

Boiler modifications. No.1 bogie, 1013, replaced by 1043. No.2 bogie, 1014, replaced by 1044. Boiler, 1494/J2950, replaced by 1490/J2946. The following modifications were carried out — Caustic injection to boiler feed water; Automatic blowdown equipment.

D9007/9007/55 007 Pinza (continued)

Loco Works	On Works	Off Works	Class of repair
Doncaster	07/12/63	01/01/64	General

No.1 engine, 417, replaced by 424. No.2 engine, 434, replaced by 419, due to 'C' bank camshaft no drive. No.1 bogie, 1043, replaced by 1021. No.2 bogie, 1044, replaced by 1022. Boiler, 1490/J2946, was given an Unclassified repair.

| Doncaster | 01/06/64 | 02/06/64 | Unclassified |

No.1 bogie, 1021, had transom stays cut and welded. No.2 bogie, 1022, had No.2 transom left side fractured and had transom stays cut and welded. Boiler, 1490/J2946, was given an MP11 exam. No.6 traction motor suspension pad out of position. Both main generators were cleaned, No.1 also having four brushes fitted.

| Doncaster | 11/06/64 | 18/06/64 | Light |

No.1 engine, 424 and No.2 engine, 419, were given Unclassified repairs. No.1 bogie, 1021, replaced by 1013. No.2 bogie, 1022, replaced by 1014. Boiler, 1490/J2946, was given an Unclassified repair.

| Doncaster | 30/10/64 | 07/12/64 | General |

Collision damage. No.2 end right hand side nose end stove in at front corner causing extensive damage. No.2 bogie framing and brakegear damaged. The collision damage was repaired and BR standard buffers were fitted. No.1 engine, 424, replaced by 408. No.2 engine, 419, replaced by 454. No.1 bogie, 1013, replaced by 1015. No.2 bogie, 1014, replaced by 1016. Boiler, 1490/J2946, replaced by 1496/J2952.

| Doncaster | 24/04/65 | 30/04/65 | Light |

No.1 engine, 408 and No.2 engine, 454, were given MP11 exams. No.1 bogie, 1015, replaced by 1049. No.2 bogie, 1016, replaced by 1002. Boiler, 1496/J2952, was given an Unclassified repair. The body was given an Unclassified repair.

| Doncaster | 19/08/65 | 23/08/65 | Unclassified |

Radiators to be changed. Coolant radiators and bypass valves were replaced. No.1 bogie, 1049, replaced by 9000-17. No.2 bogie, 1002, replaced by 9000-18. Boiler, 1496/J2952, was given an Unclassified repair.

| Doncaster | 17/09/65 | 20/09/65 | Unclassified |

No.1 engine, 408, replaced by 538, due to piston and con rod broken on 'C' bank. Lubricating oil tank was cleaned.

| Doncaster | 28/09/65 | 30/09/65 | Modification |

Boiler, 1496/J2952, replaced by 5087/J3238. A "NUWAY" burner was fitted.

| Doncaster | 27/11/65 | 11/12/65 | General |

No.1 engine, 538, was given an Unclassified repair. No.2 engine, 454, replaced by 414. No.1 bogie, 900017 and No.2 bogie, 9000-18, were given Unclassified repairs. Boiler, 5087/J3238, was given an Unclassified repair. The body was given a General repair including repairs to No.1 end buffer bar left hand side.

| Doncaster | 30/12/65 | 30/12/65 | Unclassified |

Boiler tube faceplate fractured. This was repaired.

| Doncaster | 02/03/66 | 03/03/66 | Unclassified |

Boiler tubes split. This was rectified. The locomotive mileage was 787,150 miles.

| Doncaster | 22/03/66 | 22/03/66 | Modification |

Experimental warning horns were removed and standard type were refitted. The locomotive mileage was recorded as 796,110 miles.

| Doncaster | 04/04/66 | 07/04/66 | Light |

No.2 main generator down to earth. No.1 engine, 538, was given an Unclassified repair. No.2 engine, 414, replaced by 410. No.1 bogie, 9000-17, replaced by 9000-37. No.2 bogie, 9000-18, replaced by 9000-38. Boiler, 5087/J3238, replaced by 1491/J2947. The body was given an Unclassified repair. The locomotive mileage was recorded as 799,880 miles.

| Doncaster | 06/05/66 | 08/05/66 | Unclassified |

No.1 bogie, 9000-37, No.3 axle fractured both sides. The axle was replaced.

| Doncaster | 04/06/66 | 07/06/66 | Modification |

Warning horns were repositioned.

| Doncaster | 27/10/66 | 28/10/66 | Modification |

Experimental Syphonic warning horns were fitted.

D9007/9007/55 007 Pinza (continued)

Loco Works	On Works	Off Works	Class of repair
Doncaster	01/12/66	12/01/67	General

No.1 engine, 538, replaced by 409. No.2 engine, 410, replaced by 436. No.1 bogie, 9000-37, replaced by 9000-25. No.2 bogie, 9000-38, replaced by 9000-26. Boiler, 1491/J2947, was given a General repair. The body was given a General repair. Full yellow nose ends were applied. The locomotive was fitted with experimental E.T.H. equipment.

Doncaster	27/07/67	29/07/67	Unclassified

No.2 traction motor suspension tube end cover set bolts fractured and loose. No.1 bogie, 9000-25, had No.2 wheelset replaced.

Doncaster	18/08/67	22/08/67	Unclassified

No.5 traction motor armature insulation down to earth. No.2 main generator had some repair and Nos.4, 5 & 6 traction motors were replaced.

Doncaster	12/09/67	24/10/67	General

*No.1 engine, 409, replaced by 440 (this engine is also recorded in the files as being carried by D9015 at the same time as it was fitted in D9007!). No.2 engine, 436, replaced by 449. No.1 bogie, 9000-25, replaced by 9000-13. No.2 bogie, 9000-26, replaced by 9000-14. Boiler, 1491/J2947, was given a General repair. The body was given a General repair and repainted into **blue livery with full yellow nose ends**.*

Doncaster	15/11/67	16/11/67	Unclassified

Slight flashover damage on No.1 main generator and all traction motors flashed over. All flashover damage was repaired.

Doncaster	28/11/67	28/11/67	Unclassified

Defective exhausters. Exhauster speed was checked in high position and adjustments made to obtain correct speeds.

Doncaster	15/12/67	16/12/67	Modification

The compressor stand was modified.

Doncaster	04/01/68	05/01/68	Unclassified

No.1 engine, 440, replaced by 405. Exhausters arcing badly in weak field. No.2 auxiliary generator drive coupling sheared. The defects were rectified.

Doncaster	01/04/68	05/04/68	Light

No.1 engine, 405 and No.2 engine, 449, were given Unclassified repairs. No.1 bogie, 9000-13, replaced by 9000-37. No.2 bogie, 9000-14, replaced by 9000-38. Boiler, 1491/J2947, was given an Unclassified repair. The body was given an Unclassified repair.

Doncaster	30/10/68	14/12/68	General

No.1 engine, 405, replaced by 412. No.2 engine, 449, replaced by 456. No.1 bogie, 900037, replaced by 9000-1. No.2 bogie, 9000-38, replaced by 9000-2. Boiler, 1491/J2947, replaced by 5090/J3241. The body was given a General repair. The locomotive was fitted for dual braking.

Doncaster	05/08/69	07/08/69	Unclassified

No.1 engine, 412, replaced by 418, due to crankcase fractured, No.4 'C' bank con rod broken.

Doncaster	12/08/69	18/08/69	Light

No.1 engine, 418, was given an Unclassified repair. No.2 engine, 456, passing oil into drum tanks, bad fire risk. This was given an Unclassified repair. No.1 bogie, 9000-1, replaced by 9000-17. No.2 bogie, 9000-2, replaced by 9000-18. Boiler, 5090/J3241, was given an Unclassified repair. The body was given an Unclassified repair.

Doncaster	31/12/69	02/01/70	Unclassified

No.2 engine, 456, replaced by 458, due to an internal coolant leak. No.2 end lubricating oil tank and radiators were cleaned.

Doncaster	15/01/70	21/01/70	Unclassified

Both right hand side fuel tanks and both boiler water tanks holed. All repairs were carried out.

Doncaster	04/02/70	06/02/70	Unclassified

No.1 main generator armature winding down to earth. This defect was rectified.

Doncaster	03/03/70	05/03/70	Unclassified

No.1 engine, 418, replaced by 456, due to breathing badly.

234 DELTICS ON WORKS

D9007/9007/55 007 Pinza (continued)

Loco Works	On Works	Off Works	Class of repair
Doncaster	06/04/70	24/04/70	Intermediate

No.2 main generator flashover damage, Nos.4 & 6 traction motors slight flashover damage and water damage in No.2 cab cubicle (Fire Brigade pumped water into cubicle). No.1 engine, 456, replaced by 423. No.2 engine, 458, replaced by 406. No.1 bogie, 9000-17 and No.2 bogie, 9000-18, were given General repairs. Boiler, 5090/J3241, replaced by 5093/J3244. The body was given an Intermediate repair.

Doncaster	23/06/70	26/06/70	Unclassified

No.2 engine, 406, replaced by 446.

Doncaster	15/07/70	17/07/70	Unclassified

No.1 engine, 423, replaced by 447, due to oil leaks.

Doncaster	31/08/70	02/09/70	Unclassified

No.2 engine, 446, sump tank fractured. A new sump plate was fitted and a fracture in a boiler water tank was repaired.

Doncaster	14/09/70	18/09/70	Unclassified

No.1 main generator cables from generator to cubicle No.1 end burnt. AWS cables broken. No.1 main generator was repaired and cabling and wiring renewed. Both bogies had flashover damage repaired and traction motor brushes replaced.

Doncaster	12/10/70	14/10/70	Unclassified

No.1 engine, 447, replaced by 434, due to liner seals leaking. Oil leaks on load regulator vane motors were repaired.

Doncaster	09/11/70	13/11/70	Unclassified

Collision damage, both bufferbeams bent. This was repaired, as was a fracture in No.1 boiler water tank. Oil leaks on Nos.1 & 2 load regulators were also rectified.

Doncaster	04/12/70	05/12/70	Unclassified

 No.2 engine, 446, replaced by 424, due to coolant in 'B' bank manifold.

Doncaster	04/01/71	04/02/71	Light

No.1 engine, 434, replaced by 405. No.2 engine, 424, replaced by 457, due to water in sump. No.1 bogie, 9000-17, replaced by 9000-49. No.2 bogie, 9000-18, replaced by 9000-50. Boiler, 5093/J3244, was given an Unclassified repair. The body was given a Light repair.

Doncaster	07/05/71	18/12/71	Intermediate

No.1 engine, 405, replaced by 429. No.2 engine, 457, replaced by 411. No.1 bogie, 9000-49, replaced by 9000-33. No.2 bogie, 9000-50, replaced by 9000-34. Boiler, 5093/J3244, replaced by 5092/J3243. The body was given an Intermediate repair. The locomotive was fitted with E.T.H. equipment.

Doncaster	01/06/72	02/06/72	Unclassified

No.1 engine, 429, persistent high water temperature. All radiator elements were replaced, as were coolant thermostats. Nos.1 & 2 primary fan shafts were also replaced.

Doncaster	18/08/72	22/08/72	Unclassified

No.2 engine, 411, replaced by 441, due to sump full of water. No.2 end lubricating oil tank and radiators were replaced.

Doncaster	23/08/72	24/08/72	Rectification

No.2 engine, 441, overspeeding. This was rectified.

Doncaster	12/09/72	21/09/72	Light

Collision damage to No.1 bogie, 9000-33, caused by striking cattle on the line. No.1 engine, 429, was given a Light repair. No.1 bogie, 9000-33, replaced by 9000-7. No.2 bogie, 9000-34, replaced by 9000-8. Boiler, 5092/J3243, was given an Unclassified repair. The body was given a Light repair and had minor collision damage repaired.

Doncaster	18/01/73	22/01/73	Unclassified

No.1 engine, 429, replaced by 424, due to crankcase holed.

Doncaster	14/02/73	16/02/73	Unclassified

Collision damage to No.1 end. This was repaired. No.1 engine, 424, had primary shaft drive flange repaired.

Doncaster	30/04/73	30/04/73	Unclassified

No.1 engine, 424, breathing badly and No.2 engine, 441, water pump spindle spline worn. All defects were rectified.

D9007/9007/55 007 Pinza (continued)

Loco Works	On Works	Off Works	Class of repair
Doncaster	02/07/73	05/07/73	Unclassified

No.2 engine, 441, replaced by 444, due to a coolant leak.

| Doncaster | 09/08/73 | 06/09/73 | Intermediate |

No.1 engine, 424, replaced by 430. No.2 engine, 444, replaced by 452. No.1 bogie, 9000-7, replaced by 9000-33. No.2 bogie, 9000-8, replaced by 9000-34. Boiler, 5092/J3243, replaced by 5095/J3246. The body was given an Intermediate repair.

| Doncaster | 18/10/73 | 25/10/73 | Unclassified |

No.2 engine, 452, replaced by 434, due to a fractured liner.

| Doncaster | 07/12/73 | 10/12/73 | Unclassified |

No.1 main generator armature banding burst. The main generator was replaced.

| Doncaster | 24/01/74 | 24/01/74 | Modification |

Earth fault relay modification.

| Doncaster | 01/02/74 | 06/02/74 | Unclassified |

No.1 engine, 430, replaced by 455, due to No.3 'CA' piston through bedplate both sides. All lubricating oil tanks and radiators were replaced.

| Doncaster | 04/04/74 | 11/04/74 | Unclassified |

No.1 engine, 455, replaced by 408, due to a fractured liner. A boiler water tank fracture was repaired. No.2 main and auxiliary generators were replaced. Both bogies had centre segments repaired and flashover damage on all traction motors was cleaned up.

| Doncaster | 16/06/74 | 21/06/74 | Unclassified |

No.1 end radiators to be replaced. A water tank fracture was repaired and a fracture in the floor plate under the boiler was welded. E.T.H. and coolant modifications were fitted.

| Doncaster | 10/07/74 | 12/07/74 | Unclassified |

All traction motors flashed over. Nos.2 & 5 traction motor 'Vee' rings badly burnt. No.1 load regulator tips to renew. Traction motor contactor tips were cleaned and realigned. Flashover damage was cleaned up. No.1 bodyside footstep surround was repaired. Both main generators were given three monthly repairs. Nos.2 & 5 traction motors were replaced.

| Doncaster | 18/07/74 | 25/07/74 | Unclassified |

No.1 engine, 408, replaced by 410, due to test point near water pump leaking. Both main generators and all traction motors had slight flashover damage. A boiler water tank was repaired. No.2 main generator was given a three monthly repair. Nos.2 & 5 traction motors were replaced. All other traction motors had flashover damage cleaned up.

| Doncaster | 22/08/74 | 26/09/74 | Light |

DSD fault at No.1 end, DSD pedal micro switch defective and No.2 bogie, 9000-34, No.5 wheelset with flats and right hand side tyre holed causing rough riding. No.1 engine, 410, replaced by 413. No.2 engine, 434, replaced by 457. No.1 bogie, 9000-33, replaced by 9000-23. No.2 bogie, 9000-34, replaced by 9000-30. Boiler, 5095/J3246, was given a standard repair. The body was given a Light repair. All defects were rectified. Experimental window wiper motors fitted.

| Doncaster | 05/12/74 | 08/12/74 | Unclassified |

No.1 engine, 413, replaced by 423, due to aerating. No.2 engine, 457, suspected to be aerating. No defect found.

| Doncaster | 18/01/75 | 26/01/75 | Unclassified |

No.1 engine, 423, replaced by 440, due to con rod through 'BC' crankcase. No.2 engine, 457, replaced by 449, due to repeatedly cutting out — reported low oil pressure at idling speed. Also reported to be leaking coolant — suspected defective liner. No.1 boiler water tank was repaired and No.1 end lubricating oil tank and radiators were cleaned.

| Doncaster | 21/02/75 | 22/02/75 | Unclassified |

No.1 engine, 440, replaced by 411, due to 'BC' crankcase fractured.

| Doncaster | 10/04/75 | 16/04/75 | Unclassified |

No.1 engine, 411, replaced by 405, due to 10" fracture in crankcase. No.1 end lubricating oil tanks and radiators were cleaned. No.2 primary cardan shaft was replaced.

| Doncaster | 21/04/75 | 22/04/75 | Unclassified |

No.2 bogie, 9000-23, No.2 axle hot. Bolts missing from No.2 traction motor suspension tube. No.2 wheelset was replaced.

D9007/9007/55 007 Pinza (continued)

Loco Works	On Works	Off Works	Class of repair
Doncaster	19/08/75	04/12/75	Intermediate

No.1 engine, 405, replaced by 438. No.2 engine, 449, replaced by 448, due to high spectrographic analysis. No.1 bogie, 9000-23, replaced by 9000-47. No.2 bogie, 9000-30, replaced by 9000-22. Boiler, 5095/J3246, replaced by 1494/J2950. Speedometer fluctuating between 80 and 100 mph and all brakeblocks flanging badly. The body was given an Intermediate repair and all defects rectified.

Doncaster	05/01/76	07/01/76	Unclassified

No.2 engine, 448, replaced by 440, due to 'A' bank camshaft moved or sheared. No.2 boiler water tank had a leak rectified.

Doncaster	25/02/76	26/02/76	Unclassified

No.1 engine, 438, replaced by 419, due to knocking badly and aerating.

Doncaster	01/06/76	03/06/76	Unclassified

No.1 engine, 419, replaced by 451, due to no drive between engine and main generator. Both boiler water tanks had leaks rectified.

Doncaster	06/07/76	08/07/76	Unclassified

No.2 engine, 440, replaced by 441, due to 'A' cambox No.1 fuel pump housing fractured causing fuel dilution, scavenger blower noisy, aerating, hunting and low revs.

Doncaster	17/07/76	03/08/76	Unclassified

No.1 engine, 451, replaced by 419, due to no drive, suspected gearing defect in underspeed unit. No.2 engine, 441, replaced by 442.

Doncaster	08/11/76	22/11/76	Light

No.1 engine, 419 and No.2 engine, 442, were given Light repairs and refitted. No.1 bogie, 9000-47, replaced by 9000-37. No.2 bogie, 9000-22, replaced by 9000-38. Boiler, 1494/J2950, was given an Unclassified repair. The body was given a Light repair. The locomotive was weighed at 104t 16cwt.

Doncaster	16/12/76	23/12/76	Unclassified

No.1 engine, 419, replaced by 428, due to aerating. No.2 engine, 442, replaced by 421, due to aerating, suspected fractured liner. All cab doors and windows to overhaul, not closing properly and draughty. Repeated flashovers on both main generators. Both main generators were replaced.

Doncaster	30/12/76	31/12/76	Unclassified

No.1 engine, 428, replaced by 455, due to a suspected fractured liner. Rectification was carried out to wheelslip relay No.4.

Doncaster	15/03/77	08/04/77	Unclassified

No.1 engine, 455, replaced by 451, due to con rod broken and crankcase holed. No.1 end lubricating oil tank and radiator were cleaned and collision damage to No.1 end was repaired. Mainframe and bogie bolster were realigned. No.2 traction motor nose suspension wear plate was replaced. All traction motors were checked for flashover damage and all bogie brake cylinders were replaced.

Doncaster	18/04/77	30/05/77	Unclassified

No.1 engine, 451, replaced by 409. No.2 engine, 421, replaced by 439, due to 'BC' crankcase fractured. Experiment DL/543 "Electrically operated windscreen washer pump" was fitted.

Doncaster	30/07/77	01/08/77	Unclassified

No.1 engine, 409, replaced by 406, due to being dephased. Primary gearbox badly worn, radiator fan output drive also badly worn and overspeed switch missing. No.1 fan gearbox was replaced, as was No.1 boiler water tank.

Doncaster	02/01/78	04/01/78	Unclassified

No.2 engine, 439, replaced by 423, due to low resistance readings on No.2 main generator. No.2 main generator also replaced due to continual flashovers.

Doncaster	31/01/78	03/02/78	Unclassified

Nos.1 & 6 traction motors with flashover damage. Traction motor and power circuits were checked. Flashover damage to both main generators was repaired and all traction motors were replaced.

Doncaster	27/04/78	03/05/78	Unclassified

No.2 engine, 423, replaced by 422, due to being dephased. No.1 boiler water tank had a leak repaired and all load regulator tips were replaced.

Doncaster	18/05/78	23/05/78	Unclassified

No.2 end 'B' side main fuel tank holed at top adjacent to filler and under steam pipe. This was repaired.

D9007/9007/55 007 Pinza (continued)

Loco Works	On Works	Off Works	Class of repair
Doncaster	17/07/78	25/11/78	Intermediate

No.1 engine, 406, replaced by 426. No.2 engine, 422, replaced by 445. No.1 bogie, 9000-37 and No.2 bogie, 9000-38, were given standard repairs. Boiler, 1494/J2950, replaced by 1497/J2953. The body was given an Intermediate repair. The locomotive was weighed at 105t 12cwt.

Doncaster	06/01/79	01/02/79	Unclassified

No.1 engine, 426, replaced by 538, due to sump holed on 'CA' crankcase. No.2 engine, 445, replaced by 418, due to passing oil into exhaust system. No.2 exhaust drum tank had a fracture repaired.

Doncaster	08/02/79	11/02/79	Unclassified

No.1 engine, 538, throwing oil. This was rectified. No.2 engine, 418, exhaust silencer fractured, pumping oil over boiler and engine room creating a fire hazard. No.2 silencer was replaced and silencer drains were cleaned.

Doncaster	04/06/79	07/06/79	Unclassified

No.2 engine, 418, replaced by 405, due to being dephased.

Doncaster	08/08/79	14/08/79	Unclassified

No.1 engine, 538, had the camshaft timing checked, scavenger pump chip trap removed and checked for debris. No.2 engine, 405, had suspected exhaust drum tank split causing fire on free end. All coolant hoses burnt. No.1 boiler water tank had a fracture repaired. Oil leaks on both load regulators were rectified.

Doncaster	05/10/79	09/10/79	Unclassified

No.2 engine, 405, replaced by 453, due to aerating, suspected fractured liner.

Doncaster	25/10/79	29/10/79	Unclassified

No.1 engine, 538, replaced by 408, due to being dephased. An oil leak on No.2 load regulator was rectified.

Doncaster	10/11/79	16/11/79	Unclassified

No.2 engine, 453, replaced by 418, due to a piston through crankcase. Both load regulators had oil leaks rectified. No.2 end lubricating oil tank and radiators were cleaned. No.4 traction motor was replaced due to oil contamination.

Doncaster	19/02/80	22/02/80	Unclassified

No.1 engine, 408, replaced by 454, due to defective Dowty pump and flashover damage on No.1 main generator.

Doncaster	11/06/80	12/06/80	Unclassified

No.1 engine, 454, replaced by 423, due to main generator armature bandings burst damaging field coils. An oil leak on No.2 load regulator was rectified.

Doncaster	28/08/80	19/09/80	Light

No.1 engine, 423, replaced by 453, due to being dephased. No.2 engine, 418, was given a Light repair. No.1 bogie, 9000-37, replaced by 9000-21. No.2 bogie, 9000-38, replaced by 9000-41. Boiler, 1497/J2953, was given an Unclassified repair. A boiler water tank had a fracture repaired. The locomotive was weighed at 102t 18cwt.

Doncaster	26/09/80	26/09/80	Rectification

A speedometer defect was rectified.

Doncaster	03/10/80	06/10/80	Rectification

No.2 traction motor jumper cable burned and No.4 traction motor commutator slightly scored on inner track. Both defects were rectified.

Doncaster	23/10/80	27/10/80	Unclassified

No.1 engine, 453, replaced by 448, due to phasing case bearing failure.

Doncaster	07/11/80	11/11/80	Unclassified

No.2 engine, 418, replaced by 453, due to being dephased.

Doncaster	17/11/80	19/11/80	Rectification

Boiler water tank split, engine stop lights not working correctly and no exhauster speed up. No.1 engine, 448, had a fuel pump leak rectified. All defects were rectified.

Doncaster	05/05/81	07/05/81	Unclassified

No.1 engine, 448, replaced by 404, due to being dephased.

Stratford D.R.S.	23/10/81	30/10/81	Depot

No.2 engine, 453, replaced by 423, due to a fractured cylinder liner.

238 DELTICS ON WORKS

D9007/9007/55 007 Pinza (continued)

Loco Works	On Works	Off Works	Class of repair
Doncaster	04/01/82	-	-

The locomotive arrived on Works after withdrawal with the following main components fitted. No.1 engine, 404, aerating. No.2 engine, 423, losing coolant. No.1 bogie, 9000-21. No.2 bogie, 9000-41. Boiler, 1497/J2953.

Empty stock for Eastern Region Sheffield Division's 'Merrymaker' railtour — (1Z36) 09.18 Chesterfield-Newcastle/Carlisle. Class 55, 55007 Pinza is seen arriving at Chesterfield on July 10, 1977. The Deltic's last train proved to be the (1A08) 08:07 York-King's Cross but 'Pinza' failed at Doncaster and was assisted forward by 47 146. Two defective engines brought about her withdrawal. Picture: L. P. Gater.

D9008/9008/55 008 The Green Howards

Loco Works	On Works	Off Works	Class of repair
Doncaster	07/07/61	Not recorded	Acceptance trials

New locomotive fitted with the following main components; No.1 engine, 424. No.2 engine, 423. No.1 bogie, 1017. No.2 bogie, 1018. Boiler, 1493/J2949.

R.S.H. Darlington	25/08/61	05/09/61	Not recorded

No details recorded.

Doncaster	13/12/61	15/12/61	Unclassified

No.1 engine, 424, radiator fan drive shaft and clutch drum removed for examination. Clutch shoes adjusted.

R.S.H. Darlington	26/04/62	10/05/62	General

No.1 engine, 424, replaced by 432, due to scavenge oil pump drive defective. No.2 engine, 423, replaced by 433.

Doncaster	10/05/62	10/05/62	General (continued)

No.1 bogie, 1017, replaced by 1033. No.2 bogie, 1018, replaced by 1034. A new cab window was fitted at the left hand side of No.1 end.

Doncaster	06/11/62	08/11/62	Light

No.1 bogie, 1033, replaced by 1017, due to No.2 axle horn cracked. No.2 bogie, 1034, replaced by 1018. Boiler tubes blocked due to bad combustion. No.1 exhaust collector tank inspection door was rejointed. The body was given a six monthly exam. The following modifications were carried out Drawgear; Driver's vacuum brake; Steam gauge pipe. The locomotive mileage is recorded as 153,430 miles.

Doncaster	14/11/62	15/11/62	Unclassified

No.3 traction motor overheated due to obstruction in blower vent. The traction motor was replaced.

Doncaster	23/11/62	27/11/62	Unclassified

No.1 engine, 432, leaking oil badly at phasing gearcase cover 'CA' crankshaft. Both coolant header tanks were fitted with new gauges. No.1 engine, 432, was repaired. The locomotive mileage is recorded as 158,150 miles.

Doncaster	10/01/63	10/01/63	Unclassified

Nos.1 & 2 traction motors flashed over and No.6 traction motor 'Vee' ring to retape. No.2 bogie, 1018, inner spring plank out of position. The leading transom beam on No.2 bogie was reseated on swing link and Nos.4, 5 & 6 traction motor commutators were cleaned. The locomotive mileage is recorded as 174,160 miles.

Doncaster	09/03/63	11/03/63	Unclassified

Shopped for bogie change due to fractures on inner and outer transoms. No.1 bogie, 1017, replaced by 1041. No.2 bogie, 1018, replaced by 1042.

Doncaster	18/04/63	07/05/63	General

No.1 engine, 432, replaced by 410. No.2 engine, 433, replaced by 415. No.1 bogie, 1041, replaced by 1043. No.2 bogie, 1042, replaced by 1044. Boiler, 1493/J2949, replaced by Clayton boiler 5260. The body was given an annual repair. The following modifications were carried out Exhaust collector tank drains; Lubricating oil tank filler strainers; Oil and water coolant sampling cock; Radiator fan grills; Soundproofing; Cubicle seals and additional exhauster filter.

R.S.H. Darlington	Not recorded	30/09/63	Unclassified

'The Green Howards' nameplates fitted.

Doncaster	09/10/63	12/10/63	Light

No.1 bogie, 1043, replaced by 1045, due to horn guide side liners loose. No.2 bogie, 1044, replaced by 1046. The boiler smokestack was modified. The body was given a six monthly exam.

Doncaster	13/12/63	19/12/63	Unclassified

Inoperative Clayton Boiler, 5260. Boiler coil defective.

Doncaster	14/02/64	15/02/64	Unclassified

Bogie frame fractures and the mileometer had to be cleaned, as it was unreadable. No.1 bogie, 1045, replaced by 1025. No.2 bogie, 1046, had transom fractures welded. Clayton Boiler, 5260, was given an Unclassified repair, the water pump valves and seats being overhauled

D9008/9008/55 008 The Green Howards (continued)

Loco Works	On Works	Off Works	Class of repair
Doncaster	20/03/64	24/03/64	Unclassified

Boiler stack distorted causing sparks and smoke to blow back into engine room. The WRI contactor was originally chattering and had been renewed. The boiler exhaust outlet sealing on the roof section was repaired. No.1 bogie, 1025 and No.2 bogie, 1046, both had all traction motors cleaned and each had three brushes replaced. Clayton Boiler, 5260, was given an Unclassified repair. Stack fractures were welded and raised hexagon cap nuts were fitted to the water pump.

Doncaster	30/04/64	27/05/64	General

No.1 engine, 410, replaced by 414. No.2 engine, 415, replaced by 420. No.1 bogie, 1025, replaced by 1043. No.2 bogie, 1046, replaced by 1044. Clayton boiler, 5260, was given a General repair and the boiler stack was modified. The body was given a General repair.

Doncaster	21/11/64	21/11/64	Unclassified

Main fuel tank split. This was replaced.

Doncaster	20/12/64	29/12/64	Light

No.1 engine, 414 and No.2 engine, 420, were given MP11 exams. No.1 bogie, 1043, replaced by 1013. No.2 bogie, 1044, replaced by 1014. Clayton Boiler, 5260, was given an Unclassified repair. The body was given an Unclassified repair.

Doncaster	29/04/65	29/05/65	General

No.1 engine, 414, replaced by 416. No.2 engine, 420, replaced by 436. No.1 bogie, 1013, replaced by 1039. No.2 bogie, 1014, replaced by 1040. Clayton Boiler, 5260, replaced by 1488/J2944. The body was given a General repair.

Doncaster	12/07/65	15/07/65	Unclassified

No.1 engine, 416, replaced by 442, due to liner seals leaking, water in sump oil.

Doncaster	26/08/65	31/08/65	Unclassified

No.1 engine, 442, replaced by 404, due to internal coolant leak. Lubricating oil tank was cleaned.

Doncaster	02/11/65	04/11/65	Unclassified

No.2 engine, 436, replaced by 428, due to being dephased.

Doncaster	05/01/66	11/01/66	Light

No.1 engine, 404 and No.2 engine, 428, were given Unclassified repairs. No.1 bogie, 1039, replaced by 9000-43. No.2 bogie, 1040, replaced by 9000-44. Repairs were carried out to No.1 end right hand side nose superstructure and No.1 end buffer bar gussets were welded. Coolant radiators were replaced.

Doncaster	19/03/66	21/03/66	Unclassified

No.1 engine, 404, replaced by 426, due to a suspected fractured liner. The water pick up scoop was defective and was replaced.

Doncaster	01/05/66	14/05/66	General

No.1 engine, 426 and No.2 engine, 428, were given Unclassified repairs. No.1 bogie, 9000-43, replaced by 9000-49. No.2 bogie, 9000-44, replaced by 9000-50. Boiler, 1488/J2944, replaced by 5089/J3240. The body was given a General repair.

Doncaster	06/10/66	11/10/66	Unclassified

All radiators were changed. All traction motor commutator edges were cleaned and 'Vee' rings were cleaned and painted.

Doncaster	14/10/66	21/10/66	Unclassified

No.1 engine, 426, replaced by 406.

Doncaster	28/11/66	30/11/66	Unclassified

Nos.3 & 4 axles and an exhaust silencer were changed.

Doncaster	16/01/67	21/01/67	Light

No.1 engine, 406, replaced by 427. No.2 engine, 428, was given an Unclassified repair. No.1 bogie, 9000-49, replaced by 9000-7. No.2 bogie, 9000-50, replaced by 9000-8. Boiler, 5089/J3240, was given an Unclassified repair. The body was given an Unclassified repair.

Doncaster	07/03/67	07/03/67	Not recorded

No details recorded.

Doncaster	03/04/67	07/04/67	Unclassified

No.2 engine, 428, dephased. Engine removed for repairs. The phasing gearcase was replaced and the engine was refitted.

D9008/9008/55 008 The Green Howards (continued)

Loco Works	On Works	Off Works	Class of repair
Doncaster	01/05/67	04/05/67	Unclassified

No.2 engine, 428, replaced by 405.

| Doncaster | 02/06/67 | 01/07/67 | General |

*No.1 engine, 427, replaced by 430. No.2 engine, 405, replaced by 413. No.1 bogie, 9000-7, replaced by 9000-37. No.2 bogie, 9000-8, replaced by 9000-38. Boiler, 5089/J3240, replaced by 5090/J3241. Regimental crests were fitted to the bodyside and the nameplates were lowered as a result. The body given a General repair and repainted into **blue livery with full yellow nose ends**.*

| Doncaster | 19/12/67 | 22/12/67 | Light |

No.1 engine, 430 and No.2 engine, 413, were given Unclassified repairs. No.1 bogie, 9000-37, replaced by 9000-25. No.2 bogie, 9000-38, replaced by 9000-26. Boiler, 5090/J3241, was given an Unclassified repair. The body was given an Unclassified repair.

| Doncaster | 29/01/68 | 29/01/68 | Unclassified |

No.1 engine, 430, was adjusted and run on load bank to expel oil.

| Doncaster | 18/03/68 | 19/03/68 | Unclassified |

No.1 engine, 430, exhaust drum fractured adjacent to left hand exhaust pipe flange. The drum tank was changed.

| Doncaster | 16/04/68 | 17/05/68 | General |

No.1 engine, 430, replaced by 407. No.2 engine, 413, replaced by 435. No.1 bogie, 9000-25, replaced by 9000-17. No.2 bogie, 900-026, replaced by 9000-18. Boiler, 5090/J3241, replaced by 5098/J3249. The body was given a General repair. The locomotive was fitted for dual braking.

| Doncaster | 27/05/68 | 28/05/68 | Unclassified |

Oil was cleaned from No.1 main generator and slight flashover damage repaired. Flashover damage to No.2 main generator was also repaired. On both bogies, 'Vee' rings and insulators were cleaned.

| Doncaster | 02/09/68 | 04/09/68 | Unclassified |

No.2 engine, 435, replaced by 448.

| Doncaster | 26/11/68 | 28/11/68 | Unclassified |

Flashover damage to No.2 engine and slight flashover damage to No.1 main generator and all traction motors. The flashover damage on No.1 main generator was repaired, as was that on all traction motors. No.2 engine, 448, replaced by 405.

| Doncaster | 29/12/68 | 30/12/68 | Unclassified |

No.2 engine, 405, replaced by 427, due to a suspected fractured liner. Both header tank gauges renewed and locomotive exterior cleaned.

| Doncaster | 06/01/69 | 14/01/69 | Light |

No.1 engine, 407 and No.2 engine, 427, were given Unclassified repairs. No.1 bogie, 9000-17, replaced by 9000-47. No.2 bogie, 9000-18, replaced by 9000-48. Boiler, 5098/J3249, was given an Unclassified repair. The body was given an Unclassified repair.

| Doncaster | 11/03/69 | 19/03/69 | Unclassified |

No.2 engine, 427, replaced by 452, due to crankcase holed and No.5 con rod broken.

| Doncaster | 04/07/69 | 07/07/69 | Unclassified |

No.1 engine, 407, replaced by 439, due to breathing badly from 'CB' crankcase breather. Engine also losing lubricating oil and throwing oil out of exhaust pipe. No.1 engine silencer fractured around plug boss at base of silencer.

| Doncaster | 22/09/69 | 15/10/69 | Intermediate |

No.1 engine, 439, replaced by 424. No.2 engine, 452, replaced by 404. No.1 bogie, 9000-47, was given a General repair and refitted. No.2 bogie, 9000-48, replaced by 9000-22. Boiler, 5098/J3249, replaced by 1486/J2942. The body was given an Intermediate repair and the water tank modification was carried out.

| Doncaster | 06/04/70 | 10/04/70 | Unclassified |

All traction motors and both main generators flashed over. Repairs were carried out to No.1 silencer and to cab footsteps at No.1 end. Both main generators were replaced, as was No.5 traction motor. All other flashover damage was cleaned up and brake block cotters were renewed.

| Doncaster | 15/05/70 | 22/05/70 | Light |

No.1 engine, 424 and No.2 engine, 404, were given Light repairs and refitted. No.1 bogie, 9000-47, replaced by 9000-24. No.2 bogie, 9000-22, replaced by 9000-48. Boiler, 1486/J2942, was given a Light repair. The body was given a Light repair.

D9008/9008/55 008 The Green Howards (continued)

Loco Works	On Works	Off Works	Class of repair
Doncaster	20/08/70	21/08/70	Unclassified

No.1 engine, 424, replaced by 432, due to suspect dephased. Exhaust fumes coming out of air intake.

| Doncaster | 31/08/70 | 03/09/70 | Unclassified |

No.2 engine, 404, bad oil leak from 'CA' crankcase phasing gear bearing housing. A replacement phasing case was fitted.

| Doncaster | 10/10/70 | 11/10/70 | Unclassified |

All traction motors and both main generators repeated flashovers. No.1 main generator had flashover damage cleaned up. No.2 engine, 404, replaced by 420. Flashover damage was cleaned up on both bogies.

| Doncaster | 06/11/70 | 08/11/70 | Unclassified |

Both bogies had repairs to swing link pins.

| Doncaster | 24/11/70 | 26/11/70 | Unclassified |

No.2 engine, 420, replaced by 447, due to breathing heavy. New swing link bolts were fitted to No.2 bogie, 9000-48.

| Doncaster | 12/03/71 | 02/10/71 | Intermediate |

All traction motors and both main generators flashed over. No.1 engine, 432, replaced by 433. No.2 engine, 447, replaced by 406. No.1 bogie, 9000-24, replaced by 9000-31. No.2 bogie, 9000-48, replaced by 9000-32. Boiler, 1486/J2942, replaced by 5086/J3237. The body was given an Intermediate repair. The locomotive was fitted with E.T.H. equipment.

| Doncaster | 29/11/71 | 01/12/71 | Unclassified |

No.1 engine, 433, had the governor changed. No.2 engine, 406, replaced by 445, due to breathing heavy.

| Doncaster | 25/01/72 | 27/01/72 | Unclassified |

No.3 traction motor armature down to earth. No.3 traction motor was changed.

| Doncaster | 18/05/72 | 23/05/72 | Unclassified |

No.2 engine, 445, replaced by 425, due to coolant leaks.

| Doncaster | 13/06/72 | 14/06/72 | Unclassified |

No.1 engine, 433, replaced by 539, due to breathing heavy.

| Doncaster | 15/06/72 | 15/06/72 | Rectification |

No.1 engine, 539, had a Martinair fault rectified.

| Doncaster | 03/07/72 | 08/07/72 | Light |

No.1 bogie, 9000-31, replaced by 9000-47. No.2 bogie, 9000-32, replaced by 9000-22. Boiler, 5086/J3237, was given an Unclassified repair.

| Doncaster | 19/03/73 | 20/03/73 | Unclassified |

No.2 boiler water tank was repaired.

| Doncaster | 22/03/73 | 27/03/73 | Unclassified |

No.2 engine, 425, replaced by 431, due to being time expired. All sliding doors and seals were repaired. No.2 end lubricating oil tanks and radiators were removed, cleaned and refitted.

| Doncaster | 01/05/73 | 26/05/73 | Intermediate |

No.1 engine, 539, replaced by 452. No.2 engine, 431, replaced by 422. No.1 bogie, 9000-47, replaced by 9000-49. No.2 bogie, 9000-22, replaced by 9000-50. Boiler, 5086/J3237, replaced by 5096/J3247. The body was given an Intermediate repair.

| Doncaster | 09/08/73 | 10/08/73 | Unclassified |

No.1 engine, 452, replaced by 444, due to high spectrographic analysis.

| Doncaster | 15/08/73 | 15/08/73 | Rectification |

No.1 engine, 444, heavy oil leak. The sump plug was replaced.

| Doncaster | 02/10/73 | 06/10/73 | Unclassified |

No.1 engine, 444, 'AB' crankshaft damper detached. 'AB' crankshaft was replaced and a new damper fitted.

| Doncaster | 02/11/73 | 10/11/73 | Unclassified |

No.1 engine, 444, no output from phasing gear to primary fan cardan shaft. The engine was given an Intermediate repair.

| Doncaster | 09/01/74 | 10/01/74 | Modification |

Earth fault relay modification carried out.

D9008/9008/55 008 The Green Howards (continued)

Loco Works	On Works	Off Works	Class of repair
Doncaster	11/02/74	20/02/74	Light

No.1 engine, 444 and No.2 engine, 422, were given Light repairs. No.1 bogie, 9000-49, replaced by 9000-37. No.2 bogie, 9000-50, replaced by 9000-38. Boiler, 5096/J3247, was given an Unclassified repair. The body was given a Light repair.

| Doncaster | 04/03/74 | 09/03/74 | Unclassified |

No.1 engine, 444, replaced by 415, due to aerating.

| Doncaster | 22/03/74 | 28/03/74 | Unclassified |

No.2 engine, 422, replaced by 444, due to Dowty pump drive defective.

| Doncaster | 09/05/74 | 16/05/74 | Unclassified |

No.1 engine, 415, replaced by 406, due to crankcase holed. Boiler water tank leaking and engine room window broken. E.T.H. and coolant modifications carried out.

| Doncaster | 30/09/74 | 03/10/74 | Unclassified |

No.2 engine, 444, replaced by 448, due to con rod through crankcase. No.2 boiler water tank was repaired, as was the boiler mounting pad deck.

| Doncaster | 11/12/74 | 17/12/74 | Unclassified |

No.1 engine, 406, replaced by 455, due to '5A' piston through crankcase. No.2 engine, 448, replaced by 456. No.1 bogie, 9000-37, had fractured swing link studs replaced. Boiler water tank repairs were carried out and No.1 end lubricating oil tank and radiator elements were cleaned.

| Doncaster | 20/12/74 | 03/01/75 | Unclassified |

No.1 engine, 455, replaced by 420, due to aerating and loss of coolant.

| Doncaster | 08/03/75 | 12/03/75 | Unclassified |

No.6 wheelset tyres under last turning size and right hand tyre holed. No.1 bogie, 9000-37, had traction motor nose suspension plates welded. On No.2 bogie, 9000-38, No.6 wheelset changed and Nos.4 & 5 traction motor nose suspension checkplate set screws renewed.

| Doncaster | 20/03/75 | 07/09/75 | Intermediate |

No.1 engine, 420, replaced by 446. No.2 engine, 456, replaced by 415. No.1 bogie, 9000-37 and No.2 bogie, 9000-38, were given standard repairs and refitted. Boiler, 5096/J3247, replaced by 1497/J2953.

| Doncaster | 12/01/76 | 14/01/76 | Unclassified |

No.2 engine, 415, replaced by 425, due to suspected fractured liner. No.2 boiler water tank leaking and No.1 load regulator oil leak. Coolant checks were carried out and No.2 end radiators were changed.

| Doncaster | 15/05/76 | 17/05/76 | Unclassified |

No.2 boiler water tank repaired. An oil leak was rectified.

| Doncaster | 20/05/76 | 24/05/76 | Unclassified |

No.2 engine, 425, replaced by 449, due to showing rising copper content.

| Doncaster | 28/06/76 | 01/07/76 | Unclassified |

No.1 engine, 446, replaced by 419, due to high copper content.

| Doncaster | 12/07/76 | 17/07/76 | Unclassified |

No.2 engine, 449, main bearing collapsed. Both water tanks leaking. No.1 end load regulator contact tips to renew. Side windows set screws to fit to frame. No.1 main generator flashover damage and arc horn to replace. All traction motors to be examined and necessary repairs carried out. No.1 main generator and No.2 engine, 449, repaired. No.2 main generator was replaced.

| Doncaster | 29/07/76 | 30/07/76 | Unclassified |

No.1 engine, 419, replaced by 420, due to No.1 main generator armature banding burst.

| Doncaster | 23/09/76 | 11/10/76 | Light |

No.1 engine, 440, replaced by 422. No.2 engine, 449, was given an Unclassified repair. No.1 bogie, 9000-37, replaced by 9000-17. No.2 bogie, 9000-38, replaced by 9000-18. Boiler, 1497/J2953, was given an Unclassified repair. The locomotive was weighed at 105t 3cwt.

| Doncaster | 03/02/77 | 05/02/77 | Unclassified |

No.1 engine, 422, replaced by 438, due to being dephased. No.1 boiler water tank was repaired.

244 DELTICS ON WORKS

D9008/9008/55 008 The Green Howards (continued)

Loco Works	On Works	Off Works	Class of repair
Doncaster	19/02/77	25/03/77	Unclassified

Collision damage incurred at Darlington. No.1 end right hand side panels etc. damaged, right hand buffer knocked off, right hand air reservoir cock broken. Right hand E.T.H. socket knocked off and nose end equipment to be examined for damage. Minor damage to fuel and water tanks and underside of locomotive. No.1 bogie, 9000-17, right hand No.1 brake cylinder knocked off. Right hand No.1 axle box cover missing and No.2 bogie, 9000-18, No.5 traction motor cover also missing. All damage was repaired. The locomotive was weighed at 104t 6cwt.

Doncaster	16/05/77	20/05/77	Unclassified

No.2 engine, 449, replaced by 418, due to a suspected fractured liner. No.1 boiler water tank was repaired. Experiment DL/543 "Electrically operated windscreen washer pump" was fitted.

Doncaster	25/06/77	27/06/77	Rectification

No.1 boiler water tank porous at the bottom. No.2 load regulator vane robbed. No.2 engine, 418, repeated bookings for shutting down. No.1 load regulator tips to be renewed. No.1 boiler water tank was replaced. All repairs were carried out.

Doncaster	02/09/77	07/09/77	Unclassified

No.2 engine, 418, alignment of exhaust expansion bellows. Control circuit breaker and cab heater circuit breaker trips when E.T.H. switched on. No.2 engine, 418, had exhaust bellows, drum tank and mounting feet changed. All other repairs were carried out.

Doncaster	10/09/77	17/09/77	Unclassified

A.W.S. will not cancel and reverser EP valve leaking. No.2 engine, 418, deflector plates to be fitted to exhaust system. No.2 main generator armature to earth. No.2 main generator was changed. All repairs were carried out.

Doncaster	21/09/77	23/09/77	Unclassified

No.2 engine, 418, replaced by 408, due to 'B5' piston disintegrated. Reported loss of power with E.T.H. on. No.2 end lubricating oil tank and radiators removed for cleaning and refitted.

Doncaster	23/09/77	29/09/77	Unclassified

Both bogie centre pivot studs and nuts renewed.

Doncaster	14/01/78	18/01/78	Unclassified

Both boiler water tanks leaking. No.2 load regulator oil leak. No.1 bogie, 9000-17, to be examined. No.2 bogie, 9000-18, had No.6 traction motor nose suspension pad broken. Both boiler water tanks removed, repaired and refitted. The load regulator rectified. No.1 bogie, 9000-17, had No.1 traction motor suspension pad repaired as were Nos.4 & 6 on No.2 bogie, 9000-18.

Doncaster	25/01/78	28/01/78	Unclassified

No.2 engine, 408, replaced by 430, due to metal bearing particles in lubricating oil strainer.

Doncaster	06/02/78	07/02/78	Unclassified

No.1 engine, 438, scavenge oil pump defective. Oil leak on No.2 load regulator. No.1 load regulator burnt tips. No.1 engine, 438, had a replacement scavenge oil pump fitted, all other repairs were carried out.

Doncaster	15/03/78	03/08/78	Intermediate

No.1 engine, 438, replaced by 538, due to being time expired. No.2 engine, 430, replaced by 407, due to being time expired. No.1 bogie, 9000-17, replaced by 9000-21. No.2 bogie, 9000-18, replaced by 9000-41. Boiler, 1497/J2953, replaced by 1491/J2947. Both main generators had flashover damage repaired. The locomotive was weighed at 103t 18cwt.

Doncaster	11/01/79	24/05/79	Unclassified

No.1 engine, 538, replaced by 406, due to output shaft sheared. No.2 engine, 407, replaced by 439, due to a fractured liner. The engine hour recorder was changed. No.2 primary gearbox had a fault rectified.

Doncaster	17/12/79	18/12/79	Unclassified

No.2 engine, 439, replaced by 538, due to being time expired.

Doncaster	21/03/80	24/03/80	Unclassified

No.1 engine, 406, replaced by 442, due to being time expired. A boiler water tank fracture repaired.

Doncaster	07/07/80	09/07/80	Unclassified

No.2 engine, 538, replaced by 457, due to a suspected fractured liner.

D9008/9008/55 008 The Green Howards (continued)

Loco Works	On Works	Off Works	Class of repair
Doncaster	17/07/80	19/07/80	Unclassified

No.1 engine, 442, exhaust collector tank leaking at plate cover. The exhaust drum tank was replaced.

| Doncaster | 05/08/80 | 26/08/80 | Light |

No.1 engine, 442 and No.2 engine, 457, were given Light repairs. No.1 bogie, 9000-21, replaced by 9000-19. No.2 bogie, 9000-41, replaced by 9000-20. Boiler, 1491/J2947, was given an Unclassified repair. The locomotive was weighed at 104t 10cwt.

| Doncaster | 20/01/81 | 23/01/81 | Unclassified |

No.1 engine, 442, replaced by 432, due to a suspected fractured liner.

| Doncaster | 03/03/81 | 09/03/81 | Unclassified |

No.2 engine, 457, replaced by 415, due to a suspected fractured liner.

| Stratford D.R.S. | 01/11/81 | 12/11/81 | Depot |

No.1 engine, 432, replaced by 430, due to auxiliary generator drive sheared causing damage to main generator air manifold cooling system.

| Doncaster | 23/01/82 | - | - |

The locomotive arrived after withdrawal with the following main components fitted; No.1 engine, 430. No.2 engine, 415. No.1 bogie, 9000-19. No.2 bogie, 9000-20. Boiler, 1491/J2947.

A superb shot of D9012 Crepello leaving King's Cross with the down "Flying Scotsman" in July 1963. All the atmosphere of the Deltics in their heyday is encapsulated in this study. Picture: P. Caley Collection.

D9009/9009/55 009 Alycidon

Loco Works	On Works	Off Works	Class of repair
Doncaster	21/07/61	Not recorded	Acceptance trials

New locomotive fitted with the following main components; No.1 engine, 428. No.2 engine, 427. No.1 bogie, 1019. No.2 bogie, 1020. Boiler, 1486/J2942. 'Alycidon' nameplates fitted.

| Vulcan Foundry | 31/08/61 | 07/09/61 | Unclassified |

No details recorded.

| R.S.H. Darlington | 27/10/61 | 31/10/61 | Unclassified |

No.3 traction motor armature burst, flashover on all traction motors and both main generators.

| R.S.H. Darlington | 30/11/61 | 15/12/61 | Unclassified |

No.2 engine, 427, replaced by 452, due to a broken con rod. The locomotive mileage was recorded as 42,000 miles.

| R.S.H. Darlington | 03/01/62 | 12/01/62 | Unclassified |

No.1 engine, 428, replaced by 450, due to 'B2' con rod broken. No.2 engine, 452, replaced by 425.

| R.S.H. Darlington | 11/04/62 | 26/04/62 | Unclassified |

No.2 engine, 425, replaced by 407, due to header tank split. The locomotive mileage was recorded as 76,300 miles.

| Doncaster | 07/05/62 | 08/05/62 | Light |

No.1 bogie, 1019, replaced by 1001. No.2 bogie, 1020, replaced by 1050. The body was given a six monthly examination.

| Doncaster | 27/08/62 | 28/08/62 | Unclassified |

No.1 bogie, 1001, replaced by 1009, due to frame fractured adjacent to right hand No.2 horn guide. No.2 bogie, 1050, replaced by 1010. No.1 end left hand buffer was renewed. The locomotive mileage was recorded as 141,960 miles.

| Doncaster | 13/11/62 | 16/11/62 | Unclassified |

No.1 bogie, 1009, replaced by 1003, due to No.2 axle horn right side cracked. No.2 bogie, 1010, replaced by 1004. No.4 radiator fan grill was modified, as was the drawgear. Both exhaust collector tank inspection lids were rejointed.

| Doncaster | 23/11/62 | 28/11/62 | Unclassified |

No.1 engine, 450, replaced by 438, due to 'A2' cylinder liner cracked and exhaust collector drum fractured. No.2 engine, 407, fractured exhaust collector drum repaired. The locomotive mileage was recorded as 183,400 miles.

| Doncaster | 02/03/63 | 20/03/63 | General |

No.1 engine, 438, replaced by 437. No.2 engine, 407, replaced by 427. No.1 bogie, 1003, had a fracture repaired. Boiler, 1486/J2942, replaced by 1487/J2943. The following modifications were carried out — Engine air intake ducting; AWS position; Control cubicle seals; Radiator fan guards; Exhaust drainpipes. The locomotive mileage was recorded as 228,640.

| Doncaster | 29/04/63 | 01/05/63 | Unclassified |

The Deadman's application valve was removed and a replacement fitted. Bogies and bogie beams were fitted with studs for adaptation of Wooodhead Munro shock absorbers.

| Doncaster | 28/05/63 | 29/05/63 | Unclassified |

Flashover to traction motors. No.2 engine, 427, had a new primary shaft fitted. No.1 bogie, 1003, replaced by 1029. No.2 bogie, 1004, replaced by 1030. These bogies were fitted with Woodhead Munro shock absorbers Type 'B'.

| Doncaster | 19/08/63 | 20/08/63 | Unclassified |

No.1 bogie, 1029, replaced by 1037. No.2 bogie, 1030, replaced by 1038. Modifications were carried out to brake hanger brackets.

| Doncaster | 30/09/63 | 05/10/63 | Light |

No.1 bogie, 1037, replaced by 1001. No.2 bogie, 1038, replaced by 1050. Boiler, 1487/J2943, replaced by 5095/J3246. The following modifications were carried out Caustic injection and modified air ducting to boiler; Injector seats modified. The body was given a six monthly exam. The locomotive mileage was recorded as 330,000 miles.

| Doncaster | 25/11/63 | 27/11/63 | Unclassified |

Flashover to traction motors. No.1 main generator foot fracture was welded. All traction motors were replaced.

D9009/9009/55 009 Alycidon (continued)

Loco Works	On Works	Off Works	Class of repair
Doncaster	07/12/63	12/12/63	Unclassified

Collision damage at No.1 end. No.1 end nose and body skin and air pipework was repaired.

Doncaster	12/02/64	13/02/64	Unclassified

No.1 engine, 437, replaced by 450, due to coolant leaking past a liner seal and a suspected sheared water pump shaft. No.1 bogie, 1001, had transom fractures welded. No.2 bogie, 1050, had traction motors cleaned.

Doncaster	10/03/64	26/03/64	General

No.1 engine, 450, replaced by 416. No.2 engine, 427, replaced by 417. No.1 bogie, 1001, replaced by 1027. No.2 bogie, 1050, replaced by 1028. Boiler, 5095/J3246, replaced by 1497/J2953. Bodyside fractures required welding. The following modifications were carried out — Nose end access doors; Lagging of air pipes; Boiler panel fuses. The locomotive mileage was recorded as 409,470 miles.

Doncaster	10/08/64	11/08/64	Unclassified

No.1 bogie, 1027, replaced by 1037, due to a fractured transom. No.2 bogie, 1028, replaced by 1038, due to a fractured transom. The following modification was carried out — Exhauster cutout valve.

Doncaster	26/10/64	03/11/64	Light

No.2 engine, 417, had a cardan shaft repaired. No.1 bogie, 1037, had No.2 axle liner adrift, this was rectified. Boiler, 1497/J2953, received attention having failed in service. The locomotive mileage was recorded as 523,560 miles.

Doncaster	18/02/65	18/02/65	Unclassified

A burst boiler tube was replaced.

Doncaster	02/04/65	24/04/65	General

No.1 engine, 416, replaced by 410, due to being dephased. No.2 engine, 417, was given a six monthly overhaul. No.1 bogie, 1037, replaced by 1041. No.2 bogie, 1038, replaced by 1042. Boiler, 1497/J2953, replaced by 1492/J2948. The following modifications were carried out — Spiders; Transom radius; Centre gussets; Cold pins in headstocks; Horn liners; Steel plate to brake hanger rubbing brackets; Nose suspension. The locomotive mileage was recorded as 605,150 miles.

Doncaster	08/05/65	14/05/65	Unclassified

No.1 engine, 410, had temperature probes changed. No.2 engine, 417, had excessive play in clutch shaft primary fan gearbox. No.2 fan gearbox, primary and secondary fan shafts were replaced. The water coolant radiator elements and bypass valves were changed.

Doncaster	16/06/65	19/06/65	Unclassified

No.2 main generator positive brush box connector ring burnt. This was repaired. A new 'NUWAY' burner unit was fitted to the boiler, 1492/J2948.

Doncaster	24/07/65	28/07/65	Unclassified

No.2 engine, 417, replaced by 456, due to water pump drive sheared. Note No.2 engine was originally replaced by 435, however, this failed on test.

Doncaster	25/08/65	30/08/65	Unclassified

No.1 bogie, 1041 and No.2 bogie, 1042, left leading and left intermediate axlebox horn liners fractured at weld in horn plate. These were welded.

Doncaster	12/10/65	17/10/65	Light

No.1 bogie, 1041, replaced by 9000-31. No.2 bogie, 1042 replaced by 9000-32. Brakegear was overhauled. New traction motors were fitted and tyres were turned. Both main generators received new brushes. The following modification was carried out — Protection bars for EP valve. The locomotive mileage was recorded as 669,297 miles.

Doncaster	17/12/65	18/12/65	Unclassified

Split boiler tubes were repaired.

Doncaster	05/01/66	07/01/66	Unclassified

No.1 engine, 410, replaced by 433, due to being time expired. Repairs were carried out to split boiler tubes.

Doncaster	02/02/66	04/02/66	Unclassified

No.1 end primary fan shaft was changed.

Doncaster	10/02/66	13/02/66	Unclassified

Boiler, 1492/J2948, replaced by 5092/J3243, due to split tubes.

D9009/9009/55 009 Alycidon (continued)

Loco Works	On Works	Off Works	Class of repair
Doncaster	13/03/66	26/03/66	General

No.1 engine, 433 and No.2 engine, 456, were given Unclassified repairs. No.1 bogie, 9000-31, replaced by 9000-35. No.2 bogie, 9000-32, replaced by 9000-36. Boiler, 5092/J3243 was given a General repair. The following modifications were carried out — Cab footstep stiffening plates; Oil resisting compounds in sand chutes and water pickup scoop mouthpiece. The body was given a General repair. The locomotive mileage was recorded as 762,520 miles.

Doncaster	12/04/66	14/04/66	Unclassified

No.1 engine, 433, replaced by 450, due to being time expired. No.2 engine, 456, replaced by 446, due to water pump drive shaft fractured.

Doncaster	01/05/66	03/05/66	Unclassified

No.2 bogie, 9000-36, had No.4 axle gear side fractured. This was replaced.

Doncaster	08/09/66	09/09/66	Unclassified

No.1 bogie, 9000-35, replaced by 9000-45. No.2 bogie, 9000-36, replaced by 9000-46, due to No.6 axle flawed.

Doncaster	22/09/66	22/09/66	Unclassified

Boiler, 5092/J3243, water tank split, boiler holding down legs fractured, two broken off and boiler removed. The boiler water tank was replaced, the feet were reset and welded.

Doncaster	31/10/66	04/11/66	Light

No.1 engine, 450 and No.2 engine, 446, were given Unclassified repairs. No.1 bogie, 9000-45, replaced by 9000-47. No.2 bogie, 9000-46, replaced by 9000-48. Boiler, 5092/J3243, was given an Unclassified repair. All radiators were replaced. The body was given an Unclassified repair.

Doncaster	05/12/66	07/12/66	Unclassified

No.2 end lubricating oil radiators were exchanged and flashover damage to both main generators and all traction motors was repaired.

Doncaster	11/01/67	13/01/67	Unclassified

Boiler tubes split. Two tubes were renewed. No.1 end secondary gearbox was changed. Both main generators were cleaned.

Doncaster	20/02/67	15/03/67	General

No.1 engine, 450, replaced by 442. No.2 engine, 446, replaced by 421. No.1 bogie, 9000-47, replaced by 9000-39. No.2 bogie, 9000-48, replaced by 9000-40. Boiler, 5092/J3243, replaced by 5086/J3237. The body was given a General repair and full yellow nose ends applied. The locomotive mileage was recorded as 902,249 miles.

Doncaster	10/04/67	13/04/67	Unclassified

No.2 engine, 421, replaced by 432, due to a broken con rod. Lubricating oil elements and vane meter were changed.

Doncaster	03/05/67	04/05/67	Unclassified

No.1 bogie, 9000-39, replaced by 9000-29, due to loose tyres. No.2 bogie, 9000-40, replaced by 9000-30, due to loose tyres. A bogie restraint bracket was fitted, load regulators were cleaned of oil and No.1 primary fan shaft was changed.

Doncaster	08/08/67	11/08/67	Unclassified

No.2 engine, 432, replaced by 452. Radiator elements were changed and exhaust silencers were cleaned.

Doncaster	15/08/67	17/08/67	Unclassified

Collision damage. No.1 buffer beam bent left hand side. Repairs were carried out to the buffer beam and skirting and new buffers were fitted.

Doncaster	21/08/67	22/08/67	Unclassified

No.1 engine, 442, replaced by 450, due to being time expired. The oil tank and radiators at No.1 end were washed out.

Doncaster	03/10/67	07/10/67	Light

No.1 engine, 450, was given an Unclassified repair. No.2 engine, 452, replaced by 426, due to a leaking liner seal. No.1 bogie, 9000-29, replaced by 9000-25. No.2 bogie, 9000-30, replaced by 9000-26. Boiler, 5086/J3237, was given an Unclassified repair.

Doncaster	10/10/67	11/10/67	Unclassified

No.1 engine, 450, had load checks and governor adjustments.

D9009/9009/55 009 Alycidon (continued)

Loco Works	On Works	Off Works	Class of repair
Doncaster	20/10/67	23/10/67	Unclassified

Collision damage. Five engine room windows broken and distorted, also side panelling (from No.1 end) damaged and distorted. The collision damage was repaired and both main generators had slight flashover damage cleaned up.

Doncaster	28/11/67	30/11/67	Unclassified

Power earth fault. Oil was cleaned from No.3 traction motor connection box and a new seal was fitted on the cover. No.4 traction motor was replaced.

Doncaster	11/12/67	14/06/68	General

*Severe fire damage. No.1 engine, 450, replaced by 452. No.2 engine, 426, replaced by 445. No.1 bogie, 9000-25, replaced by 9000-11. No.2 bogie, 9000-26, replaced by 9000-12. Boiler, 5086/J3237, replaced by 5095/J3246. The body was given a General repair which included new cab doors and new control cubicle at No.1 end, renewal of No.1 cab instruments, heaters and switches. No.1 cab interior was totally renewed and repainted and the locomotive was rewired. The locomotive was fitted for dual braking and was repainted into **blue livery with full yellow nose ends**. The locomotive mileage was recorded as 1,020,049 miles.*

Doncaster	02/07/68	03/07/68	Unclassified

All traction motors and both main generators flashed over. All flashover damage was repaired.

Doncaster	20/11/68	21/11/68	Unclassified

Main fuel tank holed underneath and water tank outer covering damaged. Boiler water tank and fuel tanks were changed.

Doncaster	10/02/69	17/02/69	Light

No.1 engine, 452, replaced by 419, due to auxiliary generator flexible drive shaft sheared. No.2 engine, 445, was given an Unclassified repair. No.1 bogie, 9000-11, replaced by 9000-15. No.2 bogie, 9000-12, replaced by 9000-16. Boiler, 5095/J3246, was given an Unclassified repair. The body was given an Unclassified repair.

Doncaster	08/08/69	09/08/69	Unclassified

No.1 engine, 419, replaced by 450, due to being time expired.

Doncaster	17/09/69	18/09/69	Unclassified

No.2 engine, 445, replaced by 436, due to an internal coolant leak. Lubricating oil tank and radiators were removed for cleaning.

Doncaster	27/09/69	01/10/69	Unclassified

No.1 engine, 450, replaced by 439, due to turbocharger screaming and pulsating, suspect internal damage or sheared drive.

Doncaster	24/10/69	07/11/69	Intermediate

No.1 engine, 439 and No.2 engine, 436, were given Unclassified repairs. No.1 bogie, 9000-15, replaced by 9000-23. No.2 bogie, 9000-16, replaced by 9000-30. Boiler, 5095/J3246, replaced by 5088/J3239. The body was given an Intermediate repair and a water tank modification was carried out. The locomotive mileage was recorded as 1,219,219 miles.

Doncaster	07/11/69	12/11/69	Rectification

Flashover damage and a field divert fault were rectified.

Doncaster	06/12/69	07/12/69	Unclassified

No.1 engine, 439, replaced by 417, due to being dephased.

Doncaster	04/02/70	07/02/70	Unclassified

Both main generators flashed over. No.1 main generator was repaired and No.2 main generator was replaced. All traction motors were cleaned and repaired as necessary.

Doncaster	07/04/70	08/04/70	Unclassified

No.2 boiler water tank holed. This was repaired.

Doncaster	01/05/70	02/05/70	Unclassified

No.1 engine, 417, replaced by 441, due to water in sump. No.2 bogie, 9000-30, had a loose horn liner repaired.

Doncaster	10/06/70	17/10/70	Light

No.1 engine, 441, replaced by 428. No.2 engine, 436, replaced by 439. No.1 bogie, 9000-23, replaced by 9000-7. No.2 bogie, 9000-30, replaced by 9000-8. Boiler, 5088/J3239, was given an Unclassified repair. The body was given a Light repair. The locomotive was fitted with E.T.H. equipment. The locomotive mileage was recorded as 1,305,219 miles.

D9009/9009/55 009 Alycidon (continued)

Loco Works	On Works	Off Works	Class of repair
Doncaster	07/11/70	08/11/70	Unclassified

Modification to control cubicle to assist cooling.

| Doncaster | 14/12/70 | 20/12/70 | Unclassified |

No.2 engine, 439, dephased. It was removed, given an Unclassified repair and refitted.

| Doncaster | 26/01/71 | 27/01/71 | Unclassified |

Both left hand side fuel tank outer covers damaged and No.1 boiler water tank leaking. The fuel tanks were changed and the boiler water tank repaired.

| Doncaster | 25/02/71 | 04/03/71 | Unclassified |

Traction motors and both main generators flashed over. No.1 main generator was replaced; No.2 main generator was repaired, as was all traction motor damage. No.5 traction motor was replaced.

| Doncaster | 11/03/71 | 12/03/71 | Rectification |

Both engines were load checked.

| Doncaster | 30/04/71 | 01/05/71 | Unclassified |

No.2 engine, 439, replaced by 406, due to being dephased.

| Doncaster | 20/09/71 | 22/10/71 | Intermediate |

No.1 engine, 428, replaced by 423. No.2 engine, 406, replaced by 409. No.1 bogie, 9000-7, replaced by 9000-29. No.2 bogie, 9000-8, replaced by 9000-10. Boiler, 5088/J3239, replaced by 1487/J2943. The body was given an Intermediate repair. The locomotive mileage was recorded as 1,460,719 miles.

| Doncaster | 25/11/71 | 26/11/71 | Unclassified |

No.1 engine, 423, low oil pressure. This was repaired. No.1 lubricating oil radiator element was changed.

| Doncaster | 07/01/72 | 12/01/72 | Unclassified |

No.2 engine, 409, replaced by 438, due to 'CA3' piston and con rod adrift. No.2 end lubricating oil tank and radiators were removed for cleaning.

| Doncaster | 13/04/72 | 18/04/72 | Unclassified |

No.1 engine, 423, dephased. 423 was tested and repairs were carried out to the scavenge blower. An air filter was also changed.

| Doncaster | 28/08/72 | 02/09/72 | Light |

No.1 engine, 423, replaced by 409. No.2 engine, 438, replaced by 436. No.1 bogie, 9000-29, replaced by 9000-13. No.2 bogie, 9000-10, replaced by 9000-14. Boiler, 1487/J2943, was given an Unclassified repair. The body was given a Light repair. The locomotive mileage was recorded as 1,600,719 miles.

| Doncaster | 02/09/72 | 05/09/72 | Rectification |

No details .

| Doncaster | 09/09/72 | 14/09/72 | Unclassified |

Collision damage at No.1 end having struck cattle. This was repaired, as was damage to both bogies. No.2 bogie, 9000-14, also had loose bolster segments attended to.

| Doncaster | 13/11/72 | 16/11/72 | Unclassified |

No.2 engine, 436, replaced by 412, due to 'AB' crankshaft No.3 cylinder con rod through crankcase side. Lubricating oil tanks and radiators were removed for cleaning at No.2 end. The locomotive was load tested and graphed.

| Doncaster | 05/02/73 | 08/02/73 | Unclassified |

No.2 engine, 412, replaced by 411, due to being dephased. Both main generators were replaced due to flashover damage. Numeric route indicators replaced by two white dots at No. 2 end. No. 1 end done by Finsbury Park.

| Doncaster | 16/05/73 | 17/05/73 | Unclassified |

Both boiler water tanks leaking at top seams of end plates. These were repaired.

| Doncaster | 09/07/73 | 02/08/73 | Intermediate |

No.1 engine, 409, replaced by 412. No.2 engine, 411, replaced by 455. No.1 bogie, 9000-13 and No.2 bogie, 9000-14, were given standard repairs and refitted. Boiler, 1487/J2943, replaced by 1490/J2946. Experiment DL/446 "Outer sanders to be inoperative" was fitted. The body was given an Intermediate repair. The locomotive mileage was recorded as 1,741,719 miles.

| Doncaster | 03/08/73 | 06/08/73 | Rectification |

Field divert faults, which were rectified.

D9009/9009/55 009 Alycidon (continued)

Loco Works	On Works	Off Works	Class of repair
Doncaster	02/10/73	03/10/73	Unclassified

No.2 engine, 455, replaced by 417, due to high copper and aluminium content in oil sample. No.2 end lubricating oil tank and radiators were removed for cleaning.

| Doncaster | 19/12/73 | 21/12/73 | Unclassified |

No.2 engine, 417, replaced by 453, due to phasing gears defective, whine from the blower drive. No.2 cardan shaft was replaced, as was No.2 primary fan gearbox. No.2 oil thermostat was repaired.

| Doncaster | 27/12/73 | 27/12/73 | Rectification |

No.2 engine, 453, sump plug leaking. This was rectified.

| Doncaster | 25/01/74 | 25/01/74 | Modification |

Earth fault relay modification.

| Doncaster | 11/02/74 | 14/02/74 | Unclassified |

No.2 engine, 453, replaced by 458, due to a severe internal knock.

| Doncaster | 05/04/74 | 22/04/74 | Light |

No.1 engine, 412, replaced by 446, due to auxiliary generator drive shaft bolts sheared engine flywheel casing broken, breathing badly and oil leaking from jacking screw holes on phasing case. No.2 engine, 458, was given a Light repair and refitted. No.1 bogie, 9000-13, replaced by 9000-19. No.2 bogie, 9000-14, replaced by 9000-20, due to rough riding and wheels grinding on power at low speed with excessive vibration above No.4 axle. Boiler, 1490/J2946, was given an Unclassified repair. The body was given a Light repair. The loco mileage was recorded as 1,873,149 miles.

| Doncaster | 06/05/74 | 13/05/74 | Modification |

E.T.H. and coolant modifications.

| Doncaster | 01/07/74 | 04/07/74 | Unclassified |

No.1 engine, 446, hose '9E' oil feed from 'BC' crankcase to underspeed switch to renew. Boiler, 1490/J2946, replaced by 1497/J2953, due to boiler tubes and wiring burnt.

| Doncaster | 13/07/74 | 15/07/74 | Unclassified |

No.2 engine, 458, replaced by 438, due to being dephased.

| Doncaster | 29/07/74 | 31/07/74 | Unclassified |

No.2 engine, 438, replaced by 432, due to drive between engine and generator sheared.

| Doncaster | 21/08/74 | 25/08/74 | Unclassified |

No.1 engine, 446, replaced by 434. No.2 engine, 432, replaced by 410, due to a suspected fractured liner. The coolant header tank was tested for leaks.

| Doncaster | 25/09/74 | 27/09/74 | Unclassified |

No.1 engine, 434, replaced by 427, due to being dephased. No.2 boiler water tank had leaks repaired.

| Doncaster | 28/10/74 | 01/11/74 | Unclassified |

No.2 engine, 410, replaced by 452, due to being dephased. Nos.2 & 4 traction motor nose suspension spring block bearing plates broken off and intermittent positive earth on No.2 engine start circuit. The earth fault was rectified and Nos.2 & 4 traction motor nose suspension packing plates were secured. No.1 main generator also received repairs.

| Doncaster | 11/01/75 | 13/01/75 | Unclassified |

No.1 engine, 427, replaced by 409, due to con rod through crankcase. No.1 end lubricating oil tank and radiators were removed for cleaning.

| Doncaster | 11/03/75 | 05/02/76 | Intermediate |

No.1 engine, 409, replaced by 455. No.2 engine, 452, replaced by 432. No.1 bogie, 9000-19, replaced by 9000-23. No.2 bogie, 9000-20, replaced by 9000-30. Boiler, 1497/J2953, replaced by 1496/J2952. The boiler water tanks required repair and strengthening. Note The original release date was anticipated as being 18/04/75, however, due to a severe shortage of spares to make up power units the date was subsequently amended in excess of ten times! The locomotive was weighed at 104t 13cwt. The locomotive mileage was recorded as 1,963,149 miles.

| Doncaster | 10/02/76 | 11/02/76 | Rectification |

No.1 end cab door will not remain closed. Rollers and slides badly worn, locks and catches worn and door frames distorted. No.2 cab doors to draught proof. All seat adjusters to ease. No.1 secondman's seat catching on rear panel. All repairs were carried out.

| Doncaster | 22/03/76 | 23/03/76 | Unclassified |

No.2 engine, 432, replaced by 437, due to crankcase fractured.

D9009/9009/55 009 Alycidon (continued)

Loco Works	On Works	Off Works	Class of repair
Doncaster	14/04/76	16/04/76	Unclassified

No.1 engine, 455, replaced by 415, due to suspected bearing broken up in phasing case. The accelerator air pipe was fractured. This was repaired.

| Doncaster | 10/05/76 | 12/05/76 | Unclassified |

No.2 engine, 437, replaced by 433, due to crankcase holed. No.2 end lubricating oil tanks and radiators were removed for cleaning.

| Doncaster | 29/06/76 | 01/07/76 | Unclassified |

No.1 engine, 415, replaced by 436, due to con rod and crankcase broken.

| Doncaster | 02/08/76 | 04/08/76 | Unclassified |

No.2 engine, 433, replaced by 435, due to knocking and noisy, suspected piston breaking up.

| Doncaster | 08/09/76 | 14/09/76 | Unclassified |

No.1 engine, 436, replaced by 453.

| Doncaster | 23/11/76 | 28/11/76 | Unclassified |

No.1 engine, 453, replaced by 405, due to high spectrographic analysis and breathing heavy. No.1 boiler water tank had leaks repaired.

| Doncaster | 31/01/77 | 20/02/77 | Light |

No.1 engine, 405, was given a Light repair and refitted. No.2 engine, 435, replaced by 423, due to being dephased. No.1 bogie, 9000-23, replaced by 9000-19. No.2 bogie, 9000-30, replaced by 9000-20. Boiler, 1496/J2952, was given an Unclassified repair. No.2 right hand side buffer beam was distorted. Both cabs required draught proofing, all doors, windows, catches and locks needed renewal. Control cubicles required cleaning. All repairs were carried out. The locomotive was weighed at 103t 7cwt. The locomotive mileage was recorded as 2,135,299 miles.

| Doncaster | 02/08/77 | 11/08/77 | Unclassified |

No.1 engine, 405, replaced by 417, due to breathing heavy. No.2 engine, 423, replaced by 452, due to being dephased. No.1 bogie, 9000-19, had No.1 right hand side brake rod safety bracket to fit. No.2 bogie, 9000-20, had No.6 right hand side leading horn liner to secure. No.1 and No.2 radiator primary fan drive shaft splines worn, these were rectified.

| Doncaster | 11/10/77 | 16/10/77 | Unclassified |

No.2 engine, 452, had 'C' bank camshaft quillshaft cover leaking badly, this was rectified. Bogie centre pivot studs and nuts required renewal. The control circuit breaker was reported to be continually tripping out, fault on instrument panel. No.2 end lighting was defective. All repairs were carried out.

| Doncaster | 05/12/77 | 08/12/77 | Unclassified |

No.1 engine, 417, replaced by 455, due to scavenger blower defective. Boiler, 1496/J2952, had fumes entering engine room and cyclic tests were carried out.

| Doncaster | 29/12/77 | 03/01/78 | Unclassified |

No.2 engine, 452, had output drive to primary shaft repaired. No.3 traction motor was changed due to interpole to earth. Both bogies had magnesium liners secured.

| Doncaster | 17/01/78 | 19/01/78 | Unclassified |

No.1 engine, 455, governor to change due to hunting badly. No.2 engine, 452, left hand side oil radiator element to renew. Both load regulators leaking oil. All repairs were carried out and No.2 traction motor was changed due to interpole to earth. Locomotive weighed at 104t 7cwt.

| Doncaster | 29/03/78 | 26/04/78 | Unclassified |

No.1 traction motor armature to earth, Nos.1 & 6 traction motors isolated, No.2 primary cardan shaft to renew and No.1 fan clutch slipping. No.1 traction motor was replaced and all other repairs were carried out.

| Doncaster | 02/05/78 | 02/05/78 | Unclassified |

No.1 bogie, 9000-19, replaced by 9000-47, due to No.3 right hand side axle end bolts worked out. No.2 bogie, 9000-20, replaced by 9000-22. No.1 load regulator had oil leaks rectified.

| Doncaster | 17/07/78 | 20/07/78 | Unclassified |

No.2 engine, 452, replaced by 406, due to leaking oil from a seal on the phasing gearcase between 'AB' and 'CA' crankcase. No.1 bogie, 9000-47, had No.2 traction motor nose suspension pad adrift. This was rectified.

D9009/9009/55 009 Alycidon (continued)

Loco Works	On Works	Off Works	Class of repair
Doncaster	04/10/78	06/10/78	Unclassified

No.1 engine, 455, replaced by 446, due to breathing heavy. No.2 end right hand side axlebox end cover had been robbed. No.1 end secondman's and No.2 end driver's side windscreen wipers were defective. No.2 bogie, 9000-22, had 'R4' axlebox cover and WWC cover to secure with plain nuts and spring washers. All defects were rectified.

Doncaster	18/10/78	19/10/78	Unclassified

No.2 auxiliary generator was replaced - fire damage. No.1 load regulator had an oil leak rectified.

Doncaster	19/10/78	21/10/78	Unclassified

No.3 traction motor was to earth - replaced and an oil leak from No.1 load regulator cleaned up.

Doncaster	01/12/78	24/03/79	Intermediate

No.1 engine, 446, replaced by 436. No.2 engine, 406, replaced by 433. No.1 bogie, 9000-47, replaced by 9000-35. No.2 bogie, 9000-22, replaced by 9000-36. Boiler, 1496/J2952, replaced by 1494/J2950. No.3 traction motor suspension bearing was defective, No.2 boiler water tank was leaking, No.3 traction motor had been robbed by Haymarket. All these defects were rectified. Experiment DL/590 "Fitting of 'T' cab seats" was fitted. The locomotive was weighed at 104t 16cwt. The locomotive mileage was recorded as 2,366,099 miles.

Doncaster	02/04/79	02/04/79	Rectification

No.1 engine, 436, will not shut down on occasions, suspect faulty governor. No.1 compressor fails to run when governor cuts in. Left hand fuel gauge defective and No.1 load regulator leaking oil. All defects were rectified.

Doncaster	10/04/79	12/04/79	Rectification

No.1 engine, 436, will not shut down and leaking oil. No.2 engine, 433, leaking oil from various locations. Both main generators and all traction motors had flashover damage. All defects rectified.

Doncaster	18/04/79	18/04/79	Rectification

No.1 engine, 436, will not shut down. The engine run solenoid was replaced.

Doncaster	31/05/79	04/06/79	Rectification

No.2 engine, 433, had heavy fuel dilution. No.1 bogie, 9000-35, had a loose traction motor pad. These defects were rectified.

Doncaster	25/07/79	26/07/79	Unclassified

No.2 engine, 433, replaced by 427, due to main generator drive sheared.

Doncaster	19/10/79	24/10/79	Unclassified

No.1 engine, 436, will not run. No.2 main generator replaced because of flashover damage. Both load regulators leaking oil and boiler water pump defective. All defects were rectified.

Doncaster	30/05/80	11/06/80	Unclassified

No.1 engine, 436, had an injector change and a check for any ingress of water. No.2 engine, 427, replaced by 444, due to a defective scavenger, this in turn had caused a fire. Inlet pipe, filters and bodyside battery box had been on fire on right hand side.

Doncaster	04/07/80	09/07/80	Unclassified

No.2 traction motor bearing end plate bolts sheared. This was rectified and No.2 wheelset was changed. The locomotive was weighed at 104t 7cwt.

Doncaster	24/11/80	19/12/80	Light

No.1 engine, 436 and No.2 engine, 444, were given Light repairs and refitted. No.1 bogie, 9000-35, replaced by 9000-33. No.2 bogie, 9000-36, replaced by 9000-34. Boiler, 1494/J2950, was given an Unclassified repair. The body was given a Light repair. The locomotive was weighed at 100t 2cwt. The locomotive mileage was recorded as 2,611,199 miles.

Doncaster	30/06/81	03/07/81	Unclassified

No.1 engine, 436, replaced by 417, due to 'C' bank crankcase smashed.

Stratford D.R.S.	10/08/81	19/08/81	Depot

No.1 boiler water tank was holed. This was repaired.

Doncaster	14/09/81	18/09/81	Unclassified

No.2 engine, 444, replaced by 419, due to a suspected fractured cylinder liner.

Doncaster	05/01/82	20/08/82	-

The locomotive arrived after withdrawal with the following main components fitted; No.1 engine, 417. No.2 engine, 419. No.1 bogie, 9000-33. No.2 bogie, 9000-34. Boiler, 1494/J2950. The locomotive mileage was estimated as 2,755,600 miles. The locomotive was subsequently sold for preservation and was weighed at 102t 9cwt.

254 DELTICS ON WORKS

D9010/9010/55 010 The King's Own Scottish Borderer

Loco Works	On Works	Off Works	Class of repair
Doncaster	24/07/61	Not recorded	Acceptance trials

New locomotive fitted with the following main components; No.1 engine, 443. No.2 engine, 447. No.1 bogie, 1021. No.2 bogie, 1022. Boiler, 1490/J2946.

| Doncaster | 04/04/62 | 06/04/62 | Light |

No.1 bogie, 1021, replaced by 1029. No.2 bogie, 1022, replaced by 1030. The body was given a six monthly exam.

| R.S.H. Darlington | 13/06/62 | Not recorded | Unclassified |

No.2 engine, 447, replaced by 448, due to using excessive oil. The locomotive mileage was recorded as 131,250 miles.

| Doncaster | 08/10/62 | 12/10/62 | General |

No.1 engine, 443, replaced by 424. No.2 engine, 448, replaced by 451. No.1 bogie, 1029, replaced by 1005. No.2 bogie, 1030, replaced by 1006. Boiler, 1490/J2946, replaced by 5089/J3240. No.1 boiler water tank was repaired. The body was given an annual repair.

| Doncaster | 14/12/62 | 18/12/62 | Unclassified |

No.2 traction motor armature defective and No.1 bogie, 1005, anchor link to renew. No.2 traction motor was replaced. A bracket was fitted to the compressor outlet pipe, an additional vacuum pipe filter was fitted and fuelraising pipework was removed. The locomotive mileage was recorded as 224,000 miles.

| Doncaster | 13/03/63 | 14/03/63 | Unclassified |

Boiler, 5089/J3240, replaced by 5098/J3249.

| Doncaster | 08/04/63 | 10/04/63 | Light |

No.1 bogie, 1005, replaced by 1025. No.2 bogie, 1006, replaced by 1018. The body was given a six monthly exam.

| Doncaster | 23/05/63 | 25/05/63 | Unclassified |

Fire damage. No.1 end engine and boiler roof sections were removed; No.1 exhaust collector tank and exhaust silencer tank were replaced. One new flexible hose was fitted between water pump and exhaust manifold and two pieces were fitted to coolant pipe pump to radiator.

| Doncaster | 13/07/63 | 19/07/63 | Unclassified |

No.2 engine, 451, replaced by 430, due to a fractured liner. Boiler, 5098/J3249, replaced by 5092/J3243. Water treatment modification was fitted to the boiler. The locomotive mileage was recorded as 339,900 miles.

| Doncaster | 25/07/63 | 26/07/63 | Unclassified |

No.1 bogie, 1025, replaced by 1007. No.2 bogie, 1018, replaced by 1008.

| Doncaster | 07/10/63 | 20/10/63 | General |

No.1 engine, 424, replaced by 425. No.2 engine, 430, replaced by 431. The body was given an annual repair. The following modifications were carried out — Soundproofing; Cab draught sealing; Low water contents gauge; Header tank overflow tank.

| Doncaster | 31/03/64 | 03/04/64 | Light |

No.2 engine, 431, replaced by 406. No.1 bogie, 1007, replaced by 1049. No.2 bogie, 1008, replaced by 1002. Bodyside fractures were welded. The following modifications were carried out — Antifrost precautions (Lagging of pipes, Auto drain valve, Steam heat valve); Bogie transom patches; Speedometer clocks.

| Doncaster | 22/04/64 | 23/04/64 | Unclassified |

No.1 bogie, 1049, replaced by 1019. No.2 bogie, 1002, replaced by 1020.

| Doncaster | 20/06/64 | 21/06/64 | Unclassified |

No.2 auxiliary generator replaced due to field coil burnt.

| Doncaster | 04/08/64 | 06/08/64 | Unclassified |

Main generators flashed over and No.3 traction motor interpole to earth. A new cab window was fitted to the driver's side at No.2 end, cab door runners were overhauled and No.2 boiler water tank was welded. Both main generators were cleaned out and both bogies had new brakeblocks fitted. No.3 traction motor was replaced and the modification to the exhauster cutout valve was carried out.

| Doncaster | 02/09/64 | 03/09/64 | Unclassified |

No.1 engine, 425, replaced by 411, due to an internal coolant leak.

DELTICS ON WORKS 255

D9010/9010/55 010 The King's Own Scottish Borderer (continued)

Loco Works	On Works	Off Works	Class of repair
Doncaster	10/09/64	04/10/64	General

No.1 engine, 411, replaced by 455. No.2 engine, 406, replaced by 446. No.1 bogie, 1019, replaced by 1001. No.2 bogie, 1020, replaced by 1050. Boiler, 5092/J3243, replaced by 5086/J3237. The following modifications were carried out — Nose end door for access to exhausters; Engine supports.

Doncaster	17/03/65	23/03/65	Light

No.1 bogie, 1001, replaced by 1021. No.2 bogie, 1050, replaced by 1022. Boiler, 5086/J3237, replaced by 5087/J3238. The following modifications were carried out — Spiders; Transom radius; Centre gussets; Cold pins in headstocks; Horn liners; Steel plates to brake hanger rubbing brackets; Nose suspension.

Doncaster	31/03/65	01/04/65	Unclassified

Water coolant radiator elements were changed. The burner motor on the Boiler, 5087/J3238, was replaced and the circuit rewired.

Doncaster	29/04/65	29/04/65	Unclassified

No.1 bogie, 1021 and No.2 bogie, 1022, had transom fractures cut, welded and dressed.

Doncaster	16/08/65	18/08/65	Unclassified

No.1 engine, 455, replaced by 405, due to No.4 'BC' con rod fractured.

Doncaster	02/09/65	12/09/65	Unclassified

Both main generators and all traction motors flashed over. Axlebox liners were also fractured. No.1 main generator had flashover damage repaired. All traction motors were overhauled and No.1 bogie, 1021 and No.2 bogie, 1022, both had axlebox horn blocks welded. Boiler, 5087/J3238, replaced by 5095/J3246.

Doncaster	05/11/65	07/11/65	Unclassified

No.2 main generator severely flashed over. No.2 main generator brush boxes were overhauled and new insulators were fitted. No.1 bogie, 1021, had No.1 wheelset replaced.

Doncaster	04/12/65	17/12/65	General

No.2 engine, 446, replaced by 406. No.1 bogie, 1021, replaced by 9000-41. No.2 bogie, 1022, replaced by 9000-42. The following modifications were carried out — Protection bar for EP valves; Toilet hopper; Fire alarm bell; Cab footstep stiffening plate; Oil resisting compound to sand chutes.

Doncaster	27/02/66	02/03/66	Unclassified

Boiler tubes split. Defective boiler tubes were expanded and welded and the Passenger/Goods switch modification was carried out.

Doncaster	14/04/66	19/04/66	Light

No.1 engine, 405 and No.2 engine, 406, were given Unclassified repairs. No.1 bogie, 9000-41, replaced by 9000-15. No.2 bogie, 9000-42, replaced by 9000-16. Boiler, 5095/J3246, was given an Unclassified repair. The body was given an Unclassified repair.

Doncaster	02/08/66	02/08/66	Unclassified

No.1 engine, 405, replaced by 416.

Doncaster	08/08/66	09/08/66	Unclassified

No.1 engine, 416, replaced by 405, due to suspect seized or sheared drive shaft. Boiler, 5095/J3246 had modified damper gear fitted.

Doncaster	29/09/66	03/10/66	Unclassified

No.2 engine, 406, had a sheared output shaft and was given an Unclassified repair. No.1 end radiator elements were changed.

Doncaster	18/10/66	23/12/66	General

No.1 engine, 405, replaced by 430. No.2 engine, 406, replaced by 417. No.1 bogie, 9000-15, replaced by 9000-35. No.2 bogie, 9000-16, replaced by 9000-36. Boiler, 5095/J3246, was given a General repair. The body was given a General repair including repairs to 'extensive collision damage'. **Full yellow nose ends were applied.**

Doncaster	13/01/67	15/01/67	Unclassified

Both main generators, auxiliary generators, all traction motors and commutator edges were cleaned of flashover damage.

Doncaster	16/01/67	17/01/67	Rectification

Both main generators had repairs to flashover damage.

D9010/9010/55 010 The King's Own Scottish Borderer (continued)

Loco Works	On Works	Off Works	Class of repair
Doncaster	20/01/67	24/01/67	Rectification

Both main generators had 'Vee' rings cleaned and painted and other flashover damage cleaned up. All traction motors were cleaned up and flash marks were removed from commutators.

Doncaster	14/03/67	16/03/67	Unclassified

No.1 engine, 430, replaced by 451, due to piston through crankcase. No.2 main generator and all traction motors had flashover damage repaired.

Doncaster	22/03/67	01/04/67	Light

No.2 water pump drive shaft suspect defective. Engine keeps shutting down due to bad fluctuation of coolant. No.1 engine, 451, was given an Unclassified repair. No.2 engine, 417, replaced by 424. No.1 bogie, 9000-35, replaced by 9000-33. No.2 bogie, 9000-36, replaced by 9000-34. Boiler, 5095/J3246, was given an Unclassified repair.

Doncaster	07/04/67	07/04/67	Unclassified

Positive, negative and field wires were renewed from No.2 auxiliary generator to the cubicle and other burn damage was cleaned.

Doncaster	16/11/67	20/11/67	Unclassified

No.1 engine, 451, replaced by 445. No.1 main and auxiliary generators were replaced. No.2 main and auxiliary generators were given a 3 monthly exam. All axles were ultrasonically tested.

Doncaster	28/12/67	01/02/68	General

*No.1 engine, 445, replaced by 425. No.2 engine, 424, replaced by 404. No.1 bogie, 9000-33, replaced by 9000-23. No.2 bogie, 9000-34, replaced by 9000-24. Boiler, 5095/J3246, replaced by 1493/J2949. The locomotive was fitted for dual braking and repainted into **blue livery with full yellow nose ends**.*

Doncaster	27/02/68	28/02/68	Rectification

Nos.3 & 4 traction motors flashed over. No.3 traction motor was repaired and Nos.1 & 2 traction motor nose suspension bracket set screws were renewed. No.4 traction motor had flashover damage repaired.

Doncaster	23/04/68	23/04/68	Unclassified

No.1 engine, 425, replaced by 422, due to No.4 cylinder con rod broken.

Doncaster	21/06/68	26/06/68	Unclassified

No.1 engine, 422, replaced by 419, due to piston through crankcase. No.1 end lubricating oil tank and radiators were flushed out.

Doncaster	27/09/68	02/10/68	Light

No.1 engine, 419 and No.2 engine, 404, were given Unclassified repairs. No.1 bogie, 9000-23, replaced by 9000-33. No.2 bogie, 9000-24, replaced by 9000-34. Boiler, 1493/J2949 was given an Unclassified repair. The body was given an Unclassified repair.

Doncaster	09/10/68	11/10/68	Unclassified

No.2 engine, 404, replaced by 446, due to a fracture across 'A1' blank adaptor face. Fuel tanks examined for reports of continuous low fuel light. No.1 main generator brush box section and arc horn were renewed.

Doncaster	12/12/68	12/12/68	Unclassified

No.2 engine, 446, radiator roof header tank split bottom seam. The header tank was replaced.

Doncaster	11/02/69	07/03/69	Intermediate

No.1 engine, 419, replaced by 424. No.2 engine, 446, replaced by 457. No.1 bogie, 9000-33, replaced by 9000-11. No.2 bogie, 9000-34, replaced by 9000-12. Boiler, 1493/J2949, replaced by 1488/J2944. The body was given an Intermediate repair including collision damage repairs to No.2 cab skin.

Doncaster	13/03/69	14/03/69	Unclassified

No.4 traction motor was replaced due to it's armature being down to earth.

Doncaster	19/06/69	20/06/69	Unclassified

No.1 engine, 424, replaced by 442, due to exhaust tank full of water indicating internal fracture in coolant system. No.1 end lubricating oil radiator replaced and the lubricating oil tank flushed out.

Doncaster	24/11/69	29/11/69	Light

No.1 engine, 442 and No.2 engine, 457, were given Unclassified repairs. No.1 bogie, 9000-11, replaced by 9000-7. No.2 bogie, 9000-12, replaced by 9000-8. Boiler, 1488/J2944, was given an Unclassified repair. The boiler water tank capacity modification was carried out. The body was given an Unclassified repair.

D9010/9010/55 010 The King's Own Scottish Borderer (continued)

Loco Works	On Works	Off Works	Class of repair
Doncaster	30/01/70	04/02/70	Unclassified

No.2 engine, 457, replaced by 420, due to sump full of coolant.

| Doncaster | 13/03/70 | 18/03/70 | Unclassified |

No.1 engine, 442, replaced by 439, due to piston through side of engine at 'B5' position.

| Doncaster | 05/05/70 | 07/05/70 | Unclassified |

Main steam pipe joint under locomotive between tanks leaking and horn plate liner bolts loose on both bogies. The boiler blowdown pipe discharge was causing erosion of water tank and needed to be extended below fuel tank and equalising pipe. These were all repaired and No.1 main generator was cleaned of oil.

| Doncaster | 08/06/70 | 10/06/70 | Unclassified |

No.1 engine, 439, replaced by 538, due to 'BC' crankshaft out of phase. Flashover damage to No.2 main generator and all traction motors was repaired.

| Doncaster | 24/08/70 | 07/11/70 | Intermediate |

No.1 engine, 538, replaced by 449. No.2 engine, 420, replaced by 444. No.1 bogie, 9000-7, replaced by 9000-33. No.2 bogie, 9000-8, replaced by 9000-34. Boiler, 1488/J2944, replaced by 5087/J3238. The body given an Intermediate repair. The locomotive fitted with E.T.H. equipment.

| Doncaster | 10/12/70 | 11/12/70 | Unclassified |

No.2 engine, 444, replaced by 427, due to breathing heavy.

| Doncaster | 17/02/71 | 23/02/71 | Unclassified |

No.1 engine, 449, keeps shutting down and both main generators repeatedly flashing over. No.2 main generator also had insulators broken. Wheelslip problems had also been reported. All flashover damage was repaired and all traction motors were replaced.

| Doncaster | 07/04/71 | 08/04/71 | Unclassified |

No.2 engine, 427, replaced by 434, due to breathing heavy.

| Doncaster | 14/04/71 | 15/04/71 | Rectification |

No.5 traction motor terminal box connections burnt out. Main steam pipe porous. No.2 traction motor was replaced. The main steam pipe was repaired.

| Doncaster | 14/05/71 | 15/05/71 | Unclassified |

No.1 engine, 449, replaced by 425. No.2 engine, 434, 'CA' crankcase joint blown out. 434 was removed to effect sump joint repair and was refitted.

| Doncaster | 17/05/71 | 18/05/71 | Unclassified |

No.1 engine, 425, header tank fractured at weld, coolant in sump. No.1 end secondman's warning horn valve defective, to be renewed. This was done and the coolant header tank was repaired.

| Doncaster | 01/06/71 | 09/06/71 | Unclassified |

No.1 engine, 425, coolant leak from 'C3' injector housing when injector removed. No.2 engine, 434, replaced by 424.

| Doncaster | 23/10/71 | 30/10/71 | Light |

No.1 engine, 425 and No.2 engine, 424, were given Light repairs. No.1 bogie, 9000-33, replaced by 9000-9. No.2 bogie, 9000-34, replaced by 9000-42. Boiler, 5087/J3238, was given an Unclassified repair. The body was given a Light repair.

| Doncaster | 07/02/72 | 09/02/72 | Unclassified |

No.1 engine, 425, replaced by 439, due to a liner seal defective. No.2 engine, 424, had the governor changed. No.2 end left cab footstep was repaired. No.2 main generator had cracked insulation changed and commutator slots cleaned. The safety valve on the boiler was replaced.

| Doncaster | 20/03/72 | 21/03/72 | Unclassified |

No.2 engine, 424, had adjustments made to the damper on the flexible drive.

| Doncaster | 06/06/72 | 07/06/72 | Unclassified |

No.2 engine, 424, replaced by 450, due to aerating, suspected fractured liner.

| Doncaster | 31/07/72 | 30/08/72 | Intermediate |

No.1 engine, 439, replaced by 443. No.2 engine, 450, replaced by 448. No.1 bogie, 9000-9 and No.2 bogie, 9000-42, were given General repairs and refitted. Boiler, 5087/J3238, replaced by 1495/J2951. The body was given an Intermediate repair.

| Doncaster | 07/11/72 | 08/11/72 | Unclassified |

No.1 engine, 443, output shaft phasing gear defective. No.2 engine, 448, repeated reports of low power. No.1 primary fan shaft was repaired and No.1 collector drum changed when it was found to be fractured when the locomotive went on test in the weighouse.

258 DELTICS ON WORKS

D9010/9010/55 010 The King's Own Scottish Borderer (continued)

Loco Works	On Works	Off Works	Class of repair
Doncaster	16/11/72	17/11/72	Unclassified

No.2 engine, 448, 'B' cambox to remove and overhaul and cab body pillar fractures in both cab ends. These were rewelded. The 'B' cambox on No.2 engine, 448, was replaced.

| Doncaster | 30/01/73 | 02/02/73 | Unclassified |

No.1 engine, 443, replaced by 457, due to auxiliary generator drive sheared in phasing case. Metal particles in thermostat. Experimental wheelslip circuit defective. No.1 end lubricating oil tank and radiators were cleaned. No.2 main generator was replaced and all other defects were rectified.

| Doncaster | 09/02/73 | 09/02/73 | Unclassified |

No.1 engine, 457, suspect dephased. No fault was found but the governor was changed.

| Doncaster | 14/03/73 | 16/03/73 | Unclassified |

Flashover damage. No.1 load regulator oil leak was rectified and the control cubicle cleaned out. No.6 traction motor contactor was repaired, as was all flashover damage to main generators. Nos.2 & 3 traction motors were replaced.

| Doncaster | 19/03/73 | 23/03/73 | Unclassified |

No.2 engine, 448, replaced by 434.

| Doncaster | 26/03/73 | 30/03/73 | Unclassified |

No.1 engine, 457, had the scavenge blower repaired. Flashover damage on both main generators was cleaned up.

| Doncaster | 16/04/73 | 18/04/73 | Unclassified |

No.2 engine, 434, replaced by 450, due to suspect dephased.

| Doncaster | 02/06/73 | 07/06/73 | Light |

No.1 engine, 457 and No.2 engine, 450, were given Light repairs. No.1 bogie, 9000-9, replaced by 9000-47. No.2 bogie, 9000-42, replaced by 9000-22. Boiler, 1495/J2951, was given an Unclassified repair. The body was given a Light repair.

| Doncaster | 26/09/73 | 27/09/73 | Unclassified |

No.1 boiler water tank holed. This was repaired.

| Doncaster | 23/10/73 | 26/10/73 | Unclassified |

No.2 engine, 450, replaced by 415, due to 'BC' crankshaft damper adrift and cover fractured.

| Doncaster | 25/01/74 | 25/01/74 | Modification |

Earth fault relay modification was carried out.

| Doncaster | 04/03/74 | 16/06/74 | Intermediate |

No.1 engine, 457, replaced by 451. No.2 engine, 415, replaced by 439. No.1 bogie, 9000-47 and No.2 bogie, 9000-22, were given standard repairs and refitted. Boiler, 1495/J2951, was replaced by 5093/J3244. The body was given an Intermediate repair.

| Doncaster | 26/06/74 | 28/06/74 | Unclassified |

No.6 traction motor to earth, this was replaced.

| Doncaster | 12/09/74 | 12/09/74 | Unclassified |

No.2 engine, 439, replaced by 433, due to '6C' injector pocket fractured. On No.2 cab, a replacement doorframe and sliding window were fitted.

| Doncaster | 11/11/74 | 12/11/74 | Unclassified |

No.2 engine, 433, replaced by 412, due to being dephased.

| Doncaster | 14/11/74 | 19/11/74 | Unclassified |

No.2 engine, 412, replaced by 421, due to siphoning water. No.2 end coolant radiators were replaced.

| Doncaster | 18/12/74 | 22/12/74 | Unclassified |

No.1 engine, 451, replaced by 411. No.1 end lubricating oil tank and radiators were removed for cleaning. Leaking fuel tanks were repaired.

| Doncaster | 06/01/75 | 24/01/75 | Unclassified |

No.1 engine, 411, replaced by 439, due to throwing oil out of exhaust manifold. This defect was in fact repaired, however, 411 failed on test in Works with a con rod broken and crankcase holed. No.2 engine, 421, replaced by 408. No.1 end lubricating oil tanks and radiators were removed for cleaning. No.1 end silencer was changed.

| Doncaster | 09/07/75 | 15/07/75 | Unclassified |

No.1 engine, 439, replaced by 429, due to 'AC' crankcase door joint burst and leaking oil. No.1 bogie, 9000-47, replaced by 9000-45. No.2 bogie, 9000-22, replaced by 9000-46. Both bogies needed tyres reprofiling.

D9010/9010/55 010 The King's Own Scottish Borderer (continued)
Loco Works	On Works	Off Works	Class of repair
Doncaster	29/07/75	08/08/75	Light

No.1 engine, 429, replaced by 423. No.2 engine, 408, replaced by 427. Boiler, 5093/J3244, was given an Unclassified repair. The regimental crests were replaced.

Doncaster	01/10/75	02/10/75	Unclassified

No.1 bogie, 9000-45, had bolster segments renewed. Persistent earth faults on Nos.2 & 5 traction motors. No.5 traction motor was replaced. The locomotive was weighed at 102t 10cwt.

Doncaster	18/11/75	19/11/75	Unclassified

No.1 engine, 423, had 'B' air manifold drain exuding coolant/oil mixture. This was rectified.

Doncaster	09/12/75	13/12/75	Unclassified

No.1 engine, 423, replaced by 430, due to high spectrographic analysis and breathing heavy. Both load regulators had leaks rectified.

Doncaster	05/02/76	10/02/76	Unclassified

No.2 engine, 427, replaced by 416, due to high spectrographic analysis and breathing heavy.

Doncaster	22/03/76	25/03/76	Unclassified

No.2 engine, 416, replaced by 410, due to breathing heavy.

Doncaster	12/04/76	15/04/76	Unclassified

No.2 engine, 410, replaced by 448, due to 'A6' con rod fractured and through crankcase. No.2 end lubricating oil tank and radiators were removed for cleaning.

Doncaster	21/04/76	23/04/76	Unclassified

No.1 engine, 430, replaced by 417, due to a seized piston.

Doncaster	20/07/76	19/08/76	Unclassified

No.1 engine, 417, replaced by 427. No.2 engine, 448, replaced by 452, due to breathing heavy and knocking. Cab window frames had fractures repaired and cab windows were secured. Both bogies had brake gear overhauled.

Doncaster	21/09/76	17/12/76	Intermediate

No.1 engine, 427, replaced by 437. No.2 engine, 452, replaced by 404. No.1 bogie, 9000-45, replaced by 9000-35. No.2 bogie, 9000-46, replaced by 9000-36. Boiler, 5093/J3244, replaced by 5092/J3243. Route indicator panels were plated over. The locomotive was weighed at 103t 6cwt.

Doncaster	15/01/77	16/01/77	Rectification

No.1 vacuum exhauster was renewed.

Doncaster	09/06/77	13/06/77	Unclassified

No.2 engine, 404, replaced by 434, due to auxiliary generator drive broken and air duct holed.

Doncaster	27/07/77	29/07/77	Unclassified

No.2 engine, 434, replaced by 444, due to main generator drive defective. Exhaust drain pipes to repair and secure.

Doncaster	06/08/77	08/08/77	Unclassified

No.1 boiler water tank holed. This was repaired.

Doncaster	09/08/77	10/08/77	Rectification

No.2 engine, 444, had fuel dilution. This was rectified.

Doncaster	19/09/77	21/09/77	Unclassified

No.1 engine, 437, replaced by 430, due to breathing heavy and throwing oil. No.1 bogie, 9000-35, had 'L2' brake pull rod safety bracket to fit. No.2 bogie, 9000-36, had 'L4' and 'R6' brake pull rod safety brackets to fit.

Doncaster	01/12/77	06/12/77	Unclassified

Suspect short circuit on battery charge diode. Blower motors running when engines shut down. New studs and nuts fitted to bogie centre pivots. Nos.1 & 6 traction motors were replaced. The locomotive was weighed at 105t 12cwt.

Doncaster	05/01/78	11/01/78	Unclassified

No.1 engine, 430, replaced by 413, due to being dephased.

Doncaster	14/02/78	19/02/78	Unclassified

No.1 main generator armature banding burst. No.2 main generator flashed over. Reported persistent control circuit breaker tripping and earth fault relay operating. Nos. 1-4 traction motors were replaced. All defects were rectified.

Doncaster	24/05/78	25/05/78	Unclassified

No.1 engine, 413, primary driveshaft renewed. No.6 traction motor replaced due to earth fault on field cables. No.6 wheelset replaced due to suspension tube defective.

D9010/9010/55 010 The King's Own Scottish Borderer (continued)

Loco Works	On Works	Off Works	Class of repair
Doncaster	06/07/78	19/08/78	Unclassified

No.1 engine, 413, replaced by 444 (after Unclassified repair ex No.2 engine), due to suspected fractured liner. No.2 engine, 444, replaced by 424, due to being dephased. No.1 primary gearbox repaired. No.2 boiler water tank repaired.

Doncaster	23/09/78	24/10/78	Light

No.1 engine, 444, replaced by 430, due to aerating. No.2 engine, 424, replaced by 451, due to requiring gudgeon pin housing examination. No.1 bogie, 9000-35, replaced by 9000-17. No.2 bogie, 9000-36, replaced by 9000-18. Boiler, 5092/J3243, was given an Unclassified repair. The locomotive was weighed at 105t 19cwt.

Doncaster	09/04/79	19/04/79	Unclassified

No.2 engine, 451, replaced by 422, due to oil leak at free end on 'A' bank at coolant probes. No.1 primary shaft splines worn. No.2 driver's side window catch defective. These defects were rectified.

Doncaster	18/06/79	20/06/79	Unclassified

No.1 engine, 430, replaced by 427, due to being time expired. No.2 bogie, 9000-18, had 'L6' swing link pin renewed. The locomotive was weighed at 105t 18cwt.

Doncaster	25/07/79	05/08/79	Unclassified

No.1 engine, 427, replaced by 457. No.2 engine, 422, replaced by 420, due to a fractured liner.

Doncaster	13/10/79	16/10/79	Unclassified

No.2 engine, 420, replaced by 429, due to high spectrographic analysis.

Doncaster	09/12/79	13/12/79	Unclassified

No.1 engine, 457, had two commutator covers to fit. No.2 engine, 429, replaced by 438, due to 'C' bank crankcase fractured, suspect piston and con rod broken. No.2 load regulator leaking oil. One nameplate to be removed due to numerous fractures.

Doncaster	05/02/80	11/02/80	Unclassified

No.1 engine, 457, replaced by 426, due to scavenge blower drive sheared. No.2 engine, 438, had primary shaft drive coupling loose. This was rectified.

Doncaster	29/02/80	04/03/80	Unclassified

No.2 engine, 438, replaced by 408, due to No.2 main generator field to earth.

Doncaster	10/07/80	16/07/80	Unclassified

No.1 engine, 426, had a cardan shaft to renew. No.2 main generator field windings to earth. 426 was repaired and No.2 main generator was replaced.

Doncaster	28/08/80	17/10/80	Intermediate

No.1 engine, 426, replaced by 427. No.2 engine, 408, replaced by 419. No.1 bogie, 9000-17, replaced by 9000-37. No.2 bogie, 9000-18, replaced by 9000-38. Boiler, 5092/J3243, replaced by 1486/J2942. Both main generators and all traction motors had flashover damage. The locomotive had been cannibalised prior to despatch to Works. The locomotive was weighed at 103t 6cwt.

Doncaster	27/02/81	05/03/81	Unclassified

No.2 engine, 419, replaced by 454, due to blower failure.

Doncaster	18/08/81	27/08/81	Unclassified

No.1 engine, 427, replaced by 438, due to No.1 main generator flashover damage, armature bandings burst and hole blown in armature.

Doncaster	28/09/81	01/10/81	Unclassified

No.1 engine, 438, had exhaust collector drum fracture. The collector drum was replaced.

Doncaster	24/12/81	-	-

The locomotive arrived after withdrawal with the following main components fitted; No.1 engine, 438, fractured lubricating oil pipe. No.2 engine, 454, aerating. No.1 bogie, 9000-37. No.2 bogie, 9000-38. Boiler, 1486/J2942.

D9011/9011/55 011 The Royal Northumberland Fusiliers

Loco Works	On Works	Off Works	Class of repair
Doncaster	24/08/61	Not recorded	Acceptance trials

New locomotive fitted with the following main components; No.1 engine, 429. No.2 engine, 430. No.1 bogie, 1023. No.2 bogie, 1024. Boiler, 1496/J2952.

Doncaster	11/04/62	12/04/62	General

No.2 engine, 430, replaced by 405. No.1 bogie, 1023, replaced by 1021. No.2 bogie, 1024, replaced by 1022. The body was given a six monthly examination.

Doncaster	23/10/62	26/10/62	Light

No.1 bogie, 1021, replaced by 1011. No.2 bogie, 1022, replaced by 1012. A new demister window was fitted at No.1 end driver's side. New bellows were fitted on No.1 traction motor. The following modifications were carried out — Drawgear and driver's brake valve; Boiler gauge steam pipe.

Doncaster	27/12/62	28/12/62	Unclassified

No.1 exhaust drum tank split, No.2 traction motor blower bearing failed, flashover on all traction motors and slight flashover damage on both main generators. No.1 exhaust collector drum replaced, as was No.2 traction motor blower. The loco mileage was recorded as 159,000 miles.

Doncaster	04/01/63	04/01/63	Unclassified

No.1 bogie, 1011, outside spring plank out of position at both sides. The leading transom beam was reseated on swing link. A traction motor door catch was fitted. The locomotive mileage was recorded as 159,560 miles.

Doncaster	25/02/63	28/02/63	Unclassified

Leaking Boiler tubes. Coolant water leaks on both engines. Boiler, 1496/J2952 had tubes welded and was acid washed. The locomotive mileage was recorded as 169,030 miles.

Doncaster	12/03/63	12/03/63	Unclassified

No.1 bogie, 1011, replaced by 1035, due to transom beam frames fractured. No.2 bogie, 1012, replaced by 1036, due to transom beam frames fractured. The locomotive mileage was recorded as 171,150 miles.

Doncaster	25/03/63	06/04/63	General

No.1 engine, 429, replaced by 408. No.2 engine, 405, replaced by 454. No.1 bogie, 1035, replaced by 1002. No.2 bogie, 1036, replaced by 1049. Boiler, 1496/J2952, replaced by 1486/J2942. The body was given an annual repair. The following modifications were carried out — AWS positioning; Sand trap positioning; Soundproofing; Cubicle sealing; Side air ducting; Exhaust tank drains; Radiator fan grills; Extra exhaust filter; Water contents gauge.

R.S.H. Darlington	20/05/63	25/05/63	Unclassified

'The Royal Northumberland Fusiliers' nameplates fitted.

Doncaster	16/09/63	18/09/63	Light

No.1 bogie, 1002, replaced by 1033. No.2 bogie, 1049, replaced by 1034. No.1 traction motor armature down to earth. The body was given a six monthly exam.

Doncaster	28/10/63	03/11/63	Unclassified

All traction motors to be overhauled and for boiler modifications. Boiler, 1486/J2942, replaced by 5096/J3247. The following modifications were carried out — Brush type buffers; Modified cowlings; Caustic injection to boiler; Modified air ducting to boiler. The locomotive mileage is recorded as 220,000 miles.

Doncaster	19/11/63	19/11/63	Unclassified

No.4 traction motor holed. All traction motors examined, Nos.3 & 4 badly flashed over. No.4 traction motor was replaced.

Doncaster	04/01/64	05/01/64	Unclassified

No.1 bogie, 1033, replaced by 1011. No.2 bogie, 1034, replaced by 1012.

Doncaster	31/01/64	31/01/64	Unclassified

Batteries were changed.

Doncaster	08/04/64	30/04/64	General

No.1 engine, 408, replaced by 445. No.2 engine, 454, replaced by 448. No.1 bogie, 1011 and No.2 bogie, 1012, were given General repairs. Boiler, 5096/J3247, replaced by 5095/J3246. The following modifications were carried out — Antifrost precautions; Access door to exhausters.

Doncaster	25/08/64	26/08/64	Unclassified

No.1 bogie, 1011 and No.2 bogie, 1012 had transom fractures welded. The following modifications were carried out — Boiler pump resistance; Boiler fuses; Exhauster cutout valve.

D9011/9011/55 011 The Royal Northumberland Fusiliers (continued)

Loco Works	On Works	Off Works	Class of repair
Doncaster	19/09/64	23/09/64	Unclassified

No.1 engine, 445, replaced by 431, due to a suspected fractured cylinder liner. No.1 bogie, 1011 and No.2 bogie, 1012 both had transom fractures welded.

Doncaster	23/01/65	31/01/65	Light

No.2 main generator interpole burnt. No.2 engine, 448, replaced by 430. No.1 bogie, 1011, replaced by 1017. No.2 bogie, 1012, replaced by 1026.

Doncaster	09/03/65	09/03/65	Unclassified

A coolant leak was rectified.

Doncaster	24/06/65	09/07/65	General

No.2 engine, 430, replaced by 424. No.1 bogie, 1017, replaced by 9000-1. No.2 bogie, 1026, replaced by 9000-2. Boiler, 5095/J3246, replaced by 5089/J3240. The following modification was carried out — Fire bell gong.

Doncaster	05/10/65	08/10/65	Unclassified

No.1 engine, 431, replaced by 450, due to liner seals leaking. The burner motor on the boiler was replaced.

Doncaster	13/12/65	18/12/65	Light

No.1 engine, 450, replaced by 439. No.1 bogie, 9000-1, replaced by 9000-9. No.2 bogie, 9000-2, replaced by 9000-10. The following modifications were carried out — Protection bar for EP valves; Cab footstep stiffening plates; Oil resisting compound to sandbox fillers.

Doncaster	29/12/65	02/01/66	Unclassified

Oil and coolant radiators and No.5 traction motor were replaced.

Doncaster	25/02/66	28/02/66	Unclassified

No.3 commutator badly damaged by flashover. Slight flashover on Nos.1, 2 & 4 traction motors and both main generators. No.2 end secondary fan shaft was replaced. Flashover damage was cleaned up on both main generators. All traction motors had flashover damage cleaned up except for No.3, which was replaced.

Doncaster	14/04/66	26/04/66	General

No.1 engine, 439 and No.2 engine, 424, were given Unclassified repairs. No.1 bogie, 9000-9, replaced by 9000-17. No.2 bogie, 9000-10, replaced by 9000-18. Boiler, 5089/J3240, replaced by 5090/J3241. The body was given a General repair.

Doncaster	26/04/66	26/04/66	Unclassified

A defect on No.1 main generator was rectified.

Doncaster	14/05/66	18/05/66	Unclassified

Nos.3 & 4 wheelsets were replaced due to fractures.

Doncaster	11/07/66	14/07/66	Unclassified

No.2 bogie, 9000-18, had defective horn liners repaired.

Doncaster	05/10/66	06/10/66	Unclassified

No.1 bogie, 9000-17, had a defective axlebox repaired.

Doncaster	27/10/66	28/10/66	Unclassified

No.2 engine, 424, replaced by 405. Both exhaust silencers were replaced.

Doncaster	17/12/66	21/12/66	Unclassified

Both main generators had flashover damage repaired.

Doncaster	04/01/67	10/01/67	Light

No.1 engine, 439 and No.2 engine, 405, were given Unclassified repairs. No.1 bogie, 9000-17, replaced by 9000-37. No.2 bogie, 9000-18, replaced by 9000-38. Boiler, 5090/J3241, was given an Unclassified repair. The body was given an Unclassified repair.

Doncaster	12/01/67	12/01/67	Not recorded

No details recorded.

Doncaster	17/01/67	18/01/67	Unclassified

Both main generators and all traction motors except No.4 had flashover damage cleaned up. No.4 traction motor was replaced.

Doncaster	17/03/67	22/03/67	Unclassified

All traction motors and one main generator burnt out. Both main generators and all traction motors had extensive flashover damage cleaned up and repaired. No.5 wheelset was replaced due to a fracture.

D9011/9011/55 011 The Royal Northumberland Fusiliers (continued)

Loco Works	On Works	Off Works	Class of repair
Doncaster	04/04/67	07/04/67	Unclassified

No.1 main generator to earth, brush pigtails coming out and flashed over badly. All traction motors to earth and throwing solder. No.1 main generator was replaced. Flashover damage to No.2 main generator and all traction motors was cleaned up.

Doncaster	24/04/67	11/05/67	General

No.1 engine, 439, replaced by 438. No.2 engine, 405, replaced by 407. No.1 bogie, 9000-37, replaced by 9000-39. No.2 bogie, 9000-38, replaced by 9000-40. Boiler, 5090/J3241, replaced by 1497/J2953. The body was given a General repair and full yellow nose ends were applied.

Doncaster	29/08/67	31/08/67	Unclassified

Nos.4 & 5 wheelsets end bearing bolts broken. No.1 load regulator was cleaned and the cover repaired. Nos.4 & 5 wheelsets were replaced.

Doncaster	06/09/67	07/09/67	Unclassified

No.1 engine, 438, replaced by 539, due to a fractured cylinder liner. An exhaust silencer replaced.

Doncaster	07/12/67	13/12/67	Light

No.1 engine, 539, replaced by 405. No.2 engine, 407, replaced by 421. No.1 bogie, 9000-39, replaced by 9000-7. No.2 bogie, 9000-40, replaced by 9000-8. Boiler, 1497/J2953, was given an Unclassified repair. The body was given an Unclassified repair.

Doncaster	04/01/68	05/01/68	Unclassified

No.1 engine, 405, replaced by 424, due to a fractured cylinder liner. Flashover damage to No.2 main generator was repaired.

Doncaster	19/03/68	20/03/68	Unclassified

No.1 engine, 424, replaced by 458, due to water in sump.

Doncaster	08/05/68	08/07/68	General

*Persistent loss of power. No.1 engine, 458, replaced by 431. No.2 engine, 421, replaced by 453. No.1 bogie, 9000-7, replaced by 9000-41. No.2 bogie, 9000-8, replaced by 9000-42. Boiler, 1497/J2953, replaced by 5092/J3243. The body was given a General repair and repainted into **blue livery with full yellow nose ends**. The locomotive was fitted for dual braking.*

Doncaster	24/02/69	28/02/69	Light

No.1 engine, 431 and No.2 engine, 453, were given Unclassified repairs. No.1 bogie, 9000-41, replaced by 9000-33. No.2 bogie, 9000-42, replaced by 9000-34. Boiler, 5092/J3243, was given an Unclassified repair.

Doncaster	06/03/69	06/03/69	Unclassified

Being 'down on power'. The locomotive was load tested and no fault found.

Doncaster	02/04/69	10/04/69	Unclassified

No.1 engine, 431, replaced by 440, due to being dephased.

Doncaster	06/10/69	09/10/69	Unclassified

No.2 engine, 453, replaced by 450, due to coolant in sump. No.1 bogie, 9000-33, had No.1 traction motor and Nos.1 & 3 wheelsets replaced due to motor pinions and road wheel gears damaged.

Doncaster	21/10/69	23/10/69	Unclassified

No.2 engine, 450, replaced by 419, due to governor defective and breathing heavy fumes when hot. Engine also was swaying badly at idling speed.

Doncaster	20/11/69	06/12/69	Intermediate

No.1 engine, 440 and No.2 engine, 419, were given Unclassified repairs. No.1 bogie, 9000-33 and No.2 bogie, 9000-34, were given General repairs. Boiler, 5092/J3243, replaced by 5098/J3249. The boiler water tank modification was fitted. The body was given an Intermediate repair.

Doncaster	08/12/69	09/12/69	Rectification

Both main generators had flashover damage repaired.

Doncaster	24/12/69	02/01/70	Rectification

Flashover damage on No.2 main generator. Flashover damage on both main generators was repaired and all traction motors were replaced. Field divert contactors were overhauled and both load regulators were cleaned and checked.

Doncaster	05/01/70	07/01/70	Unclassified

Flashover damage. No.2 engine, 419, replaced by 445. No.1 main generator had flashover damage cleaned up. No.2 main generator was replaced. All traction motors were checked and cleaned.

D9011/9011/55 011 The Royal Northumberland Fusiliers (continued)

Loco Works	On Works	Off Works	Class of repair
Doncaster	01/04/70	03/04/70	Unclassified

No.1 engine, 440, replaced by 450, due to sump full of coolant. No.2 end buffers to renew (taken for 9018). No.2 end windscreens, driver's side cracked and was replaced, secondman's side was resealed. Lubricating oil tanks and radiator elements were cleaned.

Doncaster	15/07/70	31/07/70	Light

No.1 engine, 450, had injectors replaced. No.2 engine, 445, was given a Light repair. No.1 bogie, 9000-33, replaced by 9000-13. No.2 bogie, 9000-34, replaced by 9000-14. Boiler, 5098/J3249, was given an Unclassified repair. The body was given a Light repair.

Doncaster	14/08/70	15/08/70	Unclassified

No.2 engine, 445, replaced by 451, due to 'B6' exhaust piston seized. Lubricating oil tanks were cleaned.

Doncaster	23/10/70	08/11/70	Unclassified

Collision damage at No.2 end, bent buffer beam and damaged pipework. All collision damage was repaired. No.1 engine, 450, replaced by 423. No.2 engine, 451, replaced by 445. No.3 wheelset was replaced.

Doncaster	29/12/70	31/12/70	Unclassified

No.2 engine, 445, replaced by 409, due to being dephased. No.1 end silencer had a fracture repaired.

Doncaster	02/03/71	04/03/71	Unclassified

No.2 engine, 409, had a governor change due to linkage out of adjustment. All lubricating oil radiator elements were replaced and cab footstep panels were renewed.

Doncaster	08/03/71	10/03/71	Unclassified

No.1 engine, 423, replaced by 455, due to 'AB' crankcase fractured. No.1 end lubricating oil radiators were replaced and the tank cleaned internally.

Doncaster	10/03/71	11/03/71	Unclassified

A boiler water tank fracture was repaired.

Doncaster	13/04/71	06/08/71	Intermediate

No.1 engine, 455, replaced by 457. No.2 engine, 409, replaced by 430, due to a piston through crankcase. No.1 bogie, 9000-13, replaced by 9000-27. No.2 bogie, 9000-14, replaced by 9000-28. Boiler, 5098/J3249, replaced by 1490/J2946. The body was given an Intermediate repair. The locomotive was fitted with E.T.H. equipment.

Doncaster	11/08/71	12/08/71	Rectification

E.T.H. defective. E.T.H. circuit breaker was rectified.

Doncaster	21/09/71	23/09/71	Unclassified

No.1 engine, 457, replaced by 440, due to a suspected fractured cylinder liner. No.2 boiler water tank had a leak on seam repaired.

Doncaster	22/12/71	31/12/71	Unclassified

No.2 engine, 430, had 'AB' crankshaft replaced.

Doncaster	26/01/72	02/02/72	Unclassified

No.2 engine, 430, replaced by 456, due to 'A5' inlet gudgeon pin housing pulled away from piston. Both coolant header tanks were repaired.

Doncaster	10/02/72	15/02/72	Unclassified

No.1 engine, 440, replaced by 412, due to crankcase holed. Lubricating oil tanks and radiators were repaired.

Doncaster	05/04/72	07/04/72	Unclassified

No.2 boiler water tank split at top seam. This was repaired.

Doncaster	14/04/72	16/04/72	Unclassified

No.2 bogie, 9000-28, right side spring plank support bracket. Nos.4 & 5 traction motors bolt working out, securing stud broken. All repairs were carried out.

Doncaster	01/06/72	09/06/72	Light

No.1 engine, 412 and No.2 engine, 456, were given Unclassified repairs. No.1 bogie, 9000-27, replaced by 9000-19. No.2 bogie, 9000-28, replaced by 9000-20. Boiler, 1490/J2946, was given an Unclassified repair. The body was given a Light repair.

Doncaster	03/10/72	11/10/72	Unclassified

No.1 engine, 412, replaced by 435, due to internal coolant leaks. Lubricating oil tank and radiators were cleaned.

D9011/9011/55 011 The Royal Northumberland Fusiliers (continued)

Loco Works	On Works	Off Works	Class of repair
Doncaster	18/01/73	23/01/73	Unclassified

No.1 engine, 435, suspect fractured liner. 435 was run on the load bank and no fault found. The swan neck casting for vacuum pipe on No.1 end buffer beam broken off. Boiler water tank split along top seam. These repairs were carried out.

Doncaster	16/02/73	16/02/73	Unclassified

No.1 engine, 435, had the fan gearbox renewed.

Doncaster	20/02/73	21/02/73	Unclassified

No.1 engine, 435, replaced by 434, due to being dephased.

Doncaster	15/03/73	11/04/73	Intermediate

No.1 engine, 434, replaced by 423. No.2 engine, 456, replaced by 407. No.1 bogie, 9000-19, replaced by 9000-45. No.2 bogie, 9000-20, replaced by 9000-46. Boiler, 1490/J2946, replaced by 1496/J2952. The body was given an Intermediate repair.

Doncaster	16/08/73	17/08/73	Unclassified

No.2 engine, 407, replaced by 443, due to piston through 'BC' crankcase.

Doncaster	17/10/73	24/10/73	Unclassified

No.2 engine, 443, replaced by 419, due to phasing gears and drive shaft damaged and main generator banding burst. No.1 main generator slight flashover damage. Radiator fan gearbox damaged. A boiler water tank was repaired, as was No.2 primary fan gearbox.

Doncaster	26/10/73	26/10/73	Unclassified

No.2 engine, 419, replaced by 445, due to a suspected fractured liner.

Doncaster	30/11/73	04/12/73	Unclassified

'HC2' contactor and associated wiring burnt. This was repaired and both main generators cleaned out.

Doncaster	19/12/73	21/12/73	Unclassified

No.1 bogie, 9000-45, No.3 axle bent. All axles checked as locomotive had been derailed on two occasions. Derailment damage to the body was repaired and No.3 wheelset was changed.

Doncaster	14/01/74	23/01/74	Light

No.1 engine, 423 and No.2 engine, 445, were given Light repairs. No.1 bogie, 9000-45, replaced by 9000-17. No.2 bogie, 9000-46, replaced by 9000-18. Boiler, 1496/J2952, was given an Unclassified repair. The body was given a Light repair and the earth fault relay modification was carried out.

Doncaster	01/02/74	11/02/74	Unclassified

No.1 engine, 423, replaced by 419, due to a seized piston.

Doncaster	15/03/74	20/03/74	Unclassified

No.1 engine, 419, replaced by 407, due to gear idler governor bearing collapsed.

Doncaster	31/05/74	08/06/74	Unclassified

Nos.2 & 5 traction motors flashed over. E.T.H. and coolant modifications were carried out. No.1 main and auxiliary generators were replaced, No.2 main generator had a three monthly repair and all traction motors were replaced.

Doncaster	11/07/74	16/07/74	Unclassified

No.4 traction motor throwing solder and all traction motors with flashover damage. No.1 cardan shaft was repaired and load regulator, traction motor contactor and tips were cleaned and realigned at No.1 end. Nos.3, 4 & 6 traction motors were changed, Nos.1, 2 & 5 had flashover damage repaired.

Doncaster	27/07/74	31/07/74	Unclassified

Wheelslip at 90 mph. No.1 engine, 407, repeated bookings for high water temperature, coolant test point hose chafing on fuel lift pump. No.2 engine, 445, coolant test point hose chafing on fuel lift pump. No.1 traction motor armature 'Vee' ring to retape. No.4 traction motor throwing brown substance from the armature ring. Nos.1, 4 & 5 traction motors were replaced.

Doncaster	05/08/74	09/08/74	Unclassified

No.1 engine, 407, replaced by 454, due to piston through crankcase. No.2 main generator had flashover damage repaired.

Doncaster	19/08/74	22/08/74	Unclassified

Wheelslip at 80 mph. No.1 traction motor throwing brown, glutinous material. No.2 traction motor commutator has bar markings. Nos.1 & 2 traction motors were replaced.

Doncaster	02/10/74	04/10/74	Unclassified

No.1 engine, 454, replaced by 434 - crankcase holed. Lubricating oil tank and radiators replaced.

D9011/9011/55 011 The Royal Northumberland Fusiliers (continued)

Loco Works	On Works	Off Works	Class of repair
Doncaster	13/11/74	14/11/74	Unclassified

Nos.2 & 5 traction motors to be replaced due to wheelslip.

Doncaster	06/12/74	11/12/74	Unclassified

No.2 engine, 445, replaced by 440, due to high spectrographic analysis. Driver's brake valve defective, no overcharge. No.2 end lubricating oil tank and radiators were cleaned.

Doncaster	22/01/75	22/04/75	Intermediate

No.1 engine, 434, replaced by 458, due to breathing heavy. No.2 engine, 440, replaced by 428. No.1 bogie, 9000-17, replaced by 9000-35. No.2 bogie, 9000-18, replaced by 9000-36. Boiler, 1496/J2952, replaced by 1491/J2947. The body was given an Intermediate repair.

Doncaster	13/05/75	20/07/75	Unclassified

No.1 engine, 458, replaced by 418. No.2 engine, 428, replaced by 416 - suspect fractured liner.

Doncaster	12/08/75	12/08/75	Unclassified

No.1 engine, 418, primary fan disintegrated and cowling badly damaged. No.1 end cardan shaft, fan and gearbox were replaced.

Doncaster	01/11/75	06/11/75	Unclassified

No.2 engine, 416, replaced by 406, due to scavenge blower drive sheared.

Doncaster	22/11/75	25/11/75	Unclassified

No.2 axle road wheel and bearing cone and cover bolts sheared and boiler water tank leaking. No.2 wheelset was changed and boiler water tank repaired. The locomotive was weighed at 105t 4cwt.

Doncaster	07/01/76	10/01/76	Unclassified

No.1 engine, 418, replaced by 423, due to 'AB' crankcase fractured at free end. No.1 main generator had flashover damage repaired and bogie side bearers were repaired.

Doncaster	26/03/76	24/06/76	Light

No.1 engine, 423, replaced by 427, due to requiring a 'Light' repair. No.2 engine, 406, replaced by 411, due to No. '5C' con rod broken and crankcase fractured. No.1 bogie, 9000-35, replaced by 9000-24. No.2 bogie, 9000-36, replaced by 9000-48. Boiler, 1491/J2947, was given an Unclassified repair.

Doncaster	26/07/76	28/07/76	Unclassified

No.1 engine, 427, replaced by 454, due to being disengaged from main generator. An oil leak on No.2 load regulator was rectified.

Doncaster	24/08/76	26/08/76	Unclassified

No.1 engine, 454, replaced by 538, due to aerating, suspect fractured liner.

Doncaster	25/01/77	26/01/77	Unclassified

No.2 engine, 411, replaced by 453, due to 'CA' crankcase 'A' side tie bolt broken, leaking oil. No.2 main generator was replaced.

Doncaster	16/02/77	17/02/77	Unclassified

No.1 engine, 538, replaced by 426. No.1 main generator replaced.

Doncaster	18/06/77	04/08/77	Unclassified

Rough riding. No.1 engine, 426, replaced by 430. No.2 engine, 453, replaced by 445. Batteries and both main generators were replaced. No.1 bogie, 9000-24 and No.2 bogie, 9000-48, were overhauled.

Doncaster	22/08/77	06/09/77	Rectification

No.1 engine, 430, replaced by 423, due to 'A' side crankcase fractured. No.1 main generator was replaced. Field divert and loss of power faults rectified. Locomotive was lifted for examination of bogie swing links; pins and bushes renewed as required.

Doncaster	15/12/77	22/12/77	Unclassified

No.1 engine, 423, replaced by 433, due to being dephased. No.2 end left hand cab floor collapsed. Boiler exhaust stack badly corroded.

Doncaster	09/01/78	22/05/78	Intermediate

No.1 engine, 433, replaced by 416. No.2 engine, 445, replaced by 458, due for General repair. No.1 bogie, 9000-24, replaced by 9000-7. No.2 bogie, 9000-48, replaced by 9000-8. Boiler, 1491/J2947, replaced by 1489/J2945. Route indicator panels were plated over. The loco weighed at 105t 3cwt.

Doncaster	25/07/78	31/07/78	Unclassified

No.1 engine, 416, had gudgeon pin housing exam carried out.

D9011/9011/55 011 The Royal Northumberland Fusiliers (continued)

Loco Works	On Works	Off Works	Class of repair
Doncaster	15/09/78	18/09/78	Unclassified

No.1 engine, 416, replaced by 418, due to suspected fractured liner and Dowty pump quillshaft missing (this had been robbed for No.2 engine, 458).

| Doncaster | 06/10/78 | 12/10/78 | Unclassified |

No.1 engine, 418, replaced by 422, due to main generator open circuit. No.2 bogie, 9000-8, required No.4 traction motor suspension tube pin bush, which was adrift, to be repaired.

| Doncaster | 26/02/79 | 07/03/79 | Unclassified |

No.2 engine, 458, had a gudgeon pin housing exam. No.2 main generator was replaced due to having badly flashed over. No.1 primary shaft was renewed.

| Doncaster | 22/03/79 | 05/04/79 | Unclassified |

No.1 engine, 422, replaced by 455, due to low oil pressure. No.2 engine, 458, replaced by 423, due to suspect fractured liner. No.1 end lubricating oil radiators and thermostat valve replaced.

| Doncaster | 03/08/79 | 08/08/79 | Unclassified |

No.1 engine, 455, replaced by 433, due to suspect fractured liner and time expired.

| Doncaster | 31/10/79 | 18/11/79 | Light |

No.1 engine, 433, replaced by 424, due to suspect fractured liner. No.2 engine, 423, replaced by 405, for use in 55 004. No.1 bogie, 9000-7, replaced by 9000-39. No.2 bogie, 9000-8, replaced by 9000-40. Boiler, 1489/J2945, was given an Unclassified repair. The locomotive weighed 104t 9cwt.

| Doncaster | 22/01/80 | 29/01/80 | Unclassified |

No.1 engine, 424, collector drum fire at Newark. Fire Brigade had hosed down exhaust. Fire alarm system was checked and recharged. No.1 engine, 424, had injectors and drum tank replaced.

| Doncaster | 30/01/80 | 31/01/80 | Not Recorded |
| Doncaster | 05/02/80 | 07/02/80 | Unclassified |

Not Recorded

No.1 engine, 424, replaced by 447, due to persistent fires in collector drum tank and exhaust system.

| Doncaster | 29/07/80 | 30/07/80 | Unclassified |

No.2 engine, 405, had the exciter flange renewed due to radiator fan shaft drive damaged in auxiliary drive gearbox.

| Doncaster | 05/08/80 | 07/08/80 | Unclassified |

No.1 engine, 447, replaced by 449, due to a fractured liner. No.1 bogie, 9000-39, had swing link 'R1' locking plate missing; Nos.1 & 3 traction motor nose suspension plates needed securing. No.2 bogie, 9000-40, had swing link 'L8' set screws broken. The locomotive was weighed at 103t 13cwt.

| Doncaster | 03/12/80 | 08/12/80 | Unclassified |

No.1 engine, 449, had main generator flashover damage repaired. No.2 engine, 405, replaced by 452, due to requiring a General repair.

| Doncaster | 30/06/81 | 03/07/81 | Unclassified |

No.1 bogie, 9000-39, replaced by 9000-46. No.2 bogie, 9000-40, replaced by 9000-42, due to both bogies tyres too thin to turn.

| Doncaster | 30/07/81 | 06/08/81 | Unclassified |

No.1 engine, 449, replaced by 434, due to collector drum tank fractured, engine throwing oil.

| Stratford D.R.S. | 06/11/81 | 23/11/81 | - |

No.1 engine, 434, replaced by 421. This replacement was carried out to allow 55 022 to return to traffic.

| Doncaster | 24/11/81 | - | - |

The locomotive arrived after withdrawal with the following main components fitted. No.1 engine, 421. No.2 engine, 452. No.1 bogie, 9000-46. No.2 bogie, 9000-42. Boiler, 1489/J2945.

D9012/9012/55 012 Crepello

Loco Works	On Works	Off Works	Class of repair
Doncaster	04/09/61	12/09/61	Acceptance trials

New locomotive fitted with the following main components. No.1 engine, 434. No.2 engine, 435. No.1 bogie, 1025. No.2 bogie, 1026. Boiler, 5087/J3238. 'Crepello' nameplates fitted.

Doncaster	19/12/61	23/01/62	Light

Collision damage repairs. No.1 traction motor casting broken and Nos.1 & 2 traction motor covers missing. No.1 bogie, 1025, cross stay bent and brake gear damaged. No.1 end nose was repaired, No.1 end buffer bar, outer frames, boxes and gussets were repaired. Nos.1 & 2 ends superstructure casing was repaired. New buffers, horns, horn guards and sand chutes were fitted to No.1 end. New screw couplings were fitted at both ends. Both engine and radiator fan gearboxes were removed, returned to the makers for modification and refitted. Exhauster stand and fire extinguisher bases were removed, repaired and refitted. No.1 bogie, 1025 and No.2 bogie, 1026, were removed, repaired and refitted. 1025 had new right hand leading brake cylinder, right hand leading brake hanger, pull rods and life guards fitted. The body was given a six monthly examination. The locomotive mileage was recorded as 34,230 miles.

R.S.H. Darlington	01/05/62	18/05/62	Modification

No.1 engine, 434 and No.2 engine, 435, received modifications.

Doncaster	28/08/62	29/08/62	Unclassified

No.2 bogie, 1026, headstock rivets loose. These were renewed and modified brake lever pins were fitted. Water scoop snouts were repaired and No.2 water tank was welded. The locomotive mileage was recorded as 119,500 miles.

Doncaster	05/11/62	07/12/62	General

No.1 engine, 434, replaced by 444, due to internal coolant leak. No.2 engine, 435, replaced by 409. No.1 bogie, 1025, replaced by 1001. No.2 bogie, 1026, replaced by 1050. Boiler, 5087/J3238, replaced by 5092/J3243. The following modifications were carried out — Drawgear; Radiator fan grills; Additional vacuum pipe filter. The locomotive mileage was recorded as 154,620 miles.

Doncaster	26/03/63	27/03/63	Unclassified

No.2 bogie, 1050, headstock rivets loose right hand side and cracks in transoms. Both bogies were chipped and welded. Bottom cock of Mowbrey blowdown valve defective, this was replaced. Conduit bracket to weld, No.1 end nose. Nos.1 & 2 water level switches were removed and cleaned.

Doncaster	04/06/63	13/06/63	Light

No.1 bogie, 1001, replaced by 1039. No.2 bogie, 1050, replaced by 1040. Boiler, 5092/J3243, replaced by 5093/J3244. The body was given a six monthly examination. The following modifications were carried out — Boiler independent air supply; Boiler caustic injection; Exhaust collector tank drains; Bogie brake rod safety brackets.

Doncaster	29/06/63	02/07/63	Unclassified

No.1 engine, 444, replaced by 412. No.2 boiler water tank and suction pipe elbow repaired

Doncaster	14/08/63	16/08/63	Unclassified

No.1 engine, 412, replaced by 406, due to 'C4' cylinder leaking. No.1 bogie, 1039, replaced by 1041. No.2 bogie, 1040, replaced by 1042.

Doncaster	21/10/63	22/10/63	Modification

Boiler modifications. Automatic blowdown was fitted and caustic filler and drainpipes were rerouted. The fuel tanks were fibre glassed.

Doncaster	26/11/63	10/12/63	General

No.1 engine, 406, replaced by 441, due to breathing heavy. No.2 engine, 409, replaced by 411. No.1 bogie, 1041, replaced by 1013. No.2 bogie, 1042, replaced by 1014. Boiler, 5093/J3244, replaced by 5094/J3245. The body was given an annual repair. The following modifications were carried out — Main generator mounting feet; Draught sealing; Sound proofing; Coolant gauges; Header tank overflow tank fitted; Oil and water roof hoses were removed. The locomotive mileage was recorded as 313,070 miles.

Doncaster	08/04/64	09/04/64	Unclassified

No.1 engine, 441 and No.2 engine, 411, had replacement air manifolds fitted. No.1 bogie, 1013, had headstocks riveted. No.1 traction motor gearcase replaced and all traction motors cleaned. No.2 bogie, 1014, had transom fractures welded, traction motors cleaned and fiftysix new brushes fitted. Boiler, 5094/J3245, was given an MP11 exam and had the blow down handle repaired. All main and auxiliary generators were cleaned. Conduiting to the exhausters was renewed.

D9012/9012/55 012 Crepello (continued)

Loco Works	On Works	Off Works	Class of repair
Doncaster	06/06/64	11/06/64	Light

No.1 engine, 441 and No.2 engine, 411, were given MP11 exams. No.1 bogie, 1013, replaced by 1003. No.2 bogie, 1014, replaced by 1004. Boiler, 5094/J3245, was given an Unclassified repair. The body was given an Unclassified repair including repairs to the corner panel at No.1 end. Both main generators were cleaned. The following antifrost precautions were carried out — Lagging of pipes; Auto drain valve and steam heater valve.

Doncaster	Not recorded	25/08/64	Not recorded

No.2 engine, 411, replaced by 451.

Doncaster	18/09/64	25/10/64	General

No.1 engine, 441, replaced by 421, due to high water temperature. No.2 engine, 451, replaced by 415. No.1 bogie, 1003, replaced by 1045, due to axle horn liner adrift. No.2 bogie, 1004, replaced by 1046. Boiler, 5094/J3245, replaced by 1495/J2951. No.2 main generator had severe flashover damage and was replaced.

Doncaster	26/10/64	27/10/64	Non Classified

Warning horn adjustments and MP11 exams. These were carried out. The boiler blow down valve was also adjusted.

Doncaster	19/01/65	20/01/65	Unclassified

Flashover damage to all traction motors. No.1 bogie, 1045, traction motor supports on transom fractured. No.2 bogie, 1046, to be examined for fractures. Fractures on both bogies were cut and welded. Boiler, 1495/J2951, was given a Light repair. The flashover damage was cleaned up.

Doncaster	20/03/65	26/03/65	Light

No.1 engine, 421 and No.2 engine, 415, were given MP11 exams. No.1 bogie, 1045, replaced by 1033. No.2 bogie, 1046, replaced by 1034. Boiler, 1495/J2951, was given an MP11 exam. The main and auxiliary generators were cleaned and had new brushes and isolators fitted.

Doncaster	05/08/65	10/08/65	Unclassified

Radiators to be replaced, engines heating up and new cast steel bogies to be fitted. No.1 bogie, 1033, replaced by 9000-13. No.2 bogie, 1034, replaced by 9000-14. The brakegear was overhauled. All coolant radiators were replaced, as was No.1 primary fan shaft. The locomotive mileage was recorded as 617,150 miles.

Doncaster	30/09/65	06/10/65	Unclassified

No.1 oil radiator leaking badly, No.2 load regulator oil pipe and primary and secondary shafts to replace. Boiler, 1495/J2951, replaced by 5091/J3242. The main and auxiliary generators were cleaned and new brushes were fitted. No.4 traction motor was replaced and all other traction motors were cleaned. The following modifications were carried out — Protection bar for EP valves; Toilet hopper; NUWAY burner; Fire alarm bell; Low water Mowbrey shroud.

Doncaster	03/11/65	04/11/65	Unclassified

No.1 engine, 421 and No.2 engine, 415, to be load tested. This was done and no repair work was found necessary.

Doncaster	01/01/66	08/01/66	Unclassified

No.1 engine, 421, suspected fractured cylinder liner. 421, was removed, overhauled and refitted.

Doncaster	10/01/66	14/01/66	Unclassified

No.1 engine, 421, cutting out. A new phasing case was fitted.

Doncaster	18/01/66	22/01/66	Unclassified

No.1 engine, 421, water pump drive shaft broken. This was repaired.

Doncaster	24/01/66	10/02/66	General

No.1 engine, 421, replaced by 443. No.2 engine, 415, replaced by 447. No.1 bogie, 9000-13 and No.2 bogie, 9000-14, were given General repairs. Boiler, 5091/J3242, replaced by 1487/J2943. The body was given a General repair. The locomotive mileage was recorded as 684,540 miles.

Doncaster	28/03/66	31/03/66	Unclassified

Repairs were carried out to a defective header tank.

Doncaster	30/04/66	02/05/66	Unclassified

No.2 engine, 447, replaced by 456.

Doncaster	11/05/66	12/05/66	Unclassified

The locomotive was lifted for access to fractured axles. Boiler, 1487/J2943, had a safety valve fitted.

D9012/9012/55 012 Crepello (continued)

Loco Works	On Works	Off Works	Class of repair
Doncaster	30/09/66	10/10/66	Light

No.1 engine, 443, replaced by 416. No.2 engine, 456, was given an Unclassified repair. No.1 bogie, 9000-13, replaced by 9000-1. No.2 bogie, 9000-14, replaced by 9000-2. Boiler, 1487/J2943, was given an Unclassified repair. The body was given an Unclassified repair.

Doncaster	31/10/66	01/11/66	Unclassified

No.1 engine, 416, output shaft oil seal defective. This was repaired. Both bogies and all traction motors were examined and cleaned.

Doncaster	04/11/66	07/11/66	Unclassified

No.1 engine, 416, replaced by 447, due to a suspected piston defect.

Doncaster	19/01/67	19/01/67	Unclassified

Boiler tubes split. These were repaired.

Doncaster	07/02/67	02/03/67	General

No.1 engine, 447, replaced by 450. No.2 engine, 456, replaced by 446. No.1 bogie, 9000-1, replaced by 9000-5. No.2 bogie, 9000-2, replaced by 9000-6. Boiler, 1487/J2943, replaced by 1490/J2946. The body was given a General repair. Full yellow nose ends were applied.

Doncaster	02/05/67	03/05/67	Unclassified

No.1 engine, 450, replaced by 419, for examination by Napier representatives.

Doncaster	21/06/67	27/06/67	Unclassified

No.2 engine, 446, replaced by 455, due to phasing gear defective.

Doncaster	12/08/67	12/08/67	Unclassified

No.2 primary shaft was replaced and a new flange drive fitted.

Doncaster	09/10/67	14/10/67	Light

No.1 engine, 419 and No.2 engine, 455, were given Unclassified repairs. No.1 bogie, 9000-5, replaced by 9000-29. No.2 bogie, 9000-6, replaced by 9000-30. Boiler, 1490/J2946, was given an Unclassified repair. The body was given an Unclassified repair.

Doncaster	04/11/67	05/11/67	Unclassified

No.4 traction motor suspension tube moved. No.4 wheelset was replaced.

Doncaster	05/12/67	06/12/67	Unclassified

Defective speedometer. The speedometer generator on No.2 bogie was replaced.

Doncaster	12/02/68	20/03/68	General

*No.1 engine, 419, replaced by 447, due to coolant water pump shaft suspected fractured. No.2 engine, 455, was given an Unclassified repair. No.1 bogie, 9000-29, replaced by 9000-3. No.2 bogie, 9000-30, replaced by 9000-4. Boiler, 1490/J2946, replaced by 1494/J2950. The body was given a General repair and repainted into **blue livery with full yellow nose ends**. The locomotive was fitted for dual braking.*

Doncaster	10/06/68	13/06/68	Unclassified

No.2 engine, 455, replaced by 421, due to exhaust gas and coolant venting from header tank overflow pipe, suspect liner or exhaust manifold fracture. A vacuum brake fault was rectified.

Doncaster	15/10/68	23/10/68	Light

No.1 engine, 447, was given an Unclassified repair. No.2 engine, 421, replaced by 429, due to a broken con rod on 'A' bank. No.1 bogie, 9000-3, replaced by 9000-49. No.2 bogie, 9000-4, replaced by 9000-50. Boiler, 1494/J2950, was given an Unclassified repair. The body was given an Unclassified repair.

Doncaster	11/12/68	12/12/68	Unclassified

No.1 engine, 447, replaced by 442, due to 'A' bank crankcase holed. No.1 end lubricating oil radiators were replaced and lubricating oil tank flushed out.

Doncaster	09/01/69	09/01/69	Unclassified

No.2 engine, 429, replaced by 444.

Doncaster	03/02/69	04/02/69	Unclassified

No.1 engine, 442, replaced by 437, due to breathing badly both on and off load.

Doncaster	18/02/69	18/02/69	Unclassified

An oil leak in the roof section was repaired.

Doncaster	04/03/69	11/03/69	Unclassified

No.2 engine, 444, replaced by 434, due to coolant in sump, suspect 'AB' crankcase. Lubricating oil radiators were replaced.

D9012/9012/55 012 Crepello (continued)

Loco Works	On Works	Off Works	Class of repair
Doncaster	12/05/69	04/06/69	Intermediate

No.1 engine, 437, replaced by 451. No.2 engine, 434, replaced by 538. No.1 bogie, 9000-49 and No.2 bogie, 9000-50, were given General repairs. Boiler, 1494/J2950, replaced by 1493/J2949. The body was given an Intermediate repair.

Doncaster	30/01/70	07/02/70	Light

No.1 engine, 451, replaced by 538, due to requiring a Light repair. No.2 engine, 538, replaced by 451, due to radiator oil element leaking badly and requiring a Light repair. No.1 bogie, 9000-49, replaced by 9000-9. No.2 bogie, 9000-50, replaced by 9000-42. Boiler, 1493/J2949, was given an Unclassified repair. Right hand side body breaking up badly adjacent to nameplate and sand boxes. The body was given a Light repair and modified water tanks were fitted.

Doncaster	09/02/70	13/02/70	Rectification

Flashover damage to both main generators. This was repaired.

Doncaster	24/04/70	25/04/70	Unclassified

No.2 engine, 451, replaced by 431, due to a suspected fractured liner, coolant in sump. No.1 bogie, 9000-9, footsteps were secured and right hand leading brakeblock key checked.

Doncaster	19/05/70	22/05/70	Unclassified

No.1 engine, 538, replaced by 411. No.2 engine, 431, replaced by 435. No.1 bogie, 9000-9, No.1 wheelset and horn liners replaced. No.2 bogie, 900042 - No.6 wheelset - loose horn liners replaced.

Doncaster	27/05/70	30/05/70	Unclassified

No.2 engine, 435, replaced by 425. No.2 main generator replaced due to being down to earth

Doncaster	24/08/70	27/08/70	Unclassified

No.1 engine, 411, replaced by 420, due to 'B6' piston defective and No.1 silencer drum fractured. Bogie restraining slings were also renewed.

Doncaster	26/09/70	22/01/71	Intermediate

No.1 engine, 420, replaced by 444. No.2 engine, 425, replaced by 445. No.1 bogie, 9000-9, replaced by 9000-15. No.2 bogie, 9000-42, replaced by 9000-16. Boiler, 1493/J2949, replaced by 1488/J2944. The body was given an Intermediate repair. The loco was fitted with E.T.H. equipment.

Doncaster	26/01/71	26/01/71	Rectification

No.2 engine, 445, fuel starvation. The transfer pump was tested and the filter cleaned. Field divert faults were rectified.

Doncaster	06/03/71	07/03/71	Unclassified

No.1 engine, 444, replaced by 448, due to trace of water in lubricating oil and breathing heavy. No.2 engine, 445, replaced by 431, due to lead and coolant in lubricating oil and breathing heavy. Both cabs to be draughtproofed after serious complaints.

Doncaster	10/03/71	10/03/71	Rectification

Adjustments to No.2 engine, 431.

Doncaster	30/03/71	01/04/71	Unclassified

Flashover damage to traction motors and both main generators. All repaired and No.2 motor replaced.

Doncaster	20/04/71	21/04/71	Unclassified

No.2 engine, 431, replaced by 455. No.2 primary fan shaft was replaced. No.1 bogie, 9000-15, received attention to swing link pins and a sheared locking plate stud was replaced.

Doncaster	13/06/71	18/06/71	Unclassified

No.1 eng. 448, replaced by 404 - coolant in sump. No.2 eng. 455, replaced by 450 - coolant in sump.

Doncaster	29/07/71	04/08/71	Unclassified

No.1 main generator to earth. No.2 main generator to clean and all traction motors to be examined. Both main generators were replaced, as was No.3 traction motor.

Doncaster	21/08/71	26/08/71	Unclassified

All axles to undergo ultrasonic test after derailment damage. Bogies to be checked for correct alignment. Fire bottles to be renewed. The main steam pipe was repaired. No.1 bogie, 9000-15 and No.2 bogie, 9000-16, had derailment damage repaired.

Doncaster	17/09/71	21/09/71	Unclassified

No.1 engine, 404, revs to adjust and No.1 main generator commutator damaged and badly scored. No.2 engine, 450, revs to adjust and suspected earth leakage on No.2 main generator or traction motors. All necessary repairs were carried out. No.1 main generator was replaced, as were Nos.1 & 5 traction motors.

D9012/9012/55 012 Crepello (continued)

Loco Works	On Works	Off Works	Class of repair
Doncaster	10/11/71	11/11/71	Unclassified

No.1 engine, 404, 'A' bank fuel camshaft not being driven. 'A' bank cambox was replaced.

| Doncaster | 17/11/71 | 25/11/71 | Light |

Persistent flashovers. No.1 engine, 404 and No.2 engine, 450, were given Light repairs. No.1 bogie, 9000-15, replaced by 9000-11. No.2 bogie, 9000-16, replaced by 9000-12. Boiler, 1488/J2944, was given an Unclassified repair. The body was given a Light repair. All flashover damage rectified.

| Doncaster | 29/02/72 | 07/03/72 | Unclassified |

No.2 engine, 450, dephased. It was given an Intermediate repair and refitted.

| Doncaster | 24/03/72 | 28/03/72 | Unclassified |

No.2 engine, 450, replaced by 428.

| Doncaster | 13/04/72 | 13/04/72 | Unclassified |

No.1 engine, 404, sparge jet oil filter in 'BC' crankcase oil gallery stripped out. 'BC' sparge jet oil filter thread was repaired and a replacement high water temperature gauge was fitted.

| Doncaster | 21/04/72 | 25/04/72 | Unclassified |

No.1 engine, 404, 'B' bank fuel pump camshaft adrift. This was repaired. No.2 engine, 428, was load tested.

| Doncaster | 15/05/72 | 17/05/72 | Unclassified |

No.1 engine, 404, replaced by 416, due to a liner seal leaking.

| Doncaster | 23/05/72 | 26/05/72 | Unclassified |

Collision damage. No.2 nose end dented above heater cock, paintwork cracked and chipped. No.2 bogie, 9000-12, main reservoir pipe flattened, vacuum train pipe damaged, auto air brake pipe fractured and screw coupling guard bent. All damage was repaired and both bogies had bolster segments repaired.

| Doncaster | 30/06/72 | 05/07/72 | Unclassified |

No.1 main generator fire damaged. No.1 engine, 416, replaced by 406. Damaged traction motor cables were repaired. No.1 bogie, 9000-11, had No.3 traction motor replaced and brakegear repaired. No.2 bogie, 9000-12, also had brakegear repaired.

| Doncaster | 24/08/72 | 26/08/72 | Unclassified |

No.1 engine, 406, replaced by 414, due to a cracked cylinder liner.

| Doncaster | 28/10/72 | 25/11/72 | Intermediate |

No.1 engine, 414, replaced by 453. No.2 engine, 428, replaced by 434. No.1 bogie, 9000-11, replaced by 9000-24. No.2 bogie, 9000-12, replaced by 9000-48. Boiler, 1488/J2944, replaced by 1492/J2948. The body was given an Intermediate repair.

| Doncaster | 13/02/73 | 15/02/73 | Unclassified |

No.2 engine, 434, replaced by 412, due to being dephased.

| Doncaster | 21/06/73 | 26/06/73 | Unclassified |

No.2 engine, 412, replaced by 430, due to being dephased.

| Doncaster | 27/08/73 | 13/09/73 | Light |

No.1 engine, 453, replaced by 427. No.2 engine, 430, replaced by 435, due to primary cardan shaft adrift. Guards and engine damaged. No.1 bogie, 9000-24, replaced by 9000-39. No.2 bogie, 9000-48, replaced by 9000-40. Boiler, 1492/J2948, was given an Unclassified repair. The body was given a Light repair.

| Doncaster | 16/01/74 | 17/01/74 | Modification |

Earth fault relay modification was carried out.

| Doncaster | 25/03/74 | 30/03/74 | Unclassified |

No.2 engine, 435, replaced by 422, due to a con rod through crankcase.

| Doncaster | 14/06/74 | 05/07/74 | Unclassified |

No.2 engine, 422, replaced by 457, due to piston through crankcase. E.T.H. and temperature probe modifications were carried out and radiators and thermostat bypass valve replaced.

| Doncaster | 18/09/74 | 30/10/74 | Intermediate |

No.1 engine, 427, replaced by 419. No.2 engine, 457, replaced by 439. No.1 bogie, 9000-39 and No.2 bogie, 9000-40, were given standard repairs and refitted. Boiler, 1492/J2948, replaced by 5087/J3238. The body was given an Intermediate repair.

| Doncaster | 30/12/74 | 04/01/75 | Unclassified |

No.1 engine, 419, reported high water temperature. No.2 engine, 439, replaced by 442, due to suspected fractured liner.

D9012/9012/55 012 Crepello (continued)

Loco Works	On Works	Off Works	Class of repair
Doncaster	03/06/75	05/06/75	Rectification

No.1 engine, 419, replaced by 437, due to breathing heavy.

| Doncaster | 20/06/75 | 24/06/75 | Unclassified |

No.2 engine, 442, replaced by 429, due to a number of crankcase fractures between Nos.4 & 5 pistons, 'BC' crankcase, in an area with many previous welded repairs.

| Doncaster | 30/06/75 | 07/07/75 | Unclassified |

No.1 engine, 437, replaced by 539. No.2 engine, 429, replaced by 538, due to being dephased. No.1 traction motor had ducting fractures repaired.

| Doncaster | 08/07/75 | 09/07/75 | Rectification |

No.1 blower motor vibrating badly. This was replaced.

| Doncaster | 11/09/75 | 12/09/75 | Unclassified |

No.2 engine, 538, replaced by 453, due to being dephased.

| Doncaster | 20/10/75 | 22/10/75 | Unclassified |

No.1 engine, 539, replaced by 440, due to suspected dephased, heavy smoke from exhaust and strange noises from 'A' bank. Intermittent fault when the compressors cut out at 140 psi. A boiler water tank was repaired. Both bogies had nose suspension plates repaired, bolster segments replaced and swing link studs renewed.

| Doncaster | 18/11/75 | 01/12/75 | Light |

No.1 engine, 440 and No.2 engine, 453, were given Light repairs. No.1 bogie, 9000-39, replaced by 9000-29. No.2 bogie, 9000-40, replaced by 9000-10. Boiler, 5087/J3238, was given an Unclassified repair. The body was given a Light repair. The locomotive was weighed at 101t 15cwt.

| Doncaster | 12/12/75 | 13/12/75 | Rectification |

No.1 end drivers side door and frame distorted. This was rectified.

| Doncaster | 06/01/76 | 26/01/76 | Unclassified |

No.1 engine, 440, replaced by 437. No.2 engine, 453, replaced by 448, due to 'BC' crankcase damper housing fractured.

| Doncaster | 19/03/76 | 08/04/76 | Unclassified |

No.1 engine, 437, replaced by 413. No.2 engine, 448, replaced by 416, due to piston through crankcase. Both lubricating oil tanks and radiators were cleaned.

| Doncaster | 09/10/76 | 10/10/76 | Unclassified |

No.2 boiler water tank holed. This was repaired.

| Doncaster | 23/10/76 | 26/10/76 | Unclassified |

No.1 engine, 413, replaced by 455, due to high spectrographic analysis and breathing heavy. No.2 engine, 416, replaced by 451, due to high spectrographic analysis and breathing heavy.

| Doncaster | 20/12/76 | 27/04/77 | Intermediate |

No.1 engine, 455, replaced by 416. No.2 engine, 451, replaced by 538. No.1 bogie, 9000-29 and 9000-10, were given standard repairs. Boiler, 5087/J3238, was given a standard repair. Experiment DL/543 was fitted "Electrically operated windscreen washer pump". The body was given an Intermediate repair. Route indicators were plated over. The loco weighed 104t 11cwt.

| Doncaster | 14/06/77 | 16/06/77 | Rectification |

No.2 engine, 538, fuel racks vibrating badly on full load, suspect engine governor defective and No.1 bogie, 9000-29, rough riding, three shock absorbers defective. An exchange governor was fitted and all horn liners were checked and secured on No.1 bogie.

| Doncaster | 23/07/77 | 28/07/77 | Unclassified |

Rough riding, several dampers reported defective. All dampers removed and sent for testing. Both bogies were rectified. The locomotive was weighed at 103t 13cwt.

| Doncaster | 10/08/77 | 16/08/77 | Unclassified |

Very rough riding at No.2 end. Noted that the locomotive is not fit for main line work in excess of 60 mph. The suspension on both bogies was overhauled. The locomotive was weighed at 104t 4cwt.

| Doncaster | 19/08/77 | 31/08/77 | Unclassified |

Rough riding at 80 mph and above. No.1 bogie, 9000-29, replaced by 9000-31. No.2 bogie, 9000-10, replaced by 9000-32. The locomotive was weighed at 104t 10cwt.

| Doncaster | 17/12/77 | 22/12/77 | Unclassified |

No.1 boiler water tank fractured under skin in three places. Centre pivot studs and nuts require renewal. No.1 fan primary shaft drive worn. Both secondman's sliding window catches to repair. All defects were rectified.

D9012/9012/55 012 Crepello (continued)

Loco Works	On Works	Off Works	Class of repair
Doncaster	19/01/78	21/01/78	Unclassified

No.2 engine, 538, replaced by 457, due to aerating badly, losing coolant and Dowty pump quill shaft to renew. Primary fan drive replaced.

Doncaster	23/01/78	24/01/78	Rectification

Battery ammeter showing discharge with No.2 engine, 457, running. The battery charging system was rectified.

Doncaster	16/03/78	22/03/78	Unclassified

No.1 engine, 416, replaced by 405, due to a suspected fractured liner. No.2 engine, 457, 'B' bank exhaust bellows replaced. No.2 boiler water tank had repairs to outer skin.

Doncaster	08/06/78	15/06/78	Unclassified

No.1 engine, 405, replaced by 451, due to con rod through 'BC' crankcase. No.2 engine, 457, had a gudgeon pin housing examination. No.2 boiler water tank had a leak rectified. No.1 coolant radiators were cleaned.

Doncaster	04/09/78	06/09/78	Unclassified

No.1 engine, 451, replaced by 442, due to 'CA' crankcase holed. Also cardan shaft and clutch was loose. Windscreen wiper linkage at both ends needed renewal. No.1 bogie, 9000-31, No.1 right hand leading axle box liner was loose. All defects were rectified.

Doncaster	28/10/78	31/10/78	Unclassified

No.2 engine, 457, replaced by 455, due to being time expired. No.2 load regulator had an oil leak rectified.

Doncaster	02/11/78	02/11/78	Rectification

No.2 engine, 455, scavenge pump defective. Sump drainpipe found adrift. These defects were rectified.

Doncaster	01/03/79	31/03/79	Light

No.1 engine, 442, replaced by 429. No.2 engine, 455, replaced by 425, due to being dephased. No.1 bogie, 9000-31, replaced by 9000-45. No.2 bogie, 9000-32, replaced by 9000-46. Boiler, 5087/J3238, was given an Unclassified repair. All traction motors were replaced.

Doncaster	02/04/79	07/04/79	Rectification

Loss of power. This was rectified. The locomotive was weighed at 106t 5cwt.

Doncaster	12/04/79	13/04/79	Rectification

No.1 end cut out switch burnt out. Both load regulators leaking oil. Oil to be cleaned from back of No.2 cubicle. No.2 bogie, 9000-46, No.4 traction motor throwing solder — foreign body found in machine. All traction motor sealing ducting contaminated with oil. No.4 traction motor was replaced. All defects were rectified.

Doncaster	24/04/79	02/05/79	Unclassified

No.1 engine, 429, replaced by 435, due to 'C2' piston through crankcase. No.2 engine, 425, reported high water temperature. Boiler, 5087/J3238, reported locking out. Both load regulators leaking oil. All defects were rectified.

Doncaster	05/06/79	13/06/79	Rectification

No.1 engine, 435, engine hours recorder full of oil. The recorder was replaced. No.2 engine, 425, drive shaft to main generator sheared. A replacement phasing case was fitted. No.2 main generator had flashover damage and was replaced.

Doncaster	12/07/79	13/07/79	Unclassified

Fault in earth detection unit. Not picking up above earth thus causing main generators and traction motors to flashover. The power earth fault protection resistance was replaced and earth fault relay adjusted.

Doncaster	19/07/79	26/07/79	Unclassified

Both main generators and all traction motors to be checked for flashover damage. Earth fault relay rechecked, adjusted and resistance replaced. No.1 main generator overhauled to three monthly standard. No.2 main generator was replaced. Nos. 1, 2, 5 & 6 traction motors were repaired. Nos.3 & 4 traction motors were replaced. The locomotive was weighed at 105t 6cwt.

Doncaster	28/07/79	10/08/79	Rectification

No.2 main generator flashed over badly. Commutator blackened under No.2 bogie, 9000-46. No.1 main generator also flashed over. Flashover damage on both bogies was repaired. Field divert resistances were repaired. Both main generators and all traction motors were overhauled.

D9012/9012/55 012 Crepello (continued)

Loco Works	On Works	Off Works	Class of repair
Doncaster	15/08/79	30/08/79	Unclassified

Both main generators and all traction motors severe flashover damage. All traction motors removed and a reconditioned set fitted. All circuits were meggered, meter boards fitted for trial. No.1 main generator was replaced.

Doncaster	03/09/79	09/09/79	Rectification

Severe flashover damage to No.2 main generator. Cause of flashover problems to be investigated. E.T.H. contactors and circuitry to be checked. Function of E.T.H. to be checked on load bank. Locomotive weights to be checked on weighbridge. On completion of repairs a test to be arranged. Test meters to be incorporated in circuits to indicate out of balance voltage, main generator voltage and E.T.H. voltage. No.1 main generator was overhauled. No.2 main generator was replaced. The locomotive was weighed at 106t 3cwt.

Doncaster	12/09/79	14/09/79	Unclassified

No.3 traction motor contactor continually dropping out. Circuits to be checked. Test lamps to be put on locomotive and load bank test to be run. The air pipe to motor contactor was repaired. Interlocks in motor circuit were checked and adjusted. The locomotive was load tested and a fully loaded test run completed.

Doncaster	16/01/80	22/01/80	Unclassified

No.2 engine, 425, replaced by 421, due to suspect fractured liner. Boiler water tank leaking and both load regulators leaking. These defects were rectified.

Doncaster	20/05/80	22/05/80	Unclassified

No.1 engine, 435, replaced by 434, due to being dephased. No.2 engine, 421, was given a replacement engine hour recorder and the radiator fan was loose on the shaft at No.2 end. This was secured.

Doncaster	05/06/80	10/06/80	Rectification

No.1 engine, 434, auxiliary generator connector box burnt out and cables burnt. The auxiliary generator was replaced. No.1 radiator roof fan on secondary gearbox needed repair, both load regulators had oil leaks and engine room floor required cleaning. All repairs carried out.

Doncaster	21/08/80	27/08/80	Unclassified

No.1 engine, 434, unable to get power, it was given an Unclassified repair. No.1 main generator separate field open circuit. The main generator was replaced. The locomotive was weighed at 105t 5cwt.

Doncaster	17/09/80	23/09/80	Rectification

No.1 main generator interpole burnt out. No.1 engine, 434, replaced by 413. The locomotive had suffered three flashovers in one week. All traction motors had flashover damage. No.1 main generator was replaced. The locomotive was load bank tested.

Doncaster	29/09/80	22/10/80	Unclassified

Flashover damage. Wheelslip relays to be checked. Both main generators and all traction motors flashed over. Reported intermittent wheelslip indications. All components were checked, repaired as necessary and tested.

Doncaster	24/10/80	29/10/80	Rectification

Rectification of flashover damage on both main generators and all traction motors. 'M1' contactor was renewed.

Doncaster	15/12/80	18/12/80	Unclassified

No.2 engine, 421, replaced by 438, due to aerating badly, suspected fractured liner.

Doncaster	13/04/81	24/04/81	Unclassified

No.1 engine, 413, replaced by 419, due to suspect dephased. No.2 cab secondman's window broken and flashover damage to No.2 main generator. The broken window and flashover damage were marked for depot attention.

Doncaster	15/06/81	-	-

The locomotive arrived on Works after withdrawal with the following main components fitted. No.1 engine, 419. No.2 engine, 438. No.1 bogie, 9000-45. No.2 bogie, 9000-46. Boiler, 5087/J3238.

D9013/9013/55 013 The Black Watch

Loco Works	On Works	Off Works	Class of repair
Doncaster	14/09/61	Not recorded	Acceptance trials

New locomotive fitted with the following main components. No.1 engine, 436 (not confirmed). No.2 engine, 412 (not confirmed). No.1 bogie, 1027. No.2 bogie, 1028. Boiler, 5089/J3240.

Doncaster	21/03/62	22/03/62	Light

No.1 bogie, 1027, replaced by 1015, due to headstock rivets loose. No.2 bogie, 1028, replaced by 1016. No.1 water tank was removed, welded, tested and refitted.

R.S.H. Darlington	03/04/62	01/05/62	Unclassified

No.1 engine, 436, replaced by 431. No.2 engine, 412, replaced by 436, due to fan gearbox defective.

Doncaster	12/09/62	23/09/62	General

No.1 engine, 431, replaced by 423. No.2 engine, 436, replaced by 447. No.1 bogie, 1015 and No.2 bogie, 1016, were modified with stiffening plates. Boiler, 5089/J3240, replaced by 1489/J2945. A modified type of flexible exhaust pipes was fitted. The body was given an annual repair.

Doncaster	10/11/62	10/11/62	Unclassified

Flashover damage on all traction motors. No.1 bogie, 1015, inner headstock fractured. 'Vee' ring tapes damaged. Both main generators flashed over and oil on No.2 main generator. All defects were rectified. The locomotive mileage was recorded as 162,150 miles.

Doncaster	11/12/62	13/12/62	Unclassified

No.1 bogie, 1015, replaced by 1009. No.2 bogie, 1016, replaced by 1010. No.2 water coolant radiator was replaced.

Doncaster	20/12/62	20/12/62	Unclassified

No.2 engine, 447, radiator leaking 'A' bank. No.2 right hand coolant radiator was replaced. The locomotive mileage was recorded as 178,600 miles.

Doncaster	02/01/63	09/01/63	Unclassified

No.1 engine, 423, had a new flexible drive shaft fitted. No.1 exhaust collector tank inspection lid was rejointed and new studs fitted.

Doncaster	11/03/63	12/03/63	Unclassified

No.1 bogie, 1009, replaced by 1025. No.2 bogie, 1010, replaced by 1018.

Doncaster	25/03/63	28/03/63	Light

No.1 bogie, 1025, replaced by 1019. No.2 bogie, 1018, replaced by 1020. The body was given a six monthly examination. Modifications were carried out to exhaust drum drainpipes.

Doncaster	11/04/63	11/04/63	Unclassified

No.1 engine, 423, replaced by 413, due to drive shaft broken. The loco mileage was 238,210 miles.

Doncaster	22/05/63	22/05/63	Unclassified

Water tank split. No.2 boiler water tank was replaced. The locomotive mileage was 260,380 miles.

Doncaster	23/09/63	07/10/63	General

Both left hand side intermediate horn guide liners loose and others to be examined. No.1 engine, 413, replaced by 451. No.2 engine, 447, replaced by 444. No.1 bogie, 1019 and No.2 bogie, 1020, were overhauled. Boiler, 1489/J2945, replaced by 5090/J3241. The body was given an annual repair. The following modifications were carried out — Boiler caustic injection; Air ducting; Automatic blowdown valve; Cab soundproofing; Draught sealing; Low water contents gauge; Header tank overflow tank. The locomotive mileage was recorded as 336,240 miles.

Doncaster	28/01/64	28/01/64	Unclassified

No.1 bogie, 1019, replaced by 1015. No.2 bogie, 1020, replaced by 1016.

Doncaster	08/04/64	14/04/64	Light

No.1 engine, 451 and No.2 engine, 444, were given MP11 exams. No.1 bogie, 1015, replaced by 1023. No.2 bogie, 1016, replaced by 1024. Boiler, 5090/J3241, was given a six monthly repair. Bodyside fractures were welded. Both main generators and auxiliary generators were cleaned out and new brushes and insulators fitted as required. The following modifications were carried out — Anti frost precautions; Lagging of pipes; Bogie transoms; Speedometer clocks; Boiler fuses.

Doncaster	27/05/64	28/05/64	Unclassified

No.1 engine, 451 and No.2 engine, 444, were given MP11 exams. No.1 bogie, 1023, headstock rivets loose. These were renewed on the outer left hand side. No.2 bogie, 1024, had shock absorber bolt missing between Nos.4 & 5 traction motors. No.5 traction motor suspension spring was renewed. Boiler, 5090/J3241, was given an MP11 exam. All traction motors and both main and auxiliary generators were cleaned out and had new brushes fitted where necessary.

D9013/9013/55 013 The Black Watch (continued)

Loco Works	On Works	Off Works	Class of repair
Doncaster	08/08/64	12/08/64	Unclassified

No.1 engine, 451, replaced by 408. No.2 engine, 444, replaced by 454.

| Doncaster | 30/09/64 | 03/10/64 | Unclassified |

No.1 engine, 408, and No.2 engine, 454, were given MP11 exams. No.1 bogie, 1023, was given a Light repair. No.2 bogie, 1024, had a horn liner welded. Boiler, 5090/J3241, was given an MP11 exam. Both main generators and all traction motors were cleaned.

| Doncaster | 21/11/64 | 17/12/64 | General |

No.1 engine, 408, replaced by 457. No.2 engine, 454, replaced by 407. No.1 bogie, 1023, replaced by 1039. No.2 bogie, 1024, replaced by 1040. Boiler, 5090/J3241, replaced by 5093/J3244.

| Doncaster | 12/01/65 | 12/01/65 | Unclassified |

Exhauster replacement. This was done.

| Doncaster | 30/04/65 | 06/05/65 | Light |

No.1 engine, 457 and No.2 engine, 407, were given MP11 exams. No.1 bogie, 1039, replaced by 1023. No.2 bogie, 1040, replaced by 1024. Boiler, 5093/J3244, was given an MP11 exam. Both main and auxiliary generators were cleaned out and new brushes were fitted. No.2 end lubricating oil radiators were replaced. Collision damage to the left hand bodyside was repaired.

| Doncaster | 10/05/65 | 18/05/65 | Unclassified |

Water coolant radiators were replaced. The locomotive was run up and water coolant temperatures checked.

| Doncaster | 21/06/65 | 21/06/65 | Unclassified |

No.2 end fire damage, air intake and one fire bottle discharged. Repairs were carried out to the bodyside air ducting, air filters and exhaust silencer bellows. The boiler roof was repainted.

| Doncaster | 12/07/65 | 13/07/65 | Unclassified |

No.1 engine, 457, replaced by 435, due to 'CA' crankshaft dephased. Boiler, 5093/J3244, had a new "NUWAY" burner fitted. The locomotive mileage was recorded as 100,490 miles.

| Doncaster | 19/07/65 | 21/07/65 | Unclassified |

No.1 engine, 435, replaced by 539, due to 'CA' crankshaft dephased. No.1 bogie, 1023, replaced by 9000-7. No.2 bogie, 1024, replaced by 9000-8. The loco mileage was recorded as 102,010 miles.

| Doncaster | 14/08/65 | 17/08/65 | Unclassified |

Coolant radiators were replaced. The locomotive mileage was recorded as 112,540 miles.

| Doncaster | 08/02/66 | 22/02/66 | General |

No.1 engine, 539, was given an Unclassified repair. No.2 engine, 407, replaced by 422. No.1 bogie, 9000-7, replaced by 9000-27. No.2 bogie, 9000-8, replaced by 9000-28. Boiler, 5093/J3244, replaced by 1486/J2942. The body was given a General repair. The loco mileage 200,420 miles.

| Doncaster | 24/04/66 | 29/04/66 | Unclassified |

No.1 engine, 539, replaced by 448, due to con rod adrift, crankcase and liner fractured. No.1 secondary and No.2 primary fan shafts were replaced and the main fuel tank and steam pipe repaired. Nos.1 & 6 wheelsets, which were fractured, were replaced.

| Doncaster | 02/05/66 | 04/05/66 | Unclassified |

No.2 bogie, 9000-28, derailment damage, sand pipe, brakework and rail guards damaged. The damage was repaired. No.1 bogie, 9000-27, had thimbles resoldered on No.2 traction motor cables.

| Doncaster | 21/05/66 | 24/05/66 | Unclassified |

No.2 engine, 422, replaced by 425.

| Doncaster | 15/09/66 | 23/09/66 | Light |

No.1 engine, 448, replaced by 445. No.2 engine, 425, replaced by 457. No.1 bogie, 9000-27, replaced by 9000-19. No.2 bogie, 9000-28, replaced by 9000-20. Boiler, 1486/J2942, was given an Unclassified repair. The body was given an Unclassified repair.

| Doncaster | 14/12/66 | 15/12/66 | Unclassified |

Boiler, 1486/J2942, replaced by 5097/J3248.

| Doncaster | 02/01/67 | 27/01/67 | General |

No.1 engine, 445, replaced by 434. No.2 engine, 457, replaced by 454. No.1 bogie, 9000-19 and No.2 bogie, 9000-20, were given General repairs. The body was given a General repair. Full yellow nose ends were applied.

D9013/9013/55 013 The Black Watch (continued)

Loco Works	On Works	Off Works	Class of repair
Doncaster	13/04/67	19/04/67	Unclassified

No.1 engine, 434, replaced by 410, due to aerating. No.2 exhaust silencer was replaced as were No.1 end lubricating oil elements. The interior lights intermediate switch link wire was renewed and other burnt wires were taped up until next repair. No.2 main generator had flashover damage cleaned up.

Doncaster	07/06/67	08/06/67	Unclassified

No.2 primary fan gearbox defective. This was replaced.

Doncaster	08/08/67	09/08/67	Unclassified

No.1 bogie, 9000-19, replaced by 9000-7, due to No.2 traction motor suspension bearing distance piece loose, studs sheared. No.2 bogie, 9000-20, replaced by 9000-8.

Doncaster	20/11/67	18/12/67	General

No.1 engine, 410, replaced by 433. No.2 engine, 454, replaced by 437. No.1 bogie, 9000-7, replaced by 9000-41. No.2 bogie, 9000-8, replaced by 9000-42. Boiler, 5097/J3248, replaced by 1488/J2944. The body was given a General repair and repainted into **blue livery with full yellow nose ends**. *The locomotive was fitted for dual braking.*

Doncaster	03/05/68	03/05/68	Unclassified

No.2 boiler water tank punctured. The tank was replaced.

Doncaster	13/05/68	17/05/68	Light

No.1 engine, 433 and No.2 engine, 437, were given Unclassified repairs. No.1 bogie, 9000-41, replaced by 9000-9. No.2 bogie, 9000-42, replaced by 9000-10. Boiler, 1488/J2944, was given an Unclassified repair. The body was given an Unclassified repair.

Doncaster	05/08/68	06/08/68	Unclassified

A fractured boiler water tank. The tank was replaced.

Doncaster	25/10/68	25/10/68	Unclassified

Control earth fault, circuit breaker continually tripping. This was rectified.

Doncaster	18/12/68	20/12/68	Unclassified

Flashover damage to both main generators. No.2 engine, 437, replaced by 440. No.1 main generator was repaired. No.2 main and auxiliary generators were replaced. Both bogies had flashover damage cleaned up.

Doncaster	23/12/68	23/12/68	Unclassified

No.2 engine, 440, replaced by 428, due to scavenge blower defective, complete engine overspeed unit required as this had been taken for 9015.

Doncaster	09/01/69	31/01/69	Intermediate

No.1 engine, 433, replaced by 429. No.2 engine, 428, replaced by 458. No.1 bogie, 9000-9, replaced by 9000-29. No.2 bogie, 9000-10, replaced by 9000-30. Boiler, 1488/J2944, replaced by 1492/J2948. The body was given an Intermediate repair.

Doncaster	13/08/69	14/08/69	Unclassified

No.1 engine, 429, replaced by 437. Radiators were removed, flushed out and refitted.

Doncaster	03/10/69	04/10/69	Unclassified

A replacement water tank was fitted.

Doncaster	20/10/69	28/10/69	Light

Bad flashover damage to both main generators and traction motors. No.1 engine, 437, was given an Unclassified repair. No.2 engine, 458, replaced by 421. No.1 bogie, 9000-29, replaced by 9000-25. No.2 bogie, 9000-30, replaced by 9000-26. Boiler, 1492/J2948, was given an Unclassified repair. The body was given an Unclassified repair and the water tank modification was carried out.

Doncaster	29/10/69	30/10/69	Rectification

Bad flashover damage, all traction motors to be checked and reason for flashover to be determined.

Doncaster	04/11/69	06/11/69	Rectification

Field divert contactors were realigned and checked and load regulators adjusted. The governor on No.1 engine, 437, was replaced and racks reset.

Doncaster	26/02/70	27/02/70	Unclassified

No.1 bogie, 9000-25, replaced by 9000-19, due to rough riding. No.2 bogie, 9000-26, replaced by 9000-20, due to rough riding.

Doncaster	23/03/70	25/03/70	Unclassified

No.5 traction motor to be replaced. This was done and all traction motor brushes were renewed.

D9013/9013/55 013 The Black Watch (continued)

Loco Works	On Works	Off Works	Class of repair
Doncaster	25/03/70	26/03/70	Unclassified

No.2 engine, 421, replaced by 455.

| Doncaster | 04/04/70 | 04/04/70 | Rectification |

No.2 engine, 455, had a governor replaced.

| Doncaster | 08/05/70 | 10/05/70 | Unclassified |

No.1 engine, 437, replaced by 425, due to 'B6' piston seized and crankcase holed. Lubricating oil tank and radiators were cleaned.

| Doncaster | 27/05/70 | 18/06/70 | Intermediate |

No.1 engine, 425, replaced by 441. No.2 engine, 455, replaced by 436. No.1 bogie, 9000-19 and No.2 bogie, 9000-20, were given General repairs. Boiler, 1492/J2948, replaced by 5089/J3240. The body was given an Intermediate repair.

| Doncaster | 07/07/70 | 09/07/70 | Unclassified |

No.2 engine, 436, replaced by 417, due to primary cardan shaft defective.

| Doncaster | 07/09/70 | 15/09/70 | Unclassified |

No.2 main generator windings burnt. The main generator was replaced. No.5 traction motor was also replaced.

| Doncaster | 09/10/70 | 10/10/70 | Unclassified |

Oil to be cleaned from locomotive interior. No.2 engine, 417, leak from cambox drive oil feed on 'C' bank. All repairs were carried out.

| Doncaster | 17/10/70 | 18/10/70 | Unclassified |

No.2 engine, 417, replaced by 413, due to 'B' bank piston through crankcase. Lubricating oil tank and radiators were cleaned.

| Doncaster | 02/11/70 | 04/11/70 | Unclassified |

No.2 engine, 413, replaced by 451, due to suspected fractured liner. Batteries unable to hold charge.

| Doncaster | 19/11/70 | 22/11/70 | Unclassified |

Both exhaust drums fire damaged and water pumped in by Fire Brigade. No.1 drum also fractured. Both were removed and repaired.

| Doncaster | 24/11/70 | 24/11/70 | Unclassified |

Load bank test. This was done.

| Doncaster | 25/11/70 | 10/12/70 | Unclassified |

No.1 engine, 441, replaced by 425, due to loss of power. No.2 engine, 451, replaced by 420.

| Doncaster | 02/01/71 | 07/01/71 | Unclassified |

No.1 engine, 425, replaced by 456, due to aerating, suspected fractured liner.

| Doncaster | 09/01/71 | 15/05/71 | Light |

Nos.1 & 6 traction motors isolated. No.1 engine, 456, replaced by 421. No.2 engine, 420, replaced by 453, due to being full of coolant. No.1 bogie, 9000-19, replaced by 9000-47. No.2 bogie, 9000-20, replaced by 9000-22. Boiler, 5089/J3240, was given an Unclassified repair. The body was given a Light repair. The locomotive was fitted with E.T.H. equipment.

| Doncaster | 24/05/71 | 30/06/71 | Unclassified |

No.1 engine, 421, replaced by 429. No.2 engine, 453, replaced by 438. Damaged wiring in No.1 control cubicle was replaced.

| Doncaster | 02/07/71 | 04/07/71 | Rectification |

No.1 engine, 429, had the governor changed.

| Doncaster | 15/09/71 | 17/09/71 | Unclassified |

Jumper plugs and sockets were replaced and the main steam pipe renewed at No.2 end.

| Doncaster | 29/10/71 | 04/11/71 | Unclassified |

No.1 engine, 429, replaced by 457, due to damaged piston and crankcase. No.2 boiler water tank leaking and No.1 left hand side horn trumpet to repair. All repairs were carried out.

| Doncaster | 08/11/71 | 19/11/71 | Unclassified |

No.1 engine, 457, replaced by 437. No.2 engine, 438, replaced by 447, due to being dephased. Desk light on when controller off both ends. This was rectified.

| Doncaster | 23/12/71 | 24/12/71 | Unclassified |

No.1 engine, 437, high crankcase pressure and coolant header tank fractured. No.1 header tank and No.2 end fan clutch were repaired.

D9013/9013/55 013 The Black Watch (continued)

Loco Works	On Works	Off Works	Class of repair
Doncaster	14/01/72	22/01/72	Unclassified

Repeated complaints about draughts in cabs. Doors at both ends to be made tight fit with body draughtproofing to be brought up to present standards. No.1 left hand main fuel tank was repaired and cab draughtproofing carried out to nose end doors. All wheelsets on both bogies were replaced.

Doncaster	21/02/72	24/02/72	Unclassified

No.1 engine, 437, replaced by 432. No.1 end lubricating oil tank and radiators were cleaned.

Doncaster	01/03/72	03/03/72	Unclassified

No.2 bogie, 9000-22, guard irons at No.2 end to replace, No.4 traction motor gearcase smashed and field winding belt sheared off. No.2 end boiler water tank holed, this was repaired. No.1 bogie, 9000-47, had bolster segments replaced and ground up and swing link pin studs replaced. No.4 traction motor and gearcase were also replaced.

Doncaster	10/03/72	11/03/72	Unclassified

No.1 engine, 432, suspect liner seal leaking inlet end. Excessive power from both engines in notch 1. No.1 engine, 432, was part dismantled to investigate the leaking liner seal and a load check was carried out.

Doncaster	24/04/72	05/08/72	Intermediate

No.1 engine, 432, replaced by 439. No.2 engine, 447, replaced by 405. No.1 bogie, 9000-47, replaced by 9000-23. No.2 bogie, 9000-22, replaced by 9000-30. Boiler, 5089/J3240, replaced by 5091/J3242. The body was given an Intermediate repair.

Doncaster	01/09/72	04/09/72	Unclassified

No.1 engine, 439, replaced by 420.

Doncaster	06/09/72	08/09/72	Unclassified

Earth fault on No.1 traction motor. Insulation on No.1 main generator was repaired. No.1 traction motor was replaced.

Doncaster	24/04/73	26/04/73	Unclassified

No.2 engine, 405, replaced by 415, due to 'CA' crankcase tie bolt broken between 5 & 6 bearings. No.2 boiler water tank was repaired and No.2 fan gearbox replaced.

Doncaster	15/05/73	19/05/73	Light

No.1 engine, 420, replaced by 406. No.1 bogie, 9000-23, replaced by 9000-19. No.2 bogie, 9000-30, replaced by 9000-20. Boiler, 5091/J3242, given Unclassified repair. Body given a Light repair.

Doncaster	21/05/73	24/05/73	Rectification

Nos.3 & 5 traction motors were replaced.

Doncaster	14/09/73	18/09/73	Unclassified

No.1 engine, 406, replaced by 446, due to breathing heavy.

Doncaster	11/10/73	19/10/73	Unclassified

No.2 engine, 415, replaced by 455, due to throwing oil. Lubricating oil tank and radiators were replaced.

Doncaster	25/01/74	25/01/74	Modification

Earth fault relay modification carried out.

Doncaster	29/01/74	28/02/74	Intermediate

No.1 engine, 446, replaced by 424. No.2 engine, 455, replaced by 410. No.1 bogie, 9000-19, replaced by 9000-45. No.2 bogie, 9000-20, replaced by 9000-46. Boiler, 5091/J3242, replaced by 5088/J3239. Regimental crests were to be replaced and cabs to be draughtproofed. The body was given an Intermediate repair.

Doncaster	08/07/74	11/07/74	Unclassified

No.2 engine, 410, replaced by 414, due to being dephased. No.1 boiler water tank was repaired, as was No.1 right hand cab footstep. E.T.H. and temperature probe modifications were carried out.

Doncaster	27/07/74	01/08/74	Unclassified

No.1 engine, 424, replaced by 405, due to con rod broken and crankcase holed.

Doncaster	31/12/74	08/01/75	Unclassified

No.1 engine, 405, replaced by 410, due to crankcase holed. No.1 end boiler water tank was repaired. No.1 end lubricating oil tank and radiators were cleaned. E.T.H. operation was checked on the load bank.

D9013/9013/55 013 The Black Watch (continued)

Loco Works	On Works	Off Works	Class of repair
Doncaster	20/01/75	09/05/75	Light

No.1 engine, 410, replaced by 418. No.2 engine, 414, replaced by 411, due to a suspected fractured liner. No.1 bogie, 9000-45, replaced by 9000-49. No.2 bogie, 9000-46, replaced by 9000-50. Boiler, 5088/J3239, was given an Unclassified repair or replaced.

| Doncaster | 19/05/75 | 22/05/75 | Unclassified |

No.1 engine, 418, replaced by 426, due to a suspected fractured liner.

| Doncaster | 03/07/75 | 05/07/75 | Unclassified |

No.2 engine, 411, replaced by 436. No.1 boiler water tank was replaced.

| Doncaster | 22/07/75 | 30/07/75 | Unclassified |

No.2 engine, 436, dephased and was given an Intermediate repair.

| Doncaster | 19/08/75 | 20/08/75 | Unclassified |

Right hand fuel tank fractured at bottom inspection cover. Floor fractured in engine room at 'L1' boiler foot. The fuel tank was replaced and all other repairs were carried out.

| Doncaster | 30/08/75 | 03/09/75 | Unclassified |

No.1 main generator interpole to earth and Nos.4 & 5 traction motors contaminated with lubricating oil. Both traction motors and No.1 main generator were replaced.

| Doncaster | 08/09/75 | 09/09/75 | Unclassified |

No.1 engine, 426, replaced by 417, due to a suspected fractured liner.

| Doncaster | 27/01/76 | 29/01/76 | Unclassified |

No.2 engine, 436, replaced by 418, due to being dephased. Exhaust outlet elbow fractured.

| Doncaster | 03/02/76 | 07/02/76 | Unclassified |

No.1 engine, 417, replaced by 457, due to 'CA' crankcase through bolt broken.

| Doncaster | 25/03/76 | 26/03/76 | Unclassified |

No.2 engine, 418, replaced by 432, due to a suspected fractured liner. Body damage was also repaired.

| Doncaster | 12/04/76 | 15/04/76 | Unclassified |

No.2 engine, 432, replaced by 405. No.2 end lubricating oil tank and radiators were cleaned.

| Doncaster | 25/05/76 | 12/12/76 | Heavy General |

Shopped with collision damage. No.2 buffer beam distorted and buffers damaged. No.2 E.T.H. junction box and cable to be repaired. No.1 engine mountings to examine. All damage was repaired. No.1 engine, 457, replaced by 446. No.2 engine, 405, replaced by 414. No.1 bogie, 9000-49, replaced by 9000-33. No.2 bogie, 9000-50, replaced by 9000-34. Boiler, (unknown), replaced by 5098/J3249. Route indicator panels plated over. The locomotive was weighed at 104t 5cwt.

| Doncaster | 05/01/77 | 07/01/77 | Unclassified |

No.3 traction motor and wheelset to be renewed due to worn pinion and gearwheel teeth. These were renewed. No.1 engine, 446, had injectors changed to rectify fuel dilution. The locomotive was weighed at 102t 11cwt.

| Doncaster | 10/02/77 | 11/02/77 | Unclassified |

No.2 engine, 414, dephased. No repair is shown in the file.

| Doncaster | 26/02/77 | 07/03/77 | Rectification |

No.1 engine, 446, fuel dilution. This was rectified.

| Doncaster | 07/03/77 | 08/03/77 | Unclassified |

Window washer bottles fitted as per Engineering Instruction G/1684.

| Doncaster | 30/04/77 | 02/05/77 | Unclassified |

No.1 boiler water tank split. No.2 end right hand side engine room double doorframe to secure and door catch to fit. Both bogies had right hand side footsteps secured.

| Doncaster | 13/05/77 | 21/07/77 | Unclassified |

Derailment damage. No.1 engine, 446, replaced by 442. No.2 engine, 414, was donated to 55 002 so it could return to traffic and then later returned to the No.2 position. No.2 end E.T.H. jumper cable junction box and conduit broken. No.1 bogie, 9000-33, had lifeguards to renew, No.1 vacuum pipe damaged below nose end and side check ferodo pads and brackets damaged. No.2 bogie, 9000-34, had steam heater pipe damaged, screw coupling to renew, side check ferodo pads and brackets damaged and No.2 left footstep broken. No.1 traction motor had cable conduit damaged. No.2 had suspension bearing cap bolt loose. No.6 traction motor had a suspension bolt loose. All damage was repaired and new tyres were fitted.

D9013/9013/55 013 The Black Watch (continued)

Loco Works	On Works	Off Works	Class of repair
Doncaster	27/09/77	05/10/77	Unclassified

No.2 engine, 414, replaced by 413, due to a suspected fractured liner. No.2 bogie, 9000-34, the right hand footstep required welding. Body floor fractured at four points around both generator end engine mounting feet pedestals.

Doncaster	13/12/77	16/12/77	Unclassified

No.2 engine, 413, replaced by 418, due to a fractured liner. No.2 boiler water tank leaking. No.1 end body centre pivot studs and nuts to renew. No.4 traction motor brush box to renew. All repairs carried out.

Doncaster	03/02/78	07/02/78	Unclassified

No.1 engine, 442 replaced by 412, due to aerating.

Doncaster	19/03/78	30/04/78	Unclassified

No.1 engine, 412, replaced by 419, due to main output shaft sheared and coolant found in left hand side lubricating oil filler pipe. No.2 engine, 418, had defective phasing case output drive to fans. This was repaired. Defective E.T.H. wiring was renewed.

Doncaster	13/05/78	14/06/78	Light

No.1 engine, 419, replaced by 420. No.2 engine, 418, replaced by 439, due to suspected blower drive failure. No.1 bogie, 9000-33, replaced by 9000-24. No.2 bogie, 9000-34, replaced by 9000-48. Boiler, 5098/J3249, was given an Unclassified repair. The loco was weighed at 105t 1cwt.

Doncaster	23/09/78	29/09/78	Unclassified

No.2 engine, 439, replaced by 415, due to a suspected fractured liner.

Doncaster	17/11/78	22/11/78	Unclassified

No.1 bogie, 9000-24, brake gear problems. Right hand side back brake gear adrift, safety bracket for brake rod missing, inside brake rod broken off and missing. Fuel tank holed adjacent to brake gear. No.1 end speedometer defective. No.2 boiler water tank leaking. All repairs were carried out.

Doncaster	17/01/79	22/01/79	Unclassified

No.1 engine, 420, replaced by 446, due to aerating.

Doncaster	01/03/79	09/03/79	Unclassified

No.1 engine, 446, replaced by 407. No.2 engine, 415, replaced by 445, due to metal in chip trap.

Doncaster	01/10/79	09/10/79	Unclassified

No.2 engine, 445, suspected piston breaking up. Debris in chip trap. 445 was given an Intermediate repair and refitted.

Doncaster	24/11/79	08/12/79	Unclassified

No.1 end right hand side fuel tank punctured. The following material had been robbed for 55 009 Auxiliary generator casing top; Shaft coupling; Flange coupling drive; Engine room lamp; Radiator fan secondary gearbox. No.2 engine, 445, had a broken Dowty pump quill drive. No.1 bogie, 9000-24, was lifted for cleaning and underbody fire damage at No.1 end right hand side. All repairs were carried out.

Doncaster	17/12/79	18/12/79	Unclassified

No.5 traction motor to earth. Boiler water tank holed. No.2 engine, 445, overspeed trip to fit. All repairs were carried out. No.5 traction motor was replaced. The locomotive was weighed at 105t 19cwt.

Doncaster	07/01/80	23/02/80	Intermediate

No.1 engine, 407, replaced by 429. No.2 engine, 445, replaced by 420. No.1 bogie, 9000-24, replaced by 9000-1. No.2 bogie, 9000-48, replaced by 9000-2. Boiler, 5098/J3249, replaced by 5096/J3247. Fuel tank level float switch defective. This was replaced. The locomotive was weighed at 104t 16cwt.

Doncaster	25/02/80	26/02/80	Rectification

Overspeed trip mechanism fitted and tested.

Doncaster	27/02/80	04/03/80	Rectification

No.1 engine, 429, continuous loss of power. The air brake pipe governor was replaced.

Doncaster	08/03/80	09/03/80	Rectification

No.1 axle right hand brake shoe fast on hanger.

Doncaster	22/03/80	26/03/80	Rectification

Fuel dilution on No.2 engine, 420. No.2 engine, 420, had 'C' cambox removed and pressure tested, two faulty pumps were replaced, as were engine mounting feet.

DELTICS ON WORKS 283

D9013/9013/55 013 The Black Watch (continued)

Loco Works	On Works	Off Works	Class of repair
Doncaster	29/04/80	01/05/80	Unclassified

No.1 engine, 429, header tank filling tank holed between solebar and tank. Hose removed to fill header tank then fitted with plug to prevent coolant draining back. No.2 engine, 420, replaced by 412, due to aerating badly.

| Doncaster | 15/09/80 | 18/09/80 | Unclassified |

Boiler water tank split. Floor fractured near main generator support bracket No.1 end right hand side. No.2 main generator had brushes replaced. The locomotive was weighed at 103t 9cwt.

| Doncaster | 25/11/80 | 28/11/80 | Unclassified |

No.2 engine, 412, replaced by 416, due to being time expired. No.1 traction motor nose pad was loose. This was secured.

| Doncaster | 20/01/81 | 27/01/81 | Unclassified |

No.1 engine, 429, fan drive output shaft splines worn and coolant flow switch and primary fan shaft robbed. No.2 engine, 416, had also had the coolant flow switch robbed. No.1 engine, 429, was repaired. No.2 engine, 416, was left for the depot to replace the switch.

| Doncaster | 02/02/81 | 04/02/81 | Unclassified |

No.1 engine, 429, replaced by 422, due to a suspected fractured liner. No.1 exhaust drum tank was replaced. No.1 primary gearbox was renewed.

| Doncaster | 25/03/81 | 31/03/81 | Unclassified |

No.1 engine, 422, replaced by 441, due to a suspected fractured liner.

| Doncaster | 08/07/81 | 14/07/81 | Unclassified |

No.1 engine, 441, auxiliary drive output bearing collapsed. The auxiliary drive was renewed.

| Doncaster | 13/08/81 | 14/08/81 | Unclassified |

No.1 engine, 441, suspected fractured liner. The locomotive was load bank tested and no fault found.

| Doncaster | 23/01/82 | - | - |

The locomotive arrived on Works after withdrawal fitted with the following main components. No.1 engine, 441, fractured liner. No.2 engine, 416, split header tank and radiator fan clutch slipping. No.1 bogie, 9000-1. No.2 bogie, 9000-2. Boiler, 5096/J3247.

A side study view of 55013 Black Watch at Doncaster on June 27, 1979. The locomotive's last working was the (1B26) 07:23 Peterborough-King's Cross on December 16, 1981but 55013 failed at Wood Green and had to be assisted forward by 31 292. Picture: J. Davenport Collection.

D9014/9014/55 014 The Duke of Wellington's Regiment

Loco Works	On Works	Off Works	Class of repair
Doncaster	29/09/61	03/10/61	Acceptance trials

New locomotive fitted with the following main components. No.1 engine, 437. No.2 engine, 439. No.1 bogie, 1029. No.2 bogie, 1030. Boiler, 5086/J3237.

Vulcan Foundry	03/10/61	06/10/61	Not recorded

Not recorded.

Doncaster	06/10/61	16/10/61	Acceptance trials

Not recorded

R.S.H. Darlington	24/01/62	17/02/62	Modification

Modifications to engines.

Doncaster	29/03/62	04/04/62	Light

No.2 traction motor gearcase damaged and No.3 traction motor cover and studs missing. Boiler water tank split and No.1 bogie, 1029, to be examined, the locomotive having struck an object. No.1 bogie, 1029, replaced by 1013. No.2 bogie, 1030, replaced by 1014. Warning horn trumpet, guard, footstep and screw coupling guard were repaired at No.2 end. The steam pipe to No.2 end cab gauge was repaired. Micro pumps on both engines were replaced. The locomotive mileage was recorded as 50,770 miles.

Doncaster	08/05/62	10/05/62	Unclassified

No.2 bogie, 1014 and frames to be examined. No.2 end driver's side leading brake cylinder and bracket damaged, blower motor filter grid damaged, driver's side window frame twisted, nose end split at left hand side, buffer flange bent. No.6 wheel air supply pipe to brake cylinder blanked off. No.2 end right hand superstructure and cab window were repaired.

Doncaster	13/07/62	14/07/62	Unclassified

No.1 bogie, 1013, replaced by 1039. No.2 bogie, 1014, replaced by 1040.

Doncaster	06/08/62	08/08/62	Unclassified

Left hand trailing fuel tank and boiler water tank burst. No.6 traction motor gearcase broken. All defects were rectified.

Doncaster	02/01/63	21/01/63	General

No.1 engine, 437, replaced by 440. No.2 engine, 439, replaced by 442. No.1 bogie, 1039, replaced by 1007. No.2 bogie, 1040, replaced by 1008. Boiler, 5086/J3237, replaced by 1488/J2944. The body was given an annual repair. The following modifications were carried out - Drawgear; Drivers vacuum brake valve; Radiator fan grills; Compressor outlet pipe bracket; Exhaust collector tank drains; Oil and water sampling cocks.

Doncaster	22/02/63	22/02/63	Unclassified

No.2 bogie, 1008, anchor link bolts missing.

Doncaster	22/05/63	23/05/63	Unclassified

No.2 left hand fuel tank level switch joint was renewed and No.5 traction motor was replaced.

Doncaster	06/06/63	16/06/63	Light

No.1 bogie, 1007, replaced by 1009. No.2 bogie, 1008, replaced by 1010. Boiler, 1488/J2944, replaced by 1497/J2953. The body was given a six monthly examination. The following modifications were carried out — Caustic injection; Boiler independent air supply; Bogie brake rod safety brackets fitted.

Doncaster	15/07/63	16/07/63	Unclassified

No.1 bogie, 1009, replaced by 1023. No.2 bogie, 1010, replaced by 1024.

Doncaster	07/08/63	08/08/63	Unclassified

Fuel tank holed on side due to the action of 'Liquor 8' leaking from inlet and outlet pipes of dosing tank. No.1 end 'A' side fuel tank was replaced. Caustic filler and drainpipes were re-routed and the fuel tank was covered with fibreglass. The locomotive mileage was recorded as 320,500 miles.

Doncaster	30/08/63	04/09/63	Unclassified

No.1 engine, 440, replaced by 432, due to broken con rod and crankcase. No.2 engine, 442, replaced by 445, due to overheating. No.1 bogie, 1023, replaced by 1027. No.2 bogie, 1024, replaced by 1028. Nos. 1 & 2 oil tanks were cleaned. No.1 coolant fan and radiator were replaced. Steam train pipes were re-jointed and lubricating oil tanks fitted with modified filler filters.

Doncaster	05/09/63	05/09/63	Unclassified

No.6 traction motor was replaced.

D9014/9014/55 014 The Duke of Wellington's Regiment (continued)

Loco Works	On Works	Off Works	Class of repair
Doncaster	22/01/64	23/01/64	Unclassified

Four boiler tubes were renewed.

Doncaster	02/02/64	19/02/64	General

No.1 engine, 432, had an injector nozzle renewed. No.2 engine, 445, had 'B' bank exhaust pistons removed for examination by Napier representatives. No.1 bogie, 1027, replaced by 1039. No.2 bogie, 1028, replaced by 1040. Boiler, 1497/J2953, replaced by 5087/J3238. The following modifications were carried out - Bodyside air intake; Soundproofing; Coolant header tank and overflow tank; Speedometers.

Doncaster	01/04/64	03/04/64	Unclassified

No.2 engine, 445, replaced by 434. No.2 bogie, 1040, had a replacement outer transom plank fitted. Anti frost precautions to the steam heater valve were carried out.

Doncaster	23/05/64	26/05/64	Unclassified

Window wipers defective on secondman's side in both cabs, No.2 traction motor blower motor commutator burnt, No.1 engine, 432, required two grease nipples on the cardan shaft renewing and No.2 engine, 434, required one grease nipple on cardan shaft renewing. All defects were rectified.

Doncaster	17/11/64	26/11/64	Light

No.1 engine, 432, replaced by 424, due to a broken con rod. No.2 engine, 434, had MP11 exams. No.1 bogie, 1039, replaced by 1031. No.2 bogie, 1040, replaced by 1032. Boiler, 5087/J3238, was given a six monthly exam. Frost precautions, lagging of pipes and auto drain valve carried out.

Doncaster	02/02/65	27/02/65	General

No.1 engine, 424, replaced by 419. No.2 engine, 434, replaced by 411. No.1 bogie, 1031, replaced by 1027. No.2 bogie, 1032, replaced by 1030. Boiler, 5087/J3238, replaced by 5097/J3248. B.R. standard buffers were fitted, as was the modification for exhauster access doors.

Doncaster	19/05/65	22/05/65	Unclassified

No.1 engine, 419, replaced by 425, due to a suspect liner or seal defective. No.2 bogie, 1030, had an anchor link pin fitted.

Doncaster	17/07/65	17/07/65	Unclassified

No.1 bogie, 1027, replaced by 9000-5. No.2 bogie, 1030, replaced by 9000-6.

Doncaster	11/08/65	11/08/65	Unclassified

No.1 control cubicle defects. These were rectified.

Doncaster	14/09/65	15/09/65	Unclassified

No.1 fuel tank holed by leak from boiler main steam pipe causing fuel to be contaminated with water (behind No.1 bogie, left hand side). The tank was replaced and train heater pipe repaired.

Doncaster	16/10/65	18/10/65	Modification

Boiler, 5097/J3248, replaced by 1496/J2952, fitted with a new "NU-WAY" burner.

Doncaster	12/01/66	21/01/66	Light

Collision damage at No.2 end. No.1 engine, 424 and No.2 engine, 411, were given Unclassified repairs. No.1 bogie, 9000-5 and No.2 bogie, 9000-6, were given Unclassified repairs. Boiler, 1496/J2952, given an Unclassified repair. The right hand corner of the nose end and the buffer were badly damaged. The sand trap, filter tube and right hand marker light were broken and No.2 rubber vacuum pipe split. The body given an Unclassified repair and damage was repaired.

Doncaster	15/05/66	27/05/66	General

No.1 engine, 425, replaced by 438. No.2 engine, 411, replaced by 421. No.1 bogie, 9000-5, replaced by 9000-43. No.2 bogie, 9000-6, replaced by 9000-44. Boiler, 1496/J2952, replaced by 5087/J3238. The body was given a General repair.

Doncaster	28/06/66	30/06/66	Unclassified

No.2 engine, 421, replaced by 447. Excessive oil was cleaned from underside of locomotive. No.2 lubricating oil tank was cleaned.

Doncaster	30/08/66	31/08/66	Unclassified

No.2 engine, 447, replaced by 407, due to having seized, defective piston ('A6' exhaust). No.2 lubricating oil tank was cleaned.

Doncaster	15/12/66	20/12/66	Unclassified

No.1 bogie, 9000-43 and both main generators to be examined for flashover damage. No.1 bogie equalising beam back liner missing on left-hand side also stop block on equalising beam missing. Right hand side leading and middle bottom axlebox horn plate bolt distance pieces all slack. All repairs were carried out.

D9014/9014/55 014 The Duke of Wellington's Regiment (continued)

Loco Works	On Works	Off Works	Class of repair
Doncaster	30/01/67	04/02/67	Light

No.1 engine, 438 and No.2 engine, 407, were given Unclassified repairs. No.1 bogie, 9000-43, replaced by 9000-49. No.2 bogie, 9000-44, replaced by 9000-50. Boiler, 5087/J3238, was given an Unclassified repair. The body was given an Unclassified repair.

Doncaster	01/05/67	09/06/67	General

No.1 engine, 438, replaced by 456. No.2 engine, 407, replaced by 406. No.1 bogie, 9000-49, replaced by 9000-37. No.2 bogie, 9000-50, replaced by 9000-38. Boiler, 5087/J3238, replaced by 5091/J3242. Full yellow nose ends were applied.

Doncaster	10/06/67	12/06/67	Rectification

No.1 bogie, 9000-37, replaced by 9000-23. No.2 bogie, 9000-38, replaced by 9000-24.

Doncaster	11/10/67	12/10/67	Unclassified

Water scoop ram broken off and boiler water tank holed. This was rectified.

Doncaster	31/10/67	02/11/67	Unclassified

No.2 nose end damaged. This was repaired.

Doncaster	01/01/68	08/01/68	Light

No.1 engine, 456 and No.2 engine, 406, were given Unclassified repairs. No.1 bogie, 9000-23, replaced by 9000-35. No.2 bogie, 9000-24, replaced by 9000-36. Boiler, 5091/J3242, was given an Unclassified repair.

Doncaster	11/01/68	11/01/68	Rectification

Loss of power. Load regulator motor pipes were repaired.

Doncaster	01/05/68	06/06/68	General

No.1 engine, 456, replaced by 411. No.2 engine, 406, replaced by 538. No.1 bogie, 9000-35, replaced by 9000-7. No.2 bogie, 9000-36, replaced by 9000-8. Boiler, 5091/J3242, replaced by 5093/J3244. The body was given a General repair. The locomotive was fitted for dual braking.

Doncaster	03/02/69	11/02/69	Light

No.1 engine, 411, was given an Unclassified repair. No.2 engine, 538, replaced by 425, due to a suspected fractured liner. No.1 bogie, 9000-7, replaced by 9000-9. No.2 bogie, 9000-8, replaced by 9000-10. Boiler, 5093/J3244, was given an Unclassified repair. The body was given an Unclassified repair. The radiators and silencers were replaced.

Doncaster	18/06/69	18/06/69	Unclassified

No.1 engine, 411, replaced by 449, due to being time expired.

Doncaster	26/06/69	27/06/69	Unclassified

No.1 engine, 449, replaced by 427.

Doncaster	27/10/69	18/11/69	Intermediate

*No.1 engine, 427, replaced by 431. No.2 engine, 425, replaced by 438. No.1 bogie, 9000-9, replaced by 9000-15. No.2 bogie, 9000-10, replaced by 9000-16. Boiler, 5093/J3244, replaced by 1487/J2943. The water tank modification was carried out. The body was given an Intermediate repair and repainted into **blue livery with full yellow ends**.*

Doncaster	26/11/69	26/11/69	Rectification

No.1 Martinair unit tripping. The Martinair valve was replaced, overspeed trip removed and refitted and racks reset.

Doncaster	28/03/70	03/04/70	Unclassified

No.2 boiler water tank holed and Nos.2 & 5 wheelsets tyres loose due to overheating. The boiler water tank was repaired, as were both exhaust silencers. Nos.2 & 5 wheelsets were replaced.

Doncaster	15/04/70	16/04/70	Unclassified

No.1 engine, 431, replaced by 458, due to phasing gear defective.

Doncaster	26/05/70	27/05/70	Unclassified

Flashover damage to both main generators and all traction motors. All repairs were carried out.

Doncaster	03/07/70	13/07/70	Light

No.1 engine, 458 and No.2 engine, 438, were given Unclassified repairs. No.1 bogie, 9000-15, replaced by 9000-31. No.2 bogie, 9000-16, replaced by 9000-32. Boiler, 1487/J2943, was given a General repair. The body was given a Light repair.

Doncaster	01/09/70	03/09/70	Unclassified

No.3 traction motor cable burnt through. No.1 engine, 458, had leaks attended to and flashover damage to both main generators was repaired. No.3 traction motor was replaced.

D9014/9014/55 014 The Duke of Wellington's Regiment (continued)

Loco Works	On Works	Off Works	Class of repair
Doncaster	06/09/70	10/09/70	Rectification

No.3 wheelset was replaced.

Doncaster	23/12/70	24/12/70	Unclassified

No.2 engine, 438, replaced by 404, due to a suspected fractured liner.

Doncaster	03/04/71	23/07/71	Intermediate

No.1 engine, 458, replaced by 427, due to aerating. No.2 engine, 404, replaced by 432. No.1 bogie, 9000-31, replaced by 9000-19. No.2 bogie, 9000-32, replaced by 9000-20. Boiler, 1487/J2943, replaced by 1494/J2950. The body was given an Intermediate repair. The locomotive was fitted with E.T.H. equipment.

Doncaster	27/09/71	01/10/71	Unclassified

Bogie and underframe damage. Both boiler water tanks were repaired. No.1 bogie, 9000-19, spring planks and pull rod safety stays were repaired. No.2 bogie, 9000-20, pull rod safety stays and nose suspension repairs were carried out.

Doncaster	07/12/71	09/12/71	Unclassified

No.1 engine, 427, suspected broken piston rings. This was rectified. No.1 boiler tank was repaired.

Doncaster	02/02/72	05/02/72	Unclassified

No.2 engine, 432, replaced by 406, due to high spectrographic analysis. No.1 boiler water tank was repaired, as were cab doors and locks.

Doncaster	02/03/72	04/03/72	Unclassified

No.2 boiler water tank holed. This was repaired.

Doncaster	12/04/72	14/04/72	Unclassified

No.1 engine, 427, replaced by 419, due to a cylinder liner seal defective. No.1 bogie, 9000-19, had swing link pins, lifeguards and footsteps repaired. No.2 bogie, 9000-20, had No.4 traction motor gearcase repaired.

Doncaster	22/05/72	26/05/72	Light

No.1 engine, 419 and No.2 engine, 406, were given Unclassified repairs. No.1 bogie, 9000-19, replaced by 9000-49. No.2 bogie, 9000-20, replaced by 9000-50. Boiler, 1494/J2950, was given an Unclassified repair. The body was given a Light repair.

Doncaster	26/05/72	28/05/72	Rectification

Not recorded.

Doncaster	21/06/72	28/06/72	Unclassified

No.2 engine, 406, replaced by 434, due to 'C' bank fuel pump camshaft disengaged.

Doncaster	22/09/72	26/09/72	Unclassified

No.1 engine, 419, replaced by 427. No.1 boiler water tank was repaired.

Doncaster	21/10/72	25/10/72	Unclassified

No.2 engine, 434, replaced by 538, due to a fractured liner.

Doncaster	06/11/72	06/11/72	Rectification

No.2 engine, 538, '4A' injector bolt broken. The injector and broken retaining stud replaced

Doncaster	20/11/72	22/11/72	Unclassified

No.2 engine, 538, replaced by 455, due to a fractured liner.

Doncaster	18/12/72	19/12/72	Unclassified

Heavy fuel leak in 'B' bank on No.2 engine, 455. Continuous bookings for high water temperature. No oil flow through oil radiators. New radiators were fitted and the fuel leak was rectified.

Doncaster	17/01/73	19/01/73	Unclassified

No.1 engine, 427, replaced by 413, due to high copper content in lubricating oil. No.1 end lubricating oil tank and radiators were replaced.

Doncaster	26/02/73	29/03/73	Intermediate

No.1 engine, 413, replaced by 429. No.2 engine, 455, replaced by 432. No.1 bogie, 9000-49, replaced by 9000-17. No.2 bogie, 9000-50, replaced by 9000-18. Boiler, 1494/J2950, replaced by 5094/J3145. The body was given an Intermediate repair.

Doncaster	13/08/73	17/08/73	Unclassified

No.1 engine, 429, replaced by 447, due to No.1 main generator ring badly burnt. No.2 engine, 432, was given an Unclassified repair.

D9014/9014/55 014 The Duke of Wellington's Regiment (continued)

Loco Works	On Works	Off Works	Class of repair
Doncaster	28/12/73	10/01/74	Light

No.1 engine, 447, replaced by 405. No.2 engine, 432, replaced by 414. No.1 bogie, 9000-17, replaced by 9000-3. No.2 bogie, 9000-18, replaced by 9000-4. Boiler, 5094/J3245, was given an Unclassified repair. The body was given a Light repair.

Doncaster	05/07/74	19/07/74	Unclassified

No.1 engine, 405, replaced by 538, due to aerating, suspected fractured liner. No.2 engine, 414, replaced by 421.

Doncaster	16/08/74	22/08/74	Unclassified

No.2 engine, 421, replaced by 420, due to a suspected fractured liner.

Doncaster	12/09/74	14/09/74	Unclassified

No.1 engine, 538, replaced by 425, due to being dephased.

Doncaster	30/12/74	19/03/75	Intermediate

No.1 engine, 425, replaced by 430. No.2 engine, 420, replaced by 437. No.1 bogie, 9000-3, replaced by 9000-17. No.2 bogie, 9000-4, replaced by 9000-18. Boiler, 5094/J3245, was given a standard repair. Body panel fractured right side above No.1 fuel tank and a fracture at corner of No.2 end right nose end filter grille. No.1 boiler water tank split on right side next to carrying bracket. This was apparently derailment damage. All damage was repaired. The locomotive was weighed at 102t 11cwt.

Doncaster	22/03/75	24/03/75	Rectification

No.1 engine, 430, fuel dilution. 'A' bank cambox was replaced.

Doncaster	29/04/75	29/04/75	Rectification

No.2 engine, 437, underspeed drive shaft sheared. This was rectified.

Doncaster	05/05/75	15/05/75	Unclassified

No.2 engine, 437, replaced by 458, due to underspeed flexible drive fretting. Dowty pump drive damaged.

Doncaster	04/06/75	09/06/75	Unclassified

Earth fault on the armature of No.1 main generator. No.2 boiler water tank was repaired. No.1 main generator was replaced.

Doncaster	08/08/75	10/08/75	Unclassified

No.1 engine, 430, replaced by 407, due to a heavy coolant leak inside between free end and phasing gear case which indicates fractured casing.

Doncaster	28/08/75	29/08/75	Unclassified

No.1 engine, 407, replaced by 456, due to a suspected fractured liner.

Doncaster	17/09/75	19/09/75	Unclassified

Collision damage. No.2 end buffer beam bent and nose end panelling fractured - repaired

Doncaster	25/09/75	02/10/75	Unclassified

No.1 engine, 456, replaced by 409. No.2 engine, 458, replaced by 443, due to breathing heavy.

Doncaster	07/01/76	08/01/76	Unclassified

High commutator bar on No.4 traction motor. No.1 bogie, 9000-17 and No.2 bogie, 9000-18, centre liners to secure. No.4 traction motor was replaced.

Doncaster	31/01/76	04/02/76	Unclassified

No.2 engine, 443, replaced by 408, due to aerating, suspected fractured liner.

Doncaster	14/04/76	16/06/76	Light

No.1 engine, 409, replaced by 407, due to 'BC' bottom piston circlip loose. No.2 engine, 408, replaced by 425. No.1 bogie, 9000-17, replaced by 9000-25. No.2 bogie, 9000-18, replaced by 9000-26. Boiler, 5094/J3245, was given an Unclassified repair. The locomotive was weighed at 103t 10cwt.

Doncaster	09/07/76	15/07/76	Unclassified

No.2 engine, 425, fuel dilution. A boiler water tank was repaired, as were sliding windows and door pillars. No.2 engine, 425, had camboxes, fuel pumps and fuel injectors replaced. Dirty boiler tubes were cleaned and adjusted.

Doncaster	12/10/76	17/10/76	Unclassified

No.2 main generator low insulation reading. No.1 engine, 407, had a knock on the engine when starting. No.1 engine radiator clutch fan noisy. Earth fault sensing circuit to be examined. No.2 main generator was replaced. All defects were rectified.

D9014/9014/55 014 The Duke of Wellington's Regiment (continued)

Loco Works	On Works	Off Works	Class of repair
Doncaster	02/03/77	10/03/77	Unclassified

No.1 engine, 407, replaced by 458, due to high spectrographic reading and breathing heavy. No.1 boiler water tank had a leak repaired.

Doncaster	26/03/77	29/03/77	Unclassified

No.2 boiler water tank leaking. This was repaired.

Doncaster	19/04/77	22/04/77	Unclassified

No.2 engine, 425, replaced by 435, due to having seized. No.1 bogie, 9000-25, had a nose suspension pad loose on No.3 traction motor. No.2 bogie, 9000-26, had similar defects. Both bogies also had repairs to loose segments in bolsters. No.1 main generator had an arc horn to renew and oil to clean from commutator and brush gear.

Doncaster	27/04/77	29/04/77	Unclassified

No.1 engine, 458, auxiliary generator drive fractured. The auxiliary generator drive was repaired.

Doncaster	02/05/77	06/05/77	Unclassified

No.1 engine, 458, replaced by 432, due to a suspected fractured liner. No.1 end coolant radiators and thermostat were replaced. An E.T. H. defect was rectified.

Doncaster	02/11/77	09/11/77	Unclassified

No.2 engine, 435, replaced by 437, due to main drive shaft sheared. Both boiler water tanks were leaking. New studs and nuts fitted in both bogie centre pivots. The boiler water tanks were removed and not refitted. The locomotive was weighed at 99t 18cwt.

Doncaster	19/11/77	23/11/77	Unclassified

No.1 engine, 432, replaced by 433, due to con rod through 'AB' crankcase. Both boiler water tanks were refitted. Both load regulators had tips replaced. Control circuit breaker tripping, circuits checked for earth faults.

Doncaster	12/12/77	28/04/78	Intermediate

No.1 engine, 433, replaced by 417. No.2 engine, 437, replaced by 443. No.1 bogie, 9000-25, replaced by 9000-1. No.2 bogie, 9000-26, replaced by 9000-2. Boiler, 5094/J3245, was given a standard repair. Route indicator panels were plated over.

Doncaster	08/05/78	11/05/78	Rectification

Repeated fuel starvation on No.1 engine, 417. A washer was caught under the flange coupling allowing air to enter the system.

Doncaster	24/05/78	30/05/78	Rectification

Fuel starvation on No.1 engine, 417. A fuel suction pipe was refitted inside the tank.

Doncaster	03/10/78	05/10/78	Unclassified

No.1 engine, 417, exciter gearbox defect. This was replaced. No.2 engine, 443, replaced by 453, due to aerating. No.2 boiler water tank was leaking. No.1 primary fan shaft was defective. The tank and fan shaft were repaired.

Doncaster	17/10/78	19/10/78	Unclassified

No.1 bogie, 9000-1, right hand side spring plank bracket locking studs broken. A swing link pin lock plate was fitted in position 'R1'. The locomotive was weighed at 106t 17cwt.

Doncaster	07/12/78	09/12/78	Unclassified

No.1 bogie, 9000-1 and No.2 bogie, 9000-2, had attention to all swing link pins. Both primary cardan shafts were renewed.

Doncaster	17/01/79	22/01/79	Unclassified

No.1 engine, 417, was given a gudgeon pin housing examination. No.2 engine, 453, had a start fault rectified.

Doncaster	21/06/79	18/07/79	Unclassified

No.1 engine, 417, replaced by 539. No.2 engine, 453, replaced by 454, due to pistons time expired. Burnt wiring - automatic voltage regulator and battery charge circuit renewed.

Doncaster	23/11/79	10/12/79	Light

No.1 engine, 539 and No.2 engine, 454, were given Light repairs and refitted. No.1 bogie, 9000-1, replaced by 9000-7. No.2 bogie, 9000-2, replaced by 9000-8, Boiler, 5094/J3245, was given an Unclassified repair. No.2 end load regulator tips repaired. The loco weighed at 105t 9cwt.

Doncaster	13/12/79	13/12/79	Rectification

No.2 axle right side end float to check. Set bolts working out and breaking axlebox cover. This was rectified.

D9014/9014/55 014 The Duke of Wellington's Regiment (continued)

Loco Works	On Works	Off Works	Class of repair
Doncaster	23/01/80	24/01/80	Unclassified

No.2 engine, 454, replaced by 445, due to a suspected fractured liner.

| Doncaster | 02/04/80 | 10/04/80 | Unclassified |

No.2 engine, 445, replaced by 419, due to a suspected fractured liner. No.2 load regulator to clean.

| Doncaster | 13/05/80 | 13/05/80 | Unclassified |

No.1 engine, 539, 'CB' crankcase threads stripped into crankcase body at free end. This was rectified. No.2 main generator had the 'Vee' ring field coils and insulators cleaned.

| Doncaster | 19/08/80 | 26/08/80 | Unclassified |

No.2 engine, 419, replaced by 538, due to scavenge blower drive sheared. A boiler water tank was repaired.

| Doncaster | 12/09/80 | 17/09/80 | Unclassified |

No.1 engine, 539, replaced by 408, due to a suspected fractured liner. No.1 bogie, 9000-7, had No.1 traction motor gear teeth worn and was 'Motak' contaminated. No.1 wheelset was replaced. No.1 boiler water tank was leaking. All defects were rectified. The loco weighed at 104t 13cwt.

| Doncaster | 03/11/80 | 06/11/80 | Unclassified |

No.1 engine, 408, replaced by 404, due to 'B' bank crankcase vibration damper smashed. No.1 primary fan gearbox was also worn. Flashover damage to No.1 main generator was rectified.

| Doncaster | 02/02/81 | 04/02/81 | Unclassified |

No.1 boiler water tank leaking. This was repaired, as was No.1 primary fan coupling and No.1 fan housing under grille.

| Doncaster | 24/02/81 | 06/03/81 | Unclassified |

No.1 engine, 404, replaced by 442 - passing oil. No.1 bogie, 9000-7, had swing link pins renewed.

| Doncaster | 16/06/81 | 18/06/81 | Unclassified |

No.2 engine, 538, replaced by 457, due to a suspected fractured liner.

| Doncaster | 13/07/81 | 15/07/81 | Unclassified |

No.2 engine, 457, replaced by 455, due to a suspected fractured liner.

| Doncaster | 07/08/81 | 11/08/81 | Unclassified |

The locomotive was load tested to check fractured liner on No.2 engine, 455. No fault was found.

| Doncaster | 23/09/81 | 28/09/81 | Unclassified |

No.2 engine, 455, replaced by 449, due to a suspected fractured liner.

| Stratford D.R.S. | 23/11/81 | 05/12/81 | - |

No.1 engine, 442 and No.2 engine, 449, removed and fitted to 55 002. Engines, 437 and 457 were fitted, however, at which end is not clear.

| Doncaster | 05/12/81 | - | - |

The locomotive arrived on Works after withdrawal with the following main components fitted. (The end each engine is fitted to is not known) Engine, 437, broken con rod through 'B' and 'C' banks. Engine, 457, main generator down to earth. No.1 bogie, 9000-7. No.2 bogie, 9000-8. Boiler, 5094/J3245.

Class 55, 55014 The Duke of Wellington's Regiment runs into York on August 28, 1979 with a down express. The locomotive's last train was the (1S14) 08:10 Newcastle-Edinburgh on November 10, 1981. However, the Deltic failed at Cramlington and was assisted forward by 37 082. 55014 was withdrawn on November 22.
Picture: C. L. Caddy.

DELTICS ON WORKS 291

A delightful study of the first Deltic to reach two million miles in service — D9010 The King's Own Scottish Borderer.

292 DELTICS ON WORKS

55002 The King's Own Yorkshire Light Infantry stands at the buffers at King's Cross with the 13.27 from Newcastle on December 16, 1977. Picture: G. Gillham.

DELTICS ON WORKS 293

D9020 Nimbus stands light engine at King's Cross on July 5, 1963. Picture: C. L. Caddy.

294 Deltics On Works

Class 55, 55005 The Prince of Wales's Own Regiment of Yorkshire makes for a fine study at York on July 3, 1976. Picture: J. C. Hillmer.

D9015/9015/55 015 Tulyar

Loco Works	On Works	Off Works	Class of repair
Doncaster	13/10/61	23/10/61	Acceptance trials

New locomotive fitted with the following known main components. No.1 engine, (Unknown). No.2 engine, 442. No.1 bogie, 1031. No.2 bogie, 1032. Boiler, 5088/J3239. 'Tulyar' nameplates fitted.

Doncaster	29/10/61	03/11/61	Not recorded

No.2 engine, 442, replaced by 458. Note - This repair may have taken place at R.S.H. Darlington.

R.S.H. Darlington	25/04/62	03/07/62	Modification

No.1 engine, replaced by 418.

Doncaster	03/07/62	05/07/62	Light

No.1 bogie, 1031, replaced by 1007. No.2 bogie, 1032, replaced by 1008. Body six monthly exam.

Doncaster	10/07/62	12/07/62	Unclassified

No.1 engine, 418, replaced by 428, due to No.1 main generator interpole burnt. No.2 radiator fan drive shaft switched to No.1 end. New radiator fan drive shaft fitted to No.2 end. The locomotive mileage was recorded as 69,000 miles.

Doncaster	15/08/62	16/08/62	Unclassified

No.6 traction motor armature down to earth. The traction motor was replaced. The locomotive mileage was recorded as 86,000 miles.

Doncaster	28/08/62	29/08/62	Unclassified

All traction motors flashed over. Water scoop snouts were repaired and all traction motors were replaced. The locomotive mileage was recorded as 89,600 miles.

R.S.H. Darlington	11/09/62	Not recorded	Not recorded

All traction motors flashed over and No.5 traction motor commutator scored. No.1 bogie, 1007, replaced by 1001. No.2 bogie, 1008, replaced by 1050. The loco mileage was recorded as 94,580 miles.

Doncaster	09/11/62	20/11/62	Light

No.1 engine, 428, replaced by 436, due to water pump defective. No.1 bogie, 1001, replaced by 1025. No.2 bogie, 1050, replaced by 1026. The body was given a six monthly examination. No.2 exhaust collector drum inspection door lid was re-jointed. Nos.1 & 2 radiator fan grills were modified. The following modifications were carried out - Drawgear; Driver's vacuum brake valve. The locomotive mileage was recorded as 137,000 miles.

Doncaster	22/01/63	25/01/63	Unclassified

Boiler, 5088/J3239, replaced by 5086/J3237, due to having overheated due to a shortage of water. The boiler fan ducting modification was carried out.

Doncaster	07/02/63	07/02/63	Unclassified

No.1 bogie, 1025, headstock rivets loose, headstock opened 1/8th inch. The headstock rivets were renewed. The locomotive mileage was recorded as 165,690 miles.

Doncaster	09/03/63	09/03/63	Unclassified

No.1 bogie, 1025, replaced by 1013, due to fractures on transoms and headstock rivets loose on left hand side. No.2 bogie, 1026, replaced by 1014. The loco mileage was recorded as 180,000 miles.

Doncaster	19/03/63	20/03/63	Unclassified

Transom fractures on No.1 bogie, 1013 and No.2 bogie, 1014. These were chipped and welded. The locomotive mileage was recorded as 185,200 miles.

Doncaster	22/03/63	22/03/63	Unclassified

No.2 bogie, 1014, transom fractured. This was repaired. The locomotive mileage 185,600 miles.

Doncaster	06/05/63	16/05/63	General

No.1 engine, 436, replaced by 446. No.2 engine, 458, replaced by 416. No.1 bogie, 1013, replaced by 1015. No.2 bogie, 1014, replaced by 1016. Boiler, 5086/J3237, replaced by 1496/J2852. The body was given an annual repair.

Doncaster	16/08/63	27/08/63	Unclassified

Collision damage to No.2 end fireman's side. This consisted of pipes in the compressor compartment damaged, large gash along side from nose to end of bogie, leading brake cylinder torn off, intermediate brake cylinder distorted, footstep badly twisted, footboard by door torn up, engine room window broken, fire alarm glass broken and case twisted, front handrail bent, sandbox lids twisted and cab door jammed. All of this was repaired. No.1 bogie, 1015, replaced by 1029. No.2 bogie, 1016, replaced by 1030. Boiler, 1496/J2952, replaced by 5091/J3242. The loco mileage was recorded as 266,210 miles.

D9015/9015/55 015 Tulyar (continued)

Loco Works	On Works	Off Works	Class of repair
Doncaster	06/12/63	10/12/63	Light

No.1 bogie, 1029, replaced by 1043, due to Nos.1 & 2 transoms fractured left side. No.2 bogie, 1030, replaced by 1044. No.2 end 'A' bank generator mounting floor fractured. The fractures were chipped and welded. The body was given a six monthly examination. The locomotive mileage was recorded as 327,000 miles.

Doncaster	03/01/64	04/01/64	Unclassified

No.2 engine, 416, replaced by 417, due to a suspect cracked liner.

Doncaster	07/01/64	08/01/64	Unclassified

No.2 engine, 417, replaced by 448, due to a suspect cracked liner.

Doncaster	15/03/64	18/03/64	Unclassified

No.1 engine, 446, replaced by 438, due to a suspect fractured liner. Modifications were carried out to the heater slide valves.

Doncaster	13/04/64	06/05/64	General

No.1 engine, 438, replaced by 538. No.2 engine, 448, replaced by 539. No.1 bogie, 1043, replaced by 1015. No.2 bogie, 1044, replaced by 1016. Boiler, 5091/J3242, replaced by 5088/J3239. Repairs were carried out to the superstructure at No.2 end.

Doncaster	14/11/64	22/11/64	Light

No.1 engine, 538, had primary and secondary fan shafts replaced. No.2 engine, 539, had the primary fan shaft replaced. No.1 bogie, 1015, replaced by 1007. No.2 bogie, 1016, replaced by 1008.

Doncaster	12/04/65	28/04/65	General

No.1 bogie, 1007, replaced by 1035. No.2 bogie, 1008, replaced by 1036. Boiler, 5088/J3239, replaced by 5086/J3237. Repairs were carried out to the right hand bodyside. The following modifications were carried out - Spiders; Transom radius; Centre gussets; Cold pins in headstocks; Horn liners; Steel plate to brake hanger rubbing brackets; Nose suspension; Fire bell gong.

Doncaster	18/06/65	21/06/65	Unclassified

No.2 engine, 539, replaced by 418, due to an internal water leak in engine sump.

Doncaster	12/07/65	14/07/65	Unclassified

No.1 engine, 538, replaced by 406, due to water in sump. Boiler, 5086/J3237, had a new "NU-WAY" burner fitted.

Doncaster	17/08/65	25/08/65	Unclassified

No.1 engine, 406, replaced by 443, due to crankcase fractured, 'A1' exhaust and 'C1' inlet. No.2 engine, 418, replaced by 432.

Doncaster	02/10/65	11/10/65	Light

No.1 engine, 443, replaced by 437, due to liner seals defective. No.1 bogie, 1035, replaced by 9000-29. No.2 bogie, 1036, replaced by 9000-30. Boiler, 5086/J3237, had the burner motor and fuel solenoids changed. Coolant radiators were replaced and No.2 primary fan shaft renewed. The following modifications were carried out - Protection bar for EP valves; Fire alarm bell.

Doncaster	21/10/65	24/10/65	Unclassified

Both main generators flashed over, No.2 traction motor burnt out and to earth. No.2 traction motor was replaced. Sand ejectors were replaced.

Doncaster	18/11/65	20/11/65	Unclassified

No.1 engine, 437 and No.2 engine, 432, both with fuel dilution, also water in No.3 axlebox left hand side. Both engines had injectors replaced. No.3 left hand axlebox bearings were renewed.

Doncaster	27/01/66	27/01/66	Unclassified

No.1 engine, 437, underspeed governor to be replaced and leaking boiler tubes. One new boiler tube was fitted and one welded.

Doncaster	04/02/66	07/02/66	Unclassified

No.2 engine, 432, replaced by 434, due to 'CA' flexible drive shaft broken.

Doncaster	17/02/66	05/03/66	General

No.1 engine, 437, replaced by 454, due to scavenge drive shaft sheared. No.2 engine, 434, was given an Unclassified repair. No.1 bogie, 9000-29, replaced by 9000-11. No.2 bogie, 9000-30, replaced by 9000-12. Boiler, 5086/J3237, replaced by 1493/J2949. The body given General repair.

Doncaster	28/04/66	01/05/66	Unclassified

No.1 bogie, 9000-11 and No.2 bogie, 9000-12, were given Unclassified repairs. The boiler safety valve was repaired.

D9015/9015/55 015 Tulyar (continued)

Loco Works	On Works	Off Works	Class of repair
Doncaster	30/08/66	31/08/66	Unclassified

No.1 engine, 454, replaced by 427, due to 'B' bank crankshaft and crankcase fractured. No.1 end lubricating oil tank was cleaned.

Doncaster	11/10/66	19/10/66	Light

No.1 engine, 427 and No.2 engine, 434, were given Unclassified repairs. No.1 bogie, 9000-11, replaced by 9000-27. No.2 bogie, 9000-12, replaced by 9000-28. Boiler, 1493/J2949, was given an Unclassified repair. The body was given an Unclassified repair.

Doncaster	04/11/66	07/11/66	Rectification

No.1 drum tank filling with oil. Both exhaust silencers were replaced.

Doncaster	06/12/66	07/12/66	Unclassified

Boiler, 1493/J2949, replaced by 1492/J2948, due to leaking tubes.

Doncaster	16/01/67	02/02/67	General

No.1 engine, 427, replaced by 452. No.2 engine, 434, replaced by 415. No.1 bogie, 9000-27 and No.2 bogie, 9000-28, were given Unclassified repairs. The body was given a General repair. Full yellow nose ends were applied.

Doncaster	09/03/67	09/03/67	Unclassified

No.2 fuel tank left side split. The fuel tank was replaced.

Doncaster	30/05/67	01/06/67	Unclassified

Repairs to derailment damage were carried out and No.1 bogie, 9000-27, had No.1 wheelset replaced.

Doncaster	25/07/67	26/07/67	Unclassified

No.1 engine, 452, replaced by 457, due to coolant pump shaft drive broken.

Doncaster	03/08/67	04/08/67	Unclassified

Leaking boiler tubes. These were repaired.

Doncaster	09/09/67	11/09/67	Unclassified

No.2 engine, 415, replaced by 440, due to quill shaft broken. (Engine 440 is also recorded in the files as being carried by D9007 at the same time as it was fitted in D9015!)

Doncaster	18/09/67	23/09/67	Light

No.1 engine, 457 and No.2 engine, 440, were given Unclassified repairs. No.1 bogie, 9000-27, replaced by 9000-19. No.2 bogie, 9000-28, replaced by 9000-20. Boiler, 1492/J2948, replaced by 1486/J2942. The body was given an Unclassified repair.

Doncaster	24/01/68	22/02/68	General

No.1 engine, 457, replaced by 426. No.2 engine, 440, replaced by 450. No.1 bogie, 9000-19 and No.2 bogie, 9000-20, were given General repairs. Boiler, 1486/J2942, replaced by 5096/J3247. The water scoop mechanism was renewed due to being inoperative. The body was given a General repair. The locomotive was fitted for dual braking.

Doncaster	27/02/68	01/03/68	Unclassified

No.1 engine, 426, continually shutting down and No.1 main generator heavy smoke coming from armature internally. The engine shutdown fault was rectified and the main generator was cleaned of oil.

Doncaster	10/05/68	10/05/68	Unclassified

No.2 exhauster defective, running at excessive RPM. The defect was rectified and the speedometer was also adjusted.

Doncaster	17/05/68	22/05/68	Unclassified

No.2 engine, 450, replaced by 412, due to a liner seal leaking. An exhauster was replaced due to a motor defect.

Doncaster	25/07/68	25/07/68	Unclassified

No.2 engine, 412, replaced by 436, due to a cylinder head liner seal defective. No.2 end lubricating oil tank and radiator were cleaned.

Doncaster	28/08/68	05/09/68	Light

No.1 engine, 426, replaced by 454, due to an unrecorded defect. No.2 engine, 436, was given an Unclassified repair. No.1 bogie, 9000-19, replaced by 9000-35. No.2 bogie, 9000-20, replaced by 9000-36. Boiler, 5096/J3247, was given an Unclassified repair. The body was given an Unclassified repair.

D9015/9015/55 015 Tulyar (continued)

Loco Works	On Works	Off Works	Class of repair
Doncaster	31/12/68	03/01/69	Unclassified

Lubricating oil in blower ducting at No.1 end and No.3 traction motor megger reading 200k, motor soaked in lubricating oil. All traction motors on No.1 bogie, 9000-35, were replaced and repairs were carried out to No.2 exhauster oil pump.

Doncaster	03/02/69	05/02/69	Unclassified

No.1 engine, 454, replaced by 414, due to con rod broken and through crankcase.

Doncaster	19/02/69	21/02/69	Unclassified

No.2 engine, 436, smoking very badly and pumping out oil. The defect was repaired.

Doncaster	24/02/69	27/02/69	Unclassified

No.2 engine, 436, replaced by 428.

Doncaster	09/04/69	02/05/69	Intermediate

No.1 engine, 414, replaced by 455. No.2 engine, 428, replaced by 420. No.1 bogie, 9000-35, replaced by 9000-41. No.2 bogie, 9000-36, replaced by 9000-42. Boiler, 5096/J3247, replaced by 5097/J3248. The body was given an Intermediate repair and repainted into **blue livery with full yellow ends**.

Doncaster	09/07/69	10/07/69	Unclassified

No.5 traction motor interpole and armature to earth. A minor defect on No.1 engine, 455, was rectified. No.5 traction motor was replaced.

Doncaster	10/11/69	11/11/69	Unclassified

No.2 engine, 420, replaced by 427, due to a coolant leak. Lubricating oil tanks and radiator elements were removed for flushing.

Doncaster	25/01/70	05/02/70	Light

No.1 engine, 455, replaced by 430. No.2 engine, 427, was given a Light repair. No.1 bogie, 9000-41, replaced by 9000-43. No.2 bogie, 9000-42, replaced by 9000-44. Boiler, 5097/J3248, was given an Unclassified repair. The body was given a Light repair. Modified water tanks were fitted.

Doncaster	07/02/70	09/02/70	Rectification

All traction motors to be cleaned and copper swarf removed. All traction motors were replaced.

Doncaster	14/02/70	14/02/70	Rectification

No.1 engine, 430, continually shutting down. Low oil pressure was rectified and the Dowty pump was replaced.

Doncaster	28/02/70	04/03/70	Unclassified

No.1 engine, 430, continually shutting down. Lubricating oil radiators were cleaned and thermostats were replaced.

Doncaster	29/05/70	30/05/70	Unclassified

No.1 engine, 430, replaced by 429, due to high crankcase pressure.

Doncaster	17/09/70	19/09/70	Unclassified

No.1 boiler water tank fractured around inspection cover. Flashover damage also needed attention. Both main generators and all traction motors had flashover damage repaired, as was the fracture in No.1 boiler water tank.

Doncaster	10/10/70	13/02/71	Intermediate

No.1 engine, 429, removed, fitted to 9018, then removed for a General repair before being returned to 9015 No.1 end. No.2 engine, 427, replaced by 452. No.1 bogie, 9000-43, replaced by 9000-35. No.2 bogie, 9000-44, replaced by 9000-36. Boiler, 5097/J3248, was given a General repair. Both main generators and all traction motors had flashed over. The body was given an Intermediate repair. The locomotive was fitted with E.T.H. equipment.

Doncaster	16/02/71	16/02/71	Rectification

Field divert faults were rectified.

Doncaster	17/03/71	18/03/71	Unclassified

Both cabs to be draughtproofed. No.2 bogie, 9000-36, repeated wheelslip, suspect No.5 traction motor defective. Wheelslip relays were checked, bolster damage repaired and No.2 traction motor was replaced.

Doncaster	02/04/71	06/04/71	Unclassified

Persistent wheelslip indications. No.1 traction motor was replaced.

Doncaster	06/05/71	07/05/71	Unclassified

 No.2 engine, 452, scavenge blower drive defective. The scavenge blower was replaced and air manifold intake filters were cleaned.

D9015/9015/55 015 Tulyar (continued)

Loco Works	On Works	Off Works	Class of repair
Doncaster	15/05/71	20/05/71	Unclassified

No.1 engine, 429, replaced by 411, due to aerating, suspected fractured liner.

| Doncaster | 24/05/71 | 26/05/71 | Unclassified |

No.2 engine, 452, replaced by 453, due to a piston through side of 'A' bank.

| Doncaster | 20/07/71 | 21/07/71 | Unclassified |

No.2 boiler water tank holed. This was repaired.

| Doncaster | 08/10/71 | 13/10/71 | Unclassified |

No.1 engine, 411, replaced by 431, due to crankcase fractured. No.1 boiler water tank fractured. This was repaired.

| Doncaster | 06/12/71 | 11/12/71 | Light |

No.1 engine, 431 and No.2 engine, 453, were given Light repairs. No.1 bogie, 9000-35, replaced by 9000-15. No.2 bogie, 9000-36, replaced by 9000-16. Boiler, 5097/J3248, was given an Unclassified repair. The body was given a Light repair.

| Doncaster | 14/02/72 | 16/02/72 | Unclassified |

No.1 boiler water tank split. This was repaired.

| Doncaster | 12/07/72 | 13/07/72 | Unclassified |

No.1 engine, 431, replaced by 426, due to 'AB' crankshaft damper adrift.

| Doncaster | 25/09/72 | 04/11/72 | Intermediate |

No.1 engine, 426, replaced by 428. No.2 engine, 453, replaced by 414, due to 'AB' crankshaft damper adrift. No.1 bogie, 9000-15, replaced by 9000-39. No.2 bogie, 9000-16, replaced by 9000-40. Boiler, 5097/J3248, replaced by 5087/J3238. The body was given an Intermediate repair.

| Doncaster | 16/02/73 | 20/02/73 | Unclassified |

No.1 engine, 428, replaced by 447, due to excessive coolant in sump. No.1 lubricating oil tank and radiators were cleaned.

| Doncaster | 25/05/73 | 30/05/73 | Unclassified |

No.2 engine, 414, replaced by 420, due to a cylinder liner defective, water in sump. Lubricating oil tanks and radiators were cleaned.

| Doncaster | 02/07/73 | 03/07/73 | Unclassified |

No.2 engine, 420, crankcase joint blowing. This was re-jointed.

| Doncaster | 13/08/73 | 21/08/73 | Light |

No.1 main generator to earth. No.1 engine, 447, replaced by 421. No.2 engine, 420, replaced by 429. No.1 bogie, 9000-39, replaced by 9000-29. No.2 bogie, 9000-40, replaced by 9000-10. Boiler, 5087/J3238, was given an Unclassified repair. The body was given a Light repair.

| Doncaster | 23/01/74 | 23/01/74 | Modification |

Earth fault relay modification was carried out.

| Doncaster | 13/05/74 | 20/05/74 | Unclassified |

No.2 engine, 429, replaced by 436, due to being dephased. E.T.H. and coolant probe modifications were carried out.

| Doncaster | 13/07/74 | 10/09/74 | Intermediate |

No.1 engine, 421, replaced by 422. No.2 engine, 436, replaced by 429. No.1 bogie, 9000-29 and No.2 bogie, 9000-10, were given standard repairs. Boiler, 5087/J3238, replaced by 5091/J3242. The body was given an Intermediate repair. E.T.H. and coolant modifications were carried out.

| Doncaster | 05/02/75 | 07/02/75 | Unclassified |

No.1 engine, 422, replaced by 457, due to 'BC' crankcase bolt broken. No.1 traction motor was replaced and No.5 traction motor nose suspension bracket was repaired.

| Doncaster | 24/02/75 | 26/02/75 | Unclassified |

No.2 auxiliary generator drive disintegrated. This was renewed.

| Doncaster | 23/05/75 | 28/05/75 | Unclassified |

No.1 engine, 457, continuous high water temperature. The radiators were replaced. No.2 engine, 429, replaced by 451, due to failure of auxiliary generator drive on three occasions. No.2 end primary gearbox was replaced.

| Doncaster | 17/06/75 | 19/06/75 | Unclassified |

No.1 engine, 457, suspected leaking cylinder liners. This was checked and no fault was found. No.1 fan gearbox and shaft were replaced.

D9015/9015/55 015 Tulyar (continued)

Loco Works	On Works	Off Works	Class of repair
Doncaster	24/06/75	25/06/75	Rectification

No.1 engine, 457, fan shaft uncoupled and overspeed trip damaged. The cardan shaft and Martinair unit were replaced.

| Doncaster | 03/07/75 | 04/07/75 | Rectification |

No.1 engine, 457, fan drive primary cardan shaft again adrift. The auxiliary drive and cardan shaft were repaired and the auxiliary drive gearbox removed for examination before refitting.

| Doncaster | 01/09/75 | 03/09/75 | Unclassified |

No.1 engine, 457, replaced by 449, due to being time expired. No.2 engine, 451, replaced by 434, due to being dephased. No.1 bogie, 9000-29 and No.2 bogie, 9000-10, were given standard repairs. Boiler, 5091/J3242, was given an Unclassified repair.

| Doncaster | 06/10/75 | 21/10/75 | Light |

No.1 bogie, 9000-29, replaced by 9000-13. No.2 bogie, 9000-10, replaced by 9000-14. Boiler, 5091/J3242, was given an Unclassified repair. No.1 main generator was repaired.

| Doncaster | 24/10/75 | 24/10/75 | Rectification |

No.2 engine, 434, hunting, suspect governor drive. This was rectified.

| Doncaster | 03/02/76 | 04/02/76 | Unclassified |

No.1 engine, 449, replaced by 451, due to 'BC' crankcase 'B5' piston breaking up and con rod bent. No.1 auxiliary generator had no output. This was rectified.

| Doncaster | 19/02/76 | 20/02/76 | Unclassified |

No.1 engine, 451, replaced by 417, due to 'CA' crankcase holed.

| Stratford D.R.S. | 14/04/76 | 15/04/76 | Depot |

No.5 wheelset was removed due to teeth broken on road gear wheel. A replacement wheelset was fitted. No.5 traction motor was also replaced.

| Doncaster | 21/04/76 | 26/04/76 | Unclassified |

No.1 engine, 417, replaced by 453. No.2 engine, 434, replaced by 443 - fractured cylinder liner.

| Doncaster | 14/08/76 | 14/08/76 | Unclassified |

Fractured boiler mounting foot adjacent to No.1 engine, 'A' side floor. This was repaired.

| Doncaster | 01/09/76 | 03/09/76 | Unclassified |

No.1 engine, 453, replaced by 445, due to Dowty pump drive bearing collapsed in phasing case. No.2 boiler water tank was repaired.

| Doncaster | 18/09/76 | 24/09/76 | Unclassified |

No.1 engine, 445, replaced by 417, due to breathing heavy. A boiler water tank was repaired.

| Doncaster | 17/10/76 | 20/10/76 | Unclassified |

No.1 engine, 417, replaced by 440, due to breathing heavy and metal particles in chip trap. No.1 bogie, 9000-13, replaced by 9000-45, due to rough riding. No.2 bogie, 9000-14, replaced by 9000-46, due to rough riding. The locomotive was weighed at 103t 2cwt.

| Doncaster | 22/11/76 | 25/11/76 | Unclassified |

No.1 engine, 440, replaced by 408, due to aerating.

| Doncaster | 15/01/77 | 21/01/77 | Unclassified |

No.2 engine, 443, replaced by 409. Oil radiators and thermostats were overhauled.

| Doncaster | 13/04/77 | 19/04/77 | Unclassified |

No.2 engine, 409, replaced by 451 - fractured liner. No.1 auxiliary generator drive repaired.

| Doncaster | 22/04/77 | 26/04/77 | Rectification |

No.2 main generator field connections burnt off, solder run into generator and flashover damage. Main generator external cables were renewed and the main generator was replaced.

| Doncaster | 27/05/77 | 02/06/77 | Unclassified |

No.1 engine, 408, replaced by 443, due to tap washers in chip trap. Body badly cracked between No.1 end secondman's side cab windscreen and quarter light. This and primary shaft repaired.

| Doncaster | 20/07/77 | 26/07/77 | Unclassified |

Flange wear Nos.4 & 6 wheels right hand side, scrap tyres. No.1 engine, 443, had radiator fan primary gearbox to renew, shaft broken. No.2 engine, 451, very noisy at phasing gearcase. Both load regulators leaking oil. All defects repaired. All tyres on both bogies replaced with new ones. The locomotive was weighed at 104t 18cwt.

| Doncaster | 19/12/77 | 22/12/77 | Unclassified |

No.1 engine, 443, replaced by 409 - main generator drive defective. Bogie centre pivot studs and nuts to renew.

D9015/9015/55 015 Tulyar (continued)

Loco Works	On Works	Off Works	Class of repair
Doncaster	10/01/78	12/01/78	Unclassified

No.1 engine, 409, replaced by 433, due to a suspected fractured liner. Both load regulators had oil leaks rectified. Battery isolating switch locking mechanism was defective. This was repaired.

Doncaster	14/01/78	18/01/78	Unclassified

No.2 engine, 451, replaced by 435, due to being dephased.

Doncaster	14/03/78	16/03/78	Unclassified

No.1 engine, 433, replaced by 425, due to aerating, suspect fractured liner. Flashover damage to both main generators. Oil leaks in No.2 roof section and on No.2 load regulator. All defects were rectified.

Doncaster	05/05/78	09/05/78	Unclassified

No.1 engine, 425, replaced by 433, due to piston through 'CA' crankcase. No.1 end lubricating oil tanks were cleaned and radiators replaced.

Doncaster	17/05/78	22/05/78	Unclassified

No.2 engine, 435, replaced by 441, due to piston through 'CA' crankcase. Both load regulators were leaking oil. Both oil and coolant radiators were replaced.

Doncaster	03/08/78	07/08/78	Unclassified

No.1 engine, 433, replaced by 452, due to being time expired. Bad steam blow under secondman's side No.2 bogie. Both load regulators were leaking oil. These defects were rectified.

Doncaster	25/09/78	27/09/78	Unclassified

No.1 engine, 452, fan drive shaft coupling defective. This was repaired. No.2 engine, 441, replaced by 424, due to scavenge blower defective. Both load regulators were leaking oil.

Doncaster	13/10/78	19/10/78	Unclassified

No.1 main generator fire damage. No.1 engine, 452, replaced by 413.

Doncaster	25/10/78	27/10/78	Unclassified

No.2 engine, 424, replaced by 443, due to a suspected fractured liner. No.2 load regulator had an oil leak rectified and tips renewed.

Doncaster	29/01/79	05/05/79	Intermediate

No.1 engine, 413, replaced by 438, due to auxiliary generator drive shaft sheared and time expired. No.2 engine, 443, replaced by 451, due to being dephased. No.1 bogie, 9000-45, replaced by 9000-31. No.2 bogie, 9000-46, replaced by 9000-32. Boiler, 5091/J3242, replaced by 1496/J2952. Note - The locomotive, as part of an experiment, had not received any classified attention since being outshopped from Doncaster on 21/10/75. This was to determine as to whether it would be possible to extend the period between classified overhauls. There now follows a report on the condition of the body when it was shopped for this repair - 1. Both sides of locomotive batten strips beneath radiator shutter rivets loose and missing. Battens coming adrift from bodysides. 2. Radiator grills fractured across corners and centre supports. Also hinges loose on numerous flaps and strained brackets. 3. Excessive lateral movement of all four cab sliding doors. 4. No.2 cab driver's side sliding window cracked. 5. Both cabs either side quarter light windows rubber surrounds and inserts badly perished. 6. Centre roof section either side of exhaust stacks support members adrift at top. 7. General condition of front cab windscreen surrounds both ends very poor. Breaking away with rust. 8. Engine room side windows badly holed and corroded away inside of framework. 9. Extensive corrosion and rust around battery vents and engine air inlet grilles. 10. Rear of sliding cab windows rotting away. 11. Both nose end route indicator mounting surrounds badly holed and corroded away at base. 12. Both nose end hatches to weld as required also calliper pins to renew. Badly worn. 13. No.1 nose end exhauster motor inspection hatch surround rusted away. 14. No.1 cab top right hand corner 10" weld fractured through. 15. General condition of paintwork chipped and cracked with numerous dents. 16. No.1 nose end left hand hatch rusting away. 17. No.1 end secondman's side bodywork fractured on weld at rear of sliding window frame. 18. No.2 nose end right hand side hatch rusting away. No.2 load regulator oil leak. Reported E.T.H. cutting out after easing controller, suspect oil pressure switch defective. All repairs were carried out. The locomotive was weighed at 105t 1 cwt.

Doncaster	16/05/79	17/05/79	Unclassified

No.1 engine, 438, would not run. The Dowty pump was repaired. No.2 engine, 451, high water temperature switch continually operating. The switch was replaced.

D9015/9015/55 015 Tulyar (continued)

Loco Works	On Works	Off Works	Class of repair
Doncaster	25/05/79	29/05/79	Unclassified

Locate and rectify coolant leak from No.1 coolant filler pipe leaking into boiler water tank. Check No.1 engine, 438, for breathing heavy. No fault found. No.1 engine coolant filler pipe and coolant temperature switch was repaired, as was No.1 load regulator.

Doncaster	24/11/79	28/11/79	Unclassified

No.1 engine, 438, replaced by 433, due to debris found in strainer. No.2 engine, 451, replaced by 443, due to being time expired.

Doncaster	02/07/80	09/07/80	Unclassified

No.1 engine, 433, main generator field to earth. 433 was given an Unclassified repair. No.2 engine, 443, replaced by 454, due to 'B1' crankcase end oil leaking down end face and front face on main crankcase joint. No.1 main generator was replaced.

Doncaster	22/07/80	25/07/80	Unclassified

No.1 main generator low readings. No.1 main generator was replaced.

Doncaster	22/09/80	25/09/80	Unclassified

No.1 engine, 433, replaced by 452, due to phasing gear drive to cooling fan sheared. Nos.3 & 6 traction motor nose pads were secured.

Doncaster	28/10/80	30/10/80	Unclassified

No.1 engine, 452, replaced by 447, due to aerating.

Doncaster	14/11/80	21/11/80	Unclassified

No.1 engine, 447, suspected fractured liner and No.2 main generator flashover damage. The locomotive was load bank tested and no fault was found.

Doncaster	05/12/80	11/12/80	Unclassified

No.2 main generator low reading after flashover repairs completed. All traction motors were inspected for flashover damage. All flashover damage repaired. The loco was weighed at 103t 4cwt.

Doncaster	12/01/81	16/01/81	Unclassified

No.2 engine, 454, replaced by 408, due to a suspected fractured liner. Both main generators had flashover damage. No.2 main generator was repaired. No.1 main generator was left for depot to repair.

Doncaster	26/08/81	31/08/81	Unclassified

No.1 engine, 447, replaced by 538, due to aerating and 'B' bank exhaust bellows blowing. Also engine speed up button defective. This was rectified.

Doncaster	05/01/82	23/11/83	-

The locomotive arrived on Works after withdrawal with the following main components fitted. No.1 engine, 538. No.2 engine, 408. No.1 bogie, 9000-31. No.2 bogie, 9000-32. Boiler, 1496/J2952. The locomotive was moved to Derby Research Centre.

D9016/9016/55 016 Gordon Highlander

Loco Works	On Works	Off Works	Class of repair
Doncaster	27/10/61	06/11/61	Acceptance trials

New locomotive fitted with the following main components. No.1 engine, 444. No.2 engine, 438. No.1 bogie, 1033. No.2 bogie, 1034. Boiler, 5092/J3243.

Doncaster	19/01/62	13/02/62	Not recorded

Not recorded.

Doncaster	26/04/62	27/04/62	Light

No.1 bogie, 1033, replaced by 1041. No.2 bogie, 1034, replaced by 1042. The body was given a six monthly examination.

Doncaster	19/09/62	19/09/62	Unclassified

No.5 axle on No.2 bogie, 1042, 3" crack. Water scoop snouts were repaired.

Doncaster	21/09/62	27/09/62	General

No.1 engine, 444, replaced by 411. No.2 engine, 438, replaced by 418. No.1 bogie, 1041, replaced by 1047. No.2 bogie, 1042, replaced by 1048. Boiler, 5092/J3243, replaced by 5095/J3246. The body was given an annual repair.

Doncaster	31/01/63	04/02/63	Unclassified

Bogie defects. No.1 bogie, 1047, had a replacement torsion bar fitted. Both bogies had headstock rivets tightened. No.1 radiator fan primary shaft was replaced. New exhaust collector tanks were fitted. The locomotive mileage was recorded as 204,000 miles.

Doncaster	28/03/63	02/04/63	Light

No.1 bogie, 1047, replaced by 1021. No.2 bogie, 1048, replaced by 1022. The body was given a six monthly examination. No.1 main generator had two new insulators fitted and three insulators anti-track painted. Exhaust drum drainpipe extension modifications were carried out.

Doncaster	09/07/63	09/07/63	Unclassified

No.1 bogie, 1021, replaced by 1001. No.2 bogie, 1022, replaced by 1050.

Doncaster	18/07/63	19/07/63	Unclassified

No.2 engine, 418, replaced by 436.

Doncaster	23/07/63	24/07/63	Unclassified

Boiler tube damage. Boiler tubes were repaired.

Doncaster	11/09/63	30/09/63	General

No.1 engine, 411, replaced by 438, due to 'C6' cylinder liner leaking to 'BC' crankcase. No.1 bogie, 1001, replaced by 1049. No.2 bogie, 1050, replaced by 1002. Boiler, 5095/J3246, replaced by 1491/J2947. The body was given an annual repair. The following modifications were carried out — Caustic injection; Soundproofing; Draught sealing; Radiator fan grills; Low water gauge fitted; Header tank overflow tank fitted.

Doncaster	10/12/63	12/12/63	Unclassified

All traction motors were replaced.

Doncaster	04/03/64	19/03/64	General

No.1 engine, 438, replaced by 439. No.2 engine, 436, replaced by 442. No.1 bogie, 1049, replaced by 1033. No.2 bogie, 1002, replaced by 1034. Boiler, 1491/J2947, replaced by 1489/J2945. The following modifications were carried out — Nose end doors for access to exhausters; Air and toilet pipes lagged; Steam heater cock slide valves.

Doncaster	20/07/64	24/07/64	Unclassified

Locomotive to be fully repainted in readiness for its naming ceremony.

Doncaster	28/11/64	07/12/64	Light

No.1 engine, 439, was overhauled. No.1 bogie, 1033, replaced by 1005. No.2 bogie, 1034, replaced by 1006. Boiler, 1489/J2945, was overhauled. Repairs were carried out to bodyside fractures.

Doncaster	12/05/65	14/05/65	Unclassified

No.1 engine, 439, replaced by 448.

Doncaster	08/07/65	14/07/65	Unclassified

No.1 engine, 448, was given a three monthly exam. No.2 engine, 442, replaced by 409. No.1 bogie, 1005, replaced by 9000-3. No.2 bogie, 1006, replaced by 9000-4. Boiler, 1489/J2945, had a "NU-WAY" burner fitted. Coolant radiators were cleaned. The locomotive mileage was recorded as 250,440 miles.

D9016/9016/55 016 Gordon Highlander (continued)

Loco Works	On Works	Off Works	Class of repair
Doncaster	24/07/65	25/07/65	Unclassified

Both main generators had flashover damage cleaned up. Tyres were turned and axles were ultrasonically tested.

| Doncaster | 24/10/65 | 13/11/65 | General |

No.1 engine, 448, replaced by 420. No.2 engine, 409, replaced by 449. No.1 bogie, 9000-3 and No.2 bogie, 9000-4, were overhauled and all wheelsets were replaced. Boiler, 1489/J2945, replaced by 5094/J3245. All traction motors were cleaned and new brushes fitted as required. The locomotive mileage was recorded as 304,460.

| Doncaster | 14/11/65 | 16/11/65 | Unclassified |

The bogie swivel limit brackets were repaired. Nos.1 & 4 traction motors were replaced. Modification was carried out to footstep plate.

| Doncaster | 26/01/66 | 27/01/66 | Unclassified |

Boiler, 5094/J3245, had a water pump changed.

| Doncaster | 01/02/66 | 02/02/66 | Unclassified |

Fire bottles discharged automatically. The fire system was checked and reset and new fire bottles were fitted.

| Doncaster | 19/02/66 | 23/02/66 | Unclassified |

The body had repairs to fire damage, the fire pull system reset and a new fire bottle fitted. Both main generators and all traction motors had flashover damage cleaned up.

| Doncaster | 16/03/66 | 19/03/66 | Light |

No.1 engine, 420 and No.2 engine, 449, were given Unclassified repairs. No.1 bogie, 9000-3, replaced by 9000-39. No.2 bogie, 9000-4, replaced by 9000-40. Boiler, 5094/J3245, was given an Unclassified repair. The body was given an Unclassified repair.

| Doncaster | 14/06/66 | 15/06/66 | Unclassified |

No.2 expansion tank split. This was repaired, as was flashover damage to both main generators and all traction motors.

| Doncaster | 09/08/66 | 11/08/66 | Unclassified |

Flashover damage on both main generators. Flashover damage on both main generators and on all traction motors was repaired.

| Doncaster | 18/08/66 | 24/08/66 | Unclassified |

Flashover damage on both main generators. No.2 engine, 449, replaced by 433. No.1 main generator was repaired. No.2 main generator was replaced. No.1 bogie, 9000-39, had Nos.1 & 2 traction motors repaired and No.3 replaced. No.2 bogie, 9000-40, had all traction motors replaced.

| Doncaster | 05/09/66 | 08/09/66 | Unclassified |

No.1 engine, 420, replaced by 416, due to No.6 'CA' con rod and crankcase fractured.

| Doncaster | 03/10/66 | 26/10/66 | General |

No.1 engine, 416, replaced by 423. No.2 engine, 433, replaced by 444. No.1 bogie, 9000-39 and No.2 bogie, 9000-40, were given General repairs. Boiler, 5094/J3245, replaced by 5098/J3249. The body was given a General repair.

| Doncaster | 20/02/67 | 24/02/67 | Light |

No.1 engine, 423 and No.2 engine, 444, were given Unclassified repairs. No.1 bogie, 9000-39, replaced by 9000-9. No.2 bogie, 9000-40, replaced by 9000-10. Boiler, 5098/J3249, was given an Unclassified repair. The body was given an Unclassified repair.

| Doncaster | 19/04/67 | 25/04/67 | Unclassified |

Flashover damage to both main generators and to all traction motors was repaired. Boiler, 5098/J3249, had four tubes renewed.

| Doncaster | 11/05/67 | 15/05/67 | Unclassified |

No.1 engine, 423, replaced by 412, due to a seized piston, con rod broken.

| Doncaster | 23/07/67 | 23/07/67 | Not recorded |

Not recorded.

| Doncaster | 14/08/67 | 07/10/67 | General |

*No.1 engine, 412, replaced by 423. No.2 engine, 444, replaced by 439. No.1 bogie, 9000-9 and No.2 bogie, 9000-10, were given General repairs. Boiler, 5098/J3249, replaced by 5089/J3240. The body was given a General repair and repainted into **blue livery with full yellow nose ends**. The locomotive was fitted for dual braking.*

D9016/9016/55 016 Gordon Highlander (continued)

Loco Works	On Works	Off Works	Class of repair
Doncaster	18/11/67	18/11/67	Modification

Modifications were carried out to dual brake pipework.

| Doncaster | 16/12/67 | 18/12/67 | Modification |

The compressor stand was modified.

| Doncaster | 06/03/68 | 14/03/68 | Light |

No.1 engine, 423 and No.2 engine, 439, were given Unclassified repairs. No.1 bogie, 9000-9, replaced by 9000-5. No.2 bogie, 9000-10, replaced by 9000-6. Boiler, 5089/J3240, was given an Unclassified repair. The body was given an Unclassified repair.

| Doncaster | 26/09/68 | 08/11/68 | General |

No.1 engine, 423, replaced by 422. No.2 engine, 439, replaced by 409. No.1 bogie, 9000-5 and No.2 bogie, 9000-6, were given General repairs. Boiler, 5089/J3240, replaced by 5091/J3242. The body was given a General repair. During this overhaul equipment not normally removed was dismantled to ascertain condition on CM&EE's instructions. This was to establish future overhaul requirements for the class.

| Doncaster | 12/02/69 | 14/02/69 | Unclassified |

No.2 exhaust drum was replaced.

| Doncaster | 05/05/69 | 09/05/69 | Light |

No.1 engine, 422 and No.2 engine, 409, were given Unclassified repairs. No.1 bogie, 9000-5, replaced by 9000-19. No.2 bogie, 9000-6, replaced by 9000-20. Boiler, 5091/J3242, was given an Unclassified repair. The body was given an Unclassified repair.

| Doncaster | 29/11/69 | 04/12/69 | Unclassified |

Flashover damage to both main generators and No.6 traction motor. All flashover damage was repaired.

| Doncaster | 22/12/69 | 23/12/69 | Unclassified |

No.2 engine, 409, lubricating oil radiator fractured and oil hose adrift. 'A' & 'B' lubricating oil radiators were replaced and a temporary repair made to burnt wiring in ducting to engine room switch and lights. The overspeed governor on No.2 engine, 409, was replaced.

| Doncaster | 29/12/69 | 16/01/70 | Intermediate |

No.1 engine, 422, replaced by 407, due to crankcase damaged and con rod broken. No.2 engine, 409, replaced by 539. No.1 bogie, 9000-19, replaced by 9000-35. No.2 bogie, 9000-20, replaced by 9000-36. Boiler, 5091/J3242, replaced by 5095/J3246. The body was given an Intermediate repair. Burnt wiring in No.1 end ducting repaired. The water tank capacity modification was carried out.

| Doncaster | 19/01/70 | 23/01/70 | Unclassified |

Both main generators and all traction motors had flashover damage repaired.

| Doncaster | 24/07/70 | 28/07/70 | Unclassified |

No.2 engine, 539, replaced by 423, due to No.2 main generator down to earth. The main generator was also replaced.

| Doncaster | 18/08/70 | 19/08/70 | Unclassified |

No.6 traction motor to be replaced, low insulation reading. Both main generators and all traction motors (except No.6 which was replaced) had flashover damage repaired.

| Doncaster | Not recorded | 10/10/70 | Light |

No.1 engine, 407 and No.2 engine, 423, were given Unclassified repairs. No.1 bogie, 9000-35, replaced by 9000-39. No.2 bogie, 9000-36, replaced by 9000-40. Boiler, 5095/J3246, was given an Unclassified repair.

| Doncaster | 01/11/70 | 03/11/70 | Unclassified |

No.2 engine, 423, replaced by 454, due to being dephased.

| Doncaster | 07/01/71 | 13/01/71 | Unclassified |

No.1 engine, 407, replaced by 456, due to coolant in sump.

| Doncaster | 31/03/71 | 06/04/71 | Unclassified |

Both main generators down to earth. No.1 main generator had flashover damage repaired whilst No.2 main generator was replaced.

| Doncaster | 21/04/71 | 12/10/71 | Intermediate |

No.1 engine, 456, replaced by 444. No.2 engine, 454, replaced by 418. No.1 bogie, 9000-39, replaced by 9000-13. No.2 bogie, 9000-40, replaced by 9000-14. Boiler, 5095/J3246, was given a General repair. The body was given an Intermediate repair. The locomotive was fitted with E.T.H. equipment.

D9016/9016/55 016 Gordon Highlander (continued)

Loco Works	On Works	Off Works	Class of repair
Doncaster	13/12/71	14/12/71	Unclassified

No.1 boiler water tank fractured. This was repaired.

| Doncaster | 21/12/71 | 22/12/71 | Unclassified |

No.2 engine, 418, replaced by 449, due to crankcase holed.

| Doncaster | 23/03/72 | 25/03/72 | Unclassified |

No.1 boiler water tank fractured, No.1 bogie, 9000-13, swing link pin broken, studs loose and brakeblock cotters to be reset. Pull rod safety stays to be renewed. No.2 bogie, 9000-14, had bolster segments to secure, swing link pins and loose studs to repair and pull rod safety stays to renew. No.4 traction motor was also to be checked. All repairs were carried out.

| Doncaster | 15/06/72 | 17/06/72 | Unclassified |

No.1 engine, 444, replaced by 432, due to a leaking liner.

| Doncaster | 21/07/72 | 28/07/72 | Light |

No.1 engine, 432 and No.2 engine, 449, were given Unclassified repairs. No.1 bogie, 9000-13, replaced by 9000-27. No.2 bogie, 9000-14, replaced by 9000-28. Boiler, 5095/J3246, was given an Unclassified repair. The body was given a Light repair.

| Doncaster | 30/08/72 | 01/09/72 | Unclassified |

No.1 engine, 432, exhaust collector drum been on fire, both engines to examine. Fire Brigade had poured water down both exhausts. Both engines were inspected and repaired as necessary. No.1 collector drum was also repaired.

| Doncaster | 27/09/72 | 30/09/72 | Unclassified |

No.1 engine, 432, had a collector drum fracture repaired. No.2 engine, 449, replaced by 421, due to coolant in sump, suspect liner seal. Boiler, 5095/J3246, had been reported locking out - checked.

| Doncaster | 27/10/72 | 30/10/72 | Unclassified |

No.1 engine, 432, replaced by 447. A fractured boiler water tank was repaired, as was No.2 load regulator.

| Doncaster | 01/12/72 | 15/12/72 | Unclassified |

Collision damage to No.1 end. The bufferbeam and cab floor were distorted and blower motor was out of line. Repairs were carried out and all fire bottles refilled.

| Doncaster | 15/02/73 | 16/02/73 | Unclassified |

No.1 engine, 447, replaced by 426, due to No.1 main generator being burnt out. No.1 main and auxiliary generators were replaced.

| Doncaster | 05/03/73 | 09/03/73 | Unclassified |

No.2 main generator down to earth. This was rectified.

| Doncaster | 21/03/73 | 22/03/73 | Unclassified |

Boiler water tanks fractured. These were repaired.

| Doncaster | 24/04/73 | 25/04/73 | Unclassified |

No.2 boiler water tank split on top front seam. This was repaired.

| Doncaster | 29/05/73 | 20/06/73 | Intermediate |

No.1 engine, 426, replaced by 440. No.2 engine, 421, replaced by 428. No.1 bogie, 9000-27, replaced by 9000-23. No.2 bogie, 9000-28, replaced by 9000-30. Boiler, 5095/J3246, replaced by 1494/J2950. The body was given an Intermediate repair.

| Doncaster | 06/10/73 | 10/10/73 | Unclassified |

No.2 main generator starting fields open circuit. The generator was given a General repair.

| Doncaster | 05/11/73 | 09/11/73 | Unclassified |

No.1 engine, 440, replaced by 452, due to being dephased. A boiler water tank was also repaired.

| Doncaster | 04/01/74 | 08/01/74 | Unclassified |

No.2 engine, 428, replaced by 439, due to No.2 main generator armature bindings damaged. The main generator was also replaced.

| Doncaster | 14/01/74 | 14/01/74 | Modification |

Earth fault relay modification was carried out.

| Doncaster | 17/01/74 | 22/01/74 | Unclassified |

No.1 engine, 452, replaced by 428, due to 'B5' piston through crankcase.

| Doncaster | 07/03/74 | 16/03/74 | Light |

No.1 engine, 428, was given a Light repair. No.2 engine, 439, replaced by 409. No.1 bogie, 9000-23, replaced by 9000-49. No.2 bogie, 9000-30, replaced by 9000-50. Boiler, 1494/J2950, was given an Unclassified repair. The body was given a Light repair.

D9016/9016/55 016 Gordon Highlander (continued)

Loco Works	On Works	Off Works	Class of repair
Doncaster	08/08/74	14/08/74	Unclassified

No.1 end radiators were replaced. No.2 end fan clutch was repaired. E.T.H. and coolant temperature probe modifications were carried out.

| Doncaster | 19/08/74 | 23/08/74 | Unclassified |

No.1 engine, 428, replaced by 446, due to 'AB' crankcase holed.

| Doncaster | 04/11/74 | 12/11/74 | Unclassified |

No.2 engine, 409, replaced by 417, due to 'C6' piston and con rod through crankcase. No.2 end lubricating oil tank and radiators were repaired.

| Doncaster | 14/02/75 | 19/02/75 | Unclassified |

No.1 engine, 446, replaced by 405. No.1 bogie, 9000-49, replaced by 9000-1. No.2 bogie, 9000-50, replaced by 9000-2. Both water tanks were repaired.

| Doncaster | 27/02/75 | 28/02/75 | Unclassified |

No.2 engine, 417, replaced by 538, due to piston through crankcase. No.2 end lubricating oil tank and radiator were cleaned. No.2 end fan gearbox and clutch were replaced.

| Doncaster | 13/03/75 | 14/03/75 | Rectification |

No.2 engine, 538, persistently losing coolant. Hoses chafing, pipes needed repositioning- rectified.

| Doncaster | 02/04/75 | 04/04/75 | Unclassified |

No.1 eng, 405, replaced by 539 - crankshaft damper bolts sheared. C/case end cover damaged.

| Doncaster | 05/07/75 | 27/04/76 | Heavy General |

No.1 engine, 539, replaced by 421. No.2 engine, 538, replaced by 458. No.1 bogie, 9000-1, replaced by 9000-7. No.2 bogie, 9000-2, replaced by 9000-8. Boiler, 1494/J2950, replaced by 5095/J3246. The regimental crests were replaced. Route indicator panels were plated over.

| Doncaster | 08/06/76 | 09/06/76 | Unclassified |

No.1 engine, 421, 'A' & 'B' banks metal bellows disintegrated at front between exhaust manifolds and collector box. Replacement bellows were fitted.

| Doncaster | 28/06/76 | 06/07/76 | Unclassified |

No.2 engine, 458, replaced by 442.

| Doncaster | 09/07/76 | 12/07/76 | Rectification |

An interlock was adjusted.

| Doncaster | 19/07/76 | 21/07/76 | Rectification |

No.2 engine, 442, replaced by 441, due to aerating.

| Doncaster | 02/10/76 | 05/10/76 | Unclassified |

No.2 engine, 441, replaced by 404. No.2 main generator had a mounting foot repaired.

| Doncaster | 19/10/76 | 24/10/76 | Unclassified |

No.1 engine, 421, replaced by 423. Both load regulators burnt and suspected earth faults. Burnt wiring was repaired and load regulator valve motor was overhauled. A boiler water tank was repaired, as was No.1 end cab footsteps.

| Doncaster | 01/11/76 | 16/11/76 | Rectification |

No.2 engine, 404, replaced by 418, due to phasing gearcase broken. Interior adjacent to No.2 main generator ruptured floor/walls/roof. Load regulator oil pipes severed, conduits and cables damaged. No.2 main generator mounting plate to engine broken, cooling fan broken, coupling and guard broken. Damage caused by compressor failure was repaired.

| Doncaster | 08/12/76 | 10/12/76 | Rectification |

No.2 engine, 418, replaced by 439, due to being dephased.

| Doncaster | 14/01/77 | 18/01/77 | Unclassified |

No.1 engine, 423, replaced by 442, due to scavenge blower suspect.

| Doncaster | 22/01/77 | 25/01/77 | Unclassified |

No.2 engine, 439, replaced by 428, due to phasing gearcase fractured and losing oil. Driver's cab window was secured and draughtproofed.

| Doncaster | 29/01/77 | 01/02/77 | Rectification |

No.2 engine, 428, low power output. Governor and spring drives were replaced.

| Doncaster | 02/02/77 | 05/02/77 | Rectification |

A no power fault was rectified.

| Doncaster | 12/03/77 | 14/03/77 | Unclassified |

No.1 bogie, 9000-7, hydraulic dampers between Nos.1 & 2 and Nos.2 & 3 wheels defective. No.2 bogie, 9000-8, similar problems between Nos.4 & 5 wheels. Overhauled components were fitted.

D9016/9016/55 016 Gordon Highlander (continued)

Loco Works	On Works	Off Works	Class of repair
Doncaster	14/06/77	20/06/77	Unclassified

No.1 engine, 442, replaced by 449, due to a suspected fractured liner.

| Doncaster | 24/06/77 | 03/07/77 | Unclassified |

No.2 engine, 428, replaced by 406, due to being dephased. No.1 end coolant radiators and thermostat were replaced.

| Doncaster | 16/07/77 | 19/07/77 | Unclassified |

No.2 engine, 406, was load bank tested. The engine governor was replaced.

| Doncaster | 19/10/77 | 10/11/77 | Light |

No.1 engine, 449, replaced by 428. No.2 engine, 406, replaced by 414. No.1 bogie, 9000-7, replaced by 9000-29. No.2 bogie, 9000-8, replaced by 9000-10. Boiler, 5095/J3246, was given an Unclassified repair.

| Doncaster | 10/02/78 | 16/02/78 | Unclassified |

No.2 main generator to earth. No.1 engine, 428, had a fan shaft coupling repaired. Both boiler water tanks were repaired, as was No.1 primary fan drive. Both bogies had horn liners secured. No.2 main generator was replaced.

| Doncaster | 26/04/78 | 27/04/78 | Unclassified |

No.2 engine, 414, replaced by 424, due to aerating. Left hand oil element leaking and five load regulator tips removed. No.2 left hand oil radiator was replaced and No.1 end left hand body footstep was repaired.

| Doncaster | 22/06/78 | 22/12/78 | Unclassified |

No.1 engine, 428, replaced by 408. No.2 engine, 424, replaced by 423, due to 'B' crankcase fractured. No.1 bogie, 9000-29 and No.2 bogie, 9000-10, had swing link pin examination. No.2 primary shaft was renewed. Both load regulators were cleaned.

| Doncaster | 10/01/79 | 26/09/79 | Rectification |

No.1 engine, 408, replaced by 404, due to suspected defective piston rings, engine pumping oil out of exhaust covering locomotive and coaches - fire hazard. No.2 engine, 423, replaced by 432.

| Doncaster | 27/02/80 | 05/03/80 | Unclassified |

No.1 bogie, 9000-29, replaced by 9000-11. No.2 bogie, 9000-10, replaced by 9000-12.

| Doncaster | 27/05/80 | 03/06/80 | Unclassified |

No.1 engine, 404, replaced by 409, due to a suspected fractured liner. No.1 bogie, 9000-11, had No.1 wheelset replaced.

| Doncaster | 16/06/80 | 17/06/80 | Unclassified |

No.1 engine, 409, with collector drum split underneath. The collector drum was replaced.

| Doncaster | 13/11/80 | 17/11/80 | Unclassified |

No.2 engine, 432, replaced by 539, due to aerating.

| Doncaster | 13/01/81 | 21/01/81 | Unclassified |

No.1 engine, 409, replaced by 424, due to scavenge blower drive sheared. A loose fan coupling was repaired.

| Doncaster | 09/03/81 | 10/03/81 | Unclassified |

No.2 engine, 539, replaced by 418, due to high iron content.

| Doncaster | 05/05/81 | 07/05/81 | Unclassified |

Collision damage repairs.

| Doncaster | 26/08/81 | 07/09/81 | Unclassified |

No.1 engine, 424, replaced by 406, due to coolant system aerating, suspect fractured cylinder liner. Collision damage and header tank repairs were also carried out.

| Doncaster | 05/01/82 | 30/07/84 | - |

Nil. The locomotive arrived on Works after withdrawal with the following main components fitted. No.1 engine, 406, build up of oil in collector drum, recently been on fire. No.2 engine, 418. No.1 bogie, 9000-11. No.2 bogie, 9000-12. Boiler, 5095/J3246. The locomotive was subsequently sold for preservation.

D9017/9017/55 017 The Durham Light Infantry

Loco Works	On Works	Off Works	Class of repair
Doncaster	10/11/61	Not recorded	Acceptance trials

New locomotive fitted with the following known main components. No.1 engine, (unknown). No.2 engine, (unknown). No.1 bogie, 1035. No.2 bogie, 1036. Boiler, 5091/J3242.

| Doncaster | 03/01/62 | 04/01/62 | Unclassified |

Fuel tank fractured. No.1 left hand side fuel tank was replaced. No.2 left hand side lifeguards were replaced. A handle was fitted to the boiler water hand pump. The locomotive mileage was recorded as 14,500 miles.

| R.S.H. Darlington | Not recorded | 22/03/62 | Unclassified |

No.1 engine, replaced by 457. No.2 engine, replaced by 421.

| Doncaster | 18/05/62 | 22/05/62 | Light |

No.1 bogie, 1035, replaced by 1002. No.2 bogie, 1036, replaced by 1042. Boiler, 5091/J3242, was overhauled. The body was given a six monthly examination. Water scoop snouts were repaired, as was the steam pipe from train pipe to cab gauge.

| Doncaster | 10/11/62 | 12/11/62 | Unclassified |

No.2 bogie, 1042, No.2 right and left hand horns cracked. These were repaired. The locomotive mileage was recorded as 130,600 miles.

| Doncaster | 27/11/62 | 30/11/62 | Light |

No.1 bogie, 1002, replaced by 1021. No.2 bogie, 1042, replaced by 1022. The body was given a six monthly examination.

| Doncaster | 01/02/63 | 05/02/63 | Unclassified |

Boiler, 5091/J3242, replaced by 5096/J3247, due to fractured tubes. The locomotive mileage was recorded as 163,190 miles.

| Doncaster | 18/03/63 | 01/04/63 | General |

No.1 engine, 457, replaced by 439. No.2 engine, 421, replaced by 414. No.1 bogie, 1021, replaced by 1011. No.2 bogie, 1022, replaced by 1012. The body was given an annual repair. The following mods were carried out - Sampling cocks; Radiator fan grills; Soundproofing; AWS positioning; Water contents gauge; Air duct on bodysides; Cubicle sealing; Silencer drain pipe extensions.

| Doncaster | 20/08/63 | 22/08/63 | Unclassified |

Both main generators and all traction motors flashed over. No.1 bogie, 1011, replaced by 1047. No.2 bogie, 1012, replaced by 1048. The flashover damage on both main generators cleaned up.

| Doncaster | 09/10/63 | 16/10/63 | Light |

No.1 bogie, 1047, replaced by 1037. No.2 bogie, 1048, replaced by 1038. Boiler, 5096/J3247, replaced by 1489/J2945. The body was given a six monthly examination.

| R.S.H. Darlington | 25/10/63 | 29/10/63 | Unclassified |

'The Durham Light Infantry' nameplates fitted.

| Doncaster | 29/11/63 | 30/11/63 | Unclassified |

No.1 engine, 439, replaced by 406, due to loss of coolant.

| Doncaster | 04/12/63 | 04/12/63 | Unclassified |

No.1 main generator feet fractures. These were welded.

| Doncaster | 17/02/64 | 07/03/64 | General |

No.1 engine, 406, replaced by 443. No.2 engine, 414, replaced by 435. No.1 bogie, 1037 and No.2 bogie, 1038, were given General repairs. Boiler, 1489/J2945, replaced by 1488/J2944. The following modifications were carried out - Coolant header tank overflow tank; Speedometer clock; Boiler panel fuses.

| Doncaster | 04/05/64 | 05/05/64 | Unclassified |

No.1 bogie, 1037, had the leading transom beam, right hand helical spring and left hand lifeguard renewed. No.2 bogie, 1038, was given a Light repair.

| Doncaster | 15/06/64 | 17/06/64 | Unclassified |

No.1 engine, 443, fan gearbox bearing defective. No.1 fan gearbox, primary and secondary cardan shafts were replaced.

| Doncaster | 15/07/64 | 15/07/64 | Unclassified |

No.2 bogie, 1038, all wheelsets to be checked for distortion following derailment. No.1 bogie, 1037, replaced by 1009. No.2 bogie, 1038, replaced by 1010. Boiler, 1488/J2944, given an MP11 exam.

D9017/9017/55 017 The Durham Light Infantry (continued)

Loco Works	On Works	Off Works	Class of repair
Doncaster	24/11/64	24/11/64	Unclassified

No.1 bogie, 1009, inner headstock fracture and boiler water pump defective. No.1 bogie, 1009, given a Light repair. No.2 bogie, 1010, had transom fractures cut and welded. Boiler, 1488/J2944, had a replacement water pump and motor fitted.

| Doncaster | 31/12/64 | 09/01/65 | Not recorded |

No.1 bogie, 1009, replaced by 1033. No.2 bogie, 1010, replaced by 1034.

| Doncaster | 06/03/65 | 01/04/65 | General |

No.1 engine, 443, replaced by 441. No.2 engine, 435, replaced by 434. No.1 bogie, 1033, replaced by 1047. No.2 bogie, 1034, replaced by 1048. Boiler, 1488/J2944, replaced by 5098/J3249.

| Doncaster | 11/09/65 | 18/09/65 | Light |

No.1 engine, 441, water relay wedged out. The engine was given an MP11 exam. No.2 engine, 434, replaced by 423, due to a suspected liner fracture or seal defective. No.1 bogie, 1047, replaced by 9000-21. No.2 bogie, 1048, replaced by 9000-22. Boiler, 5098/J3249, replaced by 5092/J3243. The following modifications carried out - Protection bar for EP valves; Low water Mowbrey shroud.

| Doncaster | 06/01/66 | 18/01/66 | General |

No.1 engine, 441, was given an Unclassified repair. No.2 engine, 423, replaced by 431. No.1 bogie, 9000-21 and No.2 bogie, 9000-22, were given General repairs. Boiler, 5092/J3243, replaced by 1489/J2945. The body was given a General repair.

| Doncaster | 14/05/66 | 21/05/66 | Unclassified |

The locomotive was lifted for access to No.2 bogie, 9000-22, fractured axles. Nos.3 & 6 traction motors removed for access to axles and refitted. No.2 end lubricating oil radiators replaced.

| Doncaster | 21/11/66 | 25/11/66 | Light |

No.1 engine, 441, replaced by 455. No.2 engine, 431, was given an Unclassified repair. No.1 bogie, 9000-21, replaced by 9000-15. No.2 bogie, 9000-22, replaced by 9000-16. Boiler, 1489/J2945, was given an Unclassified repair. The body was given an Unclassified repair.

| Doncaster | 14/12/66 | 16/12/66 | Unclassified |

No.2 engine, 431, replaced by 440.

| Doncaster | 30/03/67 | 03/04/67 | Unclassified |

No.1 engine, 455, replaced by 432. Lubricating oil radiators and an exhaust silencer replaced.

| Doncaster | 11/04/67 | 27/04/67 | General |

No.1 engine, 432, replaced by 443. No.2 engine, 440, replaced by 435. No.1 bogie, 9000-15 and No.2 bogie, 9000-16, were given General repairs. Boiler, 1489/J2945, replaced by 5093/J3244. The body was given a General repair. Full yellow nose ends were applied.

| Doncaster | 25/10/67 | 31/10/67 | Light |

No.1 engine, 443 and No.2 engine, 435, were given Unclassified repairs. No.1 bogie, 9000-15, replaced by 9000-47. No.2 bogie, 9000-16, replaced by 9000-48. Boiler, 5093/J3244, was given an Unclassified repair. The body was given an Unclassified repair.

| Doncaster | 25/03/68 | 08/05/68 | General |

No.1 engine, 443, replaced by 430. No.2 engine, 435, replaced by 413. No.1 bogie, 9000-47 and No.2 bogie, 9000-48, were given General repairs. Boiler, 5093/J3244, replaced by 1487/J2943. The body was given a General repair. The locomotive was fitted for dual braking.

| Doncaster | 12/07/68 | 15/07/68 | Unclassified |

No.2 engine, 413, replaced by 443. No.1 exhaust collector drum drainpipe connection to secure in the drum. No.2 end engine room floor plate to secure left hand side. No.2 end radiators and lubricating oil tank cleaned out. No.2 traction motor nose suspension angle brackets set screws broken. All repairs were carried out.

| Doncaster | 11/11/68 | 12/11/68 | Unclassified |

No.1 main generator suspected 'oval'. All brushes chipped and brush pigtails fractured and generator down to earth. The main generator was replaced.

| Doncaster | 23/12/68 | 07/01/69 | Light |

Derailment damage. No.1 engine, 430, replaced by 404. No.2 engine, 443, was given an Unclassified repair. No.1 bogie, 9000-47, replaced by 9000-21. No.2 bogie, 9000-48, replaced by 9000-22, due to No.4 axle suspected bent. Boiler, 1487/J2943, was given Unclassified repair. The body was given an Unclassified repair. Fuel and water tanks damaged left hand side - repaired.

| Doncaster | 10/01/69 | 13/01/69 | Unclassified |

Flashover damage to both main generators and all traction motors. This was repaired.

D9017/9017/55 017 The Durham Light Infantry (continued)

Loco Works	On Works	Off Works	Class of repair
Doncaster	27/05/69	28/05/69	Unclassified

No.2 engine, 443, replaced by 434 - top being full of coolant. No.1 end lub. oil radiator cleaned.

Doncaster	23/06/69	26/06/69	Unclassified

No.1 engine, 404, replaced by 436, due to con rod through crankcase. No.1 main generator replaced due to flashover damage. No.1 end lubricating oil and coolant systems were flushed out.

Doncaster	15/09/69	04/10/69	Intermediate

*No.1 engine, 436, replaced by 426. No.2 engine, 434, replaced by 429. No.1 bogie, 9000-21, replaced by 9000-31. No.2 bogie, 9000-22, replaced by 9000-32. Boiler, 1487/J2943, replaced by 1490/J2946. The water tank capacity modification was carried out. The body was given an Intermediate repair and repainted into **blue livery with full yellow nose ends**.*

Doncaster	18/02/70	24/02/70	Unclassified

Fuel tanks punctured due to speedometer generator coming adrift. Silencer also split. These defects were repaired, as was No.1 load regulator. Field divert contactors were also replaced. Both main generators had brushes renewed as necessary.

Doncaster	Not recorded	16/05/70	Light

No.1 engine, 426, was given a Light repair. No.2 engine, 429, replaced by 412. No.1 bogie, 9000-31, replaced by 9000-1. No.2 bogie, 9000-32, replaced by 9000-2. Boiler, 1490/J2946, was given an Unclassified repair. The body was given a Light repair.

Doncaster	30/06/70	03/07/70	Unclassified

No.2 engine, 412, replaced by 416, due to aerating, suspected fractured liner. No.2 exhauster loose on mountings. This was repaired.

Doncaster	12/11/70	14/11/70	Unclassified

No.1 engine, 426, replaced by 448 - lubricating oil sump full of water, suspected fractured liner.

Doncaster	12/01/71	14/01/71	Unclassified

No.2 engine, 416, replaced by 431, due to loss of coolant.

Doncaster	15/01/71	18/01/71	Unclassified

No.2 engine, 431, had the high water temperature probe examined and power earth fault and cut out switches were repaired.

Doncaster	23/02/71	21/05/71	Intermediate

No.1 engine, 448, replaced by 407. No.2 engine, 431, replaced by 437. No.1 bogie, 9000-1 and No.2 bogie, 9000-2, were given General repairs. Boiler, 1490/J2946, replaced by 5096/J3247. The body was given an Intermediate repair. The locomotive was fitted with E.T.H. equipment.

Doncaster	13/06/71	14/06/71	Rectification

A lighting earth fault was rectified.

Doncaster	23/06/71	24/06/71	Rectification

No.1 engine, 407, shutting down intermittently. Incorrect wiring in earth fault and engine shut down circuits. These faults were rectified.

Doncaster	24/09/71	25/09/71	Unclassified

No.1 boiler water tank was repaired.

Doncaster	22/10/71	30/10/71	Unclassified

No.2 engine, 437, suspected dephased. This engine was not replaced. Locomotive repeatedly booked for rough riding. No.1 bogie, 9000-1, had swing link pins renewed and No.1 traction motor gearcase was replaced. No.2 boiler water tank was repaired.

Doncaster	06/11/71	10/11/71	Unclassified

No.1 engine, 407, replaced by 457, due to aerating.

Doncaster	15/11/71	17/11/71	Unclassified

No.1 engine, 457, unable to start due to suspected fault in control cubicle. No.2 engine, 437, replaced by 438, due to No.2 main generator windings torn.

Doncaster	25/11/71	27/11/71	Unclassified

No.2 engine, 438, replaced by 443.

Doncaster	20/03/72	25/03/72	Light

No.1 engine, 457, was given a Light repair. No.2 engine, 443, replaced by 440. No.1 bogie, 9000-1, replaced by 9000-37. No.2 bogie, 9000-2, replaced by 9000-38. Boiler, 5096/J3247, was given a General repair. The body was given a Light repair.

D9017/9017/55 017 The Durham Light Infantry (continued)

Loco Works	On Works	Off Works	Class of repair
Doncaster	22/05/72	02/06/72	Unclassified

No.1 engine, 457, knocking, suspect phasing gear. Metal particles in scavenge oil pump strainer. No.1 engine, 457, was given an Intermediate repair.

Doncaster	10/10/72	12/10/72	Unclassified

No.1 engine, 457, replaced by 417, due to liner seal leaking, coolant in sump.

Doncaster	07/11/72	09/11/72	Unclassified

No.2 engine, 440, replaced by 411 - a suspected fractured liner, internal coolant leak in sump.

Doncaster	04/01/73	04/01/73	Unclassified

Boiler water tank leaking, No.1 bogie, 9000-37, required repairs to swing link pins and left hand footstep to be secured. The boiler water tank and bogie were repaired.

Doncaster	02/02/73	08/03/73	Intermediate

No.1 engine, 417, replaced by 413. No.2 engine, 411, replaced by 454. No.1 bogie, 9000-37 and No.2 bogie, 9000-38, were given standard repairs. Boiler, 5096/J3247, replaced by 1491/J2947. The body was given an Intermediate repair.

Doncaster	09/03/73	12/03/73	Rectification

Flashover damage to main generators and traction motors was repaired.

Doncaster	29/09/73	30/09/73	Unclassified

Boiler water tank holed. This was repaired.

Doncaster	29/10/73	03/11/73	Unclassified

No.1 engine, 413, dephased. No.1 engine, 413, was given an Intermediate repair.

Doncaster	15/12/73	22/12/73	Light

No.1 engine, 413, replaced by 449. No.2 engine, 454, was given a Light repair. No.1 bogie, 9000-37, replaced by 9000-21. No.2 bogie, 9000-38, replaced by 9000-41. Boiler, 1491/J2947, was given an Unclassified repair. The body was given a Light repair.

Doncaster	15/01/74	15/01/74	Modification

Earth fault relay modification was carried out.

Doncaster	22/04/74	25/04/74	Unclassified

No.2 engine, 454, replaced by 423, due to No.2 main generator output shaft sheared.

Doncaster	26/11/74	11/03/75	Intermediate

No.1 engine, 449, replaced by 440. No.2 engine, 423, replaced by 418. No.1 bogie, 9000-21, replaced by 9000-33. No.2 bogie, 9000-41, replaced by 9000-34. Boiler, 1491/J2947, replaced by 1489/J2945. The body was given an Intermediate repair.

Doncaster	07/04/75	15/04/75	Unclassified

No.2 engine, 418, replaced by 436, due to high spectrographic analysis. Both primary fan shafts were replaced. No.2 end lubricating oil tanks were cleaned.

Doncaster	17/04/75	17/04/75	Rectification

No.2 engine, 436, overspeeding. A replacement Martinair unit was fitted.

Doncaster	24/04/75	28/04/75	Unclassified

No.1 engine, 440, replaced by 455, due to high sodium and copper content in lubricating oil. No.1 end lubricating oil tank and radiators were cleaned.

Doncaster	04/07/75	17/07/75	Unclassified

No.1 engine, 455, replaced by 433, due to breathing heavy. No.2 engine, 436, replaced by 411.

Doncaster	15/12/75	30/12/75	Unclassified

No.1 engine, 433, replaced by 420. No.2 engine, 411, bad oil leak, 'AB' crankcase split. No.2 engine, 411, was given an Unclassified repair. No.2 boiler water tank was repaired.

Doncaster	12/03/76	26/03/76	Light

No.1 engine, 420, was given a Light repair. No.2 engine, 411, replaced by 433. No.1 bogie, 9000-33, replaced by 9000-1. No.2 bogie, 9000-34, replaced by 9000-2. Boiler, 1489/J2945, was given an Unclassified repair. The locomotive was weighed at 103t 12cwt.

Doncaster	12/04/76	13/04/76	Unclassified

No.2 engine, 433, replaced by 435.

Doncaster	12/06/76	16/06/76	Unclassified

No.1 end collision damage repairs.

Doncaster	15/07/76	20/07/76	Unclassified

No.2 engine, 435, replaced by 539, due to being dephased. No.4 traction motor contactor tips 'splashing copper'. A boiler water tank was repaired. No.4 traction motor contactor was replaced.

D9017/9017/55 017 The Durham Light Infantry (continued)

Loco Works	On Works	Off Works	Class of repair
Doncaster	25/09/76	28/09/76	Unclassified

No.1 engine, 420, replaced by 452.

| Doncaster | 04/04/77 | 08/04/77 | Unclassified |

No.1 engine, 452, replaced by 439. No.2 engine, 539, replaced by 443. No.1 main generator interpoles and fields zero. Both main generators were replaced. Nos.2, 4 & 6 traction motor nose suspension wear plates were renewed. The locomotive was weighed at 103t 17cwt.

| Doncaster | 03/05/77 | 14/05/77 | Unclassified |

No.1 engine, 439, replaced by 454, due to aerating. 454, failed on test and replaced by 407. No.2 engine, 443, replaced by 421, due to aerating.

| Doncaster | 24/05/77 | 28/05/77 | Unclassified |

No.1 main generator commutator profile uneven and commutator suspected unstable. The main generator was replaced. A leaking boiler water tank was repaired and No.1 bogie, 9000-1, had two loose liners rectified.

| Doncaster | 21/06/77 | 21/06/77 | Unclassified |

No.1 engine, 407, replaced by 453, due to aerating.

| Doncaster | 09/07/77 | 13/07/77 | Unclassified |

No.1 engine, 453, replaced by 436, due to aerating.

| Doncaster | 26/07/77 | 03/08/77 | Unclassified |

Rough riding. No.1 bogie, 9000-1 and No.2 bogie, 9000-2, examined and repaired.

| Doncaster | 03/10/77 | 19/01/78 | Intermediate |

No.1 engine, 436, replaced by 449. No.2 engine, 421, replaced by 426. No.1 bogie, 9000-1, replaced by 9000-39. No.2 bogie, 9000-2, replaced by 9000-40, due to No.5 axle flawed. Boiler, 1489/J2945, replaced by 5097/J3248. Route indicator panels were plated over.

| Doncaster | 16/05/78 | 23/05/78 | Unclassified |

No.1 engine, 449, excessive leakage of lubricating oil into main generator. Bolts missing from dome cover on 'CA' crankshaft cover. No.1 main generator was replaced due to oil contamination. No.2 boiler water tank leaking. No.1 primary drive shaft worn. No.1 load regulator tips to renew. No.1 bogie, 9000-39, 'L1' liner to secure and oil contamination. All defects were rectified.

| Doncaster | 10/08/78 | 15/08/78 | Unclassified |

A boiler water tank was leaking. This was repaired.

| Doncaster | 08/09/78 | 13/09/78 | Unclassified |

Rough riding on No.2 bogie, 9000-40. No.1 bogie, 9000-39, had No.3 left hand inner coil spring broken or out of position. No.3 spring plank striking safety brackets. No.5 traction motor suspension packing plate set bolts stripped. No.1 engine, 449, Martinair and overspeed trip to fit. No.1 bogie, 9000-39, had one equalising beam spring renewed. No.2 bogie, 9000-40, had No.4 spring plank and shock absorbers replaced.

| Doncaster | 07/10/78 | 10/10/78 | Unclassified |

No.2 engine, 426, replaced by 418, due to aerating. No.1 load regulator had an oil leak rectified. No.2 load regulator tips cleaned. No.1 bogie, 9000-39 and No.2 bogie, 9000-40, had brake adjustments made.

| Doncaster | 26/10/78 | 30/10/78 | Unclassified |

Fuel tanks contaminated with water. No.1 engine, 449, requiring gudgeon pin housing examination. No.2 engine, 418, primary fan shaft drive flange bolts loose. No.1 main generator had slight flashover damage. Boiler, 5097/J3248, reported continually locking out due to fuel contamination. No.1 left hand side fuel tank was replaced. All defects were rectified.

| Doncaster | 30/10/78 | 31/10/78 | Unclassified |

Water in main fuel tank. This was rectified, as was a defect with the main steam pipe.

| Doncaster | 28/11/78 | 29/11/78 | Unclassified |

Rough riding and No.2 bogie, 9000-40, left trailing inner bogie coil spring broken. No.2 load regulator to be set up using a radius tool. All repairs carried out. The loco weighed 106t 16cwt.

| Doncaster | 03/01/79 | 10/01/79 | Unclassified |

No.2 engine, 418, replaced by 448, due to being dephased. No.1 drum tank had a fracture repaired.

| Doncaster | 01/05/79 | 17/05/79 | Unclassified |

No.1 engine, 449, replaced by 414, due to being time expired. No.2 engine, 448, replaced by 421, due to sump oil blown out through breather.

D9017/9017/55 017 The Durham Light Infantry (continued)

Loco Works	On Works	Off Works	Class of repair
Doncaster	08/08/79	13/08/79	Unclassified

No.2 engine, 421, replaced by 458, due to bad fuel dilution, suspected 'A' bank cambox fractured. No.1 primary cardan shaft splines defective. No.2 primary gearbox defective. These were rectified.

| Doncaster | 07/09/79 | 12/09/79 | Unclassified |

No.1 main generator field windings open circuit. The main generator was replaced.

| Doncaster | 08/10/79 | 09/10/79 | Unclassified |

No.2 engine, 458, collector drum split. No.2 load regulator and engine room floor cleaned.

| Doncaster | 16/10/79 | 02/11/79 | Light |

No.1 engine, 414 and No.2 engine, 458, were given Light repairs. No.1 bogie, 9000-39, replaced by 9000-11. No.2 bogie, 9000-40, replaced by 9000-12. Boiler, 5097/J3248, was given an Unclassified repair. The locomotive was weighed at 104t 18cwt.

| Doncaster | 03/11/79 | 10/11/79 | Rectification |

No.1 engine, 414, shutting down. This was rectified.

| Doncaster | 27/11/79 | 01/12/79 | Unclassified |

No.1 engine, 414, no oil pressure. No.2 engine, 458, collector drum tank fractured, recent exhaust lagging fire. No.1 engine, 414 - pipes to oil pump cleaned out. No.2 engine, 458 - tank replaced.

| Doncaster | 18/01/80 | 28/03/80 | Unclassified |

No.1 end collision damage. No.1 bogie, 9000-11, replaced by 9000-24. No.2 bogie, 9000-12, replaced by 9000-48. Buffer beam distorted about coupling slide. Front casing from route indicator down to renew. Air pipes on buffer beam broken. E.T.H. junction box and dummy plug missing. Cables and conduit broken. Both buffers to renew. Nose end interior brake distributor pushed back and air pipes distorted. Main air reservoir pushed back and brackets broken. Fire bottles pushed out of position. Framing underneath No.1 end to examine for damage. No.1 traction motor contactor missing. All damage was repaired at a cost of £8,200.

| Doncaster | 31/05/80 | 05/06/80 | Unclassified |

No.2 engine, 458, replaced by 448, due to a suspected fractured liner.

| Doncaster | 14/06/80 | 17/06/80 | Unclassified |

No.2 engine, 448, replaced by 435, due to a suspected fractured liner.

| Doncaster | 26/09/80 | 30/09/80 | Unclassified |

No.1 engine, 414, replaced by 443, due to No.1 main generator riser banding disintegrated, suspected short circuit causing burning on armature. No.1 main generator was replaced. Primary fan shafts to renew. Both load regulators were leaking.

| Doncaster | 17/02/81 | 25/02/81 | Unclassified |

No.2 engine, 435, replaced by 409, due to being time expired. A boiler water tank was repaired. No.2 engine mounting feet to be repaired. No.2 cardan shaft and No.2 secondary shaft to repair. Both load regulators to clean and tips to reset. No.2 bogie, 9000-48, had No.5 traction motor nose suspension pad to secure, 'L7' horn liner to secure. All repairs were carried out.

| Doncaster | 24/04/81 | 01/05/81 | Unclassified |

No.2 engine, 409, replaced by 422, due to losing coolant, suspected fractured liner.

| Doncaster | 08/07/81 | 08/07/81 | Unclassified |

No.2 engine, 422, suspected fractured liner. The locomotive was load bank tested - no fault found.

| Doncaster | 13/11/81 | 17/11/81 | Unclassified |

No.1 engine, 443, replaced by 424, due to being dephased. Note - This was the last repair work carried out on the class at Doncaster.

| Doncaster | 23/01/82 | - | - |

The locomotive arrived on Works after withdrawal with the following main components fitted. No.1 engine, 424. No.2 engine, 422. No.1 bogie, 9000-24. No.2 bogie, 9000-48. Boiler, 5097/J3248.

D9018/9018/55 018 Ballymoss

Loco Works	On Works	Off Works	Class of repair
Doncaster	24/11/61	13/12/61	Acceptance trials

New locomotive fitted with the following main components. No.1 engine, 409. No.2 engine, 413. No.1 bogie, 1037. No.2 bogie, 1038. Boiler, 5093/J3244. 'Ballymoss' nameplates fitted.

| R.S.H. Darlington | 16/03/62 | 19/04/62 | Unclassified |

No.2 engine, 413, replaced by 452, due to pieces of piston and rings in chip tray. The locomotive mileage was recorded as 34,630 miles.

| Doncaster | 30/05/62 | 01/06/62 | Light |

No.1 bogie, 1037, replaced by 1035. No.2 bogie, 1038, replaced by 1036. The body was given a six monthly examination.

| Doncaster | 21/09/62 | 23/09/62 | Unclassified |

No.1 engine, 409, replaced by 412, due to breathing heavy. Flashover damage to all traction motors. The locomotive mileage was recorded as 117,220 miles.

| Doncaster | 31/12/62 | 01/01/63 | Light |

No.1 bogie, 1035, replaced by 1037. No.2 bogie, 1036, replaced by 1038.

| Doncaster | 04/02/63 | 06/02/63 | Unclassified |

No.2 engine, 452, replaced by 430, due to an unknown defect.

| Doncaster | 11/03/63 | 11/03/63 | Unclassified |

No.1 bogie, 1037, replaced by 1017, due to transom fractures. No.2 bogie, 1038, replaced by 1026, due to transom fractures. No.1 end right side oil pressure switch replaced. The locomotive mileage was recorded as 191,400 miles.

| Doncaster | 04/04/63 | 05/04/63 | Unclassified |

No.3 traction motor end suspension bearing box loose, bolts missing. Other traction motor bearing boxes loose bolts. A new axle and gear wheel were fitted to No.3 position. The locomotive mileage was recorded as 201,850 miles.

| Doncaster | 13/05/63 | 27/05/63 | General |

No.1 engine, 412, replaced by 457. No.2 engine, 430, replaced by 407. No.1 bogie, 1017, replaced by 1013. No.2 bogie, 1026, replaced by 1014. Boiler, 5093/J3244, replaced by 1495/J2951. The body was given an annual repair. The following modifications were carried out - Exhaust drain tank; Sampling cocks; Boiler air ducting; Caustic injection; Radiator fan grills; Lubricating oil tank strainers; Bodyside filters; Sound proofing; Boiler pump motor and fitting sequence.

| Doncaster | 23/07/63 | 25/07/63 | Unclassified |

Fractured boiler tubes, new clutch shoes to fit to No.1 engine fan clutch. The repairs were carried out. The locomotive mileage was recorded as 261,880 miles.

| Doncaster | 31/07/63 | 01/08/63 | Unclassified |

No.1 bogie, 1013, replaced by 1021. No.2 bogie, 1014, replaced by 1022, due to several derailments. The locomotive mileage was recorded as 264,960 miles.

| Doncaster | 20/09/63 | 21/09/63 | Unclassified |

Underframe fractures under No.1 main generator mounting 'B' side. The fractures were repaired. The locomotive mileage was recorded as 280,210 miles.

| Doncaster | 22/10/63 | 24/10/63 | Unclassified |

Repairs to a boiler water tank. No.2 main water tank was repaired. The automatic blowdown modification was fitted.

| Doncaster | 02/12/63 | 11/12/63 | Light |

No.1 bogie, 1021, replaced by 1047. No.2 bogie, 1022, replaced by 1048. The body was given a six monthly examination. Fractures to the main generator mounting floor were repaired. The locomotive mileage was recorded as 323,750 miles.

| Doncaster | 25/05/64 | 14/06/64 | General |

No.1 engine, 457, replaced by 450. No.2 engine, 407, replaced by 452. No.1 bogie, 1047 and No.2 bogie, 1048, were given General repairs. Boiler, 1495/J2951, replaced by 5089/J3240. The body was given a General repair.

| Doncaster | 24/09/64 | 27/09/64 | Unclassified |

No.1 engine, 450, was given an MP11 exam. No.1 bogie, 1047, had traction motors cleaned out and horn liners repaired. No.2 bogie, 1048, had No.5 axle horn liner broken and weld broken left side. This was repaired and ten new brushes were fitted. Boiler, 5089/J3240, was given an MP11 exam.

D9018/9018/55 018 Ballymoss (continued)

Loco Works	On Works	Off Works	Class of repair
Doncaster	15/10/64	16/10/64	Light

Flashover damage to Nos.4, 5 & 6 traction motors. No.1 engine, 450 and No.2 engine, 452, were given MP11 exams. No.1 bogie, 1047, replaced by 1025. No.2 bogie, 1048, replaced by 1018. Boiler, 5089/J3240, was given an Unclassified repair. The body was given an Unclassified repair.

Doncaster	23/10/64	26/10/64	Unclassified

No.1 engine, 450 and No.2 engine, 452, were given Unclassified repairs. No.1 bogie, 1025, left hand side axlebox liner adrift. No.2 bogie, 1018, No.4 traction motor nose suspension rubbing plate adrift. Both bogies were repaired. Boiler, 5089/J3240, was given an Unclassified repair.

Doncaster	16/11/64	20/11/64	Unclassified

Burnt wiring on compressors, exhausters and main generators. The burnt wiring was replaced and all traction motors were cleaned out.

Doncaster	12/01/65	12/01/65	Light

Slight flashover damage on all traction motors. No.1 bogie, 1025, replaced by 1028. No.2 bogie, 1018, replaced by 1029. Boiler, 5089/J3240, was given a General repair.

Doncaster	12/02/65	17/02/65	Unclassified

No.1 engine, 450 and No.2 engine, 452, were given Unclassified repairs. All traction motors were cleaned and new brushes and insulators fitted where necessary. A new boiler water tank was fitted. Boiler, 5089/J3240, was given an Unclassified repair.

Doncaster	20/03/65	20/03/65	Unclassified

All coolant radiators were replaced, as was No.1 primary cardan shaft.

Doncaster	06/04/65	06/04/65	Unclassified

No.1 bogie, 1028 and No.2 bogie, 1029, were cleaned and had transom fractures cut and welded.

Doncaster	05/05/65	04/06/65	General

No.1 engine, 450, replaced by 452. No.2 engine, 452, replaced by 427. No.1 bogie, 1028, replaced by 1037. No.2 bogie, 1029, replaced by 1038. Boiler, 5089/J3240, replaced by 1491/J2947. The body was given a General repair. The locomotive mileage was recorded as 573,220 miles.

Doncaster	20/07/65	24/07/65	Unclassified

No.2 engine, 427, replaced by 457, due to water in sump. No.1 bogie, 1037, replaced by 9000-9. No.2 bogie, 1038, replaced by 9000-10.

Doncaster	24/09/65	25/09/65	Unclassified

No.2 auxiliary generator was replaced.

Doncaster	16/11/65	17/11/65	Unclassified

Boiler, 1491/J2947, was given an Unclassified repair.

Doncaster	23/11/65	29/11/65	Light

No.1 engine, 452, replaced by 438. No.2 engine, 457, was given an Unclassified repair. No.1 bogie, 9000-9, replaced by 9000-39. No.2 bogie, 9000-10, replaced by 9000-40. Boiler, 1491/J2947, was given an Unclassified repair. The body was given an Unclassified repair.

Doncaster	05/03/66	17/03/66	General

No.1 engine, 438, replaced by 452. No.2 engine, 457, replaced by 453, due to 'BC' crankshaft inner viscous damper and quill shaft fractured. No.1 bogie, 9000-39, replaced by 9000-47. No.2 bogie, 9000-40, replaced by 9000-48. Boiler, 1491/J2947, replaced by 5086/J3237.

Doncaster	04/05/66	05/05/66	Unclassified

No.1 bogie, 9000-47, No.3 axle suspected flawed at gear side. No.2 bogie, 9000-48, No.4 axle suspected flawed at gear side.

Doncaster	04/06/66	04/06/66	Modification

Repositioning of warning horns. Westinghouse type were removed and Trico Folberth fitted.

Doncaster	24/10/66	28/10/66	Light

No.1 engine, 452 and No.2 engine, 453, were given Unclassified repairs. No.1 bogie, 9000-47, replaced by 9000-13. No.2 bogie, 9000-48, replaced by 9000-14. Boiler, 5086/J3237, was given an Unclassified repair.

Doncaster	07/11/66	08/11/66	Unclassified

No.2 engine, 453, replaced by 415, due to breathing badly, suspect loose piston crown.

Doncaster	26/01/67	15/02/67	General

No.1 engine, 452, replaced by 422. No.2 engine, 415, replaced by 447. No.1 bogie, 9000-13 and No.2 bogie, 9000-14, were given General repairs. Boiler, 5086/J3237, replaced by 1495/J2951. The body was given a General repair. Full yellow nose ends applied.

D9018/9018/55 018 Ballymoss (continued)

Loco Works	On Works	Off Works	Class of repair
Doncaster	07/03/67	08/03/67	Unclassified

Water scoop defect. No.1 fan gearbox and the water scoop were replaced.

| Doncaster | 09/06/67 | 19/06/67 | Unclassified |

No.2 engine, 447, replaced by 458 - No.5 'BC' bearing cap studs broken and bearing cap damaged.

| Doncaster | 25/09/67 | 03/10/67 | Light |

No.1 engine, 422 and No.2 engine, 458, were given Unclassified repairs. No.1 bogie, 9000-13, replaced by 9000-27. No.2 bogie, 9000-14, replaced by 9000-28. Boiler, 1495/J2951, was given an Unclassified repair. The body was given an Unclassified repair.

| Doncaster | 05/02/68 | 07/03/68 | General |

No.1 engine, 422, replaced by 457. No.2 engine, 458, replaced by 440. No.1 bogie, 9000-27, replaced by 9000-49. No.2 bogie, 9000-28, replaced by 9000-50. Boiler, 1495/J2951, replaced by 5086/J3237. The body was given a General repair. The locomotive was fitted for dual braking.

| Doncaster | 11/03/68 | 13/03/68 | Rectification |

Flashover damage on both main generators and a brake fault. All repairs were carried out.

| Doncaster | 02/04/68 | 03/04/68 | Unclassified |

Field divert resistances defective, loss of amps. This was caused by a fault on an underspeed trip, which was replaced.

| Doncaster | 09/04/68 | 09/04/68 | Unclassified |

Load tests on both engines.

| Doncaster | 23/09/68 | 27/09/68 | Light |

No.1 engine, 457, replaced by 420. No.2 engine, 440, replaced by 455. No.1 bogie, 9000-49, replaced by 9000-19. No.2 bogie, 9000-50, replaced by 9000-20. Boiler, 5086/J3237, was given an Unclassified repair. The body was given an Unclassified repair.

| Doncaster | 04/11/68 | 05/11/68 | Unclassified |

No.2 engine, 455, 'CA' crankcase cover joint to renew.

| Doncaster | 16/04/69 | 10/05/69 | Intermediate |

*No.1 engine, 420, replaced by 433. No.2 engine, 455, replaced by 417. No.1 bogie, 9000-19, replaced by 9000-35. No.2 bogie, 9000-20, replaced by 9000-36. Boiler, 5086/J3237, replaced by 5094/J3245. The body was given an Intermediate repair and repainted into **blue livery with full yellow nose ends**.*

| Doncaster | 17/10/69 | 21/10/69 | Unclassified |

No.2 engine, 417, replaced by 446, due to reported high aluminium content in lubricating oil.

| Doncaster | 31/12/69 | 31/12/69 | Unclassified |

No.1 bogie, 9000-35, replaced by 9000-19. No.2 bogie, 9000-36, replaced by 9000-20, due to No.6 axlebox liner right hand side working out.

| Doncaster | 07/02/70 | 14/02/70 | Light |

No.1 primary fan shaft to repair and high water temperature capillary tubes to re-site clear of main generator. No.1 engine, 433 and No.2 engine, 446, were given Light repairs. No.1 bogie, 9000-19, replaced by 9000-49. No.2 bogie, 9000-20, replaced by 9000-50. Boiler, 5094/J3245, was given an Unclassified repair.

| Doncaster | 05/06/70 | 06/06/70 | Unclassified |

No.2 engine, 446, replaced by 435, due to being dephased.

| Doncaster | 10/07/70 | 11/07/70 | Unclassified |

No.1 engine, 433, replaced by 406 - breathing badly. Slight flashover damage to both main generators was repaired.

| Doncaster | 28/08/70 | 29/08/70 | Unclassified |

No.1 engine, 406, replaced by 424, due to pumping air into cooling system and causing loss of coolant. It was also suspected to have a fractured liner.

| Doncaster | 26/09/70 | 27/09/70 | Unclassified |

Fitting of new swing link pin locking plate studs and welding of fractured locking plates.

| Doncaster | 14/10/70 | 16/10/70 | Unclassified |

No.2 engine, 435, replaced by 429, due to torsional vibration dampers on 'AB' crankshaft adrift. All wiring examined due to a 75-volt leak to earth when engines working. Suspect lighting circuit.

D9018/9018/55 018 Ballymoss (continued)

Loco Works	On Works	Off Works	Class of repair
Doncaster	04/11/70	23/02/71	Intermediate

No.1 engine, 424, replaced by 433. No.2 engine, 429, replaced by 438, due to a suspected fractured liner. No.1 bogie, 9000-49, replaced by 9000-9. No.2 bogie, 9000-50, replaced by 9000-42. Boiler, 5094/J3245, replaced by 1496/J2952. The body was given an Intermediate repair. The locomotive was fitted with E.T.H. equipment.

Doncaster	11/03/71	13/03/71	Unclassified

Constant wheelslip at speeds between 40 and 80 mph due to defective wheelslip relay. Suspected that Nos.3 & 4 traction motors are also defective. No.2 primary fan shaft was replaced. Wheelslip resistances and relays were checked. Nos.3 & 4 traction motors were replaced.

Doncaster	13/04/71	15/04/71	Unclassified

No.2 engine, 438, replaced by 430. No.1 boiler water tank fractured. Lubricating oil tank and radiators were cleaned.

Doncaster	26/04/71	29/04/71	Unclassified

No.2 engine, 430, replaced by 443. No.2 lubricating oil tank and oil and water radiators were cleaned, as was No.1 main generator.

Doncaster	03/07/71	07/07/71	Unclassified

No.1 engine, 433, replaced by 456, due to a suspected fractured liner, coolant in sump and high lead and water content. No.1 bogie, 9000-9, had swing link pins renewed.

Doncaster	Not recorded	21/09/71	Unclassified

No.1 bogie, 9000-9, replaced by 9000-49, due to suspension pins working out on 'A' side and studs broken and/or missing on 'B' side. No.2 bogie, 9000-42, replaced by 9000-50.

Doncaster	Not recorded	18/10/71	Unclassified

No.1 water tank leaking. This was repaired.

Doncaster	By 27/11/71	07/12/71	Unclassified

No.1 engine, 456, replaced by 416. No.2 engine, 443, replaced by 426. No.1 end lubricating oil tank and radiators were cleaned.

Doncaster	03/01/72	07/01/72	Light

No.1 bogie, 9000-49 and No.2 bogie, 9000-50, were given standard repairs. Boiler, 1496/J2952, was given an Unclassified repair. The body was given a Light repair.

Doncaster	27/04/72	28/04/72	Unclassified

No.1 bogie, 9000-49, replaced by 9000-1. No.2 bogie, 9000-50, replaced by 9000-2.

Doncaster	15/05/72	03/08/72	Unclassified

No.1 engine, 416, replaced by 431. No.2 engine, 426, replaced by 450, due to a seized piston. No.2 lubricating oil tank and radiators were cleaned.

Doncaster	08/08/72	10/08/72	Rectification

No.2 main generator replaced due to burnt cables, terminal bars and insulation.

Doncaster	15/01/73	15/02/73	Intermediate

No.1 engine, 431, replaced by 427. No.2 engine, 450, replaced by 458. No.1 bogie, 9000-1, replaced by 9000-3. No.2 bogie, 9000-2, replaced by 9000-4. Boiler, 1496/J2952, replaced by 1493/J2949. The body was given an Intermediate repair. Both cabs were draughtproofed having been reported as very draughty.

Doncaster	20/06/73	21/06/73	Unclassified

No.1 engine, 427, replaced by 442, due to a liner seal leaking. No.2 engine, 458, had flange mounting defective on auxiliary drive gearbox. This was repaired. Lubricating oil tanks and radiators were cleaned.

Doncaster	07/08/73	11/08/73	Unclassified

No.2 engine, 458, replaced by 424, due to a fractured cylinder liner.

Doncaster	05/12/73	14/12/73	Light

No.1 engine, 442, 'B' bank crankcase door blown out, this was repaired. No.2 engine, 424, replaced by 456 - breathing heavy. No.1 bogie, 9000-3, replaced by 9000-5. No.2 bogie, 9000-4, replaced by 9000-6. Boiler, 1493/J2949, was given an Unclassified repair. Body given Light repair.

Doncaster	18/01/74	18/01/74	Modification

Earth fault relay modification was carried out.

Doncaster	23/05/74	24/05/74	Unclassified

No.2 bogie, 9000-6, equalising beam coil spring broken and carrier brackets studs sheared. This was repaired, as was a fracture in No.2 boiler water tank.

D9018/9018/55 018 Ballymoss (continued)

Loco Works	On Works	Off Works	Class of repair
Doncaster	24/07/74	01/08/74	Unclassified

No.2 engine, 456, replaced by 408, due to a suspected fractured liner. All coolant radiators were replaced and coolant temperature modification was carried out.

Doncaster	15/10/74	18/10/74	Unclassified

No.1 engine, 442, replaced by 539, due to being dephased. A boiler water tank was repaired.

Doncaster	11/11/74	21/03/75	Intermediate

No.1 engine, 539, replaced by 409, due to con rod broken and crankcase fractured. No.2 engine, 408, replaced by 452. No.1 bogie, 9000-5, replaced by 9000-21. No.2 bogie, 9000-6, replaced by 9000-41. Boiler, 1493/J2949, replaced by 5097/J3248. The body was given an Intermediate repair.

Doncaster	17/04/75	19/04/75	Unclassified

No.1 engine, 409, replaced by 450, due to crankcase fractured. 'L2' bodyside window was repaired and No.1 end lubricating oil tank cleaned. No.1 radiator fan clutch was renewed.

Doncaster	22/09/75	30/09/75	Unclassified

No.2 engine, 452, replaced by 456, due to crankcase mounting broken away. No.4 traction motor nose suspension plate was replaced.

Doncaster	16/12/75	18/12/75	Unclassified

No.1 engine, 450, replaced by 433, due to aerating, priming pump lubricating oil pipe burst.

Doncaster	31/12/75	08/01/76	Unclassified

No.2 engine, 456, replaced by 419, due to 'BC' crankcase fractured, suspected due to damper bearing dropped.

Doncaster	25/02/76	13/03/76	Light

No.1 engine, 433, replaced by 429, due to breathing badly. No.2 engine, 419, replaced by 422. No.1 bogie, 9000-21, replaced by 9000-39. No.2 bogie, 9000-41, replaced by 9000-40. Boiler, 5097/J3248, was given an Unclassified repair.

Doncaster	27/08/76	08/09/76	Unclassified

No.1 engine, 429, replaced by 406, due to breathing heavy. No.2 engine, 422, replaced by 430, due to breathing heavy. No.1 bogie, 9000-39, had No.1 traction motor nose suspension pad loose and No.2 traction motor nose bracket loose. No.2 bogie, 9000-40, had No.5 right hand side pull rod safety stay missing. These defects were rectified. Nos.1 & 2 lubricating oil tanks and radiators were cleaned.

Doncaster	02/10/76	06/10/76	Unclassified

No.2 boiler water tank fractured. This was repaired, as was No.1 main generator mounting foot.

Doncaster	01/02/77	02/02/77	Unclassified

No.1 engine, 406, piston 'cracking up', aluminium in chip tray. Both engines air intake bellows to renew. No.1 boiler water tank was fractured. No.1 engine, clutch drum renewed, silencer drain repaired and Martinair and overspeed units renewed.

Doncaster	17/02/77	18/02/77	Unclassified

No.2 engine, 430, primary cardan shaft to renew. No.5 traction motor field open circuit. Flashover damage was cleaned up on both bogies. No.5 traction motor was replaced.

Doncaster	30/06/77	10/12/77	Intermediate

No.1 engine, 406, replaced by 539. No.2 engine, 430, replaced by 435, due to high copper content and breathing heavy. No.1 bogie, 9000-39, replaced by 9000-11. No.2 bogie, 9000-40, replaced by 9000-12. Boiler, 5097/J3248, replaced by 1492/J2948. The body was given an Intermediate repair. Route indicator panels were plated over.

Doncaster	15/12/77	16/12/77	Unclassified

No.2 engine, 435, replaced by 437 - aerating. Air operated window washers replaced by electric type. Mod 211/163 'Replacement of double window wipers with single type' was carried out.

Doncaster	19/07/78	28/07/78	Unclassified

No.1 engine, 539 and No.2 engine, 437, were given gudgeon pin housing examinations. No.1 bogie, 9000-11, had No.3 traction motor nose suspension pad secured. No.2 bogie, 9000-12, examination of No.5 axle bearings, left hand side is suspect. Cover discoloured and grease very black. No.5 wheelset axlebox bearings were renewed. No.1 boiler water tank had a leak rectified. Nos.1 & 2 primary fan shaft splines worn. All repairs were carried out.

Doncaster	17/08/78	20/08/78	Unclassified

No.1 engine, 539, replaced by 413, due to a suspect fractured liner.

D9018/9018/55 018 Ballymoss (continued)

Loco Works	On Works	Off Works	Class of repair
Doncaster	30/08/78	05/09/78	Unclassified

No.1 engine, 413, overspeeding - rectified. No.2 engine, 437, replaced by 404 - being dephased.

Doncaster	21/09/78	24/09/78	Unclassified

No.1 engine, 413, replaced by 437, due to scavenge blower drive broken.

Doncaster	19/10/78	25/10/78	Unclassified

No.1 engine, 437, replaced by 441, due to breathing badly. No.1 main generator field contactor was renewed and a boiler water tank was repaired.

Doncaster	12/03/79	14/03/79	Unclassified

No.2 engine, 404, replaced by 408, due to being time expired.

Doncaster	14/09/79	10/10/79	Light

No.1 engine, 441, replaced by 449, due to seizure in phasing gearcase. No.2 engine, 408, replaced by 446 - low oil pressure. No.1 bogie, 9000-11, replaced by 9000-23. No.2 bogie, 9000-12, replaced by 9000-30. Boiler, 1492/J2948, given Unclassified repair. The loco weighed 105t 3cwt.

Doncaster	22/10/79	23/10/79	Unclassified

No.1 main generator low insulation and flashover damage. This was repaired.

Doncaster	11/02/80	13/02/80	Unclassified

No.1 engine, 449, replaced by 444, due to 'A' bank end of camshaft damper and cover broken where turning over tool fits.

Doncaster	31/03/80	02/04/80	Unclassified

No.1 engine, 444, replaced by 415, due to a suspected fractured liner. No.2 primary shaft renewed.

Doncaster	15/08/80	21/08/80	Unclassified

No.1 engine, 415, replaced by 410, due to cylinder blocks to be pressure tested because of a leak.

Doncaster	28/04/81	08/05/81	Unclassified

No.2 engine, 446, replaced by 423, due to being dephased.

Stratford D.R.S.	20/10/81	23/11/81	-

No.2 engine, 423, replaced by 453, to enable 55 007 to return to traffic.

Doncaster	24/11/81	-	-

The locomotive arrived on Works after withdrawal with the following main components fitted. No.1 engine, 410, aerating. No.2 engine, 453, fractured cylinder liner. No.1 bogie, 9000-23. No.2 bogie, 9000-30. Boiler, 1492/J2948.

D9019/9019/55 019 Royal Highland Fusilier

Loco Works	On Works	Off Works	Class of repair
Doncaster	11/12/61	19/12/61 approx.	Acceptance trials

New locomotive fitted with the following main components. No.1 engine, 442. No.2 engine, 440. No.1 bogie, 1039. No.2 bogie, 1040. Boiler, 5094/J3245.

| R.S.H. Darlington | 10/05/62 | 08/06/62 | Not recorded |

Engine modifications.

| Doncaster | 12/06/62 | 14/06/62 | Light |

No.1 bogie, 1039, replaced by 1003. No.2 bogie, 1040, replaced by 1004. New flexible bellows fitted to No.2 exhaust. Compressor cylinder heads lifted and new valve strip joints fitted.

| Doncaster | 28/10/62 | 06/11/62 | General |

No.1 engine, 442, replaced by 426. No.2 engine, 440, replaced by 404. No.1 bogie, 1003, replaced by 1023. No.2 bogie, 1004, replaced by 1024. Boiler, 5094/J3245, replaced by 5090/J3241. The following modifications carried out - Radiator fan grills; Drawgear; Driver's vacuum brake valve.

| Doncaster | 05/12/62 | 07/12/62 | Unclassified |

No.2 coolant radiator was replaced. The warning horns were repositioned.

| Doncaster | 08/01/63 | 09/01/63 | Unclassified |

Earth faults to be rectified, Nos.1, 4 & 6 traction motors badly burnt. No.1 bogie, 1023, replaced by 1015. No.2 bogie, 1024, replaced by 1016. The locomotive mileage was recorded as 175,000 miles.

| Doncaster | 02/04/63 | 06/04/63 | Unclassified |

Flashover damage to all traction motors. All traction motors were replaced. The locomotive mileage was recorded as 220,840 miles.

| Doncaster | 20/04/63 | 24/04/63 | Light |

No.1 bogie, 1015, replaced by 1031. No.2 bogie, 1016, replaced by 1032. The body was given a six monthly examination.

| Doncaster | 31/07/63 | 02/08/63 | Unclassified |

No.2 engine, 404, replaced by 429. No.1 bogie, 1031, replaced by 1009. No.2 bogie, 1032, replaced by 1010.

| Doncaster | Not recorded | 12/09/63 | Unclassified |

No.1 engine, 426, replaced by 433. Boiler, 5090/J3241, replaced by 1496/J2952.

| Doncaster | 04/11/63 | 21/11/63 | General |

Underframe fractures. No.1 bogie, 1009, replaced by 1005. No.2 bogie, 1010, replaced by 1006. The body was given an annual repair. The following modifications were carried out - Main generator feet; Distance pieces under engines; Draught sealing; Soundproofing; Header tank overflow tank; Coolant gauge; New rubber oil and water hose fitted in roof section.

| Doncaster | 14/01/64 | 16/01/64 | Unclassified |

No.2 bogie, 1006, had a new anchor link pin fitted and cracks on the transom chipped and welded. No.4 wheelset was replaced.

| Doncaster | 06/05/64 | 14/05/64 | Light |

No.1 engine, 433, was given an Unclassified repair. No.2 engine, 429, replaced by 437. No.1 bogie, 1005, replaced by 1049. No.2 bogie, 1006, replaced by 1002. Boiler, 1496/J2952, was given an Unclassified repair. The body was given an Unclassified repair.

| Doncaster | Not recorded | 10/06/64 | Not recorded |

Not recorded.

| Doncaster | 30/06/64 | 01/07/64 | Unclassified |

No.2 auxiliary generator was replaced.

| Doncaster | Not recorded | 22/08/64 | Not recorded |

No.1 engine, 433, replaced by 410.

| Doncaster | 06/10/64 | 29/10/64 | General |

No.2 engine, 437, replaced by 405. No.1 bogie, 1049, replaced by 1019. No.2 bogie, 1002, replaced by 1020. Boiler, 1496/J2952, replaced by 5094/J3245. The body was given a General repair and superstructure fractures were welded.

| Doncaster | 04/11/64 | 05/11/64 | Unclassified |

No.2 traction motor cables/junction box connection burnt. No.2 traction motor cable box replaced.

| Doncaster | 28/02/65 | 05/03/65 | Unclassified |

No.1 engine, 410, replaced by 413, due to 'BC' crankshaft spline quill out of position.

D9019/9019/55 019 Royal Highland Fusilier (continued)

Loco Works	On Works	Off Works	Class of repair
Doncaster	26/03/65	26/03/65	Unclassified

Derailment damage. No.1 bogie, 1019, replaced by 1041. No.2 bogie, 1020, replaced by 1042, due to No.4 axle bent. The body had derailment damage repaired.

Doncaster	06/04/65	10/04/65	Light

No.1 engine, 413 and No.2 engine, 405 given Unclassified repairs. No.1 bogie, 1041, replaced by 1045. No.2 bogie, 1042, replaced by 1046. Boiler, 5094/J3245, was given an Unclassified repair.

Doncaster	15/04/65	15/04/65	Unclassified

No.1 engine, 413, loss of drive to scavenge blower. This was rectified.

Doncaster	20/04/65	21/04/65	Unclassified

No.1 engine, 413, had the scavenge blower replaced.

Doncaster	03/05/65	06/05/65	Unclassified

No.2 engine, 405, replaced by 422.

Doncaster	13/05/65	16/05/65	Unclassified

No.1 engine, 413, replaced by 450.

Doncaster	24/05/65	25/05/65	Unclassified

No.2 engine, 422, replaced by 428, due to excess water in sump.

Doncaster	27/07/65	29/07/65	Unclassified

No.2 engine, 428, replaced - 417 - suspected fractured liner. No.1 bogie 1045 - No.3 wheelset replaced.

Doncaster	12/09/65	14/09/65	Unclassified

No.2 engine, 417, replaced by 437.

Doncaster	02/10/65	29/10/65	General

No.1 engine, 450, replaced by 409. No.2 engine, 437, replaced by 448, due to high water temperature, suspect radiators had internal blockage. No.1 bogie, 1045, replaced by 9000-35. No.2 bogie, 1046, replaced by 9000-36. Boiler, 5094/J3245, replaced by 1494/J2950. The body was given a General repair including the repair of a cab footstep and superstructure.

Doncaster	14/02/66	16/02/66	Unclassified

Flashover damage to both main generators was cleaned up. Boiler, 1494/J2950, had repairs to defective tubes.

Doncaster	23/02/66	24/02/66	Unclassified

No.1 bogie, 9000-35 defective brakework repaired. No.1 coolant header tank repaired.

Doncaster	09/03/66	12/03/66	Light

No.1 engine, 409 and No.2 engine, 448, were given Unclassified repairs. No.1 bogie, 9000-35, replaced by 9000-33. No.2 bogie, 9000-36, replaced by 9000-34. Boiler, 1494/J2950, was given an Unclassified repair. The body was given an Unclassified repair.

Doncaster	20/03/66	22/03/66	Unclassified

No.2 engine, 448, replaced by 429, due to suspected dephased, excessive fuel oil in drum tank.

Doncaster	07/05/66	09/05/66	Unclassified

No.1 bogie, 9000-33, had No.1 axle replaced. No.1 coolant header tank was repaired.

Doncaster	23/07/66	26/07/66	Unclassified

No.1 engine, 409, replaced by 415, due to a suspected liner seal, sump full of water. No.2 engine, 429, reported to have been on fire, drum tank to repair. No.1 lubricating oil radiators were replaced. No.2 exhaust collector box was examined and lagging renewed.

Doncaster	24/10/66	25/10/66	Unclassified

No.2 collector drum was replaced due to a fracture.

Doncaster	01/11/66	18/11/66	General

No.1 engine, 415, replaced by 435. No.2 engine, 429, replaced by 411. No.1 bogie, 9000-33, replaced by 9000-11. No.2 bogie, 9000-34, replaced by 9000-12. Boiler, 1494/J2950, replaced by 5096/J3247. The body was given a General repair.

Doncaster	24/01/67	26/01/67	Unclassified

No.1 engine, 435, replaced by 458, due to a suspected fractured liner.

Doncaster	02/02/67	02/02/67	Unclassified

No.1 bogie, 9000-11, swing link bolts loose, all bottom damper bolts loose. No.2 bogie, 9000-12, left trailing bogie bearer pad liners broken out, swing link bolts loose, all bottom damper bolts loose. Waterscoop mouthpiece to renew. All repairs were carried out.

D9019/9019/55 019 Royal Highland Fusilier (continued)

Loco Works	On Works	Off Works	Class of repair
Doncaster	07/03/67	15/03/67	Light

No.1 engine, 458 and No.2 engine, 411, were given Unclassified repairs. No.1 bogie, 9000-11, replaced by 9000-17. No.2 bogie, 9000-12, replaced by 9000-18. Boiler, 5096/J3247, replaced by 1486/J2942. The body was given an Unclassified repair. Full yellow nose ends were applied.

Doncaster	14/06/67	23/06/67	Unclassified

No.1 engine, 458, replaced by 417. Both main generators and traction motors had flashover damage repaired.

Doncaster	06/07/67	11/07/67	Unclassified

No.1 auxiliary generator field coil burnt out, slight flashover damage on both main generators and all traction motors. AVRs were removed, tested and refitted. Flashover damage was cleaned up on both main and No.2 auxiliary generators. No.1 auxiliary generator was replaced, as were all traction motors. Boiler, 1486/J2942, replaced by 1489/J2945.

Doncaster	05/10/67	10/11/67	General

*No.1 engine, 417, replaced by 427. No.2 engine, 411, replaced by 428. No.1 bogie, 9000-17, replaced by 9000-15. No.2 bogie, 9000-18, replaced by 9000-16. Boiler, 1489/J2945, replaced by 5087/J3238. The body was given a General repair and repainted into **blue livery with full yellow nose ends**. The locomotive was fitted for dual braking.*

Doncaster	19/11/67	19/11/67	Modification

A modification was carried out to the dual brake auxiliary stand.

Doncaster	16/12/67	17/12/67	Modification

The compressor stand was modified.

Doncaster	01/01/68	03/01/68	Unclassified

Field divert resistances to re-balance. Wheelslip light coming bright at 82 - 92 mph - rectified.

Doncaster	13/01/68	23/01/68	Unclassified

Wheelslip at over 80 mph. Repeated bookings. Note shows loco to remain in traffic on restricted working until spares for resistance panel are on hand in Works. No.1 engine, 427, replaced by 442.

Doncaster	22/04/68	26/04/68	Light

No.1 engine, 442 and No.2 engine, 428, were given Unclassified repairs. No.1 bogie, 9000-15, replaced by 9000-31. No.2 bogie, 9000-16, replaced by 9000-32. Boiler, 5087/J3238, was given an Unclassified repair. The body was given an Unclassified repair.

Doncaster	09/12/68	03/01/69	Intermediate

No.1 engine, 442, replaced by 416. No.2 engine, 428, replaced by 423. No.1 bogie, 9000-31 and No.2 bogie, 9000-32, were given General repairs. Boiler, 5087/J3238, replaced by 1495/J2951. The body was given an Unclassified repair.

Doncaster	03/06/69	05/06/69	Unclassified

No.1 engine, 416, replaced by 413, due to a suspect cylinder liner, combustion gases in coolant. Flashover damage on No.2 main generator was cleaned up.

Doncaster	18/07/69	19/07/69	Unclassified

Traction motor bearings and boiler valve defects. No.1 bogie, 9000-31, had No.1 suspension hanger pin safety plate stud broken, No.2 axle suspension bearing flange set bolts sheared and distance piece missing. No.2 bogie, 9000-32, had No.5 axle suspension bearing flange set bolts sheared. Water pressure regulating valve renewed. Nos.2 & 5 wheelsets replaced. Repairs done.

Doncaster	01/09/69	19/09/69	Light

No.1 engine, 413 and No.2 engine, 423, were given Unclassified repairs. No.1 bogie, 9000-31, replaced by 9000-27. No.2 bogie, 9000-32, replaced by 9000-28. Boiler, 1495/J2951, was given an Unclassified repair. The body given an Unclassified repair. Water tank modification carried out.

Doncaster	14/01/70	17/01/70	Unclassified

No.1 engine, 413, replaced by 419.

Doncaster	04/02/70	05/02/70	Unclassified

No.2 engine, 423, replaced by 425, due to internal coolant leak, oil sump overflowing. Lubricating oil tank and radiators were cleaned.

Doncaster	08/04/70	09/04/70	Unclassified

No.1 engine, 419, replaced by 456, due to aerating badly and losing coolant due to a suspected fractured liner. Lubricating oil tank and radiators were cleaned. The high water temperature capillary tube was re-sited clear of main generator. The boiler blow down pipe was extended clear of the tank.

D9019/9019/55 019 Royal Highland Fusilier (continued)

Loco Works	On Works	Off Works	Class of repair
Doncaster	27/04/70	19/05/70	Intermediate

No.1 engine, 456, replaced by 413. No.2 engine, 425, replaced by 418. No.1 bogie, 9000-27 and No.2 bogie, 9000-28, were given General repairs. Boiler, 1495/J2951, replaced by 1497/J2953. The body was given an Intermediate repair.

| Doncaster | Not recorded | 08/10/70 | Unclassified |

No.2 engine, 418, replaced by 425.

| Doncaster | 12/10/70 | 14/10/70 | Unclassified |

No.1 engine, 413, replaced by 404. No.1 main generator brush ring badly burnt. No.2 main generator had flashover damage repaired.

| Doncaster | 22/10/70 | 25/10/70 | Unclassified |

No.1 engine, 404, replaced by 433, due to being dephased. Fuel coming from 'A' & 'C' manifold drains. Radiator fan shaft bearings at No.1 end replaced and leaks on steam heater pipe repaired.

| Doncaster | 26/11/70 | 24/04/71 | Light |

No.1 engine, 433, replaced by 435. No.2 engine, 425, replaced by 420. No.1 bogie, 9000-27, replaced by 9000-45. No.2 bogie, 9000-28, replaced by 9000-46. Boiler, 1497/J2953, was given a General repair. The body given a Light repair. The locomotive was fitted with E.T.H. equipment.

| Doncaster | 26/08/71 | 30/08/71 | Unclassified |

No.1 engine, 435, replaced by 409, due to water in sump.

| Doncaster | 03/09/71 | 11/09/71 | Unclassified |

No.1 engine, 409, replaced by 449, due to 'B5' con rod through crankcase. No.2 engine, 420, replaced by 455, due to suspected liner seals leaking, coolant in sump.

| Doncaster | 27/09/71 | 30/09/71 | Unclassified |

Right hand side fuel tank holed and water tank holed. Two bolts broken on No.3 traction motor and No.4 traction motor flashed over. Fuel and water tanks repaired. No.3 traction motor replaced and all other traction motors had flashover damage repaired. Pull rod safety stays were also repaired.

| Doncaster | 17/11/71 | 23/11/71 | Unclassified |

No.1 engine, 449, replaced by 421, due to con rod through crankcase. No.1 end radiator and lubricating oil tank were cleaned.

| Doncaster | 25/01/72 | 26/01/72 | Unclassified |

No.1 engine, 421, to test - continuously ruining auxiliary generator drive and coupling. The auxiliary drive shaft was repaired and re-aligned and the flexible coupling was replaced.

| Doncaster | 27/01/72 | 28/01/72 | Unclassified |

Not recorded.

| Doncaster | 16/02/72 | 16/03/72 | Intermediate |

No.1 engine, 421, replaced by 415. No.2 engine, 455, replaced by 418. No.1 bogie, 9000-45, replaced by 9000-3. No.2 bogie, 9000-46, replaced by 9000-4. Boiler, 1497/J2953, replaced by 5088/J3239. The body was given an Intermediate repair.

| Doncaster | 18/03/72 | 19/03/72 | Rectification |

Not recorded.

| Doncaster | 24/03/72 | 27/03/72 | Unclassified |

No.1 engine, 415, low lubricating oil pressure. Erratic operation of E.T.H., suspect earth fault. This was rectified. No fault found with 415.

| Doncaster | 03/05/72 | 05/05/72 | Unclassified |

Boiler water tanks fractured, No.2 end 'B' side radiator panel leaking coolant, exhauster mounting table leg fractured and oil leak at No.1 end above main generator - defects repaired.

| Doncaster | 02/06/72 | 05/06/72 | Unclassified |

All traction motors heavily flashed over. All traction motors were replaced.

| Doncaster | 05/06/72 | 08/06/72 | Unclassified |

Both main generators had flashover damage repaired.

| Doncaster | 15/12/72 | 21/12/72 | Unclassified |

No.2 engine, 418, replaced by 457, due to a suspected fractured liner, coolant in sump. No.2 end lubricating oil tank and radiators cleaned. Both bogies had repairs carried out to swing link pins.

| Doncaster | 03/01/73 | 12/01/73 | Light |

No.1 engine, 415, replaced by 430. No.1 bogie, 9000-3, replaced by 9000-35. No.2 bogie, 9000-4, replaced by 9000-36, due to rough riding, suspect loose bolts on bogie centre pivot. Boiler, 5088/J3239, was given an Unclassified repair. The body was given a Light repair.

D9019/9019/55 019 Royal Highland Fusilier (continued)

Loco Works	On Works	Off Works	Class of repair
Doncaster	12/01/73	16/01/73	Rectification

Flashover damage was repaired.

| Doncaster | 16/01/73 | 22/01/73 | Unclassified |

Both main generators were replaced. No.3 traction motor was replaced. Flashover damage was cleaned up on both bogies.

| Doncaster | 22/01/73 | 25/01/73 | Unclassified |

No.2 engine, 457, replaced by 439.

| Doncaster | 06/03/73 | 07/03/73 | Unclassified |

No.2 boiler water tank fractured at rear. No.2 load regulator had an oil leak. All defects were rectified.

| Doncaster | 28/03/73 | 28/03/73 | Unclassified |

No.2 boiler water tank fractured and No.2 load regulator leaking oil. All defects were rectified.

| Doncaster | 04/05/73 | 05/05/73 | Unclassified |

No.1 engine, 430, replaced by 434, due to a suspected fractured liner.

| Doncaster | 11/06/73 | 14/06/73 | Unclassified |

No.2 engine, 439, replaced by 410 - suspect dephased. No.2 boiler water tank had a leak rectified.

| Doncaster | 03/07/73 | 07/07/73 | Unclassified |

No.1 engine, 434, replaced by 439, along with a defective No.1 main generator.

| Doncaster | 19/10/73 | 22/11/73 | Intermediate |

No.1 engine, 439, replaced by 410, due to 'AC' lubricating filter casing face joint leaking. No.2 engine, 410, replaced by 450, due to coolant from header tank being pumped into recovery tank. No.1 bogie, 9000-35, replaced by 9000-24. No.2 bogie, 9000-36, replaced by 9000-48. Boiler, 5088/J3239, replaced by 1487/J2943. The body was given an Intermediate repair.

| Doncaster | 30/11/73 | 04/12/73 | Unclassified |

No.1 main generator was replaced due to flashover damage.

| Doncaster | 22/01/74 | 22/01/74 | Modification |

Earth fault relay modification carried out.

| Doncaster | 23/01/74 | 29/01/74 | Unclassified |

No.1 engine, 410, replaced by 431.

| Doncaster | 22/02/74 | 25/02/74 | Unclassified |

No.2 engine, 450, replaced by 413.

| Doncaster | 16/05/74 | 29/05/74 | Unclassified |

No.1 engine, 431, replaced by 453, due to con rod through crankcase. E.T.H. and coolant modifications were carried out.

| Doncaster | 04/06/74 | 06/06/74 | Unclassified |

No.1 bogie, 9000-24, '1A' bolster coil spring broken. Transom spring renewed and bolster segments were refitted and welded. No.2 bogie, 9000-48, had traction motor air ducting cleaned out and bolster segments refitted and welded. A load regulator oil leak was rectified.

| Doncaster | 16/09/74 | 17/09/74 | Unclassified |

No.2 engine, 413, replaced by 432, due to being dephased.

| Doncaster | 11/11/74 | 22/11/74 | Light |

No.1 engine, 453 and No.2 engine, 432 were given Light repairs. No.1 bogie, 9000-24, replaced by 9000-15. No.2 bogie, 9000-48, replaced by 9000-16. Boiler, 1487/J2943, was given an Unclassified repair.

| Doncaster | 08/03/75 | 08/03/75 | Unclassified |

No.2 engine, 432, 'BC' main bearing studs fractured. These were renewed.

| Doncaster | 22/03/75 | 27/03/75 | Unclassified |

No.1 engine, 453, replaced by 456, due to breathing heavy. No.2 engine, 432, replaced by 420, due to breathing heavy. A boiler water tank was repaired. No.2 traction motor nose suspension wear plates were renewed, as were No.6 traction motor nose suspension brackets.

| Doncaster | 16/05/75 | 20/05/75 | Unclassified |

No.3 traction motor earth fault on self-field. No.1 end blower motor to be changed. Blower air ducting to traction motors at No.1 end to be cleaned of oil. No.1 bogie, 9000-15, to be cleaned of oil. No.1 end blower motor was replaced and air ducting cleaned of oil. Nos.1 & 3 traction motors were replaced. No.2 traction motor was cleaned of oil.

D9019/9019/55 019 Royal Highland Fusilier (continued)

Loco Works	On Works	Off Works	Class of repair
Doncaster	28/05/75	30/05/75	Unclassified

No.2 engine, 420, 'B' bank fuel pumps not firing - camshaft adrift. 'B' bank cambox replaced.

Doncaster	12/07/75	15/07/75	Unclassified

No.1 bogie, 9000-15, replaced by 9000-1, due to worn brake gear, pins and bushes. No.2 bogie, 9000-16, replaced by 9000-2, due to worn brake gear, pins and bushes. No.1 end coolant radiators were replaced.

Doncaster	01/08/75	05/08/75	Unclassified

No.1 engine, 456, replaced by 429, due to breathing heavy. No.2 engine, 420, replaced by 408, due to breathing heavy.

Doncaster	08/08/75	11/08/75	Unclassified

No.2 end coolant radiator elements were replaced.

Doncaster	17/09/75	09/10/75	Unclassified

No.1 engine, 429, replaced by 432. No.2 engine, 408, was given an Unclassified repair. No.1 boiler water tank and No.2 fan clutch were repaired.

Doncaster	27/01/76	22/09/76	Heavy General

No.1 engine, 432, replaced by 424. No.2 engine, 408, replaced by 432. No.1 bogie, 9000-1, replaced by 9000-21. No.2 bogie, 9000-2, replaced by 9000-41. Boiler, 1487/J2943, replaced by 1486/J2942. Route indicator panels were plated over. The locomotive was weighed at 102t 18cwt.

Doncaster	21/02/77	25/02/77	Not recorded

Not recorded.

Doncaster	08/04/77	12/06/77	Unclassified

No.1 engine, 424, replaced by 445, due to con rods and crankcase fractured. No.2 engine, 432, replaced by 458, due to high spectrographic analysis. No.1 bogie, 9000-21, had No.1 traction motor cable damaged. No.1 fan drive gearbox clutch shoes to renew also primary cardan shaft to replace. All repairs were carried out.

Doncaster	22/07/77	27/07/77	Unclassified

No.1 engine, 445, replaced by 407, due to being dephased. No.1 bogie, 9000-21, had 'R2' and 'L3' horn liners loose. No.2 bogie, 9000-41, had 'L7' horn liners loose. These defects were rectified.

Doncaster	15/01/78	05/03/78	Unclassified

No.1 engine, 407, replaced by 538. No.2 engine, 458, replaced by 429, due to being dephased. Pipe fractured to D.S.D. timing. Bogie centre pivot studs and nuts to renew. No.1 load regulator burnt contacts to replace. No.2 load regulator oil leak to rectify. No.2 nose end air pipe broken. Both main generators flashover damage. All traction motors to examine for flashover damage. All repairs were carried out. The locomotive was weighed at 105t 6cwt.

Doncaster	23/03/78	24/03/78	Rectification

 No.2 engine, 429, overspeeding, suspect governor. The Martinair and overspeed trip were replaced. No.2 radiator fan primary shaft splines worn. No.1 bogie, 9000-21, had No.1 traction motor cables hanging too low. All traction motor gear cases to top up. Nos.1 & 6 right hand side friction links to secure. No.3 brake pull rod safety bracket to fit to traction motor gearcase. No.2 bogie, 9000-41, had traction motor gearcases to top up. Nos.8 & 12 right hand side friction links to secure. No.9 left hand side friction link to secure. No.1 right hand side footsteps to secure. All repairs were carried out.

Doncaster	27/04/78	18/05/78	Light

No.1 engine, 538, replaced by 453, due to 'A3' piston and con rod broken and crankcase holed. No.2 engine, 429, was given a Light repair. No.1 bogie, 9000-21, replaced by 9000-25. No.2 bogie, 9000-41, replaced by 9000-26. Boiler, 1486/J2942, was given an Unclassified repair. The locomotive was weighed at 104t 8cwt.

Doncaster	21/06/78	23/06/78	Unclassified

No.1 engine, 453, replaced by 428, due to being time expired.

Doncaster	01/09/78	05/09/78	Unclassified

No.1 engine, 428, was given a gudgeon pin housing examination. No.1 bogie, 9000-25 and No.2 bogie, 9000-26, had traction motor nose pads loose. These were rectified.

Doncaster	01/11/78	01/11/78	Unclassified

 No.2 engine, 429, aerating. No fault was found. Both load regulators had oil leaks rectified.

D9019/9019/55 019 Royal Highland Fusilier (continued)

Loco Works	On Works	Off Works	Class of repair
Doncaster	15/11/78	19/11/78	Unclassified

No.1 engine, 428, exhaust drum holed. No.2 load regulator had an oil leak rectified. The exhaust drum tank was replaced.

| Doncaster | 02/12/78 | 05/12/78 | Unclassified |

No.1 engine, 428, replaced by 432 - fractured liner. A load regulator had an oil leak rectified.

| Doncaster | 10/02/79 | 16/02/79 | Unclassified |

No.2 engine, 429, replaced by 426, due to aerating badly. Damaged route indicator panel at No.1 end was repaired.

| Doncaster | 19/04/79 | 16/05/79 | Unclassified |

No.1 engine, 432, replaced by 434, due to being time expired. No.2 engine, 426, suspected fractured liner. Injector pockets repaired and all injectors replaced. No.1 bogie, 9000-25, to be checked for collision damage. Vacuum train pipe fractured above bogie between Nos.1 & 2 brake cylinders. Collision damage to No.1 nose end left hand side. No.1 fan gearbox defective. Both load regulators leaking oil. All repairs were carried out.

| Doncaster | 22/05/79 | 23/05/79 | Unclassified |

Unable to obtain more than 500 amps. The locomotive was static tested, taken on a 'light' run and proved satisfactory.

| Doncaster | 09/08/79 | 02/09/79 | Unclassified |

No.1 engine, 434, drive flange loose on exciter gearbox. No.2 engine, 426, replaced by 413, due to ingress of water caused by Fire Brigade action to exhaust collector drum fire. Fire damage to roof and hoses. No.1 primary gearbox defective. All repairs were carried out.

| Doncaster | 02/01/80 | 06/01/80 | Unclassified |

No.2 engine, 413, cutting out in traffic and No.2 collector drum fractured on underside. Repairs were needed to No.1 end engine room/cab doorframe. Primary clutch box loose. The collector drum repaired and 413 had overspeed and Martinair units checked and rectified. Other defects rectified.

| Doncaster | 15/01/80 | 22/01/80 | Unclassified |

No.1 main generator compensating windings to earth. The No.1 main and auxiliary generators were replaced.

| Doncaster | 10/04/80 | 27/05/80 | Intermediate |

No.1 engine, 434, replaced by 451. No.2 engine, 413, replaced by 416, due to being dephased. No.1 bogie, 9000-25, replaced by 9000-15. No.2 bogie, 9000-26, replaced by 9000-16. Boiler, 1486/J2942, replaced by 5098/J3189. The locomotive was weighed at 103t 11cwt.

| Doncaster | 23/10/80 | 29/10/80 | Unclassified |

No.2 engine, 416, replaced by 428, due to aerating. No.1 bogie, 9000-15, had No.1 nose pad loose and No.2 traction motor and cables to clean. No.2 bogie, 9000-16, had No.6 nose pad loose. All repairs were carried out. The locomotive was weighed at 104t 3cwt.

| Doncaster | 09/06/81 | 17/06/81 | Unclassified |

No.1 engine, 451, replaced by 448, due to a suspected fractured liner. No.1 bogie, 9000-15, had 'R1' swing link pin refitted. The locomotive was weighed at 105t 1cwt.

| Doncaster | 23/07/81 | 06/08/81 | Unclassified |

No.1 engine, 448, replaced by 458, due to piston through crankcase.

| Doncaster | 17/08/81 | 20/08/81 | Unclassified |

No.1 engine, 458, replaced by 451 - throwing excessive oil from exhaust. Radiators were replaced.

| Doncaster | 07/10/81 | 09/11/81 | Unclassified |

No.2 engine, 428, replaced by 407, due to being dephased.

| Doncaster | 04/01/82 | 20/08/82 | - |

The locomotive arrived on Works after withdrawal with the following main components fitted. No.1 engine, 451, lubricating oil radiator leaking due to a burst element. No.2 engine, 407. No.1 bogie, 9000-15. No.2 bogie, 9000-16. Boiler, 5098/J3249. The locomotive was subsequently preserved and before leaving Works was weighed at 104t 5cwt.

D9020/9020/55 020 Nimbus

Loco Works	On Works	Off Works	Class of repair
Doncaster	12/02/62	21/02/62	Acceptance trials

New locomotive fitted with the following main components. No.1 engine, 454. No.2 engine, 453. No.1 bogie, 1041. No.2 bogie, 1042. Boiler, 5097/J3248. 'Nimbus' nameplates fitted.

Doncaster	18/04/62	18/04/62	Unclassified

No.1 bogie, 1041, replaced by 1023. No.2 bogie, 1042, replaced by 1024.

Doncaster	20/07/62	24/07/62	Light

No.4 traction motor earthed. No.1 bogie, 1023, replaced by 1031. No.2 bogie, 1024, replaced by 1032. The locomotive mileage was recorded as 67,140 miles.

Doncaster	07/08/62	08/08/62	Unclassified

Both bogies anchor pins adrift. No.1 bogie, 1031, had two new bolsters fitted. No.2 bogie, 1032, had one new bolster fitted. Anchor stay bolts also fitted. The loco mileage was recorded as 76,150 miles.

Doncaster	29/11/62	30/11/62	Unclassified

No.1 bogie, 1031, replaced by 1033. No.2 bogie, 1032, replaced by 1034. The drawgear modification was carried out.

Doncaster	13/12/62	17/12/62	Unclassified

No.2 engine, 453, replaced by 430, due to 'C5' cylinder liner cracked. The warning horns were repositioned. The locomotive mileage was recorded as 143,980 miles.

Doncaster	29/01/63	15/02/63	General

No.1 engine, 454, replaced by 435. No.2 engine, 430, replaced by 428. No.1 bogie, 1033, replaced by 1023. No.2 bogie, 1034, replaced by 1024. Boiler, 5097/J3248, replaced by 1492/J2948.

Doncaster	11/03/63	12/03/63	Unclassified

No.1 bogie, 1023, replaced by 1037. No.2 bogie, 1024, replaced by 1038.

Doncaster	29/03/63	01/04/63	Unclassified

Boiler, 1492/J2948, tubes split and leaking, boiler coil fractured. A new boiler coil was fitted and necessary tubes were repaired. The locomotive mileage was recorded as 187,160 miles.

Doncaster	10/04/63	11/04/63	Unclassified

No.3 traction motor suspension bearing to be examined, shim missing. A new Timken bearing and suspension tube were fitted to the non-gear side of No.3 traction motor. The locomotive mileage was recorded as 191,360 miles.

Doncaster	09/08/63	23/08/63	Light

No.2 manganese horn liner dropped and Nos.4 & 5 horn blocks loose. No.1 bogie, 1037, replaced by 1003. No.2 bogie, 1038, replaced by 1004. Boiler, 1492/J2948, replaced by 5097/J3248. The body was given a six monthly examination. The caustic injection to boiler feedwater modification was fitted. The locomotive mileage was recorded as 262,100 miles.

Doncaster	24/10/63	29/10/63	Unclassified

No.2 engine, 428, 'CA' flexible shaft suspected fractured. This was repaired. The locomotive mileage was recorded as 299,650 miles.

Doncaster	04/11/63	23/11/63	General

Underframe fractures. No.1 engine, 435, replaced by 440. No.2 engine, 428, replaced by 412. The following modifications were carried out - Main generator feet; Distance pieces under engines; Coolant gauge; Overflow tank to header tank. The loco mileage was recorded as 301,690 miles.

Doncaster	12/12/63	13/12/63	Unclassified

No.3 traction motor to be replaced.

Doncaster	19/05/64	23/05/64	Light

No.1 engine, 440 and No.2 engine, 412, were given Unclassified repairs. No.1 bogie, 1003, replaced by 1035. No.2 bogie, 1004, replaced by 1036. Boiler, 5097/J3248. The body was given an Unclassified repair.

Doncaster	07/11/64	07/11/64	Unclassified

 No.1 bogie, 1035, No.2 axlebox horn liner loose, other axlebox horn liners to be examined for fractures. No.2 bogie, 1036, axlebox horns to be examined for fractures. Horn liners were repaired and welded as necessary.

Doncaster	01/01/65	04/02/65	General

No.1 bogie, 1035, replaced by 1025. No.2 bogie, 1036, replaced by 1018. Boiler, 5097/J3248, replaced by 5090/J3241.

D9020/9020/55 020 Nimbus (continued)

Loco Works	On Works	Off Works	Class of repair
Doncaster	17/02/65	19/02/65	Unclassified

No.2 engine, 412, replaced by 422, due to an internal coolant leak.

| Doncaster | 23/02/65 | 23/02/65 | Unclassified |

No.1 engine, 440, coolant collection box cracked or porous. The water coolant hose was replaced. Boiler, 5090/J3241, had flue tubes cleaned externally.

| Doncaster | 26/03/65 | 27/03/65 | Unclassified |

No.2 bogie, 1018, transom fractures. These were welded and dressed.

| Doncaster | 13/04/65 | 14/04/65 | Unclassified |

No.2 bogie, 1018, No.5 axle wheels bad flats. No.5 wheelset was replaced.

| Doncaster | 01/05/65 | 03/05/65 | Unclassified |

No.1 engine, 440, replaced by 414. No.2 engine, 422, replaced by 420.

| Doncaster | 18/05/65 | 20/05/65 | Light |

No.1 engine, 414 and No.2 engine, 420, were given MP11 exams. No.1 bogie, 1025, replaced by 1029. No.2 bogie, 1018, replaced by 1014. Boiler, 5090/J3241, was given an Unclassified repair. The body was given an Unclassified repair.

| Doncaster | 23/06/65 | 24/06/65 | Unclassified |

Radiator elements were cleaned.

| Doncaster | 02/08/65 | 03/08/65 | Unclassified |

No.1 engine, 414, replaced by 412, due to a suspected fractured liner. The locomotive mileage was recorded as 604,070 miles.

| Doncaster | 12/08/65 | 19/08/65 | Unclassified |

No.2 engine, 420, replaced by 418, due to liner seal defective. No.2 primary fan shaft and coolant radiators were replaced.

| Doncaster | 11/11/65 | 20/11/65 | General |

No.1 bogie, 1029, frame fractured 7" long behind No.3 brake cylinder left side. No.1 engine, 412 and No.2 engine, 418, were given Unclassified repairs. No.1 bogie, 1029, replaced by 9000-37. No.2 bogie, 1014, replaced by 9000-38. Boiler, 5090/J3241, replaced by 5097/J3248. The body was given a General repair. The locomotive mileage was recorded as 648,840 miles.

| Doncaster | 22/11/65 | 23/11/65 | Unclassified |

No.2 traction motor was replaced.

| Doncaster | 05/02/66 | 08/02/66 | Unclassified |

No.1 engine, 412, replaced by 435, due to 'CA' flexible drive shaft fractured.

| Doncaster | 31/03/66 | 02/04/66 | Light |

No.1 engine, 435 and No.2 engine, 418, were given Unclassified repairs. No.1 bogie, 9000-37, replaced by 9000-23. No.2 bogie, 9000-38, replaced by 9000-24. Boiler, 5097/J3248, was given an Unclassified repair. The body was given an Unclassified repair.

| Doncaster | 05/05/66 | 07/05/66 | Unclassified |

No.2 bogie, 9000-24, Nos.4 & 6 axles fractured. These axles were replaced.

| Doncaster | 15/07/66 | 18/07/66 | Unclassified |

Flashover damage on No.2 main generator sustained at 100 mph. Both main generators had flashover damage cleaned up. New brush boxes were fitted to Nos.1 & 2 traction motors and both bogies had flashover damage cleaned up. A header tank coolant leak was rectified.

| Doncaster | 23/09/66 | 28/09/66 | Unclassified |

No.2 engine, 418, replaced by 411. Repairs to fire damage were carried out and the fire system checked. 'B' side air intake ducting was repaired. Soundproofing was renewed.

| Doncaster | 09/11/66 | 30/11/66 | General |

No.1 engine, 435, replaced by 448. No.2 engine, 411, replaced by 437. No.1 bogie, 9000-23, replaced by 9000-33. No.2 bogie, 9000-24, replaced by 9000-34. Boiler, 5097/J3248, replaced by 5094/J3245. The body was given a General repair.

| Doncaster | 14/03/67 | 17/03/67 | Light |

No.1 engine, 448 and No.2 engine, 437, were given Unclassified repairs. No.1 bogie, 9000-33, replaced by 9000-11. No.2 bogie, 9000-34, replaced by 9000-12. Boiler, 5094/J3245, was given an Unclassified repair. The body was given an Unclassified repair.

| Doncaster | 06/04/67 | 06/04/67 | Unclassified |

No.1 primary gearbox was replaced.

330 DELTICS ON WORKS

D9020/9020/55 020 Nimbus (continued)

Loco Works	On Works	Off Works	Class of repair
Doncaster	10/07/67	11/07/67	Unclassified

No.2 engine, 437, replaced by 421, due to breathing heavy.

Doncaster	21/11/67	30/12/67	General

*No.1 engine, 448, was given an Unclassified repair. No.2 engine, 421, replaced by 454. No.1 bogie, 9000-11 and No.2 bogie, 9000-12, were given General repairs. Boiler, 5094/J3245, replaced by 1496/J2952. The body was given a General repair and repainted into **blue livery with full yellow nose ends**. The locomotive was fitted for dual braking.*

Doncaster	20/05/68	24/05/68	Light

No.1 main generator commutator repairs, all brushes shattered. No.1 engine, 448, replaced by 406. No.2 engine, 454, replaced by 456. No.1 bogie, 9000-11, replaced by 9000-45. No.2 bogie, 9000-12, replaced by 9000-46. Boiler, 1496/J2952, was given an Unclassified repair. The body was given an Unclassified repair.

Doncaster	24/06/68	28/06/68	Unclassified

AVR cables badly burnt. Batteries have boiled, condition to be checked. Exhaust bellows on No.2 engine, 456, to be renewed. All work carried out.

Doncaster	18/07/68	22/07/68	Unclassified

No.1 engine, 406, replaced by 425, due to a suspected fractured liner.

Doncaster	09/08/68	20/08/68	Unclassified

No.2 engine, 456, replaced by 458, due to water in sump, suspect liner seal. Lubricating oil tanks and radiators were cleaned.

Doncaster	23/10/68	23/10/68	Unclassified

A defective No.1 traction motor was replaced.

Doncaster	13/11/68	14/11/68	Unclassified

No.1 engine, 425, replaced by 439, due to having seized, piston through side of engine.

Doncaster	15/01/69	07/02/69	Intermediate

No.1 engine, 439, replaced by 421. No.2 engine, 458, replaced by 441, due to cutting out and high water temperature. No.1 bogie, 9000-45, replaced by 9000-17. No.2 bogie, 9000-46, replaced by 9000-18. Boiler, 1496/J2952, replaced by 5087/J3238. The body was given an Intermediate repair.

Doncaster	24/03/69	28/03/69	Unclassified

Main fuel and water tanks holed. Traction motors damaged. Water scoop to be examined for possible damage. No.1 bogie, 9000-17, replaced by 9000-23. No.2 bogie, 9000-18, replaced by 9000-24, due to underside damage. All repairs were carried out.

Doncaster	27/08/69	27/08/69	Unclassified

No.1 engine, 421, high water temperature. The water temperature probe was rectified.

Doncaster	01/10/69	18/10/69	Light

No.1 engine, 421, replaced by 411. No.2 engine, 441, hunting and oscillating badly at high speed, was given an Unclassified repair. No.1 bogie, 9000-23, replaced by 9000-13. No.2 bogie, 9000-24, replaced by 9000-14. Boiler, 5087/J3238, was given an Unclassified repair. The body was given an Unclassified repair. The water tank capacity modification was carried out.

Doncaster	04/12/69	23/12/69	Unclassified

Wiring burnt at rear of No.1 cubicle due to loose connection on wheelslip transducer fitted on reverser. Speedometer cable to be fitted. No.1 reverser was overhauled. Burnt wiring was renewed on area of reverser. Field divert relays were checked and calibrated and the cubicle cleaned out.

Doncaster	11/02/70	12/02/70	Unclassified

No.1 engine, 411, exhaust drum tank to repair. This was repaired.

Doncaster	26/02/70	27/02/70	Unclassified

No.2 engine, 441, replaced by 435, due to being time expired.

Doncaster	01/05/70	01/05/70	Unclassified

No.1 end boiler water tank holed. This was repaired.

Doncaster	14/05/70	06/06/70	Intermediate

No.1 main generator down to earth. No.1 engine, 411, replaced by 431. No.2 engine, 435, replaced by 455. No.1 bogie, 9000-13, replaced by 9000-47. No.2 bogie, 9000-14, replaced by 9000-22. Boiler, 5087/J3238, replaced by 5090/J3241. The body was given an Intermediate repair.

Doncaster	22/10/70	24/10/70	Unclassified

No.1 engine, 431, replaced by 406, due to a suspected fractured liner, aerating badly.

D9020/9020/55 020 Nimbus (continued)

Loco Works	On Works	Off Works	Class of repair
Doncaster	21/11/70	26/11/70	Unclassified

No.2 engine, 455, replaced by 435, due to lead content increasing and slight coolant leak. Suspect liner seal defective.

| Doncaster | 15/12/70 | 08/04/71 | Light |

Flashover damage on No.1 main generator and burnt wiring in trunking. No.1 engine, 406, replaced by 447. No.2 engine, 435, replaced by 426. No.1 bogie, 9000-47, replaced by 9000-3. No.2 engine, 9000-22, replaced by 9000-4. Boiler, 5090/J3241, was given an Unclassified repair. The body was given a Light repair. The locomotive was fitted with E.T.H. equipment.

| Doncaster | 13/08/71 | 13/08/71 | Unclassified |

No.2 boiler water tank fractured. This was replaced, as was No.5 traction motor gearcase.

| Doncaster | 09/09/71 | 15/09/71 | Unclassified |

No.2 engine, 426, replaced by 446, due to high water content in engine sump, suspected fractured liner.

| Doncaster | 15/09/71 | 16/09/71 | Unclassified |

No.2 end water header tank was repaired.

| Doncaster | 17/09/71 | 22/09/71 | Rectification |

No.1 engine, 447, replaced by 428, due to suspect liner seals leaking, water in sump. No.1 end lubricating oil tank and radiators were cleaned.

| Doncaster | 04/12/71 | 09/12/71 | Unclassified |

Main generators persistently overloading when in series. Excessive power (1800-2000 amps) with both engines running and all traction motors in circuit. Persistent flashovers on both main generators. All traction motors and both main generators had flashover damage repaired. No.2 bogie, 9000-4, had No.4 spring plank safety stay repaired.

| Doncaster | 24/01/72 | 23/02/72 | Intermediate |

No.1 engine, 428, replaced by 421. No.2 engine, 446, replaced by 455. No.1 bogie, 9000-3, replaced by 9000-25. No.2 bogie, 9000-4, replaced by 9000-26. Boiler, 5090/J3241, replaced by 5098/J3249. The body was given an Intermediate repair.

| Doncaster | 06/06/72 | 08/06/72 | Unclassified |

Both boiler water tanks fractured, No.1 exhaust drum tank badly split, 'B' bank exhaust inlet bellows split. No.1 exhaust drum was replaced and all other repairs were carried out.

| Doncaster | 08/08/72 | 09/08/72 | Unclassified |

No.1 engine, 421, replaced by 413, due to large quantity of coolant in sump. Lubricating oil tanks and radiators were cleaned.

| Doncaster | 21/09/72 | 23/09/72 | Unclassified |

No.2 engine, 455, replaced by 430, due to No.2 'BC' crankshaft broken. Lubricating oil tanks and radiators were cleaned. No.1 bogie, 9000-25, had swing link pins repaired. No.2 bogie, 9000-26, had swing link pins and bolster segments repaired.

| Doncaster | 16/10/72 | 17/10/72 | Unclassified |

No.1 bogie, 9000-25, suspension link pins fractured and No.6 traction motor throwing solder. The link pins were replaced, as was No.6 traction motor.

| Doncaster | 17/11/72 | 25/11/72 | Light |

No.1 engine, 413, replaced by 438, due to a fractured liner. No.2 engine, 430, was given a Light repair. No.1 bogie, 9000-25, replaced by 9000-15. No.2 bogie, 9000-26, replaced by 9000-16. Boiler, 5098/J3249, was given an Unclassified repair. The body was given a Light repair.

| Doncaster | 12/12/72 | 14/12/72 | Unclassified |

No.2 engine, 430, replaced by 419, due to being dephased and scavenge blower defective. No.2 fan gearbox defective and No.1 boiler water tank holed. All defects were rectified.

| Doncaster | 22/01/73 | 24/01/73 | Unclassified |

No.2 nose end panelling damaged left hand side and compressor mounting damaged. All collision damage was repaired and both bogies had repairs to bolster segments and swing link pins.

| Doncaster | 20/08/73 | 22/08/73 | Unclassified |

No.1 engine, 438, replaced by 449, due to a fractured liner.

| Doncaster | 18/10/73 | 10/11/73 | Intermediate |

No.1 eng, 449, replaced by 443 - breathing badly causing heavy contamination of main generator. No.2 engine, 419, replaced by 406. No.1 bogie, 9000-15 and No.2 bogie, 9000-16 - standard repairs. Boiler, 5098/J3249, replaced by 1486/J2942. The body was given an Intermediate repair.

D9020/9020/55 020 Nimbus (continued)

Loco Works	On Works	Off Works	Class of repair
Doncaster	15/11/73	16/11/73	Unclassified

Slight flashover damage on No.1 main generator and No.1 traction motor armature banding burst. All flashover damage was cleaned up.

Doncaster	28/01/74	28/01/74	Modification

Earth fault relay modification was carried out.

Doncaster	14/02/74	15/02/74	Unclassified

No.2 engine, 406, 'C' bank cam quillshaft housing leaking oil. Suspect 'O' rings perished. The oil leaks were rectified.

Doncaster	12/03/74	15/03/74	Unclassified

No.2 engine, 406, replaced by 450, due to 'CA' crankcase holed.

Doncaster	04/04/74	05/04/74	Unclassified

No.1 boiler water tank leaking. This was repaired, as was No.2 boiler water tank bracket. Nos.1 & 2 water sight glasses were renewed. No.3 traction motor nut and stud were also renewed.

Doncaster	25/04/74	30/04/74	Unclassified

No.1 engine, 443, fuel rack seized, collector drum fire. 'A' bank cambox was replaced. No.1 boiler water tank was repaired.

Doncaster	29/05/74	05/06/74	Unclassified

No.2 engine, 450, replaced by 404, due to scavenge blower drive failed. No.2 end coolant header tank was repaired. A load regulator oil leak was rectified. E.T.H. and coolant temperature probe modifications were carried out.

Doncaster	11/06/74	18/06/74	Unclassified

No.1 engine, 443, replaced by 435, due to 'A' side crankcase fractured. No.1 thermostat by-pass valve was changed, as was No.2 left hand coolant radiator.

Doncaster	30/10/74	08/11/74	Light

No.1 engine, 435 and No.2 engine, 404, were given Light repairs. No.1 bogie, 9000-15, replaced by 9000-11. No.2 bogie, 9000-16, replaced by 9000-12. Boiler, 1486/J2942, was given an Unclassified repair. The body was given a Light repair.

Doncaster	06/12/74	12/12/74	Rectification

Traction motor contactor braids overheating and dropping out. Both main generators and all traction motors flashed over. All traction motor contactors were cleaned and all flashover damage was repaired.

Doncaster	17/02/75	19/02/75	Unclassified

No.1 main generator replaced due to flashover damage.

Doncaster	17/06/75	19/06/75	Unclassified

No.1 engine, 435, replaced by 428, due to being dephased.

Doncaster	30/06/75	01/07/75	Unclassified

No.2 engine, 404, replaced by 437, due to high spectrographic analysis and breathing badly.

Doncaster	26/07/75	28/07/75	Unclassified

No.2 buffer beam damaged, train-heating cable squashed. This was repaired.

Doncaster	04/08/75	06/08/75	Unclassified

Boiler, 1486/J2942, feet mountings fractured. This was repaired, as was collision damage to E.T.H. jumper cable box.

Doncaster	04/12/75	02/03/76	Intermediate

No.1 engine, 428, replaced by 427. No.2 engine, 437, replaced by 442. No.1 bogie, 9000-11, replaced by 9000-9. No.2 bogie, 9000-12, replaced by 9000-42. Boiler, 1486/J2942, replaced by 5086/J3237.

Doncaster	14/05/76	16/05/76	Unclassified

No.2 engine, 442, replaced by 409, due to a suspected fractured liner.

Doncaster	27/05/76	28/05/76	Unclassified

No.1 engine, 427, replaced by 457, due to a suspected con rod adrift.

Doncaster	15/06/76	16/06/76	Unclassified

No.2 engine, 409, aerating and generator foot mounting broken 'A' side. The mounting bracket was welded and a four hour load test on No.2 engine, 409, revealed no defect.

Doncaster	25/09/76	26/09/76	Unclassified

No.2 boiler water tank fractured. This was repaired.

D9020/9020/55 020 Nimbus (continued)

Loco Works	On Works	Off Works	Class of repair
Doncaster	29/09/76	01/10/76	Unclassified

No.1 engine, 457, replaced by 429, due to con rod and crankcase fractured. No.1 end lubricating oil tank and radiators were cleaned. No.1 boiler water tank was repaired. No.2 main generator mounting foot bracket was welded.

Doncaster	19/10/76	20/10/76	Unclassified

Rough riding. Excess lateral movement when No.2 end leading. No.1 engine floor plate and bolster segment on both bogies were repaired. The locomotive was weighed at 103t 6cwt.

Doncaster	12/11/76	16/11/76	Unclassified

No.2 engine, 409, replaced by 413, due to high spectrographic analysis. No.2 end lubricating oil tank was cleaned. No.2 end lubricating oil radiators were replaced.

Doncaster	16/12/76	20/12/76	Unclassified

No.1 engine, 429, replaced by 410.

Doncaster	25/04/77	27/04/77	Unclassified

No.1 engine, 410, had a coolant leak adjacent to coolant flow switch rectified. No.2 engine, 413, replaced by 427, due to piston through crankcase. No.2 boiler water tank had a leak rectified.

Doncaster	29/04/77	06/05/77	Unclassified

No.1 main generator severe flashover damage. No.2 main generator and all traction motors slight flashover damage. No.1 engine, 410, required repairs to radiator fan primary and secondary shaft and universal joints. No.1 main generator was replaced. All defects were rectified. The locomotive was weighed at 103t 19cwt.

Doncaster	09/06/77	17/06/77	Unclassified

No.2 engine, 427, fuel dilution. This was repaired. Both main generators flashed over. No.1 load regulator had an oil leak and traction control and traction circuits were to be checked for operation. All flashover damage was cleaned up and all other defects were rectified.

Doncaster	16/07/77	19/07/77	Unclassified

No.5 traction motor interpole to earth. No.1 bogie, 9000-9, Nos.1 & 4 left hand and No.3 right hand brake rod safety brackets were broken. No.2 traction motor suspension springs were weak and No.3 traction motor carcase was fractured. Nos.3 & 5 traction motors were replaced and all other defects were rectified.

Doncaster	16/08/77	11/09/77	Light

No.1 engine, 410, replaced by 424. No.2 engine, 427, repeatedly shutting down, was given a Light repair. No.1 bogie, 9000-9 and No.2 bogie, 9000-42, were given standard repairs. Boiler, 5086/J3237, was given an Unclassified repair. The locomotive was weighed at 105t 10cwt.

Doncaster	28/01/78	19/02/78	Unclassified

No.1 engine, 424, replaced by 453. No.2 engine, 427, replaced by 422, due to aerating. Nos.2 & 4 traction motor nose suspension to examine - hard on brackets. Bogie centre pivot studs were renewed and a coolant leak in No.2 end roof was rectified.

Doncaster	25/04/78	-	-

The locomotive was stopped originally at Finsbury Park on 28/03/78 with No.1 engine, 453, dephased. Also No.1 secondary cardan shaft to renew. Subsequently stopped at Gateshead on 31/03/78 with No.1 radiator fan drive gearbox to repair and refit. Various items were robbed for 55 002. The locomotive arrived on Works with the following items missing - No.2 primary fan; No.2 gearbox; Nos.1 & 2 silencer drains; Covers for ESV 1 & 2; Covers for AV and BV; No.1 secondary cardan shaft and guards; Several roof section drainpipes. No.2 engine, 422, 'A' side lubricating oil filter element to renew and casing to refit. No.1 bogie, 9000-9 was OK. No.2 bogie, 9000-42, 'L5' horn stay to secure, 'R2' lifeguard to straighten. Boiler, 5086/J3237, was OK. The locomotive was eventually withdrawn on 05/01/80 whilst still on Works.

D9021/9021/55 021 Argyll & Sutherland Highlander

Loco Works	On Works	Off Works	Class of repair
Doncaster	16/03/62	25/03/62	Acceptance trials

New locomotive fitted with the following main components. No.1 engine, 415. No.2 engine, 416. No.1 bogie, 1043. No.2 bogie, 1044. Boiler, 5098/J3249.

Vulcan Foundry	25/03/62	02/05/62	Not recorded

Not recorded. During this visit the locomotive was released to take part in high-speed trials in connection with rail end stress tests between Manchester and Crewe.

Doncaster	02/05/62	02/05/62	Acceptance trials

Not recorded.

Doncaster	27/09/62	02/10/62	Light

No.1 bogie, 1043, replaced by 1041. No.2 bogie, 1044, replaced by 1042. The body was given a six monthly examination. Both exhaust collector tanks were replaced. The following modifications were carried out - Drawgear; Driver's vacuum brake valve.

Doncaster	04/10/62	05/10/62	Not recorded

Not recorded.

Doncaster	18/02/63	07/03/63	General

No.1 engine, 415, replaced by 453. No.2 engine, 416, replaced by 456. No.1 bogie, 1041, replaced by 1033. No.2 bogie, 1042, replaced by 1034. Boiler, 5098/J3249, replaced by 1491/J2947. The body was given an annual repair. The following modifications were carried out - Radiator fan shields; Drawgear; Exhaust drum drains; Extra engine room doors fitted; AWS positioning; Air intake panel lined with foam.

Doncaster	24/08/63	30/08/63	Light

No.1 bogie, 1033, replaced by 1039. No.2 bogie, 1034, replaced by 1040. Boiler, 1491/J2947, replaced by 1492/J2948. The body was given a six monthly examination. Injector seat modifications were carried out.

Doncaster	15/11/63	16/11/63	Unclassified

No.2 engine, 456, replaced by 435, due to a suspected fractured liner.

Doncaster	30/11/63	02/12/63	Unclassified

No.2 engine, 435, replaced by 449.

Doncaster	07/01/64	06/02/64	General

No.1 engine, 453, replaced by 428. No.2 engine, 449, replaced by 426. No.1 bogie, 1039, replaced by 1029. No.2 bogie, 1040, replaced by 1030. Boiler, 1492/J2948, replaced by 5098/J3249.

Doncaster	30/07/64	31/07/64	Unclassified

No.1 bogie, 1029, replaced by 1021. No.2 bogie, 1030, replaced by 1022. Boiler, 5098/J3249, was given an MP11 exam. The boiler roof was lifted to facilitate repairs to exhaust silencer straps.

Doncaster	18/09/64	22/09/64	Light

No.1 engine, 428 and No.2 engine, 426, were given MP11 exams. No.1 bogie, 1021 and No.2 bogie, 1022, were given Unclassified repairs. Boiler, 5098/J3249, was given an MP11 exam. The body was given an Unclassified repair.

Doncaster	10/10/64	13/10/64	Unclassified

No.1 bogie, 1021 and No.2 bogie, 1022, were given Unclassified repairs. No.2 main generator received repairs.

Doncaster	17/10/64	20/10/64	Unclassified

No.2 engine, 426, replaced by 437, due to main generator interpole down to earth. No.1 bogie, 1021 and No.2 bogie, 1022, were given Unclassified repairs.

Doncaster	15/02/65	09/03/65	General

No.1 engine, 428, replaced by 424. No.2 engine, 437, replaced by 406. No.1 bogie, 1021, replaced by 1003. No.2 bogie, 1022, replaced by 1004. Boiler, 5098/J3249, replaced by 5091/J3242. The body was given a General repair. Drawgear sideblocks were welded and repairs were carried out to the left hand bodyside.

Doncaster	20/04/65	22/04/65	Unclassified

No.1 engine, 424, replaced by 435, due to a suspect liner seal leaking. High coolant content in lubricating oil.

Doncaster	19/05/65	19/05/65	Unclassified

Defective wiring was replaced.

D9021/9021/55 021 Argyll & Sutherland Highlander (continued)

Loco Works	On Works	Off Works	Class of repair
Doncaster	29/06/65	03/10/65	General

No.1 engine, 435, replaced by 458. No.2 engine, 406, replaced by 440. No.1 bogie, 1003, replaced by 9000-27. No.2 bogie, 1004, replaced by 9000-28. Boiler, 5091/J3242, replaced by 5098/J3249. The body was given a General repair. Wiring in both cabs damaged by fire. Battery charge circuits were found to be faulty causing damage to all adjacent controls and necessitating rewiring of both cubicles and engine room trunkings.

Doncaster	20/01/66	21/01/66	Unclassified

No.1 end serious oil leaks, burst oil radiator element. No.1 end lubricating oil element was replaced and other elements were cleaned.

Doncaster	01/02/66	06/02/66	Light

No.2 fuel tank holed and fire damage to No.1 bogie, 9000-27. The fuel tank was replaced. No.1 engine, 458 and No.2 engine, 440, were given Unclassified repairs. No.1 bogie, 9000-27, replaced by 9000-45. No.2 bogie, 9000-28, replaced by 9000-46. Boiler, 5098/J3249, was given an Unclassified repair. The body was given an Unclassified repair.

Doncaster	12/02/66	13/02/66	Unclassified

No.5 traction motor cables burnt in junction box adjacent to motor. A new interior was fitted to No.5 traction motor connection box and a new terminal fitted to 'A5' cable.

Doncaster	22/08/66	22/08/66	Unclassified

Replacement batteries were fitted.

Doncaster	08/09/66	03/10/66	General

No.1 engine, 458, replaced by 419. No.2 engine, 440, replaced by 408, due to fuel transfer pump and water pump drive defective. No.1 bogie, 9000-45, replaced by 9000-5. No.2 bogie, 9000-46, replaced by 9000-6. Boiler, 5098/J3249, replaced by 1496/J2952. The body given a General repair.

Doncaster	06/02/67	11/02/67	Light

No.1 engine, 419, replaced by 418. No.2 engine, 408, was given an Unclassified repair. No.1 bogie, 9000-5, replaced by 9000-43. No.2 bogie, 9000-6, replaced by 9000-44. Boiler, 1496/J2952, was given an Unclassified repair. The body was given an Unclassified repair.

Doncaster	14/02/67	22/02/67	Rectification

No.1 main generator was replaced due to armature to earth.

Doncaster	25/05/67	01/06/67	Unclassified

No.2 engine, 408, suspect scavenge blower drive shaft fractured. The scavenge blower was replaced. No.2 radiator fan shaft bearing was renewed, as were water pick up mouthpieces. Flashover damage was repaired on No.1 main generator and all traction motors.

Doncaster	20/09/67	21/09/67	Unclassified

No.1 engine, 418, air manifold drain pipes missing on 'B' bank. No.2 engine, 408, all air manifold drain pipes missing. No.2 bogie, 9000-44, loose horn liner. No.2 load regulator oil distributor block leaking at joint of vane motor.

Doncaster	06/11/67	06/12/67	General

No.1 engine, 418, replaced by 417. No.2 engine, 408, replaced by 434. No.1 bogie, 9000-43, replaced by 9000-45. No.2 bogie, 9000-44, replaced by 9000-46. Boiler, 1496/J2952, replaced by 1489/J2945. The body was given a General repair and repainted into **blue livery with full yellow nose ends***. The locomotive was fitted for dual braking.*

Doncaster	13/12/67	14/12/67	Unclassified

Flashover damage. Flashover damage to both main generators and all traction motors was repaired.

Doncaster	19/12/67	20/12/67	Modification

Air pipes to be modified. Brake defect on No.1 bogie, 9000-45, due to defective air pipe. Strengthening bracket required on distributor bracket. The modifications were carried out.

Doncaster	18/01/68	23/01/68	Unclassified

Flashover damage on No.2 main generator. Flashover damage on both main generators and all traction motors was cleaned up.

Doncaster	20/02/68	20/02/68	Unclassified

Both main generators and all traction motors flashed over. All flashover damage was cleaned up.

Doncaster	03/04/68	04/04/68	Unclassified

Nos.3 & 6 traction motors down to earth on armatures. Both traction motors were replaced.

D9021/9021/55 021 Argyll & Sutherland Highlander (continued)

Loco Works	On Works	Off Works	Class of repair
Doncaster	06/05/68	10/05/68	Light

No.1 engine, 417 and No.2 engine, 434, were given Unclassified repairs. No.1 bogie, 9000-45, replaced by 9000-25. No.2 bogie, 9000-46, replaced by 9000-26. Boiler, 1489/J2945, was given an Unclassified repair. The body was given an Unclassified repair.

Doncaster	06/09/68	18/09/68	Unclassified

Collision damage. No.1 end left hand side buffer and buffer beam damaged and underframe badly bent. This was repaired.

Doncaster	19/11/68	21/11/68	Unclassified

Traction motor brushes on Nos.1, 2, 5 & 6 traction motors to be renewed, No.3 traction motor sparking and arcing and No.4 traction motor flashed over and burnt. Flashover damage on both main generators was repaired and all traction motors were replaced.

Doncaster	10/12/68	10/12/68	Unclassified

No.1 engine, 417, replaced by 440, due to internal coolant leaks.

Doncaster	17/12/68	17/01/69	General

No.1 engine, 440, replaced by 432. No.2 engine, 434, replaced by 410. No.1 bogie, 9000-25 and No.2 bogie, 9000-26, were given General repairs. Boiler, 1489/J2945, replaced by 1491/J2947. The body was given a General repair.

Doncaster	25/09/69	26/09/69	Unclassified

No.2 engine, 410, replaced by 434, due to 'A5' exhaust con rod broken and crankcase holed. Lubricating oil radiators and tank were cleaned.

Doncaster	13/10/69	17/10/69	Light

No.1 engine, 432 and No.2 engine, 434, were given Unclassified repairs. No.1 bogie, 9000-25, replaced by 9000-24. No.2 bogie, 9000-26, replaced by 9000-48. Boiler, 1491/J2947, was given an Unclassified repair. The body was given an Unclassified repair and the water tank capacity modification was carried out.

Doncaster	24/10/69	25/10/69	Unclassified

No.1 engine, 432, had a defective rate valve replaced.

Doncaster	06/11/69	08/11/69	Unclassified

No.2 engine, 434, replaced by 425 - water in sump. Lubricating oil radiators and tank cleaned.

Doncaster	17/12/69	18/12/69	Unclassified

No.2 engine, 425, replaced by 412, due to being time expired.

Doncaster	12/03/70	16/03/70	Unclassified

No.1 engine, 432, replaced by 413, due to being time expired.

Doncaster	12/05/70	19/09/70	Intermediate

No.1 engine, 413, replaced by 421. No.2 engine, 412, replaced by 440. No.1 bogie, 9000-24, replaced by 9000-29. No.2 bogie, 9000-48, replaced by 9000-10. Boiler, 1491/J2947, replaced by 1495/J2951. The body was given an Intermediate repair. The loco was fitted with E.T.H. equipment.

Doncaster	23/10/70	23/10/70	Unclassified

No.2 engine, 440, governor defective, preventing load regulator returning to minimum field at intervals. The governor was replaced.

Doncaster	03/11/70	04/11/70	Unclassified

Boiler water tank leaking through underside rivets. Repairs to the boiler water tank and fuel tank were carried out.

Doncaster	26/03/71	02/04/71	Unclassified

No.1 engine, 421 and No.2 engine, 440, had all injectors replaced. No.2 main generator had flashover damage cleaned up. No.1 main generator and all traction motors were replaced due to flashover damage.

Doncaster	26/04/71	30/04/71	Unclassified

No.1 engine, 421, replaced by 412, due to 'BC' crankcase fractured at damper end.

Doncaster	10/05/71	12/05/71	Unclassified

No.1 engine, 412, replaced by 457, due to aerating. No.1 end lubricating oil tank and radiator elements were cleaned.

Doncaster	24/06/71	16/07/71	Light

No.1 engine, 457, had injectors replaced. No.2 engine, 440, replaced by 412, due to aerating. No.1 bogie, 9000-29, replaced by 9000-23. No.2 bogie, 9000-10, replaced by 9000-30. Boiler, 1495/J2951, was given an Unclassified repair. The body was given a Light repair.

D9021/9021/55 021 Argyll & Sutherland Highlander (continued)

Loco Works	On Works	Off Works	Class of repair
Doncaster	21/07/71	23/07/71	Unclassified

Both main generators down to earth. No.1 engine, 457, replaced by 405. Both main generators were replaced.

| Doncaster | 17/12/71 | 21/12/71 | Unclassified |

No.2 engine, 412, replaced by 441, due to a fractured liner. No.2 end lubricating oil tanks and radiators were cleaned. Both bogies had swing link studs repaired, brake block cotters reset and footsteps repaired.

| Doncaster | 11/04/72 | 11/05/72 | Intermediate |

No.1 engine, 405, replaced by 447. No.2 engine, 441, replaced by 430. No.1 bogie, 9000-23, replaced by 9000-45. No.2 bogie, 9000-30, replaced by 9000-46. Boiler, 1495/J2951, replaced by 1497/J2953. The body was given an Intermediate repair. Cab draughtproofing was carried out.

| Doncaster | 19/09/72 | 28/09/72 | Unclassified |

No.1 engine, 447, replaced by 423 - defective liner seal. No.2 engine, 430, replaced by 426. No.2 boiler water tank had a fracture repaired. No.1 end lubricating oil tank and radiators replaced.

| Doncaster | 12/02/73 | 20/02/73 | Light |

No.1 engine, 423, replaced by 444. No.2 engine, 426, replaced by 432. No.1 bogie, 9000-45, replaced by 9000-1. No.2 bogie, 9000-46, replaced by 9000-2. Boiler, 1497/J2953, was given an Unclassified repair. The body was given a Light repair.

| Doncaster | 22/02/73 | 23/02/73 | Rectification |

No.2 engine, 432, replaced by 408.

| Doncaster | 07/05/73 | 09/05/73 | Unclassified |

No.1 engine, 444, replaced by 404, due to aerating badly, suspected fractured liner.

| Doncaster | 15/05/73 | 24/05/73 | Unclassified |

Burnt wiring in No.2 control cubicle. This was repaired.

| Doncaster | 10/08/73 | 13/08/73 | Unclassified |

No.2 engine, 408, replaced by 437, due to crankcase holed, No.4 piston 'AB' crankcase, through side. Lubricating oil tanks and radiators were replaced.

| Doncaster | 17/09/73 | 25/09/73 | Unclassified |

No.1 engine, 404, had cardan shaft drive and governor replaced. No.2 engine, 437, replaced by 445, due to tie bolt on 'CA' crankcase broken. A boiler water tank was repaired. E.T.H. defective, cutting out continually, this was rectified.

| Doncaster | 22/10/73 | 26/10/73 | Unclassified |

No.1 engine, 404, replaced by 439, due to 'A' crankshaft damper adrift. No.2 engine, 445, replaced by 450, due to 'B' crankshaft damper adrift.

| Doncaster | 10/11/73 | 13/11/73 | Unclassified |

No.2 engine, 450, replaced by 411, due to 'AB' crankcase fractured at damper housing.

| Doncaster | 26/11/73 | 29/12/73 | Intermediate |

No.1 engine, 439, replaced by 416. No.2 engine, 411, replaced by 418. No.1 bogie, 9000-1 and No.2 bogie, 9000-2, were given standard repairs. Boiler, 1497/J2953, replaced by 5092/J3243. The body was given an Intermediate repair.

| Doncaster | 10/01/74 | 10/01/74 | Modification |

Earth fault relay modification was carried out.

| Doncaster | 04/02/74 | 05/02/74 | Unclassified |

A hole blown in No.4 traction motor. No.4 traction motor was replaced and all others were cleaned up and megger tested.

| Doncaster | 12/08/74 | 21/08/74 | Unclassified |

No.2 engine, 418, replaced by 411, due to a suspected fractured liner. No.2 boiler water tank was repaired, batteries renewed and coolant temperature probe and E.T.H. modifications carried out.

| Doncaster | 12/09/74 | 12/09/74 | Unclassified |

No.2 engine, 411, overspeeding. The governor was replaced.

| Doncaster | 13/12/74 | 14/12/74 | Unclassified |

Traction motor defects. No.1 bogie, 9000-1, replaced by 9000-21. No.2 bogie, 9000-2, replaced by 9000-41. A holed boiler water tank was repaired.

D9021/9021/55 021 Argyll & Sutherland Highlander (continued)

Loco Works	On Works	Off Works	Class of repair
Doncaster	19/12/74	12/02/75	Light

No.1 engine, 416, replaced by 444. No.2 engine, 411, replaced by 438. No.1 bogie, 9000-21, replaced by 9000-5. No.2 bogie, 9000-41, replaced by 9000-6. Boiler, 5092/J3243, was given an Unclassified repair. A holed boiler water tank was repaired.

Doncaster	26/02/75	28/02/75	Unclassified

No.2 engine, 438, suspect auxiliary drive out of alignment. Repairs were carried out to the auxiliary generator drive shaft.

Doncaster	04/03/75	04/03/75	Unclassified

No.2 engine, 438, underspeed defective. The underspeed governor was replaced due to a defective drive.

Doncaster	09/04/75	15/04/75	Unclassified

No.1 engine, 444, had 'CA' crankcase cover resealed. Both boiler water tanks were repaired.

Doncaster	30/04/75	01/05/75	Unclassified

No.1 engine, 444, replaced by 413, due to con rod through crankcase. No.1 end lubricating oil tank and radiators were cleaned.

Doncaster	22/10/75	11/11/75	Unclassified

No.1 eng, 413, replaced by 451. No.2 eng, 438, replaced by 539. A boiler water tank was repaired.

Doncaster	13/01/76	15/01/76	Unclassified

No.1 engine, 451, replaced by 453. No.1 boiler water tank was repaired.

Doncaster	13/02/76	17/02/76	Unclassified

No.2 traction motor bearing collapsed and disintegrated and gearwheel damaged. No.2 wheelset was replaced.

Doncaster	22/04/76	19/01/77	Heavy General

No.1 eng, 453, replaced by 417 - suspected fractured liner on 'B' bank exhaust seal. No.2 engine, 539, replaced by 418. No.1 bogie, 9000-5, replaced by 9000-13. No.2 bogie, 9000-6, replaced by 9000-14. Boiler, 5092/J3243, replaced by 5093/J3244. Route indicator panels plated over.

Doncaster	20/04/77	28/04/77	Unclassified

No.2 engine, 418, replaced by 429, due to a suspected fractured liner. Earth faults were rectified and burnt wiring was renewed.

Doncaster	11/05/77	19/05/77	Unclassified

No.2 engine, 429, 'AB' crankcase fractured at free end. This and the damper were repaired.

Doncaster	06/08/77	12/08/77	Unclassified

No.1 engine, 417, replaced by 434. No.1 main generator replaced due to persistently flashing over. E.T.H. and wheelslip faults were rectified.

Doncaster	17/08/77	20/08/77	Unclassified

No.1 engine, 434, replaced by 453, due to generator drive adrift.

Doncaster	01/12/77	05/12/77	Unclassified

No.2 engine, 429, replaced by 446, due to auxiliary fan drive shaft in phasing gearcase securing thread stripped. Bogie centre pivot studs and nuts were renewed.

Doncaster	21/01/78	02/02/78	Unclassified

No.1 engine, 453, replaced by 424, due to aerating and losing coolant. No.1 primary fan drive gearbox was replaced. No.1 bogie, 9000-13, No.3 traction motor suspension pad was secured, 'L2' brake rod safety stay was refitted and a horn liner was secured.

Doncaster	14/03/78	30/03/78	Unclassified

No.2 main generator field to earth. No.1 boiler water tank and No.1 primary cardan shaft were repaired. Both main generators and all traction motors were replaced.

Doncaster	25/04/78	05/06/78	Unclassified

No.1 engine, 424, replaced by 414. No.2 engine, 446, replaced by 418, due to 'AC' crankcase holed. Extremely bad fracture at No.1 end secondman's side cab font between windscreen and side window, over 12" long and opening out. This was repaired.

Doncaster	13/06/78	17/06/78	Unclassified

No.1 engine, 414, replaced by 454. Boiler, 5093/J3244, missing items were replaced, leaks were rectified and the boiler was made operable.

Doncaster	15/09/78	28/11/78	Unclassified

No.1 engine, 454, replaced by 539, due to aerating badly. No.2 engine, 418, replaced by 419.

D9021/9021/55 021 Argyll & Sutherland Highlander (continued)

Loco Works	On Works	Off Works	Class of repair
Doncaster	03/01/79	08/01/79	Unclassified

No.2 traction motor gear teeth sheared off. No.2 wheelset was replaced.

Doncaster	28/03/79	26/04/79	Light

No.1 engine, 539, replaced by 442, due to cardan shaft drive sheared. No.2 engine, 419, was given an Unclassified repair. No.1 bogie, 9000-13, replaced by 9000-49. No.2 bogie, 9000-14, replaced by 9000-50. Boiler, 5093/J3244, was given an Unclassified repair.

Doncaster	30/08/79	02/09/79	Unclassified

No.1 engine, 442, replaced by 448, due to being dephased.

Doncaster	30/10/79	02/11/79	Unclassified

No.2 engine, 419, replaced by 420.

Doncaster	06/12/79	13/12/79	Unclassified

No.1 engine, 448, replaced by 437, due to being dephased.

Doncaster	02/01/80	06/01/80	Unclassified

No.2 engine, 420, replaced by 455, due to a suspected fractured liner.

Stratford D.R.S.	16/02/81	20/02/81	Depot

No.1 bogie, 9000-49, replaced by 9000-27. No.2 bogie, 9000-50, replaced by 9000-28.

Doncaster	02/06/81	05/06/81	Unclassified

No.2 engine, 455, replaced by 445, due to No.2 main generator decompounding.

Doncaster	13/07/81	15/07/81	Unclassified

No.1 engine, 437, replaced by 425, due to debris in chip trap.

Doncaster	05/10/81	15/10/81	Unclassified

No.1 engine, 425, replaced by 439, due to auxiliary generator drive gears not being driven.

Doncaster	04/01/82	-	-

The locomotive arrived on Works after withdrawal with the following main components fitted. No.1 engine, 439. No.2 engine, 445, aerating. No.1 bogie, 9000-27. No.2 bogie, 9000-28. Boiler, 5093/J3244.

340 DELTICS ON WORKS

A fine study of D9015 Tulyar being re-fuelled at Finsbury Park depot in the early 1960s. Picture: P. Caley Collection.

DELTICS ON WORKS 341

Class 55, 55011 The Royal Northumberland Fusiliers undergoes attention in the paint shop at Doncaster Works on May 7, 1978. Picture: L. P. Gater.